A DOCUMENTARY HISTORY
OF THE JEWS IN ITALY

XXIV

EDITED BY

SHLOMO SIMONSOHN

THE GOREN-GOLDSTEIN DIASPORA RESEARCH CENTRE
TEL AVIV UNIVERSITY

Studia Post Biblica

General Editor

David S. Katz

Tel Aviv

VOLUME 48.3

The Jews in Sicily

VOLUME TEN

Notaries of Palermo

Part One

By

Shlomo Simonsohn

BRILL

LEIDEN • BOSTON
2007

The preparation and publication of this volume were made possible by a grant from the Memorial Foundation for Jewish Culture.

Library of Congress Cataloging-in-Publication Data is available on http://catalogue.loc.gov

ISSN: 0169-9717
ISBN-13: 978 90 04 15762 0

PRINTED IN THE NETHERLANDS

Contents

Sources

Palermo, Archivio di Stato (**ASP**)
Notaio
    Antonino de Melina, reg. 937
    Domenico Aprea, reg. 797, 797bis
    Giacomo Comito, reg. 843, 844, 845, 846, 847, 848, 849, 850, 851, 852,
        853, 854, 855, 856, 857, 858, 859, 860, 861
    Giacomo Maniscalco, reg. 342
    Giovanni Traverso, reg. 777, 778, 779, 780, 781, 782, 783, 784, 785, 786,
        787, 788, 789, 790, 791, 792, 793, 794, 795
    Guglielmo Mazzapiedi, reg. 839, 840, 841
    Luigi Terranova, reg. 1063, 1064
    Manfrido La Muta, reg. 415
    Nicolò Marotta, reg. 938
    Pietro Castelli, reg. 1044
    Pietro Goffredo, reg. 1076

Glossary

adornari — decorations
albaxore — albacore
amellano — starch
ancunia — anvil
astracum — pavement
auribello — brass
azari de raxia — cloth
ballino — ball
barduna — border
bichino — goat
bombarderius — bombardier
buctunelli, buctinori — buttons
bullonos — bolts
burnari — vessels
busunaglia (buzunaglia) — inferior quality tunny
buccaxini — cloth
calamida — tiles
calapodium — lectern or stool (?)
caratello — vat, small cask (also measure)
carmixino — crimson
carrozzata — wagon-load (measure)
cayula —*[Albanian] headdress*
centimularius — miller
chirchi/chirki — hoops for casks/barrels
cinnamorum — cinnamon
corbiseria seu zabartoria — shoemaker's business
crisinari — cloth
cubayte — sweets (almond etc.)
cuxinello — cushion
dublecti — doublets
flandini (filandini) — yarn [?]

franze de rexia — fringes
frixoni — woollen cloth
fucarolo — fireman
iarratino — barrel/sack filler
iunza — (belly) fat
machinator cannamellarum — sugar cane grinder
madono — brick
marramma — wall
naybis — playing cards
orgagni — implements, tools
parator — a labourer in a sugar refinery, winery, etc.
pisa — measure (5 *rotoli*)
plumello — lead
raubis — articles, goods, etc.
quartara — equals 13¾ litres
quartuccio — equals 1/16 of a *quartara*
roxuni — reeds, cane
salmoriare and *gubernare* (or: *salare*) *caseum* — treat cheese with salt for
    conservation (also used for tunny)
sigili dactilis — rye
sivi quagliati — hardened tallow
stalglare — coating
straczandi — scrap
stringitori — (wine) treader
tagliata — cutting (season of the tunny)
terzanelli — silk
tramutato — fortified (wine)
vanella — alley
virzillini — iron ingots
xindarelli (cindarelli) — silk
zindati (xindati) — silk veils

Not. Giovanni Traverso, Cont.

Palermo, 11 October 1434

Source: ASP, Not. Giovanni Traverso, reg. 777, c. 67v.

Simon de Mayu, a Jew, promises Antonello Manueli to sole the shoes of three of his men employed on his farm until August for one ounce. He is paid 10 tarì *on account and is promised another eight within eight days.*

Palermo, 26 November 1434

Source: ASP, Not. Giovanni Traverso, reg. 777, c. 165v.

Muxa Bonu, a Jewish citizen of Palermo, promises Iacobo de Bononia to transport with four beasts of burdens sugar cane to his press for five tarì *the quintal. He is paid 12* tarì *on account.*

Palermo, 3 December 1434

Source: ASP, Not. Giovanni Traverso, reg. 777, c. 179v.

Agreement whereby Vita de Leone and Vita Maltisi, Jews, hire themselves out to Masio Crispo to work in his sugar refinery as paratores *for one ounce a month each. They are paid 1.1.0 ounces on account. Farchono Gaczu and Salamon de Seracusia, Jews, stand surety.*

Palermo, 19 January 1435

Source: ASP, Not. Giovanni Traverso, reg. 777, cc. 241v–242r.

Notarial protest by Giovanni de Valencia against David Minchil, a Jew of Termini Imerese, who is alleged to have been late in delivering a mule. Giovanni demands damages. David lodges a similar protest against Giovanni on the ground that he had leased the mule to Giovanni safe and sound and had had it returned to him wounded. The animal had eventually succumbed to its wounds.

Palermo, 3 February 1435

Source: ASP, Not. Giovanni Traverso, reg. 777, c. 264r.

Muxa Missiria, a Jew, hires himself out to Lyotta Nigiar, a Jewish shoemaker, for two years to work in his business in Palermo and elsewhere in Sicily. He is to be paid in accordance with the work carried out.

Palermo, 2 March 1435

Source: ASP, Not. Giovanni Traverso, reg. 777, cc. 289v–290r.

Sabatinus de Amuranu, Xhanina Sacerdotu, Busacca de Gauyo, Farchonus Rabbi, Iacob and Busacca de Bono, Jews, hire themselves out to Masio Crispo to cultivate his sugarcane for 17 grana *a day each. They are paid one ounce on account.*

Palermo, 4 March 1435

Source: ASP, Not. Giovanni Traverso, reg. 777, c. 294v.

Xibiten Binassay, Salamon Balbu and Muxa Trabu hire themselves out to Masio Crispo to work in his sugar refinery for 17 grana *a day each. Xibiten is paid six* tarì *on account, Salamon, six and Muxa three.*

Palermo, 5 March 1435

Source: ASP, Not. Giovanni Traverso, reg. 777, cc. 301v–302r.

Sufen Misiria and Iacob Tunisinu hire themselves out together with six other men to Giovanni de Bononia to fertilize his sugar cane for 16 tarì *a thousand plants. They are paid 24 tarì on account.*

Palermo, 16 March 1435

Source: ASP, Not. Giovanni Traverso, reg. 777, c. 321r

Braxha Calabrisi, a Jew, hires himself out together with nine other men to Filippo de Miglacio to fertilize his sugar cane during the entire season for 17 tarì *a thousand plants. He is paid 2.3.0 ounces on account.*

Palermo, 17 March 1435

Source: ASP, Not. Giovanni Traverso, reg. 777, c. 326r.

Sabet Medui, Xamuel Nigiar, Braxhono Sicilianus and Xibiten de Vilaxi, Jews, promise Francesco de Ventimiglia to fertilize his plants and carry out other agricultural work.

Palermo, 11 April 1435

Source: ASP, Not. Giovanni Traverso, reg. 777, c. 366r.

Muxa Alluxu, Iusep Ammara, Braxhono Sichiliano and Salamon de Seracusia, Jews, hire themselves out together with two other men to Guglielmo de Xabita to work in his sugar refinery during the entire season for five ounces a month.

Palermo, 3 May 1435

Source: ASP, Not. Giovanni Traverso, reg. 777, c. 393r.

David Cipriano and Braxhono Quarteri, Jews, promise Gargano de Silvestro to transport all the red soil needed for some work in the ruga *Virdi for 10* denari *the load. They are paid six* tarì *on account.*

Palermo, 3 May 1435

Source: ASP, Not. Giovanni Traverso, reg. 777, cc. 393v–394r.

Deed whereby Lya Nigiar, a Jew, transfers his debt of one ounce which he owes Xannono Nigiar, another Jew, on account of a loan, to the guarantor who had had to pay the debt.

Palermo, 4 June 1435

Source: ASP, Not. Giovanni Traverso, reg. 777, c. 437r

Sadya Ysac, a Jew, hires himself out to Filippo de Miglacio to work as filler in his sugar refinery for two ounces a month. He is paid two ounces on account.

Palermo, 4 June 1435

Source: ASP, Not. Giovanni Traverso, reg. 777, c. 438v.

Xhayrono Gaczu and Mardoc Actuni, Jews, promise Guglielmo Xhabita to stack all the wood in his sugar refinery during the current season for one tarì *a hundred kantars.*

Palermo, 20 June 1435

Source: ASP, Not. Giovanni Traverso, reg. 777, c. 448v.

Siminto de Missina, a Jew, hires himself out to Busacca Levi, another Jew, to work on his farm from 1 September to Easter for 10 grana *a day. He is paid three* tarì *on account.*

Palermo, 27 June 1435

Source: ASP, Not. Giovanni Traverso, reg. 777, c. 457v.

Momo Gaczu, Xibiteni Virdi, Xhaymi de Liuni and Liuczu Gaczu hire themselves out together with some other Jews to Masio Crispo to work in his sugar refinery during the whole season for one ounce a month each. They are paid 2.20.0 ounces on account through the bank of Peri Gaytani. In the margin: On 21 October they were joined by Pinesi Sacerdotu and Muxa Rugila, Jews.

Palermo, 14 July 1435

Source: ASP, Not. Giovanni Traverso, reg. 777, c. 476v.

Master Antonio de Giovanni hires himself out to master Xibiten Ysaccu, a Jew, to work in the sugar refinery of Ubertino de Imperatore in his stead on Friday afternoons and Saturdays as sack filler for two tarì *for each "boiling" operation.*

Palermo, 8 June 1436

Source: ASP, Not. Giovanni Traverso, reg. 778, cc. 359v–360r.

Gallufu Xammara, Braxhono de Polici and Braxhono de Anzalono, Jews, promise Guglielmo de Xhabita to transport with eight beasts of burden 100 salme *of food from the* contrada *Falsomele to the walls of Palermo for five* grana *a* salma.

Sicily

Palermo, 19 June 1436

Source: ASP, Not. Giovanni Traverso, reg. 778, c. 371r.

Symon Palermitano, a Jew, hires himself out to Masio Crispo to work in his sugar refinery for 12 tarì.

Palermo, 27 June 1436

Source: ASP, Not. Giovanni Traverso, reg. 778, c. 385v.

Sabutu Medui and Xamuel Nigiar and another six men hire themselves out to Giovanni Lixando, acting for Francesco Ventimiglia, to fertilize the latter's sugar cane for 17 tarì *a thousand plants.*

Palermo, 4 July 1436

Source: ASP, Not. Giovanni Traverso, reg. 778, c. 396v.

Salamon Calabresi, Nissim Busuta and Lyotta de Gaczella, Jews, hire themselves out to Antonio Raimondo to work in his tunny plant at Termini Imerese during the entire season for one ounce each. They are paid 12 tarì *on account.*

Palermo, September 1436

Source: ASP, Not. Giovanni Traverso, reg. 778, c. nn.

Danieli Gaczella, a Jew, hires himself out to Filippo Bellachera to work in his tunny plant at Solanto during the entire season for one ounce. He is paid 10 tarì on account.

Palermo, 7 September 1436

Source: ASP, Not. Giovanni Traverso, reg. 778, c. nn.

Muxa de Termini, Salamon de Messina and Braxhono de Polici, Jews, promise Giovanni Bellachera to transport with 12 beasts of burden olives to his olive press for five tarì *a kantar.*

Palermo, 12 October 1436

Source: ASP, Not. Giovanni Traverso, reg. 778, c. 80r.

Agreement whereby Iacob de Termini, a Jew, promises Symone de Iacopo, acting for Antonio de Sardo to sole the latter's shoes and those of five of his men.

Palermo, 15 October 1436

Source: ASP, Not. Giovanni Traverso, reg. 778, c. 85v.

Symon de Mayu, a Jew, promises Antonello Manuele to sole his shoes and those of two other men and a boy on his farm.

Palermo, 16 October 1436

Source: ASP, Not. Giovanni Traverso, reg. 778, c. 86v.

Symon de Mayu, a Jew, promises Pino de Ferro to sole his shoes and those of two muledrivers and Antonio La Porta for a year for 16.10 tarì.

Palermo, 23 October 1436

Source: ASP, Not. Giovanni Traverso, reg. 778, c. 112r-v.

Salamon son of Levi Actuni, a Jew, promises Miano Trixona to sole his shoes and those of two of his men for 12 tarì.

Palermo, 29 October 1436

Source: ASP, Not. Giovanni Traverso, reg. 778, c. 131v.

Deed whereby David de Pulisi, a Jew, undertakes to pay 2.12.0 ounces in monthly instalments of six tarì *to Isdrael Strugu, another Jew. Simultaneously Isdrael annuls a previous undertaking by David to pay him the sum stipulated by the Jewish notary, Abram [Abenladep]. The debt arose out of the sale of 100 castrated rams (*castrati*) to Isdrael by Ilaria Talamanca, who in turn sold them to David.*

Palermo, 29 October 1436

Source: ASP, Not. Giovanni Traverso, reg. 778, c. 132r-v.

Deed whereby Isdrael Strugu and David Pulisi, Jews, declare that they have settled accounts between them to their mutual satisfaction.

6080

Palermo, 29 October 1436

Source: ASP, Not. Giovanni Traverso, reg. 778, c. 131v.

Deed whereby Isdrael Strugu, a Palermitan Jew, declares that he owes Ilaria Talamanca 4.18.0 ounces, the balance of the price for a quantity of castrati *sold Isdrael by Ilaria's representative Antonio de Lasinello. Tobia Strugu, a Jew, stands surety.*

Palermo, 5 November 1436

Source: ASP, Not. Giovanni Traverso, reg. 778, c. 144v.

Xhayrono Gaczu alias Momo hires himself out to Guglielmo Xhabitu to stack the wood in his sugar refinery for 10 tarì *a thousand kantars. He is paid 20* tarì *on account.*

Palermo, 21 January 1437

Source: ASP, Not. Giovanni Traverso, reg. 778, c. 258v.

Mastro Nixim Pulisi, a Jew, hires himself out to Busacca Levi, another Jew, until the end of August to work in his tannery for eight tarì *a month.*

Palermo, 27 February 1437

Source: ASP, Not. Giovanni Traverso, reg. 778, c. 258v.

Agreement whereby Xhayrono Gaczu, a Jew, hires himself out to Antonio Crispo to cut and harvest Antonio's sugar cane in the contrada *Turris de Bandino for nine* tarì *a thousand.*

Palermo, 28 February 1437

Source: ASP, Not. Giovanni Traverso, reg. 778, c. 316v.

Sufen Miseria, Xibiten Xammara and Iusep Ammara, Jews, promise Iuliano de Silvestri to cut the sugar cane in Iacobo de Bononia's sugar refinery for 15 tarì a thousand *and to fertilize his sugar cane for 13* tarì *a thousand.*

Palermo, 1 March 1437

Source: ASP, Not. Giovanni Traverso, reg. 778, cc. 319v–320r.

Giovanni de Arnono and Xibiteni Bambalu, a Jew, hire themselves out to Masio Crispo to work in his sugar refinery during the entire season for 3.6.0 ounces a month. Giovanni, as fireman (fucarolus), *is to receive two ounces, and Xibiteni, his helper, 1.6.0.*

Palermo, 5 March 1437

Source: ASP, Not. Giovanni Traverso, reg. 778, c. 325v.

Benedetto Cassisu, Salamon de Missina, Sabeti Busicta, Nissim Busicta and Braxhono Amarana, later joined by Pinesi Sacerdotu, all Jews, hire themselves out to Masio Crispo to work in his sugar refinery during the whole season for one ounce a month each.

Palermo, 13 March 1437

Source: ASP, Not. Giovanni Traverso, reg. 778, c. 333r.

Ansaluni Actuni, a Jew, hires himself out to Samuel Nigiar, Vita Maltisi, David Rugila and Salamone Xammara, all Jews, to work in Giovanni Omodei's sugar refinery during the whole season as helper to the paratores *for 15* tarì *a month.*

Palermo, 13 March 1437

Source: ASP, Not. Giovanni Traverso, reg. 778, c. 334r.

Sabatino Minaxhen, a Jew, hires himself out to Antonio Dulcimaschuli, acting for Giovanni Omodei, to work in the latter's sugar refinery during the whole season for the usual wages.

Palermo, 15 March 1437

Source: ASP, Not. Giovanni Traverso, reg. 778, c. 337r.

Bella et Bonu (!), Merdoc Braxhuni and Nissim Busicta, Jews, hire themselves out to Masio Crispo to fertilize his sugarcane during the entire season for 17 grana *a day. On Fridays they need work only until the afternoon. The wage on Fridays is reduced to 15* grana.

Palermo, 15 March 1437

Source: ASP, Not. Giovanni Traverso, reg. 778, c. 344r-v.

Sufeni Misseria, Xibiteni Xammara, Liuni Cuchilla, Czullus Iubara, Danieli Xhabirra and two helpers, all Jews, hire themselves out to Iacobo de Bononia to work as paratores *in his sugar refinery during the entire season.*

Palermo, 20 March 1437

Source: ASP, Not. Giovanni Traverso, reg. 778, c. 346r.

Liuni Danicholu, a Jew of Castroreale, hires himself out to Iacobo de Bononia as muledriver during the whole harvest season for 22 tari *and a pair of shoes.*

Palermo, 26 March 1437

Source: ASP, Not. Giovanni Traverso, reg. 778, c. 352r.

Xibiten Bambalu, Merdoc Xhagramuni and Braxhono Terranova, Jews, hire themselves out to Masio Crispo to fertilize his sugar cane during the entire season on the usual terms.

Palermo, 11 April 1437

Source: ASP, Not. Giovanni Traverso, reg. 778, c. 373v.

Sadya Ysac, a Jew, undertakes to transport for Ilario Talamanca 200 salme *of lime from the quarry in Misilmeri to the church of S. Maria di Gesú for 1.5* tarì *the* salma. *He is to employ eight animals.*

Palermo, 13 April 1437

Source: ASP, Not. Giovanni Traverso, reg. 778, c. nn.

Lya de Santo Marco, Ysdraeli Ysac and Siminto Aurifichi, Jews, hire themselves out to Antonio Vassallo to work in Giovanni Homodei's tunny plant in Solanto.

Palermo, 13 April 1437

Source: ASP, Not. Giovanni Traverso, reg. 778, c. nn.

Salamon de Missina, Benedetto Cafisu, Braxhono Amiranu, Sabet Busuta and

six others, all Jews, undertake to fertilize the sugar cane plants of Giovanni
Homodey for 18 tarì a thousand.

Palermo, 24 April 1437

Source: ASP, Not. Giovanni Traverso, reg. 778, c. nn.

*Salamon Xammara, Liuczu Gacxu, Xilomu Braxha and five others, all Jews,
undertake to fertilize the sugar cane plants of Bartholomeo Columba for 13* tarì
a thousand.

Palermo, 17 February 1438

Source: ASP, Not. Giovanni Traverso, reg. 779, c. nn.

*Braxhono Anzaluni, a Jew, promises Giovanni Homodey to transport water to
his tunny plant in Solanto during the entire season for one ounce. He is paid 20*
tarì *on account.*

Palermo, 20 February 1438

Source: ASP, Not. Giovanni Traverso, reg. 779, c. nn.

*Salamon Sabuchi, a Jew, hires himself out to Giovanni Homodei to work in his
sugar refinery for eight ounces. He is paid two ounces on account.*

Palermo, 26 February 1438

Source: ASP, Not. Giovanni Traverso, reg. 779, c. nn.

*Siminto Aurifichi and Iusep Balbu, Jews, promise Masio Crispo to build a well
in his sugar refinery for 24* tarì *and half a* salma *of wheat.*

Palermo, 5 March 1438

Source: ASP, Not. Giovanni Traverso, reg. 779, c. nn.

*Salamon de Missina, Benedicto Caffis, Xamuel Nigiar and Braxhono Amuram,
Jews, hire themselves out to Giovanni Homodei to work as* paratores *in his sugar
refinery for five ounces. They are paid four ounces on account.*

Palermo, 7 March 1438
Source: ASP, Not. Giovanni Traverso, reg. 779, c. nn.

Symon de Mayu dictus Rabina, a Jew, owes mastro Paolo de Li Serri the price of some leather. The date due has passed. Paolo grants Symon an extension provided he pays him instalments of four tarì *a month.*

Palermo, 8 March 1438
Source: ASP, Not. Giovanni Traverso, reg. 779, c. nn.

Merdoc de Minichi, Braxhono Sichiliano, Sabet de Minichi, Fadaluni Sacerdotu and Salamon Xunina, Jews, hire themselves out to Giovanni de Bellachera to work in his sugar refinery for one ounce a month each. They receive 2.15.0 ounces on account.

Palermo, March 1438
Source: ASP, Not. Giovanni Traverso, reg. 779, c. nn.

Xibiteni Bambalu, a Jew, hires himself out to Masio Crispo to work in his sugar refinery during the current season for two ounces a month, and is paid 1.3.0 ounces on account.

Palermo, March 1438
Source: ASP, Not. Giovanni Traverso, reg. 779, c. nn.

Manuel and Xibiten Maltis, Jews, hire themselves out to Masio Crispo to work in his sugar refinery for 15 grana *a day.*

Palermo, 14 October 1437
Source: ASP, Not. Giovanni Traverso, reg. 780, c. 85r-v.

Nissim Xidedi, a Jew, promises to pay Masio Crispo the 18 tarì *which he owes him with labour. He is to make sugar in Masio's sugar refinery.*

Palermo, 21 November 1437
Source: ASP, Not. Giovanni Traverso, reg. 780, c. 178r-v.

Contract whereby a group of Jews undertakes to supply Giovanni Bellachera with all the wood he requires for his sugar refinery until the end of August for five tarì *per hundred kantars. They are paid 29.11* tarì *on account. David Cipriani is to employ three beasts of burden; Iusep Minichi — three; Xibiteni Bambulu — three; Salamon Missina — two; Benedetto Boni — two.*

Palermo, 26 November 1437
Source: ASP, Not. Giovanni Traverso, reg. 780, c. 184r.

Xibiteni Bambalu, a Jew, hires himself out to Giovanni Bellachera to work in his sugar refinery during the whole season for 1.2 tarì *a "boiling" operation, and is paid 15* tarì *on account. Salamon de Messana stands surety for Xibiteni. Renewed on 1 October 1438.*

Die XXVI novembris prime Ind.
Xibiten Bambalu, Iudeus, coram nobis sponte se locavit cum nobilis Iohanne Bellachera pro machinator ad eius trappetum cannamellarum per totam stasionem anni presentis ad faciendum servicium per duas coctas pro qualibet septimana ad requisitionem dicti nobilis, preter in die sabati, pro stipendio tr. I et gr. II pro singula cocta. Et presenciabiliter ipse Iudeus habuit et recepit a dicto nobili pro caparro tr. XV et reliquum stipendium debet habere successivu que omnia ipse Iudeus promisit rata habere in pace, de plano...

Omissis

pro quo Iudeo circa de premissis omnibus sub servandis Salamon de Messina Iudeus coram nobis sponte fideiussit et se constituit principalem solutorem et debitorem, etc. Et fiat ritus. Et iuraverunt.
Testes: Iohannes Caxi et Manfridus de Ratinya.

Palermo, 1 October 1438
Source: ASP, Not. Giovanni Traverso, reg. 780, c. nn.

Salamon de Messina, Benedetto Bonu, Braxhono de Policio, Braxhono Ansaluni

6086

and two others, all Jews, contract with Giovanni Bellachera to transport wood from the shore at Palermo to his sugar refinery in Seracaldi until the first week in September for five tarì *per hundred kantars. They also undertake to harvest Giovanni's olives at four* grana *for six* tumoli. *They are paid 1.24.0 ounces on account.*

Palermo, 17 November 1438

Source: ASP, Not. Giovanni Traverso, reg. 780, c. 130r.

Xibiteni Gaczu, a Jew, promised Olivo de Suttil (Sottile), pretor of Palermo, to level the place were he dug for stone and gravel.

Xibiteni Gaczu, Iudeus, coram nobis sponte promisit nobili et egregio domino Olivo de Suttil, pretori felicis urbis Panormi, presenti et stipulanti nomine et pro parte universitatis Panormi, suis, videlicet dicti Iudei propriis expensis, splanare et in planum ponere illum locum ubi ipse Iudeus fodere et cavare fecit ad presens petras et truppellos bene et diligenter ad omnem simplicem requisizionem dicti domini Olivi, postquam cavari et fodere fecerunt ipsas lapides et truppellos, sub ypotheca omnium suorum bonorum ac refectione dampnorum interesse expensarum litis, etc.
Renuncians, etc. Et fiat ritus, etc.
Testes: Matheus de Sabella et Nicolaus Fanilla.

Note: On Olivo Sottile, see Bresc, *Monde Méditerranéen*, s.v.

Palermo, 20 January 1439

Source: ASP, Not. Giovanni Traverso, reg. 780, c. 215r.

Contract between Merdoc Catalano, a Jew of Ciminna, and Muxa Misiria and Lya Sadia, Jewish shoemakers and citizens of Palermo, to open a shop for the sale of shoes for one year. Merdoc invests the capital and the shop. The other two invest their labour. The profits are to be divided between the three in equal shares.

Palermo, [20] January 1439

Source: ASP, Not. Giovanni Traverso, reg. 780, c. 215v.

Accord between Vita Arami and Xhanonno Calabrensi, Jews, to settle a dispute out of court and to withdraw their respective claims. Vita is represented by his brother Manuel.

Palermo, 26 February 1439

Source: ASP, Not. Giovanni Traverso, reg. 780, c. 258r.

Daniel Cangrani, a Jewish citizen of Palermo, hires himself out to Giovanni de Bononia to work on his farm and carry out all country and urban work (servicia rusticana et urbana) demanded of him for a year at 12 tarì *a month. The wages are to be be paid to Muxa Sacerdotu until April.*

Palermo, 4 March 1439

Source: ASP, Not. Giovanni Traverso, reg. 780, c. 264v.

Contract whereby Giovanni de Bononia cedes to Busacca Levi, a Jew, ownership of a house in the Cassaro which Busacca had rented from Iacobo, Giovanni's father. The price agreed on is 6.18.0 ounces. The house is solerata *and has a pavement* (astraco), *and borders on the houses of the notary Antonino de Candela, mastro Matheo de Calanzano and Nissim Spiuni. The rent had been 1.18.0 ounces a year.*

Palermo, 5 March 1439

Source: ASP, Not. Giovanni Traverso, reg. 780, c. 268r.

Salamon de Missina, Benedetto Taps and Braxhono Amuranu, also on behalf of Sabet Busictu, hire themselves out to Giovanni Homodei to cultivate his sugarcane plantations in town and outside it and to fertilize five fields for the usual wages. They are paid four ounces on account. Salamon Benedetto, Braxhaono and Xamuel Nigiar, Jews, and another Jew hire themselves out to Giovanni to work as paratores *in his sugar refinery during the season for five ounces a month.*

Palermo, 16 March 1439

Source: ASP, Not. Giovanni Traverso, reg. 780, c. 282r.

Nissim Bussictu and Merdoc Actuni, Jews, hire themselves out to Giovanni

Homodei to stack wood in his sugar refinery for the usual wages. Each is paid 12 tarì *on account.*

Palermo, 17 March 1439

Source: ASP, Not. Giovanni Traverso, reg. 780, c. 284r.

Iosep Balbu and Manuel Maltisi, jointly, Benedetto Calabrensi and his son Xibiten, jointly, Raffael Romanu and Busacca de Tripuli, jointly, all Jews, hire themselves out to Masio Crispo to fertilize his sugar cane fields for 17 grana *a day working until 23 hours. On Fridays they are to work until vespers. Xibiten is paid four* tarì *on account, the others six each.*

Palermo, 18 March 1439

Source: ASP, Not. Giovanni Traverso, reg. 780, cc. 284v–285r.

Contract whereby Antonello de Ginnaro, on one hand, and Xibiteni Bambulu and Liuni Chuchilla, David Serruni, Jews, on the other, set up a partnership for pressing olives. Antonello invests the press, the horses and the tools. The Jewish partners invest their labour. It is agreed that at least five salme *of olives are to be processed a day. The Jewish partners cannot take oil from the press without Antonello's consent. The profits are to be divided in equal shares between Antonello and his partners.*

Palermo, 28 March 1439

Source: ASP, Not. Giovanni Traverso, reg. 780, c. 294r.

David Serruni, a Jewish citizen of Palermo, hires himself out to Giovanni Fruntilata, acting for Giovanni Homodei, to work in the latter's tunny plant at Solanto during the entire season for 24 tarì, *and is paid 12* tarì *on account.*

Palermo, 30 March 1439

Source: ASP, Not. Giovanni Traverso, reg. 780, c. 308v.

Xilomu Brixha, a Jewish citizen of Palermo, hires himself out to Masio Crispo to fertilize Masio's sugar plants during the whole season for the usual pay, and is paid 5.10 tarì *on account.*

Palermo, 30 March 1439

Source: ASP, Not. Giovanni Traverso, reg. 780, c. 310r.

Muxa Alluxu, a Jew, promises Iusep Balbu, acting for Masio Crispo, to fertilize the latter's sugar cane plants for the usual wages and is paid 1.10 tarì *on account.*

Palermo, 2 April 1439

Source: ASP, Not. Giovanni Traverso, reg. 780, c. 315v.

Symon Malti, a Jew, hires himself out to to Enrico Crispo, acting for Masio Crispo, to fertilize the sugar cane plants of the latter during the whole season for the usual pay and is paid 2.13 tarì *on account.*

Palermo, 15 April 1439

Source: ASP, Not. Giovanni Traverso, reg. 780, c. 334r.

Zullo Iubara and Salamon de Seracusia, Jews, hire themselves out to Filippo Miglacio to stack the wood needed by his sugar refinery during the entire season for 7.10 tarì *a thousand kantars.*

Palermo, 5 May 1439

Source: ASP, Not. Giovanni Traverso, reg. 780, c. 362r.

Momo Gaczu and Nissim Busictu, Jews, promise Riccardo de Bentocristo, acting for Olivo Sottile, to stack five kantars of wood in the latter's sugar refinery for eight tarì *a thousand kantars, and are paid 12* tarì *on account.*

Palermo, 13 May 1439

Source: ASP, Not. Giovanni Traverso, reg. 780, c. 366v.

Sufeni Miseria, Pinesi Sacerdotu, Xibiten Xammara, Braxhono de Politi, Daniel Xhabirra alias Cangratu and two helpers, all Jews, hire themselves out to Chicco Salisi, acting for Giovanni de Bononia, to work as paratores *in the latter's sugar refinery during the entire season for six ounces a month. They undertake to produce 17 sacks each "boiling" and are paid six ounces on account.*

Sicily

Palermo, 19 May 1439

Source: ASP, Not. Giovanni Traverso, reg. 780, c. 374r.

Pasquale Sacerdotu, Farchono, Merdoc and Lya Gaczu, also on behalf of two others, all Jews, hire themselves out to Giovanni Bellachera to work in his sugar refinery during the entire season and to process 15 sacks at each "boiling" operation for 4.21.0 ounces a month. They are paid three ounces on account.

Palermo, 22 September 1439

Source: ASP, Not. Giovanni Traverso, reg. 781, c. 34r.

Salamon Tudiscu, a Jew, hires himself out to Salamon Sabuch, [a Jew], acting for Giovanni Homodei, to work in the latter's tunny plant in Solanto for one ounce, and is paid 12 tarì *on account.*

Palermo, 23 September 1439

Source: ASP, Not. Giovanni Traverso, reg. 781, c. 43v.

Sabet Coffitor and Muxa Calabrisi, Jews, hire themselves out to Giovanni Vincentio, acting for Giovanni Homodei, to work in the latter's tunny plant at Solanto for the entire season for 1.15.0 ounces, and is paid one ounce on account.

Palermo, 28 September 1439

Source: ASP, Not. Giovanni Traverso, reg. 781, c. 59r.

Xua and Sadia Aduruti, Jews, promise Salamon Sabuchi, another Jew, acting for Giovanni Homodei, to work in the latter's tunny plant at Solanto during the whole season for 1.15.0 ounces. Xua is paid 1.2.0 ounces on account and Sadia 28 tarì. *Symon Aduruti stands surety.*

Palermo, 30 September 1439

Source: ASP, Not. Giovanni Traverso, reg. 781, cc. 64v–65r.

Iusep Terminisi, Lya Safar, Sabuc Xagaruni, Braxhono Ansaluni and Braxhono de Politi, acting also for Iusep de Minichi, all Jews, promise Giovanni Bellachera to transport wood, wheat, barley and olives until the first week in September.

They are to employ 12 beasts of burden. The wood is to be carried from the shore in Palermo to Giovanni's sugar refinery for five tarì *a hundred kantars. The other goods are to be transported from the plain of Palermo to Giovanni's house or warehouse for six* grana *the* salma.

Palermo, 30 September 1439

Source: ASP, Not. Giovanni Traverso, reg. 781, c. 65r.

Sufeni Miseria, Xibiteni Xammar and Iusep Ammara, Jewish citizens of Palermo, hire themselves out to Giovanni Bellachera to fertilize sugar cane and to stack wood for the usual wages and are paid 12 and 18 tarì *respectively on account.*

Palermo, 15 October 1439

Source: ASP, Not. Giovanni Traverso, reg. 781, cc. 111r–112v.

Deed of sale whereby the Jewess Xhaguena, widow of the late Merdoc de Tripuli, alias Barbarussa, cedes to Lya Sivena, a Jew, the lease of a solerata *house for 3.12.0 ounces. The property is situated in the* vanella *Lanza in the Cassaro, bordering on the properties of Xamueli Sala and Xannuni Nigiar and others. The rent of 1.6.0 is to be paid to Giovanni Bellachera, who agrees to the transfer.*

Palermo, 26 October 1439

Source: ASP, Not. Giovanni Traverso, reg. 781, c. 130r.

Iosep de Amato, a Jew, hires himself out to Antonio Gimmaro, acting for Giovanni Homodei, to work in the latter's tunny plant in Solanto on the terms of a filler (iarratino) *and is paid one ounce on account.*

Palermo, 27 October 1439

Source: ASP, Not. Giovanni Traverso, reg. 781, c. 135v.

David Calabrisi, a Jew, undertakes to supply water and other services to the tunny plant of Giovanni Homodei in Solanto during the entire season for one ounce.

Sicily

Palermo, 11 November 1439

Source: ASP, Not. Giovanni Traverso, reg. 781, c. 169r.

Braxhono Amiranu, a Jew, and another 11 Jews hire themselves out to Giovanni Homodei to cultivate and fertilize his sugar cane fields during the entire season on the usual terms, and are paid 24 tarì *on account.*

Palermo, 13 November 1439

Source: ASP, Not. Giovanni Traverso, reg. 781, c. 175r.

Nissim Busicta, a Jew, hires himself out to Giovanni Homodei to work in his sugar refinery and to make three "boilings" a week.

Palermo, 23 December 1439

Source: ASP, Not. Giovanni Traverso, reg. 781, c. 224v.

Salamon son of Liuni Actuni, a Jewish citizen of Palermo, undertakes to sole the shoes of two of Antonello Manueli's farm labourers until August for nine tarì.

Palermo, 13 January 1440

Source: ASP, Not. Giovanni Traverso, reg. 781, c. 248r.

Czullu Budo, a Jew of Caltabellotta, promises Guglielmo Lombardo to dig trenches for wheat with a capacity to hold 150 salme *in the* contrada *Masseria. Each trench is to hold at least 30* salme. *Guglielmo is to pay Czullu 1.15.0 ounces and food for Czullu and his assistants. He is also to supply the equipment.*

Note: See below, Doc. p. 6095.

Palermo, 27 January 1440

Source: ASP, Not. Giovanni Traverso, reg. 781, c. 260v.

Busacca de Ansalone, a Jew, hires himself out to Sufen Miseria, another Jew, to work in the sugar refinery of Giovanni de Bononia for 15 tarì *a month, and is paid 15* tarì *on account.*

Palermo, 28 January 1440

Source: ASP, Not. Giovanni Traverso, reg. 781, c. 263r.

Sufen Miseria, Xibiteni Xammara, Braxhono de Polici and Daniel Xhibirra, Jews, hire themselves out to Giovanni and Nicolò de Bononia to work as paratores *in their sugar refinery with two assistants during the entire season for six ounces a month. They promise to produce 17 sacks from every "boiling". They are paid 6 ounces on account in instalments of two each.*

Palermo, 10 February 1440

Source: ASP, Not. Giovanni Traverso, reg. 781, c. 273r.

Minto Xhagueli, a Jewish citizen of Palermo, leases an anvil to Giovanni Spina until the end of August for two tarì.

Palermo, 16 February 1440

Source: ASP, Not. Giovanni Traverso, reg. 781, c. 281v.

Salamon de Missina, Braxhono Amurani, Xamueli Nigiar, Benedetto Caffisu and two others, all Jews, hire themselves out to Giovanni Homodei to work as paratores *in his sugar refinery durng the entire season, except Saturdays, for 5.12.0 ounces, and are paid four ounces on account.*

Palermo, 22 February 1440

Source: ASP, Not. Giovanni Traverso, reg. 781, c. 299r.

Xhayruni Gaczu, Muxa de Girachi, Iacob Coffitor and Vita Simaeli, Jews, promise Masio Crispo to cut and prune all the sugar cane plants in his fields in the contrada *Turris de Brandino, and to provide them with stakes, for eight* tarì *a thousand plants and 16* tarì *a thousand stakes.*

Palermo, 10 March 1440

Source: ASP, Not. Giovanni Traverso, reg. 781, c. 337v.

Braxha Crivaru, a Jewish citizen of Palermo, promises Signorello Pezzunachi, acting for Thomeo de mastro Antoni, to cut and prune the latter's sugar cane for 18 tarì *a thousand plants, and is paid 18* tarì *on account.*

Palermo, 12 April 1440

Source: ASP, Not. Giovanni Traverso, reg. 781, cc. 383v–384r.

Declaration by Czullo Budo, a Jew of Caltabellotta, that he received from Guglielmo Lombardo the sum due to him for digging trenches for the storage of wheat as stipulated in the contract between them.

Note: See above, Doc. p. 6093.

Palermo, 19 May 1440

Source: ASP, Not. Giovanni Traverso, reg. 781, c. 426v.

Braxhuni Amiran and an assistant, Jews, promise Caczettu Iurlandu to prepare the timber for the construction of a carriage. They are to receive seven denari *for each of the smaller pieces and 10* grana *for each of the larger ones. Braxhuni is paid six tarì* on account.

Palermo, 6 June 1440

Source: ASP, Not. Giovanni Traverso, reg. 781, c. nn.

Nissim Ysac, a Jew, declares that he sold Antonio Condarulla a piece of secondhand clothing made of violet silk for 1.24.0 ounces. He receives 18 tarì *on the spot and was promised the balance within four months.*

Palermo, 20 June 1440

Source: ASP, Not. Giovanni Traverso, reg. 781, c. 466r.

Contract for setting up a partnership between David Calabrisi and Iacob Coffiter, Jews, for the sale of tunny. David invests a kantar and 10 rotoli *of fish valued at two ounces, and Iacob undertakes to sell it in Catania or elsewhere. The profits are to be shared by the partners in equal parts.*

Palermo, 19 August 1440

Source: ASP, Not. Giovanni Traverso, reg. 781, cc. 521v–522r.

Sufen Miseria, Xibiteni Xammara, Iusep Ammara and Salamon Rugila, Jews, hire themselves out to Giovanni Bellachera to stack the wood in his sugar refinery during the current season for 10 tarì *a thousand kantars. They also promise to fertilize Giovanni's sugar cane for 18* tarì *a thousand plants, and to cut and prune them for 10* tarì *out of town and 14* tarì *a thousand in town. They are paid 25.5* tarì *on account.*

Palermo, 28 June 1441

Source: ASP, Not. Giovanni Traverso, reg. 781, c. 469r-v.

Salamon de Siracusia, Xhayruni Gaczu and Vita Maltisi, Jews, hire themselves out to Fargione Gaczu, another Jew, acting for Antonio Bayamonte, to work as paratores *in the latter's tunny plant in Salanto on the usual terms, and are paid 10* tarì *each on account.*

Palermo, 28 June 1441

Source: ASP, Not. Giovanni Traverso, reg. 781, c. 470r.

Xilono Braxha and Liuczo Gaczu, Jews, hire themsleves out to Antonio Bayamonte, to work in tunny plant in Solanto during the whole season for one ounce each, and are paid 15 tarì *each on account.*

Palermo, 28 June 1441

Source: ASP, Not. Giovanni Traverso, reg. 781, c. 470v.

Charello Calabrisi, a Jew, hires himself out to Giovanni La Sala, acting for Antonio Bayamonte, to work as filler (iarratino) *in the latter's tunny plant in Solanto during the whole season for 1.6.0 ounces. He is paid 10* tarì *immediately and a* terziolo *of tunny valued at 10* tarì *on 12.9.*

Palermo, 6 July 1441

Source: ASP, Not. Giovanni Traverso, reg. 781, c. 470v.

The brothers Iacob and Lya Coffitor, Jews, hire themselves out to Farchono Caczu, acting for Antonio Bayamonte, to work as fillers in the latter's tunny plant at Solanto during the entire season until the feast of St. John the Baptist for 1.24.0 ounces and are paid one ounce on account.

Palermo, 12 October 1441

Source: ASP, Not. Giovanni Traverso, reg. 782, c. 63v.

Vita Maltisi and Iosep Coyni, Jews, undertake to transport with their beasts of burden 150 kantars of wood for Giovanni Bellachera from the port of Palermo to his sugar refinery for three tarì *a hundred kantars and are paid 12* tarì *on account.*

Palermo, 12 October 1441

Source: ASP, Not. Giovanni Traverso, reg. 782, c. 64r.

Czullu Iubara and Vita Maltisi, Jews, promise Giovanni Bellachera to stack his wood for 10 tarì *a thousand kantars. Czullu is paid 10* tarì *on account, and Vita 7.10.*

Palermo, 16 October 1441

Source: ASP, Not. Giovanni Traverso, reg. 782, c. 81r-v.

Iacobo son of Muxa de Termini, a Jew, promises the notary Pino de Ferro to sole the shoes of his six men, two slaves and five agricultural labourers until September for 1.12.0 ounces, and is paid 27 tarì *on account.*

Palermo, 17 October 1441

Source: ASP, Not. Giovanni Traverso, reg. 782, cc. 84v–85r.

Iusep de Minichi, Lya Safar and Benedetto Catalanu, Jewish citizens of Palermo, promise Giovanni Bellachera to transport wood and food with 12 beasts of burdens from the harbour of Palermo to his sugar refinery. He was to pay five tarì *for a hundred kantars of wood, six* grana *for every* salma *of food and four* grana *for every load of olives. They are paid 1.11.0 ounces on account.*

Palermo, 17 October 1441

Source: ASP, Not. Giovanni Traverso, reg. 782, cc. 87v–88r.

Sufeni Miseria, Xibiteni Xammara, Xilomu Rugila and Xibiteni Balbu, Jews, promise Chicco Salisi, acting for Nicolò de Bononia, to cut and prune his sugar cane in town and outside for 10 and 15 tarì *a thousand plants respectively.*

6097

Palermo, 20 October 1441

Source: ASP, Not. Giovanni Traverso, reg. 782, c. 96r.

The Jewish brothers Xilono and Muxa Xhalfa promise Paolo Pinnysi, acting for Filippo de Miglacio, to stack the wood in the latter's sugar refinery for 8.10 tarì a thousand kantars, and are paid 18 tarì *on account.*

Palermo, 23 November 1441

Source: ASP, Not. Giovanni Traverso, reg. 782, c. 168v.

Iacob de Termini, a Jew, promises Antonello Manueli to sole the shoes of six of his men for 1.6.0 ounces, and is paid 12 tarì *on account.*

Palermo, 15 December 1441

Source: ASP, Not. Giovanni Traverso, reg. 782, c. 192r.

Exchange of a mule for a horse between Iacobo Sufi, a Jew of Caccamo, and Antonio Lupercaro of Polizzi.

Palermo, 5 January 1442

Source: ASP, Not. Giovanni Traverso, reg. 782, c. 235r-v

Master Xibiteni Birdi, a Jew, acknowledges to Giovanni Homodei receipt of 1.3.0 ounces, 27 tarì *in tunny and six in cash, his wages for working on the wall of Giovanni for 1.10* tarì *a day.*

Palermo, 22 January 1442

Source: ASP, Not. Giovanni Traverso, reg. 782, cc. 256v–257r.

Sufeni Miseria, Daniel Xhabirra, Minto Xhaguela, Vita de Missina, Xibiteni Balbu, Xibiteni Xammara and three of their assistants, all Jews, hire themselves out to Giovanni de Bononia to work in his sugar refinery for 7.8.0 ounces a month.

Sicily

Palermo, 23 January 1442

Source: ASP, Not. Giovanni Traverso, reg. 782, c. 263v.

Braxonu Amuranu, Saduni Trapanisi alias Sayita, Xilomu Brixha, Muxa Alluxu, Muxa Aurifichi and two assistants, all Jews, hire themselves out to Giovanni Homodey to work as paratores *in his sugar refinery for 1 ounce a month each. They undertake to produce 18 sacks per "boiling", and are paid on account by Sabet Cuynu, a Jew, 1.24.0 ounces with tunny and 4.6.0 in cash.*

Palermo, 13 March 1442

Source: ASP, Not. Giovanni Traverso, reg. 782, c. 329r-v.

Iosep de Galifu, Xhairuni Gaczu alias Momo and their assistants, all Jews, hire themselves out to Pino de Ferro to fertilize his sugar cane for 16 tarì *a thousand.*

Palermo, 13 March 1442

Source: ASP, Not. Giovanni Traverso, reg. 782, cc. 330v–331r.

Siminto Xhacteni, Vita de Missina, Sansuni Candioni, also on behalf of Farrugio Sicilianu, all Jews, promise mastro Magno de Iohanne to cut and prune 3,000 sugar cane for 8 tarì *a thousand, and are paid 10* tarì *on account.*

Palermo, 23 March 1442

Source: ASP, Not. Giovanni Traverso, reg. 782, c. 343v.

Farchono Burni, Braxhono Sacerdotu, Pinesi Sacerdotu, Minto Xhactinu Farrugio Sichilianu and their assistants, all Jews, hire themselves out to Bartholomeo Columba to fertilize his sugar cane for 27 tarì *a thousand beds* (caselle), *and are paid two ounces on account.*

Palermo, 14 June 1442

Source: ASP, Not. Giovanni Traverso, reg. 782, c. 445v.

Sufen Misiria, Xibiteni Xammara, Xilomu Rugila, Muxa Muxexi, Iusep Ammara, Xibiteni Balbu and Czullu Iubara, Jews, hire themselves out to Giovanni Bellachera to fertilize his sugar for 18 tarì *a thousand beds, and to stack his wood for 10* tarì *a thousand kantars. They are paid 1.10.0 ounces on account.*

Palermo, 3 July 1442

Source: ASP, Not. Giovanni Traverso, reg. 782, c. 479r-v.

Muxa de Cathania, a Jew, together with six other Jews, hires himself out to Antonio Bayamonte to work in his tunny plant at Solanto during the entire season for 1.12.0 ounces, and is paid 9.12.0 ounces on account. Muxa pledges 47 barrels of tunny with Antonio as guarantee, to be returned on completion of the job.

Palermo, September 1442

Source: ASP, Not. Giovanni Traverso, reg. 783, c. 56v.

Master Raymundo de Ricco and Iusep Budaram, a Jews, exchange mules. Raymundo gives Iusep a mule with saddle and bridle in return for a mule and one denaro.

Palermo, 5 October 1442

Source: ASP, Not. Giovanni Traverso, reg. 783, c. 86r.

Salamon de Monso Xalutano, a Jew, hires himself out to Guglielmo Ccxina to salt and treat cheese (ad salandum, gubernandum et inbillicandum caseum et casicavallos includendum) *for 12 and 9* tarì *respectively for every hundred kantars.*

Palermo, 5 October 1442

Source: ASP, Not. Giovanni Traverso, reg. 783, c. 87r.

Sabeti Malti, a Jewish citizen of Palermo, hires himself out to Simon de Mayo and his son Mayo, master shoemakers, to work in their shop and house until Easter for 3 tarì *a month, shoes and food, and is paid five* tarì *on account.*

Palermo, 11 February 1443

Source: ASP, Not. Giovanni Traverso, reg. 783, c. 314r.

Sadya Aczaruti, a Jew, hires himself out to Giovanni Fruntilata, acting for Giovanni Homodei, to work in the latter's sugar refinery and to produce 14 sacks a *"boiling" operation for 2.15.0 ounces a month. He is paid 12* tarì *on account and need not work on Saturdays.*

Palermo, 13 February 1443

Source: ASP, Not. Giovanni Traverso, reg. 783, c. 314v.

Sadya Aczaruti, a Jew, hires himself out to Giovanni Fruntilata, acting for Giovanni Homodei, to stack wood in the latter's sugar refinery during the entire season for eight tarì *a thousand kantars. He is paid 12* tarì *on account.*

Palermo, 15 February 1443

Source: ASP, Not. Giovanni Traverso, reg. 783, c. 320r.

Pasqualis Sacerdotu, Xilomu de Siracusia, Czullu Iubara, Salamon Grecu and their assistants, all Jews, hire themselves out to Giovanni Bellachera to work as paratores *in his sugar refinery and promise to make 15 sacks a "boiling" for five ounces a month. They are paid four ounces on account by the bank of Mariano Aglata.*

Palermo, 22 February 1443

Source: ASP, Not. Giovanni Traverso, reg. 783, cc. 332v–333r.

Iusep Galifa and Vita de Messina, Jews, promise the notary Pino de Ferro to cut and prune his sugar cane in Palermo and out of town for 16 tarì *a thousand plants and nine* tarì *a thousand seedlings. They are paid 12* tarì *on account. The notary is to provide the tools.*

Palermo, 1 March 1443

Source: ASP, Not. Giovanni Traverso, reg. 783, c. 343r-v.

Muxa Galifu and Nissimi Barabarusso de Tripuli, Jews, hire themselves out to Giovanni Xixi, acting for the notary Filippo de Miglacio, to stack the wood in the latter's sugar refinery during the whole season for 8.10 tarì *a thousand kantars. They are paid 15* tarì *on account On 4 April Sansuni Condictu and Robino de Girachi, Jews, undertake to do the work in their stead.*

Palermo, 20 February 1450

Source: ASP, Not. Giovanni Traverso, reg. 783, cc. 311v–312r.

Iuda Cuchilla, Sadya Iocundi, Xilomu Brixha, Busacca de Ansaluni, Xilomu Galifa and two assistants, all Jews, hire themselves out to Nicolò de Bononia, acting also for Bartholomeo de Bononia, to work as paratores *in their sugar refinery for six ounces a month. They are to make 18 sacks a "boiling", and are paid four ounces on account.*

Palermo, 25 February 1450

Source: ASP, Not. Giovanni Traverso, reg. 783, c. 325r-v.

Iuseppi Bonu, a Jew, hires himself out to Pino Crispo to work during the whole season in his tunny plant at Arenella for one ounce. He is paid 12 tarì *on account.*

Palermo, 27 February 1450

Source: ASP, Not. Giovanni Traverso, reg. 783, c. 332v.

Braxhono Amiranu and Muxa Rugila and eight others, all Jews, hire themselves out to Giuliano de Riggio to prune and fertilize his sugar cane on the terms agreed on the previous year. They are paid three ounces on account.

Palermo, 2 March 1450

Source: ASP, Not. Giovanni Traverso, reg. 783, c. 335r.

Xibiten Xammara, Benedicto Catalanu, Czullu Iubara, Xibiten Balbu, Daniel Xhabirra and three assistants, all Jews, hire themselves out to Chicco Salici, acting for Giovanni Bononia, to work as paratores *in the latter's sugar refinery for 6.14.0 ounces a month. They are paid 6.14.0 ounces on account.*

Palermo, 17 June 1450

Source: ASP, Not. Giovanni Traverso, reg. 783, cc. 502v–503r.

Deed whereby Merdoc Farachi, a Jew, tranferred to his daughter Xhanna on her marriage the balance left of the chittubba *of Sisa, his wife and Xhanna's mother.*

Sicily

Palermo, 29 October 1443

Source: ASP, Not. Giovanni Traverso, reg. 784, c. 161v.

Pinesi Sacerdotu, Sufeni Misiria, Xibiten Xammara, Marco de Vita, Vita de Messina, also on behalf of Xibiten Balbu, and three assistants, all Jews, hire themselves out to Chicco Salisi, acting for Giovanni de Bononia, to work as paratores *in the latter's sugar refinery for 7.8.0 ounces a month. They are paid 3.19.0 ounces on account.*

Palermo, 5 November 1443

Source: ASP, Not. Giovanni Traverso, reg. 784, cc. 173v.

Iusep Terminisi, a Jew, hires himself out to Giovanni de Bononia to work in his sugar refinery for 1.6.0 ounces a month, and is paid one month's salary on account. Sabet Coffinu, a Jew, stands surety for Iusep.

Palermo, 6 November 1443

Source: ASP, Not. Giovanni Traverso, reg. 784, c. 180r.

Simon de Mayu and his son Mayu, Jews, promise Antonio Manuel to sole the shoes of three of his men until the end of August for 6.10 tarì *per person.*

Palermo, 6 November 1443

Source: ASP, Not. Giovanni Traverso, reg. 784, cc. 161v.

Salamon de Monsor, a Jew, promises Guglielmo Nixina to treat with salt his cacio *and* caciocavallo *stored in Guglielmo's warehouse for 12* tarì *the quintal for the first and 10 for the second. He is paid six* tarì *on account.*

Palermo, 27 January 1444

Source: ASP, Not. Giovanni Traverso, reg. 784, cc. 320v–321r.

Cataldo de Florio and the Jews Iusep Ammara, Salamon Grecu, Czullu Iubara and their assistants hire themselves out to Antonio Balestra, acting for Giovanni Bellachera, to work as paratores *in the latter's sugar refinery for five ounces a month. They are paid four ounces on account.*

Palermo, 28 January 1444

Source: ASP, Not. Giovanni Traverso, reg. 784, c. 321r.

Czullu Iubara and Vita Maltisi, Jews, hire themselves out to Antonio Balestra, acting for Giovanni Bellachera, to stack the wood in the latter's sugar refinery for the wages agreed on the previous year. They are paid 20 tarì *on account.*

Palermo, 1 September 1444

Source: ASP, Not. Giovanni Traverso, reg. 784, c. 2v.

Daniel Xhactu, a Jew, hires himself out to Antonio Bayamonte to work in the tunny plant in Termini Imerese for 24 tarì *a month during the entire season. He is paid 24* tarì *on account.*

Palermo, 1 October 1444

Source: ASP, Not. Giovanni Traverso, reg. 784, c. 42r.

Symon de Mayu and his son Mayu, Jews, promise Antonello Manueli to sole the shoes of six of his men until the end of August. They are paid 28 tarì *on account.*

Palermo, 2 October 1444

Source: ASP, Not. Giovanni Traverso, reg. 784, c. 43r.

Liuni Romanu, a Jew, hires himself out to Giovanni Russo, acting for Giovanni de Bononia, to work in the latter's sugar refinery for one tarì *a day in the warehouse and 1.5* tarì *outside. He is paid 18* tarì *on account.*

Palermo, 10 October 1444

Source: ASP, Not. Giovanni Traverso, reg. 784, c. 55v.

Manuel Rugila, a Jewish citizen of Palermo, hires himself out to Sabeti Coffino and Abraham Calabresi, Jews, acting for Giovanni Crispo, to work as paratores *in the latter's sugar refinery. He is paid 18* tarì *on account.*

Sicily

Palermo, 9 November 1444

Source: ASP, Not. Giovanni Traverso, reg. 784, c. 93r-v.

Galluffu Romanu, a Jewish citizen of Palermo, hires himself out to Antonio Bayamonte to work in his tunny plant at Solanto during the whole season for 27 tarì *a month, and is paid 15* tarì *on account.*

Palermo, 10 November 1444

Source: ASP, Not. Giovanni Traverso, reg. 784, c. 96v.

Momo Gaczu, Musutu Miseria, Busacca de Siracusia and assistants, Jews, hire themselves out to work as paratores *in the sugar refinery of Giovanni de Homodei for five ounces a month, and are paid five ounces on account.*

Palermo, 10 November 1444

Source: ASP, Not. Giovanni Traverso, reg. 784, c. 97r-v.

Iusep Bechu (Nechu), a Jew of Termini Imerese, declares that he surrenders to Giovanni Thuchio his lease on a house which the latter had let him for 13 tarì *a year. He also declares that he still owes Thuchio one ounce which he promises to pay in four annual instalments.*

Palermo, 24 December 1444

Source: ASP, Not. Giovanni Traverso, reg. 784, cc. 156v–157r.

Pasquale Sacerdoto, Farchonu Gaczu, Merdoc Gaczu and two assistants, Jews, hire themselves out to Nicolò de Bononia to work as paratores *in his sugar refinery for five ounces a month.*

Palermo, 12 January 1445

Source: ASP, Not. Giovanni Traverso, reg. 784, c. 172r.

Cataldo de Florio and the Jews Czullu Iubaru, Salamon Grecu and Danieli Xhaccu, as well as two assistants, hire themselves out to Pietro Bellachera to work as paratores *in his sugar refinery for five ounces a month, and receive 2.15.0 ounces on account.*

Palermo, 13 January 1445

Source: ASP, Not. Giovanni Traverso, reg. 784, c. 177r.

Xibiteni Xammara, Xibiteni Balbu, Iusep Cammara, Salamon Balbu, Daniel Xabirra and two assistants, all Jews, hire themselves out to Giovanni de Bononia to work as paratores *in his sugar refinery for 6.6.0 ounces a month, and are paid two ounces on account.*

Palermo, 28 January 1445

Source: ASP, Not. Giovanni Traverso, reg. 784, c. 198r.

Pasquale Sacerdotu, Farchonu Gaczu, Merdoc Gaczu, Liuczu Gaczu and six assistants, Jews, hire themselves out to Nicolò de Bononia to fertilize his sugar cane for 16 tarì *a thousand, and are paid two ounces on account.*

Palermo, 16 February 1445

Source: ASP, Not. Giovanni Traverso, reg. 784, c. 222r-v.

Deed whereby Paolo de Vegna sets out the payments to Onorato de Gauyu, a Jew, following judgements given in Onorato's favour. The debt amounts to 19 ounces.

Die XVI frebruarii, VIII Indicionis

Paulus de Vegna presens coram nobis sponte confessus extitit se teneri et dare debere Honorato de Gauyu, Iudeo, uncias decem et novi auri ponderis generalis, tam vigore certarum sententiarum in magna curia et in aliis iudiciis latarum. Pro qua pecunia iam fuisset carceratus, qua ex causa restitutis finalis racionis facte inter eos de omnibus quibuscumque iuribus, racionibus et causis inter eos gestis et administratis ad olim usque ad presentem diem renunciatis. Quam pecuniam dictus Paulus dare eidem Iudeo stipulanti et solvere promisit modo infrascripto, videlicet uncias duas in festo pasce surrectionis proxime future, et uncias tres per totum mensem Augusti anni presentis, et totam reliquam pecuniam inde ad annos tres, quolibet anno ipsorum trium annorum terciam partem. Et si defecerit in una solucione, possit ipse Iudeus petere totum debitum predictum, non obstante quod nondum tempus solucionis venerit. Que omnia et singula dicti contrahentes, maxime ipse Paulus, promiserunt rata habere in pace, sine lite et sub ypotheca omnium suorum bonorum habitorum et habendorum ac reficione dampnorum, interesse, expensarum, litis et extra, renunciatis moratoriis, guidatici, cessioni bonorum, privilegio agrigentino, et omnibus aliis graciis, et omnes note et scripture alie ad olim usque ad presentem diem inter eos facte, preter presens nota, sint cassa, irrita, et nullius valoris. Pro quo Paulo, etc., Iacobus et Iohannes de Vegna filiis inde premissis observandis coram nobis sponte in solidum fideiusserunt, renunciando legitime de pluribus reis debendis beneficio novarum constitucionum iuri de primo principali contraveniendo et omnia bona eorum proinde obligando, renunciantes et renunciant dictus Paulus et omnibus per dictum Paulum ut supra renunciatis.

Testes: Magnificus dominus Iohannes de Tudisco, Salvator de Iuliano et Antonellus de Panormo, scutifer dicti domini Iohannes.

Palermo, 17 February 1445

Source: ASP, Not. Giovanni Traverso, reg. 784, c. 225r-v.

Czullu Iubara, Braxhonu Simaeli, Minto Gibbe and four assistants, all Jews, promise Pietro Bellachera to fertilize his sugar cane durint the current season for 17 tarì *a thousand, and are paid six* tarì *on account.*

Palermo, 8 March 1445

Source: ASP, Not. Giovanni Traverso, reg. 784, c. 250r-v.

Lyocta Griczella and Braxhono Admiranu, a Jew, and eight other Jews hire themselves out to Giovanni de Bononia to fertilize 10,000 of his sugar cane plants for 16 tarì *a thousand. They are paid two ounces on account.*

Palermo, 4 March 1445

Source: ASP, Not. Giovanni Traverso, reg. 784, c. 262v.

Aczarono Migliarusu, master builder, and Merdoc Xhabirra, builder, Jewish citizens of Palermo, promise Pietro Maurichi to carry out construction work on his property, including foundations, walls and so forth, for four tarì *a* canna. *They are paid 9.10* tarì *on account.*

Palermo, 12 March 1445

Source: ASP, Not. Giovanni Traverso, reg. 784, c. 278r.

Farrugio Malti, a Jew of Sciacca, hires himself out to Gauyu Sardignolo, a Jew of Mussomeli, acting also for his father Sabatino, to work for him as shoemakers for two years for 1.6.0 ounces and some clothes.

Palermo, 16 March 1445

Source: ASP, Not. Giovanni Traverso, reg. 784, c. 288r-v.

Xibiteni Xammara, Xibiteni Balbu and Iusep Ammara, Jews, undertake to stack the wood in the sugar refinery of Giovanni de Bononia for 7.10 tarì a thousand kantars. They are paid 15 tarì *on account.*

Palermo, 7 April 1445

Source: ASP, Not. Giovanni Traverso, reg. 784, c. 320r.

Xua and Braxhono de Girgenti, Jews, hire themselves out with as many men as necessary to Giovanni Crispo to work in hs sugar refinery for six ounces a month, and are paid four ounces on account.

Palermo, 7 April 1445

Source: ASP, Not. Giovanni Traverso, reg. 784, c. 320v.

Salamon Monsor, a Jew, undertakes to treat all the cheese and caciocavallo *in Guglielmo Cuxina's warehouse for 12* tarì *a hundred kantars, and is paid 12* tarì *on account.*

Palermo, 12 April 1445

Source: ASP, Not. Giovanni Traverso, reg. 784, cc. 326v–327r.

Matheo de Noto, a Jew of Syracuse, hires himself out to Filippo de Bellachera to work in his tunny plant at San Giorgio during the entire season for one ounce. He is paid six tarì *on account.*

Palermo, 13 April 1445

Source: ASP, Not. Giovanni Traverso, reg. 784, c. 330r.

Vita Aram, a Jew, hires himself out to Giorgio de Piroxia, a dyer, to work in his business until the end of August for the usual wages and under the normal conditions.

Palermo, 14 April 1445

Source: ASP, Not. Giovanni Traverso, reg. 784, c. 331r-v.

Nissim Rugila, a Jew, hires himself out to Tubia Gibal, a Jewish smith, to work in his business for 18 tarì *a month until the extinction of Nissim's debt to Masio de Gilberto. Tubia is to hand Nissim's wages to Masio.*

Palermo, 30 april 1445

Source: ASP, Not. Giovanni Traverso, reg. 784, c. 355v.

Salamon, son of Liuni Actuni, a Jew, declares that he owes Antonio Faczella 1.18.0 ounces, the balance due Antonio after the final accounting of a joint venture. Salamon promises to pay in weekly instalments of two tarì.

Palermo, 30 April 1445

Source: ASP, Not. Giovanni Traverso, reg. 784, c. 356r.

Merdoc and Liuczu Gaczu, Jews, hire themselves out to Nicolò de Bononia to stack the wood in his sugar refinery for 7.10 tarì *a thousand kantars, and are paid 7.10* tarì *on account.*

Palermo, 31 May 1445

Source: ASP, Not. Giovanni Traverso, reg. 784, cc. 378v–379r.

Giovanni de Chimirella and Lya Safar, a Jew, exchange two beasts of burden for a horse and 12 tarì.

Palermo, 22 June 1445

Source: ASP, Not. Giovanni Traverso, reg. 784, c. 411r-v.

Xharono Momo, Xilomu Brixha and Iusep Ammara promise Francesco de Ventimiglia to dig trenches, each holding 50 salme *of grain, on his farm for a price agreed on. They are paid one ounce on account.*

Palermo, 22 June 1445

Source: ASP, Not. Giovanni Traverso, reg. 784, cc. 411v–412r.

Deed of sale whereby Nicolò de Lunardo, Giovanni de Oddo and Matheo Lu Gallu sell Iacob de Termini and Lya Sadia, Jews, 16 salme *of myrtle for 4.15.0 ounces the* salma. *One ounce is paid on account.*

Palermo, 25 June 1445

Source: ASP, Not. Giovanni Traverso, reg. 784, c. 412v.

Deed of sale whereby Paquale Sacerdotu, a Jewish citizen of Palermo, sells Antonio Balestra a black slave girl for 10 ounces. Antonio cedes to Pasquale six ounces owed him Aloysia de Reinaldo and 1.4.0 ounces owed him by Muxa Fima, a Jew, and pays the balance in cash. On 16 July Antonio returns the slave to Pasquale, who promises to return 8.22.0 ounces in several instalments.

Palermo, 6 July 1445

Source: ASP, Not. Giovanni Traverso, reg. 784, c. 249r.

Iuda Madocca, a Jew, hires himself out to Pietro Bellachera to work in his sugar refinery as cane grinder (machinator cannamellarum) *at one* tarì *for each "boiling", and is paid 15* tarì *on account.*

Palermo, 21 July 1445

Source: ASP, Not. Giovanni Traverso, reg. 784, c. 433r.

Sabatino Chabrellu and Braxhono Liali, Jews, hire themselves out to Antonio Bayamonte to work in his tunny plant at Termini Imerese for 13.10 tarì *each.*

Palermo, 31 August 1445

Source: ASP, Not. Giovanni Traverso, reg. 784, c. 439v.

Xharuni Gaczu, Benedictu Braxhanellu and Michilono Ysac, Jews, undertake to dig a trench in Francesco Ventimiglia's vineyard for two ounces, and are paid 22 tarì on account.

Palermo, 5 July 1444

Source: ASP, Not. Giovanni Traverso, reg. 785, c. 578r.

Deed of sale whereby Gilberto de Lugena, lord of Carini, sells David Pulisi, a Jew, the gabella di lu sagatu *for a year for 3.12.0 ounces. Gilberto promises David not to allow another shoemaker to do business in his territory. If David fails up to live to his commitment, he must pay Gilberto the entire tax and Gilberto may allow other shoemakers to ply their trade in Carini.*

Bibliography: Bresc, *Arabi*, p. 218 and n. 1034.

Palermo, 2 September 1445

Source: ASP, Not. Giovanni Traverso, reg. 785, c. 8r.

Nicolò Blundu and Enrico de Ventimiglia, rectors of the New Hospital in Palermo, let Francesco de Ventimiglia the meat stalls of the Jews for four years for 24 ounces a year.

Die secundo septembris none indictionis
Nobilis Nicolaus Blundu et Henricus de Vigintimiliis, rectores, ut dixerunt novi hospitalis, locaverunt nomine et pro parte dicti hospitalis nobili Francisco de Vigintimiglio presenti et conducenti, plancas Iudeorum seu Iudaice Panormi cum omnibus suis iuribus et pertinenciis, ut est consuetum, pro annis quattuor infrascriptis, videlicet decime, undecime, duodecime et tercie decime inditionis proxime future pro precio seu loherio unciarum vigintiquatuor pro quolibet anno ipsorum quatuor annorum. Quod loherium seu quam pensionem dictus nobilis Franciscus eisdem nobilibus Nicolao et Henrico nomine dicti hospitalis stipulanti dare et solvere promisit dicto hospitali de anno in annum, de tercio in tercium, ut est consuetum, pronmictentes dicti rectores quos supra nomine eidem nobili Francisco stipulanti predictas plancas tempore ipso

durante legitime defendere ab omni calumpniante persona, etc. Que omnia promiserunt rata habere, in pace, de plano, sine lite, sub ypotheca omnium suorum bonorum habitorum et habendorum ac refectione dampnorum, interesse, expensarum litis et cetera. Renunciantes, etc. Et fiat ritus, etc. Et iuraverunt, etc.

Testes: Dominus Bernardus de Bandino, Iacobus Lombardu, Iohannes Romanu dictus Buchardu.

Palermo, 25 September 1445

Source: ASP, Not. Giovanni Traverso, reg. 785, c. 37r-v.

Agreement whereby Musutu de Catrogiovanni alias Cheno, a Jew, is granted by Caterina, widow of Nicolò Tuczu and guardian of Giovaniella, a moratorium of five years on the payment of 12 ounces, the price of a black slave.

Palermo, 5 October 1445

Source: ASP, Not. Giovanni Traverso, reg. 785, c. 62r.

Georgio Caputo and Nicolò Cordova hire themselves out to Czullo Vidu, a Jew to work as (sack) fillers in the sugar refinery of Giovanni Crispo for 1 ounce a month each, and are paid 18 tarì *on account each. They promise to work on Saturdays and whenever Czullo is sick.*

Palermo, 5 October 1445

Source: ASP, Not. Giovanni Traverso, reg. 785, cc. 63v–64r.

Symon de Mayu alias Sufeni Rabi Iacob and his son Mayu, Jews, promise Antonello Manueli to sole the shoes of the men at his farm until the end of August for 6.10 tarì *each.*

Palermo, 14 October 1445

Source: ASP, Not. Giovanni Traverso, reg. 785, cc. 91v–92r.

Galluffu Farachi, a Jew, hires himself out to master Sufeni Rabi Iacob and his son Mayu, Jewish shoemakers, to work in their tannery inside and outside town for three months. He is to be paid 1 ounce, food, shoes and clothes for each of the first two years, and two ounces for the third.

6112

Palermo, 15 October 1445

Source: ASP, Not. Giovanni Traverso, reg. 785, c. 99r.

Braxhono lu Liali, a Jewish citizen of Palermo, hires himself out to Giovanni Crispo, a knight, acting on behalf of Giovanni de Bononia, to work in the latter's sugar refinery during the whole season. He is to perform all tasks and to make at least three "boilings" a week for one tarì *a "boiling", and is paid 15* tarì *on account.*

Palermo, 15 October 1445

Source: ASP, Not. Giovanni Traverso, reg. 785, c. 99r-v.

Xibiten Galifa, a Jewish citizen of Palermo, hires himself out to the knight Giovanni Crispo to work in his sugar refinery during the entire season and to make at least three "boilings" a week for one tarì *a "boiling". He is paid 15* tarì *on account.*

Palermo, 20 October 1445

Source: ASP, Not. Giovanni Traverso, reg. 785, cc. 113v–114r.

Master Andreas de Lu Muncti, a builder, promises Braxhono Panichello, a Jew, to build a shop in front of the Jewish quarter [in Palermo] for 3.15 tarì *a* canna. *He is paid six* tarì *on account.*

Eodem [20 Oct. 1445, IX ind.]
Magister Andreas de Lu Muncti, murator civis Panormi, coram nobis sponte promisit et convenit Braxhono Panichello, Iudeo, presenti et stipulanti, murare et facere de maramma apotecham unam a fachi la Iudeca di li fundamenti necessarii et consueti et di alticza consueta cum lu so pendenti, sencza intaglu abucactu et staglato cum omni stratu et spisi di lu Iudeu predictu, ecceptu di magisteriu et manuali, li quali divi pagari lu dictu magistru Andrea. Ad quod servicium incipere debet ad requisicionem dicti Iudei et cum inceperit debeat continuare et a lui plui tardu darila spachiata per tuctu lu misi di aprili anni presentis, pro stipendio tarenorum trium granorum quindecim pro qualibet canna. De quo stipendio dictus Iudeus presencialiter tradidit dicto magistro Andree tarenos sex, reliquum stipendium sibi solvere promisit successive. Que omnia promiserunt rata habere, etc., etc. Pro quo magistro Andrea, etc. de

premissis omnibus observandis magister Manuellus de Nicotera coram nobis fideiussit et se constituit principalem solutorem et debitorem, etc. etc.

Testes: Blasius de Deo, presbiter Bartholomeus de Virczilio, Antonius Morellu.

Palermo, 1 November 1445

Source: ASP, Not. Giovanni Traverso, reg. 785, c. 150r-v.

Sufeni Rabi Iacob and his son Mayir Rabi Iacob, Jews, promise the notary Pino de Ferro to sole the shoes of four of his slaves for a year for 25.10 tarì. *The payment includes the the sale of some leather.*

Palermo, 1 November 1445

Source: ASP, Not. Giovanni Traverso, reg. 785, c. 102v.

Iuda de Minichi, a Jew, promises Pietro Bellachera to transport with his four beasts of burden sugar cane to Giovanni's sugar refinery for seven tarì *a hundred* salme *and is paid two ounces on account.*

Palermo, 17 November 1445

Source: ASP, Not. Giovanni Traverso, reg. 785, c. 197r.

Pasquale Bulfarachi, a Jew, hires himself out to Robino de Girachio to work in the sugar refinery of Giovanni Chimencio during the whole season for 21 tarì *a month and, is paid 21* tarì *on account.*

Palermo, 13 January 1446

Source: ASP, Not. Giovanni Traverso, reg. 785, c. 349r.

Salamone de Monsor, a Jewish citizen of Palermo, hires himsefl out to Guglielmo Cuxina to treat cheese (salmoriandum et gubernandum casuem et casi cavallo) *for 10* tarì *the kantar and is paid 11* tarì *on account.*

Palermo, 8 February 1446

Source: ASP, Not. Giovanni Traverso, reg. 785, cc. 399v–400r.

Czullu Iubera, a Jew, and eight men hire themselves out to Pietro Bellachera to cut and prune the sugar cane of Giovanni Bellachera.

Palermo, 13 May 1446

Source: ASP, Not. Giovanni Traverso, reg. 785, c. 637r.

Declaration by Sabeti Missinisi, a Jew, that he received 12 tarì *from master Nicolò Failla as rent for an anvil.*

Palermo, 4 July 1446

Source: ASP, Not. Giovanni Traverso, reg. 785, cc. 713v–714r.

Nicolò de la Motta of Pollina and Gimilono Naxhay, a Jew, set up a joint business venture. Nicolò invests 30 ounces and Gimilono 29. Gimilono is to buy caciocavallo, *iron and other goods and sell them. The proceeds are to be deposited in the bank of Matheo de Crapona, to be invested in other merchandise [end of Doc. washed out].*

Palermo, 7 July 1446

Source: ASP, Not. Giovanni Traverso, reg. 785, cc. 714v–715v.

Contract for the let of a house and a shoemaker's shop in Palermo, in the Platea Marmorea, bordering on the house of Nissim Binna, by Manuel Chetibi, a Jewish citizen of Messina, also on behalf of his brother Farachio. They are the heirs of the late master Moyse Chetibi and let the property, with the consent of the guardian Iosep de Braxhono, another Jew, to master Gabriele de Villalta for an annual rent of seven ounces. Iosep, in his capacity of guardian, now relets the property on the same terms to Federico de Sinibaldi for nine years, on the condition that Federico makes the necessary repairs to the property. [Part of the Doc. is washed out].

Palermo, 17 October 1446

Source: ASP, Not. Giovanni Traverso, reg. 785, c. 40r-v.

Contract for the lease of an olive press by Robertu Titu to Benedetto Catalano,

David de Termini and Iuda de Minichi, Jews, for the entire season. The press is situated in the Kalsa quarter of Palermo. The rent agreed on is one ounce, provided the lessees undertake to renew the tools and equipment. They also undertake to press the olives of Roberto and of his son for one tarì *the* salma *and to give them the kernels.*

Palermo, 1 December 1446

Source: ASP, Not. Giovanni Traverso, reg. 785, c. 190r.

Symon Rabbi Iacob and his son Mayu, Jews, promise Antonellus Manueli to sole the shoes of three men on his farm until the end of August for 6.10 tarì *each. They need not work on holidays.*

Palermo, 24 December 1446

Source: ASP, Not. Giovanni Traverso, reg. 785, c. 210v.

Xibiteni, Farchono, Merdoc and Liuczu Gaczu as well as Lyocta Gaczella, Jews, and three assistants hire themselves out to Nicolò Bononia to work as paratores *in his sugar refinery for 6.8.0 ounces a month, and are paid 4 ounces on account. They are to be paid another two ounces on the completion of the job, and the balance at a later date.*

Palermo, 16 January 1447

Source: ASP, Not. Giovanni Traverso, reg. 785, cc. 246v–247r.

Liuczu Gaczu, Xilomu Aczara, Busacca Xagaruni, Lya de Fromento and eight others, all Jews, hire themselves out to Antonio de Nicolò, acting for Nicolò de Bononia, to fertilize his sugar cane during the entire season for 16 tarì *a thousand plant beds. They are paid two ounces on account.*

Palermo, 18 January 1447

Source: ASP, Not. Giovanni Traverso, reg. 785, cc. 248v–249v.

Deed whereby Aloisia de Raynaldo promises Pietro de Calabro to return 10 ounces which Pietro had paid for a black slave girl and which had been claimed by Yannina de Calabro. Damichu, a Jew had acted for Aloisia.

Palermo, 23 January 1447

Source: ASP, Not. Giovanni Traverso, reg. 785, c. 267r-v.

Salamon de Monsor, a Jew, promises Guglielmo Mixina to treat (salmoriare) *his cheese and* caciocavallo *during the whole year for 10* tarì *a hundred kantars and 12* tarì *for those at the warehouse.*

Palermo, 28 January 1447

Source: ASP, Not. Giovanni Traverso, reg. 785, c. nn.

Xibiteni Xammara, Xibiteni Balbu, Vita Maltisi, Czullus Iubara, Daniel Xhabirra nd three assistants, Jews, hire themselves out to Giovanni de Bononia to work as paratores *in his sugar refinery during the whole season and to make 18 sacks a "boiling" for 6.14.0 ounces a month. They are paid 2.14.0 ounces on account.*

Palermo, 25 February 1447

Source: ASP, Not. Giovanni Traverso, reg. 785, c. 344r.

Minto Gibbesi and Lya de Marsala and four assistants, all Jews, hire themselves out to Pino Ysolda [washed out].

Palermo, 6 March 1447

Source: ASP, Not. Giovanni Traverso, reg. 785, c. 357r.

Iuda Millach, a Jewish citizen of Palermo, promises Antonio Bellachera, acting for Pietro Bellachera, to grind the latter's sugar cane during the coming year for one tarì *a "boiling". He is paid 10* tarì *on account.*

Palermo, 16 March 1447

Source: ASP, Not. Giovanni Traverso, reg. 785, cc. 389v–390r.

Robino de Girachi, Mussutu Miseria, Galluf[f]u Ammara, Ysdrael de Girachi and seven assistants, Jews, hire themselves out to Antonio de mastro Antonio to hoe his sugar cane plantation for 1.6.0 ounces [washed out].

Palermo, 13 June 1447

Source: ASP, Not. Giovanni Traverso, reg. 785, c. 543r-v.

Xibiten Xammara, Iusep Xammara and Xibiten Balbu and seven assistants, Jews, hire themselves out to Iacobo Bellachera to fertilize his sugar cane for 1.6.0 ounces [washed out].

Palermo, 30 October 1447

Source: ASP, Not. Giovanni Traverso, reg. 786, c. 98r-v.

Contract whereby Salamon alias Bulxhayra Millac, a Jewish builder, hires himself out to fra Bonifacio de Bono, abbot of S. Spirito, to do such work as is required of him, as long as it is in Palermo, for 30 days for 1.15 tarì *a day. He is paid 20* tarì *on account.*

Palermo, 2 November 1447

Source: ASP, Not. Giovanni Traverso, reg. 786, c. 105r-v.

Salamon Monsor, a Jew, promises Guglielmo Cuxina to treat (salmoriare et salare) *his cheese and* caciocavallo *for 10* tarì *a hundred kantars if done in Guglielmo's shop and for 12* tarì *if carried out in Guglielmo's warehouse.*

Palermo, 8 November 1447

Source: ASP, Not. Giovanni Traverso, reg. 786, c. 112r-v.

Contract between Nicolò de La Motta and Gimilono Naguay, a Jew, for setting up a joint venture. Nicolò invested 50 ounces and Gimilono 30. The money was deposited in the bank of Mario Bonconte. Gimilono was to buy cheese, caciocavallo, *iron and other goods, and trade in them. The profits were to be divided between the partners in equal shares.*

Sicily

Palermo, 29 November 1447

Source: ASP, Not. Giovanni Traverso, reg. 786, c. 158v.

Guglielmo Bucheri and Iosep de Girachi, a Jew, agree to exchange animals. Iosep gives Guglielmo a lame mule for another beast of burden.

Palermo, 29 December 1447

Source: ASP, Not. Giovanni Traverso, reg. 786, c. 207r.

The brothers Farchono, Liuczu and Merdoc Gaczu, Sabutu Xagaruni, also on behalf of Xibiteni Gaczu their partner, as well as three assistants, all Jews, put themselves at the service of Chicco Bononia to work as paratores *in the sugar refinery of Nicolò de Bononia during the entire season for 6.8.0 ounces a month.*

Palermo, 30 January 1448

Source: ASP, Not. Giovanni Traverso, reg. 786, c. 277r-v.

Braxhono Xireribi and seven assistants, all Jews, hire themselves out to Chicco Salisi to fertilize 4,000 sugar cane beds of Giovanni de Bononia for 16 tarì *a thousand. 1.2.0 ounces are paid on account to David Serruni, a Jew.*

Palermo, 7 February 1448

Source: ASP, Not. Giovanni Traverso, reg. 786, c. 287r.

Lya de Marsala, Minto Gibbesi, Vita de Ram and three assistants, all Jews, promise to fertilize the sugar cane of Pino de Ysolda for 16.10 tarì *for a thousand beds. Pino is to furnish the requirements and pays 24* tarì *on account.*

Palermo, 9 February 1448

Source: ASP, Not. Giovanni Traverso, reg. 786, c. 293r.

Czullu Iubara, Saduni Simael, Maxhamectu de Marsali, Jews, promise Chicco Salisi to stack the wood in the sugar refinery of Giovanni de Bononia during the whole season for 7.10 tarì *a thousand kantars, and are paid 18* tarì *on account.*

Bibliography: Bresc, *Arabi*, p. 43.

Palermo, 9 February 1448

Source: ASP, Not. Giovanni Traverso, reg. 786, c. 293v.

Xhayarono Levi and seven others, all Jews, promise Chicco Salisi to fertilize 4,000 sugar cane beds of Giovanni de Bononia for 16 tarì *a thousand beds and are paid 1.2.0 ounces on account.*

Palermo, 4 March 1448

Source: ASP, Not. Giovanni Traverso, reg. 786, c. 362r.

Xamuel Balbu, a Jew, hires himself out to Giovanni Archella to work in the sugar refinery of Giovanni de Bononia on the terms of the other workers, and is paid 1.15.0 ounces on account.

Palermo, 7 March 1448

Source: ASP, Not. Giovanni Traverso, reg. 786, c. 364v.

Daniel Xhabirra, Vita Maltisi, Czullu Iubara, Xibiteni Xammara, also on behalf of Xibiteni Balbu and three assistants, all Jews, hire themselves out to work as paratores *in the sugar refinery of Giovanni de Bononia during the entire season for 6.14.0 ounces. They are paid four ounces on account through David Farachi, a Jew.*

Palermo, 8 March 1448

Source: ASP, Not. Giovanni Traverso, reg. 786, c. 367r.

Iuda Chuchilla, Xilomu Brixha, Muxa Meme, Braxhono Simael, another person and two assistants, all Jews, hire themselves out to Antonio de Antonio to work as paratores *in his sugar refinery for six ounces a month, and are paid four ounces on account.*

Palermo, 13 March 1448

Source: ASP, Not. Giovanni Traverso, reg. 786, c. 383r.

Giovanni de Sulito acknowledges to Muxa Grafari, a Jew of Mazara, receipt of 26 tarì *arising out of an earlier commitment.*

6120

Sicily

Palermo, 13 March 1448

Source: ASP, Not. Giovanni Traverso, reg. 786, c. 383r-v.

Farchono Berni and Iusep Ammara with three assistants, all Jews, hire themselves out to Giovanni Maurichi to cut and prune 4,000 new sugar cane beds in the contrada *Favara, starting work at Easter, for 8.10* tarì *a thousand, The implements are to be provided by Giovanni.*

Palermo, 18 March 1448

Source: ASP, Not. Giovanni Traverso, reg. 786, cc. 385v–386r.

Lya Safer and 10 assistants, Jews, promise Nicolò Faudali to cut and prune the sugar cane of Friderico Migliacio for 16 tarì *a thousand for old plants and three* tarì *for new ones.*

Palermo, 29 August 1448

Source: ASP, Not. Giovanni Traverso, reg. 786, c. 631r.

Muxa Catanisi and Xhayrono Levi, Jews, promise Chicco Salisi, to fertilize together with eight other Jews 2,000 sugar cane beds of Giovanni de Bononia for 16 tarì *a thousand and are paid 24* tarì *on account.*

Palermo, 2 September 1448

Source: ASP, Not. Giovanni Traverso, reg. 786, c. 1r.

Braxhono Xiraribi, a Jew, hires himself out to Chicco Salisi, to work in Giovanni de Bononia's sugar refinery as grinder for one tarì *a "boiling". He also promises to fertilize 8,000 of Giovanni's sugar cane beds together with 12 other men for six* tarì *a thousand.*

Palermo, 30 October 1448

Source: ASP, Not. Giovanni Traverso, reg. 786, c. 202v.

Contract between master Pietro de Martino, smith, and master Nissim Gerson, Jewish smith and farrier, to set up a joint venture to last a year. They agree to open a shop on the waterfront on the following terms: Pietro is to invest all the implements valued at one ounce and the shop, valued at 2.12.0 ounces; iron and coal are to be provided by both partners; they are to invest their labour; profits are to be divided at every day's end in equal shares.

Bibliography: Bresc, *Arabi*, p. 199 and n. 940 (who has 31.10).

Palermo, 31 October 1448

Source: ASP, Not. Giovanni Traverso, reg. 786, cc. 203v–204r.

Deed of sale whereby Bernardo Palo, a Catalan, sells the partners Peri de Martino and master Nixim Gerson a black horse, sick and lame, for nine tarì.

Palermo, 12 January 1449

Source: ASP, Not. Giovanni Traverso, reg. 786, c. 253r-v.

Braxhono Simael alias Gintilomo, Simon Rabibi, Xilomu Brixha, Galluffu Meme, Busacca de Ansaluni, Muxa Meme, Daniel Alluxu and a partner, all Jews, promise Nicolò, son of Giuliano de Bononia, to cut away the dry leaves of sugar cane and uproot the plants (ad exiri pagla de cannamelli et staccare plantini) *for 14* grana *a day each.*

Palermo, 17 January 1449

Source: ASP, Not. Giovanni Traverso, reg. 786, c. 269r-v.

Farchono, Merdoc and Liuczu Gaczu, Nissim Busitta and Sabet Xagaroni, Jews, hire themselves out with their assistants to Giovanni Archella, acting for the heirs of Nicolò de Bononia, to work as paratores *in the sugar refinery of the heirs on the usual terms.*

Palermo, 17 January 1449

Source: ASP, Not. Giovanni Traverso, reg. 786, cc. 269v–270r.

Xibiteni Xammara, Czullu Iubara, Daniel Xhabirra, Xibiteni Balbu, acting also for Benedetto Catalani, and three assistants, all Jews, hire themselves out to Chicco Salisi to work as paratores *in the sugar refinery of Giovanni de Bononia on the usual terms.*

Sicily

Palermo, 12 February 1449

Source: ASP, Not. Giovanni Traverso, reg. 786, c. 307r.

Daniel Alluxu and Girmini Simael, together with five others, all Jews, promise Nicolò son of Giuliano de Bononia, to fertilize 4,000 sugar cane beds for 16 tarì *a thousand.*

Palermo, 12 February 1449

Source: ASP, Not. Giovanni Traverso, reg. 786, c. 319r-v.

Xilomu Brixha, Iuda Cuchilla, Busacca Ansaluni and Busacca Xagaruni, Jews, and their assistants, hire themselves out to Antonio de mastro Antonio to work as paratores *in his sugar refinery during the entire season for six ounces a month. Muxa Meme acts as guarantor.*

Palermo, 13 February 1449

Source: ASP, Not. Giovanni Traverso, reg. 786, c. 329r.

Muxa Muxexi, a Jew, hires himself out to Giuliano Rigio to work as grinder in his sugar refinery, promising to make five "boilings" a week, for one tarì *a "boiling", and is paid 20* tarì *on account.*

Palermo, 20 February 1449

Source: ASP, Not. Giovanni Traverso, reg. 786, cc. 361v–362r.

Muxa Rugila and Braxhuno Admiranu, Jews, together with other men, promise Giuliano de Rigio to cut and prune his sugar cane for 9 tarì *a thousand new plants and 15* tarì *a thousand mature plants. They also undertake to fertilize the plantation together with another eight men for 16* tarì *a thousand.*

Palermo, 27 February 1449

Source: ASP, Not. Giovanni Traverso, reg. 786, c. 381v.

Braxhono Russo, a Jew, undertakes to work as assistant (famulo) *to Xibiteni Xammara, Czullu Iubara, Daniel Xhabirra, Xibiteni Balbu and Benedetto Catalano, Jews, in the sugar refinery of Giovanni de Bononia during the entire season for 16* tarì *a month and is paid 16* tarì *on account.*

Palermo, 23 April 1449

Source: ASP, Not. Giovanni Traverso, reg. 786, c. 445r-v.

Xibiteni Czel, a Jew, hires himself out together with his son Galluffu, aged 15, to Ubertino Russello and Minichello de Alfani to work in their ironmongery until August for 1.3.0 ounces.

Palermo, 6 June 1449

Source: ASP, Not. Giovanni Traverso, reg. 786, cc. 511v–512r.

Master Manuel de Seracusia, a Jewish builder, promises master Thommaseo Fadaluni to work on the building (marramma) *of Giovanni de Canonico for 24* tarì *a month.*

Palermo, 25 August 1449

Source: ASP, Not. Giovanni Traverso, reg. 786, c. 581r.

Xibiteni Iufaru, a Jew, lodges a notarial protest against Busacca Levi, another Jew, to make him carry out his commitment to treat leather (aptare coyramen) *[washed out].*

Palermo, 20 October 1450

Source: ASP, Not. Giovanni Traverso, reg. 787, cc. 9v–10r.

Vita Maltisi and Xhairono Gaczu, Jews, promise Iaymo Marrao, acting for the baron of Solanto, to dig a well on the grounds of the local castle, starting work on 26.10, for 3.15.0 ounces. They are paid 18 tarì *on account [washed out].*

Note: On the castle of Solanto see Bresc, *Monde Méditerranéen*, p. 877.

Palermo, 24 December 1450

Source: ASP, Not. Giovanni Traverso, reg. 787, c. 214v.

Xibiteni Xammara, Benedetto Catalanu, Czullu Iubara, Daniel Xhabirra and three famuli, *all Jews, hire themselves out to Chicco Salisi to work as* paratores *in the sugar refinery of Giovanni de Bononia during the entire season on the usual terms, and are paid two ounces on account.*

Sicily

Palermo, 31 December 1450

Source: ASP, Not. Giovanni Traverso, reg. 787, c. 224r.

Sabutu Xagaruni alias Sabara, Lya Migleni, Liuczu Gaczu, Merdoc Gaczu, Lya Sufer and two famuli, *all Jews, hire themselves out to Iacobo de Bononia to work as* paratores *in his sugar refinery for 6.8.0 ounces a month, and are paid two ounces on account.*

Palermo, 5 January 1451

Source: ASP, Not. Giovanni Traverso, reg. 787, c. 236r.

Minto Gibbesi, Iuda Millac, Xhayronus Levi, Xamuel Nigiar and six assistants, all Jews, hire themselves out to Bartholomeo Bononia to collect the dry leaves of his sugar cane during the entire season for 15 grana *a day, and are paid one ounce on account.*

Palermo, 5 January 1451

Source: ASP, Not. Giovanni Traverso, reg. 787, c. 236r-v.

Iuda Millach, Xhayrono Levi, Xamuel Nigiar, also on behalf of Galluffi Ammara, Jews, promise Bartholomeo de Bononia to fertilize his sugar cane during the whole season for 16 tarì *a thousand, and are paid one ounce on account. They also undertake to expand their workforce with eight additional Jews, if required.*

Palermo, 7 January 1451

Source: ASP, Not. Giovanni Traverso, reg. 787, c. 239v.

Xhaymi Virdi, a Jew, promises Xhairono Levi. also a Jew, to fertilize the sugar cane of Nicolò de Bononia for 16 grana *a day. Nissim Busacca assumes the same commitmnt for 12* grana *a day.*

Palermo, 8 January 1451

Source: ASP, Not. Giovanni Traverso, reg. 787, c. 240r.

Minto Xhaguela, a Jew, hires himself out to Xhayrono Levi and Iuda Millac, Jews, to fertilize the sugar cane of Nicolò de Bononia for 15 grana *a day.*

Palermo, 11 January 1451

Source: ASP, Not. Giovanni Traverso, reg. 787, c. 244v.

Nissim Medui, a Jew, hires himself out to Xhayrono Levi and Iuda Millac, Jews, to fertilize the sugar cane of Nicolò de Bononia for 15 grana *a day, and is paid six* tarì *on account.*

Palermo, 12 January 1451

Source: ASP, Not. Giovanni Traverso, reg. 787, c. 248r-v.

Master Filppo Pisano and Sabatino de Minichi, a Jew, also on behalf of their associates, hire themselves out to Nicolò de Bononia to cut and prune his sugar cane, old and new. They promise to process 2,000 plants a day for eight tarì *a thousand.*

Palermo, 12 January 1451

Source: ASP, Not. Giovanni Traverso, reg. 787, c. 248v.

Busacca Ansaluni and Sadia Sicundi, Jews, hire themselves out to Xhairono Levi, another Jew, to fertilize the sugar cane of Nicolò Bononia for 16 grana *a day, and are paid six* tarì *on account*

Palermo, 13 January 1451

Source: ASP, Not. Giovanni Traverso, reg. 787, cc. 249v–250r.

Iuda Cuchilla, Sabet Maltesi and Manuel de Tripuli, Jews, hire themselves out to Nicolò Bononia to fertilize his sugar cane during the current season for 16 grana *a day each, and are paid six* tarì *on account.*

Palermo, 25 January 1451

Source: ASP, Not. Giovanni Traverso, reg. 787, cc. 252v–253r.

Busacca Copiu and Xibiteni Trapanisi and their assistants, Jews, hire themselves out to Iuda Millac to fertilize the sugar cane of Nicolò Bononia for 16 grana *a day each, and are paid six* tarì *on account.*

Palermo, 1 February 1451

Source: ASP, Not. Giovanni Traverso, reg. 787, c. 286r-v.

Benedetto Catalano and eight helpers, all Jews, hire themselves out to Chicco Salisi to fertilize a sugar cane plantation called S. Nicola belonging to Nicolò Bononia for 16 tarì *a thousand plants and is paid six* tarì *on account.*

Palermo, 10 February 1451

Source: ASP, Not. Giovanni Traverso, reg. 787, c. 286r-v.

Iuda Millac and Xhayrono Levi, Jews, hire themselves out to Bartholomeo de Bononia to work in his sugar refinery during the entire season for the usual wages, and are paid one ounce on account.

Palermo, 1 March 1451

Source: ASP, Not. Giovanni Traverso, reg. 787, c. 337r-v.

Muxa de Rigio and David Malki, Jews, promise to work during the whole season in the tunny plant of the baron of Solanto for one ounce.

Palermo, 8 March 1451

Source: ASP, Not. Giovanni Traverso, reg. 787, c. 346r..

Nissim Busicta, a Jew, hires himself out to Antonio de Ginnaro to work in the tunny plant of the baron of Solanto during the entire season for one ounce, and is paid nine tarì *on account.*

Palermo, 2 April 1451

Source: ASP, Not. Giovanni Traverso, reg. 787, c. 410v.

Iusep de Amato alias Chaula and Salamon, son of Testanegra, Jews, hire themselves out to Antonio de Ginnaro to work in the tunny plant of the baron of Solanto during the whole season for 1.12.0 ounces each, and are paid 18 tarì *on account.*

Palermo, 8 April 1451

Source: ASP, Not. Giovanni Traverso, reg. 787, c. 395r.

Salamon de Tripuli, Iusep Misurato, Iusep Cusintini and Maxhaluffu Misurato, Jews, hire themselves out to Antonio Ginnaro to work as fillers (iarratini) *for 1.12.0 ounces and are each paid 15* tarì *on account.*

Palermo, 16 April 1451

Source: ASP, Not. Giovanni Traverso, reg. 787, c. 413r.

Xhayrono Gaczu alias Momo, a Jew, hires himself out to Antonio de Sapiolu to stack the wood in Alligrancia Crispo's sugar refinery on the usual terms, and is paid 16.15 tarì *on account.*

Palermo, 25 May 1451

Source: ASP, Not. Giovanni Traverso, reg. 787, cc. 474v–475r.

Contract for setting up a joint venture by Lya de Manueli and Donato de Bonaventura, Jews, de merchi nec et cosi de butiga. *Lya's share is three-fourths and Donato's one-fourth. The business is to last three years. Lya is to invest the merchandise. Business is to be carried on in Palermo and elsewhere.*

Palermo, 5 June 1451

Source: ASP, Not. Giovanni Traverso, reg. 787, cc. 498v–499r.

Muxa Rugila, a Jew, hires himself out to Antonio Sapiolu to work in the sugar refinery of Alligrantia de Crispo during the whole season and to make three "boilings" a week for one tarì *a "boiling".*

Palermo, 9 June 1451

Source: ASP, Not. Giovanni Traverso, reg. 787, cc. 502v–503r.

Xamuel Nigiar and Xhayrono Levi, Jews, hire themselves out to Federico Miglacio to stack all the wood in his sugar refinery during the entire season for nine tarì *a thousand kantars, and are paid 18* tarì *on account.*

Palermo, 17 June 1451
Source: ASP, Not. Giovanni Traverso, reg. 787, c. 513r-v.

Merdoc Minichi, acting also for his brother Xilomu de Minichi, Jews, sets up a joint venture with Raffael Roxidi, a Jew of Termini, for the production and sale of harnesses. The brothers' share is two-thirds and that of Raffael one-third. The partnership is to last until the end of August 1452. In addition to the division of expenses and profits, the brothers are to receive three tarì *and Raffael is to invest two ounces.*

Palermo, 12 August 1451
Source: ASP, Not. Giovanni Traverso, reg. 787, c. 571r.

Benedetto Catalano, a Jew, hires himself out to Giovanni de Bononia to fertilize his sugar cane for 16 tarì *a thousand, and is paid 18* tarì *on account.*

Palermo, 20 Ausgust 1451
Source: ASP, Not. Giovanni Traverso, reg. 787, cc. 591v–592r.

Saduni Sacerdotu, a Jew of Syracuse, hires himself out to Braxhono de Missina, another Jew, as muledriver until Easter. In return he is to receive clothes and shoes.

Palermo, 6 October 1451
Source: ASP, Not. Giovanni Traverso, reg. 788, c. 68r.

Daniel Xhabirra, a Jew, hires himself out to Luca Fanchigla, acting for the baron of Solanto, to work during the current season in the latter's tunny plant for one ounce and is paid 16 tarì *on account.*

Palermo, 14 October 1451
Source: ASP, Not. Giovanni Traverso, reg. 788, cc. 98v–99r.

The clergyman Giovanni Saponara, for half a share, and Minto Gibbesi, Lya di lu Fromento and Xhayrono Levi, Jews, for the other half, set up a joint venture for the operation of an oil press during the entire season. Giovanni invests the press and tools and the Jews their labour. The profits are to be divided daily.

Palermo, 14 October 1451

Source: ASP, Not. Giovanni Traverso, reg. 788, c. 111v.

Xibiten Gaczu, a Jew, hires himself out to Daniel Xhabirra, his fellow Jew, to work, together with three associates as paratores *in the sugar refinery of Giovanni de Bononia on the usual terms, and is paid one ounce on account.*

Palermo, 17 December 1451

Source: ASP, Not. Giovanni Traverso, reg. 788, c. 232v.

Salamon Sabuchi, a Jew, hires himself out to Luca Fanchigla to work in the tunny plant of the baron of Solanto until September for 23 tarì.

Palermo, 20 December 1451

Source: ASP, Not. Giovanni Traverso, reg. 788, cc. 240v–241r.

Muxa de Seracusia and Iusep Amatu alias Chaula, Jews, hire themselves out to Luca Fanchigla to work in the tunny plant of the baron of Solanto during the entire season for 1.18.0 each, and are paid 6 tarì *each on account.*

Palermo, 24 December 1451

Source: ASP, Not. Giovanni Traverso, reg. 788, c. 248r.

Xibiten Xammara, Saduni Simael, Iusep Ammara, Xibiten Gaczu, Farchuni Gaczu, Daniel Xhabirra, also on behalf of Czullu Iubara and an associate, all Jews, hire themselves out to Chicco Salisi to work as paratores *in the sugar refinery of Giovanni de Bononia for 6.14.0 ounces a month.*

Palermo, 30 December 1451

Source: ASP, Not. Giovanni Traverso, reg. 788, c. 254r.

Iosep de Minichi, a Jew, promises Chicco Salisi to grind sugar cane in Chicco's press during the whole season at the rate of five "boilings" a week for one ounce a month and is paid one ounce on account.

Sicily

Palermo, 13 January 1451

Source: ASP, Not. Giovanni Traverso, reg. 788, c. 262r-v.

Muxa Chancu, a Jew, with six helpers, hires himself out to Pino de Ysolda to cut and prune the sugar cane in his plantation in the contrada *Favara for 8* tarì *a thousand, and is paid 16* tarì *on account.*

Palermo, 13 January 1451

Source: ASP, Not. Giovanni Traverso, reg. 788, cc. 263v–264r.

Bartholomeo Bruschinu and Sadia Sicundi, Busacca de Ansaluni and Merdoc de Minichi, Jews, also on behalf of Vita Maltisi, a Jew, hire themselves out together with two others to work in the sugar refinery of Giovanni de Bononia for six ounces a month. They are paid three ounces on account. On 25 January Iuda Cuchilla, a Jew, joins the others as an assistant for a wage of six tarì.

Palermo, 20 January 1451

Source: ASP, Not. Giovanni Traverso, reg. 788, cc. 275v–276r.

Busacca Levi, Galluffu de Termini and Nissim de Viczini, Jews, set up a joint shoemaker business (corbiseria seu zabartoria) *in three equal shares. Busacca invests leather valued at 11 ounces, and the other two invest their labour. The business is to last until Busacca regains his investment.*

Palermo, 25 January 1451

Source: ASP, Not. Giovanni Traverso, reg. 788, c. 288r-v.

Lya Migleni, Lya Stuppa, Merdoc Gaczu, Liuczu Gaczu and Xibiteni Balbu and two assistants, all Jews, hire themselves out to Iacobo de Bononia as paratores *in his sugar refinery to work during the entire season for 6.8.0 ounces a month and are paid a month's wages on account.*

Palermo, 1 February 1451

Source: ASP, Not. Giovanni Traverso, reg. 788, c. 302r.

Xhayrono de Lentini, a Jew, hires himself out to Luca Fanchigla to work as a filler at the tunny plant of the baron of Solanto during the entire season for 1.12.0 ounces, and is paid nine tarì *on account.*

Palermo, 3 February 1451

Source: ASP, Not. Giovanni Traverso, reg. 788, cc. 303v–304r.

Salamon Sabuchi, a Jew, hires himself out to Luca Fanchigla to work as a salter of tunny during the entire season in the tunny plant of the baron of Solanto for 7 grana *per 100 barrels.*

Palermo, 17 February 1451

Source: ASP, Not. Giovanni Traverso, reg. 788, c. 337r.

Manuel and Salvator Chetibi, sons of the late master Moyses Chetibi, Jews, sell the doctor of law Bernardo Penos real estate in Palermo. This includes a shop and the rent for another shop.

Die XVII februarii XV Ind. MCCCCLII
Notum facimus et testamur quod Manuel Chetibi et Salvator Chetibi, filii quondam magistri Moyses Chetibi, Iudei, presentes coram nobis, sponte per se et eorum heredes et successores in perpetuum vendiderunt et ex causa et nomine ipsius vendicionis habere concesserunt nobili et egregio domino Bernardo Penos, legum doctori, presenti et pro se suisque heredibus et successoribus in perpetuum ementi infrascripta bona stabilia racione dominii et iura, ut infra declarabitur, videlicet apothecam unam terraneam, sitam et positam in contrata Lactarinorum ex opposito fundaci vocati de lu Arrangiu, secus apothecam que fuit Galluffi Fitira et secus tabernam heredum quondam notarii Iohannis de Grabona [repeated] et secus apothecam Iacob Taguili, censuale conventus S. Dominici Panormi, et alios confines. Item etiam vendiderunt dicto domino Bernardo utile dominium uncie unius et tarenos trium solvendorum et debendi anno quolibet in perpetuum XV augusti per Nissim Xilomu pro quadam alia apotheca terranea coniuncta et secus dictam apothecam superius venditam per dictos venditores eidem domino Bernardo venditori [=emptori], secus apothecam Muxe Russo et secus tabernam heredum quondam notarii Iohannis de Grabona predicti et alios confines, que ambe due apothece sunt subiecte in unciis duabus solvendi in pecunia numerata quolibet anno venerando domino Ardoyno de Bankerio, beneficiali

cuiusdam altaris existentis intus maiorem Panormitanam ecclesiam, vocati S. Maria de Succursu et cum dotacione census unciarum duarum que venditores vendiderunt eidem emptori, reservato consensu dicti domini Ardoyni de Bankerio beneficiali dicti altaris, cum condicione quod, si forte dictus dominus Ardoynus non esset contentu de presenti vendicioni tunc et eo totus presentis contractus sit nullus et nullius valoris ac si minime factus extitisset, et dicti conductores tunc teneantur restituere in frumenti precium ipsorum bonorum eidem emptioni. Item dictus dominus Bernardus solvere debeat canonem anni presentis ipsarum apothecarum. Et loherium ipsarum apothecarum anni presentis introytum habeat et habere debeat ipse emptor, et si aliquam pecuniam de dictis loherio et introyti apothecarum anni presentis ipsi venditores habuissent, ipsam pecuniam dicti venditores dare et restituire, ac solvere debeant dicto emptori liberi et expediti ab omni alio onere et census et cuiuslibet alterius servitutis. Ad habendum, tenendum, possidendum ab hodie in antea per eundem emptorem dicta bona, utile dominium et iura vendita cum omnibus eorum iuribus et pertinenciis, introytibus et exitibus, accessibus et egressibus iustis iudicibus debitis et consuetis, dandum, vendendum, alienandum, permutandum penam, iudicandum, utifruendum, gaudendum et faciendum de eis et in eis totum velle et desiderium suum et suisque heredum et successores absque contradicione alicuius persone, cum omni iure, actione, usu, dominio utili requisitione et potestate [empty space — 2 lines] pro precio unciarum duodecim auri ponderis generalis, quod precium dicti venditores confessi extiterunt habuisse et recepisse ab eodem emptore, renunciantes execucioni ipsius pecunie non habite non recepte speique future habicionis et recepcionis ipsius. Item ius caligarum et ius cabelle dicti contrahentes, seu partem solvere teneatur et debeant comuniter, promictentes dicti venditores in solidum eidem emptori presenti et stipulanti pro se suisque heredibus et successoribus in perpetuum dicta bona et iura, ut supra vendita, legitime defendere ab omni calumpniante, seu molestante persona cuiuscumque status, gradus vel condicionis existat ipsa bona in parte vel in toto evictere volenti, et in casu evictionis assistere iudicium ipsius cause in se suscipere, prosequi et finire eorum propriis sumptibus et expensis, appellandum, laudandum, denunciandum, requirendum et prosequendum necessitate remissa constituentes dicti venditores precario nomine et pro parte dicti emptoris predicta bona ut supra vendita, tenere et possidere donec et quousque ipse emptor corporalem vel quasi acceperit possessionem, quam intrandi, capiendi deinceps et retinendi sibi auctoritatem tribuerunt et plenariam potestatem habere concesserunt ab hodie in antea et per personam mei notarii in corporalem et realem possessionem imposuerunt et induxerunt, cedentes dicti venditores eidem emptori presenti et recipieti omnia iura omnesque actiones, reales, personales, utiles, mixtas et directas, civiles et pretorias, tacitas et expressas, que et quas dicti venditores habeant, habent et habere possint in futurum in et supra dictis bonis, iuribus superius, nominatis constituentes eundem emptorem procuratorem in re eorum propria et ponentes eum in locum proprium ut a modo liceat et licitum sit eidem emptori agere, causare, experiri, consequi et se tueri in et super premissis et qualibet premissorum et si de premissis seu aliquo premissorum vel infrascriptorum quo oriatur, quod fiat ritus secundum formam novi ritus instrumentorum magne regie curie servorum in personis et bonis ipsorum venditoris, etc. Et iuraverunt dicti contrahentes quod presens contractus fuit et est verus et non fictus nec factus in fraudem et preiudicium alicuius persone, ac quod totum est verum et iustum pretium quantum superius est declaratum premissaque omnia rata habere, unde ad cautelam dicti domini Bernardi emptoris et memoriam omnium premissorum factum est presens instrumentum scriptum per manus mei notarii Iohannis de Traversa notarii qui supra iudex et notarius, ac subscriptorum testium sub subscriptionibus meoque solito signo signatum et testium roboratum. Dat. Panormi, anno, mense, die et Ind. premissis.

Testes: Notarius Orlandus Traversa, frater Bonifacius de Bono abbas S. Iohannis, Thomeus de Bertolino.

Palermo, 1 March 1451

Source: ASP, Not. Giovanni Traverso, reg. 788, c. 373r.

Benedetto Benixhasu, a Jew of Polizzi, hires himself out to Nicolò Brando to work as filler and to carry out other jobs in his tunny plant for 12.10 tarì, and is paid 4.10 tarì on account.

Palermo, 20 March 1451

Source: ASP, Not. Giovanni Traverso, reg. 788, c. 404r-v.

Muxa de Rigio, a Jew, hires himself out to Luca Fanchigla to work as a filler in the tunny plant of the baron of Solanto during the entire season for 1.10.0 ounces and is paid nine tarì on account.

Palermo, 26 October 1452

Source: ASP, Not. Giovanni Traverso, reg. 788, c. 107r.

Daniel Calabrisi, a Jew, hires himself out to Nicolò de Bononia to work as parator *in his sugar refinery during the whole season on the the usual terms, and is paid one ounce on account. Minto Gibbesi, a Jew, stands surety.*

Palermo, 26 October 1452

Source: ASP, Not. Giovanni Traverso, reg. 788, c. 108r-v.

Minto Gibbesi and Braxhono Simael, Jews, promise Nicolò de Bononia to cut and prune his sugar cane for 16 and nine tarì *a thousand for old and new plants, respectively.*

Palermo, 29 December 1452

Source: ASP, Not. Giovanni Traverso, reg. 788, c. nn.

Lya Migleni, Lya Sufar, Merdoc Gaczu, Liuczu Gaczu, Xibiteni Balbi and their helpers hire themselves out to Iacobo de Bononia as paratores *in his sugar refinery on the usual terms, and are paid three ounces on account.*

Palermo, 6 March 1453

Source: ASP, Not. Giovanni Traverso, reg. 788, c. 274v.

Xibiteni Gaczu, Czullu Iubara, Daniel Xhabirra, Salamon Grecu and Xibiteni Xammara, Jews, hire themselves out to Chicco Salisi to cut and prune the sugar cane of Giovanni de Bononia for 16 and eight tarì *a thousand for old and new plants, respectively, and are paid one ounce on account.*

Palermo, 6 March 1453

Source: ASP, Not. Giovanni Traverso, reg. 788, c. 275r.

Czullu Iubara, Daniel Xhabirra, Salamon Grecu and Xibiteni Xammara, Jews, hire themselves out to Chicco Salisi to fertilize the sugar cane of Giovanni de Bononia for 16 tarì *a thousand, and are paid 18* tarì *on account.*

Palermo, 7 March 1453

Source: ASP, Not. Giovanni Traverso, reg. 788, c. 275r.

Muxa Chanchu and Simon Rabibi, Jews, promise Pino Ysolda, acting for the heirs of Nicolò de Bononia, to cut and prune their sugar cane on the usual terms. They undertake to cut 500 plants a day. They also promise to fertilize the plants together with ten other men for 17 tarì *a thousand, and are paid 1.6.0 ounces on account.*

Palermo, 1 August 1453

Source: ASP, Not. Giovanni Traverso, reg. 788, cc. 323r–324r.

Deed whereby fra Giovanni Iosca, abbot of S. Spirito outside the walls of Palermo and commendator of the monastery S. Maria de Cripta, appoints fra Angelo de Cardona his attorney. Angelo is to betake himself to the territory of Marsala and to replace the attorneys which the abbot had appointed previously. He is to cancel the lease (arrendacio) *granted Sabuto Alduyno, a Jew of Marsala, of the feud S. Anna in Marsala, since it is detrimental to the interests of the lessors.*

Bibliography: Bresc, *Arabi*, p. 196, and n. 902.

Palermo, 17 August 1453

Source: ASP, Not. Giovanni Traverso, reg. 788, c. 524v.

Minto de Minichi, Braxhono Simael and Nissim Danuchu, Jews, hire themselves out to Nicolò de Bononia to cut and prune his sugar cane for 1 tarì *a* carrozzata *of new plants and 16* tarì *every ten* carrozzate *of old ones. They are paid on account one ounce in wheat and cash.*

Note: *Carrozzata* = wagonload, used here to indicate a measure.

Palermo, after 17 August 1453

Source: ASP, Not. Giovanni Traverso, reg. 788, c. 529r-v.

Minto Gibbesi, Galluffu Ammaru and six assistants, all Jews, hire themselves out to Nicolò and Bartholomeo de Bononia to fertilize their sugar cane during the whole season for 16 tarì *a thousand, and are paid on account 1.16.0 ounces in wheat.*

Palermo, 19 February 1455

Source: ASP, Not. Giovanni Traverso, reg. 788, c. nn.

Xibiteni Xammara, Czullu Iubara, Daniel Xhabirra, Iuda de Minichi and Salomon Gaczu, Jews, hire themselves out to work as paratores *in the sugar refinery of Giovanni de Bononia for 5.18.0 ounces a month, and are paid 1.4.0 ounces on account.*

Palermo, 21 February 1455

Source: ASP, Not. Giovanni Traverso, reg. 788, c. nn.

Nissim Baram and Xibite Sacerdotu, Jews, hire themselves out to Simon de Mule, acting on behalf of Giovanni de Rainaldo, to transport dry sugar cane leaves for 15 tarì *a day, and are paid three* tarì *on account.*

Palermo, 21 February 1455

Source: ASP, Not. Giovanni Traverso, reg. 788, c. nn.

Vita de Medico, a Jew, promises Simon de Mule, acting for Giovanni de Bononia, to transport dry sugar cane leaves for 15 tarì *a day, and is paid three* tarì *on account.*

Palermo, 6 September 1453

Source: ASP, Not. Giovanni Traverso, reg. 789, c. 19r.

Galluffu de Termini, a Jew, hires himself out to Nicolò son of the late Giuliano de Bononia, acting also for his partner Bartholomeo de Bononia, to work in their sugar refinery during the entire season for one tarì *a day. He is paid 24* tarì *on account.*

Palermo, 22 November 1453

Source: ASP, Not. Giovanni Traverso, reg. 789, cc. 71r–72v.

Deed of sale whereby Giovanni Lancza and Pietro Bellachera, owners of the tunny plant Isola delle Femmine, sell Leon Ammara, Nissim Sansuni, Iacob de Saragusia, Iuda de Minichi and Merdoc Riczu, Jews, 2,000 kantars of tunny for six tarì *a kantar.*

Eodem XXII novembris II Ind.

Honorabilis Iohannes Lancza et Petrus Bellachera, m[.] patroni tonnarie Ysule Fimi, presentes coram nobis sponte vendiderunt Leon Ammara, Nissim Sansuni, Iacob de Saragusia, Iuda de Minichi et Merdoc Riczu Iudeis, presentibus et ementibus in solidum cantaria duomilia tonnici iarratii, pisati et anictati comu esti usu et consuetu de tonnina ki si vendi a cantarate ala logia. Et li patruni divinu pagari li paraturi et pagari unu dili iarratini per ayutari a pisari la tonnina. Quam quantitatem tonnicii, ut supra, venditam dicti patroni venditores dare et assignare promiserunt eisdem Iudeis emptoribus successive comu proventura di la dicta tonnara. Vero ki si li patruni indi vurrannu piglari cantara dechi per centinaru de cantara li poczanu piglari et non plui, perki tucti li altri pixi oy tunni divinu haviri li dicti acactaturi per fina ki ayanu havuti la dicta tonnicia venduta, videlicet lu complimentu dili dicti dui milia cantara pro precio tr. VI pro chaunu cantaru sunt tr. sei. Quod primi dicti tonnici venditi dicti Iudei emptores in solidum obligantes dare et solvere promiserunt eisdem patronibus venditoribus stipulantibus modo infrascripto, videlicet per tuctu lu misi di iugnu anni presentis unci chentu si havirannu havuti li dicti duimila cantari di tonnina, et si non li havissiru havuti pro rata de czoki havirannu mancu havutu. Et restante parte dare et solvere promiserunt successive prout vendiderunt tonnicium salatum vendendu, pagandu, et ad tardius vendito tonnino vel non solvere debeant totum precium tonnici quod tunc habuerint per totum mensem septembris proxime future. Item si li dicti Iudei vurrannu vindiri tonnina salata a cridenza la poczanu vindiri, et ki dicti patruni divinu aspictari per tuctu lu misi de octubri proximo futuro [blotted out: ..]endu dictu de bancu. Item tucta la tonnina salata ki sarra si divi mectiri in unu oy plui magaseni, et semper ad riquesta et electioni dili dicti patruni poczanu intrari in li magaseni et vidiri et cuntari la dicta tonnina. Et li chavi di li quali magaseni divi tiniri lu dictu Merdoc Riczu, vero ki non sina ki li dicti patruni hayanu havutu et receputu la prima paga ki divinu pagari li dicti Iudei ali patruni per tuctu iugnu tucta la dicta tonnina divi stari sutta dui chavi, et una indi divinu tiniri li dicti patruni et lautra lu dictu Merdoc Riczu. Item quandu li patruni anchindrannu lu sabatu oy li altri festi di li dicti Iudei li dicti patruni non poczanu constringiri ali dicti Iudei a pisari et piglari la dicta tonnina, ma la digianu piglari la matina sequenti. Item si per avintura per difectu di li porteri non si fachissi la tonnara predicta complita et furnita di li cosi necessari, li dicti patruni sianu tinuti ali dicti Iudei ali damni et interesse. Et si per avintura fachendusi la dicta tonnara fornita et complita non piscassi lu complimentu di li dicti dui milia cantari, non siano tenuti ali dicti Iudei ne ad damni ne ad interessi. Item li dicti Iudei divinu fari la logia loru complita et fornita de omni cosa necessarii, altrimenti sianu tenuti ali dicti patruni ali damni et interesse. Et haviti li dicti Iudei li dui milia cantari de tonnina sianu tenuti dari la logia et li homini di la logia ali patruni per putiri inchudiri et salari et taglari la loru tonnina ali dicti patruni, pagandu li dicti patruni ali dicti Iudei la rata di lu churma, videlicet di li homini di la logia. Item si per avintura vinendu lu ultimu iornu di sittembru li dicti Iudei non putissiru pagari tuctu lu complimentu di lu preczu dila prima vendicioni ki di czoki li dicti patruni ristirannu intandu arichipiri sindi digianu piglari tonnina intriczata per lu preczu ki li tonnini intandu vindirannu li altri patruni di tonnari in dinari contanti. Item li dicti Iudei divinu beni et diligenti salari, gubernari et guidari la dicta tonnina cum bona cura et diligencia et sollicitudini, reservatis eisdem patronibus ma[...] dicti tonnini. Item li dicti Iudei divinu portari la scana per pisari la dicta tonnina et fari li predicti per pisarila. Que omnia et singula dicti contrahenti promiserunt rata habere in pace, sine lite, sub ypotheca omnium suorum bonorum etc., in refectionem dampnorum interesse expensarum etc., renuncianti moratoriis, guidaticiis, dilacionis quinquennali et aliis regiis graciis. Et fiat ritus in personis et bonis etc. Et iuraverunt dicti contrahenti.

Testes: Guillelmus Morellu, Petrus Mariscalco, magister Iohannes de Fano, Masius de Gilberto.

Bibliography: Bresc, *Arabi*, p. 73, and n. 341.

Palermo, 10 January 1454

Source: ASP, Not. Giovanni Traverso, reg. 789, cc. 229r–230r.

Lya Migleni, Lya Sufar, Mardoc Gaczu, Liuczu Gaczu, Xibiteni Balbu and two assistants, all Jews, hire themselves out to Iacobo de Bononia as paratores *to work in his sugar refinery for 6.8.0 ounces a month. They are paid four ounces on account.*

Palermo, 30 April 1454

Source: ASP, Not. Giovanni Traverso, reg. 789, c. nn.

Contract whereby Gallufu Taguili, a Jew, undertakes to rebuild a loft over the inn which he was holding in perpetual lease from the Magione with the consent of the landlord.

Die ultimo aprilis II Ind.

Notum facimus et testamur quod cum Galluffu Taguili Iudeus per se heredes et successores suos in perpetuum habeat, teneat et possideat a Sacra Domo Mansionis Theutonicorum felicis urbis Panormi domum, seu tabernam unam magnam, sitam et positam in quarterio Cassari Panormi, in quadam vanella stricta, vocata di lu Fornaru, secus cortile domorum censualium dicte Sacre Domus Mansionis et secus introytum seu porticatum dicti cortilis et alios confines, sub onere census tr. VII gr. X, solvendum anno quolibet in perpetuum dicte Sacre Domui Mansionis in festo Sancte Trinitatis quod celebratur octavo Pentecostis, que domus seu taberna [damaged] [introytu] et exitu, tam ex parte dicti cortilis, quam ex parte dicte vanelle, et super introyti dicti cortilis erat antiquo tempore unum solare copertum pro dicta taberna et usu dicte taberne et de inde pervenit ad ruinam et fuisse dirutum, seu dirrupatum, dictusque Gallufu istis diebus preteritis, de consensu, voluntate et mandato dicti preceptoris dicte Sacre Domus Mansionis et fratrum ipsius Mansionis, incepisset ad hedificandum dictum solare et murandum ad altum supra dictum solare et faciendum domum pro dicta taberna et pro usu dicte taberne et deinde etiam ad presens hedificare et murare facit, non obstante quod hoc facere ipse Galluffu poterat, absque licencia, statu et voluntate seu mandato dicte sacre domus mansionis, ut hec omnia supradicta prefatus Galluffu et reverendus dominus Christoforus Ryeder, thesaurarius dicte sacre domus mansionis Theotonicorum et nomine et pro parte ipsius sacre domus mansionis et dicti preceptoris ipsius sacre domus mansionis, presentes coram nobis, dixerunt et confessi extiterunt vera esse. Renunciantes etc. Et pro maiori cautela et securitati dicti Galluffi, hodie presenti pretitulati die, prefatus reverendus dominus Christoforus, presens coram nobis, tam pro se quam nomine et pro parte dicti preceptoris et fratrum ipsius sacre domus mansionis, pro quibus domino preceptore et fratribus ipse dominus Christoforus proprio nomine de rato promisit sponte [damaged] et confirmavit omnia supradicta et contenta [damaged] solare et marammati hedificati et facti per dictum Galluffu supra dicto solari, et de novo licenciam, auctoritatem et potestatem dedit et concessit eidem Galluffo quod ipse Galluffu possit valeat murare ad altum et hedificare et facere domum ad eius beneplacitum pro dicta taberna, seu domo et cum ea incorporare absque contradictione dicte Mansionis. Que omnia et singula prefatus dominus Christoforus promisit rata habere, tenere et observare proprio et quo supra nomine, sub ypotheca omnium suorum bonorum, ac refectionem dampnorum, interesse, expensarum, litis et extra. Renuncians etc.

Sicily

Testes: Paulus Garofalu, Antonius de Ali et magister Iohannes de Monblanco.

Palermo, 2 September 1454

Source: ASP, Not. Giovanni Traverso, reg. 789, c. 9r.

Braxhono Luvechu, a Jew, hires himself out as a workman to Giovanni Cistortes for three months for six tarì *a month.*

Palermo, 12 September 1454

Source: ASP, Not. Giovanni Traverso, reg. 789, c. 41r.

Sabeti Fromentinu, a Jew of Sciacca, hires himself out to Lya Sadya, a Jewish shoemaker, and his partners to work as tanner from 16 to 30.9.1455 for 6.10 tarì *a month and a pair of shoes.*

Palermo, 17 September 1454

Source: ASP, Not. Giovanni Traverso, reg. 789, c. 53r.

Minto Gibbesi and Iosep Bonu, Jews, and others promise Giovanni Crispo to cut and prune his sugar cane for 16 tarì *a thousand, and are paid 24* tarì *on account.*

Palermo, 24 October 1454

Source: ASP, Not. Giovanni Traverso, reg. 789, c. 117r-v.

Minto Gibbesi, Vita Maltisi, Merdoc de Minichi, Iusep Bonu and others, all Jews, promise Nicolò de Bononia to cut and prune his sugar cane for nine tarì *a thousand new plants and 16 for old ones. They are paid 1.18.0 ounces on account.*

Palermo, 5 November 1454

Source: ASP, Not. Giovanni Traverso, reg. 789, c. 154v.

Busacca Simma, a Jew, promises Micael Quaragisima to work in the sugar refinery of Giovanni Crispo during the entire season for 21 tarì *a month, and is paid one month's wages on account.*

6141

Palermo, 3 January 1455

Source: ASP, Not. Giovanni Traverso, reg. 789, cc. 235v–236r.

Minto de Minichi and Xharuno Maxhalufu, Jews, hire themselves out to Nicolò de Bononia as paratores *in his sugar refinery for 29.12 tarì a month and 17 tarì a month for every assistant. On 29 January Michiloni Ysac joins them and is paid one ounce on account.*

Palermo, 10 January 1455

Source: ASP, Not. Giovanni Traverso, reg. 789, c. 246r.

Mussutu Misseria, Micael Abramellu and Minto de Minichi, Jews, hire themselves as parartores *to Nicolò de Bononia in his sugar refinery for the whole season for 17 tarì a month each, and are paid a month's wages on account.*

Palermo, 18 January 1455

Source: ASP, Not. Giovanni Traverso, reg. 789, cc. 268v–269r.

Fadaluni Xhabirra, a Jew, promises mastro Antonio Lu Maczu, a smith, to make horseshoes for him and for Michele de Napoli until the end of August for 1.5 tarì a kantar, and is paid six tarì on account.

Palermo, 24 March 1455

Source: ASP, Not. Giovanni Traverso, reg. 789, cc. 351–352r.

Gasena, widow of Pachino Marchili, a Jewess, and Merdoc Vignuni alias Denticutu, guardian of Xua and Ysac, sons of the late Muxa Marchili, Jews, sell Sabet Mayu, another Jew, a house with basement and courtyard in the Cassaro. The property is situated in a large court, bordering the house of Muxa and Braxha Brixha and the inn of Gallufu Taguili, also Jews. The entire property is leased to these tenants by the Magione church. The sale price agreed on is eight ounces, four of which are paid immediately. The rent due the church is one ounce.

Palermo, 24 March 1455

Source: ASP, Not. Giovanni Traverso, reg. 789, c. 360r.

Matheus Binnira, Manuel de Tripuli and Iosep Binnira, Jews, promise Giovanni

La Barbera to transport oil to Palermo for 15 grana *the kantar, and are paid nine* tarì *on account.*

Palermo, 14 April 1455

Source: ASP, Not. Giovanni Traverso, reg. 789, c. 382r-v.

Abram de Minichi, a Jew, hires himself out to Lya Sadya, a Jewish shoemaker, also on behalf of his brother Merdoc, to work in his shoeshop until the end of August for 15 tarì.

Palermo, 29 April 1455

Source: ASP, Not. Giovanni Traverso, reg. 789, c. 409r.

Iuda Cuchilla, a Jew, hires himself out to Giovanni Xixo to work in the tunny plant of Giuliano Rigio in Trabia during the entire season for 1.18 tarì.

Palermo, 19 June 1455

Source: ASP, Not. Giovanni Traverso, reg. 789, c. 476v.

Giovanni de lu Palazzu leases Fadaluni Xhabirra, a Jew, an anvil weighing 77 rotoli *for a year for one* tarì *a month.*

Palermo, 4 August 1455

Source: ASP, Not. Giovanni Traverso, reg. 789, cc. 525v–526r.

Vita Xunina and Vita Leone, Jews, set up a joint venture for the sale of oil, cheese, caciocavallo *and the like. Xunina invests a shop situated in the Cassaro and 15 ounces. Leone invests his labour. Profits are to be divided in equal shares after deduction of Xunina's 15 ounces.*

Palermo, 11 September 1455

Source: ASP, Not. Giovanni Traverso, reg. 790, c. nn.

Antonio Manueli leases to Busacca de Minichi and Braxhono Simael, Jews, an oil press with machinery and storehouse. He also sells them a horse for 1.12.0 ounces. [partly washed out].

Palermo, 13 October 1455

Source: ASP, Not. Giovanni Traverso, reg. 790, c. nn.

Minto Gibbesi, a Jew, hires himself out to mastro Manfrido Marino to stack the wood of Bartholomeo Bononia in the latter's sugar refinery during the whole season for the usual remuneration, and is paid 15 tarì *on account.*

Palermo, 22 October 1455

Source: ASP, Not. Giovanni Traverso, reg. 790, c. 112r–113r.

Xibiten Chimia, a Jewish citizen of Palermo, makes a present of all his property to his brother Siminto in Caltagirone, provided Xibiten enjoys the income and is not survived by male descendants.

Palermo, 17 November 1455

Source: ASP, Not. Giovanni Traverso, reg. 790, c. 166v.

Symon Rabibi and Iani Sacerdotu alias Iarratanu and others, all Jews, hire themselves out to Giovanni Carpaczano to cut and prune his sugar cane for 10 tarì *the thousand for new plants and 17 the old ones and are paid 15* tarì *on account.*

Palermo, 26 November 1455

Source: ASP, Not. Giovanni Traverso, reg. 790, c. 189r.

Yuda de la Pantelleria, a Jew of Marsala, sells Filippo Bellachera a white bedspread and four pieces of decorated cloth for 2.18.0 ounces. He also declares hat he received 2.12.0 ounces to buy 20 canne *of purple borders made in Sciacca and Trapani* (barduna perpigrignu de lu gettitu de Xacca et de lu gettitu de Trapani), *and to transport them during the first week of Lent for a price to be agreed on.*

Palermo, 20 January 1456

Source: ASP, Not. Giovanni Traverso, reg. 790, c. 283v.

Busacca Levi, a Jew, promises Antonio de la Lombardo to sole his shoes and those of his brother and men until the end of August for the usual wages. He also sells

Antonio a new pair of shoes for 6 tarì, to be paid in August together with the wages.

Palermo, 24 March 1456

Source: ASP, Not. Giovanni Traverso, reg. 790, cc. 370v–371r.

Lya Faylla, Abram Xagaruni, Salamon de Missina, Farchono and Momo Gaczu, Michiloni Ysac and three others, all Jews, hire themselves out to Giovanni Bayamonte to work as paratores *in his sugar refinery during the entire the season for 1.6.0 ounces a month, and are paid 4.15.0 ounces on account. Muxa Marxili, a Jew, stands surety.*

Palermo, 6 April 1456

Source: ASP, Not. Giovanni Traverso, reg. 790, cc. 381r–382r.

Vita Xunina, Muxa de Politi and Xibiteni Gibesi, Jews, and Salamon Anellu, a Jew of Cammarata, set up a joint venture for the operation of a cheese and caciocavallo *warehouse in Palermo for a year starting 1 September. Salamon invests 10 ounces and the other three 20 ounces. The money invested is to be employed to purchase* pecorino *for no more than six* tarì *the kantar,* caciocavallo *for no more than six* tarì *the kantar, and cow cheese for no more than five* tarì *the kantar. Salamon is to transport the cheese from Cammarata to Palermo, and the other three are to sell the cheese. Salamon is entitled to half the profits, and the other three to the other half.*

Palermo, 22 April 1456

Source: ASP, Not. Giovanni Traverso, reg. 790, c. nn.

Sabatino Catalanu, a Jew of Agrigento, apprentices his son Busacca with Simon Rabi Iacob, a Jewish shoemaker. Busacca is to carry out the tasks he is given by his master, whereas Simon is to provide Busacca with food and clothinsg.

Palermo, 4 May 1456

Source: ASP, Not. Giovanni Traverso, reg. 790, c. nn.

Farrugiu Minnectu, a Jew, hires himself out together with eight other men to

Antonio de Lentini to fertilize the sugar cane of Giovanni Crepanzano for 16 tarì *a thousand, and is paid six* tarì *on account.*

Palermo, 7 May 1456

Source: ASP, Not. Giovanni Traverso, reg. 790, c. 436r.

Nissim Gannuchi, Xhayruni Maxhalufu and Minto Gibbesi with five others, all Jews, hire themselves out to Pino Ysolda to fertilize his sugar cane for 18 tarì *a thousand and are paid 20* tarì *on account.*

Palermo, 11 May 1456

Source: ASP, Not. Giovanni Traverso, reg. 790, c. 438r-v.

Xillelli Rusticu, a Jew, hires himself out to Antonio Bisacza to work as parator *in the sugar refinery of Giovanni Crepanzano for 1 ounce a month. He is paid on account 18* tarì *to be handed to Daniel Xacca, a Jew, and 12* tarì *in cash.*

Palermo, 12 May 1456

Source: ASP, Not. Giovanni Traverso, reg. 790, cc. 442r–444r.

Deed of sale whereby Sadoc Sansuni, a Jew of Trapani, also on behalf of his wife Milica and his children Xhanino, Nissimi and Bulxhayra, sells to Vita Pulisi, another Jew, a group of houses, partly of one storey and partly solerate, *located in the Cassaro in the* vanella *De lu Dattilu. The property borders on the houses of Sansuni Gibel and Daniel Ysac. The annual rent amounts to 2.5.0 ounces, to be paid to the owner, Luca Bellachera. The price is 21.15.0 ounces. 1.15.0 ounces are paid on account and the balance is due in annual instalments of five ounces to be paid every August. Luca declares that he has been paid the rent regularly to date.*

Palermo, 10 September 1456

Source: ASP, Not. Giovanni Traverso, reg. 791, c. nn.

Iosep de Tripuli alias Mollemi, a Jew, hires himself out to Luca Fanchigla to treat (salmoriare) *the tunny of Manfrido de Santo Stefano at the plant of Mondello for 1.15.0 ounces. He is paid nine* tarì *on account.*

Sicily

Palermo, 29 October 1456

Source: ASP, Not. Giovanni Traverso, reg. 791, c. 148r.

Nissim Aczara, a Jew, together with another eight men, hires himself out to Nicolò Lentini to fertilize the sugar cane of Giovanni Crepanzano. He is to do a thousand beds a day for 16 tarì a thousand, and is paid one ounce on account.

Palermo, 18 March 1457

Source: ASP, Not. Giovanni Traverso, reg. 791, c. 330r.

Braxhono Russu and Minto Gibbesi, Jews, hire themselves out to Stefano Carachulo to stack the the wood of Federico de Bononia in his sugar refinery for 7.10 tarì a kantar, and are paid 15 tarì on account.

Palermo, 1 April 1457

Source: ASP, Not. Giovanni Traverso, reg. 791, c. 345r.

Merdoc de Braxhuni and another ten men, all Jews, promise Micaele Quaragesima to fertilize half the sugar cane of Giovanni Crispo for 17 tarì a thousand and are paid 1.18.0 ounces on account by the bank of Iacobo de Crapona.

Palermo, 5 April 1457

Source: ASP, Not. Giovanni Traverso, reg. 791, cc. 360v–361r.

Muxa de Gauchio and Minto Nifusi, Jews, hire themselves out to Pino Ysolda to fertilize his sugar cane for 17 tarì a thousand, and are paid 12 tarì on account.

Palermo, 6 April 1457

Source: ASP, Not. Giovanni Traverso, reg. 791, c. nn.

Iuda de Minichi, a Jew, promises Luca Fanchiglia the work of Braxhuno son of Galfuni, another Jew, as water carrier in the tunny plant of Manfrido de Santo Stefano at Mondello during the entire season. He is paid two ducats on account.

Palermo, 27 April 1457

Source: ASP, Not. Giovanni Traverso, reg. 791, c. 386r-v.

Braxhono Sichiliano and his son Farrugio, Jewish citizens of Palermo, promise Guglielmo Faraguni, acting for Giovanni Crispo, to dig four trenches to hold 200 salme *of wheat for 2.12.0 ounces, and are paid 20* tarì *on account by the bank of Iacobo de Crapona*

Palermo, 12 September 1457

Source: ASP, Not. Giovanni Traverso, reg. 791, c. 29v.

Lya Sadita, a Jewish shoemaker, promises Antonio Manueli to sole the shoes of his sons and of his slave during a year for 17 tarì, *to be paid half by Christmas and half by the middle of May.*

Palermo, 22 September 1457

Source: ASP, Not. Giovanni Traverso, reg. 791, c. 47r.

Abram de Minichi, Lya de Mineo and Busacca Cipriano set up a joint venture for the operation of an olive oil press to last the entire season.

Palermo, 27 September 1457

Source: ASP, Not. Giovanni Traverso, reg. 791, c. 54v.

Xhayrono Levi, a Jew, undertakes to press the olives of Giovanni Romeo and Marco La Valli in his press for five grana *the* salma. *He also promises to supply two salme of olive pips. He is paid 6* tarì *on account.*

Palermo, [..] November 1457

Source: ASP, Not. Giovanni Traverso, reg. 791, c. 205v.

Xibiten Czibera, a Jew, hires himself out to Stefano Carachulo to work as parator *in the sugar refinery of Federico de Bononia for one ounce a month on the usual terms. He need not work on Saturdays.*

6148

Palermo, 2 December 1457

Source: ASP, Not. Giovanni Traverso, reg. 791, c. 226r.

Braxhuni Xhayeni, a Jew of Caltabellotta, undertakes to work in the tannery and shoeshop of Salamon Czicari, a Jew, for four months for 1.2.0 ounces. He is paid eight tarì *on account.*

Palermo, [..] December 1457

Source: ASP, Not. Giovanni Traverso, reg. 791, cc. 247v–248r.

Xannuni Millach, a Jew, promises Nicolò Capublancu and Antonio Sardu to work on their farm from January to July for 10 tarì *a month, a piece of cheese and three* tumuli *of wheat. They also set up a joint venture to last until August for the exploitation of a* xhirba *belonging to Xannuni.*

Palermo, 21 March 1458

Source: ASP, Not. Giovanni Traverso, reg. 791, c. 395r.

Raffael Raxid and Salamon de Minichi, Jewish saddlers, set up a joint venture to manufacture saddlery, dividing expenses and profits in equal shares between them. Raffael invests a horse and Salamon promises to give Raffael 1.3.0 ounces by August, the proceeds of the sale of three salme *of cheese.*

Palermo, 23 March 1458

Source: ASP, Not. Giovanni Traverso, reg. 791, c. 398r.

Farrugio Siveni, a Jew, lodges a notarial protest against Gerardo de Sutera on the ground that Gerardo had allegedly sold him cheese of inferior quality. As a result Gerardo promises to exchange the cheese for one of better quality.

Palermo, 20 April 1458

Source: ASP, Not. Giovanni Traverso, reg. 791, c. 438r-v.

Aczaruni Achina, Nissim de Termini and Benedetto Canetta, Jews, set up a joint venture to manufacture rope for the tunny industry. They agree to divide the profits into three equal shares.

Palermo, 23 October 1457

Source: ASP, Not. Giovanni Traverso, reg. 792, c. 130v.

Iacob de Termini, a Jewish citizen of Palermo, promises Pino de Ferro to sole the shoes of seven of his men and of a child for a year, for the terms established the previous year. He is paid 12 tarì and a salma of wheat valued at 12 tarì on account.

Palermo, 23 October 1457

Source: ASP, Not. Giovanni Traverso, reg. 792, cc. 131v–132r.

David Gattu, a Jewish citizen of Palermo, hires himself out to the notary Pino de Ferro to work in his sugar cane plantation for 14 grana a day, and is paid six tarì on account.

Palermo, 23 October 1457

Source: ASP, Not. Giovanni Traverso, reg. 792, c. 133r-v.

Xhaymi Gaczu alias Momo, Iusep Galifu and ten others, all Jews, hire themselves out to the notary Pino de Ferro to fertilize his sugar cane for 16 tarì a thousand beds. They are paid 1.12.0 ounces on account.

Palermo, 23 October 1457

Source: ASP, Not. Giovanni Traverso, reg. 792, cc. 133v–134r.

Merdoc Saffaru, Saul Xhabirra, Gauyu de Amato, Michiloni de Ragusa and Muxa Rugila promise Xhaymi Gaczu and Iusep Galifu, Jews, to work in the sugar refinery of Pino de Ferro and his partners for 17 grana a day.

Palermo, 22 December 1457

Source: ASP, Not. Giovanni Traverso, reg. 792, c. 259r.

Iosep de Minichi and Lya de Mineo, Jews, hire themselves out to Salamone Zicari, a Jew, to work as paratores *of grapes for three tarì the kantar. They also undertake to unload the grapes. They are paid 13 tarì on account and will receive another three on Easter.*

6150

Sicily

Palermo, 22 December 1457

Source: ASP, Not. Giovanni Traverso, reg. 792, cc. 259v–260r.

Sabet Miseria, a Jew, hires himself out as a parator *to work in the sugar refinery of Federico de Bononia for 20* tarì *a month, and is paid 10* tarì *on account.*

Palermo, 6 January 1458

Source: ASP, Not. Giovanni Traverso, reg. 792, c. 274r-v.

Raffael Roxiti, a Jew, hires himself out to Giovanni de Crispo to work as a grinder in his sugar refinery during the whole season for 2.6.0 ounces, and receives 15 tarì *on account.*

Palermo, 11 January 1458

Source: ASP, Not. Giovanni Traverso, reg. 792, c. 283r-v.

Selection of arbitrators to deal with the dispute between the partners in a tunny plant. The partners are Luca Fanchiglia, Iuda de Minichi, a Jew, and Ubertino de Costa. The arbitrators are to formulate the terms for liquidating the partnership.

Palermo, 20 January 1458

Source: ASP, Not. Giovanni Traverso, reg. 792, cc. 290v–293r.

Bonaventura de Danieli, a Jewish citizen of Palermo, hires himself out to Luca de Ligotti to work in his sugar refinery for 1 tarì *a boiling. He is paid two* tarì *on account.*

Palermo, 2 May 1459

Source: ASP, Not. Giovanni Traverso, reg. 793, c. 259r.

Xibiteni Xammara, Czullus Iubara, Daniel Xhabirra alias Ornigratu, Raffaeli Miseria, Iosep Xammara and three others, all Jews, hire themselves out to Giovanni de Bononia to work as paratores *in his sugar refinery for 6.13.0 ounces a month, and are paid that amount on account.*

Palermo, 18 May 1459

Source: ASP, Not. Giovanni Traverso, reg. 793, c. 279r.

Lya de Fromento and Xibiteni Xabirra, Jews, promise Stefano Carachulo to fertilize the sugar cane of Federico de Bononia on the usual terms, and are paid 12 tarì *on account.*

Palermo, 21 March 1459

Source: ASP, Not. Giovanni Traverso, reg. 793, c. 457r.

Busacca de Xibilia, a Jew, hires himself out to Antonio Musiri to work in the tunny plant of Antonio Bayamonte in Solanto for 1.12.0 ounces a month, and is paid 12 tarì *on account.*

Palermo, [..] [..] 1459

Source: ASP, Not. Giovanni Traverso, reg. 793, c. 470r.

Gimme and Sabatino de Minichi, Jews, promise Xhayrono Aczara, a Jew, to fertilize the sugar cane of Lamberto de Flore and Bartholomeo Columba for 18 grana *a day, and are paid four* tarì *each on account.*

Palermo, 31 March 1459

Source: ASP, Not. Giovanni Traverso, reg. 793, c. 471r.

Iusep Copiu, a Jew, promises Nicolò Carusu to work in the sugar refinery of Nicolò de Bononia on the usual terms, and is paid 12 tarì *on account*

Palermo, 31 March 1459

Source: ASP, Not. Giovanni Traverso, reg. 793, c. 472r

Vita de Missina, a Jew, promises Nicolò Carusu to work in the sugar refinery of Giovanni de Bononia on the usual terms, and is paid 21 tarì *on account.*

Palermo, 31 March 1459

Source: ASP, Not. Giovanni Traverso, reg. 793, c. 472r-v.

Michiluni Ysac, a Jew, hires himself out to Salomone Greco, a Jew, to fertilize the sugar cane of Lamberto de Flore and Bartholomeo Columba for 17 grana *a day, and is paid three* tarì *on account.*

Palermo, 31 March 1459

Source: ASP, Not. Giovanni Traverso, reg. 793, c. 481r-v.

Ayeti Bulfarachi, Daniel Xabirra, Robino de Girachio, Braxhuni Simael and Minto Gibbesi alias Muntuni, Jews, promise Antonio Bayamonte to transport tunny from the plant in Solanto and the shore of Palermo to Antonio's storehouse for 2.10 tarì *a quintal of* terzaroli.

Palermo, 20 August 1459

Source: ASP, Not. Giovanni Traverso, reg. 793, c. 654r.

Minto de Minichi, a Jew, promises Giovanni de Chiaramonte to transport sugar cane (cannamelos, gitidos et stirpones) *from the* contrade *Zisa and Falsomiele to Giovanni's sugar refinery at Chilmenti for six* tarì *a hundred* salme. *He is paid two* tarì *on account.*

Palermo, 25 October 1459

Source: ASP, Not. Giovanni Traverso, reg. 793, c. nn.

Vita Ferreri and Busacca Copiu, Jews, hire themselves out to Federico de Bononia to work as paratores *in his sugar refinery during the entire season for one ounce a month, and are paid one ounce each on account.*

Palermo, 25 October 1459

Source: ASP, Not. Giovanni Traverso, reg. 793, c. 118v.

Xamuel de Girachi, a Jew of Licata, hires himself out as a paratore *to Federico de Bononia to work in his sugar refinery for 21* tarì *a month, and is paid that amount on account.*

Palermo, 8 November 1459

Source: ASP, Not. Giovanni Traverso, reg. 793, c. 120r.

Merdoc Milimetti, a Jew, promises Xamueli Rugila, another Jew, to transport with eight beasts of burden half a quintal of grapes from the contrada *dei Colli e Ambleri to Palermo, and together with other muledrivers another two quintals of grapes from Monreale to Palermo for six* tarì *a quintal. He is paid 1.20.0 ounces on account.*

Palermo, 14 November 1459

Source: ASP, Not. Giovanni Traverso, reg. 793, c. 130r.

Manuel Xunina, a Jew of Trapani, hires himself out to Luca de Ligotti for the entire oil season for wages to be established by two arbitrators. He is paid one ounce on account.

Palermo, 8 January 1460

Source: ASP, Not. Giovanni Traverso, reg. 793, c. 201r-v.

Iacob de Missina and Nissim Aurifichi, Jewish shoemakers, set up a joint venture to run a shoeshop until the end of August. They both invest in the venture, but Nissim invests an additional 3.12.0 ounces, two in cash and 1.2.0 in must. [The Doc. breaks off in the middle].

Palermo, 6 March 1460

Source: ASP, Not. Giovanni Traverso, reg. 793, c. 261r.

Iacob de Termini, a Jew, promises Pietro Maurichio to sole the shoes of four of his slaves, called Valentino, Iosep, Surrano and Iuliano, for one ounce, to be paid in three instalments.

Palermo, 18 April 1460

Source: ASP, Not. Giovanni Traverso, reg. 793, c. 298r.

Pinesi di Aron, Merdoc Sidita and Benedetto Catalano, Jews, set up a joint venture to operate during the entire season the oil press of Giovanni de Missina, situated in Palermo in the contrada *Foroveteri next to the abattoir della Magione.*

Sicily

Palermo, 5 June 1460

Source: ASP, Not. Giovanni Traverso, reg. 793, c. 351r.

Iacobo Calabresi, a Jew, promises Braxhono Czitari, a Jew, to transport on his cart 1½ kantars of grapes from the contrada *Chiavelli to Braxhono's house for five* tarì.

Palermo, 30 June 1460

Source: ASP, Not. Giovanni Traverso, reg. 793, c. 380v.

Undertaking by Yaxi de Naro, a Jew, to insure Muxa Xhalegua, a Jew, against claims by Iosep Romano on account of the lease of a warehouse by Muxa to Iosep. The lease was formulated by Benedetto de Girachi, a Jewish notary.

Palermo, 30 June 1460

Source: ASP, Not. Giovanni Traverso, reg. 793, c. 380v.

Muxa Chalegua and Yaxi de Naro, Jews, declare null and void a contract between them made by the notary Andrea de Aprea.

Palermo, 8 August 1460

Source: ASP, Not. Giovanni Traverso, reg. 793, c. 418v.

Antonio Carnugio promises Braxhono Czitari, a Jew, to transport 1½ quintals of grapes from Parisio Homodei's vineyard to Braxhono's home in Palermo for 6.2 tarì.

Palermo, 19 August 1460

Source: ASP, Not. Giovanni Traverso, reg. 793, c. 431r.

Vita Ginni, a Jew, leases to Gerardo de Sutera a herd of some 225 sheep for a year for 24 tarì *a hundred and a castrated sheep. Gerardo promises to bring the sheep to Palermo.*

Palermo, 17 November 1460

Source: ASP, Not. Giovanni Traverso, reg. 793, c. 103v.

David de Termini, a Jew, hires himself out to Ferrugio Siveni, another Jew, to work in his tunny plant Arenella during the entire season for 1.6.0 ounces, and is paid 12 tarì *on account.*

Palermo, 22 December 1460

Source: ASP, Not. Giovanni Traverso, reg. 793, c. 144v.

Antonio Carnugiu promises Braxha Czitari, a Jewish shoemaker, to transport grapes from the contrada *Balderi to Palermo for four* tarì.

Palermo, 10 February 1461

Source: ASP, Not. Giovanni Traverso, reg. 793, c. 185v.

Lya Minichi, a Jew, hires himself out to Gaspare de Calandra to work in his tunny plant as a filler for 1.18.0 ounces a la scarsa, *and is paid 24* tarì *on account.*

Palermo, 11 February 1461

Source: ASP, Not. Giovanni Traverso, reg. 793, c. 188v.

Agreeement whereby Giovanni de Arnao undertakes to keep the accounts of the Jewish meat stalls in Palermo for Merdoc Bulfarachi, a Jew, their owner. Merdoc is illiterate. The arrangement is to last a year for six ounces.

XI februarii none Ind.
Cum Merdoc Bulfarachi, Iudeus, habeat et teneat, ac tenere debeat plancas seu bucherias Iudayce Panormi et nesciat scribere neque legere neque computum facere, ideo, hodie presenti pretitulato die Iohannes de Arnao, presens coram nobis sponte promisit, convenit et se solleniter obligavit dicto Merdoc Iudeo presenti et stipulanti tenere et regere quaternionem compotum et racionem de animalibus macellandis in dictis plancis et scribere et notare omnia facta et negocia ipsarum bucheriarum, et facere compotum cum credincerio ipsarum bucheriarum tamquam personam dicti Merdoc ab hodie in antea et per annum unum et completum, pro stipendio unciarum sex. Quas quidem uncias sex dictus Merdoc dare et solvere

promisit eidem Iohanni stipulanti in pecunia numerata successive. Que omnia promiserunt rata habere in pace, sine lite et sub ypotheca omnium bonorum, ac refectionem dampnorum, interesse expensarum, litis et extra. Renuncians etc. Et fiat ritus etc., in persona et bonis etc. Et iuravit etc. Testes: Iohannes la Xharera, Honofrius de Loeri.

Palermo, 18 March 1461

Source: ASP, Not. Giovanni Traverso, reg. 793, c. 238r-v.

Iacob de Termini, a Jew, promises Pietro Maurichio to sole the shoes of seven of his slaves for a year. He is to be paid 1.15.0 ounces in three instalments.

Palermo, 30 July 1461

Source: ASP, Not. Giovanni Traverso, reg. 793, cc. 397v–398r.

Xilomu Levi, a Jew, hires himself out to Gerardo de Sutera as an odd job man for four ounces a year.

Palermo, 30 July 1461

Source: ASP, Not. Giovanni Traverso, reg. 793, c. 398r-v.

Minto Sala, a Jew, hires himself out to Gerardo de Sutera as an odd job man for 7.10 tarì a month, and is paid 15 tarì on account. Xilomu Levi, a Jew, stands surety for Minto.

Palermo, 4 November 1461

Source: ASP, Not. Giovanni Traverso, reg. 794, c. 103v.

Gallufu Catalanu, a Jew, acknowledges to Guglielmo de Cuxina receipt of the rent for a house.

Palermo, 9 November 1461

Source: ASP, Not. Giovanni Traverso, reg. 794, c. 109r.

Lya Sidita, a Jewish shoemaker, promises Enrico de Bages to sole his shoes and those of his two sons until the end of September for 20 tarì *and a quintal of grapes.*

Palermo, 9 November 1461

Source: ASP, Not. Giovanni Traverso, reg. 794, cc. 127v–128r.

Braxha Czitaru, a Jewish shoemaker, promises Nicolò Tubando to sole his shoes and those of two men on his farm until August on the usual terms.

Palermo, 10 January 1462

Source: ASP, Not. Giovanni Traverso, reg. 794, c. 155r.

Contract whereby Gerardo Sutera undertakes to supply Minto Vignuni, a Jew, with 60 large bucks from his farm to replace the 25 salme *of wheat which he had failed to deliver.*

Palermo, 18 January 1462

Source: ASP, Not. Giovanni Traverso, reg. 794, c. 164r-v.

Giovanni de Malta of Malta hires himself out to Leone Ammara, a Jew, to work in his service from 20 January until the end of May for 14 tarì *a month. [the Doc. breaks off in the middle].*

Palermo, 20 January 1462

Source: ASP, Not. Giovanni Traverso, reg. 794, c. 169r-v.

Braxhono Simael alias Gentilomu, Busacca de Ansaluni, Merdoc Xhaguela, Michiluni Xhaguela, Michiluni Ysac, Xua Simael and their assistants, all Jews, hire themselves out to Nicolò de Bononia to work as paratores *in his sugar refinery for 6.6.0 ounces a month, and are paid that sum on account by the bank of the heirs of Iacobo de Crapona.*

Palermo, 20 January 1462

Source: ASP, Not. Giovanni Traverso, reg. 794, c. 169v.

Braxhono Simael alias Gentilomu, a Jew, together with enough men to employ two blocks, promises Nicolò de Bononia to cut and prune his sugar cane for eight tarì a thousand new ones and 15 tarì a thousand old ones. He is paid 1.6.0 ounces on account.

Palermo, 29 January 1462

Source: ASP, Not. Giovanni Traverso, reg. 794, cc. 178v–179r.

Simon Rabibi, a Jew, hires himself out to Nicolò de Bononia to work in his sugar refinery for 1.10 tarì a "boiling".

Palermo, 29 January 1462

Source: ASP, Not. Giovanni Traverso, reg. 794, c. 179r.

Iosep de Minichi, a Jew, hires himself out to Nicolò de Bononia to work in his sugar refinery for one tarì a "boiling".

Palermo, 29 January 1462

Source: ASP, Not. Giovanni Traverso, reg. 794, c. 179v.

Lya Sacerdotu, a Jew, hires himself out to Nicolò de Bononia to make three "boilings" a week in his sugar refinery for one tarì a "boiling", and is paid 15 tarì on account by the bank of Iacobo de Crapona.

Palermo, 10 February 1462

Source: ASP, Not. Giovanni Traverso, reg. 794, c. 190v.

Matheo Bindira, a Jew, hires himself out to Nicolò de Bononia to work as fireman (fucarolu) in his sugar refinery for 3.6.0 ounces a month. Matheo promises to provide Christian substitutes to work on Saturdays in his stead. He is paid two ounces on account.

Palermo, 10 February 1462

Source: ASP, Not. Giovanni Traverso, reg. 794, cc. 190v–191r.

Abram de Siracusia alias lu Raysi, a Jew, hires himself out to Nicolò de Bononia

6159

to work in his sugar refinery for one tarì a "boiling", and is paid 15 tarì on account.

Palermo, 10 February 1462

Source: ASP, Not. Giovanni Traverso, reg. 794, c. 204r.

Agreement between Leone Ammara and Xilomo Mizoc, Jews. They had bought tunny for 11.20.0 ounces from Antonio de Axin, royal treasurer, to be paid for half by April and half by the opening of the tunny plant at Trabia. They now decide that having sold the fish, half the proceeds are to go to Leone, who is to pay 5.25.0 ounces to Antonio.

Palermo, 11 May 1462

Source: ASP, Not. Giovanni Traverso, reg. 794, c. 293v.

Deed of sale whereby Raimondo Calimata de Monforte sells a horse to Xannuni Millac, a Jew, for 1.15.0 ounces.

Palermo, 11 May 1462

Source: ASP, Not. Giovanni Traverso, reg. 794, c. 294r-v.

Merdoc Xhactuni, Iusep Ammara, Iuda Sacerdotu, Sabet Levi and three others, all Jews, hire themselves out to Pino de Isolda to fertilize his sugar cane for 16 tarì *a thousand, and are paid 18* tarì *on account.*

Palermo, 11 May 1462

Source: ASP, Not. Giovanni Traverso, reg. 794, c. 305v.

Contract between Manuel Xunina, a Jew of Trapani in Palermo, and Giovanni Capello for the production of 1,500 hoops for barrels (miliaria vera et dimidium chircorum de vegeti longorum). *Manuel is to make the bands and is to be paid 20.10* tarì *a thousand by Giovanni. Manuel is to sell them and the proceeds are to be divided between the two.*

Sicily

Palermo, 26 May 1462

Source: ASP, Not. Giovanni Traverso, reg. 794, cc. 305v–306r.

Deed of sale whereby Gerardo de Sutera sells Sabeti de Termini, a Jew, a kantar of curd for 2.1.0 ounces, and receives 19 tarì on account. The balance is due within eight days.

Palermo, 16 June 1462

Source: ASP, Not. Giovanni Traverso, reg. 794, c. 326v.

Xilomu Levi, a Jew of Trapani, hires himself out to Gerardo de Sutera to work with his herd for four ounces a year. He is paid two ounces on account.

Palermo, 15 July 1462

Source: ASP, Not. Giovanni Traverso, reg. 794, c. 354v.

Joint venture between Muxa Sacerdotu alias Candiotu, a Jew of Caltagirone, and Andolino Bonifanti. Andolino gave Muxa 1.24.0 ounces to buy goods, to be returned within two months. The proceeds from the sale of the goods are to be divided between the partners in equal shares.

Palermo, 30 July 1462

Source: ASP, Not. Giovanni Traverso, reg. 794, cc. 369r–370r.

Deed of sale whereby Xilomu Xhalifa and his wife Xhanna, Jews, with the consent of their of age son Abrae and their minor sons, sell a house solerata *in the Cassaro to Merdoc Sidita, a Jew. The house is one of two properties which the couple hold in lease from Iacobo de Playa for an annual rent of 20 tarì due in August. The sale price is five ounces, three of which are paid on the spot and two by August.*

Palermo, 18 August 1462

Source: ASP, Not. Giovanni Traverso, reg. 794, cc. 388v–389r.

Agreement whereby Muxa Medui, a Jew, cedes all his property to his cousin Gallufo Miseria on condition that Gallufo provides for his maintenance.

Palermo, 1 September 1463

Source: ASP, Not. Giovanni Traverso, reg. 794, c. nn.

Giuliano Lu Sardu promises to deliver to Salamon Czitari, a Jew, a quintal of grapes on demand.

Palermo, 9 September 1463

Source: ASP, Not. Giovanni Traverso, reg. 794, c. 20v.

Lia Sidita, a Jewish shoemaker, promises Aloisio de Sutera to sole his shoes and those of his employee until the end of August for 14 tarì, *to be paid in three instalments.*

Palermo, 9 September 1463

Source: ASP, Not. Giovanni Traverso, reg. 794, c. 20v.

Iosep Lu Crivaru, a Jew, hires himself out to [..] Suvararo to work in his sugar refinery as fireman (fucarolo) *for 1.24.0 ounces.*

Palermo, 13 October 1463

Source: ASP, Not. Giovanni Traverso, reg. 794, cc. 58v–59r.

Contract whereby Gerardo de Sutera and Leone and Iusep Romano, Jews, exchange 10 salme *of barley and ten of wheat for a mule and a quintal of grapes.*

Palermo, 31 October 1463

Source: ASP, Not. Giovanni Traverso, reg. 794, c. nn.

Gerardo de Sutera declares that he owes Muxa Xifuni, a Jew, 12 ounces. Seven are the balance of the price of cheese, and five are on account of the surety he had stood for Antonio Bayamonte. Gerardo undertakes to settle the debt with 60 quintals of cheese.

Palermo, 17 November 1463

Source: ASP, Not. Giovanni Traverso, reg. 794, c. 113v.

Notarial quittance issued by Manuel Xunina, a Jew, to Bulxhayra Abbate, another Jew, and declaration that he has no further claims on Bulxhayra.

Palermo, 20 December 1463

Source: ASP, Not. Giovanni Traverso, reg. 794, cc. 138v–139r.

Girmia Xammara, a Jew, declares that he owes Francesco Homodei one ounce for having cut wood on his property without permission. He undertakes to pay 15 tarì *within a month and the balance by May.*

Palermo, 5 January 1464

Source: ASP, Not. Giovanni Traverso, reg. 794, c. nn.

Minto Sala, a Jew, hires himself out to Gerardo de Sutera to curd milk and transport wood on his cattle farm for 10 tarì *a month. He is paid six* tarì *on account.*

Palermo, 27 February 1464

Source: ASP, Not. Giovanni Traverso, reg. 794, c. nn.

Aron de Missina and Sabatino Calabresi, Jews, hire themselves out to Leonardo Heder Scorfet, lieutenant of the Sacra Mansione della Magione dei Teutonici, as builders for 18 tarì *a month.*

Palermo, 9 April 1464

Source: ASP, Not. Giovanni Traverso, reg. 794, c. nn.

Xhayrono de Busacca, a Jew, hires himself out to Lya Sidita, another Jew, to work as shoemaker (ad faciendum omnia servicia artis corbiserie) *for 10* tarì *a month.*

Palermo, 4 July 1464

Source: ASP, Not. Giovanni Traverso, reg. 794, c. 334r.

Farrugio de Gauyo, a Jew, hires himself out to Domenico Bulgarino to make hoops for the tunny industry (a chitari chirki aiutari a fari logia e mictiri chirki a mollu et gittariki aqua) *for five* tarì *a thousand. He is paid 10* tarì *on account.*

Palermo, 8 November 1462

Source: ASP, Not. Giovanni Traverso, reg. 795, cc. 94v–95r.

Lya Minichi, a Jew, promises Blasio Bonfiglu to dig a well and fortify the walls in his house for 1.1.80 ounces.

Palermo, 18 November 1462

Source: ASP, Not. Giovanni Traverso, reg. 795, c. 110v

Maxhalufo di Lu Presti, a Jew, withdraws the accusation of theft he had lodged with the captain's court in Palermo against Salamon Bonavia alias de la Gricigna. Manuel Abram, a Jew, with the approval of Nissim de Medico, had stood surety for Salamon.

Palermo, 10 March 1463

Source: ASP, Not. Giovanni Traverso, reg. 795, c. 194r.

Giulianu Lu Sardu promises Salamon Czitari, a Jew, to transport a quintal of grapes at the next vintage for six tarì.

Palermo, 11 July 1463

Source: ASP, Not. Giovanni Traverso, reg. 795, c. 328v.

Muxa Barbarussa and Manuel de Tripuli, Jews, promise Orlando de Cathania to measure and transport during the olive season all Orlando's oil in Palermo for 15 grana *the kantar. They are paid six* tarì *on account.*

Palermo, 11 July 1463

Source: ASP, Not. Giovanni Traverso, reg. 795, cc. 328v–329r.

Deed of sale whereby Giovanni Cappa sells Gimiluni Naxhay, a Jew, the entire cheese production of his cow herd for 10 ounces, to be paid in instalments.

Palermo, 27 July 1463

Source: ASP, Not. Giovanni Traverso, reg. 795, c. 347v.

Musutu Malti and two partners, Jews, hire themselves out to master Michele de Napuli to make horse and mule shoes for three tarì *a hundred. They are paid 12* tarì *on account.*

Palermo, 1 August 1463

Source: ASP, Not. Giovanni Traverso, reg. 795, c. 358r-v.

Nissim Barbutu and Merdoc Sacerdotu, Jews, promise Gabriele de Napoli to dig a well in Gabriele's vineyard in the contrada *Cambrisu. The dimensions agreed on are five palms long and three palms wide, 10* tarì *the* canna. *They are to begin work on 8.8 and to continue without interruption until completion. They are paid six* tarì *on account.*

Note: A Sicilian palm measured 25 cm.

Palermo, 29 August 1463

Source: ASP, Not. Giovanni Traverso, reg. 795, c. 390v–391r.

Franciscu Bonfiglu promises Salamon Zicari, a Jew, to transport two quintals of grapes of the next vintage to Salamon's house and tavern for five tarì, *paid on the spot.*

Palermo, 30 August 1463

Source: ASP, Not. Giovanni Traverso, reg. 795, c. 395r.

Agreement whereby Farchono Sacerdotu and Xamuel Abentabarelli, Jews, undertake to sell for Iacob de Napuli some cloth of various colours valued at five to seven tarì *the* canna. *They undertake to sell the cloth at the best possible price and to hand over to Iacob the proceeds. On 18.11.1463 Iacob declares he received the money due to him.*

Source: ASP, Not. Giovanni Traverso, reg. 765

Date and Page	Debtor	Amount	Reason	Remarks
2.3.1418 c. nn	Iosep Romanu and Benedicto Giburra, Jews	1.20.0 ounces		creditor: Donna Garina de Conello; guarantor Salamon Romanus, a Palermitan Jew

Date and Page	Lender or Seller	Amount	Payment	Remarks
15.11.1417 c. nn.	Bernardo Blasco	2.12.0 ounces	by January; paid 16.2.1418	sale of honey to Busac Xhamayam, a Jew
31.12.1417 c. nn	Vita Ysac, a Palermitan Jew	a third of the price agreed		sale of a third of some cows sold to Bartholomeo de Todaro
20.1.1418 c. nn.	Donna Flos Luchusu	2 ounces		sale of grapes to Iacob Sabbuchi, a Palermitan Jew
3.2.1418 c. nn.	Donna Gioa de Meo	2.9 *tarì*	1 *tarì* a week; paid 7.2.1419	sale of a tunic to Symon de Mayu, a Jew

Date and Page	Tenant	Location and Description	Rent and duration	Remarks
20.1.1418 c. nn.	Sabbeti Taguili, a Palermitan Jew	Cassaro, bordering on inn and shop of Calogero; shop	1.15.0 ounces a year; 2 years	landlord: Calogero de Iohanne

Source: ASP, Not. Giovanni Traverso, reg. 766

Date and Page	Lender or Seller	Amount	Payment	Remarks
20.9.1418 c. 19r	Nardo de Ursino and Donna Flos, widow of Pietro de Lukisio	12 *tarì*	within 15 days; paid 5.10.1418	sale of grapes to Conino Sabuchi, a Jew

22.9.1418 c. 27r	Francesco de Labrama	1.2.0 ounces	within 4 months; paid 20.2.1419	sale of wheat to Simon Ysacco, a Palermitan Jew
27.9.1418 c. nn	Francesco de Labrama	1.18.0 ounces	within 4 months; paid 27.2.1419	sale of wheat to Busacca Xachamia, a Jew
28.9.1418 c. nn	Angelo de Labrama for Francesco de Labrama	1.2 *tarì*	within 4 months; paid 28.2.1419	sale of wheat to Merdoc Xhacchitano, a Palermitan Jew
28.9.1418 c. nn	Angelo de Labrama for Francesco de Labrama	1.2.0 ounces	within 4 months; paid 28.2.1419	sale of wheat to Busacca de Tripoli, a Jew
28.9.1418 c. nn	Angelo de Labrama for Francesco de Labrama	1.2.0 ounces	within 4 months; paid 21.2.1419	sale of wheat to Lya Siveni, a Jew
28.9.1418 c. nn	Francesco de Labrama	1.2.0 ounces	within 4 months; paid 21.2.1419	sale of wheat to Busacca Xacarono, a Palermitan Jew
28.9.1418 c. nn	Francesco de Labrama	1.2.0 ounces	within 4 months; paid 16.2.1419	sale of wheat to Rabbi Castellano, a Jew
10.10.1418 c. 54v	Conello Macza of Trapani	8 ounces	1 ounce on account, balance in monthly instalments of 1 ounce	sale of coal to Braxhono Russo, a Jew
25.10.1418 c. 69v	Giovanni Sinagra	2 ounces	by May	sale of *pecorino* and wheat to Vita and Gauyu Xua, Jews
25.10.1418 c. 70r	Angelo de Rogerio	1.3.0 ounces	12 *tarì* on account, balance within 15 days; paid 5.12.1418	sale of grapes to Vita and Sadono Ruggila Jews
3.11.1418 c. 78r	Iacobus Caczecta	28.10 *tarì*	paid	sale of grapes tro Muxa Russu, a Jew

8.11.1418 c. 83r	Andrea Lumbardo	4 ounces	weekly instalments of 12 *tarì*	sale of sugar to Sufen de Medico, a Palermitan Jew
16.11.1418 c. 88r	Lya Bambulu, a Palermitan Jew	2.21.0 ounces		sale of a horse with saddle and bridle
22.11.1418 c. 93r	Pino Manganario	1.5.0 ounces	within a month; paid 15.10.1419	sale of glass to Benedetto Spagnolo, a Jew
8.3.1419 c. 156v	Nissim Ysaya, a Jew of Trapani	within the current month		sale of wine
14.3.1419 c. 161v	Andrea de Lombardo	2.12.0 ounces	by October	sale of a horse to Bulxhayra Cusintinu, a Jew
15.5.1419 c. 217r	Valenti di Nicola and Nichu de Flore	2.6.0 ounces	by September	sale of a mantle to Vita Ysac, a Palermitan Jew
30.5.1419 c. 230v	Giovanni de Gentili	2 ounces	paid	sale of grapes to Braxhono Russo, a Jew

Date and Page	Tenant	Location and Description	Rent and Duration	Remarks
2.11.1418 c. 76v	Fariono de Ayeti, a Jew	Palermo, *contrada* Fereveteris, bordering on house of mastro Santi and of notary Giovanni Traverso; shop	1.3.0 ounces for 1 year; 15 *tarì* on account, balance in instalments	landlord: Sancto de Alexio
21.6.1419 c. nn	Xhaymi and Bussaca Levi, Jews	Palermo, *contrada* Fereveteris; shop and use of well	1.6.0 ounces for one year	landlord: Antonio Faczella

Source: ASP, Not. Giovanni Traverso, reg. 767

Data and Page	Principal	Attorney	Purpose	Remarks
24.10.1419 c. nn	Donna Giglia de La Barbera	Sabet de Armona and Graciano Taxhariatu, Jews	to collect the debt to Giglia from the property of the late Vita de Messina and his son Salamone	

Date and Page	Lender or Seller	Amount	Payment	Remarks
5.9.1419 c. nn	Rogerio de Urso	24 *tarì*	3 *tarì* on account, balance by first half of November	sale of a beast of burden to Iuda de Mineo, a Palermitan Jew
14.9.1419 c. nn	Bulxhayra Rabbi, a Palermitan Jew	4 ounces	2 ounces within a month, balance by Christmas; paid 7.3.1420	sale of an anvil
23.10.1419 c. nn	Iacobo de Yoya	1 ounce	15 *tarì* by soling his shoes, balance: half by Christmas, half 40 days later	sale of grapes to Salamon Xammara, a Palermitan Jew
23.10.1419 c. nn	Pasquale de Burrano	1.6.0 ounces	1 ounce on account	sale of grapes to Symon de Maya and Aczarono Riczio, Jews
2.5.1420 c. nn	Vita Ysac, a Palermitan Jew	1 ounce	20 *tarì* on account	sale of manure
26.6.1420 c. nn	Rogerio Pignataru	1 ounce	by December	sale of wheat to Valenczinu Sacerdotu and Benedetto Ysac, Palermitan Jews

Date and Page	Tenant	Location and Description	Rent and Duration	Remarks
16.4.1420 c. nn	Salamon Xammara, a Palermitan Jew	Palermo; shop	12.10 *tarì*	landlord: Antonio de Consilio

16.7.1420	Sabet	Palermo; shop	14 *tarì* a month for	landlord: Guarnerio
c. nn	Xammara, a		1 year	de Ru
	Palermitan Jew			

Source: ASP, Not. Giovanni Traverso, reg. 768

Date and Page	Lender or Seller	Amount	Payment	Remarks
28.10.1420 c. 45v	Tuchio de Flore	1.11.10 ounces	by February; paid 4.3.1421	sale of wheat to Mardoch Xillac, a Jew of Palermo
28.10.1420 c. 45v	Tuchio de Flore	1.11.10 ounces	by February; paid 17.3.1421	sale of wheat to Muxa Bulgidi, a Jew of Palermo
28.10.1420 c. 45v	Ubertino Abbatellis	1 ounce	15 *tarì* on account	sale of grapes to Salamon Sarritano, a Jew
30.10.1420 c. 47r	Iusep Achina, a Palermitan Jew		by November; paid 11.12.1420	sale of wheat to Vegnamino de Minichi, a Jew of Castronovo
6.11.1420 c. 57r	Tuchio de Flore	15 *tarì*	5 *tarì* a month	sale of wheat to Salamon Xammara, a Jew of Palermo
10.12.1420 c. 83r	Andrea de Milia	21 *tarì*	by May; paid 18.12.1421	sale of wheat to Xibbiteni Xammara, a Palermitan Jew
7.2.1421 c. 138v	Tuchio de Flore	1.12.0 ounces	within 3 months; paid 24.6.1421	sale of wheat to Salomone Sufer, a Palermitan Jew
2.4.1421 c. 198r	Pino Barbuczia	17.10 *tarì*	by October; paid 2611.1421	sale of goods to Iacob Medui, a Jew of Palermo
7.4.1421 c. 205v	Iohannes Muraturi	18.10 *tarì*	3 *tarì* on account, balance 4 *tarì* a month	sale of wheat to Aczarono Rigio, a Jew of Palermo

18.4.1421 c. 225v	Sadonu Russu, a Palermitan Jew	3.5.0 ounces	1.10 *tarì* on account, balance on delivery	sale of *caciocavallo* to Friderico Russello
17.7.1421 c. nn	Braxhono Russu, a Jew			loan of a sum of money
27.9.1424 c. nn	Antonia de Piczinca	2.12.0 ounces	part at Easter and part by 24.6; paid 11.10.1424	sale of grapes to Ximinco Aurifichi, a Palermitan Jew
27.9.1424 c. nn	Antonia de Piczinca	2.12.0 ounces	part at Shrovetide, part at Easter and part by 24.6	sale of grapes to Bulchayra Sansuni, a Palermitan Jewess
27.9.1424 c. nn	Antonia de Piczinca	2.12.0 ounces	part at Shrovetide, part at Easter and part by 24.6; paid 19.10.1424	sale of grapes to Murdaxhay Binna, a Palermitan Jew
3.11.1414 c. nn	Masio de Guarnota	4.6.0 ounces	part at Shrovetide, part at Easter and part by May; paid 10.8.1425	sale of grapes to Aczarono Riczio
17.11.1424 c. 134r	Merchione de Berto for Andreotta de Lumbardo	within 2 months	paid 19.1.1425	sale of 25 tables and 30 dozen forks to Leone la Iudeca and Nissim Binna, Palermitan Jews
21.12.1424 c. 142r	Andrea de Lumbardo	1.18.0 ounces	monthly instalments	loan of certain amount to Sufen de Medico, a Jew of Palermo
24.11.1424 c. 167v	Ubertino de Abbatellis	1 ounce	by July; paid 30.8.1425	sale of wheat to Muxa de Minichi, a Palermitan Jew
23.1.1425 203r	Giovanni Martino de Spallicta	3.6.0 ounces	paid	sale of a thousand tiles (*calamidarum*) and a thousand bricks (*madonum*)
7.3.1425 c. 261v	Salamon and Iusep Aurifichi, Jews of Palermo	16.24.0 ounces	6.12.0 ounces on account	sale of *confezionum*

13.3.1425 c. 269v	Andreocta Lumbardo	4.6.0 ounces	9 *tarì* a week	sale of thin silk and Bologna tafetta to Musutu Brixha, a Jew in Palermo
1.4.1425 c. 304v	Braxhono Mangiavacca, a Jew of Palermo	24 *tarì*	9 *tarì* on account	sale of manure
11.4.1425 c. 311v	Symon de Ansalono, a Jew of Palermo	1.3.0 ounces	by August	sale of a young beast of burden
14.4.1425 c. 317r	Ubertino de Abbatellis	2.12.0 ounces	by April	sale of oil to Xhayruna, wife of Nissim Medui, a Palermitan Jewess; guarantor: Sabutu Medui, a Jew
12.4.1425 c. 317r	Andreocta de Lumbardo	1.12.0 ounces	by April	sale of a piece of tafetta to Musutu Brixha, a Palermitan Jew

Date and Page	Tenant	Location and Description	Rent and Duration	Remarks
26.2.1421 c. 168r	Iacob Medui, a Palermitan Jew	Cassaro, bordering on the church of S. Dimitri; house	1 year for 1 ounce	landlord: master Moyses Chetibi, a Palermitan Jew

Source: ASP, Not. Giovanni Traverso, reg. 769

Date and Page	Debtor	Amount	Reason	Remarks
12.5.1422 c. nn	Busacca de Missina, a Jew	4 ounces	paid	creditor: Alfonso de Valladolit

Date and Page	Lender or Seller	Amount	Payment	Remarks
[..].9.1421 c. nn	Mariano Benedicto	2.27.0 ounces	3 instalments	sale of grapes to Ysdrael Medui, a Jew of Palermo

30.9.1421 c. nn	Mariano Benedicto	1.13.10 ounces	3 instalments, at Christmas, Shrovetide and Easter; paid 11.5.1422	sale of grapes to Muxa Sacerdotu, a Jew
30.9.1421 c. nn	Mariano Benedicto	1.13.10 ounces	3 instalments, at Christmas, Shrovetide and Easter	sale of grapes to Nixim Sacerdoto, a Jew
22.11.1421 c. nn	Valluni de Siracusia, a Jew		paid	sale of a wooden wheel
30.12.1421 c. nn	Tuchio de Flore	3.8.0 ounces	by April; paid 4.5.1422	sale of wheat to Czaccono Minczani, a Jew
23.2.1422 c. nn	Siminto Benassay	1.3.0 ounces	by March	sale of some goods
12.5.1422 c. nn	Sabbeti Xammara, a Jew	12 *tarì*	within 2 months	sale of goods to Sufen de Mayu, a Palermitan Jew
16.7.1422 c. nn	Alfonso de Valladolit	1 ounce	by August; paid 5.2.1423	sale of saffron to Busac Misiria and Xhufeni Mani, Jews
[..].7. 1422	Pino Manganario	4.24.0 ounces	3 instalments at Christmas, Easter and May	sale of grapes to Xhaymi Levi and Aczarono Riczu, Jews

Source: ASP, Not. Giovanni Traverso, reg. 770

Date and Page	Debtor	Amount	Reason	Remarks
2.12.1423 c. nn	Antonio de Iacob and his wife Lucia, for Leone Barba, a Jew	1.24.0 ounces	debt	creditor: Nardo de Yambertone

28.5.1424 c. nn	Braxhono Mizoc, a Jew of Palermo	1.3.0 ounces and 9 *tarì*	expenses for issue of deed and for appeal to *magna regia corte*	creditor: Andrea Columba; 7 *tarì* paid, balance in instalments
Date and Page	**Lender or Seller**	**Amount**	**Payment**	**Remarks**
17.12.1422 c. 90r	Andreotta de Lumbardo	6.5.0 ounces	within 4 months	sale of oil to Gauyo and Salamon Rabibi, Palermitan Jews
1.2.1423 c. 126r	Alfonso de Valladolit	15 *tarì*	by March	sale of saffron to Busac Misiria, a Palermitan Jew
15.2.1423 c. 134r	Alfonso de Valladolit	1 ounce	by May	sale of barley to Busac Misiria, a Palermitan Jew
20.5.1423 c. 227v	Chono Litterio	16 *tarì*	by August	sale of wheat to Symon Minichi, a Palermitan Jew
23.9.1423 c. 48r	Andrea de Columba	12 *tarì*	within a month; paid 5.11.1423	sale of an anchor to Muxa Russu and Daniel Rugila, Jews
1.10.1423 c. 58r	Ubertino Abbatellis	1.15.0 ounces	by 15.5.1424	sale of grapes to Xamuel Sala, a Palermitan Jew
13.10.1423 c. 83r	Giovanni de Sclafani	12 *tarì*	by February 1424; paid 19.5.1424	sale of wheat to Symon de Mayu, a Jew in Palermo
3.11.1423 c. 135v	Pietro de Magno for Thomeo de mastro Antonio	26 *tarì*	on demand; paid 7.11.1425	sale of tunny to David Malluczu, a Jew of Trapani
17.11.1423 c. 259r	Iuliano de Bonafede	15 *tarì*	within a year; paid 17.10.1427	sale of goods to Sabbatino de Girachio, a Jew of Palermo
15.12.1423 c. 203r	Filippo Xhareri	13 ounces	paid	sale of a white Saracen slave to Nissim Saya, a Jew

Date and Page	Lender or Seller	Amount	Payment	Remarks
17.4.1424 c. 372r	Iacob de Gauyu, a Jew	9 ounces	half by June, balance by August; paid 12.7. and 25.10.1424	sale of three mules
18.5.1424 c. 419r	Sabbeti Cusintinu, a Jew	2 ounces	12 *tarì* a month starting in June	loan
22.5.1424 c. 412r	Alfonso Valladolit	24 *tarì*	by August	sale of a metal candelabrum to Abram Castellanu, a Jew of Marsala

Date and Page	Tenant	Location and Description	Rent and Duration	Remarks
23.6.1424 c. nn	Busacca Levi and Muxa Cohen alias Sacerdotu, Jews	Cassaro, Platea Marmorea, bordering on houses of Giovanni Inveges and Sadoni Russu and public road; house *solerata* and 2 shops, 4 *catodio*, small courtyard and a well	3 ounces a year	leaseholder: Iohannes de Accayra; owner: Pietro de Afflicto, entitled to rent of 12½ florins

Source: ASP, Not. Giovanni Traverso, reg. 771

Date and Page	Lender or Seller	Amount	Payment	Remarks
26.8.1425 c. 45v	Francesco de Branna	2.12.0 ounces	by Easter	sale of merchandise to Daniele Ruggila, a Jew
14.11.1425 c. 153v	Iuliano Patella for Andreocta Lumbardo	1.15.0 ounces	by June	sale of lambs to Salamon Sabuchi and Manuel de Armona, Jews

28.11.1425 c. 177v	Tommaso de Bellachera, abbot of San Giovanni degli Eremiti	10.12.0 ounces	by May	sale of barley to Saddono Russu, a Jew
11.12.1425 c. 196r	Sadono Russu, a Jew, for Tommaso de Bellachera, abbot of San Giovanni degli Eremiti	11.6.0 ounces	within 6 months	sale of wheat to Giovanni Boychellu
22.1.1426 c. 243v	Machono Scavu, a Jew	2.24.0 ounces	1.27.0 ounces on account, balance by Easter	sale of grapes
19.2.1426 c. 271r	Ubertino Abbatellis	1.25.0 ounces	by June; paid 8.10.1426	sale of goods to Manueli Veru, a Palermitan Jew
26.4.1426 c. 353r	Thomeo de mastro Antonio	11.20.0 ounces	3 ounces on account	sale of tunny to Vita Pancza. a Jew
27.4.1426 c. 354v	Amato Xhamirichi, a Jew	18 *tarì*		sale of grapes
3.6.1426 c. 394r	Sadono Russu, a Palermitan Jew	1 ounce	by September	sale of two young beasts of burden
4.6.1426 c. 395r	Ubertino de Abbatellis	1.6.0 ounces	within a year; paid 6.6.1427	sale of 2 young beasts of burden to Amato Xhamirichi, a Palermitan Jew
4.7.1426 c. 428r	Muxa Achina, a Palermitan Jew	1.11.0 ounces	by August	sale of a young beast of burden
16.8.1426 c. 485r	Chicco de Basilicu		paid	sale of grapes to Azarono Riczu, Vita Levi and Vita de Maczara, Jews

28.8.1426 c. 537v	Giovanni de Homodei	10 *tarì*		sale of tunny to Sabet Xagaruni, a Jew

Date and Page	Tenant	Location and Description	Rent and Duration	Remarks
21.8.1426 c. nn	Guido Cappuni	Polizzi, bordering on house of Andrea de Mule; house	12 *tarì*; 1 year	landlord: Manuele Spagnolu, a Jew of Agrigento

Source: ASP, Not. Giovanni Traverso, reg. 772

Date and Page	Lender or Seller	Amount	Payment	Remarks
19.9.1426 c. 45v	Farchono Sacerdoto and Xhaguina, widow of Leone de Medico, Jews	4.15.0 and 11.7.10 ounces	10 ounces on account	sale of light and heavy rope
27.9.1426 c. 66v	Bundo de Campo	2.15.0 ounces	three instalments at Christmas, Shrovetide and Easter; paid 18.8.1427	sale of grapes to Xhaymi Levi, a Jew
10.10.1426 c. 108v	Busacca de Tripuli, a Palermitan Jew	1.17.0 ounces a thousand, 27 *tarì* a thousand respectively	10.20.0 ounces on account; paid 30.4.1427	sale of light and heavy rope
16.10.1426 c. 128r	Sadonu Russu, a Jew	17 *tarì*	by September; paid 15.10.1427	sale of a beast of burden
16.10.1426 c. 128v	Sadonu Russu, a Jew	1.19.0 ounces	by September; paid 15.10.1427	sale of 2 beasts of burden
16.10.1426 c. 129r	Braxono Bambalu, a Jew	1.18.0 ounces	four monthly rates	sale of a blue mantle to Salamon Actuni, a Jew
8.11.1426 c. 211r	Momo Gaczu, a Palermitan Jew	1.24.0 ounces	paid	sale of a horse

6177

8.11.1426 c. 211v	Leone Xhaguen and his son Lya, Palermitan Jews	1.27.0 ounces		sale of a horse
11.11.1426 c. 215v	Filippo Bellachera	2.28.0 ounces	half by Christmas, balance 20 days later	sale of goods to Xhaymi Sikili, a Jew
27.11.1426 c. 268r	Enrico de Caccabi	24 *tarì*	11 *tarì* on account	sale of grapes to Busacca Levi a Palermitan Jew
27.1.1427 c. 329v	Bono de Iacobo for Andreotta Lumbardo	18 *tarì*		sale of oil to Pinesi Sacerdotu and Salamon Missina, Palermitan Jews
27.1.1427 c. 330r	Bonectu and Busacca de Seracusia, Palermitan Jews	9 *tarì*	2 *tarì* on account	sale of oil
21.3.1427 c. 429r	Orlando Pinczuni	1.12.0 ounces	within 8 months	sale of a horse to Xibiten Virdi, a Jew
28.4.1427 c. 435r	Filippo Bellachera	11.5 *tarì*	by June	sale of chestnuts to Simon Malti, a Jew
17.7.1427 c. 524v	Francesco Ventimiglia	13.4 *tarì*		sale of manure to Vita Ysac, a Jew
11.8.1427 c. 620r	Giovanni Russu	27 *tarì*	13.10 *tarì* on account	sale of grapes to Symon de Xilomo, a Jew
21.8.1427 c. 641r	Giovanni Lombardo	2.12.0 ounces	bu September	sale of goods to Symon Benassay, a Jew

Date and Page	Tenant	Location and Description	Rent and Duration	Remarks
5.12.1426 c. 268v	Siminto Maltisi, a Jew	Palermo, bordering on prison and on house of Iacobo de Florencia; one storey house	4 years at 1.9.0 ounces a year	landlord: Iacobo de Vitaglano

6178

Sicily

Source: ASP, Not. Giovanni Traverso, reg. 773

Date and Page	Debtor	Amount	Reason	Remarks
3.5.1429 c. nn	Xilomo and Mardoc Rustico, Palermitan Jews	1.4.0 ounces		due by August to Aloisio de Campo

Date and Page	Lender or Seller	Amount	Payment	Remarks
17.10.1427 c. nn	Enrico de Caccabo	1.18.0 ounces	paid 12.1.1429	sale of grapes to Busacca Levi, a Jew
27.11.1427 c. nn	Thomasio de Giliberto	8.23.5 ounces	3 instalments	sale of white goat (*bichinorum alborum*) hides to Muxa de Gauyo a Jew of Castellammare
12.12.1427 c. nn	Filippo Bellachera	29.5 *tarì*	within 2 months; paid 28.1.1429	sale of saffron to Nixim Xidedi and Xilomo de Pichuni, Palermitan Jews
22.1.1428 c. nn	Riccardo Vitellu	1.6.0 ounces	1 *tarì* a week	sale of wheat to Vita Levi and Salamon Actuni, Jews of Palermo
4.3.1428 c. 348v	Thomeo de mastro Antonio	1.18.0 ounces	by August; paid 9.9.1428	sale of tunny to Iuda de Natali, a Jew
15.3.1428 c. 358r	Aloisio Milacio for Thomeo de mastro Antonio	24 *tarì*		sale of merchandise to Asisa La Mamma, a Jewess
18.4.1428 c. 404v	Andreocta Lumbardo	1.6.0 ounces	by August	sale of tunny to Braxhono Sufer, a Jew
18.4.1428 c. 405r	Andreocta Lumbardo	1.6.0 ounces	by August	sale of tunny to Salamon de Messina, a Jew
18.4.1428 c. 406v	Andreocta Lumbardo	1.6.0 ounces	by August; paid 23.11.1428	sale of tunny to Busacca Turri, a Jew

18.4.1428 c. 406v	Andreocta Lumbardo	29 *tarì*	by August	sale of tunny to Xilomo Xhalluli, a Jew
30.4.1428 c. 426r	Busacca de Tripuli, a Palermitan Jew	32 ounces	paid 18.4.1429	sale of heavy and light rope
2.5.1428 c. 430r	Aloisio Campo	1.4.0 ounces	by August	sale of goods to Xilomo and Mardoc Rusticu, Jews of Palermo
5.5.1428 c. nn	Andreocta Lumbardo	1.13.0 ounces	by August; paid by 12.10.1429	sale of tunny to Salamon Xammara and Sufen Messeria, Jews
8.6.1428 c. 478r	Pietro de Catania	1.18.0 ounces	27.10 *tarì* on account	sale of grapes to Syminto Benassay, a Jew
10.6.1428 c. 481v	Don Luca de Lygocti	3 ounces	by July	sale of silk to Vita Lu Russu and Sadono de Mayu, Jews
12.6.1428 c. 520r	Donatu Russu	1.18.0 ounces	by August; paid 17.91429	sale of soles to Vita Levi and Salamon Actuni, Jews
20.7.1428 c. nn	Iunta Bulcza and Stephanus Ianuysi of Palermo	2 ounces		sale of wood
29.7.1428 c. nn	Symon de Mayu, a Palermitan Jew	1.12.0 ounces	paid	sale of grapes; guarantor: Vita de Liuni, a Jew
18.8 1428 c. nn	Bundo de Campo	2.12.0 ounces	3 instalments	sale of grapes to Xhaymi Levi, a Palermitan Jew
25.8.1428 c. nn	Tommaso de Bellachera, abbot of San Giovanni degli Eremiti	1.15.0 ounces	within 4 months	sale of wheat to Manuel Verru, a Palermitan Jew; guarantor: Busacca, son of Lya Sala, a Jew

9.9.1429 c. 10r	Muxa Xammara, a Jew of Palermo	5 ounces	paid	sale of 7 pregnant cows and some young cattle
23.9.1429 c. 30v	Ubertino Abbatellis	2 ounces	by 15.8.1430; paid 17.8.1430	sale of grapes to Lya Sofer, a Jew of Palermo
5.10.1429 c. 41r	Ubertino Abbatellis	3 ounces	by August 1430; paid 17.8.1430	sale of grapes to Muxa Levi, a Jew
5.10.1429 c. 41r	Ubertino Abbatellis	3 ounces	by August 1430; paid 17.8.1430	sale of grapes to Aczarono Riczio, a Palermitan Jew
6.10.1429 c. 44r	Ubertino Abbatellis	2 ounces	by 15.8.1430	sale of grapes to Muxa de Tripuli, a Jew of Palermo
7.10.1429 c. nn	Ubertino Abbatellis	1 ounce	by 15.8.1430	sale of grapes to Vita de Liuni, a Palermitan Jew
20.10.1429 c. 81r	Braxhono Mizoc, a Jew of Palermo			sale of heavy rope; guarantor: Sadono Mizoc
20.10.1429 c. 83r	Iacob de Pranniti	15 *tarì*	within 3 months	sale of iron to Lya Copiu and Danieli Barramellu, Jews
21.11.1429 c. 140r	Iuda de Vita, a Jew of Mazara	17 ounces	by August	sale of 100 *salme* of wheat
	Bibliography: Bresc, *Arabi*, p. 196, and n. 910			
23.11.1429 c. 152v	Enrico de Caccabo	24 *tarì*	15 *tarì* on account, balance within 11 days	sale of grapes to Busacca Levi, a Jew
1.12.1429 c. 158v	Nicolò de Manso	1.18.0 ounces	24 *tarì* on account; balance by April	sale of grapes to Busacca Levi, a Jew
12.12.1429 c. 176r	Pietro de Pilligrini and Raysio Abbidutu of Syracuse	37 ounces	10 ounces on account	sale of timber
14.12.1429 c. 179r	Mardoc Avignuni, a Jew of Palermo	11 *grana* a *rotolo*	1 ounce on account	sale of iron ornaments

9.1.1430 c. 203v	Aczarono de Medico, a Jew	2.6.0 ounces	within a month; paid 12.11.1430	sale of a mule
10.1.1430 c. 208r	Paolo Lombardo	1.1.0 ounces	paid 5.9.1430	sale of wheat to Salamon Actuni, a Jew
27.1.1430 c. 228r	Xamueli Russu, a Palermitan Jew	5.10 *tarì* a piece	7.10.0 ounces on account; paid 27.4.1430	sale of calves
7.2.1430 c. 245v	Xibiten de Muxarella, a Jew of Trapani	10 ounces	5 ounces on account, balance by June; paid 23.10.1431	sale of a silk curtain
8.2.1430 c. 248v	Antonio Luchisi	1.10.10 ounces	by May; paid 26.6.1430	sale of a silk curtain to Nissim Ysacco, a Jew
23.2.1430 c. 273v	Andreocta Lumbardo	2 ounces	by August	sale of goods to Valentino Sacerdotu, a Jew
1.3.1430 c. 284v	Farrugio Russu, a Jew of Agrigento	6.6.0 ounces	4 annual instalments in August of every year	sale of an ox and 4 *salme* of wheat
2.3.1430 c. 289v	Braxhono de Daniele Sacerdotu, a Palermitan Jew	2.12.0 ounces	paid	sale of 2 beasts of burden
13.3.1430 c. 306v	Simon Xilomu, a Jew of Palermo	1.12.0 ounces	within 7 months; paid 21.1.1431	sale of a horse
24.3.1430 c. 333r	Sufen de Donarrigu, a Jew	1 ounce	paid	sale of tow
16.5.1430 c. 414r	Xamuel Russu, a Jew	1.22.0 ounces	by June; paid 21.7.1430	sale of butter
19.6.1430 c. 460v	Francesco Ventimiglia	1.28.0 ounces	paid 29.10.1430	sale of iron to Muxa Xabba, a Jew
19.6.1430 c. 460r	Francesco Ventimiglia	1.27.13 ounces	by August	sale of iron to Muxa Vignuni, a Jew

Date and Page		Amount		Remarks
19.6.1430 c. 461v	Francesco Ventimiglia	1.28.0 ounces	by August; paid 15.8.1432	sale of goods to Muxa Russu
19.6.1430 c. 461v	Giovanni de Lixandro for Francesco Ventimiglia	2.28.0 ounces	by August; paid 12.12.1432	sale of iron to Nicolò de Luca Valeri and Leone Sacerdotu, a Jew

Date and Page	Tenant	Location and Description	Rent and Duration	Remarks
18.7.1428 c. 472v	master Iusep Abudarcham, a Jewish tailor	Cassaro, ruga Magna, entrance from Natale de Marino alley, bordering on the landlady's house, that of master Muxa Bulgit, a Jewish	perpetual lease; annual rent 2.15.0 ounces	landlady: Donna Caterina de Ventimiglia

Bibliography:of Castellana Bresc, *Arabi*, p. 54, and n. 213.

bookseller, master Tommasio de Craparia and public road; row of houses *solerata* and a shop

19.6.1430 c. 459v	Daniel de Vita, a Jew	Palermo, *contrada* Ferrarie, bordering on	shop; 1 year at 15 *tarì*	landlord: Donato Russo

shop of mastro Donato and inn of Federico Russello

Source: ASP, Not. Giovanni Traverso, reg. 774

Date and Page	Debtor	Amount	Reason	Remarks
5.1.1429 c. 205r	Amaran Gibbesi, a Palermitan Jew	4 ounces	to buy some houses from Xibite Balaxi, a Jew	creditor: Vita Catalano, a Jew; to be paid within 4 years
21.7. 1429 c. 492r	Matheo de Daunisio	5.12.0 ounces	for a court order against Matheo	creditor: Farrugio Russo, a Jew; paid in instalments

Date and Page	Lender or Seller	Amount	Payment	Remarks
10.9.1428 c. 26v	Andreocta de Lumbardo	2.12.0 ounces	by February	sale of tunny to Sufen Misiria and Salamon Xammara, Jews
17.9.1428 c. 40v	Filippo de Bellachera	2.25.0 ounces	3 *tarì* a week; paid 8.3.1429	sale of soles to Symon de Mayu and Vita de Liuni, Jews
17.9.1428 c. 41r	Bono de Iacobo	1.6.0 ounces	by March	sale of saffron to Xibbiteni Gaczu and Sadono Bachularu, Jews
28.9.1428 c. 49r	Antonia de Piczinga	1 ounce	on Easter	sale of grapes to Muxa Bulgit, a Jew
2.10.1428 c. 54r	Rogerio de Paruta	1 ounce	by June; paid 15.11.1429	sale of grapes to Iuncta Bulcza, a Jew
6.10.1428 c. 68v	Vita Aczara, a Palermitan Jew	21 ounces	10 ounces on account, balance by Christmas	sale of light and heavy rope
14.10.1428 c. 73r	Petrucio de Bellachera	4.15.0 ounces	within 4 months; paid 18.4.1429	sale of wheat to Benchamin de Minichi, a Palermitan Jew
14.10.1428 c. 73r	Bono de Iacobo	1.22.0 ounces	within 5 months	sale of saffron to Sabbatino Calabrense and Czullo Markeki, Jews
5.11.1428 c. 118r	Xhayrono Russo, a Jew	7.10 *tarì*		sale of merchandise
10.11.1428 c. 126v	Andreotta de Lumbardo	24 *tarì*	by March	sale of tunny to Bernardo Capsi and Sabbet Xagarino, a Palermitan Jew
1.12.1428 c. 158r	Braxhono Mizoc, a Palermitan Jew	4 ounces	3.12.0 ounces on account, balance on delivery; paid 19.12.1430	sale of rope to Andreotta de Lumbardo
9.12.1428 c. 165v	Andreotta de Lumbardo	3.23.0 ounces	1 ounce by January, balance by March	sale of goods to Xhayrono and Busacca Medui, Jews

14.12.1428 c. 169v	Leone Xhunina, a Jew, acting for Pino de Monaco	10.15.0 ounces	by April; paid 28.7.1429	sale of oil and barley
22.12.1428 c. 186v	Giovanni de Randacio	1 ounce	on demand	loan to Muxa Russu, a Jew
14.1.1429 c. 215r	Guarnerio de Ventimiglia	3.27.0 ounces	within 6 months; paid 12.3.1430	sale of wheat to Abram Xalena, a Jew
26.1.1429 c. 233v	Adreotta de Lumbardo	3 ounces	within 2 months; paid 12.12.1429	sale of bronze cups to Xhayrono and Busacca Medui, Palermitan Jews
10.2.1429 c. 257v	Iacobo Bellassay, a Jew	20.28.0 ounces	to be paid as sales progress; paid 22.2.1430	sale of wine
14.2.1429 c. 260v	Braxhono Taguili, a Jew, for Pino de Monaco	25 ounces	by 15 March	loan
15.2.1429 c. 263v	Ysolda de Asta	1.6.0 ounces	within 6 months	sale of iron to Braxhono Xireribi, a Palermitan Jew; guarantor: Braxhono Miczoc, a Jew
18.2.1429 c. 275r	Andreocta de Lumbardo	10 *tarì* the kantar	15 ounces on account, balance after sale of cheese	sale of cheese to Michilono Minachem and Sufen de Minichi, Jews
25.2.1429 c. 291r	Ysolda de Asta	3 ounces	within 10 months; paid 29.7.1430	sale of iron to Braxhono Miczoc, a Jew
1.3.1429 c. 298v	Andreotta de Lumbardo	1.6.0 ounces	within 4 months	sale of tunny to Busacca Turri, a Jew
1.3.1429 c. 299v	Andreotta de Lumbardo	2.27.10 ounces	by July	sale of olive oil to Salamon Xammara, Sufen Misseria and Iuda Bramuni, Jews

8.3.1429 c. 318r	Andreotta de Lumbardo	1.22.10 ounces	within 5 months; paid 23.11.1429	sale of olive oil to Salamon Ruggila, a Jew; guarantors: Galluffu and Salamon de Missina, Jews
8.3.1429 c. 318v	Andreotta de Lumbardo	1.5.0 ounces	within 5 months	sale of olive oil to Muxa Rugila, a Jew
8.3.1429 c. 318v	Andreotta de Lumbardo	1.5.0 ounces	within 5 months	sale of oil to Vita Siven, a Jew
11.3.1429 c. 326v	Braxhono Mizoc for Ysolda de Asta	2.24.0 ounces	within 6 months	sale of olive oil to Momo and Xibiten Gaczu, Jews
5.4.1429 c. 356v	Tuchio Xamarella and Tuchio de Castagna	6.20.0 ounces	3 ounces on account	sale of cheese to Nixim de Benedicto, a Jew
11.4.1429 c. 373r	Ysolda de Asta	1.7.0 ounces	within 6 months	sale of olive oil to Iusep Ammara, a Jew
11.4.1429 c. 373v	Ubertino de Abbatellis	9.5 *tarì* the kantar	paid 18.8.1429	sale of cheese to Muxa de Siracusia, Iusep de Minichi and Michilono Minaxhem, Jews
13.4.1429 c. 376r	Braxhono Miczoc for Ysolda de Asta	1.7.0 ounces	within 6 months	sale of olive oil to Graciano and Braxhono de Medico, Jews
14.4.1429 c. 379v	Braxhono Miczoc for Ysolda de Asta	1.7.0 ounces	within 6 months	sale of olive oil to Muxa Ammara, a Jew
18.4.1429 c. 383r	Braxhono Miczoc for Ysolda de Asta	2 ounces	within 4 months; paid 17.3.1430	sale of silk to Graciano Taxhariatu, a Jew
20.4.1429 c. 293r	Iacob de Gauyu	1.24.0 ounces	15 *tarì* by July, balance on demand	sale of a beast of burden
22.4.1429 c. 395r	Guarnerio de Ventimiglia	9.5. *tarì* the kantar	paid 16.1.1430	sale of cheese to Sufen de Minichi, Muxa de Siracusia and Michilono Minaxhem, Jews

6.5.1429 c. 409v	Ysolda de Asta	1.6.0 ounces	within 6 months; paid 28.7.1430	sale of olive oil to Braxhono Miczoc, a Jew
11.5.1429 c. 413v	Merdoc Calabrisi, a Jew, for Ysolda de Asta	18.10 *tarì*	within 6 months	sale of olive oil; guarantor: Sufen de Misiria
11.5.1429 c. 414v	Merdoc Calabrisi, a Jew, for Ysolda de Asta	1 ounce	within 6 months	sale of iron
18.5.1429 c. 421r	Bonconte de Bonnano	2 ounces	paid	sale of olive oil to Sadono Miczoc, a Jew, for Ysolda de Asta
24.5.1429 c. 430v	Sadia Ysac, a Jew	1.18.0 ounces	1.10.0 ounces on account, balance on delivery	sale of bricks (*madonum de modalo*)
24.5.1429 c. 431r	Manfrido de Frankino	1.10.0 ounces	1 ounce on account, balance on delivery	sale of bricks to Sadia Ysac, a Jew
1.6.1429 c. 438v	Sadono Miczoc, a Jew, for Ysolda de Asta	1.6.0 ounces	within 6 months; paid 18.1.1430	sale of paper
3.6.1429 c. 439v	Braxhono Miczoc, a Jew, for Aloisio de Campo	10 ounces	within 6 months; paid 20.9.1430	sale of oil and paper to Gandolfo de Lando
7.6.1429 c. 444r	Chicco de Georgio	3.6.0 ounces	paid	sale of a mule with saddle to Levi de Sancto, a Jew
17.6.1429 c. 452v	Symon de Mayu, a Palermitan Jew	1.12.0 ounces	in exchange for the rent of some houses	sale of grapes to Xilomo Virdi, a Jew
20.6.1429 c. 456r	Pisana de mastro Antonio	1.20.0 ounces	within 1 month	sale of tunny roe to Aczarono Sabatino, a Jew

27.6.1429 c. 462r	Muxa Achina, a Jew	2.6.0 ounces	paid	sale of a bronze vessel
1.7.1429 c. 483r	Nicolò Ferreri	25 *tarì*	12.10 *tarì* on account, balance on delivery	sale of hay to Vita Ysac, a Jew
4.7.1429 c. 463v	Andreotta de Lumbardo	3.15.0 ounces	by November	sale of sheep and rams to Momo and Xibiteni Gaczu, Jews
5.7.1429 c. 466v	Vita Ysac, a Palermitan Jew	3 ounces	2 ounces on account	sale of manure
21.7.1429 c. 487r	Farrugio Russo, a Jew	5.12.0 ounces	instalments until October 1430	sale of merchandise
31.8.1435 c. nn	Antonio de Milacio	1.2.0 ounces		sale of a horse with bridle to Busacca de Tripoli, a Jew
7.9.1435 c. nn	Giovanni Falamuri	1.9.0 ounces		sale of a horse to Busacca Levi, a Jew
12.9.1435 c. nn	[..] Cusintino, a Jew	1.27.0 ounces	paid 24.9.1436	sale of grapes
13.9.1435 c. nn	Antonio Sardo	1.15.0 ounces	within 4 months	sale of iron to Muxa de Butera, a Jew
26.9.1435 c. nn	Giovanni de La Turri	1.18.10 ounces		sale of barley to Galluffo de Minichi, a Jew
30.9.1435 c. nn	Nicolò de Nicolia	2.3.0 ounces	paid 12.10.1435	sale of wheat to Symon de Mayu, a Jew
4.10.1435 c. nn	Bartholomeo de Columba	32.15.0 ounces	14 ounces through the bank of Antonio de Settimo, 6 ounces within 15 days, 12.15.0 ounces later	sale of various goods to Leone de La Iudeca, a Jew
5.10.1435 c. nn	Nicolò de Nicolia	1.2.0 ounces	by April	sale of wheat to Salamon Actuni, a Jew

7.10.1435 c. nn	Muxa Sacerdotu, a Jew	10 *grana* the *rotolo*	1 ounce on account, 4 *tarì* a month; paid 11.5.1437	sale of iron
7.10.1435 c. nn	L[..] de Puglisi, a Jew	2 ounces	on Easter; paid 20.6.1436	sale of goods
8.11.1435 c. nn	Giovanni de Ventimiglia	9.18 *tarì*	paid 23.10.1436	sale of grapes to Iuda Siven, a Jew
14.11.1435 c. nn	David de Quinu, a Jew	1 ounce	paid	sale of a horse
29.11.1435 c. nn	Masio de Gilberto	14 ounces	instalments until January 1437	sale of honey and sugar to Leone de La Iudeca
19.12.1436 c. nn	Nicolò de Puma	2.11.0 ounces	29 *tarì* on account, balance within a month	sale of cheese to Xua Aurifichi, a Jew
30.12.1435 c. nn	Iuda Sark, a Jew of Syracuse	19.15.0 ounces	paid	sale of two black slaves
11.1.1436 c. nn	Sadono de Medico, a Jew	4 ounces	2 ounces on account, another 2 at Easter; paid 24.4.1436	sale of a bedspread with silk border
14.2.1436 c. nn	Contessa Ventimiglia	8 ounces	4 ounces by August 1437, balance on following Christmas; paid 17.4.1437	sale of a bedspread to Lya and Salamon de Missina, Jews
15.2.1436 c. nn	Giovanni de Insinga	20 *tarì*		sale of a blind ox to Xhaymi Gaczu, a Jew
28.2.1436 c. nn	Sufen de Donarrrigu, a Jew	1 ounce	15.8 *tarì* on account	sale of tow
28.2.1436 c. nn	Muxa de Danieli	6 ounces	4 ounces within 4 months, balance 2 months later; paid 13.8.1436	sale of a kantar of tin to Xibiten Virdi, a Jew

Date and Page	Tenant	Location and Description	Rent and Duration	Remarks
3.1.1429 c. 202v	Amaram Gibesi, a Jew	Cassaro, bordering on courtyard of Musutu Skinelli, houses of Xagarono Busacca and Galluffi Cuynu, all Jews	a house *solerata* and a courtyard; 6 ounces, 2.6.0 ounces on account	landlord: Xibite Balaxi, a Palermitan Jew
20.4.1429 c. 388r	Iacob Medui, a Jew	Palermo, quarter dell'Albergheria, Platea Marmorea, bordering on the properties of Masio de Maligno and Andrea de Noaria; shop *solerata*	from 1.9 for 3 ounces, 1.6.0 ounces on account	rent of 6 *tarì* due to Olivo de Sottile
29.11.1435 c. nn	Symon de Mayu, a Jew	Palermo, bordering on Maczullo's inn and the notary's stall	shop; 1 year for 24 *tarì* monthly	landlord: Maczullu Castronovo, a Jew
29.11.1436 c. nn	Leone de La Iudeca, a Jew	Palermo, bordering on the houses of Aloisio de Milacio and Masio Burgisi; storehouse	1 year for 1 ounce	landlord: Masio de Gilberto

Source: ASP, Not. Giovanni Traverso, reg. 775

Date and Page	Debtor	Amount	Reason	Remarks
26.1.1431 c. nn	Yuda Bramono, a Jew	7 florins		creditor: Andrea de Lumbardo, who grants a rebate of 18 *tarì*; guarantors: Nixim Xidedi and Gallufu Bramuni, Jews

Date and Page	Lender or Seller	Amount	Payment	Remarks
11.4.1431 c. nn	Nicolò de Missina	18 *tarì*		creditor: Sadya Ysac, a Jew
18.11.1433 c. 95r	Busacca de Minichi, a Jew of Sciacca	13 *tarì*	paid as guarantee	creditor: Symone de Mayo, a Jew
22.9.1430 c. nn	Aczarono de Cusintino, a Jew	7 ounces		sale of goods (Doc. damaged)
11.10.1430 c. nn	[Rogerio] de Paruta	3.6.0 ounces	within 4 months	sale of goods to Leone Sacerdotu. a Jew
24.10.1430 c. nn	Girardo de Alba	24 *tarì*	12 *tarì* on account, 6 *tarì* on Christmas, 6 *tarì* by 6.5; paid 15.2.1431	sale of grapes to Busacca Levi, a Jew
27.10.1430 c. nn	Busacca de Tripuli and Vita Pancza, Jews	106.18.0 ounces	paid by bank of Pietro de Afflicto	sale of a considerable quantity of tunny
30.10.1430 c. nn	Ubertino de Abbatellis	1 and 1.3.10 ounces	within 3 months	sale of grapes to Benedicti Misiria, for Muxa de Tripuli, Jews; guarantors: Benedictus and Xibiteni Xatarra, Jews
1.11.1430 c. nn	Rogerio Spaventa	2.12.0 ounces	within 4 months	sale of iron to Muxa Xabbi, a Jew
8.11.1430 c. nn	Michael Riczius and his wife Graczona	8 florins	paid	sale of grapes to Muxa Russu, a Jew
13.11.1430 c. nn	Pietro de Monaco	18 *tarì*	by 3.1431	sale of goods to Benedicto Coffisi, a Jew
22.11.1430 c.nn	Giovanni Omodei	1.12.0 ounces	within 2 months; paid 12.9.1431	sale of cloth to Salamon Benassay, a Jew

19.12.1430 c. nn	Braxhono Mizoc, a Palermitan Jew	4 ounces	paid	sale of plant tying rope (*disa*)
20.12.1430 c. nn	Braxhono de Anzalono also for Xanini de Siracusia, Jews	5 ounces	12 *tarì* on account, balance on delivery	sale of manure
2.1.1431 c. nn	Sadia Xhacten, a Palermitan Jew	15 ounces	by first half of March	sale of plant tying rope (*disa*)
26.1.1431 c. nn	Filippo Bellachera	1 ounce	by Easter; paid 21.10.1432	sale of chestnuts to Xibiteni Lu Presti, a Jew
30.1.1431 c. nn	Bertullo Landulo	4 ounces	1 ounce on account, balance by Easter; paid 23.4.1432	sale of goods to Busacca Romano, a Jew; guarantor: Leone Romano
14.3.1413 c. 324v	Sadia Xhacten, a Palermitan Jew	1.28.0 ounces	by July; paid 20.2.1432	sale of plant tying rope (*disa*)
21.3.1431 c. 338r	Lancza de Sindico for Rogerio de Paruta	4 ounces	by August; paid 23.1.1432	sale of iron to Muxa Russu, a Jew; guarantor: his brother, Brachono
10.4.1431 c. 377r	Iusep Brixha, a Jew	1 ounce	6 *tarì* on account	sale of cloth
11.4.1431 c. nn	Lya Siven, a Jew	10 ounces	within a year; paid 1.9.1432	sale of nails
13.4.1431 c. nn	Giovanni de Sconzu and Giovanni de Lu Licari	24 *tarì*	paid	sale of grapes to Busacca Levi, a Jew
29.5.1431 c. nn	Muxa Russu, a Jew	1.14.17 ounces	by 24.6; paid 15.10.1431	sale of canvas
11.6.1431 c. nn	P[..] Xhanini, a Jew	1 ounce	paid	sale of wheat

22.6.1431 c. 415r	Iacob Medui, a Jew, for Thomeo de mastro Antonio	5 ounces	2.6.0 ounces on account, 24 *tarì* 15.5., balance 23.6	sale of tunny to Iacob de Danieli, a Jew
7.5.1431 c. 14r	Iacobo Riczu	1 ounce		sale of grapes to Busacca Levi, a Jew
9.11.1433 c. 76v	Giovanni de Albertino	1.12.0 ounces	21 *tarì* on account, balance first half of January	sale of a horse to Matheo Sacerdoto, a Jew of Mineo
1.12.1433 c. 117r	Salamon Xammara, a Jew	1.7.10 ounces	paid	sale of a horse
1.12.1433 c. 118r	Giovanni de Rugila	8 ounces	at vintage time; paid 8.12.1433	sale of grapes to Iuda Siven, a Jew
8.12.1433 c. 126r	Giovanni de Ferro	14 *tarì*	within 4 months	sale of wheat to David Ciprianu and Iusep Terminisi, Jews
16.12.1433 c. 143v	Giovanni Grassu	8 ounces	2 ounces on account, balance on delivery; paid 16.11.1434	sale of grapes to Iuda Siven, a Jew
16.12.1433 c. 145v	Salamon de Missina, a Jew	3.21.0 ounces	within a month; paid 15.4.1434	sale of merchandise
24.12.1433 c. 152v	Iacoba, wife of Antonio de Sardo	6 ounces		sale of leather to Leone de La Iudeca and Salamon Muxa, Jews
29.12.143 c. 160v	Nicolò Bini	8.15.0 ounces	1 ounce on account	sale of sheep to Xua Aurifichi and Xhaymi Gaczu, Jews
30.12.1433 c. 161v	Lemmo Damuni	3 ounces	paid	sale of grapes to Iuda Siven, a Jew
8.1.1434 c. 169v	Nicolò Rasu	1.12.0 ounces	paid	sale of grapes to Iuda Siven, a Jew
11.1.1434 c. 171v	Sadia Xhacten, a Jew of Palermo	16.10.0 ounces	9.12.0 ounces on account	sale of light and heavy rope

3.2.1434 c. 198r	Angelo Carbuni	1.12.0 ounces	paid	sale of grapes to Iuda Siven, a Jew
8.2.1434 c. 200v	Andrea de Aprea, notary, for the monastery S. Maria de Valverde	11 ounces		sale of a curtain to master Moyse Chetibi, a Jew of Palermo
18.2.1434 c. 219r	Symon de Rubeo	1.12.0 ounces	paid	sale of grapes to Iuda Siven, a Jew
22.2.1434 c. 223v	Antonello Manueli	26 *tarì*	by May	sale of wheat to Symon de Mayu and his son Mayu, Jews
5.3.1434 c. 239r	Giovanni Ferro	13 *tarì*	by May; paid 25.5.1434	sale of wheat to Salamon Aurifichi, a Jew
5.3.1434 c. 239r	Giovanni Ferro	13 *tarì*	by May; paid 11.6.1434	sale of wheat to David Termini and Salamon de Missina, Jews
16.3.1434 c. 258v	Antonio Sardo	20.10 *tarì*		sale of goods to Symon Accanu, a Jew
18.3.1434 c. 271r	Giovanni Ferro	1.1.10 ounces	by June	sale of wheat to Braxha Crivaru and Merdoc de Vita, Jews
6.4.1434 c. 297r	Iosep Brixha, a Jew	2 ounces	1 ounce on account	sale of cloth
7.4.1434 c. 300r	Braxhono Sufen, a Jew	3 *tarì* a thousand	12 *tarì* on account	sale of stoppers to Iacob Medui, a Jew
24.4.1434 c. nn	Vita Catalano, a Jew	27.10 *tarì*	2.10 *tarì* a month; paid 19.2.1437	sale of a lathe
22.5.1434 c. 374v	Antonio Sardo	4.17.0 ounces	1 ounce within a month, balance in instalments; paid 18.3.1438	sale of linen to Daniel Baramellu, a Jew; guarantor: Braxhono Bambalu, a Jew
1.6.1434 c. 383r	Angelo Mirmirichi	4 ounces	within 4 months; paid 5.11.1434	sale of indigo to Manuel de Arami, a Jew

Sicily

22.6.1434 c. 416r	Braxha Crivaru and Muxa Sacerdotu, Jews	6 ounces	3 ounces on account	sale of manure
25.6.1434 c. 418r	Thomeo de mastro Antonio	2 ounces	by May	sale of tunny roe to Xirello de Seracusia, a Jew
25.6.1434 c. 418v	Thomeo de mastro Antonio	1 ounce	by May; paid 25.6.1435	sale of tunny roe to Muxa de Catania, a Jew; guarantor: Iusep de Amato, a Jew
25.6.1434 c. 419v	Thomeo de mastro Antonio	1 ounce	by May	sale of tunny roe to Sabatino Xafitera, a Jew

Date and Page	Tenant	Location and Description	Rent and Duration	Remarks
2.6.1431 c. nn	abbess of Santa Maria del Cancelliere	Palermo, *contrada* Porta Busuldeni, Cassaro, bordering on houses of Lorenzo de Balbo and Enrico de Baccarellis; a *solerata* house		landlady: Altadonna, wife of Fariono Appili, a Jewess
10.6.1434 c. nn	Salamon Aurifici and Xaymi Gaczu, Jews	Palermo, *contrada* Ballarò, bordering on landlord's inn; stall	1 year for 3 ounces	landord: Giovanni de Omodei

Source: ASP, Not. Giovanni Traverso, reg. 776

Date and page	Principal	Attorney	Purpose	Remarks
20.11.1431 c. 1067r	Simon Xalomo, a Palermitan Jew	Ysac de Guillelmo and Nissim Binna, Palermitan Jews	to deal with the letting and rent of all his houses in Palermo	

6195

| 28.2.1432 c. 2068r | Aron de Compagna, a Jew of Messina | Sadono de Medico, a Palermitan Jew | to obtain payment from debtors |
| 14.4.1432 c. 3033r | Perna, widow of Muxa Chamisu, a Jewess | Iosep Chamisu, a Jew | to travel to Agrigento and elsewhere in Sicily to collect outstanding debts and to sell property |

Date and Page	Debtor	Amount	Reason	Remarks
19.6.1433 c. 428r	Muxa Russu, a Jew	1 ounce	loan	creditors: Gigla de Guarnerio
5.3.1432 c. 2073v	Busacca de Minichi, a Jew of Sciacca	13 *tarì*	paid as guarantor	creditor: Simone de Mayo

Date and Page	Lender or Seller	Amount	Payment	Remarks
16.3.1433 c. 301v	Iusep Brixha, a Jew	1 ounce	21 *tarì* on account; paid 28.4.1433	sale of cloth to Iacob Medui, a Jew
16.3.1433 c. 302r	Braxhono Sofer, a Jew	18 *tarì*	9 *tarì* on account	sale of tunny to Iacob Medui, a Jew
3.6.1433 c. 405r	Pino de Ferro	19 *tarì*	13 *tarì* on account; balance by August; paid 22.9.1433	sale of wheat to Symon de Mayu, a Jew
17.6.1433 c. 426r	Enrico de Ventimiglia	1.3.0 ounces	within 4 months	sale of a beast of burden to Xibiten Bambalu, a Jew
19.6.1433 c. 428r	Gigla de Guarnerio	1 ounce	paid 16.3.1434	loan to Muxa Russu, a Jew
16.7.1433 c. 463v	Pietro de Galati	2 ounces	1.6.0 ounces on account	sale of coal to Isdraele Medui, a Jew
27.7.1433 c. 470r	Antonio Pigueri	20 ounces	within 6 months; paid 5.3.1434	sale of goods to Iacob Taguili, a Palermitan Jew

12.8.1433 c. 489r	Giovanni de Bellachera	10 ounces	within the year of the XIII indiction	loan to Xamuel Gididia, a Jew
21.8.1433 c. 490r	Pino de Ferro	1.2.0 ounces	within 4 months; paid 6.1.1434	sale of wheat to Xannuni Migar, a Jew
30.10.1432 c. 106r	Pino de Ferro	1.10.0 ounces	within 4 months; paid 9.3.1432	sale of wheat to Czullo Markeki, Braxhono Amirami and Xibiteni Bambalu, Jews
31.10. 1432 c. 109v	Pino de Ferro	1.22.0 ounces	within 4 months; paid 12.3.1433	sale of wheat to Xannuni Migar and Muxa Sacerdotu, Jews
10.12.1432 c. 186r	Giovanni Crispu	12 ounces	within a year; paid 3.2.1433	sale of a silk curtain to Iacob Xunina, a Jew
16.12.1432 c. 193v	Giovanni de Ferro	1.2.0 ounces	within 4 months	sale of wheat to Braxha Calabrisi and Sabet Xagaruni, Jews
12.10.1431 c. 166v	Isdraeli Medui, a Palermitan Jew	6.24.14 ounces	1.19.0 on account	sale of heavy rope
12.10.1431 c. 166v	Sadya Xhacten, a Palermitan Jew	13 ounces	1.19.0 and 1.11.0 ounces on account; paid 20.2.1433	sale of light and heavy rope
16.11.1431 c. 134r	Rogerio de Paruta	2.24.10 ounces	within 8 months	sale of iron to Muxa de Butera
22.11.1431 c. 148r	Xibitini Maltisi, a Jew of Termini	1.15.0 ounces	by August	sale of wheat
14.12.1431 c. 184r	Giovanni Bankeri	1.18.0 ounces	on delivery	sale of grapes to Muxa Achina, a Jew
27.2.1432 c. 289r	Filippo de Scamacha	2.9.0 ounces		sale of a mule to David Mizar, a Jew
21.2.1432 c. 2047r	Symon Lu Bagliu	1.24.0 ounces	18 *tarì* on account; paid 2.10.1432	sale of grapes to Iuda Siveni, a Jew

21.2.1432 c. 2049r	Guglielmo Scaffitura	1.7.10 ounces	12 *tarì* on account	sale of cheese to Michilono Mennacham, a Jew of Palermo
22.2.1432 c. 2060r	Antonio de La Matina	1.2.0 ounces	within 6 months; paid 10.9.1432	sale of oil to Salamon Actuni, a Palermitan Jew
26.2.1432 c. 2063	Giovanni Lu Boi	1.21.0 ounces	6 and 12 *tarì* on account, balance by April; paid 14.3.1432	sale of grapes to Vita Cathalano, a Jew
28.2.1432 c. 2067v	Marono de Dannichella	5 ounces	3 ounces on account; paid 10.4.1432	sale of cork tree coal to Xibiteni Barbutu, a Palermitan Jew
28.2.1432 c. 2068r	Filippo de Laurencio	12 *tarì* the kantar		sale of tallow to Muxa Achina, a Palermitan Jew
28.2.1432 c. 2069v	Antonio de Mumpileri and Gerardo de Castronovo	2 ounces	1 ounce on account; paid: 29.10 1432	sale of cork tree coal to Xibiteni Barbutu, a Palermitan Jew
1.3.1432 c. 2070r	Antonio de Gimbesio	3.3.0 ounces	within 4 months; paid 6.10.1432	sale of oil to Iona de Usueli, a Palermitan Jew; guarantor: Xamuel Sacerdoto, a Jew of Palermo
1.3.1432 c. 2070v	Guglielmo Cito	2 ounces		sale of oil to Mardoc de Missina, a Jew of Trapani
1.3.1432 c. 2071r	Richello de Andrea	1.12.10 ounces	paid	sale of manure to Isdrael Medui, a Jew
5.3.1432 c. 2074v	Lemmo Palumbu	1.15.0 ounces		sale of grapes to Daidono Ricza, a Jew of Palermo
6.3.1432 c. 2077r	Battista de Termini	1.13.0 ounces	19.10 *tarì* on account	sale of tallow to Muxa Achina, a Palermitan Jew
10.3.1432 c. 2081r	Stefanu Lu Piczutu	1 ounce	paid	sale of cork tree coal to Xibiteni Barbutu, a Palermitan Jew

11.3.1432 c. 2083v	Mono de Marco	4.24.0 ounces	paid	sale of grapes to Iuda Sivena, a Palermitan Jew
11.3.1432 c. 2085r	Xamuele Premu, a Palermitan Jew	1.24.0 ounces	by August; paid 1.4.1435	sale of leather to Muxa Tasmuni, a Palermitan Jew
14.3.1432 c. 2086v	Giovanni Fatarcha	8 ounces	3 ounces on account, 1 ounce at end of April, balance on delivery	sale of cheese to Michilono Mennacham, a Palermitan Jew
17.3.1432 c. 2088r	Antonio de La Matina	1 ounce	within 4 months; paid 25.6.1432	sale of olive oil to Fariono de Ayeti, a Palermitan Jew; guarantor: Muxa de Ayeti, a Jew of Palermo
31.3.1432 c. 3008v	Channono Calabrense, a Palermitan Jew	3 ounces	by October; paid 7.4.1433	sale of a silk curtain to Sabet Gillebi, a Jew of Palermo
31.3.1432 c. 3010v	Nicolò de Lamberto	22 *tarì*	paid	sale of grapes to Iuda Sivena, a Palermitan Jew
31.3.1432 c. 3011r	Giovanni Gattararu	24 *tarì*		sale of grapes to Iuda Sivena, a Palermitan Jew
1.4.1432 c. 3011r	Giovanni de Castrogiovanni	1 ounce	paid	sale of grapes to Vita Catalano, a Palermitan Jew
1.4.1432 c. 3012v	Israele Medui, a Palermitan Jew	17.10 *tarì*	within 15 days	sale of a mule
1.4.1432 c. 3013v	Tobia Strugo, a Jew	2.24.10 ounces	within 4 months	sale of soles to Salamon Actuni, a Palermitan Jew
2.4.1432 c. 3014r	Antonio de La Francha	13 *tarì*	6 *tarì* on account, balance on Easter	sale of tallow to Muxa Achina, a Jew of Palermo

3.4.1432 c. 3015v	Xamuele Sacerdotu, a Jew of Palermo	4.12.0 ounces	2.6.0 ounces on Easter, balance by May; paid 10.4.1433	sale of gold
7.4.1432 c. 3019r	Antonio de La Matina	2.17.10 ounces	within 5 months	sale of olive oil to Bracha Crivaru and Xibiteni Gazcu, Palermitan Jews
8.4.1432 c. 3020v	Andrea de La Mantia	24 *tarì*	paid	sale of grapes to Charono Sacerdotu, a Jew of Palermo
8.4.1432 c. 3021r	Nicolò Russo	3.6.0 ounces	24 *tarì* and 2.12.0 ounces on account	sale of grapes ro Daidono Riczu, a Jew of Palermo
8.4.1432 c. 3024r	Matheo de Sancto Georgio	1.12.0 ounces	12 *tarì* on account, balance on delivery	sale of myrtle to Charorono Sacerdotu, a Jew of Palermo
11.4.1432 c. 3031v	Siminto Aurifichi, a Palermitan Jew	2.24.0 ounces	by July	sale of heavy rope
15.4.1432 c. 3034v	Nicolò de Sinagra	7.10 *tarì* the kantar	1 ounces on account, paid 17.11.1432	sale of cheese to Michilono Minnacham, a Palermitan Jew
15.4.1432 c. 3035v	Guarnerio de Pactis	1.18.0 ounces	paid	sale of grapes to Nissim Crivaru, a Jew of Palermo
16.4.1432 c. 3037v	Lando de Homodei	20 ounces	within a month; paid	sale of sugar to Sadono and Moyse, Jews of Palermo
16.4.1432 c. 3038r	Nicolò di Li Fonti	15 *tarì* a kantar	7.10 *tarì* on account; balance on delivery	sale of tallow to Ysac Actina, a Jew of Palermo
16.4.1432 c. 3038r	Filippo Testaverdi	5.10 *tarì*	2 *tarì* on account	sale of *disa* to Sadia Chanen, a Jew of Palermo
16.4.1432 c. 3039v	Petro Lu Iutirratu of Castelvetrano	1 ounce	paid	sale of coal to Xibiten Barbutu, a Palermitan Jew

16.4.1432 c. 3040r	Giovanni de Ventimiglia	1.18.0 ounces	paid	sale of grapes to Daidono Riczu, a Jew of Palermo
16.4.1432 c. 3040r	Antonio de La Calacara	4 ounces	2 ounces on account, balance on delivery; paid	sale of coal to Xibiten and Elia Barbutu, Palermitan Jews
24.4.1432 c. 3043v	Isdraele Iaracti and Muxa de Seragusia, Jews	10 ounces	within a months paid	sale of sugar to Chayruni Brachuni and Busac Medui, Jews of Palermo
24.4.1432 c. 3044r	Nicolò Galocta	24 *tarì*	6 *tarì* on account	sale of grapes to Daidono Riczu, a Jew
20.11.1431 c. 1067v	Enrico de Pinichello	22.10 *tarì*	2 *tarì* a month starting 27.12	sale of nag to Merdoch de Minnichi, a Jew
20.11.1431 c. 1069v	Guglielmo de Mauricti	1.12.0 ounces	6 *tarì* on account	sale of grapes to Nissim Lu Crivaru, a Jew
21.11.1431 c. 1073v	Samuele Sacerdotu, a Palermitan Jew	1.7.0 ounces the kantar		sale of linen to Brachono Sabatu, a Jew of Trapani
21.11.1431 c. 1074r	Iacobo de Chifalu	1.1.10 ounces	paid	sale of grapes to Daidono Riczu, a Jew of Palermo
26.11.1431 c. 1077r	Nicolò de Parisio	agreed (unspecified) price	paid	sale of grapes to Vita Cathalanu, a Jew
26.11.1431 c. 1077v	Nicolò de Xacca	1 ounce	paid	sale of grapes to Daidono Riczu, a Jew of Palermo
26.11.1431 c. 1078r	Lodato de Mariano	24 *tarì*	paid	sale of grapes to Daidono Riczu, a Jew of Palermo
27.11.1431 c. 1079v	Lodato de Mariano	24 *tarì*	paid	sale of grapes to Vita Cathalanu, a Jew

29.11.1431 c. 1081v	Sapora, a Jewess	16.13.0 ounces	1 ounce within a week, another ounce when sale of wine begins; balance in due course; paid 8.4.14[..]	sale of fortified (*tramutato*) wine to Rubino Gibra, a Jew
1.12.1431 c. nn	Filippo de Lu Poi	2 ounce	6 *tarì* on account, balance by middle of June; paid	sale of grapes to Vita Cathalanu, a Jew
3.12.1431 c. nn	Bernardo de Tricocta	1.12.0 ounces	within a month	sale of a mule to Muxa Russo, a Palermitan Jew
3.12.1431 c. 1090r	David Ysac and David Miglar, Jews of Palermo	2 ounces	within 2 months; paid 7.2.1432	sale of merchandise
3.12.1431 c. 1090v	Antonio de La Matina	5 ounces	by May; paid 4.8.1432	sale of olive oil to Fariono Faruco, a Jew
4.12.1431 c. 1091r	Enrico La Manna	16.10 *tarì*	7.2 *tarì* on account	sale of *disa* for the tying of tunny to Sadia Chanen, a Palermitan Jew
17.12.1431 c. 203v	Nicolò de Aprea	1.7.10 ounces	within 6 months; paid 22.10.1432	sale of pepper to Manuel Malti, a Palermitan Jew
20.12.1431 c. 206r	Chicco de notar Simone	24 *tarì*	paid	sale of grapes to Nissim Binna, a Palermitan Jew
20.12.1431 c. 206v	Andrea de Parisi	27 *tarì*	20 *tarì* on account	sale of grapes to David Ysac and David Mi[gl]ar, Palermitan Jews
21.12.1431 c. 207r	Salamon Azzaru, a Jew of Palermo	1.2.0 ounces	by Easter	sale of goods to Muxa Menezel, a Jew of Caccamo

24.12.1431 c. 208v	Giovanni de Ramecta and Giovanni Lu Scaritu	2 ounces	1 ounce on account, balance on delivery	sale of *disa* to Vita Ammar, a Palermitan Jew
3.1.1432 c. 2011r	David de Minnichi, a Jew of Palermo	1.6.0 ounces	paid	sale of a nag with bridle
8.1.1432 c. 2021r	Federico de Sinibaldis	1.2.0 ounces	within 4 months; paid 5.6.1432	sale of oil to Zudu Marchet, David Ruggila and Salamon de Missina, Palermitan Jews
8.1.1432 c. 2021v	Mono Muntichello	27 *tarì*	paid	sale of grapes to Farionu Gaczu, a Jew of Palermo
10.1.1432 c. 2022v	Vita Catalano, a Jew	1 ounce	within 5 months	sale of olive oil to Xibiteni Xammara and Iacop Tunis, Palermitan Jews
11.1.1432 c. 2023v	Antonio de La Matina	3 ounces	by June; 19.12.1432	sale of olive oil to Vita Ammar, a Palermitan Jew
14.1.1432 c. 2023v	Enrico de Vincio	25.10 *tarì*	paid	sale of grapes to Daidono Riczu, a Jew of Palermo
14.1.1432 c. 2024r	Thomeo de Damiano	21 *tarì*	9 *tarì* on account; paid 31.1.1432	sale of grapes to Nissim Crivaru, a Jew of Palermo
15.1.1432 c. 2025v	Siri Pietro de La Pulla	22.10 *tarì*	paid	sale of grapes to Vita Catalano, a Jew of Palermo
15.1.1432 c. 2026r	Vita Catalano, a Palermitan Jew	1 ounce	within 5 months; paid 28.7.1432	sale of oil to Iacop de Termini, a Jew of Palermo
16.1.1432 c. 2026v	Antonio de La Matina	1 ounce	within 4 months; paid 30.5.1432	sale of oil to Vita de Minichi, a Jew of Caccamo

21.1.1432 c. 2029r	Benedetto Xacaruni, a Jew, for Antonio de La Matina	4.15.0 ounces	within 4 months; paid 9.1.1433	sale of oil
21.1.1432 c. 2030r	Lodato de Mariano	1 ounce	by May; paid 10.4.1432	sale of oil to Lia de Benedicto, a Jew of Palermo
21.1.1432 c. 2030r	Cataldo Scarchella	9.16.0 ounces	2 ounces on account; paid 1.4.1432	sale of *pecorino* to Vita Catalano, a Palermitan Jew
21.1.1432 c. 2030v	Benedetto Xacharuni, a Jew, for Antonio de La Matina	6 ounces	within 2 months; paid	sale of barley
25.1.1432 c. 2034r	Benedetto Xacharuni, a Jew, for Antonio de La Matina	2 ounces	within 4 months; paid 16.9.1432	sale of olive oil
25.1.1432 c. 1034v	Xamuele Sacerdotu, a Jew	1.27.0 ounces	3 *carlini* a week; paid 17.7.1433	sale of goods to Sadonu Barasen, a Palermitan Jew
25.1.1432 c. 2035r	Michilono Minacham, a Jew of Palermo	1.4.0 ounces	within 2 months; paid 14.5.1432	sale of calf hides to Simon de Accano, a Jew, and Domenicu de Apoczu
1.2.1432 c. 2041v	Busacca de Tripoli, a Palermitan Jew	1.10.4 ounces	by August	sale of olive oil to Muxa Achina, a Jew of Palermo
6.2.1432 c. 2042v	Muxa Achina, a Palermitan Jew	3.18.0 ounces	paid	sale of 5 barrels of salted sardines and 4 of tunny bellies
6.2.1432 c. 2043r	Vita Catalano, a Palermitan Jew	1 ounce	within 4 months	sale of olive oil to Sabet Millac, a Jew of Palermo

Sicily

1.2.1432 c. 2045v	Masio Iacopu	24 *tarì*	paid	sale of grapes to Xamuele Sacerdoto, a Jew
12.2.1432 c. 2047r	Benedetto Xacharuni, a Jew, for Antonio de La Matina	1 ounce	within 4 months; paid 12.8.1432	sale of oil to Mardoc Vignuni, a Jew in Palermo
14.2.1432 c. 2048v	Antonio de La Matina	2.2.0 ounces	within 4 months; paid 7.7.1432	sale of olive oil to Muxa Sacerdotu and Xannonu Migiar, Palermitan Jews
14.2.1432 c. 2048v	Antonio de La Matina	1 ounce	within 4 months; paid 23.7.1432	sale of olive oil to Emurusu Gilefi and Sabeti Vignuni, Jews of Palermo
16.11.1432 c. nn	Muxa Sacerdoto, a Palermitan Jew	19.10 *tarì*	half within a month, half within 2 months	sale of a nag
12.12.1432 c. nn	Salamon Azzaru, a Jew of Palermo	5.10.6 ounces	1.18.0 ounces on account; balance as the wine is being disposed off	sale of wine to Muxa Xech de Calabria, a Palermitan Jew
11.5.1432 c. nn	David Ysac and David Migiar, Jews in Palermo	1.2.0 ounces	26 *tarì* by August, balance by September	sale of assorted merchandise
12.5.1432 c. 263r	Benedetto Xacharuni, a Jew, for Antonio de La Matina	1 ounce	within 4 months; paid 30.10.1432	sale of olive oil to Musutu de Missina, a Palermitan Jew
19.5.1432 c. 365r	Muni Lu Scarvagliu	at market price in Palermo	two payments on account of 10.8 *tarì* each, balance on delivery	sale of wheat to Isdrael Medui, a Jew of Palermo
20.5.1432 c. 367r	Nissim Binna, a Jew of Palermo	2.26.10 ounces	by September	sale of oil

20.5.1432 c. 367r	Daidono Riczu, a Jew of Palermo	10 ounces	by June	sale of wine to Czuto Manet, a Palermitan Jew
20.5.1432 c. 367v	Sapora, a German Jewish Jewess in Palermo	21 *tarì*	paid	sale of a nag ro Isdrael Medui, a Palermitan Jew
23.5.1432 c. 371v	Salamone Calabrense, a Jew	8.25.0 ounces	by June; paid 17.7.1432	sale of sugar to Donato and Manuel Daram, Palermitan Jews
28.5.1432 c. 375v	Iacop Taguil, a Jew of Palermo	9 ounces	within 2 months; 13.10.1432	sale of a black slave girl to Muxa Russu, a Palermitan Jew
28.5.1432 c. 376r	Iosep Abudaram, a Palermitan Jew	12.6.0 ounces	paid	sale of a black slave girl to Matafiono Cuinu, a Jew of Trapani
28.5.1432 c. 377r	Antonio de La Matina	1 ounce	within 4 months; paid 7.10.1432	sale of oil to Vita de Minichi, a Palermitan Jew; guarantor: Xamuel Nigiar, a Jew of Palermo
28.5.1432 c. 378r	Iacobo de Monte	current market price	24 *tarì* on account; paid 23.6.1432	sale of wheat to Chanino Farmuni, a Jew of Palermo
2.6.1432 c. 381r	Benedetto Xacharuni, a Jew, for Antonio La Matina	1.15.0 ounces	by September; paid 1.10.1432	sale of olive oil to Yuda and Muxa Zacca, Palermitan Jews
2.6.1432 c. 382r	Guglielmo de Romanazzo	1.16.0 ounces		sale of oil to Vita Catalano, a Palermitan Jew
3.6.1432 c. 384r	Vita Catalano, a Jew of Palermo	2 ounces	within 4 months; paid 12.6.1433	sale of olive oil

3.6.1432 c. 384v	Iuliano de Raia	83.10.0 ounces	on delivery	sale of 100 rams to Muxa Sacerdotu and Sabet Farmuni, Jews of Palermo
4.6.1432 c. 385r	Vita Catalano, a Jew of Palermo	1.6.0 ounces	within 4 months	sale of olive oil
4.6.1432 c. 386v	Nissim Binna, a Jew of Palermo	1 ounce	within 4 months	sale of olive oil
12.6.1432 c. 393v	Lia de San Marco, a Palermitan Jew	13 *tarì*	1 *carlino* a week starting the following Sunday	loan to Salamon de Missina, a Palermitan Jew
12.6.1432 c. 393v	Matheo de Anselmo	27 *tarì*	paid	sale of grapes to Daidono Riczu, a Jew of Palermo

Date and Page	Tenant	Location and Description	Rent and Duration	Remarks
[...].1432 c. 1045r	Tobia Strugu, a Jew	Cassaro, *vanella* Li Santi Setti, bordering on the houses of Sadia Sacerdotu and Busacca Sala and public road; part of a house	1 ounce annually	landlord: Samuel Sala, a Palermitan Jew
20.11.1431 1068r	Challuxia, wife of Gallufo Taguil, a Jewess	Cassaro, *vanella* Di Mastru Moyses Chetibi, bordering on house of Lya Layeni, courtyard of Moyse Chetibi, house of [..] de Lu Medicu, public road; part of a block of houses	perpetual lease	landlady: Chazena, widow of Sabet Cusintinu, a Palermitan Jewess

3.12.1431 c. 1088r	Guglielmo de Bongiovanni	Cassaro, *contrada* Santa Marina, bordering on the houses of Muxa Millac and Sabutu Millac and public road; ground floor house	5 ounces	landlord: Manuel Rugila, a Palermitan Jew
1.1.1432 c. 2041v	Muxa Achina, a Jew of Palermo	Cassaro, *vanella* Lu Bagnu; 2 houses and two storehouses	2 ounces a year	landlord: Guglielmo Bertono
12.5.1432 c. 360r	Maciocta de Calathagirone	Cassaro, Platea Marmorea, bordering on shop of Busacca Xacharuni; shop	1 year for 1.27.0 ounces to be paid in monthly instalments	landlord: Chayrona widow of Gallufo Misiria, a Jewess
16.5.1432 c. 364r	Muxa Sacerdotu and Channon Migiar, Palermitan Jews	Palermo, *contrada* Macello dei Giudei, bordering on shop of Simone Xalomo; shop	5 years for 1.6.0 ounces a year	landlord: Francesco de Castellamari

Source: ASP, Not. Giovanni Traverso, reg. 777

Date and Page	Lender or Seller	Amount	Payment	Remarks
2.9.1434 c. 6r	Consumano de Pilocta	13 *tarì*		sale of goods to Farcono Momo, a Jew; guarantor: Paquale Sacerdotu, a Jew
7.9.1434 c. 13v	Antonio de Iacobo	agreed price	paid 29.5.1440	sale of oil Sadya Ysac, a Jew
7.9.1434 c. 14v	Antonio de Iacobo	1 ounce	paid 29.5.1440	sale of oil Sadya Ysac, a Jew
15.10.1434 c. 83v	Xannono Nigiar, a Jew	10 *grana* a *rotolo*	1 ounce on account; paid 5.10.1435	sale of wrought iron

23.10.1434 c. nn	Symon de mastro Angelo, a Jew	3.6.0 ounces	1.18.0 ounces on account, balance in 2 months; paid 4.12.1434	sale of grapes
17.11.1434 153v	Bartulillo de Lalicata	1.10.0 ounces	paid	sale of fine salt to Salamone Actuni, a Jew
23.11.1434 c. 154r	Xibiteni Bambulu, a Palermitan Jew	1.21.0 ounces	within 6 months	sale of a beast of burden
26.11.1434 c. 163v	Giuliano Grasso	12 ounces	4 ounces on account, another 4 by January, balance in April; paid 24.2.1435	sale of grapes to Iuda Sivena, a Jew
3.12.1434 c. 178v	Stefano Sanchiscoschi	5 ounces	within 4 months	sale of wheat to Benedetto Brunu, a Jew
17.12.1434 c. 200v	Ubertino Ventimiglia	4.25.0 ounces	within 4 months; paid 6.7.1435	sale of indigo to Manuel de Aram, a Jew
22.12.1434 c. 205r	Brandino de Lu Presti, a Palermitan Jew	10 ounces	paid	sale of grapes
13.3.1435 c. 315r	Sufen de Donarrigu, a Jew	1.25.0 ounces	16 *tarì* on account	sale of tow
16.5.1435 c. 411v	Iulianu Grassu	1.15.0 ounces	paid	sale of grapes to Iuda Siveni, a Jew
17.5.1435 c. 413r	Antonio Grado	1.3.0 ounces	by 15 October; paid 2.6.1436	sale of coal to Muxa Russu, a Jew
19.5.1435 c. 415r	Lia de Missina, a Jew	1 *salma* of wheat		sale of a horse saddle
1.7.1435 c. 462v	Muxa de Butera, a Jew	1.20.0 ounces	1 ounce on account; paid 19.7.1436	sale of horseshoes; guarantor: Daniel Ruggila, a Jew
16.7.1435 c. nn	David Dagua, a Jew	1.9.0 ounces	by February	sale of a beast of burden

1.8.1435 c. 503v	Iacobo de Pisano	3 ounces	by 15.6.1436	sale of goods to Muxa Russu, a Jew

Source: ASP, Not. Giovanni Traverso, reg. 778

Date and Page	Lender or Seller	Amount	Payment	Remarks
22.6.1436 c. 377v	Ubertino Cammarata	1 ounce	paid 15.7.1436	sale of coal to Muxa Actuni, a Jew
23.6.1436 c. 381v	Bonifacio de Bono	20 *tarì*	on demand	sale of wheat to Sabet Xagaruni, a Jew
[..]9.1436 c. nn	Mastro Paolo	2.10.0 ounces	4 *tarì* a week	sale of soles to Symon de Mayu and Salamon Actuni, Jews
5.9.1436 c. nn	Gargano Silvestro	2.13.0 ounces	within 4 months; 19.2.1437	sale of sugar to Samuel Sacerdotu, a Jew
15.9.1436 c. nn	Pietro de Agati	2.10.0 ounces	paid	sale of wheat to Iacob Sabatinu, a Jew
6.10.1436 c. nn	Nicolò de Taya	1 ounce	12 *tarì* by October, 18 *tarì* by Christmas	sale of a horse to Xibiten Bambalo, a Jew
6.10.1436 c. nn	Antonio de Orofino	14 *tarì*	paid with labour	sale of wheat to Isdrael de Strugo, a Jew
6.10.1436 c. 70v	Aloisia de Pompina	2.15.0 ounces	3 instalments, at Christmas, Easter and Pentecost; paid 3.6.1437	sale of grapes to Muxa Levi, a Jew
6.10.1436 c. 70v	Aloisia de Pompina	2.15.0 ounces	3 instalments, at Christmas, Easter and Pentecost; paid 1.7.1437	sale of grapes to Farchono Nifusi, a Jew
12.10.1436 c. 86v	Rogerio de Capua	19 *tarì*	by Christmas; paid 24.9.1437	sale of grapes to Busacca Levi, a Jew
23.10.1423 c. 108v	Giovanni de Ventimiglia	11.6.0 ounces	paid 10.10.1437	sale of grapes to Iuda Sivani, a Jew

2.11.1436 c. 137v	Merdoc Malti, a Jew	1 *tarì* for 8 bean-shaped receptacles	12 *tarì* on account	sale of bean-shaped receptacles
13.11.1436 c. 159v	Antonio Baiamonte	2.1.13 ounces	3 instalments, at Carnival time, Lent and Easter	sale of grapes to Muxa Russu, a Jew
22.11.1436 c. 181v	Iacobo de Argiono	1.20.0 ounces	by May; paid. 22.7.1437	sale of wheat to Farchono Gaczu and Merdoc Actuni, Jews
5.12 1436 c. 202v	Iacobo de Argiono	1 ounce	by May 1437	sale of wheat to Farchono Sichilianu, a Jew
31.1.1437 c. 272v	Pietro de Monaco	14.5 *tarì*	by Easter	sale of roof tiles to Nissim Busacca, a Jew
28.2.1437 c. 316v	Masio Crispo	[..] ounces	within 4 months; paid 15.10.1438	sale of cotton to Nissim Xidoch, a Jew
4.5.1437 c. 360r	Filippo Bellachera	1.16.0 ounces	by April; paid 5.7.1437	sale of linen to Vita Siven and Iosep Xammusu, Jews
9.5.1437 c. 368r	Mandania Chitarrella	1.12.0 ounces	half within 2 months, other half within another 2 months; paid 23.10.1437	sale of a used lined skirt to Braxhono Amurano, a Jew
22.5.1437 c. nn	Liuni Sacerdotu, a Jew	5 *grana* a pair	1 ounce on account	sale of horseshoes
24.5.1437 c. nn	Paolo de Ferri	2.17.0 ounces	half by July, balance by September	sale of soles to Symon de Mayu and his son Mayu, Jews
4.6.1437 c. nn	Francesco Ventimiglia	24 *tarì*	by August	sale of wool to Xibiteni Xammara, a Jew; guarantor: Sabutu Medui, a Jew
13.8.1437 c. nn	Giovanni Bellachera	12 *grana* a container	by April; paid 11.12.1438	sale of 87 containers of manure to Vita Ammara, a Jew

Source: ASP, Not. Giovanni Traverso, reg. 779

Date and Page	Lender or Seller	Amount	Payment	Remarks
20.1.1438 c. nn	Giovanni Pescu	1 ounce	within a month; paid 3.3.1438	sale of goods to Salamon Actuni and Iacob Termini, Jews
23.1.1438 c. nn	Rogerio de Sinisio	1.24.0 ounces	within 2 months; paid 11.6.1438	sale of silk to Muxa Daniel, a Jew
15.2.1438 c. nn	Masocta de Castellucio	3.12.0 ounces		sale of wheat to Iosep Xhammara, a Jew
8.3.1438 c. nn	Giovanni de Laburi	9.15.0 ounces	paid	sale of a black slave girl to Iacob Sabatino, a Jew
8.3.1438 c. nn	Muxa de Francza, a Jew	14 *tarì* a quintal	5 ounces on account; balance during coming tunny season	sale of barrels
[..].[..].1438 c. nn	Lemmus Levi, a Jew	1.18.0 ounces	1 ounce on account	sale of coarse salt [washed out]
[..].[..].1438 c. nn	Isolda de Asta	2 ounces	20 *tarì* during the present month, another 20 during the following month, balance in June; paid 29.7.1438	sale of goods to Braxono Mizoc, a Jew
[..].[..].1438 c. nn	Xhaninu de Liuni, a Palermitan Jew	1.1.10 ounces	within a month; paid 28.7.1438	sale of a horse

Source: ASP, Not. Giovanni Traverso, reg. 780

Date and Page	Principal	Attorney	Purpose	Remarks
10.10.1437 c. 75r	Salamon Gaczu, a Jew	Busacca Achina, a Jew	collection from various people of property inherited following the death of his mother	

6212

5.6.1439 c. nn	Salamon Aurifichi, a Jew	Giovanni Minecti	collection of revenues of cattle farm from Federico Calumia, formerly manager of the farm	

Date and Page	Debtor	Amount	Reason	Remarks
3.12.1438 c. 155v	Braxhono de Polici and Braxhono Amiranu, Jews	9 ounces	court order	to be paid in monthly instalments of 9 *tarì* starting the following month; creditor: Pino de Ferro, notary

Date and Page	Lender or Seller	Amount	Payment	Remarks
1.10.1437 c. 47v	Giovanni Bellachera	4.12.0 ounces	half during Holy Week, balance in August	sale of grapes to Merdoc Barbarusso, a Jew
1.10.1437 c. 54r	Caterina Ventimiglia	1.8.0 ounces		sale of a mule to Xibiten Bambalu, a Jew; guarantor: Salamon Xammara, a Jew
17.10.1437 c. 91v	Masio Crispo	6.7.10 ounces	within 3 months; paid 4.3.1438	sale of goods to Isdrael and Busacca Medui, Jews
22.10.1437 c. 99r	Masio de Giliberto	1 ounce	within 3 months; paid 12.3.1438	sale of iron to Nissimi Cassata, a Jew of Ciminna
22.9.1438 c. nn	Altadonna de Manueli and Xibiten de Tritula, Jews	1.6.0 ounces	paid	sale of rope to Salamon Sabuchi, a Jew
26.9.1438 c. nn	Muxa de Tripuli, a Jew	1 ounce	24 *tarì* on account	sale of rope to Salamon Sabuchi, a Jew, on behalf of Giovanni Homodei

7.10.1438 c. 58v	Nissim Xidedi, a Jew	1 ounce	24 *tarì* on account	sale of rope to Salamon Sabuchi, a Jew
7.10.1438 c. 59r	David Rugila, a Jew	1 ounce	24 *tarì* on account	sale of rope to Salamon Sabuchi, a Jew
25.10.1438 c. 92r	Pietro de la Sala	27 *tarì*	paid	sale of grapes to Busacca Levi, a Jew
25.10.1438 c. 92v	Giovanni Bellachera	5 ounces	by January	sale of lady's skirt to Braxha Minaxha, a Jew
11.11.1438 c. 102v	Antonello Manueli	12 *tarì*	by January; paid 23.4.1439	sale of wheat to Merdoc Malti, a Jew
11.12.1438 c. 161r	Vita Ammara, a Jew	2 ounces	1.4.6 ounces on account, balance on demand	sale of manure
14.12.1438 c. 187v	Rogerio de Sinisio	26.7.10 ounces	1 ounce on the following day, balance in instalments until 15 April	sale of sugarloaves to Sabet Dina and Samuel Bambalu, Jews
20.1.1439 c. 214r	Salamon Minichi, a Jew	2.12.0 ounces	2 ounces on account	sale of salt
26.1.1439 c. 220v	Nissim Aduruni, a Jew	4.21.0 ounces	2 ounces on account, balance on Easter; paid 2.9.1439	sale of a white bedspread
28.1.1439 c. 221v	Lando Homodey	7.10 *tarì*	within 2 months	sale of bells (*zimbiliorum*) to David Ciprianu and Braxhono Gualteri, Jews
2.3.1439 c. 261v	Symon Sacerdotu, a Jew	30 ounces	13 ounces on account; balance later	sale of rope
2.3.1439 c. 261v	Bulfarachi Magazenu, a Jew of Messina	3.9.0 ounces		loan

6214

30.3.1439 c. 308v	Vita de Liuni, a Palermitan Jew	24 *tarì*	by 15 May	sale of ground salt
13.4.1439 c. 327v	Antonio Dulchimasculo	12 *tarì* by June		sale of inferior parts of tunny (*busunaglia* = *busunagghia*) to Samuel Nigiar, a Palermitan Jew
13.4.1439 c. 327v	Muxa Butera, a Jew	25 *tarì* a hundred pairs	1 ounce on account; paid 6.5.1439	sale of horseshoes
27.4.1439 c. 355v	Aczarono Levi, a Palermitan Jew	28 *tarì*	paid	sale of salt
29.4.1439 c. 357v	Iordano de Sperliaga	1.8.0 ounces	10 *tarì* on account, balance in instalments	sale of a horse to Vita de Liuni, a Jew of Palermo
11.5.1439 c. 364r	Aczarono Levi, a Jew	6.8 *tarì*	paid	sale of six cart loads of hay
3.6.1439 c. nn	Muxa de Gauio, a Jew	4.1.8 ounces	within 4 months	sale of linen
30.6.1439 c. nn	Antonio Corbaya	6 ounces	paid 27.8.1442	sale of linen to Braxhuni Xunina, a Jew

Source: ASP, Not. Giovanni Traverso, reg. 781

Date and Page	Principal	Attorney	purpose	Remarks
[..].7.1440 c. 486v	Lya Sivena, a Jew	notary Antonio de Iordano	to represent Lya in a lawsuit with Ysac de Guglielmo, Merdoc Levi, Samuele Balbu and other Jews, who lodged an appeal against a previous ruling	

Date and Page	Debtor	Amount	Reason	Remarks
13.11.1439 c. 164v	Musuto de Castrogiovanni, a Jew	7.6.0 ounces		creditor: Nicolò de Bracco of Corleone; guarantors Braxhono Summatu and Aieti Sacerdotu, Jews
20.11.1439 c. 186v	Agnesia de Spidirni	18 *tarì*	expenses incurred for building wall between houses	creditor: Busacca Levi, a Jew; sum to be deducted from rent which Busacca owes Agnesia for a shop
26.1.1440 c. 264v	Czaccaria Achina, a Jew	1 ounce	on account of sale of candles	paid by Muxa, Czaccaria's brother

Date and Page	Lender or Seller	Amount	Payment	Remarks
22.9.1439 c. 35v	Muxa Sacerdotu, a Palermitan Jew	5 ounces	paid	sale of 250 cart loads of manure
22.9.1439 c. 35v	Braxhuni Summatu and his wife and Pasqualis Sacerdotu and his wife Asisa, Jews	10 ounces	4 ounces on account	sale of 50 *canne* of red cotton borders
23.10.1439 c. 126v	Antonio Gimaro	1.6.0 ounces	by Easter	sale of tunny to Chirillo de Seracusia, a Jew
26.10.1439 c. 130v	David Calabrisi, a Jew	1 ounce	paid	sale of tow
2.11.1439 c. 143v	Braxhunu Panichella, a Jew	10½ *grana* the *rotolo*	1 ounce on account	iron for equipping carts
10.11.1439 c. 157r	Giovanni Homodey	18.23.12 ounces	3 ounces on account, balance in 4 months; paid 16.3.1444	sale of *lixandrini* linen to Salamon de Missina and Leone Ammari, Jews

17.11.1439 c. 182v	Giovanni Quartarella	20 *tarì*	paid 14.12.1440	sale of oil to Busacca Levi, a Palermitan Jew
7.12.1439 c. 205r	Giovanni Homodey	24 *tarì*		sale of tunny to Xua de Nifusi, a Jew
30.12.1439 c. 226v	Iosep de Medico, a Jew	3 ounces	within 3 months	loan to Braxha Minaxham, a Jew
5.1.1440 c. 233r	Braxha Minaxham, a Jew	2.18.0 ounces	by August	sale of a lady's lined coat to Muxa Actuni, Gaudiu Ferraru and his son Manuel, Jews
5.1.1440 c. 233r	Braxha Minaxham, a Jew	1.18.0 ounces	within 2 months; paid 23.3.1440	sale of lined and hooded mantle (*chappa*) to Manuel Actuni, a Jew; guarantor: Muxa Actuni
[..].1.1440 c. 234r	Giovanni Quartarella	15 *tarì*		sale of grapes to Busacca Levi, a Jew
8.1.1440 c. 237v	Antonello Manueli	26 *tarì*	by 15.4.1440	sale of nuts to Sabutu Medui, a Jew
8.1.1440 c. 238r	Antonello Manueli	26 *tarì*	by 15.4.1440	sale of almonds and nuts to Siminto Nafusi, a Palermitan Jew
26.2.1440 c. 313v	Bertullo Landolo	1 ounce	within 4 months; paid 18.7.1440	sale of scarlet lady's gowns (*cucetti*) to Vanni Ysac, a
				Palermitan Jew; guarantor: Iacob, Vanni's father, and David, his uncle
[..].3.1440 c. 323r	Antonello de Ginnaro	18 *tarì*	within 4 months	sale of tunny to Levi de Tripoli, a Palermitan Jew
10.3.1440 c. 340r	Braxha and Farchono Berni, father and son	8.15.0 ounces	by September; paid 25.12.1441	sale of a black slave girl

12.4.1440 c. 389r	Muxa Sacerdotu, a Jew of Palermo	1.25.0 ounces	in 4 instalments until July	sale of 2 beasts of burden
17.6.1440 c. 463r	Busacca de Tripuli, a Jew	26.20.0 ounces	15 ounces on account	sale of rope
1.7.1440 c. 474r	Giovanni Fruntilata	2 ounces	by October	sale of tunny to Salamon de Missina, Sabet Busicta and Benedetto Caffisi, Jews
27.7.1440 c. 501r	Giovanni Homodey		3 ounces by 15.9, balance by October	sale of linen to Lya de Missina and his son Sabet, Jews; guarantors: Muxa de Miseria and Ayam Muxa, Jews
19.8.1440 c. 522r	Leone Crichilla, a Jew	1 ounce	by January; paid 14.4.1441 by Xhanino father of Mardoc Achina, a Jew	sale of tunny to Fadaluni Xhabirra and Mardoc Achina, Jews
26.9.1440 c. 612r	Benedetto Xammara, a Jew of Termini	6.2.0 ounces	by August 1441	sale of hardened tallow (*sivi quagliati*)
28.11.1440 c. 665r	Andrea Aprea	3.9.0 ounces	by Easter; paid 23.6.1444 Minaxham, Jews; Minaxham, a Jew	sale of lady's hooded mantle to David Nigiar and Braxha guarantor: Michilono
15.12.1440 c. 692r	Antonio Monteleone	1 ounce	2 days before Passover	salle of tunny to Xhaimi Gaczu, a Jew; guarantor: Merdoc Actuni, a Jew
12.5.1441 c. 727r	Merdoc Saullu, a Jew	24 *tarì*		sale of horseshoes
16.5.1441 c. 425r	Guglielmo Nixina	20 *tarì*	by June	sale of cheese to Ysdrael Strugu and Salamon de Amari, Jews

Date and Page	Lender or Seller	Amount	Payment	Remarks
19.6.1441 c. 459r	Muxa Sacerdotu, a Palermitan Jew	20 ounces	10 ounces on account, 5 ounces with cloth, balance by August	sale of manure
[..].6. 1441 c. 465r	Busacca de Tripuli, a Palermitan Jew	43.10.0 ounces	half with tunny half in cash	sale of rope
11.7.1441 c. 474r	Busacca de Tripuli, a Palermitan Jew	2 ounces		sale of manure

Date and Page	Tenant	Location and Description	Rent and Duration	Remarks
26.1.1440 c. 262v	Ysai de Ysay, a Jew	Cassaro, bordering on the houses of Nissim Binna and Braxhono Miczoc, Jews; *solerata* house and courtyard	9 years starting 1.9 for 2 ounces annually paid in 2 instalments	landlord: Iusep Braxhono, a Palermitan Jew, acting for Siminto Miczoc, a Jew of Syracuse

Source: ASP, Not. Giovanni Traverso, reg. 782

Date and Page	Lender or Seller	Amount	Payment	Remarks
13.11.1441 c. 149r	David Ysac and Bulxhaira Sansuni, Jews of Trapani	5.15.0 ounces	2 ounces on account, balance by Christmas; 26.1.1442	sale of a new curtain
13.11.1441 c. 149r	Giovanni Homodey	1.6.0 ounces	within 3 months	sale of tunny to Xibiten de Minnichi, a Jew
4.12.1441 c. 188r	Mundaxam de Parat, a Jew of Mazara	1.24.0 ounces	paid	sale of a horse; guarantor: Pasqualis Sacerdotu, a Jew
5.12.1441 c. 192r	Iacob Sufi, a Jew of Caccamo	1.6.0 ounces	by August	sale of a horse

14.12.1441 c. 204v	Antonello de Ginnaro	1.6.0 ounces	by the carving [of fish] (*taglata*) at the tunny plant in Solanto	sale of tunny to Xirello de Seracusia, a Jew
11.1.1442 c. 249v	Paolo Lombardo	1 ounce	within 5 months; paid 24.10.1442	sale of wheat to Xhayruni Maltisi and Xauruni Sofer, Jews
18.1.1442 c. 253r	Antonio Muxulinu	1.24.0 ounces	1 ounce on account, balance by 15.2.1442; paid 25.2.1442	sale of grapes to Yacob de Termini, a Jew
8.3.1442 c. 318r	Robino Gibira, a Palermitan Jew	13 ounces	11.9.0 ounces on account, balance at harvest time	sale of a black slave
8.3.1442 c. 319r	Giovanni Fruntilata	1.1.10 ounces	by July	sale of tunny to Saduni Trapanisi, Farcono Gazu and Salamon Sabuchi, Jews
12.3.1442 c. 322r	Antonello Manueli	6.16. *tarì* a kantar	5 ounces on account	sale of 60 kantars of cheese to Vita Catalano, a Jew
16.3.1442 c. 365v	Caterina wife of Ubertino Bongiovanni	27 *tarì*	paid	sale of grapes to Xibiteni di Gibira, a Jew
24.4.1442 388v	Manuel Xunnina, a Jew of Trapani	12 ounces	24 *tarì* on account, balance within 15 days; paid 19.7.1442	sale of a black slave
6.5.1442 c. 404r	Siminto Benassay, a Palermitan Jew	1 ounce	by October	sale of oil to Nissim Panichella, a Jew
9.5.1442 c. 407v	Sufen Miseria, a Palermitan Jew	1.6.0 ounces	paid	sale of oil to Siminto Benassai, a Jew of Palermo
6.7.1442 c. 484r	Braxha Crivaru, a Palermitan Jew	20 *tarì*	paid	sale of oil to Xhairono Malti, a Jew of Palermo

Source: ASP, Not. Giovanni Traverso, reg. 783

Date and Page	Lender or Seller	Amount	Payment	Remarks
[..].5. 1442 c. 412r	Nicolò Bono	12 ounces	within 2 months	sale of cloth to Gracianu Taxharianu, a Palermitan Jew
[..].5. 1442 c. 412r	Nicolò Bono	3 ounces	within 2 months; paid 11.7.1443	sale of cloth to Salamon Benassay, a Jew
[..].5. 1442 c. 412v	Nicolò Bono	3 ounces	within 2 months; paid 5.7.1444	sale of cloth to Busacca de La Magna, a Jew
16.5.1442 c. 417r	Pasqualis Sacerdotu, a Palermitan Jew	4 ounces	2 ounces on account, balance on delivery	sale of manure
28.5.1442 c. 434r	Giovanni Asta	1.2.0 ounces	within 4 months	sale of oil to Merdoc Levi, a Jew
25.2.1443 c. 336r	Guglielmo Nixina	1.6.0 ounces	by May	sale of wheat to Salamon Actuni, a Jew
26.2.1443 c. 338v	Xhayrono Xalomu, a Jew	1.10.0 ounces		sale of rope
18.3.1443 c. 375v	Antonio Muxulinu	1.24.0 ounces	6 *tarì* and then 1 ounce on account, balance at vintage time	sale of grapes to Yacob de Termini, a Jew
15.10.1449 c. nn	Iosep Braxha, a Jew	1.3.0 ounces a kantar	1.14.0 ounces on account, balance on delivery	sale of 2 kantars of tow
5.1.1450 c. 207v	Andrea Sinibaldo	3 ounces		sale of oil to Minto Gibbesi, a Jew
5.1.1450 c. 208r	Andrea Sinibaldo	15 *tarì*	within 2 months	sale of oil to Salamon Barba, a Jew
15.1.1450 c. 230r	Guglielmo Cuxina	14 *tarì*	by Easter	sale of salted sardines and tunny to Muxa Minczil, a Jew; guarantor: Xhayrono Malti, a Jew

15.1.1450 c. 230v	Rogerio Nisio	1.6.0 ounces	14 *tarì* on account, balance in a month	sale of sheepskins to Lya Sadya, a Jew
30.1.1450. c. 261v	Enrico de La Manna			sale of grapes to Gabriele de Medico. a Jew; guarantor: Filippo Bellachera
10.2.1450 c. 289r	Giuliano La Turri	1.6.0 ounces	within 4 months	sale of tunny to Merdoc Actuni, a Jew
19.5.1450 c. 460v	Guglielmo Cuxina	2.23.8 ounces	by August	loan to Xhairono Malti, a Jew
6.7.1450 c. 523r	Braxhono de Missina, a Jew	2.4.0 ounces	19 *tarì* on account, balance by 15.8	sale of tunny roe
15.7.1450 c. 537r	Busacca Ysac, a Jew	2 ounces	paid 14.91451	sale of grapes
23.7.1450 c. 550v	Iacobo de Napuli, a Jew	1 ounce	within a month	loan to Xhairono Malti, a Jew

Date and Page	Tenant	Location and Description	Rent and Duration	Remarks
19.8.1450 c. 583r	Iacobo de Termini, a Jew	Palermo, *contrada* Foriveteris, bordering on landlord's shop	shop; 1 year for 1 ounce, in 3 instalments	landlord: Guglielmo Bucheri

Source: ASP, Not. Giovanni Traverso, reg. 784

Date and Page	Debtor	Amount	Reason	Remarks
6.11.1443 c. 180v	G[...] and Xibiten Minichi, Jews	3.18.0 ounces		creditor: Cristofaro Pyader, treasurer of Sacre Domus Mansionis [Theotonicorum], acting for Donna Eleonora de Millina; to be paid in instalments of 4 *tarì* every 4 months

Date and Page	Lender or Seller	Amount	Payment	Remarks
4.11.1443 c. 171r	Filippo de La Mantia	24 *tarì*		sale of grapes to Ferrugio Ysac and Bulxhayra Fusisa, Jews
4.11.1443 c. 171v	Filippo de La Mantia	1.2.0 ounces	12 *tarì* on account	sale of oil to Ferrugio Ysac, a Jew
7.11.1443 c. 178r	Iacob Malki, a Jew	1.20.0 ounces	12 *tarì* on account, balance on demand	sale of bricks (*pietre cotte*)
8.11.1443 c. 179r	Gimiluni Mixhan, a Palermitan Jew	5 ounces	by August	sale of wheat and barley
10.11.1443 c. 183v	Merdoc Malti, a Jew of Palermo	1 *tarì* for 8 bundles	11 *tarì* on account, balance by February	firewood
10.11.1443 c. 207v	Antonio Bayamonte	15 *tarì*	at the end of tunny season of Solanto	sale of goods to Braxhagna de Ansalone, a Jew
10.11.1443 c. 207v	Giovanni de Ferro	1.28.5 ounces	by 15.3	sale of goods to Iosep de la Iudeca, a Jew
4.12.1443 c. 236v	Nicolò Guarnerio	28 *tarì*	6 *tarì* by January	sale of oil to Sufeni Miseria and Iusep Ammaru, Jews
5.12.1443 c. 238r	Guglielmo Nixina	2.6.0 ounces	by February	sale of wheat to Salamon Actuni, a Jew
12.12.1443 c. 248r	Omodei Puchio	20 ounces	within six months	sale of Verona clothes to Iosep Braxhuni, a Jew
15.1.1444 c. 304v	Xhaymi Czitarì, a Jew	1 ounce	15 *tarì* on account; balance by April	sale of cloth
4.3.1444 c. 509r	Giovanni Bellachera	4.5.0 ounces	1 ounce every 4 months	sale of merchandise to Xamuel Gididia, a Jew
6.3.1444 c. 516r	Giovanni de Ferro	1 ounce	by March	sale of iron to Graciano Abate, a Jew

6223

27.5.1444 c. 541v	Siminto Kimicti, a Jew	15 *tarì*	paid	sale of candles
3.6.1444 c. 547r	Siminto Kimicti, a Jew	7.15.0 ounces	by April	sale of tallow to Xibiten Xhabirra, a Jew
7.9 1444 c. 10v	Antonio de Gregorio de Cammarata	1.21.0 ounces	paid	sale of 2 oxen to Gallufo Cuyno, a Jew
11.9.1444 c. 14v	Gimilono de Naxhan, a Jew	21 *tarì*	by August	sale of wheat
12.10.1444 c. 58v	Xhayrono de Xalon, a Palermitan Jew	4 ounces	paid	sale of thin rope
29.10.1444 c. 76v	Giovanni de Asta	6.12.0 ounces	within 4 months	sale of cloth to Manuel Chetibi, a Jew; guarantor: Farcono Sala, a Jew
13.11.1444 c. 100v	Donna Flori Miczullo	1.9.0 ounces	6 *tarì* a month	sale of goods to Luna de Accurano de Tripoli, a Jewess; guarantor: Muxa de Xacca, a Jew
19.11.1444 c. 110r	Giovanni de Homodei	51 ounces	15 ounces within a day, 5 ounces by Christmas, balance by June	sale of sundry goods to Donato Aurifichi, a Jew
24.11.1444 c. 118v	Garita de Simone	27 *tarì*	within 6 months; paid 14.11.1445	sale of cloth to Iusep Brixha, a Jew
9.12.1444 c. 134r	Pino de Ferro	14.27.7 ounces	within 4 months; paid 20.8.1445	sale of sugar and honey to Salamon Aurifichi and Siminto de Benedetto, Jews
22.12.1444 c. 151r	Bulxhaira de Termini, a Jew	1.18.0 ounces	paid	sale of grapes to Gauyu de Bono, a Jew
8.1.1445 c. 167v	Caterina de Yuvenco	1.6.0 ounces	by June; paid 21.5.1445	sale of merchandise to Muxa Turri, a Jew
12.1.1445 c. 173v	Giovanni de Bartholomeo	27 *tarì*	18 *tarì* on account, balance by 15.3	sale of grapes to Robino Misiria, a Jew

12.1.1445 c. 173v	Bulxhaira de Termini, a Jew	3.6.0 ounces	paid	sale of grapes
15.1.1445 c. 176v	Salamon de Missina, a Jew	1.2.0 ounces	6 *tarì* on account	sale of elongated tiles (*calamidarum de striczono*)
16.1.1445 c. 184r	Siminto Kimicti, a Jew	1.27.0 ounces	by 15.2	loan
17.2.1445 c. 224v	Manuel de Candia	2 ounces	by July; paid 13.9.1445	sale of soles to Symon de Mayu and his son Mayu, Jews
7.4.1445 c. 319v	Lya Ammara, a Jew	4 ounces	by harvest time	loan
19.4.1445 c. 338v	Sabatino Sufi, a Jew of Messina	8.10 *tarì*	paid	sale of an anvil; guarantor: Sadono de Ubi, a Jew
4.5.1445 c. 360r	Conino Riczu, a Jew	24 *tarì*	by August	sale of a beast of burden
20.5.1445 c. 369r	Braxhono Cusintinu, a Jew	6.15.0 ounces	by July; paid 26.8.1445	sale of soles
2.6.1445 c. 384r	Pino lu Crispu	2.12.0 ounces	paid	sale of a horse to Busacca de Ansaluni, a Jew
4.6.1445 c. 386v	Xibiten Chura, a Jew	27 *tarì* a hundred	1 ounce on account	sale of horseshoes
30.6.1445 c. 419v	Muxa Sacerdotu, a Palermitan Jew	5 ounces	3 ounces on account, balance last week of June	sale of manure
9.8.1445 c. 478r	Chicco de Mauro	1.5.0 ounces	paid	sale of grapes to Lya Sadya, a Palermitan Jew
13.8.1445 c. 492v	Braxha Crivaru, a Jew	15 *tarì*	paid	sale of olive pips
23.8.1445 c. 512r	Giovanni Sinagra	1.1.0 ounces	paid	sale of grapes to Lya Sadya, a Jew

Date and Page	Tenant	Location and Description	Rent and Duration	Remarks
14.5.1444 c. 526v	Xibiten Barbuti, a Jew	Cassaro, bordering on the houses of Muxa Situra and Xibiten Vignuni, Jews; *solerata* house and shop	3 years for 2.3.0 ounces a year; 6 *tarì* on account	landlord: notary Nicolò de Fossatellis; tenant promises not to have metal work done to the property
3.10.1444 c. 149v	Salvo Muxano, a Jew	Palermo; mill called La Paraturi; from 7.10.1444 to 31.8.1445	for 8 ounces a year in weekly instalments	owner: Giovanni de Asta
30.4.1445 c. 356r	Simone de Mayu and his son Mayu	Palermo, *contrada* Foriveteris; shop, until end of August	for 2 *tarì* a month and from September for a year at 1 ounce	landlord: Antonio Faczalla
14.6.1445 c. 302r	Iacob Sabatino, a Jew	Palermo, *contrada* Lattarini, bordering on shop of Sadono de Medico and Moyses Chetibi, Jews; shop	6 years starting September for 1.6.0 ounces annually	landlord: David Xifuni, a Palermitan Jew; guarantors: Manuele Chetibi and Iusep Braxhuni, Jews
23.7.1445 c. 454v	Xibite de Malta, a Jew	Polizzi; a group of houses	3.15.0 ounces annually	landlady: Berta de Paternio
3.8.1445 c. 474v	Syminti Nifusi, a Jew	Cassaro, bordering on the house of Giovanni de Bononia; shop	1 year for 3.3.0 ounces in monthly instalments	landlord: Antonio de Sala, a Carmelitan

Source: ASP, Not. Giovanni Traverso, reg. 785

Date and Page	Principal	Attorney	Purpose	Remarks
14.11.1446 c. 326v	Bulxhaira Sansuni, a Jew of Trapani	Abram Laxhedub, a Jew	to collect from Rogerio Sinisio a debt of 2.3.0 ounces owed him for a curtain	Rogerio had deposited a pawn of silver and gold

Date and Page	Debtor	Amount	Reason	Remarks
9 June 1447 c. 535v	Giovanni de Orio	1.1.0 ounces	expenses incurred in obtaining possession of a small orchard in *contrada* Falsomiele	creditor: mastro David Xifuni, a Jew

Date and Page	Lender or Seller	Amount	Payment	Remarks
1.9.1445 c. nn	Salamon de Liuno, a Jew	7.6..0 ounces	paid	sale of grapes
29.10.1445 c. 139v	Xilomu Xagul, a Jew of Mazara	10 ounces	2 ounces on account; paid 4.2.1446	sale of a curtain with silk borders
4.1.1446 c. 304r	Iacob Malki, a Palermitan Jew	1 ounce	paid	sale of bricks
10.1.1446 c. 312r	Bulxhayra Sansuni, a Jew of Trapani	5 ounces	paid	sale of curtain
4.2.1446 c. 389r	Francesca Sala	3 ounces	by August; paid 17.10.1447	sale of a lady's mantle of cloth
7.2.1446 c. 394v	Pietro Mauricio	8.1.0 ounces	by June	loan to Muxa and Sabeti Russu, Jews
8.2.1446 c. 397v	Pietro Mauricio	2.4.0 ounces	by July	sale of barley to Xayrono Russu, a Jew
16.5.1446 c. 646r	Masio de Campora	1.15.0 ounces	paid	sale of grapes to Lya Sadya, a Jew

18.7.1446 c. 730r	Sansuni de Taormina and Xibiten Achina, Jews	10 *grana* a *rotolo*	1 ounce on account	sale of wrought iron
18.7.1446 c. 732r	Bulxhayra Sansuni, a Jew of Trapani	12 ounces	:	sale of a black slave; guarantor: Ysac Naxhua, a Jew
12.11.1446 c. nn	Guarnerio de Monaco	1.6.0 ounces	within 4 months	sale of wheat to Contissa de Malti, a Jewess; guarantor: her son David Malki
7.12.1446 c. 166r	Giuliano de la Turri	1.6.0 ounces	by February	sale of tunny to Merdoc Actuni and Xhayruni Gaczu, Jews
7.1.1447 c. 215v	Giuliano de la Turri	1.9.10 ounces	by May	sale of tunny barrels to Iosep Ammara, a Jew; guarantor: Salamon Sabuchi, a Jew
9.1.1447 c. 226r	Giuliano de la Turri	1.15.0 ounces	by May	sale of tunny to Salamon Gaczu, a Jew
9.1.1447 c. 227v	Giuliano de la Turri	1.15.0 ounces	by May	sale of tunny to David Serruni, a Jew
12.1.1447 c. 235v	Iacobo Draga	1.24.0 ounces		sale of tunny roe to Iacob Malki, a Jew
13.1.1447 c. 237v	Giuliano de la Turri	18 *tarì*	by May	sale of tunny to Merdoc Xhagemuni, a Jew; guarantor: Farrugiu Czivena, a Jew
16.1.1447 c. 245v	Iuda Cuchilla and Farchono Berni, Jews	1 ounce	paid	sale of oil to Lya de Minichi, a Jew
23.2.1447 c. 335r	Braxhono Simael, a Palermitan Jew	22 *tarì*	3 *tarì* on account	sale of oil; guarantor: Sabatino Minichi, a Jew

8.3.1447 c. 368v	Giuliano de la Turri	2.3.0 ounces	by July	sale of tunny barrels to Vita Maltisi and Farchono Gaczu, Jews
8.3.1447 c. 368v	Giuliano de la Turri	1.15.0 ounces	by July	sale of goods to Xibiten Gaczu, a Jew
9.3.1447 c. 373v	Giuliano de la Turri	1.1.10 ounces	by June	sale of tunny to Czullu Iubara, a Jew
9.3.1447 c. 373v	Parisio de la Turri	1 ounce	by June	sale of goods to Czullu Dido, a Jew
9.3.1447 c. 374r	Giuliano de la Turri	1.10.10 ounces		sale of tunny to Xhayronu and Merdoc Gaczu, Jews; guarantor: Farcono Gaczu, a Jew
10.3.1447 c. 378r	Giuliano de la Turri	2.2.10 ounces	by June	sale of tunny to Fadaluni Xhabirra and Braxhono Amiranu, Jews
14.3.1447 c. 380r	Giuliano de la Turri	1.1.10 ounces	by June	sale of tunny to Muxa Turri, a Jew
14.3.1447 c. 380v	Giuliano de la Turri	1.24.0 ounces	by June	sale of tunny to Muxa Minzili, a Jew
14.3.1447 c. 380r	Giuliano de la Turri	1.9.0 ounces	by June	sale of tunny to Iacob Coffitor and Busacca de Tripoli, Jews
1.6.1447 c. 524r	Busacca Ficara, a Jew	1 ounce	paid	sale of a beast of burden
5.6.1447 c. 529v	Sansuni Taormina, a Jew	10 *grana* a *rotolo*	1 ounce on account, balance on delivery	sale of wrought iron
4.7.1447 c. 577r	Braxha Crivaru, a Palermitan Jew	15 *tarì*	paid	sale of nuts
Date and Page	**Tenant**	**Location and Description**	**Rent and Duration**	**Remarks**
15.7.1446 c. 724v	Iacob Sabatinu, a Jew	Palermo, *contrada* Lattarini; shop	1.24.0 ounces annually	landlord: David Xifuni, a Jew; Iosep de Braxhuni, guardian of Manuel and Farachi Chetibi, all Jews, confirm the contract

Source: ASP, Not. Giovanni Traverso, reg. 786

Date and Page	Debtor	Amount	Reason	Remarks
8.3.1448 c. 368r	Arnao de Santa Columba	15 ounces	commitment	creditor: Iusep Magaseni, a Jew of Messina; Galluffo Cuinu, attorney for the heirs of Iusef Cuinu, Jews, accepts 3 ounces on account and concedes an extension for the payment of the debt to be settled in instalments until Easter of 1449
23.4.1449 c. 447r	Gauyu Gemin and Benedetto Czikiri of Castrogiovanni, Jews, acting for Antonio Zumbo	3 ounces	commitment	creditor: Nicolò de Lucchisio

Date and Page	Lender or Seller	Amount	Payment	Remarks
11.10.1447 c. 58v	Blasio Bonfiglio	2 ounces	1 ounce by Easter, balance by August	sale of white grapes to Mayo Rabbi Iacob, a Jew
17.11.1447 c. 134r	Antonio de Cantello	1.21.0 ounces	middle of Lent; paid	sale of a velvet skirt to Xhaimi Xicari, a Jew; guarantor: Iacob Ianni, a Jew
27.11.1447 c. 147v	Giuliano de Royo	56.27.15 ounces	5 ounces on 1.12, half in January, balance in March	sale of honey sugar loaves to Leone de La Yudeca and his son Iosep, Jews
4.12.1447 c. nn	Czullu Iubara, a Jew	10 tarì	paid 29.12.1447	sale of oil
12.12.1447 181v	Michael Tirannu	24 tarì	paid	sale of grapes to Busacca Levi, a Jew
2.1.1448 c. 213r	Yanua, wife of Andrea de Surra	1.12.0 ounces	18 tarì on account; paid	sale of grapes to Lya Sadya and Iacob de Termini, Jews

12.1.1448 c. 235v	Tifano Mezzatesta	6.15.7 ounces	2.19.10 ounces on account, balance by February; paid 1.3.1449	sale of linen to Bulxhayra Sansuni, a Jew of Trapani
15.1.1448 c. 237v	Busacca de Minichi, a Jew	2.12.0 ounces	12 *tarì* on account, balance by Easter	sale of a horse
22.1.1448 c. 242r	Antonio de Raimundo	1.3.0 ounces	paid	sale of a horse to Busacca de Minichi, a Jew
22.1.1448 c. 264r	Muxa Sacerdotu, a Jew	10 ounces	1.20.0 ounces on account; balance later	sale of manure
24.1.1448 c.269r	Costantino de Andrea Xhila	25.10 *tarì*	paid	sale of grapes to Lya Sadya and Iacob de Termini, Jews
7.2.1448 c. 286r	Vita de Terranova, a Jew of Castrogiovanni	12 ounces	1.21.0 ounces and 27 *tarì* on account, balance within 6 months	sale of a white slave girl
18.7.1448 c. 563r	Nicolò Brando	23 *tarì*	within 4 months; paid 23.11.1448	sale of hides to Sabet de Termini, a Jew; guarantor: Busacca Rabibi, a Jew
1.4.1448 c. 249r	Iohanne Salamuni, a Jew of Termini	3.9.0 ounces	9 *tarì* on account, balance in 2 months	sale of 2 horses; guarantor: Nissim Binna, a Jew
14.6.1448 c. 513v	Iacobo de Napoli	1.24.0 ounces	paid 26.8.1448	sale of [Albanian] silk headdresses (*cayule*) to Xamueli Sacerdotu, a Jew; guarantor: Pasquale Sacerdotu, a Jew
8.7.1448 c. 517r	Ubertinu de Xixo	2.12.0 ounces	1.6.0 ounces within 15 days, balance in a month; paid 10.2.1449	sale of a boat to David Termini, a Jew
10.7.1448 c. 548v	Paolo de Pasquali	5.10.0 ounces	2 ounces by 15.7, balance in September	sale of cheese to Sabeti Russu, a Jew

23.7.1448 c. 566v	Andrea de Arena	1.9.0 ounces	instalments starting by July	sale of a horse to Iosep de Minichi, a Jew
6.9.1448 c. 18r	Gauyusa Xhammara and Xhaguerra Ammara, Jewesses	5 ounces		sale of rope for the tunny industry
6.9.1448 c. 19r	Busacca de Ansaluni and his wife Stella, Jews	1.15.0 ounces		sale of heavy rope for the tunny industry to Salamuni Sabuchi, a Jew
10/9/1448 c. 32r	Gauyusa de Iuda Guchada, a Jewess	1 ounce	paid	sale of light rope for the tunny industry to Salamuni Sabuchi, a Jew
11.9.1448 c. 33r	Regina Millac, a Jewess	1 ounce	paid	sale of heavy rope for the tunny industry to Salamon Sabuchi, a Jew
11.9.1448 c. 33r	Iacob Portan, a Jew	1 ounce	paid	sale of heavy rope to Salamon Sabuchi, a Jew
16.9.1448 c. 41r	Giovanni La Barbera	2.6.0 ounces	by January; paid 27.2.1449	sale of oil to Vita de Leone, a Jew
18.9.1448 c. 43v	Iosep Brixha, a Jew	2 ounces	1.19.11 ounces on account, balance on delivery	sale of tow for barrels to Salamon Sabuchi, a Jew
12.10.1448 c. 104v	Giovanni de la Sapoceona and his mother Ysolda	3.6.0 ounces	1.12.0 ounces on account	sale of grapes to Iacob Sabatini, a Jew
30.10.1448 c. 146r	Guglielmo Quartarello	11 *tarì*	paid	sale of olive oil to Busacca Levi, a Jew
31.10.1448 c. 203v	Bernardo Polo	9 *tarì*	on demand	sale of a horse to master Pietro de Martino and master Nixim Gerson, a Jew

29.11.1448 c. 220v	Nicolò Brando	1.15.0 ounces	within 4 months; paid 21.5.1450	sale of hides to Sabeti de Termini, a Jew; guarantor: Busacca Rabibi, a Jew
24.12.1448 c. 249r	Pasqualis Sacerdotu, a Palermitan Jew	2.9.0 ounces	2.1.0 ounces on 4.2.1449, balance on 11.7.1449	sale of a lame white slave girl
14.1.1449 c. 266r	Giovanni de Ferro and Filippo Aglata	3.22.10 ounces	1 ounce on account, balance within 5 months	sale of sheepskin to Braxhono Summatu and his son Muxaxi
14.1.1449 c. 266v	Giovanni de Ferro	2.2.16 ounces	paid	sale of sheepskin to Braxhono Summatu and his son Muxaxi
31.1.1449 cc. 299v- 300r	Milica widow of Xibiteni Barbutu and her son Moyses Barbutu, Jews	4.25.0 ounces	2.25.0 ounces on account; paid	sale of cows
12.2.1449 c. 324v	Giovanni de Bartholomeo	29 *tarì*	15 *tarì* on account	sale of white grapes to Lya Sadia, a Jew
19.3.1449 c. 392v	Giuliano de Rigio	11.6.0 ounces		sale of 7 horses to Minto de Minichi, Michilono Sacca and Vegnamino de Minichi, Jews
19.3.1449 c. 395v	Giovanni de Ferro	2.20.0 ounces	within 4 months; paid 1.12.1451	sale of sheepskin to Sabet and Merdoc Levi, Jews
3.4.1449 c. 3.4.1449	Guglielmo Cuxina	27 *tarì*	by August	sale of clean tunny to Muxa Minczil, a Jew
17.4.1449 c. 436v	Iuda Minichi, a Palermitan Jew	2.6.0 ounces	2 ounces on account	sale of ground salt of Cammarata; guarantor: Braxhono Bambolu, a Jew
17.4.1449 c. 437r	Rogerio de Nisio	18 *tarì* the kantar	1 ounce on account, balance at harvest time	sale of tallow to Minto Kimitti, a Jew

12.5.1449 c. 479v	Guglielmo Buccheri	2.121.0 ounces		sale of wheat to Lya Sadia and to his partner Iacob de Termini, Jews
7.7.1449 c. 547r	Simon de Giglia and Giovanni de Cipi	1 ounce	6 *tarì* on account, balance on delivery	sale of myrtle to Busacca Levi, a Jew

Date and Page	Tenant	Location and Description	Rant and Duration	Remarks
9.6.1448 c. nn	Xibiten de Lu Presti, a Jew	Palermo, bordering on landlord's shop; shop	1.6.0 ounces annually	landlord: Giovanni Spina

Source: ASP, Not. Giovanni Traverso, reg. 787

Date and Page	Debtor	Amount	Reason	Remarks
[..].[..]. 1450 c. nn	Enrico de Bages	payment for half a quintal of grapes	grapes not delivered	creditor: Iacob de Termini, a Jew
12.8.1451 c. 570r	Muxa Sofer, a Jew		debts arising out of concluded business	creditor: Merdoc Malti, a Jew
26.8.1451 c. 588r	Minto de Minichi, a Jew, guarantor for Merdoc de Minichi, another Jew	1 ounce	former debt	creditor: Andrea de Sinibaldo

Date and Page	Lender or Seller	Amount	Payment	Remarks
2.9.1450 c. 2v	Xilomu Levi, a Jew of Cammarata	6 *tarì* on account, balance on delivery	paid 13.4.1452	sale of iron

2.9.1450 c. 5r	Rogerio Farfagla	1.4.10 ounces	monthly instalments of 7.10 *tarì*; paid 4.5.1452	sale of oil to Gallufu de Termini, a Jew; guarantor: Busacca Levi, a Jew
17.9.1450 c. 25v	Antonio Mameli	17 *tarì* a kantar	1 ounce on account	sale of tallow to Minto Kimitti, a Jew
25.9.1450 c. 38r	Muxa Sabuchi, a Jew			sale of tow for barrels to Salamon Sabuchi, a Jew
1.10.1450 c. 52r	Iacobo Cathania	1.14.0 ounces	within 2 months	sale of wheat to Xhayrono Malti, a Jew
17.11.1450 c. 154v	Pino Lu Crispu	2 ounces	12 *tarì* on account, another 12 *tarì* by Christmas, balance on Easter	sale of a horse to Braxha Catalano, a Jew
19.11.1450 c. 160r	Giuliano de Raimondo and Braxha Catalano, a Jew	1 ounce		sale of ground salt of Cammarata
29.12.1450 c. 222r	Merdoc and Sabeti Malti, Jews	2.12.0 ounces	monthly instalments of 6 *tarì* starting in January	sale of leather to Muxa Safari, a Jew
7.1.1451 c. 239r	Sabatino Sufe, a Jew	27 *tarì*	18 *tarì* on account, balance by February; paid 28.4.1451	sale of a horse; guarantor: Xilleli Aczara, a Jew
19.1.1451 c. 262r	Busacca Ysac, a Jew	4 ounces	paid	sale of grapes to Vita Xifuni, a Jew
20.2.1451 c. 296r	Iusep Brixha, a Jew	1.3.0 ounces	1.1.0 ounces on account	sale of tow for barrels
21.2.1451 c. 298v	Busacca de Siracusia, a Jew	18.10 *tarì*	paid	sale of stoppers for barrels
30.5.1451 c. 486r	Salimbeni de Talia	1.28.10 ounces	paid	sale of grapes to Iacob de Termini and Lya Sadia, Jews

30.5.1451 c. 486r	Iacobo Maurichi	10 ounces	paid	sale of grapes to Iacob de Termini and Lya Sadia, Jews
14.7.1451 c. 547v	Nicolò Maurichi	4 ounces	3 ounces on account, balance by July	sale of grapes to Lya Sadia, a Jew
12.8.1451 c. 570r	Leone Ammara alias Pancza, a Jew	10 ounces	6.15.0 ounces on account, balance by August	sale of heavy rope for tunny plant
26.8.1451 c. 588r	Merdoc de Minichi, a Jew	1 ounce	monthly instalments of 1.10 *tarì*	earlier unpaid sale; guarantor: Minto de Minichi, a Jew

Source: ASP, Not. Giovanni Traverso, reg. 788

Date and Page	Principal	Attorney	Purpose	Remarks
20.3. 1452 c. 494r	Xibiten Malti, a Jew of Polizzi	Sadono de Medico, a Jew	to manage his affairs and to rent a shop in Polizzi belonging to the church Della Magione of Palermo	

Date and Page	Debtor	Amount	Reason	Remarks
19.4.1452 c. 452r	Simon de Mayu and his son Mayu, Jews	22.12 *tarì*	balance of rent for a shop	creditor: Bernardo Stagno
1.10.1454 c. 84r	Iuda de Minichi, a Jew	12 *tarì*	balance of debt for guarantee	creditor: Andrea Sinibaldo
30.10.1454 c. 135v	Sabatino Pernichi, a Jew of Catania	undetermined amount	previous debt	creditor: Sabatino Greco, a Jew; debt paid by sale of horse valued at 2 ounces and a cash payment of 1.24.0 ounces

Date and Page	Lender or Seller	Amount	Payment	Remarks
13.10.1451 c. 89r-v	Pietro de Nicotera	1.18.0 ounces the quintal	2.4.0 ounces on account; balance by Christmas; paid 19.1.1452	sale of grapes to Busacca Levi, a Jew
29.10.151 c. 133r	Bartholomeo de Bononia	84 ounces	25 ounces on account; balance by September	sale of grapes to Robino Gibira, a Jew
2.11.1451 c. 143r	Giovanni de Noto	1.17.0 ounces	paid	sale of a beast of burden to Busacca de Minichi, a Jew
30.12.1451 c. 253v	Luca de Ligorii	1.6.0 ounces	by April	sale of tunny barrels to Braxhono Sacerdotu, a Jew; guarantor: Salamon Sabuchi, a Jew
10.2.1452 c. 321v	Salvatore Maltisi	3 ounces	within 4 months	sale of wheat to Vita de Medico, a Jew
17.2.1452 c. 340r	Masio de Pace	3.6.0 ounces	1.3.0 ounces on account	sale of 3 beasts of burden to Iuda de Minichi, a Jew
7.4.1452 c. 437v	Xilomo Levi, a Jew of Cammarata in Palermo	1.15.0 ounces	21 *tarì* on account; balance on delivery	sale of manure; guarantor: Galluffu Levi, a Jew
17.11.1452 c. 145v	Xanono Copiu, a Jew	4.18.0 ounces	within a year	sale of a horse
18.12.1452 c. 186r	Matheo Dannisi	3.28.0 ounces	1 ounce on account, balance by middle of April; paid 2.5.1453	sale of grapes to Braxhono Panichello, a Jew
[..].1.1453 c. nn	Giovanni Ismiligli	34 ounces	10 ounces on account, 10 ounces by Easter, balance on delivery; paid 23.5.1454	sale of cow cheese to Vita Xunina, a Jew

5.1.1453 c. nn	Merdoc de Minichi, a Jew	1.12.0 ounces	3 *tarì* on account, balance by 7.1	sale of a beast of burden
12.1.1453 c. nn	Masio de Dato	9.15 *tarì* the kantar of cow cheese, 7.16 *tarì* the kantar of *caciocavallo*	6 ounces on account, balance on delivery	sale of 60 kantars of cow cheese and *caciocavallo* to Vita Xunina, a Jew
16.1.1453 c. nn	Ioanna de Brogna	1.18.0 ounces	within a year	sale of a mattress and two cases to Pasquali Sacerdotu, a Jew
14.3.1453 c. 285v	Federico de Iambruno	24 *tarì*	paid	sale of grapes to Lya Sadya and Iacob de Termini, Jews
2.4.1453 c, 370r	Matheo Dannisi	1.24.0 ounces		sale of grapes to Braxhono Panichellu, a Jew
2.4.1453 c. 380v	Leone Ammara, a Palermitan Jew	24 *tarì*	paid	sale of grapes
2.5.1453 c. 395v	Busacca de Minichi, a Jew	2.6.0 ounces	1.6.0 ounces on account, balance by June	sale of a mule
10.4.1453 c. 434r	Musutu Binna, a Jew	1.2.0 ounces	by 20.4; paid 9.5. 1455	sale of beast of burden
9.8.1453 c. 511r	Sabeti Russu, a Jew	11.15.0 ounces	3 instalments, at Christmas, May and August	sale of grapes
20.9.1454 c. 54v	Pino de Ferro	1/18.0 ounces	on demand in ironware and tools	sale of wheat to Braxhono Panichello, a Jew

Source: ASP, Not. Giovanni Traverso, reg. 789

Date and Place	Debtor	Amount	Reason	Remarks
8.1.1454 c. c. nn	Muxa Minczul, a Jew	21 *tarì*	payment due	creditor: Thomeo de Ochisu

Date and Page	Lender or Seller	Amount	Payment	Remarks
5.11.1454 c. 155r	Iusep de Minichi and Nissim Aczara, Jews	13.10 *tarì*	for guarantee	creditor: Antonio de Macza; to be paid with labour
11.9.1453 c. 32r	Braxhono Panichellu, a Jew	2 (or 9) florins the kantar	paid	sale of grapes to Vita Xifuni, a Jew
13.9.1453 c. 42r	Xammuni Calabresi and his son Salamon, Jews	24 *tarì*	paid	sale of a horse
21.9.1453 c. 169v	Giovanni Ysmiriglu	22.10.0 ounces	10 ounces on account; paid 19.7.1454	sale of *caciocavallo* to Vita Xunina, a Jew
3.12.1453 c. 189r-v	Antonio Manueli	27 *tarì*	by June; paid 11.3.1455	sale of wheat to Symon Rabbi and his son Mayu, Jews
2.1.1454 c. 220r	Signurellu Chincumanu	18 *tarì* the kantar	3.14.0 ounces on account, balance on delivery	sale of cheese to Sabeti Cuyno, a Jew
11.1.1454 c. nn	Merdoc Achina, a Jew		1.9.0 ounces on account, another 24 ounces within 8 days; balance on delivery	sale of iron ornaments for carriages
21.1.1454 c. nn	Petro de Ysira	1.6.0 ounces	12 *tarì* on 15.6, 2.4 *tarì* by 15.8; paid 10.12.1454	sale of myrtle to Symon Rabi, Iacob alias Mayu, and his son Mayu, Jews
9.5.1454 c. nn	Chicco de Li Monti			sale of salt to Iacob Sufi, a Jew
3.9.1454 c. nn	Lambertu Vaccaru	1.18.0 ounces	by October	sale of a horse to Brachono de Missina, a Jew
7.9.1454 c. 29r	Braxhono Panichellu, a Jew	3.18.0 ounces	by Easter; paid	sale of oxen

9.9.1454 c. 32r	Merdoc Sidica, a Jew	24 *tarì*	4 *tarì* on account; paid 17.7.1455	sale of rope for tunny plant
11.9.1454 c. 34r	Iuda Minichi, a Jew	6.0.10 ounces	paid	sale of tunny and inferior parts of tunny (*busunaglia*)
27.9.1454 c. 66r	Silvestro Barbari	26 *tarì*	on demand	loan to Mussutu Minczili, a Jew of Termini
21.10.1454 c. 108v	Nicolò de Noto	2 ounces	paid	sale of wool to Sabeti Russu, a Jew
12.11.1454 c. 161r	Nicolò de Englisi	1.2.0 ounces	paid	sale of grapes to Lya Sadya and Iacob de Termini, Jews
12.11.1454 c. 161r	Pino Calcaterra	1.16..16 ounces	21 *tarì* on account, 9 on Christmas, balance on delivery	sale of rams to Salamon Czigari, a Jew
19.1.1455 c. 265r	Iosep Gaskis, a Jew	1.18.0 ounces	12 *tarì* on account, 12 at Lent, 24 on Easter; paid 1.7.1455	sale of cloth; guarantor: Galluffu Consigler, a Jew
21.1.1455 c. 269r	Enrico de Politi	2.6.0 ounces	1.6.0 ounces on account, balance on Easter; paid 17.4.1456	sale of wheat to Lya Sadya and Iacob de Termini, Jews
23.1.1455 c. 272v	Farrugiu Bellu, a Jew of Castrogiovanni	4 ounces	paid	sale of a bedspread in 5 sections
23.1.1455 c. 273r	Girmia Xammara, a Jew	1.9.0 ounces	paid	sale of a beast of burden
3.2.1455 c. 286v	Giovanni Romeo	24 *tarì*	9 *tarì* on account	sale of grapes to Lya Sadya and Merdoc Sitani, Jews
7.2.1455 c. 294r	Symon Rabbi Iacob alias Mayu, a Jew	8 *tarì*	by April	sale of a pair of shoes

11.2.1455 c. 300r	Muxa Xireribi and his mother Ricca, Jews	22 *tarì*	1 *tarì* on account	sale of a beast of burden
17.2.1455 c. 305r	Symon Rabbi Iacob alias Mayu, a Jew	11 *tarì*	by May	sale of a pair of shoes
6.3.1455 c. 328v	Filippo Lu Mussu	1.6.0 ounces	5 *tarì* a month	sale of soles to Simon Rabbi Iacob, a Jew
17.4.1455 c. 387v	Giovanni Vitali	1 ounce	at harvest time	sale of an implements (*orgagni*) to Merdoc Farachi and Nissim Gannuchu, Jews
17.4.1455 c. 388v	Giovanni de Lu Presti	1.6.0 ounces	paid	sale of a horse to Sabatino de Minichi, a Jew
24.4.1455 c. 405r	Muxa Ysac, a Jew	1.9.0 ounces	paid	sale of oil to Farrugio Siveni, a Jew; guarantor: Sabatino de Minichi, a Jew
30.4.1455 c. 410r	Braxhono Simael alias Gentilomo, a Jew	1 ounce	paid	sale of oil to Ferrugio Siveni, a Jew
9.5.1455 c. 415r	Matheo de Monteleone	1 ounce	24 *tarì* on account; paid 24.10 1455	sale of grapes to Salamon Czitari, a Jew
3.6.1455 c. 452v	Isdrael Rugila, a Jew	1.6.5. ounces	paid	sale of leather to Yuda de la Pantelleria, a Jew; guarantor: Mayu de Rabbi Iacob, a Jew
3.6.1455 c. 453v	Iuda de La Pantelleria, a Jew of Marsala	1.6.5. ounces	paid	sale of ox leather to Lya Sidica and Iacob de Termini, Jews
6.6.1455 c. 454r	Antonio Zaffarana	1.15.0 ounces	paid	sale of grapes to Manueli de Aram, a Jew

10.6.1455 c. 462v	Antonio de Lentini	1 ounce	18 *tarì* on account	sale of myrtle to Salamon Czirari, a Jew
19.6.1455 c. 477r	Giovanni Bulcza	1.6.0 ounces	10 *tarì* on account; balance in instalments	sale of myrtle to Lya Sidita and Iacob de Termini, Jews
19.6.1455 c. 477r	Consulu and Nicolò de La Panittera	1 ounce	paid	sale of oil to Ferrugio Siveni, a Jew
23.6. 1455 c. 483v	Maria Ventimiglia	4 ounces	within 6 months	sale of iron to David Xhaguela, a Jew; guarantor: Iuda Sacerdoto, a Jew
30.6.1455 c. 488v	Gilberto de Brucato	26 *tarì*	12 *tarì* on account, balance later	sale of myrtle to Lya Sidita and Iacob de Termini, Jews
23.7.1455 c. 520v	Bartholomeo Mirabella	24 *tarì*	15 *tarì* on account	sale of grapes to Abram de Minichi, a Jew

Source: ASP, Not. Giovanni Traverso, reg. 790

Date and Page	Debtor	Amount	Reason	Remarks
24.12.1455 c. nn	Iuda de La Pantelleria, a Jew of Marsala	5.6.0 ounces	sum entrusted to him by other debtors	creditor: Giovanni Suriano

Date and Page	Lender or Seller	Amount	Payment	Remarks
18.9.1455 c. nn	Giovanni de Lista		3 instalments	sale of the tax on meat, eggs and sausages to Busacca Naxhani, a Jew
24.9.1455 c. nn	Bernardo Penos			sale of cheese to Donato Bonaventura, a Jew

[..].10.1455	Iacobo de	4 ounces		sale of a white
c. nn	Napuli			bedspread to Sisa,
				wife of Pasqualis
			Sacerdoto, a Jewess; guarantor: the husband	
21.10.1455	Parisio	market price	13 *tarì* on account	sale of grapes to
c. 110v	Homodei			mastro Salamoni
				Czicari, a Jewish
				shoemaker
5.12.1455	Matheo			sale of grapes to
c. nn	Dannisi			Braxhono Panicello,
				a Jew
16.12.1455	Luca Fanchigla	1.12.0 ounces	paid 9.8.1457	sale of white curtain
c. nn				to Muxa Mira, a Jew;
				guarantor: Xibiteni
				Aczara, a Jew
23.12.1455	Matheo	24 *tarì*	paid	sale of grapes to Lya
c. nn	Dannisi			Sadya, a Jew
19.1.1456	Girardo de	6.15.0 ounces	by 10.12.1456	sale of curd to Sabet
c. 278r	Sutera			de Termini and
				Sabet Malti, Jews;
				guarantor: Gallufu
				Berni, a Jew
27.1.1455	Giovanni	3.6.0 ounces	16 *tarì* on account,	sale of casks to Muxa
c. nn	Xharcha		balance in	Xilomu, a Jew
			instalments until	
			May	
19.3.1455	Friderico	5.12.0 ounces	paid	sale of a slave to
c. 36r	Lignami			Siminto Kimitti, a Jew
7.4.1455	Girardo de	8.10 *tarì* the	2 ounces on	sale of cheese to
c. 382r	Sutera	kantar	account, 8 *tarì*	Fadaluni Sacerdotu,
			by middle of	a Jew
			May, 10 at end of	
			July, balance on	
			delivery	
14.4.1455	Andreas de lu	19 *tarì*	paid	sale of grapes to
c. 389v	Muntu			Braxhono Panichello,
				a Jew
14.4.1455	Antonio	1 ounce	2 *tarì* a week; paid	sale of linen to Lya
c. 391v	Ragusia			Sadia, a Jew

28.4.1455	Nicolò de	8.10 *tarì* a kantar	5 ounces on	sale of cheese to
c. nn	Oddo	of cheese, 9.10	account, another	Fadalono Sacerdotu
		the *pecorino*	5 by end of	and Merdoc de
			August, balance	Minichi, Jews
			on delivery	

Bibliography: Bresc, *Arabi*, p. 71

| 12.5.1455 | Farrugio | 2.12.0 ounces | within 6 months | sale of oil to Xilomu |
| c. 345r | Siveni, a Jew | | | Sacerdotu, a Jew |

Source: ASP, Not. Giovanni Traverso, reg. 791

Date and Page	Debtor	Amount	Reason	Remarks
22.10.1456 c. nn	Enrico and Angelo Maltisi	4 ounces	result of a previous contract	creditor: Merdoc de Minichi, a Jew; debt settled with a mule and 24 *tarì*
21.3.1456 c. nn	David Lu Presti, a Jew	6.18.0 ounces	loan	creditor: Giovanni La Matina
23.3.1456 c. 400r	Giuliano de Raimondo	sum not mentioned	loan	creditor: Muxa Sacerdotu, a Jew

Date and Page	Lender or Seller	Amount	Payment	Remarks
7.9.1456 c. nn	Merdoc Catalano, a Palermitan Jew	19.18.0 ounces	1 ounce a month	loan to Salamon Catalano, a Jew
10.9.1456 c. nn	Filippo de Nisi	8.15.0 ounces	1.15.0 ounces by November, balance on delivery	sale of cheese to Merdoc de Minichi and Manueli Siveni, Jews
11.10.1456 c. nn	Gabriel de Medico, a Jew	1 ounce a thousand heavy ropes , 20 *tarì* a thousand light ropes	1 ounce on account; balance in instalments	sale of 5,000 ropes
27.10.1456 145r	Giovanni de Crispo	2.3.0 ounces	by Christmas	sale of hay to Merdoc de Minichi, a Jew

29.10.1456 c. 147v	David Naxhay, a Jew	3.18.0 ounces	2.12.0 ounces on account	sale of a white curtain
7.3.1457 c. 314r	Nicolò Baczu	1 ounce	by April	sale of candles to Xhayrono Malti, a Jew
17.3.1457 c. 329r	Virgognusa de Leo	24 *tarì*	paid	sale of grapes to Lya Sadia and Iacob Termini, Jews
22.3.1457 c. 334r	Giovanni de Sarzana	14.6.0 ounces	7.6.0 ounces within 4 months, balance in 2 months	sale of cloth to Grasinu de Narra Dinaru, a Jew
22.3.1457 c. 334v	Xua de Missina, a Jew	1.6.0 ounces	paid with funds provided by Sadono Ubi, a smith, and Deulusa, Jews	sale of a book entitled *chitubeti* = כתובים or כתובות bound in red leather to Muxa de Pulizzi, a Jew
16.4.1457 c. 377r	Iosep de Palermo, a Jew of Syracuse	1 ounce	12 *tarì* a month	sale of a beast of burden
5.5.1457 c. 399r	Raymundu de Bages	current price	12 *tarì* on account, balance on delivery	sale of wheat to Lya Sadica, a Jew
13.5.1457 c. 412r	Giovanni de Polizi	24 *tarì*	within 4 months	sale of a coat to Xua de Messina, a Jew; guarantor: Muxa Marxili, a Jew
29.5.1457 c. 489r	Farchono Sala, a Jew	3.12.0 ounces	1 ounce on account paid by Xamueli Caro, a Jew	sale of a mule to Ioseph Xhammusu, a Jew
1.6.1457 c. 453v	Raffaeli Provinzanu, a Jew		15 *tarì* on account	sale of wheat
15.6.1457 c. 471v	David Farachi and Iuda de Minichi for Iacob de Seracusia, Jews	56.20.0 ounces	5 ounces by 15.10, balance on delivery	sale of rope

30.6.1457 c. nn	Giovanni Spagnolo	7 *tarì*	1.5 *tarì* a week	sale of goods to Sansuni de Gauyu, a Jew
2.7.1457 c. 483r	Pietro Maurichio	1.23.8 ounces	within 4 months; paid 28.6.1458	sale of iron to Gallufo Levi, a Jew
23.8.1457 c. 561v	Busacca de Bono, a Jew of Trapani	1.23.5 ounces	by September; paid 27.10.1457	sale of cloth
5.9.1457 c. 9v	David Ramecta, a Jew	1.8.5 ounces	paid	sale of a horse to Braxhono de Missina, a Jew
7.10.1457 c. 85v	Micael de Napoli	2 ounces	1 ounce by October, another by December	sale of a horse to Merdoc de Minichi, Salamon de Rigio and Musuto Minaxhani, Jews
13.10.1457 c. nn	Enrico de Bages	1.24.0 ounces	17 *tarì* on account	sale of grapes to Salamon Czitari, a Jew
19.10.1457 c. 121v	Salimbeni de Ytalia	2 ounces	by Easter; paid 17.4.1458	sale of grapes to Iacob de Termini, a Jew
26.10.1457 c. 143v	Iacobo de Lamia	1.24.0 ounces	2 pairs of boots and 1 ounce on account; balance, a promise to sole boots	sale of grapes to Salamon Czitari, a Jew
[..].10.1457 c. 144v	Micael Riczu	27 *tarì*	paid	sale of grapes to Salamon Czitari, a Jew
29.11.1457 c. 221r	Giovanni Romeo	1.24.0 ounces	18 *tarì* on account, balance on 11.1.1458; paid 29.11.1459	sale of grapes to Lya Sadica for Merdoc Sadica, Jews
8.3.1458 c. 347r	Antonio de Chambris	12 *tarì*	by April	sale of wheat to Michael Burati, a Jew
8.3.1458 c. 347v	Antonio de Chambris	18 *tarì*	half in April and half in June	sale of wheat to Fadalono Xhabirra and Sabeti Raffaeli, Jews

13.3.1458 c. nn	Pietro Maurichio	1.25.0 ounces	by June	sale of wheat to Muxa Sofer, a Jew
12.4.1458 c. 410r	Nicolò Boy	1.9.0 ounces	17 *tarì* on account	sale of myrtle to Lya Sadica, acting for Merdoc Sadica, Jews
26.4.1458 448r	Paolo Basilio	1.10.0 ounces	half by May and half by June; paid 2.6.1458	sale of honey to Lya de Benedicto, a Jew

Source: ASP, Not. Giovanni Traverso, reg. 792

Date and Page	Lender or Seller	Amount	Payment	Remarks
29.10. 1457 c. 146r	Sadya Ysac, a Palermitan Jew	29 *tarì*	15.10 *tarì* on account	sale of a beast of burden; guarantor: Salamon de Liucio, a Jew
2.11.1457 c. 160v	Enrico de Balczamo	2.5.0 ounces	1.24.0 ounces on account	sale of ground salt to Leone Ammara, a Jew
3.11.1457 c. 164v	Aloisio de Gambara	6.15.0 ounces	1 ounce on account, balance by August	sale of a black slave girl to Vita de Medico, a Jew
2.1.1458 c. 284r	Sabeti Russu, a Jew	2.6.0 ounces a quintal	paid 19.2.1460	sale of grapes to Xhairono Xunina, a Jew
11.1.1458 c. 284r	Giovanni de Brancato	27 *tarì*		sale of grapes to Muxa de Politi, a Jew

Date and Page	Tenant	Location and Description	Rent and Duration	Remarks
2.1.1458 c. 270v	Xhairono Xunina, a Jew	Cassaro, bordering on houses of the notary and Aloisio de Terranova and and Benedetto de Canno; tavern	1 year, 2 ounces in 3 instalments, afterwards 3.15.0 ounces	landlord: Sabeti Russu, a Jew; landlord is entitled to the use of an exit leading to the *vanella* mastro Moyse Chetibi; the premises are equipped for winemaking

Source: ASP, Not Giovanni Traverso, reg. 793

Date and Page	Debtor	Amount	Reason	Remarks
19.9.1459 c. nn	Muxa de Girachi, a Jew of Licata	2.25.0 ounces	contractual obligations arising out of administration of wife's property	creditor: Antonio Mino; payment in instalments
15.7.1460 c. 391v	Braxha Catalano, a Jew	2.6.0 ounces	purchase of mule resold to Giovanni Bordonaro of Sortino	creditor: Pino de Caro; the *Corte Pretoriana* of Palermo assigns the amount to Pino, making the second purchaser pay
22.1.1461 c. 170v	Fadaluni Xhagegi, a Jew	2.10.0 ounces	result of previous contract	creditor: Giovanni Spagnolo
20.3.1461 c. 240r	Xibiten de Benedicto, a Jew	2.27.0 ounces	result of previous contract and collection expenses	creditor: Pietro Luca of Viterbo; payment in instalments; guarantors: Lia de Benedicto and Merdoc Riczu, a Jews
3.6.1461 c. 341r	Abramono Sidita, a Jew	24.10 *tarì*		creditor: Michael Bonafini, a Jew; to be paid within a month by Lya, Abramono's brother

Data and Page	Lender or Seller	Amount	Payment	Remarks
4.5.1459 c. 263v	Pietro Maurichio	2.12.0 ounces	within 6 months	sale of oil to Iosep de Boemia, a Jew
22.5.1459 c. 287v	Nicolò Boy	15 *tarì*	9 *tarì* on account; balance in instalments	sale of myrtle to Iacob de Termini, a Jew
22.5.1459 c. 288r	Nicolò de Contissa	1 ounce	half in June and half in August	sale of a horse to Merdoc Binna, a Jew

22.5.1459 c. 288v	Iacobo de Bonanno	5.12.0 ounces	2.12.0 ounces on account; paid 22.11.1460	sale of a horse with harness to Nissim de Leone, a Jew of Sciacca
25.5.1459 c. 295r	Sadia de Acri, a Jew	current price	3 ounces on account; paid 2.10.1459	sale of 15 *salme* of wheat to Iacob de Napoli, a Jew
30.3.1459 c. 469v	Xibiten Xabirra, a Jew of Marsala	6 ounces	3 ounces on account; paid 3.6.1459	sale of tallow to Siminto Kimit, a Jew of Cammarata
31.3.1459 c. 471r	Giovanni de Ferro	1 ounce	5 *tarì* a week	sale of iron to Muxa Xobbu, a Jew
15.10.1459 c. nn	Contissa de Porto	2 ounces in *disa* rope for tunny	4 rolls of heavy rope and 2 of light rope a week	sale of mattresses to Manuela Suyeli, a Jewess
17.10.1459 c. nn	Lemmu Mondello	35 [45] ounces	3 ounces on account, balance in instalments; paid 24.11.1460	sale of sheep cheese to Xibiteni Gibel and Vita Xunina, Jews
17.10.1459 c. nn	Gerardo de Sutera	6.10 *tarì* a kantar	2.ounces on account, balance in instalments	sale of *ricotta* to Nissim de Tripuli, a Jew
22.10.1459 c. nn	Antonio de Rossino	1 ounce	paid 17.3.1460	sale of grapes to Braxhono Czitari, a Jew
8.11.1459 c. 120r	Pietro Maurichio	1.20.0 ounces	by May	sale of 5 salme of wheat to Xamuel Rugila, a Jew
8.11.1459 c. 121v	Pietro Maurichio	1.12.12 ounces	by April	sale of Pisan iron vessels (*burnarii*) to Gallufo Levi, a Jew
12.11.1459 c. 128v	Giovanni di S. Giovanni	25 *tarì*	within 4 months	loan to Busacca de Benedicto, a Jew
20.11.1459 c. nn	Iacobo de La Biola	24 *tarì*	12 *tarì* on account; paid 11.12.1459	sale of grapes to Braxhono Czitari, a Jew
22.11.1459 c. 155v	Pietro Maurichio	4.16.16 ounces	by May; paid 20.1.1461	sale of Pisan vessels to Merdoc Vignuni, a Jew

5.12.1459 c. 162r	Pietro Maurichio	1 ounce	by May	sale of vessels to Galluffu Levi, a Jew
6.12.1459 c. 166r	Giovanni Petra	2 ounces	within 4 months	sale of one cask of wine to Vita de Medico, a Jew
11.12.1459 c. 172v	Simon de Comitunangelo	1.18.0 ounces	paid	sale of grapes to Lya Sidita, a Jew
23.1.1460 c. 213v	Contissa de Porto	3.3.0 ounces	paid	sale of 2 woollen mattresses to Braxha Cuyno and Iacob Sabatino, Jews
29.1.1460 c. 223r	Salvatore de Graffeo	current price	18 *tarì* on account	sale of barley to Iacobo de Missina, a Jew
30.1.1460 c. 225v	Antonio de Chambris	1.25.0 ounces	half by April, balance by May	sale of wheat to Nissim Medui, a Jew
1.2.1460 c. 228v	Antonio de Chambris	2.6.0 ounces	by May; paid 12.6.1460	sale of wheat to Vita de Aram and Xamueli Actuni, Jews
7.2.1460 c. 232r	Marco de Rosa	1.15.0 ounces	paid	sale of barley to Iacob de Missina, a Jew
8.2.1460 c. 233v	Antonio Bernini			sale of grapes to Salamon Zicari, a Jew
10.2.1460 c. 238r	Andrea de Mannina	8.10.0 ounces	within 4 months	sale of wheat to Muxa Ysac and Braxha Brixha, Jews
18.2.1460 c. 240v	Maczullu de Alfano	1.18.0 ounces	19 *tarì* on account; paid 17.3.1460	sale of grapes to Iacob de Termini, a Jew
21.2.1460 c. 246v	Luca de Ligotti	12 *tarì* and 1 kantar of oil	within 4 months	loan to Manuel Xunina; guarantor: Iuda Xunina, a Jew
3.3.1460 c. 256v	Federico Birczilio	1 ounce	paid 24.4.1460	loan to Iosep de Gauio, a Jew; guarantor: Iacob de Gauio, a Jew
17.3.1460 c. 270r	Filippo Patrintino	20 *tarì*		sale of must to Iacob de Missina, a Jew

19.3.1460 c. 276v	Giovanni de Naso	24 *tarì*	paid	sale of grapes to Braxhono Czitari, a Jew
26.3.1460 c. 280r	Blasio Bonfiglio	2 ounces	within 6 months	sale of oil to Sabet de Termini, a Jew; guarantor: Gabriel de Medico, a Jew
16.4.1460 c. 295r	Giovanni de Palacio	1.22.0 ounces	24 *tarì* on account, balance by August	sale of a horse to Busacca Cipriano, a Jew
16.4.1460 c. 299v	Giovanni de Augustino	1.16.0 ounces	6 *tarì* on account, balance in instalments	sale of merchandise to Sabeti Raffaele and Fadaluni Xabirra, Jews
20.5. 1460 c. 327v	Blasio Bonfiglio	4 ounces	by December; paid 25.6.1462	sale of oil to Merdoc and Busacca de Minichi, Jews
20.5. 1460 c. 328r	Simingto Bulfarachi, a Jew of Sciacca	6.11.0 ounces	in instalments over 3 years	loan to Pinesi de Aron, a Jew; guarantors: Vita Vitrano and Abram de Aron, Jews
16.7.1460 c. 392r	Nicolò Pantigla	15 ounces	within 10 months; paid 14.8.1460	sale of silk clothes to Iosep Braxhuni, a Jew
16.7.1460 c. 398r	Girardo de Sutera	4.24.0 ounces	1 ounce on account; paid 20.10.1461	sale of cheese to Muxa Xunina, a Jew
18.7.1460 c. 398v	Andrea de Salemi	12 *tarì*	within 1 year	sale of 6 casks of wine to Iosep Braxhuni, a Jew
5.8.1460 c. 415r	Busacca Pinichello, a Jew	10 *grana* a *rotolo*	1 ounce on account, balance on delivery	sale of iron for carriages
5.8.1460 c. 415v	Minto Vignuni, a Jew	6 ounces		sale of barley
5.8.1460 c. 416r	Xamuel Russo, a Jew, for Luca de Lombardo	3.22.10 ounces	on Christmas; paid 9.6.1462	sale of lime

Date / c.	Name	Amount	Terms	Description
25.8.1460 c. 449v	Giovanni Spagnolu	2.9.0 ounces	2 *tarì* on account, balance in instalments	sale of a mule to Braxha Catalano, a Jew
5.9.1460 c. 12v	Girardo de Sutera	6 *tarì* a kantar	2 ounces on account	sale of *ricotta* to Nissim de Tripuli and Nissim Sansuni, Jews

Bibliography: Bresc, *Arabi*, p. 71

Date / c.	Name	Amount	Terms	Description
[..].10.1460 c. 73r	Minto Kimitto, a Jew	18 *tarì* a kantar		sale of tallow
24.10.1460 c. 77v	Giovanni de Catania	1.18.0 ounces	paid 17.11.1460	sale of grapes to Lya Sidita, a Jew
30.10.1460 c. 83v	Salvatore Bracco	7.10 *tarì* a kantar		sale of cow cheese to Benedicto Caseni, a Jew
3.11.1460 c. 86r	Giovanni Milia	1 ounce	with labour	sale of grapes to Braxha Czitari, a Jew
6.11.1460 c. 89r	Giovanni Gangi	24 *tarì*	2 *tarì* on account; paid 4.12.1460	sale of grapes to Braxha Czitari, a Jew
8.11.1460 c. 94r	Florencia de Binchi	12 *tarì*	by Christmas	sale of clothes to Manuel Xunina, a Jew
24.11.1460 c. 110r	Aloisio de Sutera	1.24.0 ounces	1.6.0 ounces by January, balance with labour	sale of grapes to Brazha Czitari, a Jew
24.11.1460 c. 110v	Giovanni de Naso	24 *tarì*	12 *tarì* on account, balance in weekly instalments of 3 *tarì*	sale of grapes to Braxha Czitari, a Jew
23.12.1460 c. 145v	Ysdrael de Minichi, a Jew	1.18.0 ounces	15 *tarì* on account, balance in instalments	sale of a horse
23.12.1460 c. 146r	Ysdrael de Minichi, a Jew	1.3.0 ounces	half by January, other half a month later	sale of wheat
26.1.1461 c. 174r	Antonio Bontempo	2.6.0 ounces	6 *tarì* on account, balance in instalments	sale of a mule to Merdoc de Minichi, a Jew

26.1.1461 c. 175r	Giovanni Capello	10 ounces	by August; paid 8.10.1461	sale of 4 pounds of gold wire to Xhayrono Xunina, a Jew
5.3.1461 c. 220r	Girardo de Sutera	6 ounces	paid	sale of cow hides t Minto Vignuni, a Jew
17.3.1461 c. 235r	Braxha Czitari, a Jew	6 ounces	by 15.5	sale of leather to Merdoc Rabibi, a Jew of Cammarata
13.4.1461 c. 264v	Girardo Sutera	6 ounces	instalments until Easter	sale of curd to Sabet de Termini, a Jew
15.4.1461 c.272r	Pinesi de Aron, a Jew	1.9.0 ounces	paid	sale of a horse
21.4.1461 c. 269v	Antonio de Girgenti	1 quintal and 5 *pise* (=5 *rotoli* each) of grapes		sale of a mule to Sadya Aczaruti, a Jew
24.4.1461 c. 288v	Andrea Le Nati	1.24.0 ounces	by October	sale of a cask of wine to Muxa Miseria, a Jew; guarantor: Donato Bonaventura, a Jew
4.5.1461 c. 300r	Siminito Kinniti, a Jew	18 *tarì*	within 15 days	sale of goods
3.7.1461 c. 365v	Iosep de Minichi, a Jew	6 ounces	1 ounce on Christmas; balance within 3 years; paid 8.1.1464	sale of some mules
9.7.1461 c. 378v	Sabeti Abbati, a Jew	7.19.0 ounces	2 ounces on delivery, balance by August; paid 26.5.1462	sale of castrated sheep (*castrati*) to Merdoc Bulfarachi and Muxa Ysac, Jews
19.8.1461 c. 410r	Pietro Maurichio	2.9.0 ounces	by 15.12	sale of merchandise to Merdoc Vignuni, a Jew
19.8.1461 c. 410v	Pietro Maurichio	23 *tarì*	by 15.12	sale of steel balls (*balloni di aczaru*) to Stranu di Ciminna, a Jew

Date and Page	Tenant	Location and Description	Rent and Duration	Remarks
23.6.1460 c. 370r	Nissim Medui, a Jew	Cassaro, *contrada* hospicii Domini Masi de Crispo, bordering on the *xherba* of Francesco Ventimiglia and on the tenant's houses; *solerata* house	2 years for 1.15.0 ounces annually in 3 instalments	landlord: Rosa de Trani
14.7.1460 c. 391v	Vita Xunina, a Jew	Palermo, *contrada* Biffarda, bordering on houses of Iacob Trusconi and Braxhono Sacerdoto, a Jew; *solerata* house		landlord: Vita Siveni, a Jew; contract may be extended for another 3 years; tenant may make repairs
29.5.1461 c. 323v	Merdoch Xariribi and Fazella Aczaruti, Jews	Cassaro, bordering on house of Francesco Ventimiglia; *solerata* house	3 years for 1.12.0 ounces annually	landlord: Rosa de Trani
29.5.1461 c. 329v	Salamon Czicari, a Jew	Palermo, *contrada* Foriveteri, bordering on shop of master Bernardo; shop	9 years for 2 ounces annually	landlord: Bernardo Stagno; shop must be sublet; may use water from landlord's well

Source: ASP, Not. Giovanni Traverso, reg. 794

Date and Pge	Principal	Attorney	Purpose	Remarks
17.4.1464 c. c. 225r	Ximon Sunina, a Jew	Ximilonu Naxhay, a Jew	to collect various debts, acting also at the *pretura* of Palermo and other courts	

Date and Page	Lender or Seller	Amount	Payment	Remarks
2.9.1461 c. 6r	Giovanni Scurradadi and Andrea Lu Piczu	3.18.0 ounces	24 *tarì* on account, balance on delivery	sale of goods to Braxuni Simaeli and Merdoc Azaroni, Jews
4.9.1461 c. 11v	Blasio Infantino	current price	1.10 *tarì* on account, 9 *tarì* by 11.11; paid 10.5.1462	sale of grapes to Braxha Zicari, a Jew
10.9.1461 c. 21r	Garita de Pesto	8 *tarì*	paid	sale of a bedspead to Iacob de Termini, a Jew
11.9.1461 c. 23r	Pino de Bentivegna	1.8.10 ounces	within 6 months	sale of goods to Xamuel Rugila, a Jew
11.9.1461 c. 25r	Sabeti Russo, a Jew	10 ounces	instalments over 2 years	sale of grapes
15.9.1461 c. 27r	Braxhono de Missina, a Jew	2.12.0 ounces	15 *tarì* on account,balance at of month	sale of mule to Braxha Catalanu, a Jew
12.10.1461 c. 61v	Braxhono de Missina, a Jew	2.6.0 ounces	6 *tarì* on account, balance in instalments	sale of a horse
12.10.1461 c. 63v	Salimbeni Bulcze	18 *tarì*	paid	sale of olive oil to Sadono Lu Liali, a Jew; guarantor: Braxhono de Missina and Minto Romano, Jews
22.10.1461 c. 80r	Thomeo de Rosta	2.12.0 ounces	paid	sale of goods to Muxa Conti, a Jew

30.10.1461 c. 92v	Iorlando Scarparu	21 *tarì*	9 *tarì* on Christmas, balance with labour	sale of grapes to Braxha Czicari, a Jew
9.11.1461 c. 108v	Giovanni de Milia	27 *tarì*	paid	sale of grapes to Braxha Czicari, a Jew
16.11.1461 c. 119v	Salamon de Seracusia, a Jew	1.15.0 ounces	15.10 *tarì* on account, balance within 3 months	sale of a horse
26.11.1461 c. 122v	Filippo de Geremia	1.9.0 ounces	paid	sale of grapes to Braxha Czicari, a Jew
24.12.1461 c. 143v	Aloisio de Sutera	26 *tarì*	17.10 *tarì* on account, balance with labour	sale of goods to Lia Sidita, a Jewish shoemaker
29.12.1461 c. 147v	Iacob Galifu, a Jew	1.24.0 ounces	12 *tarì* on account, balance in instalments until sugar processing time	sale of a horse
8.1.1462 c. 154r	Iacob de Tavurmina, a Jew	27.10 *tarì*	by June	sale of goods to Maxallufu Miseria, a Jew of Polizzi
18.1.1462 c. 164r	Nicolò de Mainerio	93.10.0 ounces	25 ounces on account, balance on delivery	sale of tunny to Iosep Termini, a Jew
18.1.1462 c. 166r	Francesco Iambruno	1.18.0 ounces	paid	sale of goods to Lia Sidita, a Jew
25.1.1462 c. 173r	Pietro Nigro	1 ounce	within 1 month	loan to Salamon Cuyno
22.2.1462 c. 204r	Antonio de Axin	11.20.0 ounces	5.25.0 ounces on account, balance on sale of merchandise	sale of goods to Leone Ammara and Xilomu Merczoc, Jews
11.3.1462 c. 220v	Minto Vignuni, a Jew	value of 6 *salme* of barley	paid	sale of goods
7.4.1462 c. 248v	Xibiteni Gibel, a Jew	30 ounces	on delivery	sale of *pecorino*

14.6.1462 c. 324r	Giovanni Mandica	13.10.0 ounces	4 ounces on account; balance in instalments	sale of Cammarata salt to Muxa de Politi, a Jew
21.6.1462 c. 328r	Iacobo de Bonanno	19.6.0 ounces	by February	sale of wine to to Abram Bambassu, a Jew; broker: Iosep de Braxuni, another Jew
21.6.1462 c. 329r	Antonio Manueli	13 ounces	6 ounces on account, balance on delivery	sale of goods to Muxa Xifuni
25.6.1462 c. 330r	Blasio de Bonfiglio	1.6.0 ounces	within 4 months	sale of oil to Busacca de Minichi, a Jew
25.6.1462 c. 330v	Xilomo de Anello, a Jew of Cammarata	3 ounces	paid	sale of a mule to Xhayrono Gaseni, a Jew
5.7.1462 c. 341r	Sabeti Raffaeli and Fadaluni Xhabirra. Jews	10½ *grana* the *rotolo*	1 ounce on account, balance on delivery	sale of iron for carriages
9.7.1462 c. 346v	Giovanni Favaro	13 *tarì*	paid	sale of barley to Muxa de Polici, a Jew; guarantor: Braxha Czitari, a Jew
24.7.1462 c. 362r	Gerardo de Sutera	2 ounces	paid	sale of goods to Minto Vignuni
11.8.1462 c. 380r	Antonio Manueli and Gerardo de Sutera	13 ounces	8 ounces on account, balance on delivery	sale of merchandise
19.8.1462 c. 391v	Bartolo de Cristina	10.10.0 ounces	4 ounces on account, balance later; paid	sale of *pecorino* to Minto Vignuni, a Jew
5.9.1463 c. 13v	Nicolò de Iacona	24 *tarì*	paid	sale of grapes to Benedetto Catalano, a Jew
14.9.1463 c. 27v	Gimiluni Naxai, a Jew	3 ounces	half a quintal of grapes annually	sale of goods to Iuda de Minichi, a Jew

14.9.1463 c. 27v	Francesco de Vitali	2.24.0 ounces	2 ounces on account, balance on delivery	sale of goods to Iuda de Minichi, a Jew
22.9.1463 c. 37r	Giovanni de Anzalono	current price	18 *tarì* on account	sale of wheat to Merdoc Catalano, a Jew
13.10.1463 c. 60r	Blasio Bonfiglio	2 ounces	within a month, also with oil	sale of a horse to Muxa Sufeni, a Jew
24.10.1463 c. 74v	Xibiteni Gibel, a Jew	12.2 *tarì* a kantar	on delivery	sale of cheese
24.10.1463 c. 75v	Abram de Missina, Sadia Sacerdotu and Minto Romanu, Jews	2.8.0 ounces	7 *tarì* on account, balance on delivery	sale of olive pips
22.11.1463 c. nn	Salamon de lu Castru, a Jew	2.12.0 ounces	paid	sale of a mule
2.1.1464 c. nn	Giovanni de Lapi	12.6.0 ounces	24.12 *tarì* on account	sale of grapes to Braxha Czitari and Busacca di Trapani, Jewish shoemakers
3.1.1464 c. nn	Giovanni Capello	4.15.0 ounces	within 4 months	sale of gold to Merdoc Catalani, a Jew
18.1.1464 c. nn	Azarello de Gauyo	1.6.0 ounces a *canna*	each purchaser pays 10 *grana* a week	sale of cloth to Lucio Sidita, Braxha Czitari and Xhairono de Busacca, Jews
27.2.1464 c. 185r	Giovanni de Gangi	18 *tarì*	6 *tarì* on account, balance with labour	sale of grapes to Braxha Czitari, a Jew
4.3.1464 c. 187v	Braxhono Pinichello, a Jewish smith	12 *grana* a rotolo	payment with wheat	sale of iron
5.3.1464 c. 191v	Braxhono de Missina, a Jew	3.18.0 ounces	3 ounces on account, balance in 15 days	sale of a mule

6.3.1464 c. 192r	Giovanni and Benedetto Galesi	1 ounce	paid	sale of *disa* for rope to Sadia Azara, a Jew
14.3.1464 c. 199r	Blasio Bonfiglio	1.6.0 ounces	within 4 months	sale of oil to Busacca de Minichi, a Jew
5.4.1464 c. 214v	Gerardo de Sutera	6 ounces	3.24.0 ounces on account, balance by the guarantor	sale of butter to Iosep de Xilomo, a Palermitan Jew; guarantor: Machalufo Berni, a Jew
13.4.1464 c. 222r	Lemmu Mundellu	30 ounces	10 ounces on account, balance on delivery; paid 26.7.1465	sale of goods to Xibiteni Gibel, a Jew
2.5.1464 c. 237v	Antonio Buxema, Chicco lu Presti, Rainero and Matheo Tirnidainu	current price		sale of 17 *salme* of salt to Salamon and Braxhono Czitari, Jews
17.5.1464 c. 254r	Gauyusa, wife of Braxhuno Ansaluni, a Jewess	1 ounce	paid	sale of rope for tunny
17.5.1464 c. 254r	Donatu Russu	1.12.0 ounces	7.10 *tarì* on account, balance to Gimilono Maxoni, a Jew	sale of grapes to Siminto Kimitti, a Jew
23.5.1464 c. 259v	Braxha Czitari, a Jew	1 *salma* of wheat		sale of a spade
14.6.1464 c. 285v	Lya Sidita, a Jew	2.2.10 ounces	paid	sale of salted tunny
Date and Page	**Tenant**	**Location and Description**	**Rent and Duration**	**Remarks**
4.11.1461 c. 103v	Guglielmo Cuxina	Palermo, Albergheria, bordering on	12 *tarì* annually	landlord: Galluffu Catalanu, a Jew

houses of Isac Vechi and Pietro Sigia; house

16.11.1461	Xibiteni di	Palermo,	3 years with
c. 118v	Gibel, a Jew	*contrada*	possibility of
		Burdelli,	extension for
		bordering on	2.24.0 ounces
		landlord's shop;	annually
		ground floor	
		warehouse	
12.4.1464	Iacobo de	Palermo,	5 years for 1.24.0
c. 221r	Termini, a Jew	*contrada*	ounces a year
		Foriveteri; shop	

Source: ASP, Not. Giovanni Traverso, reg. 795

Date and Page	Lender or Seller	Amount	Payment	Remarks
6.9.1462 c. 20r	Betus La Ricza	7 *tarì* a kantar	2 ounces on account. balance on delivery	sale of cheese to Xibiten Gibel, a Jew
4.11.1462 c. 40v	Enrico de Bages	27 *tarì*	with labour	sale of grapes to Iacob de Termini, a Jew
5.11.1462 c. 92v	Andrea Cuczu	1.18.0 ounces	24 *tarì* on account, balance by Christmas; paid 1.2.1463	sale of a mule to Braxhono de Missina, a Jew
15.11.1462 c. 104r	Giovanni de Naso	21 *tarì*	paid 14.3.1463	sale of grapes to Salamon Czitari, a Jew
15.11.1462 c. 104v	Giovanni de Blasi	1.12.0 ounces	paid	sale of a horse to Iuda Millac, a Jew
20.11.1462 c. 115v	Clemente de Catania	1.6.0 ounces	by December	loan to Abram de Minichi, a Jew
27.11.1462 c. 122v	Giuliano Paulillo	2.12.0 ounces	by Easter; paid 21.4.1463	sale of barrels of sardines to Nissim Sansuni and Minto Xhactani, Jews

1.12.1462 c. 124r	Antonio Cordaro	1.2.0 ounces	6 *tarì* on account, balance in instalments until 6.12; paid 16.8.1463	sale of ground salt to Salamon Czitari, a Jew
1.12.1462 c. 125r	Vita de Gebbi, a Jew	6.15.0 ounces	1.15.0 ounces on account, balance in instalments until May; paid 12.3.1464	sale of a silk bedspread
2.12.1462 c. 130r	Ubertino de Guchardino	10-13 *tarì* a head	10 ounces on account, balance half on delivery and half by Christmas	sale of calves and cows to Samueli Russo, a Jew; guarantor: Sabeti Russo, a Jew
11.12.1462 c. 148r	Antonio de Chirino	1.10.0 ounces	in a week	sale of a beast of burden to Manueli Xunina, a Jew
3.1.1463 c. 154v	Giovanni de Gangi	24 *tarì*	7 *tarì* on account; paid 30.6.1465	sale of grapes to Braxha Czitari, a Jew
14.2.1463 c. 161r	Maczullu de Alfano	21 *tarì*	7 *tarì* on account; paid 1.7.1463	sale of grapes to Busacca Levi, a Jew
17.2.1463 c. 164r	Micael Quaragisima	2 ounces	by May	loan to David Daynu, a Jew
17.2.1463 c. 164v	Giovanni de Laczi	18 *tarì*	12 *tarì* on account; paid 8.6.1463	sale of grapes to Braxha Czitari, a Jew
2.3.1463 c. 184v	Pino Tenicholo	27 *tarì*	8.10 *tarì* on account	sale of grapes to Braxha Czitari, a Jew
4.3.1463 c. 185v	Masio Trupia	21 *tarì*	9 *tarì* and a pair of shoes on account, balance with labour	sale of grapes to Salamone Czitari, a Jew
10.3.1463 c. 193v	Braxha Suse, a Jew	1 ounce		sale of a mule
30.3.1463 c. 217v	Cusumano Tetralonga	19 *tarì* the kantar		sale of tallow to Minto Kinitti, a Jew
13.5.1463 c. 272r	Muxa Minczil, a Jew	2.1.10 ounces	within 15 days	sale of a mule
18.5.1463 c. 278v	Nicolò Boy	price current at vintage time	1.6.0 ounces on account	sale of grapes to Lya Sidita, a Jew

6261

Date	Name	Amount	Terms	Description
23.5.1463 c.287r	Muxa Xunina, a Jew	10 ounces		sale of cow cheese
2.6.1463 c. 296r	Girardo de Sutera	7 ounces	1 ounce on account; paid	sale of cow and *caciocavallo* cheese to Benedetto Czichili, a Jew of Messina
14.6.1463 c. 308v	Francesco Xhilatu	2.17.0 ounces	monthly instalments of 7.10 *tarì*	sale of a mule to Geremia Xammara, a Jew
4.7.1463 c. 325v	Merdoc Fadali, a Jew	1.15.0 ounces	1.6. ounces on account, balance by August; paid 29.8.1463	sale of a mule
11.7.1463 c. 328v	Giovanni Cappa	7 *tarì* a kantar	10 ounces on account	sale of cow cheese to Gimiluni Naxhay, a Jew
12.7.1463 c. 333r	Aczaruni and Xamueli Bambalu, Jews	1.10.0 ounces	paid	sale of olive oil
20.7.1463 c. 344r	Bero La Ricza	9 *tarì* a kantar	2 ounces on account	sale of cheese to Xibiten Gibel, a Jew
20.7.1463 c. 344v	Andrea Lumbardu	1.15.0 ounces	paid	sale of a horse to Michiloni Ysac, a Jew
28.7.1463 c. 351v	Giovanni de Naso	18 *tarì*		sale of grapes to Braxha Czitari, a Jew
9.8.1463 c. 363r	Iacob Coffiter, a Jew	10 *tarì*	paid	sale of oil
22.8.1463 c. 379r	Salamon de Rigio, Iacob Coffiter and Iosep de Rayusio, Jews	21.10 *tarì*	paid	sale of oil
22.8.1463 c. 380v	Giovanni de Guardia	6 ounces	paid 22.9.1463	sale of grapes to Salamon Czitari, a Jew
29.8.1463 c. 390r	Salamon Fataxi, a Jew	10.15 *tarì*	paid	sale of oil
30.8.1463 c. 394v	David Xhaguela. a Jew	2 *grana* a *rotolo*	24 *tarì* on account	sale of iron fittings for a carriage

Not. Guglielmo Mazzapiedi

Palermo, 28 September 1418

Source: ASP, Not. Guglielmo Mazzapiedi, reg. 839, c. 14r.

Contract for setting up a partnership between Busacca Cathalano and Sabeti Cuynu, Jewish citizens of Palermo, for pressing olives. Busacca invests a press belonging to Nixim Yelo, another Jew, in the contrada *della Giudecca. Sabeti invests a mule and his labour.*

Note: Repeated in reg. 840, c. 41v.

Palermo, 28 September 1418

Source: ASP, Not. Guglielmo Mazzapiedi, reg. 839, c. 14v.

Notarial quittance by Leone Maltisi, a Jewish physician of Polizzi, whereby he declares to have been paid the 50 ounces owed him by Iuffre de la Matina, master racionale *and administrator of Giovanni Ventimiglia, count of Geraci. The payment was carried out by Vitale Frigola,* secreto *of Palermo, debtor of the count of Geraci, to Bartholomeo de Manuel, a Catalan merchant, creditor of Leone.*

Palermo, 24 October 1418

Source: ASP, Not. Guglielmo Mazzapiedi, reg. 839, c. 33v.

Deed of sale whereby Musa Sansarius, a Jewish citizen of Cefalù, sells a third of his boat, the Santa Maria, currently at anchor in the harbour of Palermo, to Battista Fossanova, and another third to Costanzo de La Mandino, for 5.25.0 ounces each. Costanzo stands surety for both purchasers.
In the left margin: on 15.2.1419, Leone Maltisi, a Jewish physician in Polizzi, acknowledges receipt of four ounces from Battista. Musa owed him that amount.
In the right margin: On 23.8.1419, Musa acknowledges receipt of 1.25.0 ounces

6263

from Battista. On 7.2.1420 Nicolò de Pinolo, creditor of Musa, acknowledges receipt of the balance from Battista.

Eodem XXIIIII° Octubris

Musa Sansarius, Iudeus civis civitatis Cephaludi, dominus et patronus, ut dixit, unius navigii nunc existens in porto Panormi vocatum S.ta Maria, ac dominus, ut dixit, unius vele, duorum ferri et unius ancori, nec non et omnibus illorum corredorum rerum et guarnimentorum ad opus dicti navigii, que res et guarnimenta sunt descripte et notate in quondam inventario facte manu messeri Nicolai de Picorella et presente in posse dicte Muse, coram nobis sponte per se heredes et successores suos in perpetuum vendidit etc. Baptiste de Fossanova, civi Panormi, presenti et ab eo per se etc., solleniter ementi tertiam partem et pro indiviso dicti navigii, rerum et guarnimentorum supra dictorum existencium descriptorum in dicta scriptura. Idem venditor similiter per se etc., vendidit etc., Constancio de Lamandino de maiori precii et ab eo solleniter ementi aliam terciam partem etc. pro indiviso dicti navigii, rerum et guarnimentorum descriptorum in dicta scriptura. Reliqua vero tercia parte dicti navigii, rerum, guarnimentorum pro se et ad sui opus idem Muse retinuit, quas predictas duas tercias partes et pro indiviso dicti navigii et rerum, ut supra, dicti emptores coram nobis presentem et hoc ab eis petentes dicto venditori sponte et solleniter confessi sunt se ab eodem venditori habuisse et recepisse. Renunciantes etc. Ad habendum etc., pro precio et nomine certi precii unciarum auri quinque et tarenorum vigintiquinque pro singula tercia parte vendita, ut supra. Promictentes dicti emptores et quilibet eorum pro sua tercia parte dicto venditori solemniter stipulanti dare et solvere ipsi venditori etc. in pecunia numerata etc., in hinc modum videlicet terciam partem dicti precii hinc ad mensem IIII^or, alia terciam hinc ad mensem octo et reliquam terciam hinc ad annum unum proximum venturum presentes dictus venditori eisdem emptoribus et cuiuslibet in solidum solleniter stipulanti dantes duas tercias partes dicti navigii et rerum singulo pro tercia parte ut supra vendite, semper et omni venturo tempore legitime defendere. Que omnia et singula predicte et inferte dicte partes sibi invicem promiserunt rata et firma habere in omnem eventum, in pace, sine lite et sub ypotheca et obligatione omnium bonorum et habendorum. Pro quo Constancio, altero ex emptoribus supradicti erga eundem venditorem de dando, solvendo et integre assignando dictam pecuniam modo, forma et termino quibus supra, ac de baraptaria prefatus Baptista coram nobis sponte se constituit fideiussor principalem pagatorem et debitorem. Renunciando iuri de primo et principali con[venen]do bonis omnibus et ipsius fid[eiussor] pro causa predicta eidem venditori et creditori pro causa predicta efficaciter obligavit. Et hac fiat ritus in persona et bonis parte convenutis. Et iuravit omnes tres etc., et idem Iudeus ad legem Moysi more solito etc.

Testes: Orlando de Cavallerio, Micael de Galgana, Bonanno de Nubula et Antonius Henrici de La Matina.

Note: Repeated in reg. 840, c. 48r.

Palermo, 28 October 1418

Source: ASP, Not. Guglielmo Mazzapiedi, reg. 839, c. 34r.

Notarial deed whereby Battista Fossanova and Musa Sansarius, a Jewish citizen of Cefalù, each owning a third of the boat Santa Maria, appoint Costanzo de La Mandino, owner of the remaining third and master of the vessel, to administer the boat's business on their behalf. He is to travel aboard the boat and engage in trade.

Eodem

Cum hoc publico instrumento sit omnibus manifestum quod Baptista Fossanova, civis Panormi, dominus et patronus pro una tercia parte et Musa Sansarius, Iudeus de civitate Chefalude, dominus et patronus pro una alia tercia parte, ut dixerunt, unius navigii nunc exitentis in portu Panormi vocatum S.ta Maria et certarum rerum et guarnimentorum navigii prelibati, coram nobis confisi de fide, prudencia et legalitate Costancii de Lomandino de maiori patronum reliqua tercie parte dicti navigii, rerum et guarnimentarum presenti et omni inserti patronatus in se voluntarie suscipienti sponte eundem Constancium constituerunt, fecerunt, statuerunt et ordinaverunt et proposuerunt dictarum duarum partium dicti navigii, corredorum rerum et assistorum et guarnimentorum dominum et patronum, ac gubernator et administrator ex nunc in antea donec et quo usque eisdem Baptiste et Muse placuerit dantes et concedentes, dicti Baptista et Musa eidem patrono proposito licentiam et liberam potestatem, ac liberam et generalem administracionem dictarum duarum partium dicti navigii, rerum et guarnimentorum, ut supra, per marem per quacumque loca mundi ducendi et cum eodem navigio navigandi ad marinandi in totum dictas duas partes et in parte naulizandi, locandum, dislocandum mercibus et rebus et vinarum onerandum et exonerandum naulum et naula, ac redditus et proventus petendum, habendum et recipiendum ipsaque omnia habuisse conficendum pro quocumque vel quibuscumque naulis, cuicumque, vel quibuscumque conducere, volentibus quomodocumque qualitercumque eidem proposito visum fuerit et sibi melius videbitur expedire, ipsumque navigium si opus fuerit a[d]ptandi ad conducendum et dislocandum ponendum, amovendum marinaios et homines quoscumque ad opus dicti navigii pro illis solidis quibus eidem patrono proposito placuerit, presentes dictus Baptista et mihi se eidem proposito solleniter stipulanti pro sese mihi notario publico ad opus omnium quorum interest solleniter stipulanti rata et firma habere omnia et singula predicta, que per ipsum propositum fuerit gesta, procurata et administrata fuit [....] omnium bonorum eorum habitorum et habendorum, ac refectionem dampnorum interesse et expensarum, litis etc. Et equo dictus Constancius propositus promisit, convenit eisdem Baptista et Muse et cuisulibet in solidum solleniter stipulanti dictam ducionem, navigationem, ammarinacionem, nauligacionem, locacionem, onerationem, exonerationem, naulos proventum et redditum dictarum duarum partium dicti navigii etc. Et omnia et singula predicta bene, solliciter et diligenter, sine dolo et negligentia, facere, procurare pro eisdem Baptista et Musa, prout ei melius videbitur expedire, dum eisdem Baptista et Muse placueri[n]t ut supra. Et statim dictus propositus teneatur ad ad omnem ipsorum Baptista et Muse simplicem requisitionem ponere, facere atque monstrari ipsis Baptisti et Muse, seu aliis pro eidem, finalem computum, rationum, legalem de omnibus gestas et administratas per eum, sub ypotheca et obligationem omnium bonorum suorum habitorum et habendorum, ac refectionem dampnorum, interesse, expensarum litis etc. Et ad maiorem cautelam omnium premissorum pro missionibus actendentes modo, forma, ac terminis quibus omnes tres [!] ad Sancta Dei Evangelia corpore tactis scripturis iuraverunt.

Testes: Orlandus de Cavalerio, Micael de Galgana, Bonannus de Nubola et Antonius Henrici de la Matina.

Palermo, 6 February 1420

Source: ASP, Not. Guglielmo Mazzapiedi, reg. 839, cc. 120v–121r.

Accord between Donna Allegrancia, widow of Pietro de Vanni Bellachera, citizen of Palermo, and Graciano Nachagui, acting also for Leone de lu Medicu, Sabet and *Azarono Cusintino, her Jewish fellow citizens, in regard to 100 ounces which they owe her. She had received 37 ounces paid with cloth. Graciano promised to pay Allegrancia another 16 ounces in instalments until August. He pawned some articles with Allegrancia to provide security for this promise. She agreed to separate Graciano from the others, against whom she were to proceed separately.* In the margin: *Paid.*

Palermo, 9 February 1420

Source: ASP, Not. Guglielmo Mazzapiedi, reg. 839, cc. 127v–128r.

Notarial deed whereby Chonus de Litterio, a Palermitan citizen, is appointed by the captain's court to act as arbiter in a financial dispute between Sabet Cusintinus and Amoroso de Vita, his Jewish fellow citizens, to present their accounts.

Palermo, 10 March 1421

Source: ASP, Not. Guglielmo Mazzapiedi, reg. 839, c. 118r-v.

Agreement between Elia, son of Fariono de Bono, a Jew of Marsala, acting for his father, and Antonio de la Mannina. Antonio had been sentenced by the captain's court in Marsala to pay Fariono 7.10.0 ounces, being the balance in favour of Fariono in an accounting with the latter. Antonio had appealed to the Gran Corte *in Palermo. Now the parties agree to appear by April before the notary Giovanni La Liotta in Marsala, present their accounts under oath, and settle the dispute. Done in the presence of Xamuele Aczaro, a Jew.*

Palermo, 8 April 1421

Source: ASP, Not. Guglielmo Mazzapiedi, reg. 839, c. 150r.

Deed of sale whereby Nucius Marchisonus of Ciminna undertakes to carry 10 salme *of must from Termini Imerese to the home in Palermo of Muxa Missini, a Jewish citizen of Palermo, for 10* tarì. *He also sells him 1* salma *of barley for 5.10* tarì.

Palermo, 1 October 1421

Source: ASP, Not. Guglielmo Mazzapiedi, reg. 839, c. 14r.

Agreement whereby Charufus de Siracusia and Gauyu Terru, Jews of Syracuse,

6267

hire themselves out to Iacobo Camache Zoppu and Sabeti Catalanu, a Jew, for the entire tunny season, to work in the tunny plant in Cefalù for 1.18.0 ounces.

Palermo, 28 November 1421

Source: ASP, Not. Guglielmo Mazzapiedi, reg. 839, c. 143r.

Agreement between the heirs of the late Sarra, wife of Vita Sacerdotu, a Jew of Termini Imerese. Sarra had bequeathed her property to her brother Xibiten de Binna, except for certain bequests to others. Brother and husband now reach an agreement for the division of the estate, setting aside Sarra's will.

Palermo, 28 November 1421

Source: ASP, Not. Guglielmo Mazzapiedi, reg. 839, c. 143r.

Settlement of accounts between Beninatus de Belpuchi, a merchant of Valencia, and Elia Misiria, a Jewish citizen of Palermo. Elia now owes two ounces to Beninato.

Note: On c. 147v Beninatus is described as consul of Castile in Palermo.

Palermo, 5 December 1421

Source: ASP, Not. Guglielmo Mazzapiedi, reg. 839, c. 147r.

Declaration by Moyses Chetibi, a Jewish physician and citizen of Palermo, that he received 73.10.0 ounces from Ximeni de Filippo, royal tax collector, through the treasurer Nicolò Speciali. These were 500 florins of Aragon which Moyses had lent together with Antonio de Morosino to finance half the 3,000 florins which the Jewish community of Messina had to pay the Crown.

Ex hoc publico instrumento sit omnibus manifestum quod in presentia mei notari et testium subscriptis magister Moyses Chetabi [Chetibi] fisicus, Iudeus civis Panormi, ad instanciam mei notarii est confessus habuisse et recepisse a Ximeni de Philippo collectorem pro parte regie curie, seu a aliquorum Iudeorum Messane certam quantitatem pecunie [in the right margin: de summa mille et quingentorum florenos de Aragonia quos idem magister Moyses mutuavit cum Antonio de Murusino [Morosini] ad complementum trium mille florenorum dantes domino regi pro Iudayci

6268

civitatis Messane] a Iudaycis regni Sicilie [in the left margin: per mandatum magistri domini Nicolao de Speciali regii thesaurari] uncias auri septuaginta tres et tarenos decem quas et quos idem magister Moyses mutuavit, ut dixit, regie curie in florenis quingentis ad requisitionem et rogamina domini magistri thesaurario. Execucioni dicte pecunie non habite et recepte et doli. Idem magister Moyses solleniter recepisse. Renuncians. Unde ad cautelam dicte regie curie et dicti Ximeni et dictum m[agistrum] interest sibi fieri fecit presentem apocham de soluto, volens et mandans per me infrascriptum notarium scripti publicis dicti pro eis fieri fecit de premissis unum et pluria [...]. Dat. in urbe felicis Panormi, anno D. M°CCCC° XXI, mensis Decembris, die V° eiusdem mensis, XV° Ind.

Presentibus Antonio de Caramagna de Notho, Antonio de Marchisio de Messana, et Iacobo Paratollis de Barchinone.

Palermo, 16 March 1425

Source: ASP, Not. Guglielmo Mazzapiedi, reg. 839, c. 318r.

Contract for the establishment of a partnership between master Guglielmo Gumar, leather worker of Barcelona, and master Gauyu Gibel, a Jewish citizen of Palermo, for the sale of leather. Guglielmo invests his labour and Gauyu the shop and 1.24.0 ounces in goods. He also lends Guglielmo one ounce. The profit is to be divided in equal shares.

Palermo, 20 March 1425

Source: ASP, Not. Guglielmo Mazzapiedi, reg. 839, c. 329r.

Contract whereby Challufu Binna and Challufu Bramuni, Jewish builders and citizens of Palermo, undertake to build a small house in the contrada *Terre Rosse for Nicolò Craparo, their fellow citizen. The house is to measure two by two* canne (i.e., approximately 16 square metres) *at 2.10* tarì *a* canna.

Palermo, 15 May 1425

Source: ASP, ASP. Not. Guglielmo Mazzapiedi, reg. 839, c. nn.

Declaration by Gauyu Taguili, a Jew of Polizzi, that he received from Raynerio Aglata, a Pisan merchant in Palermo, a quantity of clothes in accomanda, valued at 136.29.13 ounces. Taguil undertakes to retail the goods, to be paid for in instalments, at his risk. The partnership is to last for one year, at the end of which one-third of the profits are to go to Taguil and two-thirds to Aglata.

Palermo, 12 October [1433?]
Source: ASP, ASP. Not. Guglielmo Mazzapiedi, reg. 840, c. 35v.

Contract whereby master Muxa Rugila, a Jewish builder and citizen of Palermo, undertakes to build fermentation vats and smaller vessels (palmentos et tinellos) *for Philippo de Pontecorona, his fellow citizen, for 24 tarì. The contract spells out the manner of construction, dimensions and location of the vats and vessels.*

Palermo, 5 November [1436?]
Source: ASP, ASP. Not. Guglielmo Mazzapiedi, reg. 840, c. 112v.

Promise by Abdella Bumusa of Tripoli in Barbary, slave of Benedetto Chaseni, a Jewish citizen of Palermo, to pay him 19 ounces in the course of two years for his emancipation. In the margin: quittances made out at various dates.

Palermo, 8 March 1436
Source: ASP, ASP. Not. Guglielmo Mazzapiedi, reg. 841, c. 263v.

Declaration by Manuel Daram, a Jew of Sciacca, acknowledging receipt from Guglielmo Scales of 265 [!] salme of wheat in accomanda. *Manuel stored the wheat in his shop in in Sciacca.*

Palermo, 24 May 1436
Source: ASP, ASP. Not. Guglielmo Mazzapiedi, reg. 841, c. nn.

Antonio de La Mantina grants Siminto Maltisi, a Jew of Polizzi, a year's moratorium on the payment of of a debt amounting to 13.2.0 ounces.

Palermo, 21 November [..]
Source: ASP, ASP. Not. Guglielmo Mazzapiedi, reg. 841, c. nn.

Declaration by Bernardo Sardo that he had been paid in full by Xamuel Sala, a Jew.

Palermo, 7 May 1436

Source: ASP, ASP. Not. Guglielmo Mazzapiedi, reg. 841, c. 344r.

Muxa and Bulchayra Millach, Jewish citizens of Palermo, undertake to build a house for Simone de Cavaciis in his vineyard for 2.10 tarì *the* canna.

Palermo, 21 January [..]

Source: ASP, ASP. Not. Guglielmo Mazzapiedi, reg. 841, c. nn.

Declaration by Elia Nixim, a Jewish citizen of Palermo, that he received from Capuano de Latorina 1.10.0 ounces, the balance of a larger sum owed for the sale of some goods.

Palermo, 28 May [..]

Source: ASP, ASP. Not. Guglielmo Mazzapiedi, reg. 841, c. nn.

Perpetual lease granted by fra Paolo de Yordano, abbot of the monastery Santa Maria degli Angeli di Baida, to Xamuele Xalomo, a Jewish citizen of Palermo, of a house in the Cassaro of Palermo occupied by Banno de Termis, subject to an annual rent of nine tarì, *for two ounces.*

Palermo, 2 October [..]

Source: ASP, ASP. Not. Guglielmo Mazzapiedi, reg. 841, c. nn.

Declaration by Manuel de Dormuna, a Jewish citizen of Palermo, that he received some goods from Ricio de Andrea.

Palermo, 31 March [..]

Source: ASP, ASP. Not. Guglielmo Mazzapiedi, reg. 841, c. nn.

Lease by Antonio de Caligis of an olive oil press to Iosep Amar, Salamon Zacca and Zullo [..], Palermitan Jews. They undertake to maintain the press in good order.

Palermo, 30 August [..]

Source: ASP, ASP. Not. Guglielmo Mazzapiedi, reg. 841, c. nn.

Declaration by Beninato de Belpuchi of Palermo that he received one ounce from Balluni de Seracusia, a Palermitan Jew, the purchase price of a coat.

Palermo, 14 March [..]

Source: ASP, ASP. Not. Guglielmo Mazzapiedi, reg. 841, c. nn.

Agreement whereby Nachuni Rugila, Muxa de Mantuxi, Natali Thabirra and Benedetto Cabisi, Palermitan Jews, hire themselves out to the Palermitan notary Giovanni Bellachera to work his sugar cane plantation in Plano Sancti Patris in the contrade Archimuski and La Guadagna. They are promised a salary of 18 tarì *a thousand canes.*

Palermo, 29 January [..]

Source: ASP, ASP. Not. Guglielmo Mazzapiedi, reg. 841, c. nn.

Declaration by sister Margherita de Mecca, abbess of the convent Santa Chiara in Palermo, whereby she confirms the grant of a moratorium to Axexi Xaxarono and Sufen Gillebi, Palermitan Jews, on the repayment of a loan of 50 ounces.

Palermo, 1 August [..]

Source: ASP, ASP. Not. Guglielmo Mazzapiedi, reg. 841, c. nn.

Agreement whereby Muxa Calibusi, a Palermitan Jew, hires himself out to Bono de Iacopo to salt tunny and cheese (ad salamoriandum tonenam et caseum) *for 24* tarì a month. *He is paid 12* tarì *on account.*

Palermo, 19 February [..]

Source: ASP, ASP. Not. Guglielmo Mazzapiedi, reg. 841, c. nn.

Contract whereby Salamon Gaczu, a Palermitan Jew, undertakes to cut tallow for making candles (taglare vel incidere totam quantitatem sepi ad opus faciendi candelas) *at a salary of eight* grana *the kantar.*

6272

Sicily

Palermo, 2 March [..]

Source: ASP, ASP. Not. Guglielmo Mazzapiedi, reg. 841, c. nn.

Agreement whereby Siminto de Missina and Brachono Sichilianu, Palermitan Jews, promise Giovanni de Aldobrandinis to stack all the wood in his sugar refinery during the entire season for six tarì *a thousand pieces.*

Source: ASP, Not. Guglielmo Mazzapiedi, reg. 839

Date and Page	Principal	Attorney	Purpose	Remarks
8.1.1421 c. 71r	Xanonus Mizoc, a Palermitan Jew	Brachono Ginni, a Palermitan Jew	to represent him in the dispute with Brachono and Sadono Mizoc and Muxa de Ram, all Jews	
10.1.1421 c. 73r	Siminto Maltisi, a Palermitan Jew	Azarono Maltisi, a Jew of Polizzi	to defend him in the lawsuit with Pino Larante over a tavern in Polizzi let to Pino	
22.5.1425 c. nn	Noray de Gauyu, a Spanish Jew in Palermo	Yona ben Uziel and Yosep Ben Azaru, Palermitan Jews	to administer his property during his absence	
5.9.1428 c. nn	Ximonello de Aczaru, a Jew of Marsala	Muxa Achina, a Palermitan Jew	to collect a debt of 2.3.0 ounces	

Date and Page	Debtor	Amount	Reason	Remarks
4.12.1420 c. 51v	Siminto Maltisi, a Palermitan Jew	24 *tarì*	balance of a larger sum	creditors: Damiano Mazola; paid to Bonamico Testa, a notary in Polizzi, creditor of Damiano

6273

Date and Page	Lender or Seller	Amount	Payment	Remarks
17.4.1433 c. 239v	Paolo Samer	2.24.0 ounces	within 4 months; paid 20.10.1433	sale of Catalan cloth to Honorato de Sayn, a Palermitan Jew
17.4.1433 c. 240r	Simone de Lacsi, a Jew of Palermo	1 ounce	within 4 months	sale of wheat to Manueli Mayr, a Palermitan Jew
17.4.1433 c. 242v	Simone de Lacsi, a Jew of Palermo	1 ounce	by August; paid 7.9.1433	sale of wheat to Sufeni de Minixi, a Jew in Palermo
17.4.1433 c. 245r	Raynerio Aglata	1.19.0 ounces	within 3 months; paid 9.9.1433	sale of iron to Elia de Missina, a Jew of Palermo
3.9.1427 c. nn	Paolo de Sobua	3.2.5.10 ounces	within 6 months; 27.12.1427	sale of poniards to Busacca Sabatinu, a Jew of Palermo
5.9.1427 c. nn	Narciso de Bundill	24 *ounces*	10 ounces on account through Chayrono Taguil, a Jew, balance in 6 months; paid 16.7.1428	sale of purple cloth to Gauyo Taguil, a Jew of Polizzi
5.9.1427 c. nn	Guillelmo Gilba	16.3.0 ounces	within 4 months	sale of "village" cloth to Gauyu Taguil, a Jew
8.9.1427 c. nn	master Lamberto de Vaccaro	2.6.0 ounces	3 instalments: Christmas, Carnival and Easter; paid 20.4.1428	sale of grapes to to Sufeni Minixi, a Palermitan Jew
9.9.1427 c. nn	Gauyu Taguil, a Jew of Polizzi	17.18.0 ounces	within 6 months	sale of Verviers (*vervey*) cloth
3.9.1427 c. nn	Galcerano de Aquilo	15.12.0 ounces	within 4 months	sale of Barcelona and Valencia cloth to Gauyu Taguil, a Jew of Polizzi

10.9.1427 c. nn	Lamberto Vaccaro	2.6.0 ounces	3 instalments: Christmas, Carnival and Easter; paid 15.4.1428	sale of grapes to Nixim Isac, a Jew
11.9.1427 c. nn	Galcerano de Aquilo	16.24.0 ounces	within 6 months	sale of Catalan cloth to Sema de Partanna, a Jew of Sciacca
12.9.1427 c. nn	Narciso de Bundill	31.4.0 ounces	by January; paid 3.8.1428	sale of purple cloth to Sema de Partanna, a Jew of Sciacca
16.9.1427 c. nn	Antonio de Pedunillo	1 ounce	within a month	sale of a horse to Iosep Lu Medicu, a Palermitan Jew
16.9.1427 c. nn	[...] de Termini and Merdoc Simal, Palermitan Jews	15 to 25 *tarì* a 100	1 ounce on account, balance on delivery	sale of white and black sheepskin
17.9.1427 c. nn	Gabriele Roden	5 ounces	by October; paid 9.1.1428	sale of poniards to Siminto Aurifichi, a Jew of Palermo
30.9.1418 c. nn	Gregorio de Urso	5.29.0 ounces	within 4 months; paid 22.3.1419	sale of stout cloth to Brachono de Lu Medicu and Michilono Xunina, Palermitan Jews
[..].10.1418 c. 17v	Giovanni de Manella	3.4.1 ounces	by May 1419; paid 25.10.1419	sale of iron to Muxa de Sansaru, a Jew of Cefalù
6.10.1418 c. 19r	Bartholomeo de Manella	4.25.0 ounces	within 4 months; paid 4.7.1419	sale of saffron to Brachono de Lu Medicu, a Jew of Palermo
12.10.1418 c. 24r	Iaymo Ferreri	35.15.0 ounces	10 ounces in 4 months, balance in 6	sale of Languedoc cloth to Vegnamino Chilfa, a Jew of Trapani

17.10.1418 c. 29r	Antonio de Bruna	1.15.0 ounces	a third by Christmas, a third by Lent and the balance by Easter; paid 18.6.1419	sale of grapes to Faryuni Cafisu, a Jew of Palermo
24.10.1418 c. 34v	Antonio de Bruna	4.3.0 ounces	a third by Christmas, a third by Lent and the balance by Easter; paid 21.5.1421	sale of grapes to Merdoc Sillac, a Jew of Palermo
7.11.1418 c. 40v	Simone de mastro Andrea	2.3.0 ounces	by November	sale of wine to Machuni Saba, a Jew of Palermo
31.1.1420 c. 116r	Iaymo Ferreri	3.12.0 ounces	within 4 months; paid 22.11	sale of Perpignan cloth to Xirello Balbu, a Jew of Trapani
31.1.1420 c. 117v	Nicolò de Lu Castilluzu	1.12.0 ounces	by 15.8	sale of wheat to Elya Missina, a Jew of Palermo
26.2.1420 c. 140r	Francesco Villanova	22 *tarì*	in 2 months; paid 8.4	sale of assorted goods to Simon Minichi, a Jew of Palermo
[... 1420] c. nn	Calzarono de Aquilo	2.12.0 ounces	in 4 months	sale of Catalan cloth to Brachono Taguil, a Jew of Palermo
7.9.1420 c. nn	Gauyu Xua, a Jew of Palermo	a quintal for 15 and 28 *tarì* respectively	on delivery	sale of sheepskin
14.11.1420 c. 34v	Iaimo Ferreri of Perpignan	6.18.0 ounces	within 6 months; paid 24.10.1421	sale of Perpignan cloth to Chirello Balbu, a Jew of Trapani
27.11.1420 c. 43r	David Rizu, a Jew of Palermo	15 ounces	3 ounces on account, 3 more by December; paid 8.10.1321	sale of sheep cheese

29.11.1420 c. 46r	Sabet Gilebi and Banni Xiba, Jews of Palermo	7.4.0 ounces	25 *tarì* on account	sale of Valencia cloth
11.12.1420 c. 56v	Giovanni de Caligis	1 ounce	within 2 months	sale of violet cloth to Muxa and Vita Amara, Jews of Palermo
28.1.1421 c. 84r	Siminto de Aurifichi, a Jew of Palermo	2.8.12 ounces		sale of double sacks
29.1.1421 c. 85r	Pietro Palau	7.18.0 ounces	paid	sale of a black slave to Nixim Saya, a Jew of Trapani
29.1.1421 c. 85r	Sabet Xunina, a Jew of Palermo	1.21.15 ounces		sale of double sacks
29.1.1421 c. 85v	Salamon Azaru, a Jew of Palermo	20 *tarì*		sale of double sacks
7.2.1421 c. 89v	Faciu de Moyses, a Jew of Cagliari	1.6.0 ounces		sale of red cloth
7.2.1421 c. 90r	Salamon Azaru, a Jew of Palermo	1.4.0 ounces		sale of a piece of silk (*terzanello*)
7.2.1421 c. 90r	David Xifuni, a Jew of Palermo	1.21.10 ounces		sale of a piece of silk (*terzanello*)
7.2.1421 c. 90v	Sabet Xunina, a Jew of Palermo	1.4.3 ounces		sale of 30 canne of double sacks
11.2.1421 c. 94v	Calzarono de Aquilo	4.24.0 ounces	within 4 months; paid 24.10.1422	sale of Barcelona cloth to Xirello Balbu, a Jew of Trapani
2.4.1421 c. 145v	Calzarono de Aquilo	3.6.0 ounces	within 5 months; paid 10.1.1422	sale of scales to Azaruni de Lu Medicu, a Palermitan Jew

11.4.1421 c. 152v	Pericono Giovanni and Bernardo Andrea	3.15.0 ounces	within 6 months	sale of Perpignan cloth to Chaym de Sabatu, a Jew of Trapani, and Iosep de Fagilla, a Jew of Alcamo
22.4.1421 c. 182v	Giovanni Columbo	4.16.0 ounces	within 4 months	sale of oil to Salamuni Actuni, a Jew of Palermo
24.4.1421 c. 184v	Francesco Mercer	3.23.8 ounces	within 4 months; paid 31.4.1423	sale of deerskins to Iacob de Termini, a Jew of Palermo
2.5.1421 c. nn	Calzarono de Aquilo	19.15.0 ounces	in 4 months; paid 3.12.1422	sale of deerskins to Iuda Sibeni and Daiduni Rizu, Jews of Palermo
2.5.1421 c. nn	Nicolò Olivier	1.3.0 ounces	in 2 months; paid 31.7	sale of cloth to Sabet Gindusio, a Jew of Sciacca
21.5.1421 c. nn	Yaymo Serafina	1.29.0 ounces	in 8 months	sale of ground salt to Iuda Cuyno, a Jew of Palermo
23.9.1421 c. 45r	Matheo Baruchi	5.10.0 ounces	in 4 months	sale of assorted goods to Elia Missini and Musuto Bricha, Jews of Palermo
23.9.1421 c. 46v	Matheo Baruchi	4 ounces	in 4 months; paid 11.3.1422	sale of assorted goods to Simon Benassai, a Jew of Palermo
23.9.1421 c. 47v	Sabet Dinar, a Jew of Messina	15 ounces	paid	sale of a black slave girl and her son
24.9.1421 c. 48v	Guglielmo Marci	4.14.15 ounces	within 6 months; paid 14.4.1424	sale of iron to Isdrael Medui, a Jew of Palermo
25.9.1421 c. 50r	Salvatore Falcuni	1 ounce	on demand; paid 14.11	loan to Simon Minnichi, a Jew of Palermo

2.10.1421 c. 54v	Gauyu Xua, a Jew of Palermo	28 *tarì*	10 *tarì* on account, balance on delivery	sale of sheepskin; guarantor: Simone de Minnichi, a Palermitan Jew
13.10.1421 c. 68v	Agabito de Bartholomeo	6.6.0 ounces	2 ounces on account, balance 4 months later; paid 17.2.1424	sale of gold wire to Graciano Tachariato, a Jew of Palermo
30.10.1421 c. 92r	Agabito de Bartholomeo	6.28.10 ounces	within 4 months; paid 28.12.1422	sale of canvas to Benedetto Azeni, a Palermitan Jew
30.10.1421 c. 92r	Agabito de Bartholomeo	6.28.10 ounces	within 4 months; paid 28.12.1422	sale of canvas to Vita Azaru, a Palermitan Jew
30.10.1421 c. 92v	Ysdrael Medui, a Jew of Palermo	4.11.6 ounces		sale of keys
30.10.1421 c. 93r	Elia Sufer, a Palermitan Jew	1.8.0 ounces		sale of merchandise
30.10.1421 c. 93v	Perri Ponzi	1.12.0 ounces	within 7 weeks; paid 2.1.1423	sale of silk to Salamon Aurifichi, a Jew of Agrigento
31.10.1421 c. 97v	Thomeo Andrea, son of Simone	5.16.10 ounces	by Easter	sale of tunny to Charrufo de Siracusia, a Jew of Syracuse
5.11.1421 c. 102v	Agabito de Bartholomeo	5 ounces	1 ounces in 2 months, 4 ounces in 4; paid 4.5.1422	sale of gold wire to Salamon Azaru, a Jew of Palermo
20.11.1421 c. 132r	Pino de Avellino	23 *tarì*		loan to Pipo Amar, a Jew
20.11.1421 c. 132r	Moyse Chetibi, a Palermitan Jew	17 *tarì*		loan to Pipo Amar, a Jew
2.12.1421 c. 146r	Sabet Xunina, a Palermitan Jew	3.7.0 ounces		sale of keys, hemp rope and spun yarn

2.12.1421 c. 146r	Sabet Xunina and Salamon Aczaru, Palermitan Jews	25.15 *tarì*	paid	sale of rope
2.12.1421 c. 146r	Sabet Xunina and Salamon Aczaru, Palermitan Jews	1.17.0 ounces	paid	sale of rope
2.12.1421 c. 146v	Sabet Xunina, a Palermitan Jew	19 *tarì*	paid	sale of nails
5.12.1421 c. 148v	Giovanni Guillelmu	12 ounces	half with cash and half with a black slave girl aged 30	sale of a Hebrew Bible, containing 24 books, written by Sali Dari, a Jew of Messina
9.12.1421 c. 151v	Perri Serra	1.25.0 ounces	within 4 months; paid 4.5.1422	sale of saffron to Salamon de Muxa, a Jew of Palermo
9.12.1421 c. 151v	Perri Serra	2.18.0 ounces	within 4 months; paid 4.5.1422	sale of saffron to Leone de la Iudeca, a Jew of Palermo
10.12.1421 c. 153r	Perri Serra	4.16.0 ounces	within 4 months; paid 3.10.1423	sale of saffron to Brachono Taguil, a Jew of Palermo
15.12.1421 c. 159v	Nicolò Oliveri	2.12.0 ounces	by February; paid 21.1.1422	sale of green cloth to Sabet Gindusio, a Jew of Sciacca
18.12.1421 c. 163r	Perri Serra	8.5.10 ounces	within 4 months; paid 4.3.1423	sale of saffron and canvas yarn to Vita Azaru, a Jew of Palermo
15.3.1425 c. 317r	Pietro Palau	1.26.5 ounces	within 4 months; paid 29.8.1425	sale of deerskins to Brachuni lu Aurifichi, a Jew of Alcamo

16.3.1425 c. 317v	Bartholomeo de Fasana	current price	18 *tarì* on account	sale of grapes to Gaudio Gibel, a Palermitan Jew
16.3.1425 c. 320r	Michele Vives	3.6.0 ounces	in 4 months; paid 30.10.1425	sale of San Lorenzo cloth to Salamon de Canet, a Jew
12.6.1425 c. nn	Giovanni Zabbateni	3.1.15 ounces	on demand; paid 2.1.1426	loan to Iosep Gilpa, a Jew of Alcamo
12.10.1429 c. nn	Sufen de Minnichi, a Palermitan Jew	4.15.0 ounces	on demand; paid 14.11.1429	sale of a Bible to Honorato de Gaudio, a Jew
7.2.1430 c. 327v	Giovanni Abbatellis and Raynerio de Risignano	5.12.0 ounces	in 4 months	sale of cloth to Iosep Abudaram, a Jew of Palermo
23.2.1430 c. nn	Paolo Samer	14.21.0 ounces	within 6 months	sale of Catalan cloth to Iosep Maltisi, a Jew of Polizzi
1.3.1430 c. 347r	Nicolò de Bayolo	6.1.6 ounces	within 2 months; paid 6.9.1430	sale of iron to Musuto Nixim, a Palermitan Jew
10.3.1430 c. 368r	Giovanni Abbatellis and Raynerio de Risignano	1 ounce	in a month; paid 11.5	sale of merchandise to Gauyu Gibel, a Palermitan Jew
20.3.1430 c. nn	Paolo Samer	2.15.0 ounces	in a month; paid 16.5.1430	sale of cloth Machachiuni de Benedetto, a Jew of Marsala

Date and Page	Tenant	Location and Description	Rent and Duration	Remarks
12.9.1427 c. nn	Sabeti Chohino, a Jew of Palermo	Palermo	a mill called Di La Loggia; for 3 years at 13 ounces a year; in weekly instalments	owner: Antonio Iacobi

Bibliography: Bresc, *Arabi*, p. 193

Source: ASP, Not. Guglielmo Mazzapiedi, reg. 840

Date and Page	Principal	Attorney	Purpose	Remarks
5.2.1437 c. 218r	Arnaus Porta	Pietro Serra	to collect his credits from Muxa Xillemi, a Jew of Sciacca	

Date and Page	Lender or Seller	Amount	Payment	Remarks
31.10.1432 c. 55r	Elia Sibeni, a Jew of Palermo	1 ounces	within 3 months	sale of canvas to Muxa Vignuni, a Jew of Palermo, acting for Rafael Calabrisi, a Jew of Caccamo
4.11.1432 c. 55v	Raynerio de Risignano	5.18.0 ounces	within 4 months; paid 15.12.1435	sale of Valencian clothes to Faryono Sala, a Jew of Palermo
12.11.1432 c. 61r	Paolo Samer	8.27.0 ounces	within 2 months; paid 20.10.1433	sale of Catalan cloth to Honorato de Gaudio, a Palermitan Jew

Bibliography: Trassetti, Mercato dei panni, p. 150.

Date and Page	Lender or Seller	Amount	Payment	Remarks
21.11.1432 c. 67v	Andrea de Gentili	3.12.0 ounces	within 4 months; paid 28.5.14	sale of Genoese cloth to Muxa Nissim and David Niyar, Palermitan Jews
24.11.1432 c. 68v	Petro Malvil	12.24.0 ounces	by March; paid 10.6.1433	sale of cloth to Honorato de Gaudio, a Palermitan Jew
9.12.1432 c. nn	Paolo Samer	2.8.0 ounces	within 2 months; paid 20.10.1433	sale of cloth to Honorato de Gaudio, a Palermitan Jew
11.12.1432 c. nn	Pietro Admairik	3.6.0 ounces	within 3 months; paid 17.6.1433	sale of Perpignan cloth to Vita Azar, a Jew of Palermo
10.1.1433 c. 53v	Giovanni Giordano	31.15.0 ounces	within 6 months	sale of cloth to Faryono Bonu, a Jew of Marsala

30.9.1433 c. 42r	Gregorio de Urso	5.29.0 ounces	within 4 months	sale of cloth to Brachono de Medico and Michilono Xunina, Palermitan Jews
12.10.1433 c. 42r	Iaymo Ferreri	31.15.0 ounces	within 4 months	sale of various cloths to Vegnamino Chilpa, a Jew of Trapani
17.10.1433 c. 46v	Antonio de Bruna	1.15.0 ounces	in 3 instalments at Christmas, Shrovetide and Easter	sale of grapes to Fariuni Cafisu, a Jew of Palermo
24.10.1433 c. 48v	Antonio de Bruua	4.3.0 ounces	in 3 instalments at Christmas, Shrovetide and Easter	sale of grapes to Merdoc Sillac, a Jew of Palermo
5.9.1436 c. nn	Peri Amar	19.6.0 ounces	within 4 months of which 4 ounces by 7.11.1436; paid 8.1.1437	sale of Barcelona cloth to Salamon Maltisi, a Jew of Polizzi
5.9.1436 c. nn	Benedetto Torquo	11.18.0 ounces	within 4 months, of which 10 ounces by 20.12.1436; paid 29.11.1437	sale of Barcelona cloth to Iosep Maltisi, a Jew of Polizzi

Bibliography: Trassetti, *Mercato dei panni*, p. 149.

5.9.1436 c. nn	Peri Amar	12 ounces	within 4 months, 6 ounces by 22.1.1437; paid 23.2.1437	sale of Barcelona cloth to Iosep Maltisi, a Jew of Polizzi
5.9.1416 c. 18v	Antonio de Caligis	12.7.10 ounces	within 4 months	sale of cloth to Honorato Gauyu and Iosep Abudaram, Palermitan Jews
6.9.1436 c. 20r	Domenico Lyeru	12 ounces	within 4 months; paid 3.5.1437	sale of silk and fustian to Salamon de Musu, a Palermitan Jew
7.9.1436 c. 20v	Simone and Raynerio de Risignano	1.1.16 ounces	within 2 months; paid 26.4.1437	sale of iron to Merdoc Bignuni, a Jew of Palermo

7.9.1436 c. 21v	Benedetto Torquo	6 ounces	within 4 months	sale of cloth to Iosep Abudaram, a Palermitan Jew
10.9.1436 c. 24r	Laurino de Diana	6 ounces	on demand; paid 15.1.1437	sale of cheese to Vita Catalano, a Palermitan Jew
13.9.1436 c. 27v	Brachono Taguil, a Jew of Palermo	25 ounces	on demand; paid 14.3.1437	sale of wheat
29.9.1436 c. 39r	Benedetto Villar	7.6.0 ounces	within 4 months; paid 21.2.1437	sale of cloth to Iosep Maltisi, a Jew of Polizzi

Bibliography: Trassetti, *Mercato dei panni*, p. 149.

29.9.1436 c. 39v	Benedetto Serdas	13.26.0 ounces	within 4 months; paid 21.2.1437	sale of cloth to Iosep Maltisi, a Jew of Polizzi
8.10.1436 c. 60r	Baldassare Bortone and Domenico de Trigona	6.6.0 ounces	half within a month, balance within 2 months; paid 10.12.1436	sale of gold wire to Nixim Azanite, a Jew in Palermo
11.10.1436 c. 77v	Benedetto Villar	5 ounces	within 4 months; paid 6.4.1437	sale of Catalan cloth to Iusep Abudaram, a Jew of Palermo
22.10.1436 c. 86v	Chaninus Farmuni, a Palermitan Jew	9 ounces	paid	sale of a Moorish slave from Tripoli
23.10.1436 c.91v	Simone de Risignano	33 ounces	within 4 months; paid 9.11.1437	sale of Florentine and Barcelona cloth to David Nachagui and Xibiten De Yona, Jews of Alcamo
25.10.1436 c. 94v	Manuele Daram, a Jew of Sciacca	1.20.0 ounces	1 ounce on account; balance on delivery	sale of cheese
26.10.1436 c. 95v	Benedetto Torquo	14 ounces	within 4 months; paid 12.11.1437	sale of Barcelona cloth to Azarono de Minichetulu, a Jew of Marsala

Date	Name	Amount	Terms	Description
26.10.1436 c. 96r	Antonio de Crapona	26.6.0 ounces	within 5 months; paid 8.4.1437	sale of Catalan cloth to Muxa Silleni, a Jew of Sciacca
26.10.1436 c. 96v	Antonio de Crapona	3.2.0 ounces	within 5 months; paid 4.3.1437	sale of Languedoc cloth to Muxa Silleni, a Jew of Sciacca. Paid by Salon son of Muxa and by Challufu lu Medico, both Jews
26.10.1436 c. 97r	Guglielmo Bonfill	24.25.0 ounces	within 5 months; 3 ounces on account; paid 9.4.1437	sale of cloth to Muxa Silleni, a Jew of Sciacca
26.10.1436 c. 97v	Guglielmo Bonfill	7.6.0 ounces	by March; paid 23.5.1437	sale of cloth to Busacca de Alfazar, a Palermitan Jew
26.10.1436 c. 98r	Arnao Porta	12.15.0 ounces	within 2 months; paid 6.3.1437	sale of cloth to Azaruni de Minichetulu, a Jew of Marsala
30.10.1436 c. 100r	Arnao Porta	5.15.0 ounces	within 3 months, 3.15.0 ounces on account; paid 29.2.1437	sale of Catalan cloth to Muxa Xilleni, a Jew of Sciacca
30.10.1436 c. 100v	Giovanni Aspla	7.5.5 ounces	within 3 months, 3.5.5 ounces by 10.1.1437; paid 28.2.1437	sale of Gerona cloth to Muxa Xilleni, a Jew of Sciacca
5.11.1436 c. 109r	Antonio de Crapona	6.8.0 ounces	within 4 months; paid 18.4.1437	sale of pieces of curtain and gold wire to Iosep Benazere, a Jew of Palermo
5.11.1436 c. 111r	Simone and Rainerio de Risignano	3.6.0 ounces	15 *tarì* a week; paid 8.2.1437	sale of gold wire to Elia de Missina, a Jew of Palermo
5.11.1436 c. 111r	Benedetto Torquo	2 ounces	by Christmas; paid 8.6.1439	loan to Muxa de Tripuli, a Palermitan Jew

9.11.1436 c. 118r	Simone and Rainerio de Risignano	3.6.0 ounces	12 *tarì* a week; paid 24.12.1436	sale of gold wire to donna Dulci de Gauyu, a Jewess of Palermo
15.11.1436 c. 124r	Xuse de Xuse, a Jew of Agrigento	1.9.0 ounces	on delivery	sale of sheepskin
21.11.1436 c. 127r	Benedetto Torquo	5.27.0 ounces	within 4 months	sale of Catalan cloth to Abram Abagard, a Jew in Palermo
3.12.1436 c. 138r	Simone and Rainerio de Risignano	24.18.0 ounces	within 6 months; paid 11.9.1437	sale of Florentine cloth to Mento de Musarella, a Jew of Marsala
3.12.1436 c. 139v	Antonio de Sempo	12.18.0 ounces	within 6 months; paid 16.9.1437	sale of Florentine cloth to Mento de Muxarella, a Jew of Marsala
2.1.1437 c. 159r	Simone de Blanchiis	2.15.0 ounces	instalments of a third by Shrovetide, Easter and Pentecost; paid by 28.1.1437	sale of grapes to David Isac, a Palermitan Jew
8.1.1437 c. 168r	Benedetto Torquo	27 ounces	within 4 months; paid 19.4.1437	sale of Barcelona and S. Lorenzo cloth to Salamon Maltisi, a Jew of Mazara
8.1.1437 c. 169r	Goffredo La Vineda	22 ounces	within 5 months	sale of Majorcan cloth to Iosep Sala, a Jew of Mazara
8.1.1437 c. 169v	Saldoni Ferrer	6.18.0 ounces	within 4 months; paid 24.4.1437	sale of cloth to Iosep Saul, a Jew of Mazara
8.1.1437 c. 170r	Guglielmo Serra	17.15.0 ounces	within 4 months; paid 7.11.1437	sale of cloth to Iosep Saul, a Jew of Mazara
8.1.1437 c. 170v	Fortugno Manarellu	18.6.0 ounces	within 4 months; paid 19.4.1437	sale of Catalan cloth to Liuczu Cohino, a Jew of Trapani

8.1.1437 c. 175r	Benedetto Villar	7 ounces	within 4 months	sale of Catalan cloth Liuczu Cohino, a Jew of Trapani
9.1.1437 c. 176v	Benedetto Torquo	12 ounces	within 4 months; paid 25.10.1437	sale of deerskin to Elia de Mazaria, a Jew in Palermo
9.1.1437 c. 177r	Saldoni Ferrer	28.15.10 ounces	within 4 months, 12 ounces by 11.3.1437; paid 26.9.1437	sale of Catalan cloth to Liuczu Cohino, a Jew of Trapani
14.1.1437 c. 245r	Salamon de Messana, a Jew in Palermo	11.7.10 ounces	within 4 months, on 3.2.1438 Iosep's share, on 18.3.1438 Salomon's share; paid 4.7.1438	sale of deerskin to Muxa Levi, Iosef Coriz and Salamon de Missina, Jews in Palermo
14.1.1437 c. 182v	Benedetto Torquo	4.24.0 ounces	within 4 months	sale of deerskin to Gauyu Fuxisa, a Jew of Mazara
15.1.1437 c. 184r	Simone and Raynerio de Risignano	34.9.15 ounces	13 ounces by April, balance within 6 months; paid 15.7.1437	sale of Florentine cloth to Muxa Xilleni, a Jew of Sciacca
18.1.1437 c. 194v	Benedetto Torquo	4.15.0 ounces	within 4 months, 2.10.7 ounces by 9.5.1437; paid 12.11.1437	sale of deerskin to Strugu de Amoranu and Bulchayra de Benedictu, Jews of Mazara. Guarantor: Xibiten Gibia, a Palermitan Jew
21.1.1437 c. 293r	Antonio Galigis	12 *tarì*	by March	sale of Perpignan cloth to Brachuni Sagaru, a Palermitan Jew
30.1.1437 c. 211r	Giovanni Displa	4.12.0 ounces	within 2 months; paid 28.1.1438	sale of Perpignan cloth to Iosep Abudaram, a Jew of Palermo

1.2.1437 c. 214r	Peri Amar	9.26.0 ounces	within 4 months; paid 2.12.1438	sale of Barcelona cloth to Elia Amar, a Palermitan Jew
1.2.1437 c. 214v	Benedetto Torquo	6 ounces	within 4 months; paid 4.7.1438	sale of deerskin to Vita Azaru, a Jew of Palermo
18.2.1437 c. 226v	Nicolò Pinzolo	6.13.8 ounces	by June, 4 ounces on 17.7.1437; paid 3.12.1437	sale of nails to Muxa Sacerdotu, a Jew of Palermo
20.2.1437 c. 229v	Benedetto Villar	17 ounces	within 4 months; paid 13.8.1437	sale of S. Lorenzo and Gerona cloth to Iosep Maltisi, a Jew [of Polizzi]
20.2.1437 c. 230r	Guglielmo de Bonfill	23 ounces	within 4 months; paid 13.8.1437	sale of Barcelona cloth to Iosep Maltisi, a Jew [of Polizzi]
28.2.1437 c. 244v	Guglielmo Scales	3.10.16 ounces	within 4 months; paid 20.3.1438	sale of deerkin to Sadia Gindusio, a Jew of Sciacca. Guarantor Sabutu de Benedictu, a Jew of Sciacca
28.2.1437 c. 245r	Giovanni Despla	7.15.0 ounces	within 2 months; paid 28.1.1438	sale of cloth to Iosep Abudaram, a Palermitan Jew
20.2.1437 c. 245v	Giovanni Despla	12.3.0.ounces	within 3 months; paid 19.7 1437	sale of Catalan cloth Muxa Sacerdotu, a Jew in Palermo
3.4.1437 c. 316r	Rainerio Ricasti	3.11.5 ounces	15 *tarì* a week; paid 30.7.1438	sale of oil to Iaskeri de Minnixi, a Palermitan Jew
5.4.1437 c. 319r	Giovanni Caner	10 ounces	within 4 months	sale of cloth to Onorato de Gauyu, a Palermitan Jew
5.4.1437 c. 321r	Giovanni Caner	5.24.0 ounces	within 4 months; paid 14.11.1437	sale of Perpignan cloth to Onorato de Gauyu, a Palermitan Jew

5.4.1437 c. 323v	Giovanni de Despla	8.18.0 ounces	within 2 months; paid 19.1.1441	sale of S. Lorenzo cloth to Onorato de Gauyu, a Palermitan Jew
8.4.1437 c. 327v	Giovanni Ripoll	40.8.0 ounces	within 4 months, 24.8.0 ounces on 19.8.1437; paid 10.9 1437	sale of cloth to Muxa Xilleni, a Jew of Sciacca
9.4.1437 c. 330r	Guglielmo Scales	9.15.0 ounces	within 4 months; paid 30.9.1437	sale of deerskin to Sabet de Aurifichi, a Jew of Alcamo
9.4.1437 c. 331r	Simone and Rainerio de Risignano	12 ounces	by August	sale of Valencia cloth to Muxa Xilleni, a Jew of Sciacca
10.4.1437 c. 331v	Martino Gual	45.28.0 ounces	within 4 months, 33 ounces on 20.8.1437; paid 21.1.1438	sale of Catalan cloth to Muxa Xilleni, a Jew of Sciacca
20.4.1437 c. 332r	Nicolò de Bayolo	3.2.0 ounces	within 4 months; in instalments; paid 2.4.1438	sale of iron to Ysdrael Medui, a Palermitan Jew
22.4.1438 c. nn	Giovanni Servec	6 ounces	within 4 months	sale of deerskin to Xibiten de Sadonu, a Jew of Sciacca
24.4.1438 c. nn	Baldassare de Boton and Antonio de Crapona	6.18.0 ounces	within 3 months; paid 10.10.1438	sale of silk (*terzanelli*) to Graziano Tachariato and Salamon Benasai, Jews of Palermo
29.4.1438 c. nn	Benedetto Torquo	11.22.16 ounces	within 4 months	sale of deerskin to Charuni Sacerdotu, Muxa Actuni and Bulchayra Frisisa, Palermitan Jews
15.9.1439 c. nn	Simone and Rainerio de Risignano	5.0.16 ounces	within 4 months	sale of iron to Liuni Sacerdotu, a Jew in Palermo

4.9.1439 c. nn	Pietro de Santo Paolo	5.10.0 ounces	by December; paid 28.4.1440	sale of cloth to Xibiten Gibel, a Palermitan Jew
17.9. 1439 c. nn	Iacob de Acri, a Palermitan Jew		3 *tarì* on account, balance by October	sale of 24 vats (*caratelli*)
22.9.1439 c. nn	Pietro de Santo Paolo	5 ounces	within 4 months; paid 5.4.1440	sale of Catalan cloth to Moyse Sacerdotu, a Jew of Palermo
23.9.1439 c. nn	Pietro de Santo Paolo	7.10 *tarì* a week		sale of Catalan cloth to Iosep Taguil, a Palermitan Jew
23.9.1439 c. nn	Baldassare de Casasaya	9.18.0 ounces	within 4 months	sale of cloth to Iosep Taguil, a Jew of Palermo
23.9.1439 c. nn	Gabriel Verneda	2 ounces	within 3 months; paid 28.4.1440	sale of two pieces of cloth to Xibiten Gibel, a Jew of Palermo
23.9.1439 c. nn	Pietro de Santo Paolo	4.24.0 ounces	within 4 months; paid 18.4.1440	sale of cloth to Bellomu Sacerdotu, a Palermitan Jew
25.9.1439 c. nn	Gabriel Verneda	6 ounces	within 4 months; paid 13.6.1441	sale of deerskin to Iosep Cori and Sabet Levi, Palermitan Jews
25.9.1439 c. nn	Gabriel Verneda	19.6.3 ounces	within 4 months; paid 13.3.1441	sale of deerskin to Xirellu de Fariuni, a Jew in Palermo
25.9.1439 c. nn	Gabriel Verneda	6.28.13 ounces	within 4 months; paid 25.8.1441	sale of deerskin to Charuni Sacerdotu, a Jew of Palermo
25.9.1439 c. nn	Gabriel Verneda	5.22.10 ounces	within 4 months; paid 10.2.1441	sale of deerskin to Charuni Sacerdotu and Gallufu Actuni, Jews of Palermo
27.9.1439 c. nn	Benedetto Aglata	4 ounces	within 4 months; paid 16.2.1441	sale of goods to Saduni Rugila, a Palermitan Jew

27.9.1439 c. nn	Giovanni Damiani	2 ounces	within 2 months; paid 24.11.1440	sale of resin and paper to Iosep Xillac and Moyse Xunina, Palermitan Jews
29.9.1439 c. nn	Simone de Risignano	3 ounces	within 4 months; paid 2.12.1441	sale of Valencia cloth to Moyse Sacerdotu, a Jew of Palermo
29.9.1439 c. nn	Giovanni Caner	15.6.0 ounces	within 5 months	sale of Perpignan cloth to Brachuni Taguili, a Jew of Palermo; guarantor Iacob Taguili, another Jew
1.6.1439 c. nn	Berengario Carreris	33.18.0 ounces	within 4 months	sale of Catalan cloth to Salamon Maltisi, a Jew of Polizzi
2.6.1439 c. nn	Guglielmo Baroles	17.17.17 ounces	within 4 months, paid 29.11.1440	sale of deerskin to Iosep Curi, Sabeti Levi and Bulchayra Frisisa, Jews of Palermo
2.6.1439 c. nn	Gabriele Verneda and Benedetto Torquo	19.7.11 ounces	within 4 months	sale of deeerskin to Muxa Sacerdotu, Salamon de Missina and Xibiten Gilebi, Jews in Palermo
3.6.1439 c. nn	Georgio de Georgio	50.26.5 ounces	by June	loan to Zaccaria Achina, a Palermitan Jew
3.6.1439 c. nn	Georgio de Georgio	32 ducats	within 4 months; paid 1.6.1442	sale of breeches to Zaccaria Achina, a Jew of Palermo
3.6.1439 c. nn	Zullo de Gregori	5.6.0 ounces	by September; paid 29.10.1440	sale of Calabrian tables to Raffaele de Danieli, a Palermitan Jew
3.6.1439 c. nn	Gabriel Verneda	3.1.9 ounces	within 3 months; paid 3.7.1441	sale of cloth to Xibiten Gibel, a Jew of Palermo
7.6.1439 c. nn	Giovanni de Vinaya	48.13.0 ounces	paid 5.9.1441	sale of cinnamon and gold wire to Salamon Acaninu, a Jew of Messina

Source: ASP, Not. Guglielmo Mazzapiedi, reg. 841

Date and Page	Debtor	Amount	Reason	Remarks
31.7.14[..] c. nn	Iosep Turiot, a Jew of Palermo	4 ounces		creditor: Pietro de Frankis; paid
29.11.14[..] c. nn	Moyses Lu Medicu on behalf of Siminto de Muxarella. Palermitan Jews	8.12.0 ounces	sale of cloth	creditor: Paolo Saccu; paid after 4 months
2.10.14[..] c. nn	Sabet Taguili and Ysdrael Farachi, Palermitan Jews	10 ounces	business transaction	creditor: Vita Sacerdotu, a Jew of Termini; paid at the end of a year

Date and Page	Lender or Seller	Amount	Payment	Remarks
4.3.1436 c. 250v	Filippo Almareki	2.26.0 ounces	within 2 months	sale of deerskin to Nachuni Milecta, a Jew of Mazara
4.3.1436 c. 251r	Baptista Aglata	41.27.17 ounces	within 6 months; paid 21.8.1436	sale of Florentine cloth to Elya Cuyno, a Jew of Trapani
4.3.1436 c. 253r	Bartholomeo Formiga	10 ounces	within 4 months; paid 6.6.1437	sale of Catalan cloth to Muxa de Musticu, a Jew of Monte San Giuliano
5.3.1436 c. 257r	Baldassare de [Casasaya]	13.6.0 ounces the quintal	3 instalments: 1.6., 1.10., 1.2	sale of sugar to Xua and Siminto Aurifichi, Jews of Palermo
8.3.1436 c. 264r	Benedetto Torquo	5 ounces	within 4 months	sale of cloth to Busacca Misiria, a Jew in Palermo

6292

8.3.1436 c. 267v	Bartholomeo de Rau	20.24.0 ounces	by June; paid 1.7.1436	sale of Barcelona cloth to Rubino de Muxarella, a Jew of Marsala
12.3.1436 c. 274v	Battista Aglata	9.16.3 ounces	within 6 months; paid 22.4.1437	sale of indigo to Manuel Daram, a Jew of Sciacca
12.3.1436 c. 275v	Peri Traval	1.12.0 ounces	by April	sale of cloth to Mayr Chassini, a Jew of Nicosia
13.3.1436 c. 276v	Bartholomeo Fortugno	24.21.0 ounces	within 4 months	sale of Barcelona cloth to Mayr Chassini, a Jew of Nicosia
13.3.1436 c. 278r	Filippo Alvaru	4.15.0 ounces	paid 26.11.1436	sale of deerskin to Chamuni de Chaulu, Iosep Marzucu and Raffael Gazella, Jews of Mazara
14.3.1436 c. 284r	Nicolò de Bononia	1 ounce	by 15.4	sale of cloth to Salamon Minixi, a Palermitan Jew
14.3.1436 c. 286v	Raynerio de Casale	4 ounces	by April; paid 2.5.1436	sale of oil to Challufu Coynu, a Jew of Palermo
14.3.1436 c. 287v	Guglielmo Scales	13 ounces	by August; paid 6.5.1436	sale of goods to Honorato de Gauyu, a Jew of Palermo
14.3.1436 c. 288v	[Simon] and Raynerio de Risignano	9 ounces	within 4 months	sale of cloth to Brachono Taguili, a Palermitan Jew
15.3.1436 c. 292r	Battista Aglata	39 ounces	instalments	sale of indigo to Donato Daram, a Jew in Palermo
24.5.1436 c. nn	Iacobo Vernagallu	3.28.0 ounces	by August	sale of iron to Merdoc and Nixim Gilebi, Palermitan Jews

24.5.1436 c. nn	Iacobo Vernagallu	2.28.0 ounces	by August	sale of iron to Vegnamin de Girachio, a Jew in Palermo
[..]6.1436 c. nn	Simone de Caligis	2.22.10 ounces	within 4 months	sale of iron to Leone de Medico, Benedetto Chaseni and Fariono de Medico, Jew of Palermo
3.9.[1436] c. nn	Antonio de Tinirello	4 ounces	by 15.10; paid 29.10.1436	sale of ox leather to Chamuni, a Jew of Paola in Calabria
30.10.[1436] c. nn	Leone Maltisi, a Jewish physician in Polizzi	39 ounces	paid	sale of wheat and barley to Donato de Salamone, a Jew in Termini Imerese
2.12.[1436] c. 62v	Nicolò de Maniscalco	1 ounce	by March	sale of oil to Sufeni [..], a Palermitan Jew
9.12.[1436] c. 69r	Iacobo de Blanco	1.16.0 ounces	within 4 months	sale of wine to Sabet de Azaro, a Palermitan Jew
16.12.[1436] c. 70r	Bartholomeo de Navel	3.6.0 ounces	within 4 months	sale of cloth to Brachono Taguili, a Palermitan Jew
21.1.[1437] c. 344r	Baldassare Bonconte	4 ounces	within 1 month	sale of goods to Brachono de Medico and Pichono de Vita, Palermitan Jews
19.3.[1437] c. nn	Bernardo Flexantis	10.24.10 ounces	within 4 months;	sale of corals to Nixim Binna, a Jew in Palermo
14.6.[1436] c. nn	Galcerano de Aquilo	5.3.0 ounces	within 5 months	sale of wheat to Vita Azar, a Palermitan Jew
[...] c. nn	Yaymo [..]	2.15.0 ounces	within 6 months	sale of cloth to Leone de Medico, a Jew in Palermo
12.12.14[36] c. nn	Andrea Gentili	5.8.0 ounces	within 4 months	sale of gold wire to Gauyu de Malta, a Jew of Messina

6294

29.5.14[..] c. nn	Benedetto Torquo	1.24.0 ounces	within 3 months	sale of cloth to Iosep de Tripuli and Busacca Medui, Jews of Palermo
29.5.14[..] c. nn	Benedetto Torquo	3.25.0 ounces	within 4 months	sale of deerskin to Bulchayra de Benedicto and Strugu Damiranu, Jews of Marsala
31.5.14[..] c. nn	Benedetto Torquo	2 ounces	within 3 months	sale of cloth to Iosep Abudaram, a Palermitan Jew
5.4.14[..] c. nn	Beninato de Belpuchi	2 ounces	within 2 months	sale of spun cotton to Elia de Missina, a Palermitan Jew
2.4.14[..] c. nn	Bernardu Curtu	27.6.0 ounces	by September	sale of goods to Salomon de Messina, a Jew of Palermo
26.1.14[..] c. nn	Baldassare de Bonconte	1.18.0 ounces	paid 7.4	sale of cloth to Elia Nixim, a Jew of Palermo
[....] c. nn	Alfonso Vagugles	4.24.0 ounces		sale of Barcelona cloth to Iosep Abudaram, a Jew of Palermo
30.12.14[..] c. nn	Guglielmo Fabre	11 ounces	within 4 months; paid 26.8	sale of tables to Merdoc Sillac and Vita Azar, Palermitan Jews
19.1.14[..] c. nn	Chirello Friolo	18.15 *tarì*	10 *tarì* on account, balance later	sale of *disa* to Busacca de Tripuli, a Jew of Palermo
18.11.14[..] c. nn	Agostino de Latorina	1.24.0 ounces	within 3 months	sale of honey to Elia de Benedicto, a Palermitan Jew
22.1.14[..] c. nn	Simone de Risignano	13.8.0 ounces	within 4 months	sale of cloth to Muxa Xillemi, a Jew of Sciacca

[....] c. nn	Antonio de Crapona	5 ounces	within 4 months	sale of goods to Nixim Alurutu, a Jew in Palermo
[....] c. nn	Sabet Gilebi, a Palermitan Jew	1.15.10 ounces	within 2 months; paid 4.1	sale of ox leather
17.9.[..] c. nn	Paolo Samer	30.6.0 ounces	within 4 months; paid 15.10	sale of Catalan cloth to Donato Genni, a Jew of Nicosia
13.6.[..] c. nn	Pietro de Gaetano and Antonio de Settimo	10 ounces	within 2 months	sale of goods to Saduni de Lu Medicu, a Jew of Palermo
25.10.[..] c. nn	Martino Poalles	15 ounces	7.15.0 ounces by November, balance by June	sale of cloth to Raffael Lu Presti, a Jew of Sciacca
2.5.[..] c. nn	Filippo de Almariki	11.10.0 ounces	within 4 months; paid 2.12	sale of deerskin to Muxa Sacerdotu and Xibiten Gibel, Palermitan Jews
[....] c. nn	Giovanni de Vinaya	15.7.10 ounces	within 4 months	sale of gold thread to David Magaseni, a Jew of Messina
2.3.[..] c. nn	Francesco Marter	7.15.0 ounces	within 4 months; paid 12.3	sale of deerskin to Merdoc Farachi, a Jew of Palermo
[....] c. nn	Peri Catalano	11.12.0 ounces the quintal	within 6 months	sale of deerskin to Muxa Sacerdotu, Robino Gibra, Musutu Binna, Xibiten Gibay and Salamon de Missina, Jews of Palermo
17.2.[..] c. nn	Gabriele Verneda	35.15.0 ounces	within 4 months	sale of goods to Minto de Muxarella, a Jew of Marsala
17.2.[..] c. nn	Gabriele Verneda	2.15.0 ounces	within 4 months	sale of leather to Charuni Sacerdoto, a Palermitan Jew
17.2.[..] c. nn	Benedetto Agleri	25.18.0 ounces	within 8 months	sale of goods to Minto de Muxarella, a Jew of Marsala

17.2.[..] c. nn	Baldassare C[asa]	8.24.0 ounces	within 4 months	sale of Catalan cloth to Xibiten de Iona, a Jew of Alcamo
18.2.[..] c. nn	Benedetto Torquo and Gabriele Verneda	10.22.6 ounces	within 4 months; paid 22.3	sale of deerskin to Muxa Sacerdotu, Salamon de Vanni de Messina and Faryono Nifusi, Palermitan Jews
19.2.[..] c. nn	Simone de Risignano	37 ounces	within 6 months	sale of Florentine cloth to Xibiten de Iona, a Jew of Palermo
19.2.[..] c. nn	Giovanni Bonetta	2 ounces	1 ounce on account	sale of grapes to Gallufu Taguili, a Jew in Palermo
22.2.[..] c. nn	Minto de Muxarella, a Jew of Marsala	41.9.0 ounces	within 4 months; paid 18.1	sale of Catalan cloth
22.2.[..] c. nn	Guglielmo Bardes	25.8 ounces	within 4 months	sale of cloth to Muxa Cassuni and Azaruni Xikeri, Jews in Nicosia
23.2.[..] c. nn	Thomeo de Magistro Antonio	6.28.0 ounces	by July; paid 18.7	sale of oil to Xibiten de Minnichi, a Palermitan Jew
23.2.[..] c. nn	Gerardo Aglata	2.27.0 ounces	within 4 months	sale of gold wire to Muxa Sacerdotu, a Palermitan Jew
23.2.[..] c. nn	Antonio Alu	7.1.6 ounces	within 4 months; paid 13.8	sale of cloth to Abram de Portugammo, a Palermitan Jew
24.2.[..] c. nn	Baldassare Casa	3.7.10 ounces	paid 19.7	sale of goods to Xibiten Gibel, a Jew of Palermo

3.12.1441 c. nn	Pachio Russo	2 ounces	within 5 months	sale of Pisan iron to Muxa and David Alluxu, Palermitan Jews
3.12.1441 c. nn	Lorenzo de Laurencio	3.15.0 ounces	within 4 months; paid 31.8	sale of spun cotton to Isac Machagui, a Jew of Palermo
28.2.1442 c. nn	Adinolfo de Fornaris	2.24.0 ounces	within 4 months; paid 24.6	sale of gold wire to Raffaele de Danieli, a Jew in Palermo
1.3.1442 c. nn	Peri Amar	20.27.17 ounces	within 4 months; paid 24.11	sale of cloth to Iosep Abudaram, a Jew in Palermo
2.3.1442 c. nn	Benedetto Villar	2.19.0 ounces	within 4 months	sale of iron to Faryunu de Liuzo, a Jew of Palermo
2.3.1442 c. nn	Giovanni Lanza	7.6.8 ounces	within 4 months; paid 11.8	sale of goods to Muxa Sacerdotu, a Palermitan Jew
12.3.1442 c. nn	Battista Aglata	9.16.0 ounces	within 4 months	sale of indigo to Manuel Daram, a Jew in Sciacca
27.6.14[..] c. nn	Benedetto Villar	4.15.0 ounces	monthly instalments	sale of iron to Brachuni Panichellu, a Palermitan Jew
5.11.14[..] c. nn	Baldassare de Grillo	23.29.5 ounces	within 4 months	sale of Valencia wool to Naten de Manikettulu, a Jew in Marsala
5.4.14[..] c. nn	Raffaele Carrega	112.0 ounces	within 1 month	sale of gold wire to Iosep Cariot, a Palermitan Jew
5.9.14[..] c. nn	Calzarono de Aquilo	2.2.13 ounces	within 4 months	sale of cloth to Simon Benassay, a Jew in Palermo
18.2.14[..] c. nn	Benedetto de Villafranca	1 ounce	within 6 months; paid 28.1	sale of oil to Vita Rugila, a Palermitan Jew

Not. Domenico Aprea

Palermo, 2 November 1418

Source: ASP, Not. Domenico Aprea, reg. 797, c. 11r.

Gallufus Binna and Nixim Missiria, Jewish masons and citizens of Palermo, promise Carlo Sprenerio, a merchant, their fellow citizen, to build a wall in his tavern situated in the Cassaro in the Piazza Marmorea. They are to begin work when David Sicundi, another Jew, finishes his work in the building. They are to be paid 1.10 tarì *a day.*

Palermo, 3 November 1418

Source: ASP, Not. Domenico Aprea, reg. 797, c. 11r-v.

Contract whereby Antonio Cullura, a Palermitan citizen, promises to supply to the merchant Busacha Xacarono, his Jewish fellow citizen, black grapes from his vineyard in the contrada *Faxineri, to be delivered at the next vintage time, for 1.6.0 ounces paid on the spot.*

Palermo, 10 November 1418

Source: ASP, Not. Domenico Aprea, reg. 797, cc. 15v–16r.

Agreement whereby Barchianus saracinus, *a Jewish citizen of Palermo, hires himself out to Salamonello de Medico, his Jewish fellow citizen, to grind the sugar cane and* gididas *in Salamonello's sugar refinery during the entire season. His salary is to be one ounce a month. He is paid 15* tarì *on account.*

Note: *Saracinus* is perhaps a curtain maker/merchant.

Palermo, 15 November 1418

Source: ASP, Not. Domenico Aprea, reg. 797, c. 18v.

Deed of sale whereby Roberto Garuni, a Palermitan citizen, sold Sabet Cuyno, miller (centimularius), *his Jewish fellow citizen, two* salme *of salt,* salis macinati, boni, utili, mercantibilis ac receptibilis et necti, *for 8.10* tarì *the* salma. *Sabet pays on the spot and Roberto undertakes to make delivery at Sabet's warehouse in Palermo.*

Palermo, 15 November 1418

Source: ASP, Not. Domenico Aprea, reg. 797, cc. 18v–19r.

Agreement whereby Salamon Suffer, a Jewish citizen of Palermo, hires himself out to Salamonello de Medico, his Jewish fellow citizen, to fill sacks together with two fellow workers with the sugar from four presses belonging to Salamonello. The work is to last the entire sugar pressing season for four ounces a month. Salamon is paid one ounce on account.

Palermo, 23 November 1418

Source: ASP, Not. Domenico Aprea, reg. 797, c. 22r.

Contract whereby master Manuel Verru, a Jewish mason and citizen of Palermo, promises canon Raynaldo de Buxia, his fellow citizen, to build six pillars and cover the floor tiles in the canon's house for 20 tarì. *He is paid 14* tarì *on account.*

Palermo, 23 November 1418

Source: ASP, Not. Domenico Aprea, reg. 797, c. 27v.

Deed of sale whereby Vita de Provenza, a citizen of Palermo, sold Muxa de Bulgiti, a Palermitan Jew, some white grapes for 1.18.0 ounces. Muxa paid 18 tarì *on account and promised to pay the balance on delivery.*

Palermo, 23 November 1418

Source: ASP, Not. Domenico Aprea, reg. 797, c. 27r.

Sadono de Tripoli, a Jew of Syracuse, hired himself out to Salamonello de Medico, a Palermitan Jew, to grind the sugar cane and gididas *in his sugar refinery during the entire season for one ounce a month. Sadono is paid 2.10* tarì *on account.*

Sicily

Palermo, 23 November 1418

Source: ASP, Not. Domenico Aprea, reg. 797, c. 28r.

Agreement whereby Iacu Ferru, the Jewish messenger of the prothi *of the Jewish community in Palermo, hires himself out to Salamonello de Medico, a Palermitan Jew, to work in Salamonello's sugar refinery during the entire season for one ounce a month.*

Palermo, 28 November 1418

Source: ASP, Not. Domenico Aprea, reg. 797, c. 37r.

Contract whereby Dominico de Busicta, servitor of the pretura *in Palermo, promises Zaccono Minzel, the Jewish collector of the taxes imposed by the Jewish community in Palermo, to distrain twice a week for a year those Jews who owe taxes and other payments to the community. He is empowered to imprison defaulters. He is to be paid one ounce in three instalments. Subsequently Busicta is replaced by another servitor of the* Corte Pretoriana.

Palermo, 4 September 1420

Source: ASP, Not. Domenico Aprea, reg. 797, c. 44v.

Lease whereby Gallufo Cuyno, acting for Master Moyse Chetibi, a Jewish physician in Palermo, secretary of the Jewish "church", i.e., synagogue in Palermo, lets Manfrido de Bonsaldo and Antonio Paganello a ruin or empty lot (hirbam seu terram vacuam), *inside the area of the synagogue, for one ounce annually for two years.*

Bibliography: Bresc, *Arabi*, p. 264, and n. 1270.

Palermo, 16 August 1420

Source: ASP, Not. Domenico Aprea, reg. 797bis, c. nn.

Last will and testament of Abram Safert of Aragon, a Jewish inhabitant of Palermo. He makes Donato Aben Azara, a Jewish citizen of Palermo, his universal heir, and provides for setting up a charitable fund with a capital of ten ounces or a revenue of one ounce. The proceeds are to be distributed to the poor by the chief sacristan of the Jewish community. Failing that, he makes other provisions for the distribution of that amount.

XVI mensis Augusti

Abraam Safert, Iudeus de Aragona, h[abitator] P[anormi], sanus per[!] Dei gracia corpore et mente et proprie racionis bene compos, timens divinum iudicium repentinum et casum humane fragilitatis, cum nihil certior morte et nihil incertius die mortis, volens bonis suis salubriter providere, suum presens nuncupativum condidit testamentum, cassatis prius per eum omnibus testamentis atque codicillis per eum anterius condidit atque factis, preter presens quod voluit omnimodo obtineri roboris firmitatem.

In primis quidem dictus testator suum heredem universalem instituit Donatum Aben Azara, Iudeum civem Panormi, super omnibus bonis suis mobilibus, pecunis, iuribus et actionibus quibuscumque solutis in legatis et dispositionibus infrascriptis.

Item voluit idem testator quod in sussidium sue anime ematur per eius heredem possessum una pro unciis decem, seu directum dominium et proprietatem uncia unius, que possessio sive directum dominium ematur infra tempus anni unius ad alcuis[!] post mortem testatoris in antea, quod redditus dicte possessionis recollegi debeat per maiorem sacristanum muskite Iudeorum anno quolibet et in perpetuum, et sic de anno in annum dictis venditis detur pauperibus per manus sacristani maioris et per manus dicti sui heredis et successorum suorum, et hoc fieri debeat semper in vigilia sabati sabatorum in ora vespertina et ante portam dicti testatoris habitacionis in qua suum diem claudet extremum, pacto quod si in premissis vel aliquo premissorum contrafacti seu contraventi fuerint, quod eo casu incontinenti dictus eius heres vendi debeat supradictam possessionem, seu directum dominium et ponere debeat pecuniam in banco tuto quod stare debeant per annos duos. Et si infra dictum tempus dictorum duorum annorum aliquis compareret consanguineus testatoris, voluit idem testator quod tradantur tali consanguineo dicti testatoris dictam pecuniam in banco positam. Et si nullus infra eundem tempus consanguineus compareret quod unquam stent in banco per unum alium annum ad opus alicuius Iudei supervenientis per annum retemptum super aliqua galea de nactione Aragone pro eius recaptu Panormum superveniente, et casu quo spireretur annus et nullus compareret, voluit idem testator et sic dat ex nunc pro tunc, auctoritate dicti sui heredis, quod de banco capi debeat dictas pecunias et illas, prout eius discreptione, dare debeat pauperibus pro anima dicti testatoris. Et hec est eius ultima voluntas et ultimum testamentum, et si iure testamenti non valeret, valere voluit iure codicillorum, et si iure codicillorum non valeret, valeat pro omni iure quo melius valere.

6302

Sicily

Testes: Pater Iohannes de Manganerio, Antonius de Manganerio, Bernardus de Aflicto, magister Petrus de Scarello.

Bibliography: Bresc, *Monde Méditerranéen*, p. 634, n. 261; Id., *Arabi*, p. 134, dates the Doc. 1450 and sets the amount mentioned at 100 ounces.

Palermo, 26 September 1420

Source: ASP, Not. Domenico Aprea, reg. 797, c. 56r.

Notarial protest by Nixim Xor, a Jewish citizen of Palermo, against Iacob de Termini, his Jewish fellow citizen, his partner in a shoemaker's shop. The partnership had taken loans from various parties. They had repaid one Guglielmo de Tricocta four ounces, only half of which were supposed to have been paid by Nixim. Nixim demands an accounting.

Palermo, 17 October 1420

Source: ASP, Not. Domenico Aprea, reg. 797, c. 75r.

Agreement whereby master Manuel de Minaham, a Jewish cobbler and citizen of Palermo, hires himself out to master Friderico de Bernardo, his fellow citizen, to sole shoes until the following October for one salma *and eight* tumuli *of wheat from the the new harvest to be delivered by July.*

Source: ASP, Not. Domenico Aprea, reg. 797

Date and Page	Principal	Attorney	Purpose	Remarks
30.10.1418 c. 9v	Maribinis Sullemi, a Jew in Messina	Xamuele Sacerdote, a Jew in Palermo	collection of outstandig debts in Palermo	
5.9.1420 c. 45v	Sabet Cusintini, a Palermitan Jew	Simone de Craparia	collection of all debts owed by tenants	

11.10.1420 c. 63r	Gaudio de Anello, a Palermitan Jew	Giovanni Pontecorona	collection from Iacobo de Mayda former servitor of Pontecorona of the silver objects pawned with him
11.10.1420 c. 63r	Sabet Cusintino, a Jew of Palermo	Giovanni de Oliverio, notary	collection of debts owed him in Alcamo
11.10.1420 c. 63r	Sabet Cusintino, a Jew of Palermo	Giovanni de Oliverio, notary	Collection of debts owed him in Alcamo, including Bracha and Chaym de Sacerdoto

Date and Page	Debtor	Amount	Reason	Remarks
20.10.1418 c. 1r	Vannes Caveta	¼ quintal of grapes	for grapes	creditor: Michilono Minaham
20.10.1418 c. 1v	Nicolò di Castrogiovanni	1½ quintals of grapes	for grapes	creditor: Busacca Xacharono, a Palermitan Jew
21.10.1418 c. 2r	Donna Magna, wife of Raimondo de Suneti	1.15.0 ounces	for grapes	creditor: Conino Sabuchi, a Jew
13.12.1418 c. 41v	Salamonello and Moyses de Medico, Palermitan Jews	50 ounces		creditors: Matheo Buchetta and Symon de Medico, a Jew
[..].9.1420 c. 43r	Cristoforo Petarius	3.14.0 ounces	earnings of a cattle farm	creditors: Gallufu Cuynu acting for Moyse Chetibi, Palermitan Jew, to be paid within 3 months

Date and Page	Lender or Seller	Amount	Payment	Remarks
4.9.1420 c. 44r	Palmerio Massario	27 *tarì*	earnings of a cattle farm	Galluffu Cuynu acting for Moyse Chetibi and Symon de Medico, Palermitan Jews, to be paid by the end of the month
[..].10.1420 c. 63r	Gaudio di Anello, a Palermitan Jew	1.4.0 ounces		creditor: Giovanni de Pontecorona
7.10.1420 c. 67v	Tommaso de Monteleone	a quintal of grapes	supply of grapes	creditor: Busacca Xacharono, a Palermitan Jew
15.10.1420 c. 74r	Sabet Gillebi, a Jew of Palermo	a quintal of grapes	supply of grapes	creditor: Angelo de Pagano
23.10.1420 c. 81v	Salamone de Minichi, a Jew in Palermo	7.21.0 ounces	unpaid rental	creditor: Iudas de Mineo, a Palermitan Jew, to be paid in annual instalments of 1 ounce
Date and Page	**Lender or Seller**	**Amount**	**Payment**	**Remarks**
25.10.1418 c. 5v	Andrea Pappe and Marco Yssela	1.7.0 ounces	paid 2.3.14.19	sale of silk from Calabria to Fariono Dachurono (?), a Palermitan Jew
27.10.1418 c. 6v	Antonio Speziario	6 ounces	3 ounces within 3 months, balance within another 6 months; paid 1.11.1419	sale of mule to Salamon de Minichi, a Palermitan Jew
30.10.1418 c. 9r	Ascarello de Sirio	21.10 *tarì*	monthly instalments of 5.7 *tarì*	sale of glass to David Sacerdoto, a Jew in Palermo
3.11.1418 c. 11r	Antonio Cullura	1.6.0 ounces	paid	sale of grapes to Busacca Xacharono, a Jew in Palermo

15.11.1418 c. 18v	Sabet Cuynu Sacedotu, a Palermitan Jew	17 *tarì*	paid	sale of ground salt
21.11.1418 c. 24v	Lucia de Apibus	6 ounces	2.12.0 ounces within a year, another 2.12.0 ounces within another year, balance within another 6 months	loan to Mardoc Mizoctus, a Palermitan Jew
21.11.1418 c. 25r	Lucia de Apibus	3 ounces	4 monthly instalments of 8 *tarì*	loan to Mardoc Mizoctus, a Palermitan Jew
28.11.1416 c. 35r	Giovanni Magru	1 ounce	paid	sale of grapes to Leone de Yudaica, a Palermitan Jew
9.12.1418 c. 39r	Matheo Cole	5.20.10 ounces	by April	sale of knives to Salamonello and Moyses de Medico, Palermitan Jews
12.12.1418 c. 41r	Graciano Naguay, a Jew of Trapani	5 ounces	by Easter	sale of Florentine cloth and iron wire to Elia Sala, a Jew of Trapani
[..].9.1420 c. 43r	Antonio de Cantore	2.6.0 ounces	1 ounce on delivery; 1.6.0 ounces by Christmas	sale of grapes to Gallufo Abramono, a Palermitan Jew
12.9.1420 c. 47v	Sabet Cusintino, a Jew of Palermo	2.10.0 ounces	within 4 months	sale of a mule
12.9.1420 c. 48r	Cola Sadoctu	24 *tarì* the quintal of black skins; 8 *tarì* the quintal of white skins	4 *tarì* on account; balance on delivery	sale of skins to Simone de Minichi, a Palermitan Jew
12.9.1420 c. 48r	Nicolò Gangio	15 *tarì*	paid 24.12.1420	sale of grapes to Xamuel Nixigueni, a Palermitan Jew

12.9.1420 c. 48r	Pietro Catania	1.12.0 ounces	paid 28.11.1420	sale of grapes to Salamon Suffer, a Jew of Palermo
17.9.1420 c. 51v	Suffen [...], a Jew in Palermo	18 *tarì*	paid with oil	sale of some goods
17.9.1420 c. 52v	Machono de Salemi	1.4.10 ounces	in 3 instalments at Christmas, Shrove-tide and Easter; paid 8.2.1422	sale of grapes to Ysdrael Strugu, a Palermitan Jew
17.9.1420 c. 60r	Machono de Salemi	1.3.0 ounces	in 3 instalments at Christmas, in January and at Easter; paid 8.5.1421	sale of grapes to Simon de Polizo, a Jew of Palermo
7.10.1420 c. 67r	Leone Barbutus, a Jew of Palermo	4 ounces	in 3 instalments in January, May and August; paid 1.10.1421	sale of a mule
7.10.1420 c. 67r	Antonio de Mineo	4 ounces	15 *tarì* on account, balance on delivery	sale of cork wood coal to master Ysdraeli, a Palermitan Jew
8.10.1420 c. 68r	Siri Iacob de Leonardo	2.12.0 ounces	at Easter; paid 12.4.1421	sale of grapes to Salamone Sarritano, a Jew of Palermo
19.10.1420 c. 76v	Salamon Suffer, a Palermitan Jew	22 *tarì*	by Lent	sale of a beast of burden
22.10.1420 c. 76v	Michael Lu Capu	2 ounces the kantar	1 ounce on account, another in January, and another in April; paid 21.41421	sale of grapes to Busacca Xacharono, a Palermitan Jew
22.10.1420 c. 80v	Sabet Gillebi, a Palermitan Jew			sale of grapes
23.10.1420 81r	Enrico Lombardo	1 ounce		sale of grapes to Vita Cathalano, a Jew in Palermo

25.10.1420 c. 83v	Iacob Medui, a Jew in Palermo	5.22.0 ounces		sale of grapes
25.10.1420 c. 84r	Salimbeni de Traina	1.20.0 ounces	18 *tarì* on account, balance on delivery	sale of grapes to Aron Taguil, a Palermitan Jew
29.10.1420 c. 85r	Syminto Aurefichi, a Jew of Palermo	35 *tarì*	within 4 months	sale of oil to Sabet Xammara, a Palermitan Jew
Date and Page	**Tenant**	**Location and Description**	**Rent and Duration**	**Remarks**
13.12.1418 c. 42r	Iosep Chetibi, a Jew of Palermo	Cassaro of Palermo, Piazza Marmorea, bordering on shop of Muxa Lisu and Sabet Dinar, Jews, and public road	shop; perpetual lease at 1.6.0 ounces a year	lanlord: Gallufu Cuynu, a Palermitan Jew, acting for Moyses Chetibi, another Jew
10.10.1420 c. 70v	Aron Taguil, a Palermitan Jew	Palermo, corner of *vanella* of S. Maria del Cancelliere, bordering on property of Iacob de Carascono, a Jew, shoemaker's of Emanuel, another Jew, other shops and the small house of Chaym Aczar, a Jew	house and shop; perpetual lease at 13 florins a year	and lady by Donna Salonia de Carascono, a Jewess

Not. Giacomo Maniscalco

Palermo, 18 October 1426

Source: ASP, Not. Giacomo Maniscalco, reg. 342, cc. 48r–49r.

Deed of sale whereby Ubertino de Rainaldo, a notary, sells to Zudu Nikiseuy [!], a Jewish citizen of Palermo, 43 casks of Jewish (i.e., kosher) new wine, at present in his tavern in the ruga *Balnei, in the Cassaro of Palermo. The price is 1.24.0 ounces a cask, to be paid in instalments as sales proceed. Fully paid by 22.8.1427.*

Bibliography: Bresc, *Arabi*, p. 70 and n. 318.

Palermo, 20 March 1427

Source: ASP, Not. Giacomo Maniscalco, reg. 342, c. 78v.

Salamon de Messana, Iosep Ammara, Zullus Markeki e Salamon Rugila, Jewish citizens of Palermo, promise Bundo de Campo to work as paratores *in his sugar refinery during the entire season for one ounce a month. They are paid four ounces on account by the bank of Giovanni de Abbatellis.*

Palermo, 27 March 1427

Source: ASP, Not. Giacomo Maniscalco, reg. 342, c. 81v.

Contract whereby Merdoc Calabrensi, a Jewish citizen of Palermo, acting for Ysolda, wife of Aloisio de Asta, and Xibite de Syragusa, his Jewish fellow citizen, set up a joint business venture. Ysolda, through Merdoc, invests four ounces. Xibite undertakes to travel in the country, to purchase leather and to sell it in Palermo. The profits are to be divided between the parties. The business is wound up on 8.3.1431.

Palermo, 24 April 1427

Source: ASP, Not. Giacomo Maniscalco, reg. 342, cc. 118v–119v.

Contract between Emanuele Xalla and Sabet Binna, Jewish citizens of Palermo, acting for his sister, in regard to the marriage between Emanuele and Sabet's sister, Gisa, widow of Brachono Binna, according to the custom and practice of the Jews in Palermo. The deed contains a list of the articles making up the dowry. Emanuele promises to maintain Xamuele Binna, Gisa's son, in his house.

Die XXIIII eiusdem Aprilis

Pro matrimonio contrahendo secundum morem et consuetudinem Iudeorum felicis urbis Panormi inter Emanuelem Xalla, Iudeum civem Panormi, sponsum ex una parte, et Sabet Binna, Iudeum eius concivem, contrahentem nomine et pro parte Gisie eius sororis, uxoris quondam Brachoni Binna, pro qua de rato promisit et ex altera prefatus Sabet nomine quo supra ac suo proprio et in solidum promisit et convenit eidem Manueli sponso presenti et ab eo soleniter stipulanti dare et tradere et integre assignare eidem Manueli in dotem, pro dote et nomine dote dicte eius sororis contemplacione ac decoratione matrimoni prelibati ad dictam consuetudinem nec non res et bona infrascripta, videlicet cultras duas albas unam magnam et aliam parvam, item paria duo lintheaminum alborum, item par unum lintheaminum de serico, item traverserium [washed out], item suttanas duas, item par unum cuxinellorum alborum, item mataracia duo burdi maltesi, item dublectos duos, item tobalias quatuor de tabola, duas de ramu et duas planas, item tobalias sex facie, item plomaccium unum de serico, item copertam unam de serico, item suyabuchi sex, item bacilia duo de here, item caldaria unam de here, item padellam unam, item mortarum unum de mitallo, item caxea una, item tangire unum de here, item bucalia duo de here, item cayulas quatuor albas cum rinchellis, item cayulam unam de serico et auro, item cayulam aliam de serico, item cayulam aliam de serico cum rinchellis, item faczolum unum cum auro, item faczolum unum album, item tobaliam unam albam magnam, item tobaliam unam de barba, item carpitas duas palnas[!] rubeas, item avanlectos duos, item tunicam unam de virti magnam, item tunicam unam de virti garofolatus, item clamis una de virti coloris pagonacii, item chammicias sex albas, item serchelum unum album ad ramu, nec non et uncias decem et octo pecunia numerata, de quibus presencialiter numerando idem Manuel recepit et habuit ab eodem Sabet uncias decem, reliquas vero ad complementum una cum arnesio extimando per eorum comunes amicos, ut est moris Iudeorum, hinc ad mensem unum proximum futurum; ac etiam tractare et curare ita taliter et cum effectu omni exceptionis iuris et facti remotorum, quod dicta Gisia in contracto supradicto capiet eundem Manuelem in suum maritum more

Iudeorum, et equo dictus Manuel promisit et convenit eidem Sabet nomine quo supra, et mihi notario publico ut persone publice vice et nomine ipsius Gisie absentis, sollemniter stipulantibus ipsam Gisiam in dicto contracto capere in sua uxore et cum ea dictum matrimonium contrahere, dictamque dotem regere et conservare, et in casu dissolucionis dicti matrimonii dotem predictam restituere et assignare eidem Gisie aut cui ius et casus dederit. Insuper dictus Emanuel dotavit eidem Gisie absenti, me predicto notario pro ea stipulanti, dare ei cortinam unam precii unciis novem; ac etiam promisit mihi predicto notario stipulanti vice et nomine Xamuelis Binna filii dicte Gise dum idem Xamuel stare voluit cum predicta eius matre dare ei comestionem et potu ac etiam calciora necessaria ad rationem de unciis duabus anno quolibet percipiendo, habendo per ipsum Manuelem de et super bonis dictis Xamuelis. Que omnia [empty space].

Et iuraverunt dicti contrahentes ad legem Moysi premissa servare.

Testes: Symon Calandrinus, Iacob de Bua et Gregorius de Pacti.

Palermo, 1 March 1429

Source: ASP, Not. Giacomo Maniscalco, reg. 342, c. 241r.

Deed of sale whereby Salamon Actuni, a Jewish citizen of Palermo, sells Muxa Rubeo, his Jewish fellow citizen, 653 pairs of soles for 3.16.0 ounces.

Palermo, 1 March 1429

Source: ASP, Not. Giacomo Maniscalco, reg. 342, c. 241r-v.

Contract whereby Brachono Misiria alias lu Russu, a Jewish builder (fabricator) *in Palermo, undertakes to build for master Gabriele Villanova a new one-storey house, four* canne *long and 2½* canne *wide. He is paid three* tarì *a* canna. *Building material is to be supplied by Gabriele.*

Palermo, [April, 1429]

Source: ASP, Not. Giacomo Maniscalco, reg. 342, c. 270r-v.

Zudu Markeki, a Jewish citizen of Palermo, hires himself out to Iuda Sivena, his Jewish fellow citizen, to sell wine in his tavern for 16.10 tarì *a month. He is to sell all the wine stored in Sivena's house.*

Palermo, [May, 1429]

Source: ASP, Not. Giacomo Maniscalco, reg. 342, c. 294r-v.

Master Muxa Millac, a Jewish citizen of Palermo, hires himself out to Federico Ventimiglia as builder (fabricator) *in Palermo and elsewhere for two* tarì *a day. The salary is to be deducted from a debt of seven ounces which Muxa owes Federico, at the rate of six* tarì *a week, starting the coming July. The brothers Bulchaira and Sabuc Millac, Jewish citizens of Palermo, act as guarantors for Muxa.*

Palermo, 20 July [1429]

Source: ASP, Not. Giacomo Maniscalco, reg. 342, c. 324r-v.

Deed whereby Iacob de Danieli, a Jewish citizen of Palermo, cedes to Matheo de Asmari his rights towards Giovanni Perriconi, a Catalan merchant, and his brother, Giovanni de Arens. These amount to 3.6.0 ounces, less 1.6.0 ounces paid previously.

Palermo, 9 August, [1429]

Source: ASP, Not. Giacomo Maniscalco, reg. 342, c. 334r-v.

Iosep Spagnolo, a Jew, hires himself out to Antonio d'Arpino as builder for 10 grana *a day.*

Palermo, 18 February, [1432]

Source: ASP, Not. Giacomo Maniscalco, reg. 342, c. 384r-v.

Contract whereby Salamon Xammara and Leone Cuchello, Jews, promise Bundo de Campo to carry out the following work for four days: incidere, eligere totam illam quantitatem plantaminis gitidarum, arroiarum et callonorum *on Bundo's sugar plantations in Palermo and outside. They are paid eight* tarì *a thousand* casellarum plantaminis gitidarum ad colpi XVI pro casella et calloczu octu per colpu *and 15* tarì *a thousand* casellarum plantaminis callonum a colpi XVIII pro casella et callozcu dechi per colpu. *They receive one ounce on account. Bundo undertakes to supply the tools:* chippum et gladium.

6312

Sicily

Palermo, 7 July, [1432]

Source: ASP, Not. Giacomo Maniscalco, reg. 342, c. 424r.

Charono Rubeo (Rosso), a Jewish citizen of Palermo, lodges a notarial protest against Iacobo Xunina, his Jewish fellow citizen [empty space].

Palermo, 24 January, [1441]

Source: ASP, Not. Giacomo Maniscalco, reg. 342, cc. 477r–478r.

Agreement between the monastery of the Magione in Palermo and Musuda, widow of Nixim Skinellu, and Xua Marchilli, her nephew, Palermitan Jews. Musuda gives up the courtyard houses she holds in perpetual lease from the monastery, since she is no longer able to pay the annual rent of two ounces and carry out the necessary repairs. The monastery promises to lease the property to Xua on the same terms.

Palermo, 22 March, [1441]

Source: ASP, Not. Giacomo Maniscalco, reg. 342, cc. 493v–494r.

Agreement between the monastery of the Magione and Rosa, widow of Sabet Cusintino, a Palermitan Jewess. Rosa gives up the perpetual lease she holds from the monastery of a tavern in the Cassaro, bordering on the house of Gallufu Coyno, [a Jew], and on a courtyard belonging to the monastery. She can no longer afford to pay for the improvements which she undertook to carry out under the terms of the lease.

Palermo, 13 December, [1441]

Source: ASP, Not. Giacomo Maniscalco, reg. 342, cc. 584v–587v.

Inventory of the estate of the late Minto Allul, at the request of his widow Stera. When on his deathbed, he had made her his univresal heir, and had instructed Benedetto de Girachio, Jewish notary, to implement his last will. The purpose of the present deed is to safeguard her rights from other claims on the estate, including those of creditors. The estate includes a solerata *house in Salemi bringing in 12* tarì *in rent, and chattels, including five Hebrew books on parchment, and some iron tools, including arms.*

Bibliography: Bresc, *Arabi*, p. 156, and n. 741, who describes Minto as carpenter.

Palermo, 20 June, [1442]

Source: ASP, Not. Giacomo Maniscalco, reg. 342, cc. 617r–618r.

The corte Pretoriana *orders Iosebet, widow of the late Busacca Medui, a Jewish citizen of Palermo, who had died intestate, to inventory her late husband's property. This is to be done in the interest of Xua, their minor son. Benedetto Axeni and Salamon Levi, their Jewish fellow citizens, are charged with the task. There follows the inventory, consisting mainly of household goods and clothing. There is also a credit of 16 ounces with Iosep de Tripoli, another Jew.*

Die XX eiusdem Iunii

Notum facimus et testamur quod cum Busac Medui Iudeus c. P. mortus fuisset ab intestato, relicto et superstito sibi Xua eius filio maior nato ex se et Iosebet eius uxore, quod Iosebet tamquam mater et tutrix ipsius Xue infra legitima tempora a iure statuta inventarium sollemne bonorum remanentium post ipsius quondam Busacce mortem minime fecisset in ipsius pupilli maxime dampnum, preiudicium et interesse; propter quod de ex parte dicti pupilli fuisset in regie curie preture f.u.P. petitum dictum pupillum tamquam minoris inlesum restituit confectionem dicti inventarii, qua peticione per eadem curie tamquam infra admissa constito sibi de maiori etate ipsius Xue dictum Xuam ad confectionem dicti inventarii restituisset, prout in quadam cedula in antea ipsius redapta die XVIIIIº instantis latius contineri. Nunc vero die pretitulato dicta Iosebet tamquam mater et tutrix ipsius Xue vigore et auctoritate cedule supradicte volens dicto Xue hereditate et benis paternis immiscere non inconsulte sed cum beneficio inventarii ne forte ultra vires hereditarias creditoribus dicti quondam Busacce de suo proprio teneretur, vocatis prius in curie predicta ut constitit et in domo dicti quondam Busacce eius creditoribus etiam conpentibus loco quorum assumptis Benedicto Axeni et Salamon Levi, Iudeis civibus dicte urbis Panormi, utique ydoneis et dictum defunctum cognoscentibus, in presencia [..] Antonius de Surrerius, iudicis dicte urbis hinc et ei pro tribunali sedenti in sua iudiciaria auctoritate, prestans Dei nomine pro ipsa tutrix invocato omni propterea malignitate sublata, presens inventarium seu repertorium bonorum remanentium post ipsius quondam Busacce mortem in hunc modum facere procuravit, in quo quidem inventario dicta Iosebet tutrix dixit et confessa extitit invenisse bona infrascripta, videlicet:

In primis cultram unam albam veterem allupinellu, item mensalia duo usitata, item tobaleas quatuor de facie, item tobaleas tres de serico,

item guardanappos duos, item par unum lintheaminum alborum de serico usitatum, item paria duo lintheaminum alborum usitatorum, item interulam unam albam usitatam cum maniciis [..istans], item copertam unam de perthia cum listis de serico, item guardanappos septem, item tobaleam unam de serico pro confetis, item dublectum unum veterum, item guarnachia unam de ianzillocto, item cuxinellos tres de serico, item cuxinellos tres de relaaiva [!], item thunicas duas traversiata de serico, item mataracia duo de purpurigno usitata, item traversaria duo unum xilandratum et aliud purpurignum, item bucalia quatuor, item stagnatellas quatuor de piltro usitatas, item bacilia duo parva, item mortarium unum parvum de mitallo, item caldariam unam [..], item padellam unam, item cayulam unam de auro, item cayulam una de serico cum ysmalta, item sang[.]nam unam traversiatam de serico, item chanacam unam de parnis et iohenis, item anulos tres de argento, item vegetes quatuor vacuas, item caratellos duos, item bacilem unum veteri, item tenam unam capacitatem dimidii [..], item apparatorium unum pro vini, item panes LXXXXIII saponis, item marczapani unum vacuum, item marczapani duo cum preipe, item carpitam unam usitatam, item clamidem unam muliebre de persona usitate coloris bruni, item togam unam muliebrem de Florencia usitata coloris rosati, item tunicam unam marem de Gabillino usitatam, item vegetem unam cum dimidia plenam vino, item cannam unam palmum unum de fustayno, item certam quantitatem taxillorum valoris tr. trium, item recipere debeat a Iosep de Tripuli uncias XVI et tr. [empty space], item habuisse tr. XXIIII pro precio certarum ollarum de terra et coclararum venditarum pro ipsa tutricem, item tr. XV quos ipsa tutrix habuit a quoddam Iudeo [..], item tr. octo quos habuit pro pretio unie caxie vendite pro ipsa tutrice, item tr. XVIII quos habuit a Iosep de Tripuli, item tr. duos et gr. X quos habuit pro pretio certe quantitatis char[..], item tr. XV quos habuit pro precio miliariorum novem venditorum per ipsa tutrice [empty space].
Testes: Iohannes de Virmiglia, Antonius de Napoli, Baldassar Calandra.

Palermo, 25 July, [1442]

Source: ASP, Not. Giacomo Maniscalco, reg. 342, c. 640r.

Brachono Xunina, a Jewish citizen of Palermo, lodges a protest against the Jewish notary in Palermo, Benedetto de Girachio, because he is alleged to have failed to summon master Moyse de Gaudio, another Jew, in the criminal case brought by Brachono against Leone Romano [a Jew] and his wife.

Source: ASP, Not. Giacomo Maniscalco, reg. 342

Date and Page	Principal	Attorney	Purpose	Remarks
19.12.1441 c. nn	Stera, widow of master Minto Allul, a Jewess of Palermo	Ayeti Ganuchu, a Jew of Palermo	general power of attorney	

Date and Page	Lender or Seller	Amount	Payment	Remarks
25.9.1426 c. nn	Aloisio de Ast	1.5.0 ounces	within 6 months	sale of merchandise to Nixim Xalom, a Palermitan Jew
26.9.1426 c. nn	Aloisio de Ast	1.5.0 ounces	within 6 months	sale of goods to Sufen Romano and Profucio de Moise, Jews in Palermo
1.10.1426 c. nn	Simon Benassai, a Palermitan Jew	2 ounces	monthly instalments of 6 *tarì*	sale of goods
1.10.1426 c. 24v	Antonio de Taranto	1.2.0 ounces	17 *tarì* on account, balance on delivery	sale of merchandise to Isdrael Medui, a Palermitan Jew
10.10.1426 c. 40r	Giovanni de Boichello	1.15.0 ounces	within 4 months	sale of goods. Chayrona, widow of Nixim Medui, a Jewess, stands surety
11.3.1427 c. 103v	Sadia Isac, a Palermitan Jew	2 ounces	paid	sale of goods
[..].3.1427 c. nn	Aloisio de Ast	2.10.16 ounces	by August	sale of goods to Salamon Sofer and Xanono Calabrensis, Palermitan Jews
21.5.1427 c. nn	Sabet Dinar, a Jew	1.18.0 ounces	within 7 months	Ughetto de Gimbesio owes the sum on account of an inheritance

Date and Place	Tenant	Location and Description	Rent and Duration	Remarks
10.10.1427	Symon Xalom, a Jew	1 ounce	5 *tarì* on account, half the balance by Christmas, the other at Carnival time	sale of goods
11.1.1429 c. nn	Giovanni de Dundideo	2 ounces	within 2 months	sale of goods to Musutu Brixa, a Palermitan Jew
25.2.1429 c. nn	Leone Barberio	1 ounce	15 *tarì* on account, balance on delivery	sale of goods to Nixim Xalom, a Palermitan Jew
1.3.1429 c. nn	Muxa Rubeo, a Jew	3.16.0 ounces	weekly instalments of 15 *tarì* starting the first week of Easter	sale of goods to Salamon Actuni and Vita [...], Jews
14.9.1440 c. nn	Busac de Tripuli, a Jew of Palermo	half a quintal of grapes	at vintage time	in exchange for a colt
2.12.1440 c. nn	Ubertino de Costa	1.15.0 ounces	paid	sale of goods to Merdoc Gaczu and Brachono Ammirano, Jews of Palermo
30.12.1440 c. nn	Masio de Zamparrono	22.5 florins	2.9.0 ounces on account, balance on demand	sale of goods to Nissim Serretanu, a Jew of Palermo
11.1.1441 c. nn	Aloisio de Campo	1.14.0 ounces	monthly instalments of 4 *tarì*	sale of goods to Muxa Minachem. Bracha, Muxa's father, stands surety
Date and Place	**Tenant**	**Location and Description**	**Rent and Duration**	**Remarks**
12.10.1426 c. nn	Iacob Sabatinu, a Palermitan Jew	*Contrada* Lactarini in Palermo, bordering on the shop of the landlord and others; shop	1.14.0 ounces annually for 5 years	landlord: Michilono Xunina, a Palermitan Jew

Bibliography: Bresc, *Arabi*, pp. 114, 328, n. 596

Not. Giacomo Comito

Palermo, 6 June 1428

Source: ASP, Not. Giacomo Comito, reg. 843, c. nn

Narcisco Bondello stands surety for Muxa de Vita, a Jew, who owes Liucio Cuyno, a Jew of Trapani, 10 ounces. Payment is due within eight days.

Palermo, 12 June 1428

Source: ASP, Not. Giacomo Comito, reg. 843, c. nn

Notarial protest by Gallufo Cuyno, a Jew of Palermo, against Guglielmo de Scales, a Majorcan merchant, for having failed to deliver some merchandise.

Palermo, 25 October 1427

Source: ASP, Not. Giacomo Comito, reg. 843, c. nn.

Undertaking by Salamon Gibell, a Palermitan Jew, to pay Iacobo de Serenello 2.29.5 ounces on receiving that sum from Iosep de Serafinis.

Palermo, 25 October 1427

Source: ASP, Not. Giacomo Comito, reg. 843, c. nn.

Bracha Cuyno, a Palermitan Jew, undertakes to pay two ounces to Bartholomeo de mastro Antonio, farmer of the tax on wood, being the balance of a debt of four ounces due for that tax.

Palermo, 14 January 1433

Source: ASP, Not. Giacomo Comito, reg. 843, c. 37v.

Gaudio de Aram, a Jew, declares that he received 20 ounces from the bank of Antonio de Septimo for the production of biscuits for the royal curia.

6318

Palermo, 9 April 1433

Source: ASP, Not. Giacomo Comito, reg. 843, c. nn.

Deed whereby Gaudio son of Brachono de Medico, a Jew, cedes to Chanino Balbo, another Jew, all his rights in regard to a debt owed him by Charono Chassen, a Jew of Pantelleria.

Palermo, 19 April 1433

Source: ASP, Not. Giacomo Comito, reg. 843, c. nn.

Samuel de Simon, a Jew of Ciminna, hires himself out to Pino de Bellachera to work in his tunny plant in Solanto during the entire season for 1.9.0 ounces, and is paid 18 tarì *on account.*

Palermo, 23 April 1433

Source: ASP, Not. Giacomo Comito, reg. 843, c. nn.

Iacob de Lu Furmento, Muxa Catanisi, Iacob Sufe, Sabatino [...], Muxa de Mayu, Xilomo Fitira and three assistants, all Jews, hire themselves out to Thomeo de mastro Antonio to work in his tunny plant in Solanto for between 2.12.0 and 2.18.0 ounces each.

Palermo, 24 February 1445

Source: ASP, Not. Giacomo Comito, reg. 843, c. 83r.

Commenda *contract whereby Guillelmo de Spuches, a Majorcan merchant, entrusts Azarono Monachatelu, a Jew of Marsala, with 100 ounces worth of cloth. Azarono undertakes to sell the cloth wholesale and retail, except in his shop. He is to keep book of his transactions and to report every four months. The contract is to last a year. If Guillelmo does not wish to extend the contract beyond a year, Azarono is to pay him the hundred ounces and profits.*

Bibliography: Bresc, *Arabi*, p. 225 and n. 1064; Trasselli, *Mercato dei panni*, p. 148.

Palermo, 21 April 1434

Source: ASP, Not. Giacomo Comito, reg. 844, c. nn.

Brachono Taguil, a Palermitan Jew, undertakes to transfer five ounces to Andrea de Speciali, treasurer of the realm.

Palermo, 23 April 1434

Source: ASP, Not. Giacomo Comito, reg. 844, c. 42r.

Andrea de Speciali, treasurer of the realm, acknowledges that he received from Iuda and Chayronello Balbu, Jews of Mazara, a large quantity of biscuits sold by Merdoc Cuyno. He paid them 97.15.0 ounces.

Palermo, 23 April 1434

Source: ASP, Not. Giacomo Comito, reg. 844, c. nn.

Quittance by Gaudio Rayni, a Jew of Messina, to Mardoc Cuyno, a Jew of Trapani, of 12 ounces for biscuits (ad opus fieri faciendum biscotum).

Bibliography: Ashtor, *Palermo*, p. 223 (who has 1424).

Palermo, 26 April 1434

Source: ASP, Not. Giacomo Comito, reg. 844, c. nn.

Muxa de Cathania, Sabatino Chassator, Iosep de Amato and Xirello de Siragusia, Jews of Syracuse hire themselves out to Iacobo Cassatori to work as fillers in his tunny plant in Solanto for 1.18.0 ounces a month.

Palermo, 22 September 1434

Source: ASP, Not. Giacomo Comito, reg. 844, c. nn.

Brachono Taguili, a Jew, cedes to Farrino Dalmau all of his rights with Andreotta Gentili in regard to 18.15.0 ounces.

Sicily

Palermo, 7 October 1434

Source: ASP, Not. Giacomo Comito, reg. 844, c. 81v.

Iosep Abinazara, a Jewish citizen of Palermo, acknowledges receipt of 6.16.11 ounces from Bernardo Pardo, from the will of Iaime Castellar [another Jew]. Iaime had left the amount to his daughter, who is married to Iosep.

Palermo, 7 october 1434

Source: ASP, Not. Giacomo Comito, reg. 844, c. nn.

Vita Racham, a Jew from Calabria, hires himself out to Iacobo de Perbominato for 1.19.0 ounces, and is paid 1.6.0 ounces on account.

Palermo, 15 December 1434

Source: ASP, Not. Giacomo Comito, reg. 844, c. 176r-v.

Brachono Taguil, Gallufo Cuyno, prothi *of the Jewish community in Palermo, and nine members of that community acknowledge receipt of 130 ounces as an interest free loan from Antonio de Settimo, being the balance of 150 ounces to be paid to the treasurer of the realm, Andrea de Speciali, for privileges. They promise to pay Antonio in weekly instalments of 20 ounces.*

Palermo, 13 July 1435

Source: ASP, Not. Giacomo Comito, reg. 844, c. nn.

Sabatino Cassator, Zudo de Bundo and Sabatino Calabresi, Jews, hire themselves out to Antonio Boyani to work as fillers in his tunny plant at Arenella on the usual terms. They are paid 29 tarì *on account.*

Palermo, 24 November 1435

Source: ASP, Not. Giacomo Comito, reg. 844, c. 180r.

Deed whereby Gallufo Cuyno and Salamon Azaru, Palermitan Jews, emancipate Mahamet Amer, their slave, for eight ounces. Mahamet promises to pay this amount in weekly instalments of three tarì.

Palermo, 28 November 1435

Source: ASP, Not. Giacomo Comito, reg. 844, c. 190r-v.

Deed whereby Illesio Farki, a German, acknowledges receipt of a loan of five ounces from Bulgayra Sansono, a Jew of Trapani, on behalf of Frankina, wife of Pietro Serra. Illesio undertakes to use the loan to obtain the release of prisoners: facere elemosinam cum suum adventum pro redimere captivorum in partibus Barbarie. *He undertakes to embark from Trapani to North Africa on the route taken by Trapanese merchants.*

Palermo, 28 November 1435

Source: ASP, Not. Giacomo Comito, reg. 844, c. 910r.

Elia Gazella and Muxa Alluxa, Palermitan Jews, hire themselves out to Bartholomeo de mastro Antonio to work in his sugar refinery during the entire season for one ounce a month each.

Palermo, 2 December 1435

Source: ASP, Not. Giacomo Comito, reg. 844, c. 204v.

Muxa de Daniele, a Jew of Messina, promises Guglielmo Scales to pay his debt of 20 ounces shortly.

Palermo, 5 December 1435

Source: ASP, Not. Giacomo Comito, reg. 844, c. 217r.

Chanino Balbu and Iuda de Vita, Jews of Mazara, promise Luca de Moroxini 40 salme of wheat, to be delivered in Mazara and in Sciacca, for 9.5 tarì *a salma in Mazara, and nine* tarì *in Sciacca.*
In the margin: *Delivered on 4.7.1436.*

Palermo, 5 December 1435

Source: ASP, Not. Giacomo Comito, reg. 844, c. 217v.

Contract between Luca de Morixino and the Mazarese Jews Chanino Balbo and Iuda de Vita for setting up a joint venture for the sale of cheese in Sciacca and caciocavallo *in Mazara. The Jews invest their labour and half the price of the cheese, while Luca invests the other half. Chanino and Iuda acknowledge receipt of 50 ounces from Moroxini.*

Palermo, 23 October 1436

Source: ASP, Not. Giacomo Comito, reg. 845, c. 88v.

Final accounting of the business between Mariano Aglata, acting for Francesco Moroxini, and Iuda de Vita and Chanino Balbo, Jews of Mazara. As a result Vita and Chanino owe Francesco a balance of 348 salme *of wheat which they promise to deliver on request.*

Palermo, 23 November 1436

Source: ASP, Not. Giacomo Comito, reg. 845, c. 149r.

Contract whereby Chaym Bricha and Vita Russu, Palermitan Jews, promise to pay Filippo de Ponticorona weekly instalments of three tarì *to meet the terms of an agreement between them.*

Palermo, 5 December 1436

Source: ASP, Not. Giacomo Comito, reg. 845, c. 169r.

Elia de Gazella, a Palermitan Jew, and Sabatino Minachem, a Jew of Syracuse, hire themselves out to Thomeo de mastro Antonio to work in his tunny plant in Arenella during the entire season for 1.6.0 ounces each.

Palermo, 23 April 1437

Source: ASP, Not. Giacomo Comito, reg. 845, c. nn.

Xibiten and Chayrono Gaczu, Jews, hire themselves out to Thomeo de mastro Antonio to work in his tunny plant in San Nicola for 2.12.0 ounces, and are paid 1 ounce on account.

Source: ASP, Not. Giacomo Comito, reg. 845, c. nn.

Vanni Sabuchi, a Palermitan Jew, promises Francesco de Lupo, a Napolitan merchant, to deliver the oil he had sold him by July.

Palermo, 6 May 1442

Source: ASP, Not. Giacomo Comito, reg. 845, c. nn.

Moyses de Medico, a Jew, acting for Minto de Muxarella, his Jewish fellow citizen, promises Simone de Risignano to deliver some wine in exchange for cloth.

Palermo, 3 September 1442

Source: ASP, Not. Giacomo Comito, reg. 846, c. nn.

Fariono Sala, a Jew, promises Bulchayra [...], another Jew, to repay six ounces which he had lent to Fariono within a month.

Palermo, 26 September 1442

Source: ASP, Not. Giacomo Comito, reg. 846, c. nn.

Salamon Bonacu and Ioseph Abudarcham, Palermitan Jews, lodge a notarial protest against Benedetto Saver and Roderico de Niraculo, who had sold them some cloth. The cloth had been paid for but had not been delivered.

Palermo, 11 October 1442

Source: ASP, Not. Giacomo Comito, reg. 846, c. 56v.

Ysac Sala, a Palermitan Jew, leases to Aloysio de Seragusia a vineyard in the contrada *Biscumie by the métayage system. Aloysio is to cultivate the vineyard, to sell the grapes and to give Ysac some of the proceeds. On 14 May 1446 the arrangement is brought to an end.*

Sicily

Palermo, 19 October 1442

Source: ASP, Not. Giacomo Comito, reg. 846, c. nn.

Xibiten Zullo, a Palermitan Jew, is granted a deferment by Nicolò de Ianquisto of the payment of a debt amounting to 24 tarì.

Palermo, 21 January 1443

Salamon Azara, a Jewish smith of Palermo, promises Chayrono Balbo, a Jew of Mazara, to enter his employment to refine salt for one ounce.

Palermo, 17 February 1443

Source: ASP, Not. Giacomo Comito, reg. 846, c. nn.

Busacca de Seragusia, Manuel Calabrisi and Graciano Xeni, Palermitan Jews, hire themselves out to Antonio de Bruno and Giuliano de Benedictis to work in their sugar refinery on the usual terms.

Palermo, 24 March 1443

Source: ASP, Not. Giacomo Comito, reg. 846, c. nn.

Sabatino Challuffo, a Palermitan Jew, promises to pay Giovanni Spagnolo two ounces within four months for some wood.

Palermo, 9 April 1443

Source: ASP, Not. Giacomo Comito, reg. 846, c. nn.

Fariono Sala and Gallufo Dinar, Jews, set up a joint venture for a year to run a wine shop.

Palermo, 12 June 1443

Source: ASP, Not. Giacomo Comito, reg. 846, c. nn.

Ysac and Sadono Sala, Palermitan Jews, declare that they are willing to assume responsibility for profits and losses of a joint venture for the purchase of a certain quantity of tables and beams.

Palermo, 12 June 1443

Source: ASP, Not. Giacomo Comito, reg. 846, c. nn.

Simuni Bonito, a Palermitan Jew, undertakes to work in the business of Francesco [...] for three tarì *a day.*

Palermo, 6 November 14[..]

Source: ASP, Not. Giacomo Comito, reg. 846, c. nn.

Salamon Maltisi, a Jew of Polizzi, promises Iacob Taguil, another Jew, to sole his shoes for one ounce.

Palermo, 13 November 14[..]

Source: ASP, Not. Giacomo Comito, reg. 846, c. nn.

Brachono Samueli and Salamon de Nifusi, Palermitan Jews, promise Giuliano [...] to pay their debt as soon as possible.

Palermo, 17 April 14[..]

Source: ASP, Not. Giacomo Comito, reg. 846, c. nn.

Farchono Sala, a Jew of Palermo, obtains a deferment from Arnaldo Basso on the payment of a debt.

Palermo, 23 April 14[..]

Source: ASP, Not. Giacomo Comito, reg. 846, c. nn.

Mastro Iacobo de Ponino agrees that Sadono Rubeo and Galluffo de Comenia, Jews, deliver within a year the wheat they owe him.

Palermo, 24 April 14[..]

Source: ASP, Not. Giacomo Comito, reg. 846, c. nn.

Ysac Sala and Nissim Sansuni, Palermitan Jews, set up a partnership for running a warehouse in the Cassaro of Palermo to trade in cheese during the whole year of the 12th indiction. Ysac invests 25 ounces and Nissim the building.

Sicily

Palermo, 28 January 1445

Source: ASP, Not. Giacomo Comito, reg. 846, c. 24v.

Undertaking by Giovanni de Barbera of Marsala and Azarono de Monachectulo, a Jew of that locality, to pay Davanzato Fanny of Florence 125 ounces for cloth, including cloth of Barcelona and Florence, within five months. Azarono owes 100 ounces out of the 125. They promise to pay the debt in cheese.

Bibliography: Bresc, *Arabi*, p. 225 and n. 1065.

Palermo, 3 October 1450

Source: ASP, Not. Giacomo Comito, reg. 847, c. nn.

Sabeti and Iacobo Cassator, Palermitan Jews, promise Antonio de Vita to salt tunny barrels during the entire season for two ounces.

Palermo, 9 December 1450

Source: ASP, Not. Giacomo Comito, reg. 847, c. nn.

Mussuto Binna, a Palermitan Jew, hands to Filippo Aglata his due from Iuda de Minichi, another Jew of Palermo.

Palermo, 30 December 1450

Source: ASP, Not. Giacomo Comito, reg. 847, c. nn.

Iacob and Muxa Taguil, Palermitan Jews, settle accounts in regard to their partnership. As a result Muxa owes Iacob 12 ounces which he promises to pay within two months.

Palermo, 16 January 1451

Source: ASP, Not. Giacomo Comito, reg. 847, loose page.

Bartholomeo de Altavilla, a notary, Nicolò de Augusta, a judge, and Charono Chitano, a Jew, accepted from Giovanni de Damiano, a Pisan merchant, the value of a bill of exchange drawn on Barcelona for 91.18.13 ounces, underwritten by Antonio de Bellomo, formerly lord of Augusta. The letter was not paid and the debt grew to 111.19.1 ounces including damages and expenses. Giovanni took

Antonio to court and won. Guillelmo de Moncada, count of Caltanissetta and chancellor of Sicily, stood surety for Antonio. Giovanni had the verdict executed against the property of the guarantor, including an additional 2.4.8 ounces for the court order and stamp duty. He now declares that he has no further claims and that the count is free to proceed against the other parties.

Die XVI Ianuarii XIIII Indicionis MCCCCL

Cum honorabilis notarius Bartholomeus de Altavilla, iudex Nicolaus de Augusta, Charonus Chitanus Iudeus, [empty space] ceperint ad cambium a Iohanne de Damiano, mercatore pisarum, complendas et solvendas in civitate Barchinone uncias nonaginta unam, tarenos decem et octo et granos XIII, et de dicto cambio licteras fecerint et scripserint in quibus seu in una quarum se subscripsit nobilis dominus Anthonius de Bellomo, olim dominus terre Auguste, ut principalem pagatorem et solutorem, et quod ibi dicte uncie LXXXXI, tareni XVIII et [granis] XIII non fuerunt complete et reverse, fuerunt computatis et deductis dampnis, interesse et expensis ad uncias centum undecim, tarenos XVIII et granum I, et receptis licteris recambii predicti cum protestatione per eundem Iohannem, dictus Iohannes execucionem fecerit contra dictum nobilem dominum Anthonium fideiussorem cambii et recambii predicti in magna regia curia Panormi degente, qua execucione facta, magnificus dominus Guillelmus de Moncata, comes Calatanixecte et regni Sicilie cancellarius, ut bancus se fideiussorem constituerit, ut in actis magne regie curie, die XXVIII aprilis XII Ind. proxime preterite et licteris cambii et recambii, hec et alia asseritur contineri, adversus quam executionem factam de dictis unciis centum undecim, tarenis XVIII, granis VIII contra nobilem Antonium de Bellomo per dictum Iohannem Damiano, dictus nobilis Anthonius se opposuerit et processo in dicta opposicione usque ad solutionem inclusive per dictam magnam curiam fuerit sentenciatum et declaratum dictam execucionem procedere debere in dictis unciis centum undecim tarenis XVIII et granis VIII, opposicionibus dicti opponentis non obstantibus, qua sentencia et declarationem facta per dictam magnam curiam, dictus Iohannes Damianus execucionem fecerit contra eundem magnificum dominum regiam comitem Calatanixecte, tamquam fideiussorem ut bancus dicti nobilis Antonii de Bellomo. Que execucio suum sortita extitit effectum super bonis dicti magnifici domini comitis fideiussoris usque ad integram solucionem dictarum pecuniarum, ut omnia liquent per acta dicte magne regie curie, hinc est quod hodie, pretitulato die, dictus Iohannes coram me notario et testibus infrascriptis, de mandato et ad iniuncionem sibi factam per magnam regiam curiam, ut constitit, dedit, cessit et concessit, transtulit et mandavit Marino Magdalena, procuratori magnifici domini comitis predicti presenti et dicto nomine recipienti, omnia iura omnesque actiones reales, personales, utiles, directas, mixtas, tacitas et expressas, pretorias et civiles et alias quascumque quas et que habet et sibi competunt contra et adversus dictos dominum Anthonium, notarium Bartholomeum, iudicem Nicolaum et Charonum Iudeum et quemlibet eorum, vigore et auctoritate tam licterarum cambii et recambii et aliarum quarumcumque scripturarum quantum pro unciiis centum quatuordecim tarenis III et granis VIII, computatis in hiis unciis duabus et tarenis XXVII solutis per eundem Iohannem pro iure execucionis dictarum unciarum centum undecim tarenorum XVIII et granorum VIII iure sigilli commissionis et date reservando, tamen eidem Iohanni omnia iura que habet contra superius in omnes debitores quantum pro aliis expensis factis per eum quomodocumque et quandocumque, ita ut ipsius iuribus et actionibus dictus Marinus dicto nomine uti possit, agere et experiri dictas uncias centum XIIII, tarenos IIII et granos VIII in iudiciis et extra a predictis domino Anthonio, notario Bartholomeo, iudice Nicolao et Charono Iudeo et altero eorum petere, exlugere [=exigere], recipere et habere et contra eos et eorum quemlibet et in eorum eorumque ipsorum bonis execucionem et execuciones facere et illas quietaciones et cessiones quascumque necessarias et opportunas litteras cambii, recambi et protestationes superius mencionari cum [...] in dorso restituere et dum omnia alia facere que dictus Iohannes facere poterat, potest, possit, posset et unquam melius potuit ante presentem cessionem dum... [from here on practically illegible, consisting mainly of legal formula].

Palermo, 6 March 1451

Source: ASP, Not. Giacomo Comito, reg. 847, c. nn.

Salamon de Tripoli, Elia de Rugila, Abraam [...] and Minto Barbutu hire themselves out to Giovanni Amodeo to cultivate his field for 18 tarì *a month.*

Palermo, 12 March 1451

Source: ASP, Not. Giacomo Comito, reg. 847, c. nn.

Iosep, son of Chayrono Balbo, a Jew, declares that he owes Iacobo de Crapona 6.2.0 ounces for cloth purchased by Chaym Balbo, a Jew of Mazara on 2.3.1451.

6329

Palermo, 26 February 1452
Source: ASP, Not. Giacomo Comito, reg. 847, c. nn.

Brachono de Amurano, Muxa Rugila and Danieli Calabrisi, Palermitan Jews, hire themselves out to Giuliano de Bes to fertilize his field in Palermo for 1.18.0 ounces

Palermo, 10 April 1452
Source: ASP, Not. Giacomo Comito, reg. 847, c. nn.

Iacob Formono, a Jew, hires himself out to Andrea de mastro Antonio to work in his tunny plant for three ounces.

Palermo, 4 February 1438
Source: ASP, Not. Giacomo Comito, reg. 848, c. nn.

Chanino de Balbu, a Jew of Mazara, appoints Ysach de Guillelmo, another Jew, his attorney to look after his affairs in Palermo and to collect all his outstanding debts.

Palermo, 9 December 1452
Source: ASP, Not. Giacomo Comito, reg. 848, loose page

Notarial protest lodged by Rabbi Iona de Usuel [=Uziel] of Palermo against the judge Ferdinando de Milina in the lawsuit pending between him and David de Minayem [=Menachem] alias Russu and his wife, Jews of Sciacca. Rabbi Iona wants the President of the realm to rule on his petition before the judge proceeds with the case.

Die VIIII mensis Decembris prime Ind.

Rabi Yona de Usue[l], Iudeus, constitutus in presencia nobilis et egregii domini Fredirandi de Milina, mei notarii et testium infrascriptorum, animo et intencione sibi protestandi et ius suum in futurum conservandi exposuit, dixit et fuit protestatus, quod cum in causa vertente inter eumdem exponentem et David de Minayem, dictu Russu, et eius uxorem de terra Xacce ex altera parte vertatur questio coram dicto domino Fredirando, ut iudice delegato magnifici domini Bernardi de Requisens, et in eadem causa dictus Rabi, dum intra terminum sibi indultum esset in continua producione testium, dictus dominus Fredirandus testes producendos super falsitate scripture asserte scripte per Muxam di Lu Medicu et reprobacione testium partis adverse mandavit, quod minime reciperet supplicacione decretata per dominum presedentem minime observata. Et quod dictus Rabi supplicaverit iterum dicto domino presedenti dictumque dominum Fredirandum habeat in suspectum quia alias fuit advocatus ipsius exponentis et consulit eumdem exponentem super causa predicta tamen etiam quia intendit sentenciare super premissis ipso exponente in audito indefenso. Ideo presentis serie ex parte serenissimi domini nostri regis exponens ipse eumdem dominum Frederandum presentem requisivit et requirit, sub pena florenorum mille regio fisco applicandorum et ab eo inremissibiliter extorquendorum tociens quociens per eum in premissis contrafactum fuerit quatenus non debeat annetare aliquid, nec ad ulteriora procedere donec et quousque fuerit per dominum presedentem supplicacio ipsius exponentis decretata et per eumdem exponentem sue probacionis facte. Et si per eum aliquod factum fuerit, ordine et iusticia non servatis, illud revocare debeat et annullare, aliter incidat in penam predictam quam ex nunc pro tunc renunciavit et renunciat regio fisco et pro denunciata habuit et habet submictendo se iuri voluit et vult exponens ipse quod si aliqua verba contra ius in presenti posita fuerint illa revocaret et annullaret et revocat et annullat et pro non posita habuerit et habet, et nichilominus procedatur contra dictum dominum Fredirandum de omnibus dampnis etc. constituens se etc. hanc sentenciam etc.

Note: See above, Docs. 2855, 3129. Requisens was the viceroy. The president was Simon de Bologna.

Bibliography: Gerardi-Scandaliato, *Studium Iudeorum*, p. 447; Id. *Istruzione*, p. 36; Id., Ebrei in Sicilia, pp. 129f.

Palermo, 22 December 1452

Source: ASP, Not. Giacomo Comito, reg. 848, c. 181r.

Iosep de Benedicto and Sabet Russo, Palermitan Jews, settle business accounts. As a result Iosep owes 14.15.0 ounces to Sabet, which he promises to pay within a year.

Palermo, 15 January 1453

Source: ASP, Not. Giacomo Comito, reg. 848, c. 199r.

Cristofaro de Torpiano, a Genoese merchant, grant Busacca Ysaya, a Jew of Palermo, a moratorium of 1½ years on the payment of two ounces which Busacca's wife owes Cristofaro.

Palermo, 11 August 1453

Source: ASP, Not. Giacomo Comito, reg. 848, c. 356r.

Salamon Azaru and Iosep Lu Medicu, prothi *of the Jewish community in Palermo, issue an official quittance to the notary Nicolò de Iacio for 56 ounces. The payment was made on viceregal orders, issued in Catania on 27 June of the 7ᵗʰ indiction.*

Palermo, 21 March 1454

Source: ASP, Not. Giacomo Comito, reg. 848, c. 131v.

Simon Rabibi, a Palermitan Jew, hires himself out to Giovanni de Li Muli to work as grinder in his sugar refinery during the whole season for 1.12.0 ounces.

Palermo, 9 July 1454

Source: ASP, Not. Giacomo Comito, reg. 848, c. 164r.

Salamon Azara, a Jew of Palermo, promises Gerardo de Sutera to supply him with goat's milk during the entire season for six ounces a quintal. The milk is the product of Salamon's herd.

Palermo, 2 September 1454

Source: ASP, Not. Giacomo Comito, reg. 848, c. 2r.

Notarial protest lodged by Liocta Xayuni, a Palermitan Jew, against Aron Mactuti, his Jewish fellow citizen, in regard to a window which Aron built in a wall overlooking Liocta's property in the Cassaro. Liocta hereby wishes to restrain Aron from acting in detriment to his interests.

Sicily

Eodem II mensis septembris

Liocta Xayuni, Iudeus de Panormo, in presencia magistri notarii et testium infrascriptorum constitutus coram Arono Mactuti, Iudeo suo concive, presente et audiente, animo et intencione sibi protestandi et ius suum in futurum conservandi contra et adversus eumdem Aronum exposuit dixit et fuit protestatus, quod cum dictus Liocta habeat, teneat et possideat cortile unum certarum domorum situm et positum in civitate Cassari, suis finibus limitatum, intus darbum magistri Sabuci ipseque Aron habeat tenimentum unum domorum soleratarum muro mediante dicto cortili sine aliqua ianum respondente intus cortile, in muro cuius tenimenti domorum erat una furrata per quam domus ipsius Aroni habebat lucem et eidem Liocte nullam interebat subiectionem, ipseque Aron noviter fabricaverit et aperuerit quamdam finestram pisaniscam per quam si affachia intus cortile, inferendo ibidem subiectionem que numquam fuit nec facere poterat, in preiudicium, dampnum et subiectionem cortilis predicti, iuxta tenorem et formam consuetudinis Panormitane dictantis quod nullus presumat facere aperturas aliquas in pariete sue domus contra veteram formam sui invito convicino; et noviter etiam intendit et vult facere stringituri in cortili predicto in quo tamen ipse Aron habet unam vacuam partem iam locatam et sic nichil habet facere in dicto cortili nec tamen capere loherium sue tercie partis, iam locate ab inquilinis quod facere minime potest in preiudicium dicti exponentis et inquilinorum suorum. Qua propter volens facta sua exponens ipse facere tacite et ne taciturnas in futurum habeat ei nocere et subiectionem inferre presentis serie exponens ipse requisivit et requirit dictum Aconum[=Aronum] presentem et intelligentem ex parte serenissimi domini nostri regis, sub pena unciarum viginti et magnificorum dominorum pretoris et iuratorum sub pena unciarum decem, regio fisco applicandarum et maramatis domus consilii edificandarum et ab eo inremissibiliter extorquendarum tociens quociens per eum in premissis vel aliquo premissorum contrafactum fuerit, quatenus dictam finestram noviter fabricatam conrespondentem intus cortile predictum [...] alias aperturas factas contra sui tenorem formam claudere et obturare debeat incontinenti, omni mora postposita et stringitorium minime facere numquam fuit ibi factum stringitorium, alias incidat in pena predicta, protestando nichilominus contra eumdem Aronum presentem et intelligentem de omnibus damnis, interesse, missionibus et expensis propterea factis et faciendis, que et quas extitit pati et subtineri poterit quoque modo culpa dicti Aroni facientis aperturas contra sui formam in dicto muro, constituendo in dolo, mora et culpa; et nichilominus si aliqua verba posita fuerint in presenti protestatione contra ius et iuris formam illa revocavit et revocat et quod non posita habere voluit hanc sentenciam. Die III eiusdem traddita fuit copia dicto Aroni. Actum in etc., Antonio Andrea Faldali et Maciocta Galcu.

Note: See following Doc. There the names of the parties are spelled differently.

Palermo, 3 September 1454

Source: ASP, Not. Giacomo Comito, reg. 848, cc. 6r–7r.

Xarono (Arono) Mactuti, a Palermitan Jew, rejects the notarial protest of Liocta Xaruno (Xayuno), his fellow citizen, in the matter of the window allegedly built by Xarono in their joint courtyard, and makes a number of counterclaims.

Eodem III septembris

Ad quamdam protestationem factam et publicatam per honorabilem notarium Iacobum de Comite Xaroni Mactuti Iudeo ad peticionem et instanciam Liocte Xaruni [Xayuni], Iudeo, licet non esset opus responsionis quia dicta protestacio fuit et est iniusta et contra formam iuris et in se non continet veritatem, tamen timore pene et ob reverenciam regii nominis et cautelam dicti Xaronis ita breviter respondetur et in quantum dicitur quod dictus Xaronus aperuit finestram in cortilio, contra formam consuetudinis noviter inferendum maximum dampnum et preiudicium dicti protestanti, salva pace, hoc non est verum, nam Xaronus ipse de novo ex nunc noviter nullam finestram aperuit, est bene verum quod postquam dictum Xaronus iam est annus, habuit terciam partem dicti cortilis, pro ut habet in muro dicti Xaroni erat quedam finestra que respondet in dicto cortili, que finestra fuit et erat ab antiquo et non erat mera furrata, quavis esset longa, tamen adeo erat larga qui unusquisque si chi poria affachari, quam finestram seu aperturam dictus Xaronus adaptavit reformando minime et accussi comu era longa, la fichi in pocu plui larga per haviri plui luchi, quam finestram dictus Haronus tenuit et tenet de iure firmiter potuisse illam actari facere prout fecit, et non fecit in contentum nec ad iniuriam dicti protestantis, quoniam dicta finestra non nocet dicto protestanti, premaxime cum in domo dicti Xaroni sunt alie finestre maiores corrispondentes in dicto cortili et sic quitquid fecit dictus Xaronus credidit potuisse illud facere, nichilominus si dictus protestans addit aliud dirigat in sua protesta iuris quia dictus Xaronus paratus est obedire iusticie. Ad illud vero quod dictus protestans allegat et dicit quod dictus Xaronus iam locavit domum suam et quod non debet recipere loherium etc. salva pace hoc dicente quod Xaronus locavit tamen domum et non cortile, et nichilominus quitquid dictus Xaronus fecit et facit cum voluntate et consensu dicti conductoris et vicinorum quod non ad illud quod dictusque dominus Xaronus posuit stringitorium in dicto cortili cum voluntate dicti protestantis et vicinorum, et hoc respondetur quod dictus Xaronus posuit dictum stringitorium in dicto cortili prope murum dicti Xaroni et nullum preiudicium, nec impedimentum dat nec facit dicto protestanti, et credit Xaronus ipse potuisse illud facere pro servicio suo maxime per paucos dies, scilicet ad usum vendemiarum, tamen non faciendo in cortili aliquam immondiciam, seu vinacium, sicut etiam fecit dictus protestans qui retinuit et retinet in dicto cortili quoddam strumentum magnum carpinterie et etiam alia lignamina et similiter dictus dominus Xaronus credit et tenet quitquid fecit et facit, credet de iure posse fieri et ad eius utilitatem et non ad iniuriam vicinorum, nichilominus si dictus protestans non potest illud facere, petit provideatur per iusticiam quia paratus est stare disposicioni iuris et consuetudinis, submictendo se mandato magnificorum officialium et sic respondentur ad alias aperturas, et nichilominus quia dictus protestans requisivit cum pena contra formam iuris indistinte eundem Xaronum, et sic dicta protestacio videtur iniusta dictus Xaronus retorquendo penam contro eam impositam sub eadem pena requisivit et requirit eumdem protestantem quatenus incontinenti debeat desistere a dicta protestacione et illam revocare quoniam et in quantum fuit et est et apparet iniusta contra formam iuris, quod si non fecerit, incidat in dictam penam ipso iure et ipso facto unde pro cautela dicti Xaronis dicta est presens responsio et protestacio.

Actum in banco etc. presentibus Angilo de Tirono, domino Bartholomeo de Palmerio et domino Petro de Colica.

Note: See above, preceding Doc.

Palermo, 4 October 1454

Source: ASP, Not. Giacomo Comito, reg. 848, c. 33r.

Ubertino de Guchardino and Liuzu de Cuyno, a Jew of Trapani, settle accounts in regard to the sale by Liuzu of a mantle, a bedsheet and other articles to Ubertino's wife. As a result it appears that Ubertino owes Liuzu a balance of 1.18.0 ounces.

Palermo, 6 February 1455

Source: ASP, Not. Giacomo Comito, reg. 849, c. 2r.

Contract whereby Giovanni Conconte, Iacobo de Salvo and Salamon Taguil, a Palermitan Jew, set up a joint venture for running a cheese warehouse for a year. Giovanni is to invest half the capital and Iacobo and Salamone the other half. The profits are to be divided among the partners in proportion to their investment.

Palermo, 6 February 1455

Source: ASP, Not. Giacomo Comito, reg. 849, c. 5r.

Busacca de Ansalono, Gallufo Amar, Simon Rabibi and Sadono Gazu, Palermitan Jews, hire themselves out to Giovanni de Nuch, to work in his business for one ounce a month.

Palermo, 8 May 1455

Source: ASP, Not. Giacomo Comito, reg. 849, c. 144r.

Elia Cuyno, a Jew of Trapani, promises Federico de La Matina to transport all the grapes from the latter's vineyard to his storehouse for an agreed sum.

Palermo, 4 June 1455

Source: ASP, Not. Giacomo Comito, reg. 849, c. 197r.

Enrico de Vicencio, acting for Sabet Abati, a Jew of Palermo, settles accounst with Vita Canet, his Jewish fellow citizen, in regard to the management of a cheese warehouse. As a result, Vita owes Sabet a balance of 10.6.0 ounces which he undertakes to pay by 15 July. In the margin: paid on 18.10.1455.

Palermo, 26 August 1455

Source: ASP, Not. Giacomo Comito, reg. 849, c. 223r-v.

Notarial protest lodged by Salamon Titan, a Jew of Syracuse, acting for Iacob and Sadia Dacri, Jews of Agrigento, against Marino Pisano, a Venetian merchant in the matter of a bill of exchange. The bill was for the payment of 310 ounces for wheat. Giovanni Rossolmino, a Pisan merchant, acting for Marino, had promised to pay the amount on the usual date for the payment of bills of exchange. Salamon had agreed to waive additional clauses in the bill, provided Giovanni paid for a rise in the price of wheat after the established date for payment, and without prejudice to Salamon's right to damages. The protest contained the gist of the agreement between Salamon and Giovanni.

Die XXVI mensis Augusti IIIe Ind.

Salamon Titan, Iudeus de civitate Siracusarum, in presencia mei notarii et testium infrascriptorum, nomine et pro parte Iacob et Saddie Dacrii, Iudeorum de civitate Agrigenti, obtulit et presentavit et per me notarium infrascriptum publice legi peciit coram Johannem Rossolmino, mercathorem Pisarum, quamdam lictera cambii tenoris sequentis videlicet: "Ihesus, M°CCCCLV in Saragusis pagati per questa de cambio a Iacobus et Sadia Dacra, Iudei de Agrigenti, per parti de formenti onze 310, zoè onze trixento deci, dapo richiputa da iorni dechi sic fatili e lo dover pregauna asai Marin Pisani, fio de misser Piero, adi 19 di augustu per domino Iohanni Rosolmino, data Palermo". Pro qua lictera lecta et presentata dicto Iohanni, statim dictus Iudeus, dicto nomine, requisivit dictum Iohannem quatenus dictam licteram acceptare debeat et solvere dictas pecunias tempore consueto solucionis cambiorum, iuxta tenorem contractus vendicionis frumenti inter eos celebrati, non obstante quod in dicta lictera aliter conteneatur, ita quod per presentem presentacionem nullum preiudicium generetur dictis Iudeis casu quo frumentum infra dies sex supersalvos positos in lictera cambii predicti, ultra tenorem contractus sepedicti, adscenderet ad maiorem precium quo nunc est, ad que dictus Iohannes respondidit quod dictam licteram acceptavit et acceptat et termino in eadem contenta solvere dictas uncias tricentas decem, iuxta tenorem lictere preinserte et lictere avisi, presentibus Philippo Basadonna, notario Antonio de Clarello et Raynerio de Vernagallo. Postea vero, die predicto, dictus Iudeus, dicto nomine, in presencia nobilis Aloysii de Campo, consulis venetorum in urbe Panormi commorancium et concurrencium, protestatus fuit contra dictum Marinum Pisanum, mercathorem venetum, licet absentem de omnibus dampnis et maiori precio quo forte valeret, ultra illud quod ad presens valet, infra dies sex, appositos in lictera cambii ultra tempus statutum in contractu celebratu inter dictos Iudeos et dictum Marinum.

Actum in urbe felici Panormi, presentibus quibus supra, anno, mense, die et indicione premissis.

Palermo, 2 September 1455

Source: ASP, Not. Giacomo Comito, reg. 849, c. 23v.

Mastro Iacob de Salvo lodges a protest against Salamon Taguil, a Palermitan Jew, with whom he managed a cheese warehouse together. Iacob had failed to consult Salamon, who claims damages from Iacob.

Palermo, 18 september 1455

Source: ASP, Not. Giacomo Comito, reg. 849, c. 57v.

Deed whereby Iacobo de Crapona appoints Iosep Bindira, a Palermitan Jew, to look after his interests in relation to a guarantee which he had furnished for Amato Migleni, another Jew.

Palermo, 9 October 1455

Source: ASP, Not. Giacomo Comito, reg. 849, c. 94v.

Agreement between Chayrono Sikiri, a Jew of Syracuse, and Sabet Vignuni, a Jew of Palermo, with Nicolò de Marino in regard to some property.

Palermo, 15 October 1457

Source: ASP, Not. Giacomo Comito, reg. 849, c. 40r.

Agreement whereby Graciano Dinar, a Palermitan Jew, undertakes to pay within four months 21 ounces to David Xunina, his fellow citizen. Graciano owes David that sum for a house he had purchased from him. It is situated in the Cassaro, vanella S. Ippolito.

Palermo, 10 September 1457

Source: ASP, Not. Giacomo Comito, reg. 850, c. 31r.

Merdoch Farachi, a Jew of Palermo, promises Simone de Bomberio to carry out some work [the Doc. breaks off at this point].

Palermo, 26 November 1457

Source: ASP, Not. Giacomo Comito, reg. 850, c. 53v.

Benedetto de Ierusalem, a Palermitan Jew, hires himself out to Giovanni Bayamonte to work during the entire season in his sugar refinery at Carini for 20 tarì *a month and is paid one ounce on account.*

Palermo, 14 February 1458

Source: ASP, Not. Giacomo Comito, reg. 850, c. 71r.

Minto de Vignuni, a Jew of Palermo, hires himself out to Giovanni de Bononia to work in his sugar refinery [the Doc. breaks off at this point].

Palermo, 18 February 1458

Source: ASP, Not. Giacomo Comito, reg. 850, c. 81r.

Mussuto Misiria, a Jew of Palermo, hires himself out to Giovanni Bayamonte to work during the whole season in his sugar refinery for 17 tarì *a month, and is paid 17* tarì *on account.*

Palermo, 21 February 1458

Source: ASP, Not. Giacomo Comito, reg. 850, c. 85v.

Iacobo de Messina de Mozia, acting on behalf of Vita Assuni, a Jew, promises to supply Giovanni de Capello with all of the olives produced by Vita's olive trees during the current season for 13 tarì *the kantar. Giovanni pays 26 ounces on account.*

Palermo, 3 March 1458

Source: ASP, Not. Giacomo Comito, reg. 850, c. 96v.

Master Sadono Lu Medicu, a Jewish physician in Palermo, Salamon Taguil, also a Jew of Palermo, and the Catalan merchant Giovanni de Adam, promise to pay 10 ounces each within eleven months to Abram Bass [a Jew], acting on behalf of Mario de Bonconte. In the margin: On 8 March Mario transferred his rights to Andrea Amat, a merchant of Barcelona. On 5 May Sadono paid his share.

Palermo, 17 October 1458

Source: ASP, Not. Giacomo Comito, reg. 850, c. 35r.

Daniel Calabrisi, Muxa Rabibi, Merdoc Xanchilo and Raffael Xamuel, Palermitan Jews, hire themselves out to Giovanni de Bonconte and Giovanni de Brandino to work in their sugar refinery during the whole season as paratores *for 6.12.0 ounces a month. They are paid four ounces on account.*

Palermo, 19 December 1458

Source: ASP, Not. Giacomo Comito, reg. 850, c. 53bisv.

Contract whereby Chayno Muxarella and Busacca de Iueli, Jews of Marsala, acting for the Jewish community there, agree to purchase from Giovanni Adamo, a Catalan merchant, two pieces of cloth of Barcelona for a total of 5.9.0 ounces, to be paid in Palermo within six months.

Eodem XVIIII mensis Decembris

Chaynus Muxarella et Busacca de Iueli, Iudei de terra Marsale, procuratores dicte Iudayce, ut constitit tenore cuiusdam procurationis firmate in posse notari Iacobi de Carbone, de eadem terra, olim die ultimo Novembris VII Ind. proxime preterite coram me notario et testibus infrascriptis, sponte tam nomine proprio in solidum, quam procuratorio nomine dicte Iudayce, dixerunt et confessi fuerunt teneri et dare debere nobili Iohanni Adamo, mercathori cathalano, licet absenti, me notario publico, officio publice pro eodem stipulante et recipiente, pro precio pannorum duorum de Barchinone ad uncias duas et tarenos XVIIII, granos X qualibet peccia capu cuda uncias quinque, tr. VIIII emptorum, habitorum et receptorum per dictos Iudeos procuratorio nomine quo supra a dicto Iohanne per manus Rubini Muxarella, renunciantes execucioni. Quas uncias quinque et tarenos VIIII tenentur dicti Iudei proprio et procuratorio nomine, quo supra, et sollemni stipulacione in solidum promiserunt dictis et propris nominibus dicto nobili Iohanni creditori, licet absenti, me notario publico, officio publico pro eodem stipulante et recipiente, eidem Iohanni creditori, vel persone legitime pro eo dare, solvere et integre assignare in pecunia numerata, in Panormo, hinc ad menses sex proxime venturos, dantes auctoritatem dictas pecunias, casu cessante solucionis tempore adveniente, capiendi ad cambium et currentibus cambiis et non execucionem faciendi etc., in pace, de plano etc., omni libello, moratoria etc. Renunciantes execucioni etc. ad penam duppli etc. cum refectionem omnium dampnorum, interesse et expensarum etc. et specialiter expensarum viaticarum ad tarenos tres pro quolibet etc. Obligantes in sese dictis et propris nominibus et eorum principales in solidum eorum et cuique ipsorum heredes et bona omnia habita et habenda etc. Et fiat ritus etc. in personis et bonis etc. renunciantes etc. et iuraverunt etc.

Actum in banco mei notarii infrascripti, presentibus nobili domino Bartholomeo de Faccio, Iuliano de Riccio testibus, etc.

Palermo, 15 March 1459

Source: ASP, Not. Giacomo Comito, reg. 850, cc. 118r–119r.

Peremptory request by Amatu Milieni, a Jew of Castrogiovanni, acting for Pietro de Matina, also of Castrogiovanni, from Giovanni de Rossolmino, a Pisan merchant. Pietro had bought cloth from Giovanni for 162 ounces. Pietro had entrusted the merchandise for sale to three Jewish brokers, who had sold a part. Giovanni was preventing the brokers from handing over the money to Pietro, claiming that his guarantees to ensure payment of the purchase price had been insufficient. Pietro, through Amatu, demands that Giovanni have the brokers hand over the proceeds. A similar request addressed to her brokers. Attached is the reply of the brokers. They blame Giovanni.

Eodem XV mensis Marcii

Amatus Milieni, Iudeus de terra Castri Iohannis, procurator nobilis domini Petri de Matina, habitatoris dicte terre, cum potestate infrascripta et alia faciendi, ut constitit vigore procurationis firmate in posse Raymundi Ristucha, publici dicte terre notarii, die quinto mensis Marcii presentis, constitutus in presencia nobilis Iohannis de Rosolmino, merchatoris pisani, presentis et audientis, exposuit, dixit, fuit dicto nomine protestatus quod, cum ipse nobilis Iohannes vendiderit dicto nobili domini Petro tantam quantitatem pannorum, quorum precio ascendit ad summam unciarum centum sexaginta duarum, solvendarum certo modo contento in contractu publico celebrato manu notarii Antonii de Aprea, die XXX Ianuarii proximi preteriti. Et promisit dictus dominus Petrus dictum contractum ratificari facere per nobilem dominum Franciscum de Matina, eius filium, ac dare in fideiussores certos declaratos in dicto contractu, infra certam dilacionem, dictusque dominus Petrus volens adimplere que

6341

promiserat per contractum se dictum contractum superius mencionatum per dictum nobilem, eius filium, ratificari fecerit et fideiussores, in contractu introducto, declaratos prestiterit et dederit, cum omnibus renunciacionibus in eodem contentis et declaratis, prout in quo de publico contractu celebrato in posse notarii Iohannis de Collotorto, publici dicte terre notarii, die VII Februarii proximi preteriti continetur, et presentata dicta ratificatione et prestatione fideiussione, dictus Iohannes dictos pannos et alia bona venditos et venditas dederit et assignaverit Ysace Sale, Leono Chamuso et Iosep Abodaram, publicis medianis, ut venderent illos et illa et precia ipsorum traderent dicto domino Petro aut eius procuratori, dictusque procurator, dicto nomine, requisiverit dictos medianos quod sibi tradere et solvere debeant precium ipsorum et solvere minime voluerint, allegando quod dictus Iohannes non fuit nec est contentus, in grave dampnum, preiudicium et maximum interesse dicti domini Petri. Qua propter dictus procurator, procuratorio nomine quo supra, requisivit et requirit dictum nobilem Iohannem presentem et intelligentem, quatenus non debeat impedire solucionem, tradicionem et assegnationem precii dictorum pannorum et bonorum et dictis medianis licenciam dare solvendi, tradendi et assignandi illud precium eidem protestanti, aliter protestatur contra eum de omnibus dampnis, interesse, missionibus et expensis propterea factis et fiendis, que et quas dictus suus principalis passus extitit et pati et iusticie que poterit quomodo defectu et culpa dicti Iohannis impedimentum facientis circa solucionem precii dictorum bonorum faciendam dicto nobili domino Petro. Constituens eum in dolo, mora et culpa. Hanc suam etc. Actum in banco etc.

Eodem

Dictus Amatus, Iudeus, constitutus in presencia Ysacce Sala, Lioni Chamusu et Iosep Abudaram, Iudeorum medianorum, exposuit quod cum ipsi promisissent dicto suo principali, per contractum publicum, vendere pannos et alias merces emptos per eundem dominum Petrum a Iohanne de Rossolmino infra dictum tempus, contentum in contractu facto in posse notarii Antoni de Aprea et de precio dictorum bonorum solvere uncias XXVI in una manu cuidam et uncias L^{ta} cuidam alteri prestare in adversa manu dicto suo principali, ipsique Iudei mediani vendiderint maiorem partem dictorum bonorum et minime solvere curaverint pecunias predicti cui solvere debebant de commissione dicti domini Petri, nec curant ad presentem, in grave preiudicium et interesse dicti domini Petri. Qua propter dictus procurator, nomine quo supra, requisivit et requirit dictos

Iudeos, presentes et intelligentes, quatenus solvere debeant pecunias predictas illis quibus debeant et eidem procuratori illud quod superest in manibus eorum ceterorum prout contractus et eorum quilibet in solidum de omnibus dampnis, interesse, missionibus et expensis propterea factis et fiendis quitquid dictis suis principalibus possit restitui et pati et substitui poterit quo quomodo, defectu et culpa dictorum Iudeorum [..]e ad implimentum promissa.

Ad quam dicti Iudei responderunt quatenus defecit nec deficit per eos, sed predicto suo principali qui nullo dixerit fideiussores quos promisit dare, nec fieri fecit obligationem fideiussionis, iuxta tenorem quo supra principalis Xilomus[!] requisiverit et requirere dixit procurator pro eos debeat satisfacere de iustitie aliqua.

Palermo, 6 April 1459

Source: ASP, Not. Giacomo Comito, reg. 850, c. 137v.

Mussuto Misiria, a Palermitan Jew, hires himself out to Giovanni Bayamonte to work in his tunny plant during the entire season for 17 tarì *a month. He is paid that amount on account.*

Palermo, 9 August 1459

Source: ASP, Not. Giacomo Comito, reg. 850, c. 304r.

Bonsignoro Canet, a Jew of Palermo, promises Iosep Chimisi, another Jew, to pay during the the month of August 40.20.15 ounces which he owes Iosep for Venetian tables.

Palermo, 20 December 1459

Source: ASP, Not. Giacomo Comito, reg. 850, c. 122v.

Sadia Sala, Abram Bass and Manuel Aurifichi, Palermitan Jews, acknowledge receipt from Antonio Falco, a Genoese merchant, of a bill of exchange for 50 ounces made out in favour of Antonio de Iuliano. They promise to pay the bill within three months through Azaruti de Manuel and David Xunina, Jews.

Palermo, 4 January 1460

Source: ASP, Not. Giacomo Comito, reg. 850, c. 132v.

Giovanni de Raynaldo and Marino de Bindiru, a Jew, hire themselves out to Iacobo de Crapona to work in his sugar refinery during the entire season for a fixed wage of 5.2.0 ounces

Palermo, 16 January 1460

Source: ASP, Not. Giacomo Comito, reg. 850, c. 138v.

Agreement between Ysach Sala, a Palermitan Jew, and the notary Filippo Scolaro, whereby Ysach promises the notary to pay the 1.15.18 ounces which he owes him with one ounce worth of wheat and the balance with grapes.

Palermo, 13 February 1460

Source: ASP, Not. Giacomo Comito, reg. 850, c. 171r.

Iacu Malti, a Jew of Palermo, declares under oath and aided by witnessess that he paid Matheo de Girardo, a Pisan, five ounces for and on account of Vita Gaseni, a Jew of Sciacca. The amount was the price for Vita's stay at Matheo's fondaco for 12 days.

Note: The price charged appears to be rather stiff.

Palermo, 4 April 1460

Source: ASP, Not. Giacomo Comito, reg. 850, c. 235v.

Mussuto Misiria, a Palermitan Jew, hires himself out to Giovanno Bayamonte to work in his tunny plant during the entire season for 17 tarì *a month. He is paid 11.5* tarì *on account.*

Palermo, 28 April 1460

Source: ASP, Not. Giacomo Comito, reg. 850, loose leaf

Muxa Ysach and Merdoc Bulfarachi, Palermitan Jews, present their arguments in regard to the protest lodged against them by Iaimo de Paruta over the sale of a

6344

table cloth. Iaimo protested that the cloth did not correspond to the one they had offered him.

Palermo, 30 June 1460

Source: ASP, Not. Giacomo Comito, reg. 850, c. 313r.

Chayrono Abruchezen, a Jew, appoints Antonio la Vallu to look after his interests and to collect 10 florins and two Venetian ducats from a debtor who had not paid for his purchases.

Palermo, 26 June 1460

Source: ASP, Not. Giacomo Comito, reg. 850, c. 309r.

Brachono Raxidi, a Palermitan Jew, declares that he owes Isdraeli Raxidi, his ward, some clothes, a band and some other articles, including two Hebrew books, which he is keeping in his capacity as guardian.

Palermo, 17 July 1460

Source: ASP, Not. Giacomo Comito, reg. 850, c. 330r.

Muxa de Minichi, a Palermitan Jew, hires himself out to Giovanni Bayamonte to work as a parator *in his sugar refinery for one ounce a month.*

Palermo, 26 August 1460

Source: ASP, Not. Giacomo Comito, reg. 850, c. 349v.

Machalufo Xiba, a Trapanese Jew, promises Giovanni Bayamonte to trasnport with two mules Giovanni's sugar cane during the entire season for five tarì *a* salma. *He is paid one ounce on account.*

Palermo, 29 December 1460

Source: ASP, Not. Giacomo Comito, reg. 851, c. 41r.

Minto de Muxarella, a Palermitan Jew, acting for Francesco Allegra, launches a notarial protest against Simone de Martorana to obtain payment of a debt long overdue.

Palermo, 28 March 1461

Source: ASP, Not. Giacomo Comito, reg. 851, c. 127r.

Quittance by Sabet Cuyno, a Palermitan Jew, acknowledging receipt of the linen which he had purchased for 34.18.0 ounces from Iacobo de Castro, a Pisan merchant.

Palermo, 7 April 1461

Source: ASP, Not. Giacomo Comito, reg. 851, c. 148r.

Ismael Romano, a Palermitan Jew, promises Pino de Sancto Filippo to carry out certain jobs for an agreed sum.

Palermo, 12 April 1461

Source: ASP, Not. Giacomo Comito, reg. 851, c. 157r.

Abram de Seragusia, a Palermitan Jew, hires himself out to Nicolò Mundoloni of Lipari to work in his tunny plant for 15 tarì *a month.*

Palermo, 2 June 1461

Source: ASP, Not. Giacomo Comito, reg. 851, c. 219r.

David and Simone Xunina, Palermitan Jews, promise Simon Assuni alias Copiu, another Jew, to pay their debt for the purchase of gold wire within three months.

Palermo, 23 October 1461

Source: ASP, Not. Giacomo Comito, reg. 851, c. 4v.

Chanino Farmuni, son of Nixim, a Palermitan Jew, promises to pay Siminito Salcazu, his fellow Jew three tarì *a day on behalf of his father. Siminto had stood surety for Nixim, who owed 12 ounces to the local castellan.*

Palermo, 24 October 1461

Source: ASP, Not. Giacomo Comito, reg. 851, c. 11r.

Andrea Gallo, of Malta, promises Maymone de Anello, a Jew of Agrigento, to

6346

*pay 15 tarì immediately and another 15 tarì within six months, in settlement of
a debt of one ounce, the balance of the purchase price of 2.24.0 ounces for wheat
which Maymon had sold Andrea.*

Palermo, 24 October 1461

Source: ASP, Not. Giacomo Comito, reg. 851, c. 26v.

*Agreement whereby Leone Anaffi, a Jew of Palermo, promises Granillino to return
15 tarì which he had received on account of the purchase of grapes which he had
failed to supply to Granillino. Leone is to pay the debt in weekly instalments of
2.10 tarì. Gabriel de Liucio, a Jew, stands surety for Leone.*

Palermo, 2 May 1462

Source: ASP, Not. Giacomo Comito, reg. 851, c. 141v.

*Abram Xaccarono, a Palermitan Jew, hires himself out to Giovanni Bayamonte
to work in his sugar refinery during the entire season for one ounce a month, and
is paid the same amount on account.*

Palermo, 2 May 1462

Source: ASP, Not. Giacomo Comito, reg. 851, c. 141v.

*Giaimo Bonfiglio grants Salamon Cuyno, a Palermitan Jew, a postponement on
the payment of two ounces overdue to Giaimo for the purchase of goods.*

Palermo, 12 November 1462

Source: ASP, Not. Giacomo Comito, reg. 852, c. 242r-v.

*Contract whereby Rubino Muxarella, a Jew of Marsala, a Palermitan citizen,
promises Lemmo Cucucza to pay by the end of May six ounces which the latter
had lent him free of charge. He pledges property and provides a guarantor to
Lemmo. On 1 December Gauiusa, Rubino's wife, and Gayu, his son, also stand
surety for Rubino. Rubino having failed to pay the debt, Lemmo cedes all his
rights to the guarantor for six ounces.*

Eodem

Rubinus Muxarella, Iudeus de terra Marsalie, civis Panormi, coram me notario et testibus infrascriptis sponte dixit et confessus fuit mihi notario infrascripto, ut persone publice, officio publico, vice et nomine Lemmi Cucucza absentis, stipulantis et recipientis se ab eodem Lemmo habuisse et recepisse mutuo, gratis precibus et amore uncias auri sex p[onderis] g[eneralis] renuncians execucioni etc. [empty space] Quas uncias VI tenetur dictus Iudeus debitor et sollemni stipulacione promisit dicto Lemmo creditori, licet absenti, me notario publico stipulante pro eodem, eidem creditori, vel persone legitime pro eo, dare, solvere et integre assignare, reddere et restituire in pecunia numerata in Panormo, hinc per totum mensem Madii proxime venturi, in pace, de plano etc., omni libello, moratoria regia, gracia, guidatico, dilacione quinquennali, bonorum cessionis et quibuscumque aliis provisionibus impetratis et impetrandis remotis et a dicto Iudeo debitore remissis et ex pacto sollemni renuncians ipsisque impetratis aut quomodolibet concessit promisit non uti cum iuramento. Cum refectione omnium dampnorum, interesse et expensarum et specialiter expensarum viaticarum etc. Obligando inde se suosque heredes et bona omnia habita et habenda etc. Et specialiter obligavit et ypothegavit, ac obligat et ypothegat vineam unam sitam et positam in territorio Marsalie, in contrata vocata di La Marinella, secus vineam Petri de Bellissima, viam publicam et alios confines, nec non tenimentum unum domorum situm et positum in dicta terra Marsalie, secus domos Manfre de Bandera et alios confines, ita quod specialis obligacio non deroget generali nec eo converso constituens precario possidere, promictens dictam vineam et tenimentum domorum legitime defendere etc. Pro quo Iudeo debitore et eius precibus extitit fideiussorem et se principalem debitorem, pagatorem, solutorem et omnium premissorum observatorem constituit versus dictum Lemmum, licet absentem, me notario stipulante et recipiente pro eodem Iacobus de Bonanno iuri de primo principali conveniendo et expresse renuncians, sub ipotheca et obligacione omnium bonorum suorum presencium et futurorum, ita quod liceat dicto Iacobo fideiussori, casu quo dictas uncias sex adveniente tempore solucionis non fuerint solute per dictum Iudeum debitorem, sed per ipsum fideiussorem accedere ad dictam terra Marsalie quod expensas viatica, ut supra, ipsasque vineam et domos vendendi illo precio quo poterint vendi et sibi satisfieri de pecuniis predicto Iudeo solutis dicto Lemmo quam de dampnis, interesse et expensis et de evictione vinee et dictorum domorum se fideiussorem constituit Gayu de Muxarella, filius ipsius Robini, renunciando omni iuri sibi competenti et competituro in et super dictis vinea et tenimento domorum cui dictus Robinus auctoritatem dedit dictarum vinee et domorum. Promictens de evictione dare etiam in fideiussorem in solidum cum eius filis eius uxorem, infra terminum dierum octo ab hodie continuo numerando, ita quod, elapso termino dictamque eius uxorem fideiussitricem non constituerit ut supra, liceat eidem creditori execucionem facere de toto debito ac si terminus foret decursus. Et fiat ritus in persona et bonis et quod possit variare de persona ad bona et de bonis ad personam ad electionem dicte creditricis. Renuncians privilegio fori, refugio domos. Et iuraverunt et iterum iurant ab solucionem inlincentianter non petere, etc.

Actum in vanella Carcerum Panormi, presentibus Iuliano Bonconti, Antonio de Parisi et magistro Antonio Ioczo testibus.

In the left margin: Die primo mensis Decembris Ind. predicte, Gauiusa Iudea mulier, uxor dicti Rubini, auctorizata a dicto eius viro presente et ipsam ad infrascripta auctoriczante, non protestata nec [...] ducta, sed de sua mera, pura et spontanea voluntate, ut dixit, nemine eam cogentem, coram nobis, sponte ratificavit, acceptavit et confirmavit proximum contractum et constituit se fideiubssitricem in solidum cum eius filio de [...] vinee et domorum obligata dicto Iacobo in proximo contractu renunciando omni iuri sibi competenti et competituro tam actioni sue chitube quam quocumque alia racione et iuri de primo principali conveniendo, sub ypotheca et obligatione omnium bonorum suorum supram presencium et futurorum et novarum constitucionum de pluribus rebus debendis.

Actum in domo dicti Rubini, presentibus magistro Stephano Geraci et magistro Petro Mantuva, magistro Vincencio.

Die ultimo mensis Iunii Ind. predicte dictus Lemmus, coram nobis sponte dedit, cessit et concessit dicto Iacobo fideiussori, presenti et recipienti omnia iura omnesque actiones reales, personales, utiles, directas, mixtas, tacitas et expressas, pretorias et civiles et alias quascumque quas et que habet et sibi competunt contra et adversus dictum Rubinum Iudeum pro unciis VI, quatenus vigore proximi contractus, ita ut ipsis iuribus et actionibus dictus Iacobus uti possit agere et experiri, defendere et se tueri in iudiciis et extra eum et in eius bonis execucionem facere, quietare et absolvere dictum contractum cassare et annullare et demum omnia alia facere que dictum Iacobum procuratorem constituens in premissis et in rem proprius et ponens eum in locum suum et hoc quia dictus Lemmus confessus fuit dictas uncias sex a dicto Iacobo ut fideiussore habuisse et recepisse, solvente de sua propria pecunia, animo recuperandi a dicto Iudeo ut dixit. Testes: Lambertus Vaccarus et magister Nicolaus Sinara.

Palermo, 12 November 1462

Source: ASP, Not. Giacomo Comito, reg. 852, c. nn.

Contract between Bartholomeo de Miglacio and Simon Xunina, a Palermitan Jew, for setting up a joint venture for the management of a warehouse to trade in cheese and caviocavallo. *It is to last a year. Bartholomeo invests nine ounces and Simon his labour.*

Palermo, 25 November 1462

Source: ASP, Not. Giacomo Comito, reg. 852, c. 164r.

Pasquale Sidoti and his son Iuda, Palermitan Jews, promise Sadia de Girachio, a Jew of Caltabellotta, to transport casks of wine from Caltabellotta to Palermo for 23 tarì.

Palermo, 3 November 1462

Source: ASP, Not. Giacomo Comito, reg. 852, c. 174r.

Gallufo Amar, a Jew in Palermo, hires himself out to Giovanni Bayamonte to work in his sugar refinery during the whole season for two ounces.

Palermo, 3 November 1462

Source: ASP, Not. Giacomo Comito, reg. 852, c. 174v.

Xibiten Ysach, a Jew in Palermo, hires himself out to Giovanni Bayamonte to work in his sugar refinery during the whole season for two ounces.

Palermo, 4 November 1462

Source: ASP, Not. Giacomo Comito, reg. 852, c. 177v.

Salamon de Messina and and Raffael Misiria, Jews of Palermo, hire themselves out to Giovanni Bayamonte to work in his sugar refinery during the whole season for two ounces a month.

Palermo, 8 November 1462

Source: ASP, Not. Giacomo Comito, reg. 852, c. 185r.

Salamon de Messina and and Raffael Misiria, Jews of Palermo, in addition to hiring themselves out to Giovanni Bayamonte to work in his sugar refinery during the whole season for two ounces a month, undertake to cut and prune his sugar cane for 10 tarì a bed of new plants and 15 tarì a bed of old ones. They are paid 15 tarì by Christmas and one ounce by April.

Palermo, 8 November 1462

Source: ASP, Not. Giacomo Comito, reg. 852, c. 185v.

Xamuel Sansuni, Iosep Xammara, Busacca de Seracusia and David Amiseni, Jews, hire themselves out to Giovanni Bayamonte to work in his sugar plantation at Carini for 10 tarì a bed of new plants and 15 tarì a bed of old ones. They are also to be paid one grana for fertilizing each bed. They are paid 12 tarì on account.

Palermo, 15 November 1462

Source: ASP, Not. Giacomo Comito, reg. 852, c. nn.

Contract between Robino Gibra, a Palermitan Jew, and Giovanni Homodeo in regard to the tunny plant of Solanto. Robino had leased the plant from the archbishop of Palermo for the the current season. Giovanni is co-owner of the plant.

Note: The Doc. is damaged and partly illegible.

Palermo, 3 December 1462

Source: ASP, Not. Giacomo Comito, reg. 852, c. 228v.

Notarial protest by Sabatino de Minichi, a Palermitan Jew, against Guglielmo Valdaura, a Catalan merchant. Sabatino had hired a mule to Guglielmo to travel to Syracuse. The mule had died en route. Sabatino claims damages from Guglielmo.

Palermo, 10 January 1463

Source: ASP, Not. Giacomo Comito, reg. 852, c. 242v.

Sadia Azaruti, Muxa Achina, and Benedetto Aurifichi, Palermitan Jews, hire themselves out to Giovanni Carbona to work in the sugar plantation of Nicolò de Bonfante during the entire season for 10 tarì *a bed of new plants and 15* tarì *a bed of old ones, as well as one* grana *for fertilizing each bed. They are paid two ounces on account.*

Palermo, 10 January 1463

Source: ASP, Not. Giacomo Comito, reg. 852, c. 243r.

Sadia Azaruti, a Jew of Palermo, hires himself out to Giovanni Bonfante to work during the whole season as a paratore *in the sugar refinery of Pietro Imperatore for one ounce a month.*

Palermo, 1 February 1463

Source: ASP, Not. Giacomo Comito, reg. 852, c. 283r.

Notarial protest by Iosep Camusu, a Palermitan Jew, against Gallufo de Minichi, his Jewish fellow citizen, for having caused damage to Iosep's house during work carried out there by Gallufo.

Palermo, 1 February 1463

Source: ASP, Not. Giacomo Comito, reg. 852, cc. 285r–286v.

Contract whereby Iacobo Sabatino, a Palermitan Jew, with the consent of his wife Rosa, formerly married to Pachuni Marsili, cedes to David Sandato, his Jewish fellow citizen, a shop in the ruga *Nova of the Albergaria quarter in the* contrada *Bardariorum. The shop borders on those of Sabatino de Minichi and Vita Stranu, Jews, and is situated below the monastery of S. Tomaso de Ruffo. The shop belongs to the monastery, which agrees to the transfer of the lease from Iacobo to David. The annual rent, payable to the monastery, is one ounce plus an impost of six* tarì. *In addition, David undertakes to pay Rosa 25* tarì *annually.*

Eodem

Iacobus Sabatinus, Iudeus de Panormo, coram me notario et testibus infrascriptis, sponte nomine et pro parte Rose, eius uxoris, olim uxoris Pachuni Marsili, Iudei, pro qua eius uxore de rato promisit sub ipotheca et obligatione omnium bonorum suorum presentium et futurorum in perpetuum per heredes et successores dicte sue uxoris, locavit et dedit ad emphiteosim et canone census uncie unius habere et licere concessit David Sandato, Iudeo suo concivi, presenti et recipienti pro se heredibus et successoribus suis in perpetuum apotecam unam terraneam sitam et positam in quarterio Albergarie in ruga vocata La ruga Nova, in Contrada Bardariorum, secus apotecam Sabatini de Minichi, ex una parte, sub posita et infrascripto monasterio et secus apothecam Vite Stranu, viam publicam et alios confines, cum omnibus introitibus exitibus ipsius, ingressibus, regressibus, iuribus et pertinenciis suis et cum omnibus hiis que intra se supra se, circum, circa in integrum continentur confines alios si qui forent, cum onere census tarenorum sex solvendorum quolibet anno monasterio Sancti Tomasi de Ruffo Panormi, presente nichilominus venerabili sorore Scolastica Castillar, abatissa dicti monasteri, et consensu infrascriptorum monialium, videlicet sororis Garite de Bentivegna, vicarie sororis Alionore de Blundo, sororis Ianne Apichelis, sororis Thomasine de Cardella, sororis Catherine de Cutaida, sororis Anthonie Resciti, sororis Ianne de Paruta, sororis Ianne de Blankiforti, sororis Anthonie de Nanzano, sororis Madalene de Canthuco et sororis Pine de Canthuco, congregatarum ad sonum campanelle huius conventus eorum consensium prestancium et suum consensum prestantis, animo et intencione dictam Rosam a prestacione dicti canonis liberandi et dictum David in novum emphiteotam heredem et successorem recipiendi, quam apotecam dictus Iacob asseruit ad dictam eius uxorem convenire pro rata futura liberam et expeditam ab omni alio onere census et cuiuslibet alterius servitutis, que olim fuit Pachuni Marsili, bardarii. Constituens se ex nunc pro tunc prefatus Iacobus, nomine quo supra, dictam apothecam cum omnibus suis iuribus et introitibus ipsius precario nomine tenere et pro parte dicti David emphiteote, heredum et successorum suorum in perpetuum tenere et possidere donec et quousque dictam corporalem vel quasi capere possessionem quam intrandi, capiendi deinceps et tenendi absque iussu curie et magistratorum decreto et auctoritatem dedit et pleniorem potestatem ad habendum per eumdem emphiteotam, heredes et successores suos dictam apothecam cum universis iuribus suis ex nunc in antea [empty space] intrandum, possidendum, utendum, alienandum, permutandum, pro animo iudicandum et suas ultimas et omnimodas voluntates faciendum tamquam de re propria iusto titulo acquisita, pactis emphiteuticis infrascriptis omnibus et singulis sibi a dicto monasterio et dicto utili dominio salvis penitus servatis vel quasi dictus emphiteuta promisit, convenit et se solleniter obligavit in perpetuum per se, heredes et successores suos dictum canonem uncie unius, cum onere tarenorum sex, et dicte Rose heredibus et successoribus suis in perpetuum tarenos vigintiquinque anno quolibet dare, solvere et integre assignare, aut dari, solvi et integre assignare facere die XV augusti, incipiendo die XV augusti anni presentis pro rata videlicet, dictamque apothecam beneficare et de bono in melius augmentare et non permictere deteriorari a statu quo nunc est et erit in futurum, et non liceat eidem emphiteote, nec suis heredibus et successoribus dictam apothecam vendere, nec alienare ecclesie, fisco, comiti nec alicui alteri persone privilegiate, nisi personis licitis et a iure permissis, et si vendere voluerit emphiteuta ipse et sui heredes voluerint primo dicta omnia requirere debeant dictum monasterium et dictam Rosam et successores suos, et si emere voluerit aut altera pars voluerit, preferantur et altera pars preferatur aliis emptoribus et non debeant altere partes de bonis predictis que ab aliis recipere contingunt et minime dictam unciam unam et nolentes pro se ipso dictum monasterium [...] et iure caligarium tarenos sex vice qualibet qua vendi contigerit et si dicta Rosa et successores sui [...] noluerint pro se emere dictam apothecam. Et de presenti contractu fieri facere duo publica consimilia instrumenta infra dies XV ab hodie continuo numerando, unum ad cautelam dicti emphiteute et aliud ad tuendum ipsum monasterium. Et si dictus emphioteuta cessaverit et sui successores cessaverint in solucione dicti canonis per biennium quo ad omne triennium quo ad utilem dominum liceat et si [...] precario et ultra [...] dictam apothecam cum emponema.....[imponimentibus] suis et melioracionibus ad se libere revocaret consuetudini panormitane non obstante cui consuetudini dictus emphiteota per se et successores suos et omni ipsius auxilio renuncians et renunciantes, promictens dictus utilis dominus pro dictis racionibus per se, heredes et successores suos dictam apothecam superius concessam cum omnibus iuribus suis dictum emphiteotam dictus emphiteota aut bonum ius unus pro alio semper et omni futuro tempore legitime defendere, guarentire et disbrigare ab omni calumpniante et intrigante persona loco, curie et universitatis et contra omnem calumpniantem et intrigantem personam locum, curie et universitatem, lites et questiones in se suscipiendo, permutando suis omnibus suis concessionibus propriis sumptibus [...] prosequi et finiri, etc... appellando, prosequendo et supplicando expresse universis cum pacto sollemni cum iuramento renunciantes. Quam quidem concessionem et omnia et singula supradicta et infrascripta promiserunt dicti contrahentes sibi ad ...et vicissim ... etc. etc.

6354

Sicily

Palermo, 7 February 1463

Source: ASP, Not. Giacomo Comito, reg. 852, c. 289v.

Muxa de Liuni, a Jew of Palermo, hires himself out to Giovanni Bayamonte to work in his sugar refinery for one ounce a month.

Palermo, 7 February 1463

Source: ASP, Not. Giacomo Comito, reg. 852, c. 290r.

Busacca Chifanu, a Jew of Palermo, hires himself out to Giovanni Bayamonte to work in his sugar refinery for one ounce a month.

Palermo, 29 April 1463

Source: ASP, Not. Giacomo Comito, reg. 852, c. nn.

Sabet Pulisi, a Jew of Palermo, hires himself out to Giovanni Bayamonte to work in his sugar refinery for one ounce a month.

Palermo, 14 June 1463

Source: ASP, Not. Giacomo Comito, reg. 852, c. 431r.

Busacca Panichello, a Jew of Palermo, lodges a notarial protest against Thomeo de Graciano, a Genoese merchant, for having failed to deliver the merchandise which Busacca had purchased from him for 3.10.0 ounces

Palermo, 17 June 1463

Source: ASP, Not. Giacomo Comito, reg. 852, cc. 335v–336v.

Master Sadono de Medico, a Jewish physician and citizen of Palermo, grants Nicolò Manueli, his fellow citizen, a perpetual lease of two inns and attached storehouses for an annual rent of two ounces, to be paid in three instalments. The inns are situated in Palermo in the contrada *La Pinda [!], near the enclosure of S. Giovanni and the property of the heirs of Pietro Afflicto.*

Palermo, 19 July 1463

Source: ASP, Not. Giacomo Comito, reg. 852, c. 305v.

Raffael Xunina and Minto Minachem, Palermitan Jews, hire themselves out to Nicolò Bonconte to work in his sugar plant during the entire season, and to collect the dry leaves and clean the courtyard.

Palermo, 3 august 1463

Source: ASP, Not. Giacomo Comito, reg. 852, c. 319v.

Azarono Bindira, Muxa Barbaru, Muxa de Seracusia, Busacca de Seracusia and Iosep Bindira, Jews in Palermo, hire themselves out Antonio de Amato to work in his business for one tarì *a day.*

Palermo, 30 October 1463

Source: ASP, Not. Giacomo Comito, reg. 852, c. nn.

Nixim Balbu and Chayrono de Girachio, Jews of Termini Imerese, hire themselves out to Lupo de Puchio to work in his tunny plant for one ounce a month, and are paid that sum on account.

Palermo, 18 September 1465

Source: ASP, Not. Giacomo Comito, reg. 853, c. 29v.

Notarial protest by Gimilono Naguay, a Palermitan Jew, against Aron Aseni, Busacca Sabatino and Gimilono Abdili, his Jewish fellow citizens, for having failed to pay for a piece of velvet which they had purchased from him. He demands payment forthwith.

Palermo, 18 November 1465

Source: ASP, Not. Giacomo Comito, reg. 853, c. 140r.

Minto Galifa, Sabet Magaseni and Abdila Bramellu, Palermitan Jews, hire themselves out to Iacobo Salvo to work in his sugar plant as grinders for one ounce a month.

6356

Sicily

Palermo, 29 November 1465

Source: ASP, Not. Giacomo Comito, reg. 853, c. 157r.

Muxa Sabuchi, a Jew of Palermo, hires himself out to Iacobo de Salvo to work as a paratore *in his sugar refinery during the whole season for two ounces.*

Palermo, 29 November 1465

Source: ASP, Not. Giacomo Comito, reg. 853, c. 157v.

Sabatino Bramuni, a Jew of Palermo, hires himself out to Iacobo de Salvo to work as a paratore *in his sugar refinery during the whole season for two ounces.*

Palermo, 3 December 1465

Source: ASP, Not. Giacomo Comito, reg. 853, c. 163r.

Sabet Cuyno, a Jew of Palermo, hires himself out to Iacobo de Salvo to work in his sugar refinery during the whole season for two ounces.

Palermo, 5 December 1465

Source: ASP, Not. Giacomo Comito, reg. 853, c. 165v.

Bonano de Girachio, a Jew in Palermo, hires himself out to Pietro de Imperatore to work in his sugar refinery during the whole season for 22 tarì *a month.*

Palermo, 10 December 1465

Source: ASP, Not.Giacomo Comito, reg. 853, c. 168r.

Sadono Seracusano, a Jew in Palermo, promises Iosep Camuti, his Jewish fellow citizen, to pay the 15 tarì *which he has been owing him for a long time.*

Palermo, 15 January 1466

Source: ASP, Not. Giacomo Comito, reg. 853, loose leaf.

Notarial protest lodged by Fariono Gazu, a Palermitan Jew, against Bonsignoro Canet, his fellow Jew, in the matter of the damage allegedly caused his dwelling

*in the course of work carried out by Bonsignoro for Nissim Millac, a Jew. Fariono
demands that Bonsignoro restore the previously existing state of his property.*

Palermo, 4 February 1466

Source: ASP, Not. Giacomo Comito, reg. 853, cc. 214v–215v.

*Renewal of the perpetual lease of a solerata house by the Franciscan monastery of
S. Giovanni to Muxa Levi, a Palermitan Jew, for an annual rent of 14* tarì. *The
house is situated in the* contrada *Cannarite in the Conciaria quarter of Palermo,
next to the tannery of Salamone Levi.*

Palermo, 31 January 1466

Source: ASP, Not. Giacomo Comito, reg. 853, cc. 215v–216v.

*Renewal of a perpetual lease of two shops by the Franciscan monastery of San
Giovanni to Merdoch Vignuni, a Palermitan Jew, for an annual rent of four* tarì.
The shops are situated in the Cassaro, in the ruga *Ferrariorun, next to another
shop of Merdoch and other properties.*

Palermo, 15 January 1466

Source: ASP, Not. Giacomo Comito, reg. 853, cc. 221v–222v.

Renewal of a perpetual lease of a solerata *house by the Franciscan monastery of
S. Giovanni to Muxa Si[..], a Palermitan Jew, for an annual rent of one ounce.
The house is located in the Cassaro, in the* vanella *Mamma Iacopa, next to the
properties of Fariuno Ysach and Busac Malti, Jews.*

Palermo, 4 February 1466

Source: ASP, Not. Giacomo Comito, reg. 853, c. 224r

*Deed whereby Elia Cuyno and his mother Disiata, and Rachila, daughter of the
late Xamuel Cuyno, Jews of Palermo, appoint Muxa Cuyno, another Jew, their
attorney to look after their affairs in Palermo and elsewhere and to collect their
outstanding debts.*

Palermo, 12 April 1466

Source: ASP, Not. Giacomo Comito, reg. 853, c. 276v.

Contract whereby Muxa Sufi, a Jew of Corleone and Merdoc Xirebi, a Jew of Palermo, set up a joint venture to trade in cloth for a year. Muxa invests three ounces and Merdoc a certain quantity of merchandise. The proceeds are to be divided between the partners in equal shares.

Palermo, 24 June 1466

Source: ASP, Not. Giacomo Comito, reg. 853, c. 389r.

Sabet Cuyno, a Palermitan Jew, appoints the Jewish brothers Vita and Lazaro Nifusi, his fellow citizens, to travel to Malta to collect some of his outstanding debts.

Palermo, 1 October 1461

Source: ASP, Not. Giacomo Comito, reg. 854, c. 6v.

Demand by Brachono de Messana, a Palermitan Jew, that Giovanni de Messana return forthwith a fully equipped olive press which he had leased him until the end of September, since elapsed. The press is situated in Palermo, in the contrada *Fori Veteris.*

Palermo, 25 May 1462

Source: ASP, Not. Giacomo Comito, reg. 854, c. 43r.

Declaration by Abram Xiffuni, a Palermitan Jew, widower of the late Gaudiosa, and their daughter Gaudiosa, that they received all the property listed in Gaudiosa's ketubah. *They do so at the behest of Azara Taguil, their Jewish fellow citizen.*

Palermo, 25 June 1462

Source: ASP, Not. Giacomo Comito, reg. 854, c. 78v.

Bartholomeo Bonvichini and Provido de Firrerio, in disagreement over a matter of taxes, appoint as arbitrator Salamon Cuyno, a Palermitan Jew.

Palermo, 24 January 1463

Source: ASP, Not. Giacomo Comito, reg. 854, c. 59r.

Merdoc Chaynello, a Jew of Palermo, hires himself out for a year to Iuda de Minichi, his Jewish fellow citizen, to work in his business to salt tunny for 1.20.0 ounces.

Palermo, 29 January 1463

Source: ASP, Not. Giacomo Comito, reg. 854, c. 66r.

Abram Bass, a Palermitan Jew, had ceded to Antonio Pedivillano all his rights in regard to 26 ounces which he claimed from Nicolò de Verniga. Following a dispute between the parties, they appoint Antonio Vitanze as arbitrator .

Palermo, 30 January 1463

Source: ASP, Not. Giacomo Comito, reg. 854, c. 70v.

Salamon de Missina, a Jew of Palermo, hires himself out to Giovanni Bayamonte to work as a parator *in his sugar press at Carini during the entire season for one ounce a month. He is paid 24* tarì *on account.*

Palermo, 2 May 1463

Source: ASP, Not. Giacomo Comito, reg. 854, c. nn.

Notarial protest lodged by Simone de Risignano, owner of the tunny plant in San Giorgio, against Robino Gibra and Nissim Binna, Palermitan Jews, for having failed to pay him the decima *for the lease of the plant. He demands payment forthwith.*

Palermo, 25 October 1466

Source: ASP, Not. Giacomo Comito, reg. 854, c. 24v.

Thomeo de mastro Antonio appoints Creciano Calabrisi, a Jew of Palermo, his attorney to represent his interests and collect his debts in Palermo and elsewhere.

Palermo, 31 October 1466

Source: ASP, Not. Giacomo Comito, reg. 854, c. 31v.

Notarial protest by Muxa de Medico, a Palermitan Jew, against Minto de Muxarella, a Jew of Marsala, his attorney, who had collected one of his debts but had failed to hand it over to him.

Palermo, 5 November 1466

Source: ASP, Not. Giacomo Comito, reg. 854, c. 40r.

Muxa de Medico, a Palermitan Jew, renews his protest against Minto de Muxarella, a Jew of Marsala, his attorney, for not paying him his due.

Palermo, 26 December 1466

Source: ASP, Not. Giacomo Comito, reg. 854, c. nn.

Salamon Raffaele, a Jew of Palermo, hires himself out to Giovanni de Bayamonte to work in his sugar refinery during the entire season for one ounce a month.

Palermo, 26 December 1466

Source: ASP, Not. Giacomo Comito, reg. 854, c. nn.

Merdoc Chaguela, a Jew of Palermo, hires himself out to Giovanni de Bayamonte to work in his sugar refinery during the entire season for one ounce a month. He is paid that sum on account.

Palermo, 26 December 1466

Source: ASP, Not. Giacomo Comito, reg. 854, c. nn.

Salamon de Missina, a Jew of Palermo, hires himself out to Giovanni Bayamonte to cultivate his sugar cane during the entire season for 10 grana *a bed of new plants and 15* grana *a bed of old ones.*

Palermo, 26 December 1466

Source: ASP, Not. Giacomo Comito, reg. 854, c. nn.

Vita Cathanisi, a Jew of Palermo, hires himself out to Giovanni de Bayamonte for the entire season to work in his sugar refinery as a parator *for 28* tarì *a month. He is paid six* tarì *on account.*

Palermo, 26 December 1466

Source: ASP, Not. Giacomo Comito, reg. 854, c. nn.

Sadia Niffusi, a Palermitan Jew, hires himself out to Giovanni de Bayamonte for the entire season to work in his sugar refinery as a parator *for 28* tarì *a month. He is paid six* tarì *on account.*

Palermo, 14 October 1466

Source: ASP, Not. Giacomo Comito, reg. 855, loose leaf.

Salamon Balbu, a Palermitan Jew, on his own behalf and on that of Muxa Meme, Minto Misiria and Xibiten Balbu, his Jewish fellow citizens, in the presence of Bartholomeo Franco, doctor of law and assessore iustiziario *in Palermo, start legal proceedings against Busacca Actuni, a Jew, in the matter of a theft allegedly committed by the latter. They ask for damages.*

Palermo, 27 October 1466

Source: ASP, Not. Giacomo Comito, reg. 855, c. 51r.

Vita Calabrisi, a Jew of Palermo, hires himself out to Giovanni de Bayamonte for the entire season to work in his sugar refinery as a parator *for 21* tarì *a month. He is paid 21* tarì *on account.*

Palermo, 7 February 1467

Source: ASP, Not. Giacomo Comito, reg. 855, c. 97r.

Gallufo Dinar, a Jew in Palermo, appoints his son Sabeti to look after his interests in Palermo and elsewhere and to travel to Marsala to collect some of his debts.

Palermo, 7 February 1467

Source: ASP, Not. Giacomo Comito, reg. 855, c. 51r.

Sabeti Dinar, a Jew in Palermo, following his appointment to act for his father and having to leave Palermo on business, appoints Raffaele de Danieli, a Jew, to look after his interests during his absence.

Palermo, 30 July 1467

Source: ASP, Not. Giacomo Comito, reg. 855, c. 153r.

Formal request presented to Cristofalo Iumbataro to give his consent to the sale of the lease of a house belonging to him in the vanella *Fadaloni in Trapani. Chayrono Cuyno, son of Sabeti and Carissima, had sold the lease to his brother, Iuda.*

Palermo, 13 November 1467

Source: ASP, Not. Giacomo Comito, reg. 855, c. 84r.

Sadia Niffusi, a Jew of Palermo, hires himself out to Lupo de Sivigla, owner of a tunny plant, to work there during the whole season for 24 tarì *a month. He is paid six* tarì *on account.*

Palermo, 18 November 1467

Source: ASP, Not. Giacomo Comito, reg. 855, c. 134r.

Muxa de Gallufo and Merdoc Soffer, Palermitan Jews, undertake to supply Antonio de Bruney with wood needed by his sugar refinery during the entire season for eight tarì *a thousand [logs].*

Palermo, 22 December 1467

Source: ASP, Not. Giacomo Comito, reg. 855, c. 180v.

Siminto Xalbi, a Jew of Trapani, arbiter in the dispute between Farchono Minachem and Iuda Combiressi, Jews, over business affairs, declares that Farchono had completely satisfied Iuda and that the latter had no further claims.

Palermo, 12 January 1468

Source: ASP, Not. Giacomo Comito, reg. 855, c. 194v.

Muxa Minzil, a Palermitan Jew, hires himself out to Alessandro de Settimo to *work in his tunny plant in Trabia for a year, starting the 23rd of April, to salt fish and do other jobs for six ounces.*

Palermo, 7 February 1468

Source: ASP, Not. Giacomo Comito, reg. 855, c. 237r.

Busacca Copiu, a Palermitan Jew, hires himself out to Lupo de Sivigla, owner of the tunny plant of San Giorgio, to work in his business during the entire season for 24 tarì *a month. He is paid 12* tarì *on account.*

Palermo, 2 June 1468

Source: ASP, Not. Giacomo Comito, reg. 855, c. 296r.

Salamon de Messina, a Jew in Palermo, hires himself out to Giovanni Bayamonte to cultivate his sugar cane for 12 tarì *a thousand small plants and 11* tarì *for the new plants. He is paid one ounce on account.*

Palermo, 12 January 1468

Source: ASP, Not. Giacomo Comito, reg. 855, c. 194v.

Muxa Ximexi and Muxa Copiu, Jews of Palermo, hire themselves out to Salamon de Messina, their Jewish fellow citizen, to work in the sugar cane plantation of Giovanni de Bayamonte for 15 grana *a bed of old plants and 10 a bed of new ones.*

Palermo, 15 November 1468

Source: ASP, Not. Giacomo Comito, reg. 855, c. 50r.

Master Prospero de la Bonavogla, a Jewish physician of Messina, promises Alegrecto de Perna 20 ounces for rent.

Palermo, 15 November 1468

Source: ASP, Not. Giacomo Comito, reg. 855, c. 52r.

Daniel Calabrisi and Xibiten de Liuni, Jews of Palermo, hire themselves out to

Lupo de Sivigla to work in his business for 2.6 tarì a day during the whole tunnny season.

Palermo, 8 December 1468

Source: ASP, Not. Giacomo Comito, reg. 855, c. 76v.

Abram Xaccarono, a Palermitan Jew, hires himself out to Antonio de Septimo to salt the fish in his tunny plant during the whole season for 10 ducats. He is paid 15 tarì on account.

Palermo, 12 October 1469

Source: ASP, Not. Giacomo Comito, reg. 855, c. 76v.

David Alluxu, Vita Maltisi, Salamon de Messana and Abram Xaccarono, Jews of Palermo, hire themselves out to Giovanni de Bayamonte to work as grinders in his sugar refinery during the whole season for one ounce a month.

Palermo, 14 November 1469

Source: ASP, Not. Giacomo Comito, reg. 856, c. 49v.

Manuel Calabrisi and Muxa de Chimisi, Jews of Palermo, promise Antonio Scalisi to transport grapes from his vineyard to his home for an agreed 24 tarì.

Palermo, 14 November 1469

Source: ASP, Not. Giacomo Comito, reg. 856, c. 50v.

Daniel Calabrisi, a Jew, hires himself out to Iacobo Rubeo to work in the sugar refinery of Giovanni de Bononia during the entire season for 16 grana a day, and is paid four tarì on account.

Palermo, 14 November 1469

Source: ASP, Not. Giacomo Comito, reg. 856, c. 50v.

Michael Brumellino, a Jew, hires himself out to Iacobo Rubeo to work in the sugar refinery of Giovanni de Bononia during the entire season for 16 grana a day, and is paid six tarì on account.

Palermo, 18 November 1469

Source: ASP, Not. Giacomo Comito, reg. 856, c. 52r.

Manuel Actuni, a Jew, hires himself out to Iacobo Rubeo to work in the sugar refinery of Giovanni de Bononia during the entire season for 16 grana *a day, and is paid four* tarì *on account.*

Palermo, 18 November 1469

Source: ASP, Not. Giacomo Comito, reg. 856, c. 52v.

Michilono Ysach, a Jew, hires himself out to Iacobo Rubeo to work in the sugar refinery of Giovanni de Bononia during the entire season for 16 grana *a day, and is paid four* tarì *on account.*

Palermo, 21 November 1469

Source: ASP, Not. Giacomo Comito, reg. 856, c. 57r.

Xaym de Liucio, a Jew, hires himself out to Salamon Sichira, his fellow Jew, to work in his shop until the end of August for 15 tarì *a month. He is paid one ounce on account.*

Palermo, 21 November 1469

Source: ASP, Not. Giacomo Comito, reg. 856, c. 60v.

Brachono Sichiliano, a Jew, hires himself out to Giovanni de Plumerio to work in his service for one ounce a month. He is paid 15 tarì *on account.*

Palermo, 27 November 1469

Source: ASP, Not. Giacomo Comito, reg. 856, c. 61v.

Iosep de Minichi, a Palermitan Jew, hires himself out to Giovanni de Plumerio to work in his sugar refinery during the whole season for one ounce a month.

Sicily

Palermo, 27 November 1469

Source: ASP, Not. Giacomo Comito, reg. 856, c. 62r.

Giovanni Nucella promises Braxa Cuyno, a Palermitan Jew, to transport merchandise for him until the end of August for 15 grana a work day.

Palermo, 18 November 1469

Source: ASP, Not. Giacomo Comito, reg. 856, c. 52v.

Sabatino Liparioto, a Palermitan Jew, apprentices his son Laczaru to Iacobo de Tavormina, his fellow Jewish citizen, to learn the craft of shoemaker (corbiserio). *He is to be paid 15* tarì *and provided with food and lodgings.*

Palermo, 29 November 1469

Source: ASP, Not. Giacomo Comito, reg. 856, c. 64r.

Merdoc Sofer, a Jew of Palermo, hires himself out to Iacobo Rubeo to work in the sugar refinery of Giovanni de Bononia during the entire season for 16 grana day, and is paid four tarì *on account.*

Palermo, 3 December 1469

Source: ASP, Not. Giacomo Comito, reg. 856, c. 69v.

Francisco Rampulle and Xaym Frisisa, a Jew of Palermo, barter a quantity of grapes for six cases of charcoal valued at 16 tarì.

Palermo, 3 December 1469

Source: ASP, Not. Giacomo Comito, reg. 856, c. 70r-v.

Addition to a marriage contract between Mulxayra, daughter of Nissim and Sadona Graxona, and Xamuel Caru. The contract was drawn up by the notary Nicolò de Aprea. The dowry totalled 110 ounces. The bridegroom was paid most of that sum except for some articles valued at 3.12.0 ounces. The parties now agree on the terms of payment if the bride's parents fail to hand over the articles or part of them.

Eodem

Cum contractum fuerit matrimonium inter Mulxayram, filiam Nissim
Graxona e Sadoce, mulieris iugalium, sponsam ex una parte, et Xamuelem
Carum sponsum ex parte altera, pro decoracione cuius matrimonii
fuissent [debitores] in summa uncie centum decem per dictos Nissim
et eius uxorem, prout dictus sponsus et dicti dotantes dixerunt, hodie,
vero pretitulato die, dictus sponsus coram nobis presens ad instanciam
dictorum dotancium presencium et hoc ab eo petencium sponte confessus
est se habuisse et recepisse a dictis dotantibus ex tunc uncias centum
decem dotium predictarum, tamen quod dictus sponsus restat ad
habendum ipse sponsus uncias tres in pecunia numerata nec non tarenos
XII pro uno traverserio dublectum unum, prout est illud quod habet,
item guardanappia quattuor, nova tobalias novem de facie, bacile unum
de ere, item suprachelum unum, item par unum lintheaminum alborum
preci unciarum duarum, item bacile unum preci V, item mortarium unum
de mitallo cum eius pistono, item tobaliam I, item coffiteram unam
prout est illa quam habet. Quas restantes dotes dicti dotantes in solidum
promiserunt dicto sponso stipulanti dare solvere et integre assignare ei,
iuxta formam presentis contractus, ut asseritur, facti manu notarii Nicolai
de Aprea, pro ut in ipso contractu continetur. Qui contractus in suo
robore permanere debeat cum pacto quod, si non assignaverit dictas
restantes dotes, liceat et licitum sit dicto sponso se satisfieri super loherio
domus dictorum dotantium, aut de parte superiori dicto iure domus
de restantibus dotis predictis, item ex pacto quod si non assignaverit
dictum par lintheaminum novum dicti dotantes dare, solvere et assignare
eidem sponso uncias tres in quo quidem precio dictorum lintheaminum in
omnem eventum, in pace etc., omni libello moratoria remotis sub ipotheca
et obligacione omnium bonorum eorum, cum refectione dampnorum
interesse et expensarum. Et quod fiat ritus in eorum personis et bonis. Et
iuraverunt etc.

Testes: Magister Chiccus Mercataru Matheus, magister Angilus de Gaxera
et Andreas Manueli.

Palermo, 3 December 1469

Source: ASP, Not. Giacomo Comito, reg. 856, c. 70v.

*Accord between Nixim Medui, a Palermitan Jew, and Federico de Gactelluzzo
whereby Nixim removes the obstruction to a window of Federico's cowshed.
Nixim had made some structural changes to his hovel next to Federico's property.*

Palermo, 3 December 1469

Source: ASP, Not. Giacomo Comito, reg. 856, c. 71r.

Extension for another four months of the agreement between Nixim Medui and Merdoc de Braxono, Palermitan Jews. The deed had been drawn up by the Jewish notary Benedetto de Girachio.

Palermo, 1 February 1470

Source: ASP, Not. Giacomo Comito, reg. 856, c. 103r.

Following a protest lodged by Vinichu Lo Nigru, Abram Xaccaruni, a Jew in Palermo, promises to deliver the grapes which he had promised Vinichu.

Palermo, 26 June 1470

Source: ASP, Not. Giacomo Comito, reg. 856, c. 113r

Muxa Puglisi, a Palermitan Jew, promises Nicolò de Millino to transport limestone from Nicolò's quarry to an agreed location for two grana *a* salma.

Palermo, 27 June 1470

Source: ASP, Not. Giacomo Comito, reg. 856, c. 115r-v.

Agreement whereby Frederico de Diana cedes to Daniel Xunina his rights in a well in return for the construction of a warehouse by Daniel.

Die XXVII mensis Iunii

Cum inter nobilem dominum Fredericum de Diana, c[ivem] P[anormi], et Danielem Xunina, super facto unius puthei, in quo dictus Daniel asserebat partecipare qui est in plano facto per dictum dominum Fredericum ex domibus ipsius domini Frederici diructis et in plano reductis, per eum, ex citato et deferentis vertatur, hinc est quod hodie pretitulato die, dicto dominus Fredericus cum dicto Iudeo ad convencionem infrascriptam devenerit, videlicet quod protestatus dominus Fredericus in presencia mei notarii et testium infrascriptorum, sponte ductus, putheum renunciavit et renunciat dicto Danieli presenti et acceptanti eique habere cessit, ita quod ex nunc in antea dictus putheus sit et esse debeat dicti Iudei, heredum et successoreum suorum, et eo converso dictus Iudeus promisit, convenit et se solleniter obligavit dicto domino Frederico presenti dealbari faceret et signanter de cantonis, ut est, faciat fundacum ipsius domini Friderici, suis expensis, parietes sive muros duos tenimenti domorum dicti Iudei corrispondentes in plano predicto et non faceret in pariete, sive domus per eum fabricando in dicto plano aliquas aperturas, immo si alique sint ipsas et omnia foramina existencia in parietibus dicti tenimenti suorum domorum claudere et obturare dictumque planum mundari facere et anictari, ac reducere in pristinum et hoc per totum et infra annum proximum venturum quarte Ind., aliter, elapso dicto termino, liceat eidem domino Frederico illud suis facere expensis dicti Daniel in pace, de plano et eius auxilio, moratoria etc. Renunciantes etc., cum refectionem omnium dampnorum, sub ipotheca et obligatione omnium bonorum suorum. Et fiat ritus etc. Et iuraverunt. Actum in fundaco ipsius nobilis, presentibus nobili Raymundo de Diana et Francisco.

Palermo, 12 July 1470

Source: ASP, Not. Giacomo Comito, reg. 856, loose leaf.

Notarial protest by Manuel Veru, a Palermitan Jew, against Deulusa, his Jewish fellow citizen. Deulusa had leased to him a courtyard bordering on the property of Manuel. The latter alleges that Deulusa had some construction done on the courtyard which caused the openings of Manuel's property into the courtyard to be obstructed and prevented him from using a well in the courtyard, which he had been in the habit of doing. He demands that Deulusa restore the status quo ante, *on pain of a fine.*

Die XII mensis Iulii III Ind.

Manuel Veru, Iudeus de Panormo, constitutus in presencia Deulusa, Iudei sui concivis, presentis et audientis, animo et intencione sibi protestandi et ius suum in futurum conservandi contra et adversus dictum Deulusa presentem exposuit, dixit et fuit protestatus quod cum nobilis dominus Leonardus de Lampisu, legum doctor, concesserit ad emphiteosim eidem Deulusa quoddam cortile collaterale domui dicti exponentis ad emphiteosim sibi concesse per heredes quodam domini Bernardi Pinos et in dicto cortili domus predicte exponentis habebat furracas, aperturas et putheum, quas furracas et aperturas dictus Deulusa clauserit et obturaverit, contra sui veterem formam, et putheum sibi ceperit et clauserit ipsum ex parte domus dicti exponentis dictumque cortile coperiendo, quod minime facere poterat, in preiudicium dicti exponentis, cum domus ipsius exponentis non habet, nec potest habere aliud lumen, nec lustrum extra aliqua alia parte nec ex dicto cortile et propterea dictus exponens presentis serie requisivit et requirit dictum Deulusa presentem ex parte serenissimi domini nostri regis, sub pena unciarum quinquaginta regio fisco applicandarum et ab eodem Deulusa inremissibiliter extorquendarum, tociens quociens per eum contrafactum fuerit in premissis et aliquo premissorum, quatenus omni mora post posita, omnia reducere debeat ad pristinum, dictumque cortile discoperire et in pristinum statum reducere et sic etiam diruere parietem factam in putheo et solarium et tectum, ita et taliter quod omnia sint reducta et remaneant in statu quo erant tempore quo fuit facta sibi concessio dicti cortilis, aliter incurrat et incurrere debeat in penam predicta constituens eundem Deulusa in dolo, mora et culpa. Hanc sentencia etc.

Note: See below, foll. Doc.

Palermo, 17 July 1470

Source: ASP, Not. Giacomo Comito, reg. 856, c. 137v.

Deposition by Deulusa denying the charges preferred against him by Manuel Veru in the matter of the courtyard which he had rented in perpetual lease. He proposes arbitration to solve the conflict.

Note: See above, preceding Doc.

Palermo, 17 July 1470

Source: ASP, Not. Giacomo Comito, reg. 856, c. 138v.

Quittance by Xibiten Michisen, a Palermitan Jew, to Nicolò Russo for 20 tarì, *his fee for having brokered the sale of merchandise.*

Palermo, 3 August 1470

Source: ASP, Not. Giacomo Comito, reg. 856, c. 150v.

Contract whereby Iacob Gallifa, a Palermitan Jew, undertakes to dig a well in the property La Turri of Pietro Aglata for 1.24.0 ounces. Iacob is paid six tarì on account. He is to deduct from the fee a debt of one ounce arising out of a joint venture between Pietro and Simone de San Filippo, Iacob's partner. The balance of 18 tarì is to be paid within seven days.

Palermo, 10 October 1470

Source: ASP, Not. Giacomo Comito, reg. 856, c. 22r.

Xibiten Levi, a Jew of Palermo, hires himself out to Giovanni de Bayamonte to work as a paratore *in his sugar refinery during the current season for one ounce a month.*

Palermo, 26 December 1470

Source: ASP, Not. Giacomo Comito, reg. 856, c. 38r.

David de Mazara, a Jew in Palermo, hires himself out to Giovanni Russo to do work for him until August for four ounces.

Palermo, 13 November 1471

Source: ASP, Not. Giacomo Comito, reg. 856, c. 44r.

Abram Gallifa, a Jew of Palermo, hires himself out to Giovanni de Bayamonte to work in his sugar refinery during the whole season for 14 tarì *a month.*

Palermo, 17 December 1471

Source: ASP, Not. Giacomo Comito, reg. 856, c. 44v.

Busacca Gazu, a Jew of Palermo, hires himself out to Giovanni de Bayamonte to work in his sugar refinery during the whole season for 20 tarì *a month, and is paid 16* tarì *on account.*

Palermo, 17 December 1471

Source: ASP, Not. Giacomo Comito, reg. 856, c. 80r.

Deed of sale whereby Pinesi de Aron, his wife Stella, and their children sell to Antonio Salvato a house in Palermo for 10 ounces. The house is subject to a perpetual lease rent to the convent of S. Maria de Martorana.

Palermo, 22 January 1472

Source: ASP, Not. Giacomo Comito, reg. 856, c. 112v.

Contract whereby Iacob de Rustico, a Palermitan Jew, promises Renzo de Soligo to do building work at his house in the Albergaria quarter of Palermo, in the contrada *Ballarò, next to the house of Leone de Palya, for 1.18.0 ounces. He is paid 6.1* tarì *on account.*

Palermo, 23 January 1472

Source: ASP, Not. Giacomo Comito, reg. 856, c. 114r.

Muxa Ysach, a Palermitan Jew, promises Nerone Masi, a Florentine merchant, to settle his debt of 14.29.0 ounces in monthly instalments of 2.12 tarì*. The debt arose out of the sale of merchandise. Muxa had not responded to repeated demands by Nerone.*

Palermo, 13 April 1472

Source: ASP, Not. Giacomo Comito, reg. 856, c. 177r.

Xibiten Soffer, a Jew of Palermo, hires himself out to Giovanni de Homodei to work in his tunny plant during the entire season for 11 tarì *a month.*

Palermo, 14 July 1472

Source: ASP, Not. Giacomo Comito, reg. 856, c. 233v.

Abram Lu Salvatu, Salamon Grossu, Michael Bramellu and Raffael Misiria, Jews of Palermo, hire themselves out to Lupo de Sivigla to work during the entire current season in his tunny plant for one ounce each. They are paid 20 tarì *each on account.*

Palermo, 15 July 1472

Source: ASP, Not. Giacomo Comito, reg. 856, c. 234v.

Caro de Seracusia, a Jew of Palermo, hires himself out to Iorlando de Paruta to work in his olive oil press for 22 tarì *a month.*

Palermo, 3 August 1472

Source: ASP, Not. Giacomo Comito, reg. 856, c. 246r.

Contract whereby Bulchayra Frisisa, a Palermitan Jew, lets his son Nixim a shop solerata *in the Cassaro of Palermo, in the Platea Marmorea, for 1.27.0 ounces a year. The shop is situated next to that of Antonio de Sinibaldo and to another belonging to Nixim.*

Palermo, 7 August 1472

Source: ASP, Not. Giacomo Comito, reg. 856, c. 247r.

Deed of sale whereby Iosep Talbi, a Jew of Mazara, sells Ambrogio de Virgilio 100 salme *of wheat for 13* tarì *the* salma. *He is paid 25 ducats and some articles on account.*

Palermo, 28 January 1473

Source: ASP, Not. Giacomo Comito, reg. 856, c. 78r.

Notarial protest by Raymondo Aglata againt David Actuni, a Palermitan Jew, for not having been paid his due. Raymondo had paid surety for David in the latter's transaction with Muxa Lu Presti, a Jew of Trapani, in the amount of six ounces.

Palermo, 6 July 1473

Source: ASP, Not. Giacomo Comito, reg. 856, c. 217r.

Michilono Ysach, a Palermitan Jew, hires himself out to Lupo de Sevigla to work during the entire season in his tunny plant at Arenella for 1.15.0 ounces

Palermo, 8 November 1475

Source: ASP, Not. Giacomo Comito, reg. 857, c. nn.

Aron Azeni and Sabet Cuyno, prothi *of the Jewish community in Palermo, promise to pay Nicolò de Bonfanti 1.16.0 ounces for a tax.*

Sicily

Palermo, 5 July 1477

Source: ASP, Not. Giacomo Comito, reg. 857, c. 314r.

Gallufo Balbu, a Palermitan Jew, hires himself out to Lupo de Sivigla, owner of the tunny plant in San Giorgio, to work in his business during the entire season for seven ounces. He is paid 18 tarì *on account.*

Palermo, 20 August 1477

Source: ASP, Not. Giacomo Comito, reg. 857, c. nn.

Agreement between Iosep de Fraym and Xua Simaeli, Jews in Palermo. They had bought a nag from Giovanni de Cataldo for 1.6.0 ounces and had paid 18 tarì *on account, promising to pay the balance by 8.9. Xua cedes to Iosep his share in the nag. Iosep pays Xua his part of the down payment and undertakes to pay the balance to Giovanni.*

Palermo, 23 August 1477

Source: ASP, Not. Giacomo Comito, reg. 857, c. nn.

Contract whereby Abneri Grixon, a Jew of Palermo, sells Salamon Lu Medicu, his Jewish fellow citizen, half a mule for two ounces, to be paid in monthly instalments of three tarì. *Abneri had bought the mule from Giovanni de Costanzo, for four ounces, to be paid in monthly instalments of six* tarì *starting in November. Repeated on 23 August.*

Palermo, 23 August 1477

Source: ASP, Not. Giacomo Comito, reg. 857, c. nn.

Demand by Filippo Castiglione junior of Pollina that Sabet Rugila alias Sansuni, a Palermitan Jew, repay him forthwith a loan of 3.0.9 ounces, although it was not yet due.

Palermo, 27 August 1477

Source: ASP, Not. Giacomo Comito, reg. 857, c. nn.

Benedetto Canet and Siminto Taguil, Palermitan Jews, collectors of the current

6375

carlino *tax of the Jewish community in Palermo, enjoin Benedettto Talo, their fellow citizen, to submit an exact accounting of his profits from trading in cloth, on pain of a fine of 30 ounces.*

Palermo, 15 January 1476

Source: ASP, Not. Giacomo Comito, reg. 857, c. 132v.

Muxa Millac and Azarono Azeni, Palermitan Jews, hire themselves out for a year to Masio de Naczono to quarry stone in his quarry in the contrada *Colli in Palermo for 15* tarì *a thousand [stones?].*

Palermo, 28 February 1476

Source: ASP, Not. Giacomo Comito, reg. 857, c. nn.

Nicolò Grissafi promises Muxa Millac, a Palermitan Jew, to crush his grapes for wine making for two tarì.

Palermo, 5 March 1476

Source: ASP, Not. Giacomo Comito, reg. 857, c. nn.

Power of attorney granted Muxa Verru by his brother Manuel, a Jew of Palermo, empowering him to regain possession of his mule that had been retained by Muxa de Aurifichi, a Jew of Trapani.

Palermo, 8 March 1476

Source: ASP, Not. Giacomo Comito, reg. 857, c. nn.

Busacca Copiu, a Jew of Palermo, hires out Gallufo, his twelve year-old son, to Lupo de Sivigla to work as an apprentice in the tunny plant at Arenella for 12 tarì *and food.*

Palermo, 7 December 1476

Source: ASP, Not. Giacomo Comito, reg. 857, c. nn.

Settlement of a dispute between the heirs of the late Simon Ysac, a Palermitan

Jew. Simon owned a solerata *house in the* vanella *Lu Daptilu, in the Cassaro of Palermo, bordering on the houses of Leone Amar, the heirs of Nixim Binna, Muxa Calabrisi and Xibiten Gibel, all Jewish fellow citizens of Simon. The property is subject to a annual ground rent of 1.26.0 ounces to the Jewish community in Palermo. Simon's heirs are Ismael and Farrugio, sons of Simon and Ricca, and Xamuel, Muxa, Leone and Gaudio, sons of his second marriage. The property is being let. The settlement provides for division of the rent between the two groups: 18* tarì *each.*

Note: See below, Doc. 3.1.1477.

Palermo, 9 December 1476

Source: ASP, Not. Giacomo Comito, reg. 857, c. nn.

Sadia Kimessi, Salamon Malti and Muxa de Minichi, Palermitan Jews, promise Iacobo Grasso to build a wall on his property for two ounces.

Palermo, 18 December 1476

Source: ASP, Not. Giacomo Comito, reg. 857, c. nn.

Elia Xixono, a Jew in Palermo, hires himself out to Lupo de Sivigla to work in his tunny plant at Arenella during the whole season for the ususal wages.

Palermo, 30 December 1476

Source: ASP, Not. Giacomo Comito, reg. 857, c. nn.

Muxa Niyar, a Jew in Palermo, hires himself out to Giovanni de Bayamonte to work in his sugar refinery during the entire season for 1.6.0 ounces a month, and is paid one ounce on account.

Palermo, 3 January 1477

Source: ASP, Not. Giacomo Comito, reg. 857, c. nn.

Agreement between the heirs of Simon Ysac, a Palermitan Jew, over the division of the rent of their house in the Cassaro of Palermo.

Note: See above, Doc. 11.7.1476. Some of the names are spelled differently.

Palermo, 10 January 1477

Source: ASP, Not. Giacomo Comito, reg. 857, c. nn.

Contract for setting up a joint venture between Geremia Azeni and Azarono Actuni, Jews of Palermo, to manage a shop in the contrada *Patitelli in Palermo to last four years. Azarono is to invest 50 ounces in two instalments, in January and February. Geremia is to invest his labour and is to pay the rent amounting to one ounce annually, and for the furnishings. The profits are to be divided in equal shares.*

Palermo, 26.February 1474

Source: ASP, Not. Giacomo Comito, reg. 857, c. nn.

Undertaking by Xibiten de Yona and Xibiten Abbati, Jews of Palermo, to salt all the fish produced in the tunny plant of Simon de Risignano at San Giorgio during the coming season for 20 tarì *a month.*

Palermo, 15 March 1474

Source: ASP, Not. Giacomo Comito, reg. 857, c. 233r.

Agreement whereby Donato Abenazara, a Jew of Palermo, cedes to to his father Gabriel half the property which had been given him by his grandfather, Iosep. It consists of a solerata *house and two adjoining shops, situated in the Cassaro of Palermo, in the Platea Marmorea, bordering on the the houses of the heirs of Bartholomeo de Pino and of Bonsignoro Canet, a Jew. The property is subject to an annual ground rent of 20* tarì *to the chapel of San Giacomo.*

Palermo, 31 March 1474

Source: ASP, Not. Giacomo Comito, reg. 857, c. 258v.

Alessandro de Septimo, owner of the tunny plant at Trabia, acknowledges the purchase of 30,000 ropes for tunny to be delivered in September by Benedetto Catalano, Calzarono de Tripuli and Nixim Cusintino, Jews in Palermo.

Palermo, 27 June 1474

Source: ASP, Not. Giacomo Comito, reg. 857, c. 341v.

Michilono Ysac, a Jew of Palermo, hires himself out to Lupo de Sivigla, owner of the tunny plant at Arenella, to work in his business during the entire season for 1.15.0 ounces a month.

Palermo, 27 June 1474

Source: ASP, Not. Giacomo Comito, reg. 857, c. 342r.

Manuel de Busita, a Jew of Palermo, hires himself out to Lupo de Sivigla, owner of the tunny plant at Arenella, to work in his business during the entire season for one ounce a month and is paid 9 tarì *on account.*

Palermo, July 1474

Source: ASP, Not. Giacomo Comito, reg. 857, c. nn.

Undertaking by Sabatino de Minichi, a Jew of Palermo, to pay by September for a certain quantity of tunny which he purchased from Alessandro de Septimo for 2.3.10 ounces.

Palermo, 15 July 1474

Source: ASP, Not. Giacomo Comito, reg. 857, c. nn.

Muxa Furmenti, a Jew of Palermo, hires himself out to Francesco de Xibilia to work in his tunny plant during the entire season for one ounce.

Palermo, 8 August 1474

Source: ASP, Not. Giacomo Comito, reg. 857, c. nn.

Busacca Frisisa, a Jew of Palermo, promises Martino de Parrino to pay as soon as possible his debt of 4.19.10 ounces. In the meantime he asks for a postponement.

Palermo, 13 November 1474

Source: ASP, Not. Giacomo Comito, reg. 858, c. nn.

Request by Giovanni Pietro de Rigio to apply the terms of a notarial contract he signed with the Jewish community in Palermo on 14.1.1469 for the sale of the gabella *on wine.*

Palermo, 4 December 1476

Source: ASP, Not. Giacomo Comito, reg. 858, c. 250r.

Moyses Compangira, a Jew (?) of Messina, appoints Iacobo de Richardo to act for him in regard to the sale of 200 kantars of French iron for 22.10 tarì the kantar. It is to be loaded on a Venitian boat in the port of Messina.

Palermo, 11 July 1477

Source: ASP, Not. Giacomo Comito, reg. 858, c. 201v.

Undertaking by Gauio Abdila, a Palermitan Jew, to settle his debts at his earliest convenience. He owes 10.8.0 ounces to Giovanni Canfora as well as other amounts to various debtors. These include Simone de Lala, to whom he owes the rent for the house in which Gauia lives in the Cassaro in the Platea Marmorea. Gauio also provides a guarantor.

Palermo, 8 August 1477

Source: ASP, Not. Giacomo Comito, reg. 858, c. 261v.

Gallufo Momo, a Jew in Polizzi, hires himself out to Sadono Ubi, a Jew in Palermo, for two years for 20 tarì a month.

Palermo, 10 September 1477

Source: ASP, Not. Giacomo Comito, reg. 858, c. 12v.

Saya de Salvatu, a Jew of Trapani, hires himself out to Antonio de Pietro Giovanni, manager (rayso) *of the tunny plant in Castellamare del Golfo, during the entire season as filler* (iarratino) *for one ounce.*

Palermo, 29 July 1478

Source: ASP, Not. Giacomo Comito, reg. 858, c. 218v.

Nixim Minachem and Iacob Rusticu, Jews of Palermo, hire themselves out to Antonio de Pietro Giovanni to work as builders in his estate, situated at the feud of Fitalia, for one ounce.

6380

Sicily

Palermo, 24 October 1480

Source: ASP, Not. Giacomo Comito, reg. 859, c. 78v.

Merdoc Ziczu, a Palermitan Jew, acting for Giovanni de Homodei, has recourse to the Regia Curia *against Xamuele Xilli and Xamuele Datu, Jews, in the matter of their failure to pay for a barrel of tunny.*

Palermo, 15 November 1480

Source: ASP, Not. Giacomo Comito, reg. 859, c. 96v.

Power of attorney by Muxa Millac, a Palermitan Jew, to Iacobo Farachi, a Messinese Jew, to look after his interests in Messina and to collect his outstanding debts.

Palermo, 26 November 1480

Source: ASP, Not. Giacomo Comito, reg. 859, c. 114v.

Gallufo Barbuto, a Jew of Palermo, hires himself out to Lupo de Sivigla to work in his tunny plant during the entire season for one ounce.

Palermo, 9 December 1480

Source: ASP, Not. Giacomo Comito, reg. 859, c. 127r.

Elia Cuyno, a Jew in Palermo, appoints Giovanni Fruntilata of Palermo to act for him in collecting his due from Antonino Lugarinisi.

Palermo, 28 December 1480

Source: ASP, Not. Giacomo Comito, reg. 859, c. 144r.

Xibiten de Liuni, a Jew of Palermo, hires himself out to Lupo de Sivigla to work in his tunny plant during the whole coming season for 25 tarì.

Palermo, 17 February 1481

Source: ASP, Not. Giacomo Comito, reg. 859, c. 181r.

Merdoc de Minichi, a Palermitan Jew, hires himself out to Lupo de Sivigla to work in his tunny plant during the whole coming season for one ounce.

Palermo, 24 February 1481

Source: ASP, Not. Giacomo Comito, reg. 859, c. 188v.

Muxa Mizoc, *a Palermitan Jew, hires himself out to Lupo de Sivigla to work in his tunny plant during the whole coming season for 20* tarì *a month, and is paid six* tarì *on account.*

Palermo, 13 July 1481

Source: ASP, Not. Giacomo Comito, reg. 859, c. 270r.

Iacobo de Risignano, director of the office in charge of the Jewish badge, appoints Nicolò de Forestieri his representative to act for him the territory of San Marco.

Palermo, 19 July 1481

Source: ASP, Not. Giacomo Comito, reg. 859, c. 271r.

Filippo Purchellu acknowledges to Muxa Millac, a Palermitan Jew, receipt of five ounces due him as tax collector of the Jewish community in Palermo.

Palermo, 30 July 1481

Source: ASP, Not. Giacomo Comito, reg. 859, c. 280r.

Gerardo Salvagno, a Genoese merchant, and Iacob Ladeb, a Palermitan Jew, appoint Matheo de Perlista and Antonio Galanto, Tuscan merchants, arbitrators to settle the dispute between them in regard to a donation made by Antonio Lu Blancu of Mazara.

Palermo, 28 March 1481

Source: ASP, Not. Giacomo Comito, reg. 859, c. 160r.

Settlement of accounts between Azara Taguili and Muxa Millac, Jews of Palermo, of a joint venture. As a result Azara owes Muxa 8.16.0 ounces, to be paid in two instalments by May.

Palermo, 30 May 1481

Source: ASP, Not. Giacomo Comito, reg. 859, c. 196v.

Elia Cuyno, a Jew of Trapani, appoints Nixim Cuyno, a Jew of Palermo, to act for him in Palermo and to collect the rent of two houses he owns there.

Palermo, 13 June 1481

Source: ASP, Not. Giacomo Comito, reg. 859, c. 203v.

Giaimo de Scaldato, collector of the tax on the slaughter of animals (gabella fumi) *on the Jews of Palermo, sells his rights as collector for the year of the 15th Indiction to Stefano de Iordano for 1.18.0 ounces. He is paid 20* tarì *on 1.9 and 24* tarì *on 1.1.*

Note: For the tax, see above, Doc. 342.

Palermo, 9–12 September 1481

Source: ASP, Not. Giacomo Comito, reg. 860, loose leaf and c. 11v.

1. *Protest by the* prothi *and* maggiorenti *of the Jewish community in Palermo against the* sacristani *of the community. The* sacristani *are alleged to be acting independently of each other, contrary to regulations. They are enjoined to deposit in a bank the moneys they collect, and a fine is imposed on them.*
2. *The* sacristani *reply that the accusations were unfounded and that if they did wrong, it was up to the viceroy to punish them, since it was he who had appointed them.*

1. Die nono mensis Septembris XV Ind. Dominice Incarnacionis anno Millesimo CCCCLXXXI
Manuel de Gnisu alias Barba di Stiro, Salamon Russu, Aron Asuni, Iudei proti, Isac Romanu, Achina Balbu, Salamuni de Beniosep, Muxa Amira, Xibiteni Giberi, Busacca Sala, Siminto de Pulicii et Iacob Sanu, maiurentes Iudayce felicis urbis Panormi, constituti intus eorum Iayma seu Muskita, animo et intencione protestandi et ius dicte Iudayce in futurum conservandi contra et adversus Leonem Aurifichi et Iacob Magnu, sacrestanos dicte eorum Iayme, presentes et audientes, exposuerunt, dixerunt et protestati fuerunt quod cum prefati Leonum et Iacob sacristani fuerunt et sunt creati per illustrem dominum huius regni viceregem, ut

officium eorum exercere et facere deberent, ut per eorum predecessores solitum fuit et est exercere et sacrestani predecessores simul et coniunti dictum officium exercere soliti fuerunt, prefatique Leonus et Iacob dictum officium sacristanie unus sine alio et alter sine uno faciunt, quod facere non possunt, nec debent. Propterea hodie pretitulato die prefati prothi et maiurentes, in presencia mei notarii et testium infrascriptorum ex parte serenissimi domini nostri regis requisiverunt et requirunt, prefatos sacrestanos presentes et intelligentes et eorum quemlibet in solidum, sub pena unciarum centum pro medietate applicandarum regio fisco et fossi urbis Panormi me notario officio meo publico, vice et nomine prefati regi fisci et fossi, stipulantis et recipientis et ab eis eorum altero extorquendarum tociens quociens per eos et alterum eorum in solidum contrafactum fuerit in predictis et quolibet predictorum. Qua pena exigatur et exigui debeat de et super bonis propriis ipsorum sacrestanos et non Iayme predicte, quatenus dictum eorum officium simul et semel, ac coniuncti et non separatim, facere et exercere debeant iuxta eorum morem et observanciam antiquam dicte Iayme et pro ut alii predecessores eorum in dicto officio facere consueverunt hactenus. Et quod pecunias exactas hactenus penes eos existentes et in posse cuiusvis alterius persone nec non et exigendas hinc in antea, occasione et causa offici eorum predicti sacristanie depositare debeant penes bancos urbis predicte nomine amborum, et quod alter ipsorum non possit nec valeat pecunias predictas expendere et de eis aliquid facere nisi ambo, simul et aliter incidant in penam predictam, extorquendam ab eis, ut supra. Et nichilominus, si aliqua diferencia seu destinactio, seu altercacio super predictis oriri contigerit seu oriatur inter eos, comparere debeat coram dictis prothis et maiurentibus qui parati fuerunt et sunt eorum altercacionem et differenciam dirimere et declarare pro comuni utilitate et comodo dicte Iayme seu Muskite, nec minus protestantur contra eosdem sacristanos de omnibus dampnis, interesse, missionibus et expensis propter ea factis et faciendis culpa et defectu prefatorum sacristanorum, nolencium servare ea que alii sacristani consueverunt servare, et si aliqua verba in presenti requisicione posita sunt contra ius et iuris formam, illa protestantes ipsi voluerunt et volent fore nulla ut si posita non fuissent, constituens eos etc., alter eorum in solidum in dolo, mora et culpa etc., hanc sentenciam etc. Ad quam protestationem prefati sacrestani responderunt quod, habita copia parati sunt respondere. Testes etc.

2. Die XI mensis septembris. Ad dictam protestationem pro parte dicti Leoni respondetur quod ipse et socius fuerunt criati sacriste per nobilem dominum viceregem et non sunt subiecti dictis protestantibus, et parati

sunt exercere officium prout alii sacriste exercuerunt, et si ipse Leonus non faciet debitum vel dominus vicerex habebit eum castigare et non dicti protestantes. Quo vero ad illud quod pecunias exacta aut exigenda debeant ponere in banco, ipse Leonus respondet quod ipse Leonus numquam recolligit pecuniam nisi tarenos XV aut XVI quos solvit pro arra felicis civitatis [...], de pecunia vero recolligenda paratus est ponere illam in banco aut expendere, prout consuetum est, superveniente necessitate; et hec est eius responsio. Nichilominus, si socius ipsius respondetis non facere debitum, non habet ipse Leonus eum corrigere, set requirit dictos protestantes quod debeat sibi providere cum dicto illustri domino vicerege pro indempnitate dicte Iudayce et hac ipsi protestantes constituentes in dolo, mora et culpa et teneantur ad dicta dampna, interesse et expensas. Testes etc.

Palermo, 12 October 1481

Source: ASP, Not. Giacomo Comito, reg. 860, loose leaf.

Ysac Sacerdotu, a Jewish citizen of Palermo, consigns to Salvatore Paglarinu, master of a ship at anchor in Palermo harbour, 17 thousand ropes and nine rolls for delivery to Achina Millac, a Jew.

Palermo, 5 November 1481

Source: ASP, Not. Giacomo Comito, reg. 860, c. 49v.

Settlement of accounts between Giovanni Mazarono, on one hand, and Bartholomeo de La Rocca and Muxa Millac, a Palermitan Jew, on the other, of a business transaction. It transpires that Giovanni owes the other two 24.25.0 ounces. He promises to pay them with grapes of the coming vintage.

Palermo, 22 November 1481

Source: ASP, Not. Giacomo Comito, reg. 860, c. 60v.

Alfonso de Vitali promises Muxa Millac, a Palermitan Jew, to cultivate his vineyard, formerly the property of Bartholomeo della Rocca, in the contrada *Colli of Palermo for an agreed fee based on units of a thousand plants each.*

Palermo, 28 November 1481

Source: ASP, Not. Giacomo Comito, reg. 860, c. 79v.

Azara Taguil, a Palermitan Jew, acting for Filippo de Giglia of Corleone, promises Muxa Millac, a Palermitan Jew, to transport 1,000 [kantars] of grapes from Muxa's vineyard to his house for 10 tarì.

Palermo, 4 December 1481

Source: ASP, Not. Giacomo Comito, reg. 860, c. 80r.

Chanino Balbu of Alcamo promises David Ysac, a Jew of Palermo, to transport 50 kantars of cheese from the feud Ribasisa to Palermo for five tarì.

Palermo, 28 March 1482

Source: ASP, Not. Giacomo Comito, reg. 860, c. 131v.

Notarial protest by Manuel Verru, a Palermitan Jew, against Bartholomeo de Palmerio, rector of the church S. Giacomo in Mazara, in regard to a tax collection of 1,000 florins on behalf of the Crown.

Palermo, 18 July 1482

Source: ASP, Not. Giacomo Comito, reg. 860, c. 202r.

Notarial protest by Sabet Millac, a Palermitan Jew, also on behalf of his son Muxa, against Martino de Riparolo, a Genoese merchant, for not having paid for the sugar he had supplied to Martino on 16.6.1481. The sugar had been produced by the sugar refinery of Manfrido La Muta.

Palermo, 5 August 1482

Source: ASP, Not. Giacomo Comito, reg. 860, c. 210r.

Muxa Russo, a Palermitan Jew, promises Muxa Millac, his Jewish fellow citizen, to treat 50 quintals of grapes in Muxa's vineyard situated in the contrada Colli *of Palermo for seven* tarì *a quintal.*

Palermo, 8 August 1482

Source: ASP, Not. Giacomo Comito, reg. 860, cc. 3r–4r.

Perpetual lease of a solerata *house by master Donato Abenazara, a Jewish surgeon and Palermitan citizen, inhabitant of Trapani, also on behalf of his wife Bulkaira, to Iacobo Lu Presti, a Palermitan Jew, for 2.21.0 ounces annually. The house is situated in the Cassaro, in the* vanella La Furnaca. *The property is subject to a ground rent of one ounce to the New Great Hospital of Palermo, which has to give its consent to the lease.*

VIII augusti XV Ind. anno Dominice Incarnationis MCCCCLXXXII

Testamur quod magister Donatus Abenazara, Iudeus cirurgicus, civis Panormi, et ha[bitator] civitatis Drepani, tam pro se quam nomine et pro parte Bulkaire eius uxoris de dicta civitate absentis pro qua de rato promisit etc., presens coram nobis sponte et solleniter per se et eorum in perpetuum heredes et successores locavit et ad emphiteosim et ad annum censum unciarum duarum et tarenorum XXI p[onderis] g[eneralis] habere concessit Iacobo Lu Presti Iudeo de urbe felicis Pa[normi], presenti et ab eo recipienti pro se et suis in perpetuum heredibus et successoribus ad emphiteosim et ad annuum censum predictum domum unam soleratam subtus et supra, cum quodam astraco cohoperto et uno magasinocto terraneo secus dictam domum soleratam, sitam et posita et posita dicta bona sive corpora concessa ut supra in dicta urbe felicis Pa[normi], videlicet in Cassaro et in vanella nuncupata di la Furnace, secus domum Sabet Cuyno Iudei ex una parte, et secus cortile domorum Gimiloni Achina ex altera, et secus viam publicam et alios confines. Que bona concessa predictus concedens proprio et quo supra nomine asseruit ad eum nomine quo supra pleno iure spectare et pertinere, cum onere census uncie unius debite et solvende annis singulis in perpetuum racione proprietatis magno novo hospitali Pa[normi], cuius hospitalis consensum ipse concedens in presenti contractu reservavit et reservat, ita quod si forte dictum hospitale suum consensum in presenti contractu recusaverit, seu noluerit prestare, presens concessio sit cassa et nulla, franca et libera dicta bona concessa ab omni alio onere census et cuiulibet alterius servitutis. Tota dicta bona concessa cum omnibus iuribus, iusticiis ac iustis et legitimis pertinenciis eorum et cum omnibus et singulis hiis que dicta bona concessa habens intus, intra, circum, circa et in integrum eorum continentur confines et alii si qui forent accessibus et egressibus suis etc., constituens se predictus concedens dicti emphiteote nomina predicta

6387

bona concessa precario tenere et possidere donec et quousque idem emphiteota de eisdem corporalem, actualem et civilem, vacua et expedita acceperit et intraverit possessionem quam intrandi, capiendi et habendi, prestito prius dicto consensu dicti hospitalis et proprietarii et ex nunc pro tunc [missing] potestatem tribuit et concessit ad habendum, tenendum, possidendum, dandum, vendendum, alienandum, permutandum pro anima, iudicandum, utifruendum et gaudendum ac de eis faciendum et fieri faciendum totum velle et desiderium suum suorumque heredum et successorum tamquam de rebus sibi enphiteoticatis iusto titulo et bona fide acquisitis etc., etc.

Testes: Magnifici Andreas et Nicolaus de Liages et nobilis Nicolaus de Laurencio.

Palermo, [1482]

Source: ASP, Not. Giacomo Comito, reg. 860, c. 47r.

Abram, son of David Magaseni, a Jew of Messina, appoints Iosep Sacerdoto, a Palermitan Jew, to look after his interests in Palermo and to collect his outstanding debts.

Palermo, [1482]

Source: ASP, Not. Giacomo Comito, reg. 860, c. 51v.

Xibiten Taguili, a Jew of Palermo, admits the justice of a notarial protest lodged against him by Iuda Ianini, his Jewish fellow citizen, and declares that Gimilono, Iuda's son, cannot be involved in a business exchange.

Palermo, [1482]

Source: ASP, Not. Giacomo Comito, reg. 860, c. 52v.

Angelo de Messina hires himself out to Salamon Beniosep, a Jew of Palermo, to work for him.

Note: The Doc. is defective.

Palermo, 16 August 1482

Source: ASP, Not. Giacomo Comito, reg. 860, c. 76r.

Leone Lulu promises Iosep Ginna, a Jew of Palermo, to build a door in the latter's house in the Cassaro of Palermo for 15 tarì.

Palermo, 2 October 1482

Source: ASP, Not. Giacomo Comito, reg. 860, loose leaf.

Settlement of accounts between Iuda Boniosep, a Jew, and Antonio la Taria, in regard to various business transactions, including a vineyard, a nag and so forth. As a result Antonio remains owing Iuda 1.24.0 ounces.

Die II Octobris prime Ind. anno Dominice Incarnacionis MCCCCLXXXII Facta racione finali inter Iudam Boniosep, Iudeum, ex una parte et Antonium la Taria, ex altera, de omnibus et singulis inter eos gestis et habitis, videlicet tam de omnibus per eundem Antonium habitis et contentis in quodam contractu, die III° decembris anni proxime preteriti inter eosdem contrahentes manu mei notarii celebrato, de vinea quam Antonius ipse habet ab eodem Juda ad medietatem quam de illis unciis duabus ad quas dictus Antonius se debitorem constituit eidem Iude pro parte Salvatoris la Raniocta, quam de illis tarenis VIIII et gr. X per dictum Antonium ab ipso Iuda habitis et receptis extra contractum et de illis unciis III et tarenis VIIII contentis in quodam contractu facto manu notarii Mathei de Vermiglio, ad quas et quos predictus Antonius eidem Iude tenetur pro precio cuiusdam ronczeni, per dictum Antonium empti a dicto Iuda, quam etiam de omnibus et singulis uvarum quantitatibus per dictum Antonium prefato Iude assignatis presentibus in vendemmis perventis ex vinea dicti Iude in contrata Collium, quam idem Antonium habet ab ipso Iuda ad medietatem et de porcione contingente eidem Antonio, et etiam de frumento et ordeo, ac palea per dictum Antonium ipsi Iude tradditos et assignatos anno preterito, et de illis uncia I et tr. III per Antonium Lancza et Nicolaum de Sancto Georgio pro parte dicti Antonii La Taria solutis et tradditis eidem Iude, omnibus hinc inde deductis et extenuatis, excomputatis et compensatis ab olim usque ad presentem diem per eandem rationem ut supra diligenter factam, prefatus Antonius remansit et remanet debitor et relinquator dicto Iude in una manu in uncia una de summa predictarum unciarum duarum, quas Antonius ipse, pro parte predicti Salvatoris la Raniocta predicto, solvere promiserat et se obligaverat, et in alia manu in tr. XXIII restantibus ad complimentum predictarum unciarum III et tr. VIIII precii ronczini predicti, renuncians execucioni. De quibus uncia I et tr. XXIII idem Antonius dare promisit eidem Iude presenti etc., unciam unam in vino de vinea predicta quam dictus Antonius habet ad medietatem a dicto Iuda, et de porcione uvarum dicto Antonio contingente in vendemiis proxime futuris in gassiria dicte vinee pro precio contento in dicto contractu facto manu mei notarii dicto die III° decembris predicti anni preteriti, et reliquos tr. XXIII ad complimentum predictarum unciam I et tr. XXIII idem Antonius dare et solvere promisit dicto Iuda presenti etc., ad omnem eiusdem Iude simplicem requisitionem, ex nunc in antea, in pecunia numerata. Que omnia etc., promiserunt etc., rata etc., habere etc., in omnem eventum etc., in pace etc., sub ypotheca et obligatione omnium bonorum eorum etc., ac refectionem dampnorum, interesse et expensarum, litis et extra et quod fiat ritus in persona et bonis etc. Renunciantes etc., et specialiter cum iuramento, beneficio moratorie supersessorie regii guidatici quinquennalis dilacionis refugii domus et cessionis bonorum et cuiuslibet alterius dilacionis maioris seu minoris etc. Et iuraverunt ambo dictusque Antonius iterum predicta actendere et observare etc.

Testes etc.

Palermo, 2 April 1483

Source: ASP, Not. Giacomo Comito, reg. 860, c. 116r.

Liuzo Sin and Lia Cuyno, Jews of Trapani, appoint Machaluffo Cuyno, a Jew of Palermo, to act for them in Palermo and to collect outstanding debts.

Palermo, 15 May 1483

Source: ASP, Not. Giacomo Comito, reg. 860, c. 140r.

Simone de Marchisio sells Sadia Azara a tax imposed on the Jews of Palermo for 12 ounces.

Palermo, 10 September 1483

Source: ASP, Not. Giacomo Comito, reg. 860, c. 4v.

Benedetto de Girachio, notary of the Jewish community of Palermo, lodges a protest against Raffaele de Daniel, his Jewish fellow citizen, for having let a tavern on 19.8.1483 for 1.18.0 ounces without the permission of the community.

Palermo, 10 September 1483

Source: ASP, Not. Giacomo Comito, reg. 860, c. 5r.

Settlement of accounts between Bartholomeo Michono and Iosep Talo, a Jew of Palermo, of past business transactions. As a result Bartholomeo owes Iosep 10 tarì.

Palermo, 17 September 1483

Source: ASP, Not. Giacomo Comito, reg. 860, c. 10r.

Salamon Magaseni, a Palermitan Jew, undertakes to pay Iacob de Girachio, a Jew of Polizzi, seven ounces which he owes to Beniamino de Girachio, a Jew, at present absent, by the coming month. The sum is the balance of the dowry of Xanna, daughter of Busacca Magaseni, a Jewess.

Palermo, 17 September 1483

Source: ASP, Not. Giacomo Comito, reg. 860, c. 10v.

Pietro Antonio de Lampiso leases to Iosep de Liucio, a Jew in Palermo, two large copper pots for use in a sugar refinery for a year for 1.8.0 ounces.

Palermo, 7 October 1483

Source: ASP, Not. Giacomo Comito, reg. 860, c. 15v.

Contract whereby Agnesia, widow of Xibiten Xaccarono, and her sons David and Abram, all Palermitan Jews, set up a joint venture to manage a shop for the sale of assorted merchandise and cloth at Ciminna or in Palermo. Agnesia invests 20 ounces in cash and 10 ounces in cloth, while the sons invest their labour. Profits are to be divided in equal shares.

Palermo, 4 March 1483

Source: ASP, Not. Giacomo Comito, reg. 860, c. 22r.

Settlement of accounts between Agnesia, widow of Xibiten Xaccaruni, administrator of her late husband's estate, and her son David, Palermitan Jews, in regard to the management of a shop. As a result it transpires that David owes his mother 17 ounces.

Palermo, 14 October 1483

Source: ASP, Not. Giacomo Comito, reg. 860, c. 25v.

Merdoc Xillura, a Jew of Sciacca, hires himself out to Xamuel Actuni, a Palermitan Jew, to work in his dyeing business for five years for 15 grana a day.

Palermo, 22 October 1483

Source: ASP, Not. Giacomo Comito, reg. 860, c. 32r.

Cola Cannata of Modica promises Merdoc de Minichi, a Palermitan Jew, to cultivate his land situated in the contrada *Lu Ficu of Palermo for 24 tarì, and is paid three tarì on account.*

Palermo, 3 November 1483

Source: ASP, Not. Giacomo Comito, reg. 860, c. 38r.

Merdoc di Lu Presti, a Jew of Palermo, hires himself out to Simone de Martorana to work in his vineyard situated in the contrada *La Sichiria in Palermo, for seven tarì a thousand plants, and is paid six tarì on account.*

Palermo, 4 November 1483

Source: ASP, Not. Giacomo Comito, reg. 860, c. 38v.

Following negotiations between Raynaldo Lu Canaru and Muxa Millac, a Palermitan Jew, in regard to the settlement of accounts relating to large quantity of grapes sold to Muxa in the year of the 1st Indiction for 40 ounces, it transpires that Muxa received less than the quantity stipulated. Raynaldo now agrees to make up the deficit in the course of the present vintage.

Sicily

Source: ASP, Not. Giacomo Comito, reg. 860, c. 52r.

Agreement between Guglielmo de Vinusu and Muxa Millac, a Palermitan Jew, whereby Guglielmo is to pay Muxa a sum of money due to Muxa as result of the settlement of accounts between them. Guglielmo is to pay with grapes during the current vintage and 18 tarì cash are to be paid in May.

Palermo, 30 September [1467?]

Source: ASP, Not. Giacomo Comito, reg. 861, loose leaf.

Master Sabbatino de Medico, a Palermitan Jew, lodges a notarial protest against Baldassare Bonconto in regard to a consignment of oil which turned out to defective. He demands compensation.

Palermo, 10 October 1466

Source: ASP, Not. Giacomo Comito, reg. 861, c. loose leaf.

Zullo Magaseni, a Jew in Palermo, hires himself out to Simone de Sancto Filippo to work during the current year in Simone's vineyard for 15 tarì a thousand plants, and is paid one ounce on account.

Palermo, 8 March 1482

Source: ASP, Not. Giacomo Comito, reg. 861, c. loose leaf.

Merdoc Rixab, a Jew in Palermo, hires himself out to Giovanni Homodei to work in his tunny plant during the entire season for one ounce.

Source: ASP, Not. Giacomo Comito, reg. 843

Date and Page	Principal	Attorney	Purpose	Remarks
10.4.1433 c. 38r	Iacobo de Marco	Iosep Abudaram, a Palermitan Jew	to collect debts at Bivona	

Date and Page	Debtor	Amount	Reason	Remarks
8.3.1428 c. nn	Isac de Guillelmo, a Jew of Palermo	3.6.0 ounces		creditor: bank of Pietro de Accardio; to be paid within 5 months

Date and Page	Lender or Seller	Amount	Payment	Remarks
23.8.1427 c. nn	Rainerio de Risignano	1.3.8 ounces	within 4 months	sale of iron to Nissim Carluni, a Jew
23.8.1427 c. nn	Matheo de Zampardo	7.22.0 ounces	within a month	sale of wine to Iosep Abudaram, a Jew of Palermo
23.8.1427 c. nn	Simon de Bancherio	2 ounces	by May; paid 2.5.1428	sale of grapes to Brachono and Muxa de Rubeo, Jews
23.8.1427 c. nn	Xibiteni de Muxarella, a Jew of Trapani	10 ounces		sale of a slave
23.8.1427 c. nn	Narciso de Bondello	12 ounces		sale of deerskins to Iacob Fitira, a Jew
23.8.1427 c. nn	David Xifuni, a Palermitan Jew	4 ounces	within 4 months	sale of merchandise to Busac and Chayrono Medui, Jews
27.8.1427 c. nn	Nicolò Girardi	1.28.16 ounces	within a month; paid 27.4.1429	sale of keys to Vita Azaru, a Palermitan Jew
27.8.1427 c. nn	Yaimo de Oria	2.3.0 ounces	by May; paid 27.5.1430	sale of goods to Vanni de Termini and Merdoc Simal, Jews of Palermo
27.8.1427 c. nn	Xirello de [...]	2.7.8 ounces	within 15 days	sale of merchandise to Gauiusa La Iudia, a Jewess of Palermo
27.8.1427 c. nn	Andreocta Consuli	15.12.0 ounces	paid 12.2.1429	sale of cloth to Gallufu de Lu Medicu, a Jew of Palermo

29.10.1427 c. nn	Giovanni [...]	13.6.0 ounces	within 4 months; paid 7.5.1429	sale of cloth to Chanino Balbo, a Jew of Mazara
30.10.1427 c. nn	Nicolò Ferrari	2.7.0 ounces	within 4 months; paid 28.1.1430	sale of cloth to Nachuni Milecta, a Jew of Mazara
2.11.1427 c. nn	Guglielmo de Scales	1.12.8. ounces	paid 12.8.1429	sale of cloth to Nachuni Milecta, a Jew of Mazara
10.11.1427 c. nn	Pino Gaitano	5.12.13 ounces	within 5 months; paid 5.5.1429	sale of linen to Salamon de Muxa, a Jew
10.11.1427 c. nn	Guglielmo de Scales	8.12.0 ounces	within 5 months	sale of cloth to Leone Sacerdoto, a Palermitan Jew
10.11.1427 c. 132r	Francesco Iustino	6.7.0 ounces	within 6 months; paid 6.7.1429	sale of cloth to Musuto Bricha, a Jew of Palermo
10.11.1427 c. 132r	Pietro [...]	1.15.0 ounces	within 6 months; paid 10.12.1430	sale of olive oil to Benedettto Miseria, a Jew of Palermo
10.11.1427 c. 136r	Giovanni Damiani	1.25.0 ounces	within 6 months; paid 12.7.1429	sale of deerskins to Iuda Sivena and Nissim Xor, Jews of Palermo
10.11.1427 c. 136r	Pino de Tango	1.15.0 ounces	within 3 months	sale of cloth to Nissim Azaruti, a Palermitan Jew
10.11.1427 c. 136v	Nicolò de Girardo	1.12.0 ounces	by 15 March	sale of linen to Busac Sabatino, a Jew of Palermo
10.11.1427 c. 136v	Nicolò de Girardo	2.12.0 ounces	within 6 months; paid 9.9.1428	sale of linen to Sabeti Cuino, a Jew of Palermo
14.11.1427 c. 139r	Giovanni de Damiano	25.23.0 ounces	within a year; paid 12.7.1428	sale of cloth to Siminto de Muxarella, a Jew of Marsala

14.11.1427 c. 140r	Guglielmo de Scales	2.12.0 ounces		sale of silk Fariono de Iona, a Jew of Marsala
14.11.1427 c. 140v	Raimondo Garau	1.5.0 ounces		sale of cloth Fariono de Iona, a Jew of Marsala
17.11.1427 c. 148r	Bernardo Bertolino	12.18.0 ounces	by July	sale of cloth to Siminto de Muxarella, a Jew of Marsala
9.2.1428 c. 307r	Pino Gaitano	4.17.18 ounces	paid 17.2.1429	sale of fabric to Gallufo Taguil, a Jew of Palermo
9.2.1428 c. 307v	Nicolò Omodei	3.13.17 ounces	by June; paid 2.8.1430	sale of cloth to Michilono Xunina, a Jew of Palermo
9.2.1428 c. 307r	Gerardo de Provenza	1.20.8 ounces	within 4 months; paid 12.7.1428	sale of keys to Iacob Sabatino, a Palermitan Jew
9.2.1428 c. 318v	Martino Paoli	1.12.0 ounces	within 6 months; paid 9.10.1428	sale of saffron to Michilono Xunina, a Jew of Palermo
9.2.1428 c. 319r	Martino Paoli	1.12.0 ounces	within a month; paid 12.12.1428	sale of cinnamon to Iacob Taguil, a Palermitan Jew
9.2.1428 c. 319v	Martino Paoli	1.12.0 ounces	within a month; paid 7.10.1428	sale of linen to Iacob Sabatino, a Jew of Palermo
12.2.1428 c. 321r	Martino Paoli	2.9.15 ounces	paid 5.6 1428	sale of cinnamon to Xamuel Sabatino, a Jew
12.2.1428 c. 321r	[....]	2.11.0 ounces	within a month; paid 7.6.1428	sale of deerskin to Merdoc Liuni, a Palermitan Jew
20.2.1428 c. 333r	Giovanni Damiani	32.15.0 ounces	within 5 months; paid 2.1.1429	sale of cloth to Iosep Maltisi, a Jew of Polizzi

6396

Date	Name	Amount	Term	Description
23.2.1428 c. 341r	Guglielmo Scales	4 ounces	within 4 months	sale of fabric to Muxa de Mussuto, a Messinese Jew
23.2.1428 c. 341r	Guglielmo Scales	6.18.0 ounces	within 4 months	sale of fabric to Muxa Sillac, a Palermitan Jew
23.2.1428 c. 342v	Pietro Serra	8 ounces	by June; paid 6.7.1428	sale of cloth to Nissim de Caccabo, a Jew of Caltabellotta
23.2.1428 c. 343v	Raimondo Aglata	3.10.0 ounces	within 5 months; paid 18.5.1429	sale of cloth to Lia Nissim, a Jew of Palermo
26.2.1428 c. 345v	Giaimo de Levis	2.10.0 ounces	by July	sale of cloth to Nissim Nifusi, a Jew of Mazara
26.2.1428 c. 347r	Guglielmo Salem	14.2.0 ounces	within 3 months	sale of cloth to Nissim Nifusi, a Jew of Mazara
26.2.1428 c. 348r	Guglielmo Firreri	9.6.0 ounces	by July; paid 19.9.1429	sale of cloth to Nissim Azaruti, a Palermitan Jew
8.3.1428 c. nn	Iayme [...]	9.19.0 ounces	by May; paid 26.8	sale of cloth to Geremia Cuyno, a Jew of Trapani
8.3.1428 c. nn	Giovanni de Colta	12.12.0 ounces	within 8 months	sale of cloth to Muxa and Fariono Ginni, Jews of Nicosia
8.3.1428 c. nn	Antonio Funali	3 ounces	within 15 days; paid 12.6.1429	sale of goods to Fariono Lu Medicu, a Jew of Catania
8.3.1428 c. nn	Pietro Anello	20 ounces	within 6 months; paid 17.5.1429	sale of cloth to Nissim Caccabo, a Jew of Caltabellotta
8.3.1428 c. nn	Agabito de Bartholomeo	7.26.0 ounces	by June; paid 18.4.1429	sale of cloth to Fariono Cuino, a Jew of Trapani
8.3.1428 c. nn	Nicolò Ayroldo	20 ounces	within 4 months; paid 1.12.1428	sale of cloth to Muxa and Fariono Ginni, Jews of Nicosia

8.3.1428 c. nn	Giovanni de Accardo	25 ounces	within 3 months; paid 19.2.1429	sale of goods to Lia de Benedicto, a Jew
8.3.1428 c. nn	Adinolfo de Fornaio	28.22.10 ounces	within 6 months; paid 30.5.1429	sale of cloth to Fariono Cuino, a Jew of Trapani
8.3.1428 c. nn	Iaymo Pinto	22 ounces		sale of cloth to Fariono Cuino, a Jew of Trapani
8.3.1428 c. nn	Pietro de Guillelmo	14 ounces	within 6 months; paid 1.7.1429	sale of cloth to Iacob and Michilono Xunina, Palermitan Jews
8.3.1428 c. nn	Francesco Perchanni	13.6.0 ounces	within 5 months	sale of cloth to Azarono Monachetilu, a Jew of Marsala
8.3.1428 c. nn	Sperandeo Pilar	9.21.0 ounces	within 3 months	sale of cloth to Benedetto Azarono, a Jew
8.3.1428 c. nn	Benedetto Perdicario	25.12.0 ounces		sale of cloth to Azarono Monachetilu, a Jew of Marsala
22.11.1428 c. nn	Guglielmo Scales	7.11.0 ounces	by July; paid 9.8.1429	sale of drill to Iosep Abudaram, a Jew
22.11.1428 c. nn	[...] [...]	6 ounces	within 4 months; paid 22.10.1429	sale of cloth to Muxa Cuyno, a Palermitan Jew
22.11.1428 c. nn	Andreocta Gentili	5.15.0 ounces	within 6 months	sale of cloth to Xibiten Dinar, a Palermitan Jew
22.11.1428 c. nn	Andreocta Gentili	15.20.0 ounces	within 5 months	sale of cloth to Simon Bissar, a Palermitan Jew
22.11.1428 c. nn	Nicolò Guirardi	7.9.0 ounces	within 2 months; paid 26.6.1430	sale of cloth to Iosep Abudaram, a Palermitan Jew

7.6.1429 c. nn	Andreocta Gentili	5.28.0 ounces	within 4 months; paid 18.12.1429	sale of cloth to Lia Nissim, a Jew of Palermo
7.6.1429 c. nn	Antonio de Casafranca	2.12.0 ounces	within 2 months; paid 11.10.1430	sale of cloth to Abram Abagatel, a Palermitan Jew
9.6.1429 c. nn	Nicolò Infranca	7.29.0 ounces	by August; paid 6.8.1431	sale of cloth to Simon Bissar, a Palermitan Jew
9.6.1429 c. nn	Ieronimo Pomas	7.16.10 ounces	within 4 months; paid 20.5.1430	sale of cloth to Abram and Vita de Aram, Palermitan Jews
9.6.1429 c. nn	Simon de Raia	2.7.0 ounces	within 3 months; paid 10.5.1430	sale of olive oil to Busacca Actuni, a Jew of Palermo
23.6.1429 c. nn	Antonio de Casafranca	2 ounces	by July; paid 11.11.1429	sale of cloth to Abram Abagatel, a Palermitan Jew
28.6.1429 c. nn	Andreotta Gentili	15.12.10 ounces	within 3 months; paid 28.6.1430	sale of cloth to Iosep Abudarham, a Jew of Palermo
1.7.1429 c. nn	Salamon Minichi, a Jew of Palermo	10 ounces	paid	sale of salt
4.7.1429 c. nn	Adinolfo de Fornaio	15 ounces	within a month	sale of iron to Siminto Azaruti, a Jew of Palermo
22.10.1429 c. nn	Federico de P[..]	5 ounces	by end of October; paid 20.10.1430	sale of olive oil to Vanni Sabuchi, a Palermitan Jew
22.10.1429 c. nn	Michilono Chunina, a Palermitan Jew	2 ounces		sale of grapes
23.10.1429 c. nn	Francesco de Bellachera	4.8.7 ounces	within 2 months	sale of grapes to Graciano Tachariato and Salamon Benassay, Jews of Palermo

4.11.1429 c. nn	Simon de Spuches	1.6.0 ounces	within 2 months	sale of cloth to Busacca de Tripoli, a Jew of Palermo
24.11.1429 c. nn	Iacobo de Penso	18 ounces	within 4 months; paid 22.7.1430	sale of cloth to Sabet Vignuni, a Palermitan Jew
26.11.1429 c. nn	Simone de Risignano	2.24.0 ounces	by July; paid 27.5.1430	sale of wheat to Iosep de Medico, a Palermitan Jew
27.11.1429 c. nn	Lorenzo de Li Strozzi, a Florentine nobleman	24.11.12 ounces	paid 10.11.1430	sale of Florentine cloth to Iosep de Medico, a Palermitan Jew
8.12.1429 c. nn	Giovanni Peras	6.2.0 ounces	within 6 months	sale of cloth to Manuel Chetibi, a Jew of Palermo
11.12.1429 c. nn	Giovanni Peras	2 ounces	within 6 months	sale of cloth to Manuel Chetibi, a Jew of Palermo
11.12.1429 c. nn	Filippo Aglata	12.11.0 ounces	within 6 months	sale of gold wire to Farrugio Ysac and Sabeti Cuyno, Jews of Palermo
22.12.1429 c. nn	Bartholomeo de La Oliva	12.6.0 ounces	within 4 months; paid 19.8.1430	sale of cambric (*brixa Xambraxia*) to Xibiten Azara, a Palermitan Jew
27.3.1430 c. nn	Battista Aglata	5.16.9 ounces	monthly instalments; paid 20.5.1430	sale of iron to Muxa Xabber and Busacca de Fitira, Palermitan Jews
31.3.1430 c. nn	Pietro Market	2.16.10 ounces	within 6 months; paid 5.7.1431	sale of cloth to Onorato de Gaudio, a Palermitan Jew
11.10.1431 c. nn	Bernardo Sardo	6.23.0 ounces	within 4 months; paid 14.3.1432	sale of cloth to Muxa Sivena, a Jew of Palermo

11.10.1431 c. nn	Vincenzo Colanti	5.3.0 ounces	within 4 months; paid 15.1.1432	sale of cloth to Busacca Romano, a Jew of Palermo
11.10.1431 c. nn	Giaimo [...]	2.15.0 ounces	by July; paid 10.4.1433	sale of cloth to Busacca Romano, a Jew of Palermo
11.10.1431 c. nn	Zullo de Graciano	11.29.0 ounces	within 4 months; paid 14.3.1432	sale of cloth to Salamon de Muxa, Iacob Riczu and Iosep Lu Medicu, Palermitan Jews
17.10.1431 c. nn	Battista Aglata	6.6.0 ounces	within 4 months; paid 14.4.1432	sale of linen to Iosep Abudaram, a Jew of Palermo
17.10.1431 c. nn	Antonio de C[..]	5.15.10 ounces	within 5 months; paid 14.3.1432	sale of linen to Samuel Sacerdoto, a Palermitan Jew
17.10.1431 c. nn	Battista Aglata	8 ounces		sale of fabric to Benedetto Azara, a Palermitan Jew
17.10.1431 c. nn	Giovanni Spayoll	5.8.15 ounces	paid 29.2 1432	sale of linen to Chayrono and Busacca Medui, Jews
18.10.1431 c. nn	Antonio Capulito	11 ounces	within 4 months; paid 22.1.1433	sale of linen to Vita Azara, a Jew
19.10.1431 c. nn	Nicolò Snortu	5.10.0 ounces	within 4 months; paid 10.7.1432	sale of linen to Iacob Xunina, a Palermitan Jew
19.10.1431 c. nn	Benedetto Sacerdoto, a Jew	6.29.15 ounces	within 5 months; paid 14.1.1433	sale of textiles to Siminto de Muxarella, a Jew of Marsala
19.10.1431 c. nn	Baldassare Bonconti	7.15.0 ounces	within 5 months; paid 15.1.1432	sale of linen to Siminto de Muxarella, a Jew of Marsala

19.10.1431 c. nn	Francesco Sardu	7.14.14 ounces	paid 27.1.1432	sale of cloth to Siminto de Muxarella, a Jew of Marsala
19.10.1431 c. nn	Pietro Gennaro	7.3.0 ounces	within 4 months; paid 10.1.1432	sale of cloth to Sadia Gibra, a Palermitan Jew
22.10.1431 c. nn	Baldassare Bonconti	26 ounces	within 4 months; paid 27.1.1432	sale of cloth to Brachono Sacerdoto, a Palermitan Jew
26.10.1431 c. nn	Antonio de Casafranca	7 ounces	within a month; paid 15.12.1432	sale of cloth to Abraam Abagatell, a Jew of Palermo
11.4.1432 c. nn	Giovanni Abbatellis	15.9.0 ounces	within 2 months	sale of cloth to Sadia de Partanna, a Jew of Sciacca
12.4.1432 c. nn	Francesco de Prixono	15.10.5 ounces	within 2 months; paid 12.7.1432	sale of goods to Sadia de Partanna, a Jew of Sciacca
19.4.1432 c. nn	Onorato de Florencia	2 ounces	at vintage time	sale of grapes to Iuda Simon, a Palermitan Jew
26.4.1432 c. nn	Antonio de Casafranca	7 ounces	within 2 months; paid 15.12 1432	sale of cloth to Abraam Abagatell, a Jew of Palermo
27.4.1432 c. nn	Battista Aglata	5.19.0 ounces		sale of gold wire to Simon Benassay, a Palermitan Jew
5.6.1432 c. nn	Antonio de Settimo	50.15.0 ounces	within 6 months; paid 15.15.1434	sale of cloth to David Issuni, a Palermitan Jew
15.9.1432 c. nn	Tommaso Spinula	6.12.0 ounces	within 6 months; paid 6.5.1433	sale of merchandise to Iuda de Liuni, a Jew of Palermo
19.9.1432 c. nn	[...] [...]	12 ounces	within 4 months; paid 15.11.1433	sale of linen to Iosep Abudaram, a Jew
9.1.1433 c. nn	Batholomeo de Casagrande	7 ounces	paid 27.4.1435	sale of velvet to Iosep Abudaram, a Palermitan Jew

9.1.1433 c. nn	Antonio de Crapona	27.10 *tarì*		sale of manure to Gallufo Channiti, a Jew of Palermo
9.1.1433 c. nn	Iuda de Vita and Chaym Balbu, Jews of Mazara	82.3.0 ounces	40 ounces on account, balance by February	sale of biscuits
13.1.1433 c. nn	Chaym Balbu, a Jew of Mazara	agreed price	11.16.10 ounces on account, balance in March	sale of biscuits
16.1.1433 c. nn	Damiano de Cammarata	23.28.9 ounces	paid 27.3.1434	sale of sugar to Isdrael Farachi, a Jew of Palermo
16.1.1433 c. nn	Michilono Minachem, a Palermitan Jew	2.29.14 ounces	within 15 days	sale of cheese
16.1.1433 c. nn	Baldassare Bonconti	1.1.0 ounces	within 5 months	sale of smith's bellows to Siminto Benassay and Iuda de Girachio, Palermitan Jews
19.1.1433 c. nn	bank of Francesco de Prixono	1 ounce	within a month	loan to Simon Ysac, a Palermitan Jew
26.1.1433 c. nn	Marraffo de Bandello	2.12.0 ounces	paid 14.5.1433	sale of cloth to Iosep Abudaram, a Palermitan Jew
16.2.1433 c. nn	Tommaso Spinula	1.25.10 ounces	within 2 months	sale of cloth to Lia Amar, a Jew of Palermo
17.2.1433 c. nn	Paolo Sardu	2 ounces	within 2 months; paid 23.5.1433	sale of cloth to Abraam Abagatell, a Jew
17.2.1433 c. nn	Tommaso Spinula	3.27.0 ounces	within 5 months; paid 12.1.1434	sale of cloth to Iosep Abudaram, a Palermitan Jew
18.2.1433 c. nn	Tommaso Spinula	2.7.0 ounces	by July	sale of drill to Elia Amar, a Jew of Palermo

23.2.1433 c. nn	Iacobo Italiano	2 ounces	within 15 days; paid 29.3.1434	sale of goods to Aron Campagna, a Jew of Messina and Sabatino de Medico, a Jew of Palermo
24.2.1433 c. nn	Tommaso Spinula	14.2.0 ounces	within 4 months; paid 28.8.1434	sale of cloth to Sadono de Medico, a Palermitan Jew
26.2.1433 c. nn	Paolo Sardu	17.12.0 ounces	within 4 months; paid 25.9.1433	sale of cloth to Iosep de Medico, a Palermitan Jew, acting for Siminto de Muxarella, a Jew of Marsala
26.2.1433 c. nn	Tommaso Spinula	1.9.0 ounces	within 5 months; paid 19.7. 1433	sale of linen to Leone de La Iudeca, a Palermitan Jew
26.2.1433 c. nn	Giovanni M[..]	15.22.0 ounces	within 5 months; paid 16.1.1434	sale of cloth to Iosep Maltisi, a Jew of Polizzi
26.2.1433 c. nn	Marraffo de Bandello	25.21.0 ounces	within 5 months; paid 26.10.1433	sale of cloth to Iosep de Medico, a Palermitan Jew, acting for Siminto de Muxarella, a Jew of Marsala
26.2.1433 c. nn	Paolo Sardu	8.24.0 ounces	within 5 months; paid 12.1.1434	sale of cloth to Iosep Maltisi, a Jew of Polizzi
27.2.1433 c. nn	Antonio de Bargano	24 ounces	within 4 months	sale of cloth to Chanino Balbo, a Jew of Mazara
27.2.1433 c. nn	Pietro Mal[..]	23.24.0 ounces	within 6 months; paid 12.1.1434	sale of cloth to Iosep Maltisi, a Jew of Polizzi
27.2.1433 c. nn	Chaninu Balbu, a Jew of Mazara	agreed price		sale of goods to Nissim Dinna, a Jew of Palermo
27.2.1433 c. nn	Paolo Sardu	9.15.0 ounces	within 5 months; paid 28.8.1434	sale of cloth to Iuda de Oria, a Jew of Mazara

6404

27.2.1433 c. nn	Bernardu Curtu	22.2.0 ounces	within a month; paid 30.4.1434	sale of deerskin to Iusep Theru, a Jew
27.2.1433 c. nn	Francesco de Pau	12.2.0 ounces	within a month; paid 24.6.1433	sale of cloth to Iosep Maltisi, a Jew of Polizzi
27.2.1433 c. nn	Antonio Pardo	27.21.0 ounces	within 5 months	sale of cloth to Iuda de Oria, a Jew of Mazara
2.3.1433 c. nn	Bernardu Curtu	5.15.0 ounces	within 5 months; paid 21.7.1433	sale of cloth to Chanino Farmono, a Palermitan Jew
2.3.1433 c. nn	Tommaso Spinula	33.4.10 ounces	within 5 months; paid 8.9.1433	sale of cloth to Farchono Rubeo, a Palermitan Jew
3.3.1433 c. nn	Giovanni Carbo	7.18.10 ounces	within 4 months; paid 23.12.1433	sale of cloth to Iusep Abudaram, a Palermitan Jew
3.3.1433 c. nn	Geronimo Castigliano	6.12.0 ounces	within 2 months; paid 30.7.1433	sale of cloth to Iusep Abudaram, a Palermitan Jew
3.3.1433 c. nn	Andreotta Gentili	9.21.0 ounces	within a month; paid 10.9.1433	sale of skins to Nissim Azaru, a Palermitan Jew
3.3.1433 c. nn	Antonio de Crapona	2.22.15 ounces	within a month; paid 7.9.1433	sale of iron to Muxa Rubeo, a Jew of Palermo
3.3.1433 c. nn	Paolo Sardu	7.24.0 ounces	within a month; paid 13.4.1433	sale of cloth to David Chaseni, a Jew of Nicosia
4.3.1433 c. nn	Rainerio de Risignano	17.15.0 ounces	within 5 months; paid 21.4.1434	sale of cloth to Iusep de Lu Medicu, a Jew of Palermo
9.3.1433 c. nn	Rainerio de Risignano	4.24.0 ounces	within 5 months	sale of cloth to Iusep Abudaram, a Palermitan Jew
10.3.1433 c. nn	Pietro de Gaetano	11.10.0 ounces	within 2 months; paid 8.7.1434	sale of goods to Sadono de Medico, a Jew of Palermo

6405

Date	Name	Amount	Terms	Description
10.3.1433 c. nn	Rainerio de Risignano	7.18.10 ounces	within 5 months; paid 13.1.1434	sale of cloth to Onorato de Gaudio, a Palermitan Jew
11.3.1433 c. nn	Iaymo Castellano	10.24.0 ounces	within a month	sale of cloth to Iusep Abudaram, a Palermitan Jew
11.3.1433 c. nn	Simone Audice	3.15.18 ounces	within 4 months	sale of linen to Sabatino de Lu Presti, a Jew of Palermo
11.3.1433 c. nn	Simone Audice	3.15.18 ounces	within 4 months	sale of linen to Daniel de Abramono and Lia Copiu, Jews
11.3.1433 c. nn	Simone de mastro Andrea	3 ounces	within 4 months	loan to Sabet de D[..], a Jew of Palermo
11.3.1433 c. nn	Bernardo Curtu	16.4.10 ounces	on demand	sale of cloth to Elia Cuyno, a Palermitan Jew
11.3.1433 c. nn	Pietro de Oria	6.9.0 ounces	within 3 months	sale of cloth to Iusep Abudaram, a Palermitan Jew
12.3.1433 c. nn	Geronimo Io[..]	4.6.0 ounces	within a month; paid 20.4.1433	sale of cloth to Iosep de Iona, a Jew
13.3.1433 c. nn	Andreotta Gentili	15.6.0 ounces	within a month	sale of merchandise to Nissim Azaruti, a Jew of Palermo
13.3.1433 c. nn	Bernardo Curtu	2.18.0 ounces	within 2 months	sale of cloth to Iosep de Medico, a Palermitan Jew, for Siminto de Muxarella, a Jew of Marsala
13.3.1433 c. nn	Geronimo Castellino	2.18.0 ounces	within 4 months; paid 3.2.1434	sale of gold wire to Vita Azaru, a Palermitan Jew
16.3.1433 c. nn	Francesco de Prixano	36 ounces	within 6 months; paid 14.8.1434	sale of deerskin to Xirello Farmono, Chayrono Sacerdotu and Sabet Farmono, Jews of Palermo

17.3.1433 c. nn	Rainerio de Risignano	2.12.0 ounces	within 4 months; paid 7.4.1434	sale of cloth to Abraam Abagatell, a Jew of Palermo
17.3.1433 c. nn	Rainerio de Risignano	2.24.0 ounces	within 2 months; paid 25.9. 1433	sale of goods to Abraam Abagatell, a Palermitan Jew
17.3.1433 c. nn	Bernardo [Curtu]	4 ounces	within 2 months; paid 19.6.1433	sale of cloth to Onorato de Gaudio, a Jew of Palermo
17.3.1433 c. nn	Andreotta Gentili	8.24.0 ounces	2.12.0 ounces in a week, balance in 4 months	sale of cloth to Elia Amar, a Palermitan Jew
17.3.1433 c. nn	Bernardo Curtu	1.15.0 ounces	within 4 months; paid 7.7.1433	sale of deerskin to Chanino Rindillaru, a Jew of Caccamo
18.3.1433 c. nn	Xibiteni di Saduni, a Jew of Sciacca	70.15.0 ounces	paid	sale of cheese
24.3.1433 c. nn	[...] [...]	2.6.0 ounces	within 4 months	sale of oil to Salamon Cuyno, a Palermitan Jew
27.3.1433 c. nn	Siminto de Muxarella, a Jew of Marsala	9.27.0 ounces	by August; paid 25.9.1433	sale of cloth to Iosep de Medico, a Palermitan Jew
30.3.1433 c. nn	Tommaso Spinula	7 ounces	within 4 months; paid 12.1.1434	sale of cloth to Abraam Abagatell, a Jew of Palermo
30.3.1433 c. nn	Andreotta Gentili	1.26.0 ounces	within 4 months	sale of a bale of paper to Salamon Fitira, a Palermitan Jew
1.4.1433 c. nn	Pietro Ysalla	6.21.7 ounces	to be paid with food; paid 22.4 1433	sale of merchandise to Xibiten Mayeti and Salamon Zaffarana, Jews of Palermo
18.4.1433 c. nn	Nicolò Tagliavini	2.28.0 ounces	within 4 months	sale of goods to Nissim Sansono, a Palermitan Jew

29.4.1433	Ambroxino	8.16.16 ounces	within 4 months	sale of gold wire to
c. nn	Commisso			Iosep Provinzano, a
				Jew

Source: ASP, Not. Giacomo Comito, reg. 844

Date and Page	Principal	Attorney	Purpose	Remarks
5.12.1435 c. 212v	Luca Moroxini, a Venetian	Chanino Balbo, a Jew of Mazara	to sell 2 inns, one with a cistern, and a house in Sciacca	

Date and Page	Lender or Seller	Amount	Payment	Remarks
[8].9.1433 c. 11r	Simone de Buxa	1 ounce	paid	sale of barley to Busac Sala, a Jew of Palermo
8.9.1433 c. 11v	Simone de Buxa	1.14.0 ounces		sale of wheat to Michilono Xunina, a Palermitan Jew
9.9.1433 c. 12v	Simone de Buxa	1 ounce		sale of wheat to Sadia Chacten, a Jew of Palermo
9.9.1433 c. 13v	Simone de Buxa	1.16.0 ounces		sale of wheat to Muxa Rubino, a Jew of Palermo
10.9.1433 c. 14v	Antonio de Settimo	10.15.0 ounces	within 4 months	sale of cloth to Conino Coppula, a Jew of Mazara, and Iosep Xaulo, a Jew of Palermo
10.9.1433 c. 15r	Rainerio de Ferrugio	3 ounces	paid 15.6.1433	sale of gold wire to Elia Nissim, a Palermitan Jew
10.9.1433 c. 16v	Rainerio de Risignano	1.11.0 ounces		sale of iron to Salamone Rusticu, a Palermitan Jew

Date	Name	Amount	Terms	Description
11.9.1433 c. 17v	Siminto de Muxarella, a Jew of Marsala	6.27.0 ounces		sale of cloth to Iosep de Medico, a Palermitan Jew
17.9. 1433 c. 28r	Nicolò Augusta	1 ounce	within 5 months	sale of a beast of burden to Sabet Xacaruni, a Jew
22.9.1433 c. 36r	Pietro Canelli	7.24.0 ounces		sale of cloth to Xibiten Cazuni, a Jew of Nicosia
22.9.1433 c. 36v	Pietro Pau and Iaimo de Spula	21 ounces	paid 24.11.1433	sale of cloth to Iacob Maltesi, a Jew of Polizzi
25.9.1433 c. nn	Pietro de Oria	6.11.0 ounces	within 4 months	sale of cloth to Muxa Sacerdoto, a Palermitan Jew
[..].12.1433 c. nn	Nicolò [...]	2.18.0 ounces	within 4 months	sale of gold wire to Busac Sala, a Jew
[..].12.1433 c. nn	Giovanni Oliva	8 ounces	by March	sale of cloth to Geremia Cuyno, a Palermitan Jew
[..].12.1433 c. nn	Sabet Fitira, a Palermitan Jew	12.3.6. ounces		sale of goods to Moyses de Medico, a Palermitan Jew
5.1.1434 c. nn	Pietro de Oria	3.21.0 ounces	within 4 months	sale of merchandise to Iosep Abudaram, a Palermitan Jew
8.1.1434 c. nn	Simone de Buxa	agreed price	paid	sale of cheese to Iuda de Vita and Braymi Balbu, Jews
9.2.1434 c. nn	Iacobo de Signorello	7.27.0 ounces	within 4 months	sale of merchandise to David Ysac, a Jew of Trapani
15.4.1434 c. nn	Filippo Amaludi	8.21.0 ounces		sale of cloth to Iosep Maltisi, a Jew of Polizzi
16.4.1434 c. nn	Baldassare Bonconti	39 ounces		loan to Iuda de Vita, a Jew of Mazara

16.4.1434 c. nn	Domenico de Valditera	3 ounces		sale of merchandise to Nissim Azaruti, a Palermitan Jew
16.4.1434 c. nn	Rainerio de Risignano	agreed price		sale of merchandise to Abraam Abagatell, a Palermitan Jew
17.4.1434 c. nn	Andrea de Speciali	40 ounces		sale of wheat to Iuda de Vita and Xhayanello Balbo, Jews of Mazara
20.4.1434 c. nn	Nicolò de Riczolo	agreed price		sale of merchandise to Fariono Siciliano and Salamon Actuni, Jews of Palermo
21.4.1434 c. nn	Andrea de Speciali	29.1.4 ounces	within a year	sale of iron to Brachono Taguili, a Jew of Palermo
23.4.1434 c. nn	Iacobo de Tusa	agreed price	3 ounces on account, balance on delivery	sale of wheat to Brachono Taguili, a Palermitan Jew
30.4.1434 c. nn	Baldassare Bonconte	17.16.0 ounces	within a year	sale of cloth to Iuda de Vita, a Jew
30.4.1434 c. nn	Andrea Pisano	25.18.12 ounces	by August	sale of Florentine cloth to Iuda de Vita and Chanino Balbo, Jews
4.5.1434 c. nn	Anfuso de Leydo	12 ounces	paid	sale of a Saracen slave to Siminto Aurifichi, a Palermitan Jew
15.5.1434 c. nn	Cuyno de Muxarella, a Jew	28.14.0 ounces	by August	sale of goods to Iosep de Medico, a Palermitan Jew
15.5.1434 c. nn	Guglielmo Serra	2.9.0 ounces		sale of cloth to Iosep de Medico, a Palermitan Jew
15.5.1434 c. nn	Cuyno de Muxarella, a Jew	3.24.15 ounces	paid	sale of goods Iosep de Medico, a Palermitan Jew

9.6.1434 c. nn	Pietro Bardulla	3.27.0 ounces	paid 30.10.1434	sale of alum to Iosep Sillach, a Jew of Palermo
1.9.1434 c. nn	Nicolò de Cabila	1.6.0 ounces	on delivery	sale of a horse to Xibiten Bambalu, a Jew of Palermo
7.9.1434 c. nn	Giovanni Ronira	3.2.4 ounces	within 2 months; paid 9.5.1435	sale of almonds to Samuele Rubeo, a Palermitan Jew
7.9.1434 c. nn	Pietro de Francesco de Prexano	2 ounces	paid 15.12.1434	sale of a mule to Robino Gibra, a Jew
16.9.1434 c. nn	Onorato Berto	26.12.0 ounces	within a year	sale of cloth to Siminto de Muxarella, a Jew of Marsala
16.9.1434 c. nn	Francesco de Prexano	8.21.0 ounces	by May	sale of cloth to Siminto de Muxarella, a Jew of Marsala
16.9.1434 c. nn	Yaimo Masdamunt	3.9.0 ounces	by December	sale of cloth to Brachono Taguili, a Palermitan Jew
22.9.1434 c. nn	Paolo Subiras	6.24.0 ounces	within 6 months	sale of cloth to Iosep Maltisi, a Jew of Polizzi
28.9.1434 c. nn	Bundo de Campo	3.27.12 ounces	within 4 months; paid 24.3.1435	sale of canvas to Isac de Gaudio, a Palermitan Jew
28.9.1434 c. nn	Damiano de Mari	4.24.0 ounces	within 4 months; paid 43.1435	sale of fabric to Muxa de Danieli, a Messinese Jew
28.9.1434 c. nn	Saldono Firreri	18.24.0 ounces	4.24.0 ounces on account, balance on delivery	sale of cloth to Salamon Maltesi, a Jew of Polizzi
30.9.1434 c. nn	Raimondo de Ganchi	14.12.0 ounces	within 4 months	sale of cloth to Iosep Abudaram, a Palermitan Jew

1.10.1434 c. nn	Iaymo Masdamunt	21.3.0 ounces	within 4 months	sale of cloth to Iosep Abudaram, a Palermitan Jew
5.10.1434 c. nn	Bernardo Curtu	13.9.0 ounces	within 6 months	sale of goods to Donato de Aram, a Palermitan Jew
11.10.1434 c. nn	Pietro de Oria	4 ounces	within 4 months	sale of fabric to Elia Nissim, a Jew
3.11.1434 c. nn	Nicolò de Leonardo	21.24.0 ounces	within 4 months	sale of gold wire to Leone de La Iudeca, a Jew of Palermo
3.11.1434 c. nn	Pietro Pau	30 ounces	within 4 months	sale of cloth to Brachono Taguili, a Palermitan Jew
5.11.1434 c. nn	Francesco de Prixano	7.7.15.0 ounces	within 4 months	sale of silk to Muxa de Daniel, a Jew of Messina
8.11.1434 c. nn	Antonio de Crapona	13.4.21 ounces	within 5 months; paid 14.6.1435	sale of merchandise to Muxa Rubeo, a Palermitan Jew
10.11.1434 c. nn	Pietro de Oria	6 ounces	weekly instalments of 12 *tarì*; paid 22.6.1435	sale of fabric to Abraam Ladeb, a Palermitan Jew
12.11.1434 c. nn	Bernardo Tango	10.27.0 ounces	within 4 months; paid 1.6.1435	sale of gold wire to Muxa de Daniele, a Jew of Messina
15.11.1434 c. nn	Filippo Aglata	12 ounces	within 4 months	sale of leather to Xirello Farmono and Muxa Levi, Jews of Palermo
16.11.1434 c. nn	Nicolò de Leonardi	13.15.0 ounces	paid 23.8.1435	sale of gold wire to Muxa de Daniele, a Jew of Messina
19.11.1434 c. nn	Onorato de Benedicto	15.15.0 ounces	within 6 months	sale of cloth to Moyses de Medico, a Palermitan Jew
22.11.1434 c. nn	Nicolò [...]	2 ounces	within 2 months	sale of fabric to Brachono de Lione, a Jew of Palermo

22.11.1434 c. nn	Onorato de Benedicto	24.21.0 ounces	within 4 months; paid 14.6.1435	sale of cloth to Geremia Cuyno, a Jew of Palermo
22.11.1434 c. nn	Filipppo Aglata	9.15.0 ounces	within 5 months; paid 29.7.1435	sale of cloth to Xirello Farmono, a Palermitan Jew
23.11.1434 c. nn	Giovanni Dalmau	3.24.0 ounces	by January	sale of cloth to Iosep Provinzano, a Jew of Giuliana
24.11.1434 c. nn	Onorato de Benedicto	1.12.0 ounces	within 4 months	sale of goods to Bonsat Sala, a Jew of Palermo
24.11.1434 c. nn	Guglielmo Scales	18. ounces	within 6 months	sale of cloth to Geremia Cuynu, a Jew
24.11.1434 c. nn	Iosep Provinzano, a Jew of Giuliana	17.12.0 ounces	14.12.0 ounces on account, balance on delivery; paid 22.8.1435	sale of merchandise
24.11.1434 c. nn	Luca de Moroxinis	21.10.12 ounces	within 3 months	sale of goods to Xua and Siminto Aurifici, Jews of Palermo
29.11.1434 c. nn	Arnaldo Scylla	12 ounces	by 25.3; paid 26.4.1435	sale of cloth to Iosep Maltisi, a Jew of Polizzi
1.12.1434 c. nn	Onorato de Benedicto	9.27.0 ounces	within 6 months; paid 9.6.1435	sale of cloth to Iosep Maltisi, a Jew of Polizzi
1.12.1434 c. nn	Iacobo Sagarru	3.12.0 ounces	within 4 months; paid 22.6.1435	sale of cloth to Simon Ysac, a Palermitan Jew
1.12.1434 c. nn	Antonio de Settimo	90 ounces	within a month	loan to Geremia Cuyno, a Jew of Trapani
1.12.1434 c. nn	Bernardo Curtu	12 ounces	within 4 months	sale of deerskin to Samuel Gididia, a Jew of Palermo

9.12.1434 c. nn	Filippo Aglata	1.19.7 ounces	within 4 months; paid 14.6.1435	sale of soles to Sadono Rugila, a Palermitan Jew
9.12.1434 c. nn	Iaymo Sugarru	3.12.0 ounces	by January; paid 13.4.1435	sale of cloth to Leone de La Iudeca, a Jew of Palermo
9.12.1434 c. nn	Sadono Ferreri	3 ounces	by 15.1.1435	sale of cloth to Elia Amar, a Jew of Palermo
9.12.1434 c. nn	Iaymo Santi	7.24.0 ounces	within 2 months	sale of goods to Abraam Ladeb, a Palermitan Jew
14.12.1434 c. nn	Raffaele de Viniu	3.28.0 ounces	within 4 months	sale of gold wire to Salamone Rubeo, a Palermitan Jew
14.12.1434 c. nn	Guglielmo Scales	8.1.4 ounces	within a month	sale of wine to Leone de La Iudeca, a Palermitan Jew
15.12.1434 c. nn	Lukino de Guisulfis	17.4.0 ounces	within 4 months	sale of merchandise to Brachono Taguili, a Palermitan Jew
15.12.1434 c. nn	Antonio Lignigo	8.17.0 ounces	within 24 days; paid 24.6.1435	sale of goods to Siminto de Salamone, a Jew of Trapani
16.12.1434 c. nn	Battista Aglata	4.10.0 ounces	within 4 months	sale of bolts (*bullonos*) to Nissim Binna, a Jew of Palermo
20.12.1434 c. nn	Pietro de Oria	2.18.0 ounces	within 4 months	sale of 4 steel balls (*ballinorum quattuor azari*) to Charono Rubeo, a Jew of Palermo
21.6.1435 c. nn	Antonio de Settimo	12.12.0 ounces	within 4 months; paid 24.11.1435	sale of goods to Iosep de Iona, a Jew
21.6.1435 c. nn	Filippo Aglata	1.21.0 ounces	paid 14.7.1435	sale of goods to Muxa de Mussutu, a Jew
23.6.1435 c. nn	Filippo Sportell	6.7.4 ounces	weekly instalments of 20 *tarì*	sale of olive oil to Gallufu Mayorana, a Palermitan Jew

23.6.1435 c. nn	Filippo Sportell	6 ounces	paid 16.1.1436	sale of olive oil to Busac de Tripuli, a Jew of Palermo
27.6.1435 c. nn	Giovanni Damiani	6.10.0 ounces	within 4 months	sale of merchandise to Gallufo Taguili and Benedetto Chazeni, Jews of Palermo
28.6.1435 c. nn	Battista Aglata	2.26.0 ounces	half within a month and half within 3 months	sale of iron to Isdrael Medui, a Jew
5.7.1435 c. nn	Filippo Aglata	1.0.6 ounces	within 4 months	sale of iron to Nissim Binna, a Palermitan Jew
5.7.1435 c. nn	Filippo de Sportell	6 ounces	weekly instalments of 15 *tarì*; paid 5.10.1436	sale of oil to Muxa Vignuni, a Jew of Palermo
5.7.1435 c. nn	Filippo de Sportell	5.24.0 ounces	weekly instalments of 15 *tarì*	sale of oil to Benedetto Misiria, a Palermitan Jew
6.7.1435 c. nn	Rainerio dc Risignano	14.24.0 ounces	within 4 months; paid 21.5.1436	sale of cloth to Iosep Maltisi, a Jew of Polizzi
7.7.1435 c. nn	Guglielmo Scales	5 ounces	within 4 months	sale of cloth to Iosep Maltisi, a Jew of Polizzi
7.7.1435 c. nn	Rainerio dc Risignano	21.12.0 ounces	half within a month, half on delivery; paid 7.9.1436	sale of linen to Iacob Xunina, a Palermitan Jew
7.7.1435 c. nn	Iaymo Sugarru	2.15.0 ounces	within 5 months	sale of cloth to Leone Sacerdoto, a Palermitan Jew
7.7.1435 c. nn	Iaymo Sugarru	2.22.3 ounces		sale of a paternoster to Iosep de Tripuli, a Palermitam Jew
8.7.1435 c. nn	Guglielmo Scales	1.13.0 ounces	within 4 months	sale of a paternoster to Muxa de Tripuli, a Palermitam Jew

8.7.1435 c. nn	Filippo de Sportell	1.24.0 ounces	within 20 days	sale of oil to Mussutu Medui, a Palermitan Jew
8.7.1435 c. nn	Lukino de Guisulfis	2.2.8.0 ounces	within 3 months	sale of silk veils (*zindati*) to Muxa de Danieli, a Messinese Jew
11.7.1435 c. nn	Guglielmo Scales	4.24.0 ounces	within 4 months	sale of cloth to Muxa Ginni, a Jew of Nicosia
11.7.1435 c. nn	Rainerio de Risignano	14.12.0 ounces	within 4 months; paid 31. 1 1436	sale of linen to Iosep Abudaram, a Palermitan Jew
12.7.1435 c. nn	Filippo Aglata	1.18.0 ounces	within 4 months	sale of cloth to Abraam Abagatell, a Jew of Palermo
13.7.1435 c. nn	Guglielmo Scales	1.9.0 ounces	within a month	sale of merchandise to Muxa de Tripuli, a Palermitan Jew
13.7.1435 c. nn	Guglielmo Scales	3.1.10 ounces	within 4 months	sale of cloth to Elia Amar, a Jew of Palermo
14.7.1435 c. nn	Bernardo Tango	4.18.0 ounces	within 4 months	sale of silk veils to Siminto Chirken, a Jew of Trapani
14.7.1435 c. nn	Iacobo Ser Guillelmo	2.24.0 ounces	within 6 months	sale of cloth to Siminto Chirken, a Jew of Trapani
14.7.1435 c. nn	Filippo Aglata	3.7.15 ounces	within 4 months; paid 24.6.1436	sale of deerskin to Robino Gibra and Mussuto Binna, Palermitan Jews
19.7.1435 c. nn	Bernardo Tango	11.17.0 ounces	weekly instalments of 12 *tarì*	sale of gold wire to Muxa de Daniele, a Jew of Messina
21.7.1435 c. nn	Guglielmo Scales	10.28.10 ounces	5.7.10 ounces by August; balance on delivery	sale of linen to Salamon de Muxa, a Jew of Palermo

27.7.1435 c. nn	Giovanni Damiani	1.15.6 ounces	within 4 months	sale of iron to Leone Sacerdoto, a Jew of Palermo
21.2.1435 c. nn	Pietro Pau	6.24.0 ounces	within 4 months; paid 3.8.1435	sale of cloth to Busac Romano, a Jew of Palermo
15.2.1435 c. nn	Francesco Gasparro	7.6.0 ounces	within 4 months; paid 3.8.1435	sale of cloth to Muxa Abzainas, a Jew of Palermo
16.2.1435 c. nn	Battista Lanza	2.3.5. ounces	paid 5.4.1436	sale of cloth to Fariono and Muxa de Iona, Palermitan Jews
16.2.1435 c. nn	Onorato de Gaudeo, a Jew of Palermo	14 ounces	9.6.0 ounces on account, balance on delivery	sale of a black slave girl to Xua Aurifichi, a Palermitan Jew
18.2.1435 c. nn	Raimondo Guarnerio	21 ounces	within 2 months; paid 11.7.1435	sale of merchandise to Busacca Medui, a Palermitan Jew
18.2.1435 c. nn	Pietro Pau	1.3.0 ounces	within 2 months; paid 5.5.1435	sale of paternoster to Brachono de Liono, a Palermitan Jew
23.2.1435 c. nn	Sadono Firreri	13.18.0 ounces	within 4 months	sale of cloth to Salamon Maltisi, a Jew of Polizzi
7.2.1435 c. nn	Iacobo Taguili, a Palermitan Jew	87.21.0 ounces	within 6 months	sale of cloth to Salamon Maltisi, a Jew of Polizzi
8.2.1435 c. nn	Giovanni Marrocco	6.1.10 ounces	within 6 months	sale of cloth to Isac Sala, a Jew of Palermo
10.2.1435 c. nn	Giovanni Canellis	26.27.0 ounces		sale of cloth to Mussuto Minzill, a Jew of Termini
16.2.1435 c. nn	Antonio de Settimo	35.6.0 ounces	within 4 months	sale of cloth to Iosep Taguili, a Jew of Polizzi
18.2.1435 c. nn	Benardo Oliveri	7.2.0 ounces	within 6 months	sale of cloth to David Russo, a Jew of Nicosia

18.2.1435 c. nn	Benardo Oliveri	3.6.0 ounces	within 6 months	sale of cloth to David Russo, a Jew of Nicosia
18.2.1435 c. nn	Benardo Oliveri	3.6.0 ounces	within 6 months	sale of cloth to Mussuto Minzill, a Jew of Termini
23.2.1435 c. nn	Amarono Migleni, a Jew of Castrogiovanni	4 ounces		sale of a mule
28.4.1435 c. nn	Antonio de Settimo	4.20.0 ounces	weekly instalments of 15 *tarì*	sale of merchandise to Muxa de Daniele, a Jew of Messina
28.4.1435 c. nn	Lukino de Guisulfis	6.9.0 ounces	within 2 months	sale of cloth to Bracha Minacham and Siminto Bricha, Palermitan Jews
27.5.1435 c. nn	Antonio de Settimo	105.17.4 ounces	within a year	sale of merchandise to Xua and Siminto Aurifichi, Jews
27.5.1435 c. nn	Antonio de Settimo	2.20.0 ounces	within 3 months	sale of goods to Elia Nissim, a Jew
30.5.1435 c. nn	Giovanni Grasso	9.12.0 ounces	within 4 months; paid 27.9.1435	sale of cloth to Iosep Maltisi, a Jew of Polizzi
30.5.1435 c. nn	Rainerio de Risignano	2.24.0 ounces	within 4 months; paid 27.9.1435	sale of cloth to Iosep Maltisi, a Jew of Polizzi
30.5.1435 c. nn	Iano Pau	6 ounces	within 4 months; paid 19.12.1435	sale of cloth to Xibiteni Chazeni, a Jew of Nicosia
31.5.1435 c. nn	Giovanni Aglata	2.16.0 ounces	weekly instalments of 9 *tarì*	sale of goods to Muxa de Danieli, a Messinese Jew
31.5.1435 c. nn	Iaimo Sardu	17.24.0 ounces	within 6 months; paid 20.12.1435	sale of cloth to Xibiteni Chazeni, a Jew of Nicosia

3.6.1435 c. nn	Antonio de Settimo	9.15.0 ounces	within 4 months	sale of merchandise to Muxa de Gaudeo, a Palermitan Jew
8.6.1435 c. nn	Rainerio de Risignano	3.50 ounces	by November; paid 19.1.1436	sale of cloth to Daniel Rugila and Merdoc Vignuni, Jews of Palermo
10.6.1435 c. nn	Giovanni Damiani	1.4.4 ounces	within 5 months	sale of iron to Leone de Vitrano and Muxa Sofer, Jews of Palermo
14.6.1435 c. nn	Antonio de Settimo	5.10.0 ounces	3 ounces by July; balance in weekly instalments of 15 *tarì*	sale of goods to Muxa de Daniele, a Jew of Messina
14.6.1435 c. nn	Giovanni Damiani	3.6.0 ounces	within a month	sale of iron to Muxa Sacerdoto and Xannono Nijar, Palermitan Jews
14.6.1435 c. nn	Giovanni Damiani	2.4.4 ounces	within a year	sale of iron to Isdrael Medui, a Palermitan Jew
15.6.1435 c. nn	Bernardo Serra	19.18.0 ounces	within 5 months	sale of cloth to Elia Cuyno, a Jew of Trapani
15.6.1435 c. nn	Guglielmo Scales	2.18.2 ounces	within 2 months	sale of goods to Brachono Bambolo and Vita Sivena, Jews of Palermo
17.6.1435 c. nn	Lukino de Guisulfis	11.6.0 ounces	within 5 months	sale of goods to Sabet Dinar and Leone de La Iudeca, Palermitan Jews
20.6.1435 c. nn	Antonio de Settimo	14.12.0 ounces	within 4 months	sale of goods to Muxa de Mussuto, a Jew
21.6.1435 c. nn	Filippo Aglata	5.22.10 ounces	within 4 months	sale of deerskin to to Elia de Mazara, a Jew

21.6.1435 c. nn	Giovanni Damiani	3.23.8 ounces	within 4 months	sale of merchandise to Salamon de Muxa, a Palermitan Jew
27.6.1435 c. nn	Pietro Pau	22 ounces	within 4 months	sale of cloth to Iacob Chamusi, a Jew of Agrigento
1.9.1435 c. nn	Battista Aglata	15.12.0 ounces	within 6 months	sale of cloth to Iuda de Vita, a Jew of Mazara
1.9.1435 c. nn	Rainerio de Risignano	32.6.0 ounces	1 ounce a month	sale of cloth to Chanino Balbo, a Jew of Mazara
2.9.1435 c. nn	Martino de Bilbao	3.6.0 ounces	within 2 months paid 17.4.1436	sale of fabric to Leone Amar, a Palermitan Jew
7.9.1435 c. nn	Pietro Villa	3.6.0 ounces	within 4 months	sale of cloth to Mardochay Vignuni, a Jew of Palermo
7.9.1435 c. nn	Baldassare Bonconti	1.5.0 ounces	within 6 months; paid 7.9.1436	sale of iron to Mardochay Vignuni, a Palermitan Jew
9.9.1435 c. nn	Martino de Bilbao	3.6.0 ounces	within 2 months; paid 10.5.1436	sale of fabric to Gaudio Gibel, a Palermitan Jew
9.9.1435 c. nn	Rainerio de Risignano	25 *tarì*	within a week	sale of goods to Xibiten Xaru, a Jew of Ciminna
13.9.1435 c. nn	Martino de Bilbao	1.2.0 ounces	within 2 months	sale of fabric to Xibiten Zelle, a Palermitan Jew
13.9.1435 c. nn	Giovanni Damiani	1.14.16 ounces	within a month	sale of iron to Daniel Rugila, a Palermitan Jew
15.9.1435 c. nn	Antonio de Settimo	4.6.0 ounces	within 2 months	sale of merchandise to Graciano Tachariato, a Jew of Palermo

17.9.1435 c. nn	Iesue de Lipari, a Jew of Naples	6 ounces	paid	sale of a slave
19.9.1435 c. nn	Pietro Pau	2.20.0 ounces	in 2 weekly instalments	sale of cloth to Iosep de Tripuli, a Palermitan Jew
20.9.1435 c. nn	Giovanni Damiani	3.6.0 ounces	within 5 months; paid 22.3.1436	sale of cloth to Muxa Cuynu alias Sacerdotu, a Palermitan Jew
22.9.1435 c. nn	Muxa de Sinagra, a Palermitan Jew	4.22.10 ounces	paid	sale of a curtain
22.9.1435 c. nn	Filippo Sportell	3.23.12 ounces	weekly instalments of 9 *tarì*	sale of goods to Mussuto [...], a Palermitan Jew
26.9.1435 c. nn	Battista Aglata	2 ounces	weekly instalments of 5 *tarì*	sale of iron to Salomone de Rustico, a Jew of Palermo
5.10.1435 c. nn	Rainerio de Risignano	30.24.0 ounces	12.24.0 ounces within 4 months, balance after another 2 months	sale of cloth to Siminto de Muxarella, a Jew of Marsala
5.10.1435 c. nn	Pietro Gaetano	18.24.0 ounces	within 6 months; 19.6.1436	sale of cloth to Siminto de Muxarella, a Jew of Marsala
5.10.1435 c. nn	Onorato Vinti	23.24.0 ounces	within 6 months; paid 1.6.1436	sale of cloth to Siminto de Muxarella, a Jew of Marsala
5.10.1435 c. nn	Arnaldo Servigado	2 ounces	paid 27.1.1436	sale of merchandise to Muxa Abzanias, a Jew of Palermo
17.10.1435 c. nn	Arnaldo Servigado	2.10.14 ounces	within a year	sale of goods to Abraam Baylu, a Palermitan Jew

19.10.1435 c. nn	Giovanni Damiani	2.8.8 ounces	within 3 months	sale of a paper bale to Busac and Iosep de Tripuli, Palermitan Jews
19.10.1435 c. nn	Rainerio de Risignano	7.11.0 ounces	within 4 months; paid 23.10.1436	sale of cloth to Xibiten de Iona, a Jew of Alcamo
20.10.1435 c. nn	Benedetto Aglata	6.15.0 ounces	within 4 months; paid 23.10.1436	sale of cloth to Xibiten de Iona, a Jew of Alcamo
20.10.1435 c. nn	Pietro Pau	23 ounces	within 6 months	sale of textiles to Xibiten de Iona, a Jew of Alcamo
24.10.1435 c. nn	Giovanni Grasso	3.28.2 ounces	weekly instalments of 7 *tarì*	sale of velvet to Muxa de Daniele, a Jew of Messina
24.10.1435 c. nn	Geremia Cuyno, a Jew in Palermo	13 ounces	paid	sale of a slave
24.10.1435 c. nn	Giovanni Grasso	3.28.2 ounces	weekly instalments of 7 *tarì*; paid 18.4.1436	sale of velvet to Graciano Tachariato, a Palemitan Jew
24.10.1435 c. nn	Onorato Benedicto	20.3.0 ounces	within 4 months; paid 11.4.1436	sale of cloth to Geremia Cuyno a Jew
25.10.1435 c. nn	Giovanni Damiani	2.9.0 ounces	within 3 months	sale of iron to Muxa Catalano and Iacu Sagicta, Jews of Nicosia
26.10.1435 c. nn	Bernardo Tango	4 ounces	within a month; paid 12.6.1436	sale of silk veils to Nissim Azaruti, a Palermitan Jew
31.10.1435 c. nn	Onorato Benedicto	40.24.0 ounces	within 6 months; paid 15.5.1436	sale of cloth to Chayronello Balbo and Busacca Chandarellu, Jews of Mazara
31.10.1435 c. nn	Pietro Pau	9 ounces	within 4 months	sale of cloth to Xamuel Fitira, a Jew of Agrigento

31.10.1435 c. nn	Iaimo Sardu	24.12.0 ounces	within 4 months; paid 8.3.1436	sale of cloth Chaym Balbo and Busacca Chandarellu, Jews of Mazara
2.11.1435 c. nn	Bernardo Badanis	12 ounces	within 5 months	sale of cloth to Salamon and Suffeni de Minichi, Palermitan Jews
2.11.1435 c. nn	Battista Aglata	1.15.0 ounces	within 3 months; paid 26.1.1436	sale of iron to Muxa Cauzeni, a Jew of Giuliana and Israel Medui, a Jew of Palermo
2.11.1435 c. nn	Antonio de Settimo	4.18.0 ounces	within 4 months; paid 10.5.1436	sale of merchandise to Busacca de Chandarello, a Jew of Mazara
2.11.1435 c. nn	Rainerio de Risignano	7.6.0 ounces	within 4 months	sale of cloth to Vita Zara, a Jew in Palermo
2.11.1435 c. nn	Guglielmo Scales	6.12.0 ounces	within 4 months; paid 3.5.1436	sale of cloth to Manuel Fitira, a Jew of Agrigento
7.11.1435 c. nn	Bernardo Curto	2 ounces	within 4 months; paid 14.3.1436	sale of deerskin to Sabet and Muxa de Vignuni, Jews of Monte San Giuliano
7.11.1435 c. nn	Giovanni Grasso	1.15.0 ounces	within 4 months	sale of cloth to Muxa Sacerdoto, a Palermitan Jew
7.11.1435 c. nn	Iaimo Sardu	2.12.0 ounces	paid 31.1.1437	sale of cloth to Vita Azaru, a Palermitan Jew
11.11.1435 c. nn	Bernardo Curto	9.21.0 ounces	paid 20.4.1436	sale of deerskin to Muxa Sacerdoto, a Palermitan Jew
14.11.1435 c. nn	Pietro Villa	2.6.0 ounces	within 3 months	sale of cloth to Nissim Frisisa and Salamon Minichi, Jews in Palermo

15.11.1435 c. nn	Giovanni Damiani	1.27.12 ounces	weekly instalments of 3.15 *tarì*	sale of iron to Muxa Actuni, a Jew
16.11.1435 c. nn	Pino Pau	27.19.10 ounces	within 4 months; paid 1.3.1436	sale of cloth to Samuel Fitira, a Jew of Agrigento
16.11.1435 c. 160r	Benedetto de Girachio, a Palermitan Jew	1.6.0 ounces	by Christmas	sale of a tunic
16.11.1435 c. 160v	Antonio de Settimo	11.14.0 ounces	within 5 months; paid 21.6.1436	sale of merchandise to Salamon Azaru, a Palermitan Jew
21.11.1435 c. 168r	Bernardo Sardo	9.18.0 ounces	within 5 months; paid 20.6.1436	sale of merchandise to Muxa de Xilleni, a Jew
21.11.1435 c. 168v	Bernardo Serra	3.15.0 ounces	within 5 months; paid 2.5. 1436	sale of cloth to Iosep Maltisi, a Jew of Polizzi
21.11.1435 c. 168v	Bernardo Villar	15 ounces	by February; paid 11.3.1436	sale of cloth to Iosep Maltisi, a Jew of Polizzi
22.11.1435 c. 170v	Sabet Dinar, a Palermitan Jew	10 ounces	within 4 months; paid 17.4.1436	sale of merchandise to Muxa de Xilleni, a Jew of Sciacca
22.11.1435 c. 171r	Pietro Zunart	12.10.0 ounces	by March; paid 11.4.1436	sale of cloth to Iosep Maltisi, a Jew of Polizzi
23.11.1435 c. 174r	Iaimo Sardu	31 ounces	within 5 months; by 17.4.1436	sale of cloth to Levi de Sancto, a Jew in Palermo
23.11.1435 c. 177r	Antonio de Settimo	35 ounces	11 ounces in December, balance in January	loan to Gallufo Cuyno, Salamon Azara, Gallufo Taguili and Muxa de Medico, Palermitan Jews
23.11.1435 c. 177v	Iaymo Sardu	2.15.0 ounces	within 4 months; paid 17.4.1436	sale of cloth to Busacca Sala, a Jew in Palermo

24.11.1435 c. 180r	Giovanni Damiani	2.18.0 ounces	within 3 months; paid 13.5.1436	sale of iron to Simon de Xalom, a Jew of Palermo
28.11.1435 c. 183v	Antonio de Settimo	20 ounces	10 ounces by December, another 10 in January	loan to Geremia Cuyno, a Jew of Trapani
5.12.1435 c. 217r	Chanino Balbu and Iuda de Vita, Jews of Mazara	21.20.0 ounces	paid	sale of 400 (!) *salme* of wheat to Luca de Moroxino
9.12.1435 c. 221v	Pietro Amat	23.20.0 ounces	by Easter	sale of cloth to Iosep Maltisi, a Jew of Polizzi
9.12.1435 c. 221v	Rainerio de Risignano	5.4.0 ounces	weekly instalments of 8 *tarì*; paid 27.4.1436	sale of goods to Muxa de Danieli, a Jew of Messina
9.12.1435 c. 222r	Bernardo Curtu	9.24.6 ounces	within 6 months	sale of goods to Donato de Aram, a Jew in Palermo
14.12.1435 c. 230v	Muxa de Seragusia, a Palermitan Jew	4.5.0 ounces	by October; paid 22.6.1436	sale of goods
14.12.1435 c. nn	Guglielmo Scales	5 ounces	within 4 months	sale of cloth to Abram Abbaxatell, a Jew of Portugal in Palermo
14.12.1435 c. nn	Guglielmo Scales	5 ounces	within 4 months; paid 18.4.1436	sale of cloth to Busacca Elfaza, a Jew
16.12.1435 c. 238r	Pietro Pau	3.6.0 ounces	within 4 months	sale of cloth to Samuel Sala, a Palermitan Jew
16.12.1435 c. 240r	Pietro Amat	2.10.0 ounces	within 3 months	sale of cloth to Abraam Abbagatell, a Jew in Palermo
19.12.1435 c. 246r	Antonio de Settimo	12.23.0 ounces	within 5 months	sale of pepper to Leone de La Iudeca, a Palermitan Jew

19.12.1435 c. 246v	Giovanni Damiani	6.12.0 ounces	weekly instalments of 12 *tarì*	sale of iron to Muxa Xabilu, a Jew
20.12.1435 c. 247v	Iaimo Sardo	24.9.0 ounces	by May	sale of cloth to Xibiteni Chazuni, a Jew
9.5.1436 c. nn	Rainerio de Risignano	20 ounces	10 ounces within 15 days, balance in 30 days	sale of merchandise to Iosep Maltisi, a Jew of Polizzi
9.5.1436 c. nn	Bundo [...]	3.16.3 ounces	paid 23.3.1437	sale of goods to Muxa Xeba, a Palermitan Jew
10.5.1436 c. nn	Antonio de Settimo	53.15.0 ounces	within a month	loan to Geremia Cuyno, a Jew of Trapani
14.5.1436 c. nn	Bernardo Testuchi	1.28.0 ounces	14 *tarì* a month	sale of iron to Brachono Cusintino and Gabriel de Girachio, Jews
14.5.1436 c. nn	Pietro Lorenzo de [...] and Chaym Balbo, a Jew of Mazara	155 ounces	half within 8 days, half in 2 months	sale of wheat
15.5.1436 c. nn	Bernardo Curto	15 ounces	within a month	sale of cloth to Iosep de Iona and Machaluffo [...], Jews
15.5.1436 c. nn	Chaym Balbo, a Jew of Mazara	4 *tarì* a kantar		sale of cheese
15.5.1436 c. nn	Antonio Castanesi	18 ounces	6 ounces in a month, balance in 4 months	sale of goods to Salamon Maltisi, a Jew of Polizzi
15.5.1436 c. nn	Bernardo [...]	4.10.0 ounces	weekly instalments of 8 *tarì*	sale of iron to Nissim de Trixi, a Jew of Palermo

15.5.1436 c. nn	Bernardo Curto	5.22.10 ounces	within 5 months	sale of deerskin to Elia di Mazara, a Jew in Monte San Giuliano
15.5.1436 c. nn	Francesco de Spola	11.12.0 ounces	within 4 months	sale of cloth to Iosep Maltisi, a Jew of Polizzi

Source: ASP. Not. Giacomo Comito, reg. 845

Date and Page	Principal	Attorney	Purpose	Remarks
8.11.1441 c. nn	Iacob Taguil, a Palermitan Jew	Artale Deutallevi	to collect the debt owed him by Amaru and Muxa Chazuni, Jews of Nicosia	

Date and Page	Debtor	Amount	Reason	Remarks
9.11.1436 c. 119v	Iosep de Brachono, a Jew of Palermo	2.9.19 ounces	debt of purchase price	creditor: Raynerio de Ricasuli; to be paid within 4 months
31.10.1436 c. nn	Azarono de Montechattulo, a Jew of Marsala	26 ounces	debt of purchase price	creditor: Minto de Muscarello, a Jew; to be paid within 6 months
30.4.1437 c. nn	Iacobo de Lu Nigro de Miseria, a Jew	unspecified	a debt	creditor: Bernardo Tango; to be paid within 15 days
11.12.1441 c. nn	Elia de Benedicto, a Jew of Palermo	1 ounce	price of cloth	creditor: Antonio de Settimo and Pietro Gaytano; to be paid by January
30.1.1442 c. 335v	Merdoc de Minichi, a Palermitan Jew	unspecified	purchase price of goods	creditor: Iacobo de Crapona; to be paid by May

Date and Page	Lender or Seller	Amount	Payment	Remarks
10.2.1442 c. nn	Iuda Rabibi, a Palermitan Jew	12 ounces	purchase of cloth	creditor: Marco Bonconte, Pisan merchant
20.2.1442 c. nn	Iacob de Aurichio, Brachono Lu Medicu and Busacca Naguay, Jews in Palermo	3.15.0 ounces	unpaid loan	creditor: Merdoc Malti, a Jew in Palermo; to be paid within 2 months
26.7.1442 c. nn	Muxa Russu, a Jew of Palermo	2 ounces		creditor: Guglielmo Ferrari
Date and Page	**Lender or Seller**	**Amount**	**Payment**	**Remarks**
4.9.1436 c. nn	Pietro Gaitano	5.12.0 ounces	within 2 months; paid 12.4.1437	sale of goods to Muxa de Daniele, a Jew
5.9.1436 c. nn	Antonio Baiamonte	13 ounces	within 2 months; paid 12.4.1437	sale of a black slave girl to Salamon Minichi, a Jew of Palermo
5.9.1436 c. nn	Saldono Firreri	10.6.0 ounces	within 4 months	sale of cloth to Iosep Maltisi, a Jew of Polizzi
5.9.1436 c. nn	Baldassare Bonconte	15.6.0 ounces	within 2 months; paid 28.9.1437	sale of cloth to Iosep Maltisi, a Jew of Polizzi
7.9.1436 c. nn	Battista Aglata	23.26.0 ounces	within 4 months; paid 7.10.1437	sale of wool to Samuel Sadono, a Jew in Palermo
10.9.1436 c. nn	Pietro de Campo	5.12.0 ounces	within 2 months; paid 8.2.1438	sale of merchandise to Muxa Cuyno, a Jew in Palermo
15.9.1436 c. nn	Bernardo Sardo	12.6.0 ounces	by July; paid 11.3.1437	sale of cloth to Robino Muxarella, a Jew of Marsala
15.9.1436 c. nn	Antonio de Settimo	28.12.0 ounces	within 4 months; paid 5.9.1437	sale of cloth to Robino Muxarella, a Jew of Marsala

15.9.1436 c. nn	Antonio [...]	15.22.10 ounces	within 6 months; paid 6.3.1437	sale of cloth to Robino Muxarella, a Jew of Marsala
17.9.1436 c. nn	Battista Aglata	5 ounces	within a month; paid 26.4.1437	sale of cloth to Robino de Muxarella, a Jew of Marsala
17.9.1436 c. nn	Raffaelle Michaelli	6.9.0 ounces	within 4 months	sale of cloth to Onorato de Gaudeo, a Jew of Palermo
17.9.1436 c. nn	Giovanni Iacobo, druggist	6.3.11 ounces	within 20 days	sale of iron to Sabatello de Lipari, a Jew
18.9.1436 c. nn	Battista Aglata	8.14.0 ounces	within 2 months	sale of iron to Iaco de Galiffa. a Jew of Giuliana
18.9.1436 c. nn	Nissim Binna, a Jew	4.24.0 ounces	within 4 months; paid 23.5.1438	sale of cloth
24.9.1436 c. nn	Battista Aglata	9 ounces	within 4 months	sale of hides to Muxa de Seragusia, a Palermitan Jew
28.9.1436 c. nn	Baldassare Bonconte	10.12.0 ounces	within a month; paid 23.11.1436	sale of cloth to Iosep Maltisi, a Jew of Polizzi
28.9.1436 c. nn	Bernardo Sardo	14.3.0 ounces	within 4 months; paid 18.3.1437	sale of cloth to Iosep Abenazara, a Jew of Palermo
1.10.1436 c. nn	Samuel Sacerdoto and Vita Amar, Jews in Palermo	10 ounces	paid	sale of rope
11.10.1436 c. nn	Pietro Armati	4.6.0 ounces	within 4 months; paid 28.5.1437	sale of cloth to Abraam Abagatell, a Jew in Palermo
11.10.1436 c. nn	Bartholomeo Villar	8.24.0 ounces	within 4 months; paid 29.4.1437	sale of cloth to Elia Amar, a Palermitan Jew

15.10.1436 c. nn	Manfrido de Sciacca	3.11.8 ounces	within a month	sale of soap to Sadia de Lia, a Palermitan Jew
16.10.1436 c. nn	Bernardo Sardu	6.3.0 ounces	within a month; paid 17.4.1437	sale of cloth to Muxa Sacerdoto, a Jew of Palermo
17.10.1436 c. nn	Antonio de Florencia	12 ounces	within a month	sale of deerskin to Samuel de Actono, a Jew of Palermo
17.10.1436 c. nn	Antonio de Florencia	40 ounces	within 4 months; paid 17.5.1437	sale of deerskin to Iosep Choin, Salamon de Messina and Bulchayra di Frisisa, Palermitan Jews
17.10.1436 c. nn	Antonio de Florencia	6 ounces		sale of deerskin to Chayrono Sacerdoto, a Jew of Palermo
17.10.1436 c. nn	Antonio de Florencia	6 ounces		sale of deerskin to Muxa Sacerdoto, a Jew of Palermo
17.10.1436 c. nn	Antonio de Florencia	6 ounces		sale of deerskin to Muxa Actuni, a Jew of Palermo
17.10.1436 c. nn	Bernardo de Consule	28 ounces		sale of linen to Merdoc Xarello, a Jew of Trapani
18.10.1436 c. nn	Antonio de Florencia	6.18.16 ounces	within a month	sale of deerskin to Muxa Liuni, a Jew in Palermo
19.10.1436 c. nn	Battista Aglata	10.9.12 ounces	by November; paid 29.11.1436	sale of linen to Iacob Xunina, a Jew in Palermo
22.10.1436 c. 86v	Artale D'Alagona	3.18.0 ounces	1.6.0 ounces on account, balance in 4 months	sale of a hair business (*officium pili*) to Xibiten Gibra and Nissim Binna, Jews of Palermo
22.10.1436 c. 87r	Battista Aglata	13.12.0 ounces	within 3 months	sale of wheat to Salamon and Sufeni de Minichi, Jews of Palermo

22.10.1436 c. nn	Rainero de Crisafi	1.26.6 ounces	within 8 days	sale of iron to Nissim Millac, a Palermitan Jew
22.10.1436 c. nn	Baldassare Bonconte	14.18.0 ounces	within 4 months	sale of cloth to Iuda de Vita, a Jew of Mazara
22.10.1436 c. nn	Baldassare de Bonconte	23.26.0 ounces	within 4 months; paid 10.4.1437	sale of cloth to Busacca de Chandarello, a Jew
23.10.1436 c. 91r	Bernardo Portes	20 ounces	within 4 months; paid 10.5.1437	sale of cloth to David de Noto and Xibiten de Iona, Jews of Alcamo
24.10.1436 c. 91v	Battista Aglata	25.6.0 ounces	within 6 months; paid 13.6.1437	sale of cloth to Iuda de Vita and Chanino Balbo, Jews
24.10.1436 c. 92r	Pietro Armati	5.24.0 ounces	within 2 months	sale of cloth to Xibiten de Iona and David Minachay, Jews of Palermo
24.10.1436 c. 92v	Antonio de Settimo	12 ounces	within 6 months; paid 28.5.1437	sale of cloth to Iuda de Vita and Chanino Balbu, Jews of Mazara
24.10.1436 c. 98r	Giovanni Sofer	5.6.0 ounces	within 2 months	sale of cloth to Iusep Abudarcham, a Jew
30.10.1436 c. 99v	Siminto Aurifichi, a Jew	14.24.0 ounces	within 6 months; paid 22.1.1437	sale of cloth to Muxa Xillemi, a Jew of Sciacca
30.10.1436 c. 100v	Manfrido de Sciacca	2.3.10 ounces	within 4 months	sale of soap to Fariono Gazu and Xibiten Virdi, Palermitan Jews
1.11.1436 c. nn	Antonello Bonfillo	7.20.0 ounces	within 5 months; paid 21.8.1437	sale of goods to Iosep Abudarcham, a Jew in Palermo
1.11.1436 c. nn	Antonio Baiamonte	2.1.0 ounces	within 4 months	sale of cloth to Sabatino Chalull, a Jew of Palermo

5.11.1436 c. nn	Marciano Iustu	8.29.10 ounces	within 4 months	sale of cloth to Muxa Genni, a Jew of Nicosia
7.11.1436 c. nn	Marciano Iustu	12.2.0 ounces	within 5 months	sale of cloth to Chaym and Muxa Chazuni, Jews in Nicosia
7.11.1436 c. 109v	Marciano Iustu	12.2.0 ounces	within 5 months; paid 12.3.1437	sale of cloth to Muxa Ginni, a Jew of Nicosia
7.11.1436 c. 110v	Antonio de Settimo	7.15.0 ounces	within 6 months; paidn 23.6.1437	sale of cloth to Iosep Abudarcham, a Jew in Palermo
7.11.1436 c. 110v	Baldassare de Bonconte	9.6.0 ounces	within 6 months; paid 9.6.1437	sale of cloth to Salamon Maltisi, a Jew of Polizzi
7.11.1436 c. 111r	Baldassare de Bonconte	9 ounces	within 4 months; paid 10.3.1437	sale of cloth to Chaym and Muxa Chazuni, Jews of Nicosia
9.11.1436 c. 111v	Bernardo Sardu	8.9.0 ounces	within 3 months; paid 5.1.1437	sale of cloth to Salamon Maltisi, a Jew of Polizzi
9.11.1436 c. 112r	Giovanni Barbo	7.8.0 ounces	within 6 months; paid 19.8.1437	sale of cloth to Muxa Genni, a Jew of Nicosia
9.11.1436 c. 112v	Dionisio Martino Ferrara	2.12.0 ounces	within a month	sale of cloth to Fariono Sala, a Jew of Palermo
9.11.1436 c. 113v	Battista Aglata	14 ounces	within 15 days; paid 26.8.1437	sale of cotton to Xalom de Galiffa, a Jew of Trapani
9.11.1436 c. 113v	Antonio de Settimo	7.7.0 ounces	within 4 months; paid 26.10.1437	sale of velvet to Xalom de Galiffa, a Jew of Trapani
9.11.1436 c. 117v	Mariano and Gerardo Aglata	8.20.0 ounces	within 5 months; paid 26.8.1437	sale of cloth to Iacob Xunina, a Palermitan Jew

12.11.1436 c. 124r	Bernardo Sardono	14 ounces	within 4 months	sale of cloth to Muxa Genni, a Jew of Nicosia
13.11.1436 c. 124r	Antonio Iacobi Speciali	14.15.0 ounces	within 4 months	sale of a case of mastic gum to
				Salamon Accarino, a Messinese Jew
13.11.1436 c. nn	Battista Aglata	8.14.14 ounces	by May	sale of merchandise to Donato de Aram, a Jew in Palermo
14.11.1436 c. nn	Antonio de Settimo	7.10.0 ounces	within 5 months; paid 7.5.1437	sale of goods to Abram Sacerdotu, a Jew of Palermo
14.11.1436 c. 130r	Thomeo de mastro Antonio	6.9.0 ounces	within a month	sale of olive oil to Busacca de Tripuli, a Jew of Palermo
16.11.1436 c. 135r	Battista Aglata	10.15.0 ounces	within 5 months; paid 26.11.1438	sale of cloth to Iosep Abudarcham, a Jew in Palermo
20.11.1436 c. 142v	Salvo de Salvo	15.5.8 ounces	within 2 months; 29.11.1436	sale of linen to Iusep de Brachono, a Jew of Palermo
21.11.1436 c. 146r	Thomeo de mastro Antonio	1.15.0 ounces	within 4 months; paid 24.11.1437	sale of oil to Levi Lu Puli, a Jew
21.11.1436 c. 146v	Thomeo de mastro Antonio	3 ounces	within 5 months; paid 2.4.1437	sale of oil to Isdrael Medui, a Jew of Palermo
25.11.1436 c. 150r	Mariano Aglata	15 ounces	by January	sale of cloth to Brachono Taguil, a Jew of Palermo
27.11.1436 c. 155r	Andrea [...]	2.23.0 ounces		sale of linen to Liuni Sacerdoto, a Jew of Palermo
29.11.1436 c. 159v	Siminto de Muxarella, a Jew of Marsala	11 ounces	monthly instalments of 16 *tarì*	sale of cheese
29.11.1436 c. 160r	Siminto de Muxarella, a Jew of Marsala	6 *tarì* a kantar	3 *tarì* on account, balance on delivery	sale of salt

29.11.1436 c. 161r	Iuda de Vita and Chanino de Balbo, Jews of Marsala	1 ounce		sale of wheat
29.11.1436 c. 161v	Gaudio Gibell and Iuda de Mazaria, Jews in Palermo	2.29.0 ounces	within 3 months; 10.7.1437	sale of oil
29.11.1436 c. 162v	Iuda de Vita and Chanino de Balbo, Jews of Marsala	6 ounces		sale of wheat
30.11.1436 c. 165r	Pietro Dinar	3.15.0 ounces	within 4 months	sale of cloth to Merdoc and Xillac Aurifichi, Palermitan Jews
10.12.1436 c. 173r	Giovanni [...]	3.3.0 ounces	within 4 months; paid 26.4.1437	sale of cloth to Muxa Cuyno, a Jew in Palermo
11.12.1436 c. 176v	Antonio Baiamonte	12 ounces	by August; paid 10.1.1437	sale of merchandise to Iuda Cuyno, a Jew of Palermo
12.12.1436 c. 178v	Giovanni [...]	6.18.12 ounces	within a month; paid 5.2.1437	sale of saffron to Nissim Azaruti, a Jew of Palermo
17.12.1436 c. 184v	Simone de Risignano	6.12.0 ounces	by 24 June; paid 5.6.1437	sale of gold wire to Muxa de Danieli, a Jew of Messina
23.12.1436 c. 193v	Ioffre Liminera	33 ounces	within 5 months	sale of cloth to Siminto Muxarella, a Jew of Marsala
2.1.1437 c. 194v	Guglielmo Firreri	15 ounces	within 4 months; paid 11.9.1437	sale of goods to Siminto Muxarella, a Jew of Marsala
2.1.1437 c. 195r	Guglielmo Firreri	30 ounces	within 5 months	sale of cloth to Elia Cuyno, a Jew of Trapani
3.1.1437 c. 195v	Bernardo Arau	6.15.0 ounces	within 5 months; paid 7.10.1437	sale of deerskin to Sadia Gibra, a Jew of Marsala

6434

3.1.1437 c. 196r	Saldono Firreri	33 ounces	within 4 months	sale of linen to Siminto de Muxarella, a Jew of Marsala
6.1.1437 c. 197v	Guglielmo Bonfiglio	10.15.0 ounces	within 2 months; paid 4.9.1437	sale of cloth to Muxa de Daniele, a Messinese Jew
6.1.1437 c. 198v	Antonio Castanecta	36.9.0 ounces	within a month; paid 15.5.1437	sale of cloth to Salamon Maltisi, a Jew of Polizzi
9.1.1437 c. 201v	Ioffre de Liminera	3.7.0 ounces	within 2 months; paid 26.2.1437	sale of oil to Iosep de Tripuli, a Jew of Palermo
9.1.1437 c. 205r	Antonio Oliveri	9 ounces	within a month	sale of merchandise to Muxa de Danieli, a Jew
10.1.1437 c. 205r	Antonio Oliveri	7.15.0 ounces	within a month	sale of oil to Salamone de Missina, a Jew in Palermo
10.1.1437 c. 206v	Iuffre de Liminera	22.15.10 ounces	within 4 months; paid 9.4.1437	sale of cloth to Muxa Xilleni, a Jew of Sciacca
10.1.1437 c. 207v	Guglielmo Firreri	28.5.0 ounces		sale of cloth to Elia Cuyno, a Jew of Trapani
14.1.1437 c. 210v	Giaimo Brondat	17.15.0 ounces	by May; paid 9.4.1437	sale of cloth to Muxa Xilleni, a Jew of Sciacca
14.1.1437 c. 211r	Giaimo Brondat	2.15.0 ounces	by May	sale of cloth to Gallufo de Medico, a Jew of Sciacca
14.1.1437 c. 211v	Iuffre de Liminera	12.7.10 ounces	within 5 months; paid 6.4.1437	sale of deerskin to Xamuel Gididia, a Palermitan Jew
15.1.1437 c. 213v	Saldono Firreri	25.7.0 ounces	by May; paid 8.4.1437	sale of cloth to Muxa Xilleni, a Jew of Sciacca

15.1.1437 c. 214r	Antonio Oliveri	21.29.0 ounces	within 4 months	sale of cloth to Muxa de Danieli, a Jew of Messina
16.1.1437 c. 216v	Iacobo de Ser Guillelmo	4.24.0 ounces	within 6 months; paid 8.6.1437	sale of cloth to Muxa Sacerdoto, a Palermitan Jew
16.1.1437 c. 217v	Paolo Sardu	28.5.14 ounces	within 4 months; paid 22.4.1437	sale of cloth to Iusep Maltisi, a Jew of Polizzi
18.1.1437 c. 220r	Nissim Frisisa, a Jew of Mazara	55 ounces		sale of wheat
21.1.1437 c. 226v	Iacobo Vela	5.7.10 ounces	within 4 months; paid 27.4.1437	sale of cloth to Muxa Sacerdoto, a Palermitan Jew
22.1.1437 c. 234r	Antonio de Settimo	4.9.0 ounces	within 2 months; paid 4.9.1437	sale of fabric to Muxa de Danieli, a Jew of Messina
22.1.1437 c. 235v	Matheo de Oria	10 ounces	within 4 months; paid 23.9.1437	sale of cloth to Abraam Abbagatell, a Jew in Palermo
22.1.1437 c. 236v	Bartholomeo de mastro Antonio	6.7.0 ounces	within 6 months; paid 25.9.1437	sale of oil to Benedetto Sacerdoto, a Palermitan Jew
22.1.1437 c. 237r	Saldono Firreri	5.3.0 ounces	within 6 months; paid 30.4.1438	sale of cloth to Bonaco Chetibi, a Jew of Geraci
23.1.1437 c. 239r	Antonio de Settimo	4.15.0 ounces	by May; paid 7.6.1437	sale of oil to Danieli de Aram, a Jew of Palermo
24.1.1437 c. 241r	Saldono Firreri	3.27.0 ounces	within 2 months	sale of cloth to Muxa de Danieli, a Jew of Messina
29.1.1437 c. 241r	Thomeo de mastro Antonio	1.15.0 ounces	within 4 months	sale of oil to Benedetto Misiria, a Jew
30.1.1437 c. 248v	Antonio de Settimo	15.9.0 ounces	within 4 months	sale of merchandise to Matafuni Cuyno, a Jew of Trapani

30.1.1437 c. 249r	Marco de Pilocta	25 *tarì*	within 3 months	sale of merchandise to Brachono Cusintino, a Jew in Palermo
30.1.1437 c. 249r	Giaimo Bonconti	1.29.0 ounces	within 4 months	sale of cloth to Abraam Baylu, a Palermitan Jew
31.1.1437 c. 250r	Mariano Aglata	3.15.0 ounces		sale of merchandise to Busacca Sala, a Palermitan Jew
1.2.1437 c. 252r	Pietro Catalano	4.16.0 ounces	by May	sale of cloth to Salamon de Minichi, a Jew of Palermo
13.2.1437 c. 257r	Andrea de Mares	2.4.0 ounces	within 5 months; paid 18.01.1438	sale of cloth to Merdoc and Xilleni de Rustico, Jews of Palermo
15.2.1437 c. 259r	Battista Aglata	12.18.0 ounces	within 6 months; paid 23.10.1438	sale of cloth to Xannono Sacerdoto and Nissim Azaruti, Jews of Palermo
18.2.1437 c. 262r	Bernardo Sardu	45 ounces	within 8 months	sale of cloth to Salamon de Minichi, a Jew of Palermo
20.2.1437 c. 266r	Pietro Insulano	7.22.0 ounces	within 4 months; paid 17.7.1437	sale of merchandise to Xirello Farmono, a Jew in Palermo
21.2.1437 c. 267v	Iacobo de Ser Guillelmo	7.15.0 ounces	paid 22.6.1432	sale of cloth to Iosep Abudarcham, a Jew in Palermo
21.2.1437 c. 269r	Saldono Firreri	14.7.10 ounces	within 4 months; paid 27.4.1438	sale of cloth to Salamon Maltisi, a Jew of Polizzi
25.2.1437 c. 272v	Andrea de Mares	2.11.0 ounces	within 5 months	sale of cloth to David de Aram, a Jew in Palermo
26.2.1437 c. 276v	Pietro Catalano	8.16.10 ounces	within 5 months; paid 5.3.1438	sale of cloth to Sabuto Ubi, a Jew in Palermo

27.2.1437 c. 277r	Bernardo Sardu	2.6.0 ounces	within 4 months	sale of cloth to Abraam Abbagatell, a Jew in Palermo
28.2.1437 c. 280r	Baldassare Bonconte and Antonio de Crapona	26.2.0 ounces	within 4 months; paid 4.11.1437	sale of cloth to Xalom Xilleri and Gallufo de Medico, Jews of Palermo
29.2.1437 c. 280r	Andrea Mares	15.6.0 ounces	by 15.6.1437; paid 7.9.1437	sale of cloth to Muxa Xilleni, a Palermitan Jew
1.3.1437 c. 283r	Antonio Castanisi	30.2.0 ounces	within 4 months; paid 29.8.1437	sale of cloth to Chanino Balbu, a Jew of Marsala
1.3.1437 c. 284r	Guglielmo Scales	6.12.0 ounces	within 4 months; paid 20.6.1437	sale of cloth to Iosep de Iona, a Jew of Noto
1.3.1437 c. 284v	Guglielmo Bonfiglio	10.19.0 ounces	by August; paid 5.9.1437	sale of cloth to Chanino Balbo, a Jew of Mazara
5.3.1437 c. 292r	Saldono Firreri	13.28.0 ounces	within 4 months; paid 5.4.1438	sale of cloth to Galuffu de Lu Medicu and Xalom Xilleri, Jews
5.3.1437 c. 293v	Francesco de Belmonte	2.21.0 ounces	within 2 months; paid 11.7.1438	sale of deerskin to Muxa and Iusep Ginni, Palermitan Jews
5.3.1437 c. 294r	Francesco de Belmonte	1.5.0 ounces		sale of goods to Busacca Sabatino, a Palermitan Jew
11.3.1437 c. 299r	Antonio Castanecta	9.13.0 ounces	by June; paid 1.8.1437	sale of cloth to Robino de Muxarella, a Jew of Marsala
11.3.1437 c. 299v	Saldono Firreri	6.29.0 ounces		sale of cloth to Robino de Muxarella, a Jew of Marsala
15.4.1437 c. 358r	Pietro Catalano	5.19.10 ounces	within 4 months; paid 8.10.1437	sale of merchandise to Muxa Sacerdoto, a Palermitan Jew

17.4.1437 c. nn	Battista Aglata	3.15.0 ounces	within a month	sale of gold wire to Elia Nissim, a Jew of Palermo
17.4.1437 c. nn	Antonio de Settimo	27 *tarì*	by August; paid 25.8.1437	sale of cotton to Elia Cuyno, a Jew of Trapani
23.4.1437 c. nn	Guglielmo de Luca	14.12.0 ounces	within 5 months; paid 5.9.1437	sale of cloth to Chanino Balbo, a Jew of Mazara
24.4.1437 c. nn	Martino Iustu	15.15.0 ounces	within 4 months; paid 4.11.1437	sale of cloth to Chanino Balbo, a Jew of Mazara
26.4.1437 c. nn	Salvo de Salvo	14.0.0 ounces	by 15 July	sale of linen to Liuzu Sumatu, a Jew of Mazara
26.4.1437 c. nn	Nissim Frisisa, a Jew of Mazara	exchange for textiles		sale of wheat
29.4.1437 c. nn	Filippo Aglata	3.10.0 ounces	within 5 months; paid 10.1 1438	sale of gold wire to Siminto Chiccu, a Jew of Trapani
30.4.1437 c. nn	Filippo Aymeris	12 ounces	by the feast of San Vincenzo	loan to Santono de Sanctoro, a Jew of Geraci
30.4.1437 c. nn	Battista Aglata	1.12.0 ounces	by August; paid 27.2.1438	sale of cloth to Muxa [...], a Jew of Giuliana
24.4.1437 c. nn	Battista Aglata	16.28.0 ounces	paid 16.2.1438	sale of cloth to Elia Cuyno, a Jew of Trapani
30.8.1437 c. nn	Baldassare de mastro Antonio	10 ounces	within 4 months	sale of oil to David de Azarono, a Jew
3.9.1437 c. nn	Battista Aglata	23.26.17 ounces	within 5 months; paid 30.10 1437	sale of linen to Xamuel Sacerdoto, a Jew of Palermo
12.10.1437 c. nn	Guglielmo Bonell	10 ounces	within 4 months; paid 1.2.1438	sale of oil to Iusep Sacerdoto, a Jew of Palermo

17.10.1437 c. nn	Giovanni Firreri	4.10.0 ounces	within 5 months; paid 29.5.1438	sale of deerskin to Samuel Gididia, a Jew of Palermo
17.10.1437 c. nn	Chillino de Settimo	25.6.0 ounces	within 2 months; paid 30.8.1438	sale of cloth to Aram and Xaul, Jews of Palermo
17.10.1437 c. nn	Giovanni Augusta	2.10.0 ounces		sale of goods to Isac Sala, a Palermitan Jew
31.10.1437 c. nn	Ambrosio de Alamanno	9.6.0 ounces	within 4 months	sale of cloth to Minto de Muxarella, a Jew of Marsala
2.11.1437 c. nn	Guglielmo de Iunta	72 ounces	within a year; paid 20.5.1438	sale of merchandise to Moyse Lu Medicu, a Palermitan Jew
2.11.1437 c. nn	Dionisio Sabruca	9.6.0 ounces	within 5 months; paid 28.3.1438	sale of cloth to Iosep de Iona and Elia de Mazara, Jews
3.11.1437 c. nn	Pietro Chicala	7.12.0 ounces	within 5 months; paid 13.31438	sale of cloth to Merdoc [...], a Jew of Palermo
7.11.1437 c. nn	Pietro de Cavalli	4 ounces	within 5 months	sale of fabric to Nissim Azaruti, a Jew in Palermo
7.11.1437 c. nn	Armanno Porta	15 ounces	within a month; paid 27.11.1437	sale of deerskin to Robino Gibra and Nissim Binna, Palermitan Jews
8.11.1441 c. nn	Giovanni de la Cagna	1.10.0 ounces	within a month	sale of Cammarata salt to Merdoc de Minichi, a Palermitan Jew
8.11.1441 c. nn	Antonio Tuleffi	17.15.0 ounces	within 4 months	sale of cloth to David Catalano, a Jew of Palermo
9.11.1441 c. nn	Simone de Brandino	1.29.0 ounces	within 5 months	sale of paper to Farchono Sala, a Jew of Palermo

12.11.1441 c. nn	Vita Dari, a Jew of Messina	2 ounces	within 5 months; paid 16.11 1442	sale of assorted goods to Salamon Zaffira, a Jew of Palermo
14.11.1441 c. nn	Vita Dari, a Jew of Messina	13.15.0 ounces	within 4 months; paid 14.11.1442	sale of silk to Iusep Sillac and Muxa de Muxa, Jews of Palermo
14.11.1441 c. nn	Vita Dari, a Jew of Messina	agreed price		sale of assorted goods to Iusep Sillac and Muxa de Muxa, Jews of Palermo
14.11.1441 c. nn	Guglielmo Barollo	4.2.0 ounces	within 4 months	sale of oil to Muxa Minzill, a Palermitan Jew
15.11.1441 c. nn	Guglielmo Barollo	4.6.0 ounces	within 4 months; paid 24.5.1442	sale of oil to Merdoc Binna, a Jew of Palermo
15.11.1441 c. nn	Guglielmo Barollo	8 ounces	within 2 months; paid 7.6.1442	sale of oil to Vanni Sabuchi, a Jew of Palermo
15.11.1441 c. nn	Guglielmo Barollo	8.2.0 ounces	within 2 months; paid 9.2.1442	sale of oil to Vanni Sabuchi and Muxa Taguil, Jews of Palermo
16.11.1441 c. nn	Baldassare Bonconte	32.22.16 ounces	within 5 months; paid 22.6.1442	sale of cloth to Leone de La Iudeca and Muxa de Muxa, Palermitan Jews
16.11.1441 c. nn	Giovanni Spagnolo	11.14.15 ounces	within 3 months; paid 12.1.1442	sale of linen to Iusep Sillac, a Palermitan Jew
16.11.1441 c. nn	Chillino de Settimo	27.27.0 ounces	by September; paid 30.8.1442	sale of cloth to Vita Dari, a Messinese Jew
20.11.1441 c. nn	Mussutu Minzill, a Jew	5 ounces		sale of oil
20.11.1441 c. nn	Chillino de Settimo	13.16.0 ounces	by April; paid 5.8.1442	sale of cloth to Vita Dari, a Messinese Jew

27.11.1441 c. nn	Antonio de Crapona	7.10.0 ounces	within 2 months; paid 18.1.1442	sale of oil to Leone Romano and Muxa Xunina, Jews of Palermo
29.11.1441 c. nn	Nicolò de Anello	5.5.15 ounces	within 6 months; paid 15.3.1443	sale of silk to Nissim Azaruti, a Jew in Palermo
5.12.1441 c. nn	Aron de Xaull, a Palermitan Jew	2 ounces	by June	loan
10.12.1441 c. nn	Antonio de Crapona	6 ounces	within a month	sale of merchandise to Aron de Vita Saffiri, a Jew of Palermo
12.12.1441 c. nn	Gianotto de Caro	4.25.0 ounces	within 3 months; paid 4.1.1443	sale of 2 containers filled with little wheels to mastro Manuel de Aram, a Jew of Sciacca
4.1.1442 c. nn	Guglielmo de Iunta	32 ounces	within 4 months	sale of cloth to Moyse de Medico, a Jew, acting for Elia Cuyno, a Jew of Trapani
5.1.1442 c. nn	Chillino de Settimo	16.17.2 ounces	by September; paid 5.9.1442	sale of gold wire to Iuda Rabibi and Muxa de Iosef, Jews of Palermo
9.1.1442 c. nn	Farchono Sala, a Jew of Palermo	2 ounces		sale of grapes
9.1.1442 c. nn	Pietro de Guil[lelmo]	27.2.0 ounces	by May	sale of cloth to Aron Monachatulo, a Jew of Marsala
10.1.1442 c. nn	Antonio Aiutamicristo	2.6.0 ounces	within 8 months	sale of starch (*amellanorum*) to Brachono Daguai, a Jew of Palermo
16.1.1442 c. nn	Antonio Casafranca	29 ounces	by June; 18.8.1442	sale of cloth to Xibiten Azaru, a Palermitan Jew

18.1.1442 c. nn	Gasparino Moroxini	7.10.0 ounces	within a month	sale of gold wire to Graciano Tachariato, a Palermitan Jew
18.1.1442 c. nn	Arnaldo Poma	12.15.0 ounces	by June	sale of cloth to Muxa de Medico, acting for Minto Muxarelli, Jews
19.1.1442 c. nn	Giovanni Peres	21.29.12 ounces	within 4 months; paid 22.6.1442	sale of deerskin to Xirello Farmono and Xibiten Corbay, Jews of Palermo
23.1.1442 c. nn	Giovanni Spaioll	25 ounces	by the feast of San Giovanni	sale of cloth Brachono Chetibi, a Palermitan Jew
23.1.1442 c. nn	Iacobo de Anello	63 ounces	by June; paid 15.1.1444	sale of cloth to Iosep Abudarcham, a Jew of Palermo
24.1.1442 c. nn	Baldassare Bonconte	9.2.0 ounces	within 4 months	sale of merchandise to Gallufo and Abram Aurifichi, Jews
24.1.1442 c. nn	Baldassare Bonconte	5.19.0 ounces	within 2 months; paid 6.7.1442	sale of cloth to Vita Xunina, a Jew of Palermo
24.1.1442 c. nn	Arnaldo Poma	5.18.0 ounces	within 4 months	sale of cloth to Brachono Xillatu, a Palermitan Jew
24.1.1442 c. nn	Iacob Riyna	37.19.2 ounces	within 4 months; paid 14.11.1442	sale of cloth to Iosep Abudarcham, a Jew of Palermo
24.1.1442 c. nn	Nicolò de Anello	17 ounces	within 4 months	sale of cloth to Nissim Binna and Iosep Actuni, Palermitan Jews
26.1.1442 c. nn	Giovanni Xinago	17.26.0 ounces	within 6 months; 24.11.1442	sale of gold wire to Xamuel Sacerdoto, a Jew of Palermo

26.1.1442 c. nn	Giovanni Vernengo	2.20.0 ounces	within 4 months	sale of cloth to Xamuel Fitira, a Palermitan Jew
30.1.1442 c. nn	Arnaldo Poma	4.10.19 ounces	within 4 months; paid 10.1.1443	sale of cloth to Xaul Frazu, a Jew of Palermo
31.1.1442 c. nn	Lodovico de Dino	12.6.0 ounces	within 6 months; paid 12.7.1444	sale of cloth to Iuda de Vita, a Jew of Mazara
1.2.1442 c. nn	Giovanni Damiano	7.8.0 ounces	within 6 months	sale of gold wire to Iuda Rabibi, a Jew of Palermo
6.2.1442 c. nn	Arnaldo Poma	38 ounces	within 6 months; paid 11.5.1444	sale of cloth to Elia Cuyno, a Jew of Trapani
9.6.2.1442 c. nn	Costantino de Gregorio	27.12.0 ounces	within 5 months	sale of linen to Bulchayra Sansuni, a Jew
10.2.1442 c. nn	Giovanni de Vernengo	2.6.0 ounces	within 3 months; paid 3.10.1443	sale of indigo to Xibiten Azaru, a Palermitan Jew
13.2.1442 c. nn	Arnaldo Poma	1 ounce	by July	sale of cloth to Muxa Soffer, a Jew in Palermo
13.2.1442 c. nn	Francesco Moroxino	10.16.16 ounces	within 2 months	sale of linen to Sadia Cuyno and Iosep Sillac, Palermitan Jews
14.2.1442 c. nn	Gabriele Sardu	7.29.15 ounces	within 4 months	sale of cloth to Ayrono Sacerdoto alias Cuyno, a Palermitan Jew
15.2.1442 c. nn	Egidio Aiutamicristo	1.29.8 ounces	within 4 months	sale of wheat to Minto de Muxarella, a Jew in Palermo
16.2.1442 c. nn	Arnaldo Poma	1 ounce		sale of goods to Vita Simina, a Jew in Palermo

17.2.1442 c. nn	Simone de Risignano	3.6.3 ounces		sale of cloth to Muxa de Azaruni, a Jew of Palermo
17.2.1442 c. nn	Guglielmo Barollo	9 ounces		sale of cloth to David Catalano, a Jew of Palermo
17.2.1442 c. nn	Francesco Moroxini	6.12.0 ounces	by August	sale of fabric to Fariono Sala and Busacca Actuni, Palermitan Jews
17.2.1442 c. nn	Bernardo Villar	16.15.0 ounces	by August; paid 2.7.1442	sale of cloth to Muxa and Salamon de Azarono, Jews of Nicosia
17.2.1442 c. nn	Arnaldo Poma	6.21.0 ounces		sale of cloth to Muxa and Salamon de Azarono, Jews of Nicosia
20.2.1442 c. nn	Bernardo Villar	6.19.0 ounces	within 4 months; paid 10.7.1442	sale of cloth to Gaudio and David Ginni, Jews of Nicosia
21.2.1442 c. nn	Simone de Risignano	16.15.0 ounces	within 4 months; paid 4.11.1443	sale of cloth to Gaudio and David Ginni, Jews of Nicosia
21.2.1442 c. nn	Guglielmo Barollo	9.6.13 ounces	by May	sale of oil to Muxa Minczill, a Jew in Palermo
21.2.1442 c. nn	Giovanni Capuchi	12 ounces		sale of cloth to Macaluffo Actuni, a Jew of Trapani
22.2.1442 c. nn	Pino de Barollo	39.22.0 ounces	paid 11.7.1442	sale of linen to Salamon and Siminto Cuyno, Jews
2.3.1442 c. nn	Antonio de Piperno	2.7.0 ounces	within 4 months; paid 5.9.1442	sale of soap to Liuni de La Iudeca, a Palermitan Jew

6.3.1442 c. nn	Bernardo Villar	14 ounces	paid 1.11.1442	sale of deerskin to Xirello Farmono and Xibiten Gibra, Palermitan Jews
7.3.1442 c. nn	Brachono de Aurillo, a Jew of Licata	5 ounces		sale of wheat
8.3.1442 c. nn	Giovanni Amorello	5.22.0 ounces	within 4 months; paid 22.5.1443	sale of cloth to Iosep Abudarcham, a Jew in Palermo
9.3.1442 c. nn	Bartholomeo Villar	3 ounces	paid 26.10.1442	sale of cloth to Gallufo Taguil, a Palermitan Jew
13.3.1442 c. nn	Federico de Anello	1.15.0 ounces	within 4 months	sale of goods to Sabuchi Minichi, a Jew of Palermo
14.3.1442 c. nn	Simone de Risignano	40.24.0 ounces	by July; paid 3.10 1445	sale of cloth to Xibiten de Iona, a Jew of Alcamo
22.3.1442 c. nn	Guglielmo de Scales	21.7.0 ounces	within 6 months	sale of cloth to Lia de Bono, a Jew of Marsala
22.3.1442 c. nn	Nicola de Iolu	14.6.0 ounces	within 4 months; paid 10.11.1443	sale of cloth to Iuda Sivena and Ayrono and Nissim Xua, Jews of Palermo,
23.3.1442 c. nn	Guglielmo de Scales	18.27.0 ounces	within 6 months; paid 15.11.1443	sale of cloth to Naguay de Gauiu, a Jew
23.3.1442 c. nn	Giovanni Zabactary	6 ounces	within 6 months	sale of cloth to Abraam Fillona, a Jew
23.3.1442 c. nn	Guglielmo de Scales	5.12.0 ounces	by June	sale of gold wire to Merdoc Bramello, a Jew of Palermo
23.3.1442 c. nn	Giovanni de Blundo	35.6.0 ounces	by August; paid 27.1.1443	sale of cloth to Azarono Monachatulo, a Jew of Marsala

23.3.1442 c. nn	Giovanni de Lu Bannu	12.5.3 ounces	within 9 months; paid 12.1.1443	sale of merchandise to Muxa Chiffu, a Jew of Palermo
23.3.1442 c. nn	Antonio de Valmanara	2 ounces	within 15 days; paid 14.8.1442	sale of oil to Simon Binna, a Palermitan Jew
23.3.1442 c. nn	Antonio de Valmanara	2 ounces	within 2 months; paid 3.7.1442	sale of oil to Pasquale Sacerdotu, a Jew of Palermo
23.3.1442 c. nn	Leonardo Stalmi	12.18.12 ounces	within 6 months; 293.1443	sale of cloth to Azarono Monachatulo, a Jew of Marsala
2.6.1442 c. nn	Giovanni Zambactaru	5 ounces		sale of goods to Bulchayra Sansono, a Jew of Palermo
6.6.1442 c. nn	Guglielmo de Scales	5 ounces	within a month	sale of deerskin to Gallufo de Liuzo, a Jew of Alcamo
6.6.1442 c. nn	Guglielmo de Scales	3 ounces	within 4 months	sale of cloth to Muxa Azarono, a Jew of Termini
6.6.1442 c. nn	Andreotta Xunuli	1.12.0 ounces	within 6 months	sale of cloth to Sufeni Romano, a Palermitan Jew
6.6.1442 c. nn	Guglielmo de Scales	4.12.0 ounces	within 6 months	sale of linen to Leone Sacerdoto, a Palermitan Jew
6.6.1442 c. nn	Giovanni Alzini	12.19.15 ounces	within 4 months; paid 10.11.1444	sale of oil to Busacca de Tripuli, a Jew of Palermo
1.7.1442 c. nn	Guglielmo de Scales	44 ounces in wheat		sale of cloth to Simon Xarabi, a Jew of Castrogiovanni
1.7.1442 c. nn	Nicola Xinardi	3.21.0 ounces	paid. 15.3.1444	sale of cloth to Iosep Abudarcham, a Jew of Palermo

6.7.1442 c. nn	Nicola Xinardi	2.26.7 ounces	within a month; paid 13.8.1443	sale of linen to Salamon de Muxa, a Jew
9.7.1442 c. nn	Paolo Aliamen	9.13.0 ounces	within 6 months	sale of hides to Busacca Sabatino, a Palermitan Jew
12.7.1442 c. nn	Gabriele Putade	2.12.0 ounces	within 4 months	sale of cloth to Busacca Sabatini, a Palermitan Jew
12.7.1442 c. nn	Antonio de Oria	2.6.0 ounces		sale of silk to Nissim Millac, a Jew of Palermo
12.7.1442 c. nn	Nicolò de Girardo	2.18.0 ounces	within 6 months	sale of spices and indigo to Nissim Binna, a Palermitan Jew
12.7.1442 c. nn	Nicolò de Girardo	1.27.12 ounces	within 6 months	sale of merchandise to Sabuto Lu Medicu, a Jew in Palermo
12.7.1442 c. nn	Giovanno Giordano	3 ounces	within 4 months; paid 12.6.1443	sale of deerskin to Robino Gibra, a Jew
15.7.1442 c. nn	Giovanni Iuffis	5 ounces	within 4 months; paid 25.4.1444	sale of deerskin to Busacca Sabatino and Iacob Levi, Jews in Palermo
15.7.1442 c. nn	Francesco de Piloma	6.12.0 ounces	within 4 months; paid 17.2.1444	sale of deerskin to Xirello Romano, Iosep Cuyno,
			Azarono Russo, Nissim Binna and Robino Gibra, Jews	
15.7.1442 c. nn	Francesco Parchama	7 ounces	within 6 months; paid 9.4.1444	sale of cloth to Gaudio de Xirello, a Palermitan Jew
15.7.1442 c. nn	Pino de Lampio	4.15.0 ounces	within 2 months; paid 6.6.1444	sale of cloth to Iosep Abudarcham, a Jew of Palermo
15.7.1442 c. nn	Giovanni Iuffis	4.26.13 ounces	within 4 months; paid 10.12.1442	sale of cloth Salamon de Muxa, a Jew

26.7.1442 c. nn	Pino de Lunas	21 ounces	within 2 months; paid 10.12.1443	sale of cloth to Gaudio Taguili, a Jew of Polizzi
26.7.1442 c. nn	Guglielmo de Scales	6.8.0 ounces		sale of iron to Xibiten Virdi, a Jew in Palermo
26.7.1442 c. nn	Guglielmo de Scales	2.13.18 ounces	within 6 months	sale of linen to Bulchayra Sansono, a Jew
26.7.1442 c. nn	Donato de Lunes	2.15.0 ounces		sale of wool to Nissim Millac, a Jew
20.3.1442 c. nn	Giovanni Ferrari	9.28.0 ounces	within 6 months; paid 5.9.1443	sale of gold wire to Leone de La Iudeca, a Jew
24.3.1442 c. nn	Guglielmo de Iunta	3.21.0 ounces	paid 18.8.1443	sale of cloth to Xibiten Chazuni, a Jew of Nicosia
24.3.1442 c. nn	Bartholomeo Sardu	7.6.0 ounces	paid. 10.6.1442	sale of cloth to Chayrono Xalom, a Palermitan Jew
30.3.1442 c. nn	Bartholomeo Sardu	6.11.10 ounces	within 2 months; paid; 26.8.1443	sale of gold wire to Xibiten Barbuto, a Jew in Palermo
9.4.1442 c. nn	Giovanni Dannaru	6.7.0 ounces	1 ounce a month; paid 13.11.1443	sale of gold wire to Nissim Azaruti, a Jew of Palermo
9.4.1442 c. nn	Pietro Sancto Pasquali	2.29.10 ounces	within 6 months	sale of gold wire to Leone Azara, a Jew of Palermo
9.4.1442 c. nn	Giuliano Pasquali	9.21.15 ounces	within 5 months; paid 5.1.1443	sale of saffron to Nissim Azaruti, a Jew of Palermo
16.4.1442 c. nn	Baldassare de Bonsignore	2.16.0 ounces	within a month	sale of iron to Simon Xabuti, a Jew in Palermo
16.4.1442 c. nn	Federico de [...]	44.6.8 ounces	paid 1.9.1443	sale of iron to Iosep Abudarcham, a Jew of Palermo

23.5.1442 c. nn	Chinellu Balbu, a Jew of Mazara	2 ounces	by July; paid 2.8.1442	sale of goods to Girardo Lumillino
20.4.1442 c. nn	Leonardo de Adamo	9.18.0 ounces	within 6 months; paid 18.8.1443	sale of merchandise to Nissim Azaruto, a Jew of Palermo
20.4.1442 c. nn	Altadonna [...]	1.5.0 ounces		sale of goods to Graciano Tachariato and Salamon Brixixa, Jews
20.4.1442 c. nn	Giovanni Damiani	9.25.12 ounces	paid 16.10.1443	sale of deerskin to Iusep de Medico, a Jew
21.4.1442 c. nn	Lamberto de Dario	8.23.0 ounces	within 6 months; paid 28.2.1444	sale of cloth to Busacca de Marxili, a Jew
23.4.1442 c. nn	Iaymo Gaytani	3.6.0 ounces	by 26.4.0 ounces; paid 19.8.1444	sale of linen to Samuele Sacerdoto, a Jew of Palermo
24.4.1442 c. nn	Guglielmo de Iunta	28. ounces	within 6 months	sale of cloth to Abraam Abbagatell, a Jew in Palermo
26.4.1442 c. nn	Pino de Bonsignoro	22.23.0 ounces	within 8 months	sale of oil to Sabatino de Gaudeo, a Palermitan Jew
4.5.1442 c. nn	Simone de Risignano	19 *tarì*	within a month; paid 22.10.1443	sale of iron to Muxa Sillac, a Palermitan Jew
4.5.1442 c. nn	Manuel de Aram, a Jew	exchange for wool		sale of soap
4.5.1442 c. nn	Simone de Bancherio	10.9.0 ounces within 3 months		sale of oil to Brachono de Airia and Xibiteni Sabatino, Jews
7.5.1442 c. nn	Lamberto Dario	8 ounces	within 6 months; paid 28.4.1444	sale of cloth to Iosep de Lu Medicu, a Palermitan Jew

13.5.1442 c. nn	Guglielmo Blanco	32.17.18 ounces	within 3 months; paid 28.11.1442	sale of merchandise to Iacob Xunina and Salamon de Russu, Jews
13.5.1442 c. nn	Lazaro de Francesco	3.6.0 ounces	within 3 months	sale of cloth to Iosep Taguil, a Jew of Palermo
15.5.1442 c. nn	Antonio de Settimo	29.24.0 ounces	within a month	sale of velvet to Aron de Danieli, a Jew in Palermo
27.5.1442 c. nn	Riccardo Villar	22.10.0 ounces	within 6 months; paid 17.10.1443	sale of cloth to Muxa Chazuni, a Jew of Nicosia
28.5.1442 c. nn	David de Minachem, a Jew of Sciacca	4 ounces	paid 26.7.1443	sale of salt
29.5.1442 c. nn	Iacobo Farulla	16.6.0 ounces	within 6 months; paid 20.10.1443	sale of velvet to Salamon Azaruti, a Palermitan Jew
1.7.1442 c. nn	Azarono Levi, a Palermitan Jew	18 *tarì* a *tumulo*		sale of salt
1.7.1442 c. nn	Antonio de Florencia	36 ounces		sale of linen to Merdoc Malti and Amoruso de Galifa, Jews in Palermo
1.7.1442 c. nn	Giacomo de Scales	11 ounces	within 3 months; paid 20.1.1443	sale of deerskin to Samuele Gididia, a Palermitan Jew
27.7.1442 c. nn	Giovanni Amallis	6.26.0 ounces	within 4 months	sale of deerskin to Muxa Actuni, a Jew of Palermo

Source: ASP, Not. Giacomo Comito, reg. 846

Date and Page	Principal	Attorney	Purpose	Remarks
20.5.1444 c. nn	Moyse Medico, a Jew of Palermo	Sadono de Muxarella, a Jew of Marsala	to obtain 2 ounces from Sadono de Medico, a Jew	
27.10.1447 c. nn	Iosep Taguil, a Jew of Polizzi	Iacob Taguil, a Palermitan Jew	to collect a debt of 3 ounces	

Date and Page	Debtor	Amount	Reason	Remarks
28.5.1444 c. nn	Salamon Xillilo, a Jew of Palermo	unspecified amount	a debt	creditor: Cusimanno de Pullina; to be paid by July
18.7.1444 c. nn	Zaffiro de Daniel, a Jew in Palermo	15.4 tari	for purchase of merchandise	creditor: Bono de Iacobo of Florence; to be paid by September; surety by Xibiten Calabrise, a Jew
20.11.1444 c. nn	Sabeti and Gallufo Misiria, Palermitan Jews	1 ounce	debt arising out of surety for Muxa Misiria, a Jew	to be paid within 4 months

Date and Page	Lender or Seller	Amount	Payment	Remarks
4.1.1443 c. nn	Muxa Provinzano, a Jew of Giuliana	7 ounces		sale of tunny
12.1.1443 c. nn	Guglielmo Peralta	4.26.9 ounces	within a month; paid 13.3.1443	sale of goods to Muxa de Muxa, a Palermitan Jew
14.1.1443 c. nn	Angelo Flores	4.25.6 ounces	within 7 months; paid 14.3.1443	sale of indigo to Iosep Xillatu, a Jew in Palermo

14.1.1443 c. nn	Antonio de Settimo	6.7.0 ounces	within 4 months; paid 13.6.1443	sale of gold wire to Sadono Sala, a Jew of Trapani
14.1.1443 c. nn	Guglielmo de Scales	13.8.0 ounces	within 4 months; paid 4.6.1443	sale of cloth to Iusep de Rabato, a Jew of Palermo
14.1.1443 c. nn	Benvenuto de Poppi	4.7.3 ounces	by July; paid 12.2.14445	sale of velvet to Gabriele Lu Medicu, a Palermitan Jew
15.1.1443 c. nn	Francesco Oliver	9.19.0 ounces	within 4 months; paid 14.2.1444	sale of goods to Salamon Azara, a Jew of Palermo
16.1.1443 c. nn	Goffredo de Angelo	12.9.0 ounces	within 4 months	sale of cloth to Iosep Abudarcham, a Jew in Palermo
18.1.1443 c. nn	Guglielmo de Scales	44.12.0 ounces	within 4 months; paid 3.7.1443	sale of cloth to Iusep Chamusi, a Jew of Palermo
21.1.1443 c. nn	Arnaldo Pomar	2.28.0 ounces	within 4 months; paid 27.7.1443	sale of cloth to Gimilono Naguay, a Jew of Palermo
22.1.1443 c. nn	Iacobo de Virgillito	2.25.10 ounces	within 4 months	sale of cloth to Bulchaira de Vanni and Fariono Sala, Jews of Palermo
22.1.1443 c. nn	Arnaldo Pomar	25.18.0 ounces	within 6 months; paid 13.1.1444	sale of cloth to Chaynello Balbu, a Jew of Mazara
9.9.1446 c. nn	Bernardo Oliver	54.14.0 ounces	within 6 months; paid 24.6.1447	sale of cloth to Moyse Zilini, a Jew of Polizzi
9.9.1446 c. nn	Giaimo Prates	11.12.0 ounces	within 6 months	sale of cloth to Moyse Zilini, a Jew of Polizzi
12.9.1446 c. nn	Pietro de Seragusia	13.240 ounces	within 6 months; paid 24.5.1447	sale of cloth to Moyse Zilini, a Jew of Polizzi
12.9.1446 c. nn	Bernardo Oliver	4.10.0 ounces	within 6 months; paid 26.1.1447	sale of deerskin to Bulchayra Frisisa, a Palermitan Jew

16.9.1446 c. nn	Federico [Lanza]	6.4.0 ounces	within 4 months	sale of cloth to Azarono Malti, a Jew in Palermo
20.9.1446 c. nn	Federico Lanza	3.15.0 ounces	within 6 months; paid 3.4.1447	sale of cloth to Abram Medui, a Palermitan Jew
26.9.1446 c. nn	Federico Lanza	6.21.0 ounces	within 4 months	sale of cloth to Abraam Baylli, a Jew of Palermo
26.9.1446 c. nn	[...] [...]	26.9.0 ounces	within 4 months; paid 27.1.1447	sale of cloth to Iosep Taguil, a Jew of Palermo
28.3.1448 c. nn	Arnaldo Pomar	33 ounces	within 6 months; paid 30.4.1449	sale of cloth to Vita Ginni, a Jew of Palermo
1.4.1448 c. nn	Lazaro de Francesco	4.12.0 ounces	within 6 months; paid 1.8.1449	sale of cloth to Iosep Abudarcham, a Jew in Palermo
1.4.1448 c. nn	Francesco Moroxini	3.6.0 ounces	within 4 months	sale of merchandise to Nissim Brixo, a Jew of Palermo
8.4.1448 c. nn	Iacobo de Vergillito	1.7.0 ounces	within a month	sale of soap to Xamuel Rabibi, a Jew
8.4.1448 c. nn	Iacobo de Vergillito	1.7.13 ounces	within a month	sale of soap to Tobia Azaruti, a Palermitan Jew
9.4.1448 c. nn	Iacobo de Vergillito	2.26.16 ounces	within 5 months; paid 24.10.1448	sale of cloth to Xamuel de Gididia, a Palermitan Jew
9.4.1448 c. nn	Iaimo de Guillelmo	84 ounces	within 6 months; paid 21.4.1449	sale of cloth to Sabeti Vignuni, a Palermitan Jew
9.4.1448 c. nn	Giovanni de Corona	25.6.0 ounces	within 3 months	sale of assorted goods to Chaym de Muxa and Iosep Sillac, Palermitan Jews
10.4.1448 c. nn	Bernardo Oliver	4.9.0 ounces	within 4 months	sale of cloth to Iosep Abudarcham, a Jew in Palermo

11.4.1448 c. nn	Iaimo de Guillelmo	13.4.0 ounces	within 6 months	sale of cloth to Manuele Chetibi, a Palermitan Jew
24.4.1448 c. nn	Giovanni Spagnolo	1 ounce	within 4 months	sale of wood to Brachono Levi, a Jew of Palermo
10.5.1448 c. nn	Bartholomeo de Rigio	4.2.0 ounces	within a month; paid 5.7.1449	sale of merchandise to Nissim Azaruti, a Jew
14.5.1443 c. nn	Bartholomeo Fortis	5.27.0 ounces	within 4 months; paid 21.4.1444	sale of raw silk to Gallufo Cuyno, a Jew of Palermo
13.5.1443 c. nn	Arnaldo Pomar	2.12.0 ounces	within 4 months; paid 9.11.1444	sale of cloth to Muxa Misiria, a Jew of Palermo
12.6.1443 c. nn	Giovanni Corona	3 ounces	within 6 months	sale of cloth to Azarono Cusintino, a Palermitan Jew
28.7.1443 c. nn	Guglielmo [...]	2.3.0 ounces	in instalments	sale of iron to Muxa Minzil, a Jew of Palermo
2.8.1443 c. nn	Bernardo Montorto	7.6.0 ounces	within 5 months; paid 28.2.1444	sale of cloth to Salamon Aurifichi, a Palermitan Jew
22.10.1443 c. nn	Simon Tumminellis	17.3.0 ounces	paid 14.5.1444	sale of cloth to Iosep Sillac, Farmuni, Isac and Liuni Romano, Muxa Xunina and Muxa Taguil, Jews in Palermo
28.5.1444 c. nn	Arnaldo Pomar	5.21.0 ounces	within 6 months; paid 23.4.1445	sale of cloth to Azarono Cusintino and Sabeti Vignuni, Jews of Palermo
28.5.1444 c. nn	Antonio de Settimo	11.15.0 ounces	within 6 months; paid 29.4.1445	sale of cloth to Ysac Sala and Azarono Cusintino, Jews of Palermo

28.5.1444 c. nn	Iaymo de Guillelmo	2.12.0 ounces	within 4 months; paid 9.4.1445	sale of cloth to Zudo Market, a Jew in Palermo
29.5.1444 c. nn	Iaymo de Guillelmo	2.12.0 ounces	within a month; paid 18.2.1445	sale of cloth to Sabet Vignuni, a Jew in Palermo
4.6.1444 c. nn	Iaymo de Guillelmo	5.6.0 ounces	within 4 months	sale of cloth to Muxa Minzill, a Palermitan Jew
13.6.1444 c. nn	Iaymo de Guillelmo	4.12.0 ounces	within 4 months	sale of cloth to Nissim Grixon, a Jew in Palermo
17.6.1444 c. nn	Simone de Risignano	2.6.0 ounces	within 4 months; paid 7.4.1445	sale of cloth to Iuda de Fraym, a Palermitan Jew
17.6.1444 c. nn	Bernardo Toscano	24.9.0 ounces	within 4 months; paid 10.12.1445	sale of cloth to Salamon Maltisi, a Jew of Polizzi
8.7.1444 c. nn	Masio de Giliberto	3.18.0 ounces	within a month; paid 28.4.1445	sale of cloth to Salamon Maltisi, a Jew of Polizzi
12.7.1444 c. nn	Nicolò Zumpardi	2 ounces	within 4 months; paid 9.12.1445	sale of linen to Donato de Aram, a Jew in Palermo
13.7.1444 c. nn	Antonio de Imperatore	3.24.0 ounces	within 2 months; paid 25.10.1445	sale of cloth to Iosep Abudarcham, a Jew of Palermo
8.7.1444 c. nn	Guglielmo Imperiali	14.18.0 ounces	by August; paid 12.9.1445	sale of merchandise to Iosep de Benedicto, a Jew of Trapani
8.7.1444 c. nn	Simone de Risignano	5.10.0 ounces	within a month; paid 29.9.1444	sale of cloth to Muxa Sacerdoto alias Cuyno, a Palermitan Jew
9.7.1444 c. nn	Iaimo Bonsignoro	40.24.0 ounces	within 6 months; paid 12.8.1445	sale of cloth to Salamon Maltisi, a Palermitan Jew

9.7.1444 c. nn	Bernardo Villar	16.12.0 ounces	within 6 months; paid 8.2.1445	sale of cloth to Salamon Maltisi, a Palermitan Jew
9.7.1444 c. nn	Guglielmo Salvatoris	2.6.0 ounces	by August; paid 20.2.1445	sale of wood to Samuel Cuffi, a Palermitan Jew
13.7.1444 c. nn	Giovanni Giordano	16.24.0 ounces	within 5 months; paid 12.11.1445	sale of cloth to Simon Xarabi, a Jew of Castrogiovanni
14.7.1444 c. nn	Giovanni Giordano	2.12.0 ounces	by August	sale of cloth to Simon Xarabi, a Jew of Castrogiovanni
14.7.1444 c. nn	Perrucio Spagnolo	30.15.0 ounces	within 6 months	sale of cloth to Simon Xarabi, a Jew of Castrogiovanni
16.7.1444 c. nn	Bernardo Oliver	7.9.0 ounces	within 4 months; paid 19.4.1445	sale of cloth to Iacob de Malti and Muxa Misiria, Jews of Palermo
16.7.1444 c. nn	Giovanni Spagnolo	2 ounces	within a month; paid 18.5.1445	sale of velvet to Samuel Gididia, a Palermitan Jew
17.7.1444 c. nn	Benedetto P[..]	3.27.0 ounces	within 4 months; paid 9.9.1444	sale of cloth to Farmuni Lu Medicu and Liuni de La Iudeca, Palermitan Jews
19.7.1444 c. nn	Antonio de Settimo	2.20.16 ounces	by August; paid 27.8.1444	sale of linen to Nissim Gazella, a Jew of Mazara
21.7.1444 c. nn	Antonio Gentili	4.6.0 ounces	within 6 months; paid 1.6.1445	sale of merchandise to Nissim Binna, a Palermitan Jew
23.7.1444 c. nn	Bernardo Oliver	9.2.0 ounces	within 4 months; paid 18.9.1444	sale of cloth to Sabeti Levi, Bulchayra Frisisa and Xibiten Gibra, Palermitan Jews

27.7.1444 c. nn	Iaimo Paulillo	22.8.0 ounces	within 2 months	sale of cloth to Samuel Cuffi, Azarono Cusintino and Farchono Sala, Palermitan Jews
28.7.1444 c. nn	Nicolò Airordi	1 ounce	within a month paid 8.1.1445	sale of iron to Merdoc Vignuni and Muxa de Budari, Jews of Palermo
28.7.1444 c. nn	Iaimo [...]	5.7.0 ounces		sale of velvet to Iusep Sillac, a Jew in Palermo
1.9.1444 c. nn	Nicolao [...]	11 ounces	within 4 months	sale of raw silk to Busacca Naguay, a Palermitan Jew
2.9.1444 c. nn	Francesco Corona	3 ounces	within 12 months; paid 23.6.1445	sale of cloth to Xillano and Merdoc Azara, Jews
3.9.1444 c. nn	Iacobo de Ximeto	1 ounce	within 3 months; paid 22.4.1445	sale of wheat to Chanino Balbu, a Jew in Palermo
11.9.1444 c. nn	Tobia Gibel, a Palermitan Jew	27 *tarì*		sale of rope for tunny plants
25.9.1444 c. nn	Giovanni Eleusa	2.29.0 ounces	within 4 months; paid 5.4.1445	sale of cloth to Samuel Gididia, a Jew of Palermo
25.9.1444 c. nn	[...] Bonconte	9 ounces	within 4 months; paid 15.9.1445	sale of merchandise to Xibiten and Azarono Azara, Jews in Palermo
7.10.1444 c. nn	Giuliano de Bononia	2.12.0 ounces	within 4 months; paid 7.8.1446	sale of cloth to Onorato de Gaudio, a Jew in Palermo
7.10.1444 c. nn	Giovanni de Lanza	5.18.0 ounces	within 4 months; paid 5.3.1445	sale of cloth to Xibiten Vignuni, a Palermitan Jew
7.10.1444 c. nn	Giovanni de [Lanza]	2.29.0 ounces	within 4 months	sale of cloth to Farchono Sala, a Jew of Palermo

7.10.1444 c. nn	Giovanni de Lanza	2.29.0 ounces	within 4 months; paid 29.2.1445	sale of cloth to Isac Sala, a Jew of Palermo
8.10.1444 c. nn	Giovanni de Villis	2 ounces		sale of grapes to Busacca Cuppilli, a Jew in Palermo
9.10.1444 c. nn	Bernardo Oliver	21.21.0 ounces	within 4 months; paid 12.4.1445	sale of cloth to Iosep Taguil, a Jew of Polizzi
12.10.1444 c. nn	Bernardo Oliver	22.18.0 ounces	within 6 months; paid 9.8.1445	sale of cloth to Iosep Taguil, a Jew of Polizzi
13.10.1444 c. nn	Marco de Bononia	3 ounces	within 4 months; paid 1.2.1445	sale of gold wire to Busacca Galifi, a Jew of Sciacca
13.10.1444 c. nn	Bernardo Oliver	31.20.0 ounces	within 6 months; paid 18.1.1446	sale of cloth to Moyse de Medico and Minto de Muxarella, Palermitan Jews
13.10.1444 c. nn	Pietro Armellis	10.2.0 ounces	within 4 months; paid 22.4.1445	sale of deerskin to Muxa Sacerdoto, Bulchayra Frisisa and Gallufo Actuni, Jews of Palermo
15.10.1444 c. nn	Iosep de La Iudeca, a Palermitan Jew	agreed price		sale of assorted goods
16.10.1444 c. nn	Bernardo Oliver	6.29.0 ounces	within 4 months; paid 18.6.1445	sale of cloth to Moyse de Medico, a Palermitan Jew
19.10.1444 c. nn	Elia de Benedicto, a Palermitan Jew	9 ounces		sale of a black slave
21.10.1444 c. nn	Chanino Balbo, a Jew of Mazara	29 *tarì* a kantar	50 ounces on account, balance on delivery	sale of cow and ox hides
21.10.1444 c. nn	Giovanni Channaglis	7.0.12 ounces	within 4 months; paid 5.10.1445	sale of cloth to Benedetto de Gaudio, a Jew of Palermo

14.1.1445 c. nn	Simone de Risignano	16.2.0 ounces	within 6 months; paid 19.8.1445	sale of cloth to Iosep Taguil, a Jew of Polizzi
18.1.1445 c. nn	Antonio Castagna	4 ounces	within 4 months; paid 13.9.1445	sale of cloth to Azarono Cusintino and Sabet Vignuni, Palermitan Jews
19.1.1445 c. nn	Giovanni Cannaglis	4.26.0 ounces	within 4 months; paid 11.8.1445	sale of cloth to Muxa de Policio, a Jew of Palermo
20.1.1445 c. nn	Bernardo Oliver	5.6.0 ounces	within 4 months; paid 21.6.1445	sale of hides to Xibiten Gibel, a Palermitan Jew
24.1.1445 c. nn	Pietro Villar	5.29.0 ounces	within 4 months; paid 9.8.1445	sale of goods to David Malti, a Jew in Palermo
1.2.1445 c. nn	Francesco Moroxini	5 ounces	within 4 months; paid 25.5.1445	sale of gold wire to Sadono Sala, a Jew of Trapani
12.2.1445 c. nn	Pasquale de Florio	2.27.10 ounces	within 6 months	sale of velvet to Daniel Xunina, a Jew of Palermo
5.10.1445 c. nn	Iosep de Minichi, a Palermitan Jew	25 *tarì*	paid	sale of manure
7.10.1445 c. nn	Giuliano de Bononia	11.21.0 ounces	within 4 months; paid 10.7.1446	sale of cloth to Iosep Abudarcham, a Jew in Palermo
7.10.1445 c. nn	Giovanni Provinzano	9.8.0 ounces	within 9 months	sale of cloth to Moyse de Medico, a Palermitan Jew
11.10.1445 c. nn	Iacobo de Pisis	1.2.0 ounces	by 21.10; paid 11.2.1446	sale of wheat to Manuel de Minichi, a Palermitan Jew
20.10.1445 c. nn	Giovanni Provenzano	9.2.0 ounces	within 4 months	sale of cloth to Abram Abinazara, a Jew of Palermo

27.10.1445 c. nn	Bernardo Villar	66.9.0 ounces	within 6 months; paid 28.7.1446	sale of linen to Iosep de Iona, a Jew of Monte San Giuliano
27.10.1445 c. nn	Bernardo Oliver	6.22.10 ounces	within 4 months; paid 16.10.1446	sale of cloth to Iosep Taguil, a Jew of Polizzi
27.10.1445 c. nn	Giovanni Peres	23 ounces	within 6 months; paid 19.6.1447	sale of cloth to Iosep Taguil, a Jew of Polizzi
6.11.1445 c. nn	Giovanni de Canaglis	64.24.10 ounces	by July; paid 17.12.1448	sale of cloth to Iacob Taguil, a Jew of Palermo
6.11.1445 c. nn	Pino [...]	23.22.0 ounces	by July; paid 17.12.1448	sale of cloth to Iacob Taguil, a Jew of Palermo
15.11.1445 c. nn	Bernardo Villar	7.12.0 ounces	within 6 mmonths; paid 22.3.1446	sale of cloth to Manuel and Salamone Chetibi, Jews of Palermo
15.2.1446 c. nn	Bernardo Firreri	14.15.0 ounces	within 4 months	sale of cloth to Onorato de Gaudio, a Jew of Palermo
16.2.1446 c. nn	Antonio de Settimo	5.22.0 ounces	within 6 months	sale of cloth to Xibiten Stranu, a Jew of Cammarata
26.2.1446 c. nn	Nicolò [...]	2.21.16 ounces		sale of merchandise to Iacob Tavormina, a Jew in Palermo
1.3.1446 c. nn	Nicolò Tagliacarni	5.17.0 ounces	within 4 months; paid 23.10.1447	sale of gold wire to Busacca de La Magna, a Jew
1.3.1446 c. nn	Ambrogio Bertizzo	6.12.0 ounces	within 6 months	sale of gold wire to Graciano Bulfarachi, Elia and Minto de Fitira, Jews of Palermo
6.3.1446 c. nn	Michilono Xunina, a Jew	3 ounces	within 4 months	sale of assorted goods to Chanino Balbu, a Jew of Mazara

10.4.1448 c. nn	Tommaso Spinula	12.15.0 ounces	within 6 months; paid 11.8.1449	sale of goods to Salamon Sparti, a Jew
10.4.1448 c. nn	Tommaso Spinula	3.10.0 ounces		sale of gold wire to Nissim Xalom and Farchono Sala, Jews
17.4.1448 c. nn	Tommaso Spinula	6 ounces	within a month	sale of gold wire to Nissim Sansono, a Palermitan Jew
19.4.1448 c. nn	Nicolò Tagliacarni	11 ounces	within 4 months; paid 19.1.1449	sale of gold wire to Nissim Azaruti, a Palermitan Jew
22.4.1448 c. nn	Nicolò Tagliacarni	12.24.0 ounces	within 6 months	sale of merchandise to Chayrono Malti, a Jew in Palermo
23.4.1448 c. nn	Iona Sala, a Palermitan Jew	1 ounce	by May	sale of goods
10.8.1448 c. nn	Salvatore de Auria	4.12.0 ounces	within 4 months; paid 6.8.1449	sale of goods to Salamon de Xannono, a Jew

Source: ASP, Not. Giacomo Comito, reg. 847

Date and Page	Debtor	Amount	Reason	Remarks
1.10.1450 c. nn	Muxa de Auricano and Sabatino de Tripuli, Jews	5 ounces	debt	creditor: Iuliano de Blundo; to be paid in monthly instalments
20.10.1450 c. nn	Sabatino de Vignuni, a Palermitan Jew	7 ounces		creditor: Baldassare de Raya; to be paid in a month
19.11.1450 c. nn	Iosep Lu Medicu, a Palermitan Jew	4.15.0 ounces	balance for purchase of cloth/clothes	creditor: Gerardo de Lomellino of Genoa; to be paid within 2 months
12.1.1451 c. nn	Iacob de Medico, a Palermitan Jew	5 ounces	balance of debt	creditor: Antonio Bayamonte; to be paid in August

Date and Page	Lender or Seller	Amount	Payment	Remarks
13.1.1451 c. nn	Salamon Ginni, a Messinese Jew	2.12.0 ounces	balance of debt	creditor: Vita Ginni, a Jew; to be paid in July
12.3.1451 c. nn	Iusep Balbu, a Jew of Mazara	41 ounces	unpaid purchase price	creditor: Iacobo Pedivillano; to be paid in a month
3.9.1451 c. nn	Bulchayra de Vanni, a Palermitan Jew	2 ounces	unpaid loan	creditor: Antonio de Lanizza
2.12.1451 c. nn	Bulchayra de Termini, a Palermitan Jew	7 ounces		creditor: Nicolò de Faxilla; to be paid in 2 instalments within 2 months
8.4.1452 c. nn	Salamon de Minichi, a Palermitan Jew	30 *salme* of [tunny] fat (bellies) *iunza*		creditor: Antonio Bayamonte; to be paid within 5 months

Date and Page	Lender or Seller	Amount	Payment	Remarks
1.9.1450 c. nn	Iosep de Minichi, a Palermitan Jew	agreed price		sale of goods to Leone Xunina, a Jew of Palermo
1.9.1450 c. nn	[...] [...]	17.22.10 ounces	within 4 months	sale of cloth to Iosep Taguil, a Jew of Polizzi
1.9.1450 c. nn	Giovanni Provinzano	3 ounces	within 2 months	sale of cloth to Iosep Taguil, a Jew of Polizzi
6.9.1450 c. nn	Antonio de Settimo	24 ounces	by May	sale of cloth to Iosep Taguil, a Jew of Polizzi
6.9.1450 c. nn	Paolo Viola	35.6.0 ounces	within 2 months	sale of cloth to Iosep Taguil, a Jew of Polizzi
16.9.1450 c. nn	Guglielmo Bonello	14.7.3 ounces	within 4 months; paid 23.6.1451	sale of cloth to Muxa Sacerdoto, a Jew
16.9.1450 c. nn	Antonio de Crapona	7 ounces		sale of cloth to Xibiten Gibel, a Jew of Palermo

17.9.1450 c. nn	Iusto de Feras	15.6.0 ounces	within 5 months; paid 1.6.1451	sale of cloth to Iosep Abudarcham, a Jew in Palermo
18.9.1450 c. nn	Salvo de Salvo	6.12.0 ounces	within 4 months; paid 6.2.1451	sale of linen to Merdoc Malti, a Jew in Palermo
23.9.1450 c. nn	Pietro Gaytano	5.24.0 ounces	within 4 months; paid 1.5.1451	sale of gold wire to Busacca de Girachio, a Jew of Palermo
29.9.1450 c. nn	Guglielmo Bonello	14.18.0 ounces	within 4 months	sale of cloth to Vita Impala, a Jew of Agrigento
29.9.1450 c. nn	Iaimo and Nicolò Pasquali	23.6.0 ounces	within 4 months; paid 19.4.1451	sale of cloth to Vita Impala, a Jew of Agrigento
4.10.1450 c. nn	Giaimo Surdu	10.24.0 ounces	within 4 months	sale of cloth to Ricca, wife of Abram Baylu, a Jew
20.10.1450 c. nn	Antonio Aglata	4.24.0 ounces	within a month	sale of a mule to Muxa de Isac, a Jew in Palermo
21.10.1450 c. nn	Calzarano Fornis	2 ounces	by November; paid 29.2.1452	sale of merchandise to Chayrono Russu, a Jew of Palermo
22.10.1450 c. nn	Tommaso Spinula	4.12.0 ounces		sale of gold wire to Deulusa Bonacu, a Palermitan Jew
8.11.1450 c. nn	Gabriele Sardu	29.23.14 ounces	by September; paid 1.11.1451	sale of indigo to Manuel Cazuni, a Jew of Palermo
8.11.1450 c. nn	Daminao Oliveri	3 ounces		sale of grapes to Sabeti Malti, a Palermitan Jew
10.11.1450 c. nn	Giovanni de Amodeo	2.17.10 ounces	by June; paid 16.3.1451	sale of wool to Iosep Xunina, a Jew in Palermo
12.11.1450 c. nn	Tommaso Spinola	2.27.0 ounces	within 2 months	sale of goods to David Taguil, a Jew of Palermo

12.11.1450 c. nn	Busacca Lu Presti, a Jew of Palermo	7.20.0 ounces		sale of indigo
14.11.1450 c. nn	Iosep de Brixa, a Jew of Palermo	5 ounces	by April	sale of tunny
17.11.1450 c. nn	Federico Lanza	21.4.0 ounces	within 6 months	sale of cloth to Elia de Bono, a Jew of Marsala
19.11.1450 c. nn	Manfrido Aglata	38.15.0 ounces	within 6 months	sale of cloth to Elia de Bono, a Jew of Marsala
26.11.1450 c. nn	Galeono Auria	6.18.0 ounces	within a month; paid 1.12.1451	sale of cloth to Simon de Malti, a Jew
7.12.1450 c. nn	Antonio de Crapona	12.18.16 ounces	within 6 months; paid 18.4.1452	sale of gold wire to Muxa Sacerdoto, a Jew
12.12.1450 c. nn	Calzarano Fornis	5.6.0 ounces	within 4 months	sale of cloth to Bulchayra de Termini, a Jew of Palermo
23.12.1450 c. nn	Galeono de Auria	6.27.10 ounces	within 5 months; paid 23.2.1452	sale of gold wire to Muxa Sacerdoto, a Palermitan Jew
24.12.1450 c. nn	Gerardo Lomillino	1.22.10 ounces	paid 1.4.1451	sale of iron to Iosep Cosina, a Jew of Palermo
24.12.1450 c. nn	Gerardo Lomillino	3.19.7 ounces	within 4 months; paid 23.6.1451	sale of merchandise to Leone Xunina, a Palermitan Jew
30.12.1450 c. nn	Thomeo de mastro Antonio	50.6.0 ounces		sale of salt to Salamon de Minichi, a Palermitan Jew
30.12.1450 c. nn	Thomeo de mastro Antonio	96 ounces	within 2 months; paid 22.6.1451	sale of salt to Bracha Cuyno, a Palermitan Jew
31.12.1450 c. nn	Filippo Amalisi	6.10.0 ounces	within 4 months; paid 5.7.1451	sale of merchandise to Sabeti Liuni, a Jew of Palermo

11.3.1451 c. nn	Battista Aglata	25.26.10 ounces	within 6 months; paid 25.9.1452	sale of goods to Elia Cuyno, a Jew of Palermo
12.3.1451 c. nn	Antonio Custonisi	7.16.0 ounces	by June	sale of cloth to David Nachuay, a Jew of Alcamo
13.3.1451 c. nn	Pietro Amar	3 ounces	within 2 months	sale of cloth to David Nachuay, a Jew of Alcamo
13.3.1451 c. 310v	Giovanni de Ricasuli	3.17.10 ounces	within 4 months	saole of oil to Chayrono Sacerdoto, a Jew of Palermo
19.3.1451 c. 320r	Giovanni de Ricasuli	5 ounces	by 15.6	sale of oil to Busacca de Tripuli, a Palermitan Jew
19.3.1451 c. 320r	Giovanni de Ricasuli	5.7.0 ounces		sale of oil to Muxa de Achina, a Palermitan Jew
20.3.1451 c. nn	Gabriele Xardu	7.9.13 ounces	within 2 months; paid 17.4.1452	sale of cloth to Graciano Tachariato and Muxa and Daniel de Missina, Jews of Palermo
26.3.1451 c. 327v	Pino de Impalamo	7.6.0 ounces	within 4 months; paid 31.3.1452	sale of cloth to Abraam Abagatell, a Jew in Palermo
26.3.1451 c. nn	Pietro de Amore	2.6.0 ounces	within 3 months; paid 29.8.1452	sale of cloth to Abraam Gididia, a Jew of Palermo
4.4.1451 c. nn	Giovanni de Ricasulu	28.2.0 ounces	by April; paid 29.4.1451	sale of iron to Saldono Obi, a Jew of Palermo
5.4.1451 c. nn	Giovanni Danivaru	4.15.7 ounces	within 2 months; paid 12.4.1452	sale of merchandise to Leone Azara, a Jew of Palermo
5.4.1451 c. nn	Filippo Amalisi	28.10.0 ounces	within 4 months; paid 15.10.1452	sale of deerskin to Muxa Actuni, Azarono Riczu,

Farchono Nifusi and Bulchayra Frisisa, Jews
of Palermo

5.4.1451 c. nn	Iacobo Panichello	11.15.0 ounces	within 2 months; 21.6.1452	sale of cloth to Abraam Abudarcham, a Palermitan Jew
9.4.1451 c. nn	Arcangelo [...]	8.10.0 ounces	within a month	sale of cloth to Salamon de Minichi, a Palermitan Jew
9.4.1451 c. nn	Pietro Amar	2.15.0 ounces	11 *tarì* a month; paid 27.4.1452	sale of cloth to Muxa Xilba, a Jew of Palermo
10.4.1451 c. nn	Bartholomeo Simonia	1.15.0 ounces	within 4 months	sale of oil to Elia Barbuto, a Jew of Palermo
10.4.1451 c. nn	Pietro Vela	4.25.0 ounces	within 3 months; paid 15.10. 1452	sale of paper to Farmuni Ysac, a Jew of Palermo
10.4.1451 c. nn	Giovanello de Bononia	20.14.9 ounces	by June; paid 23.9.1452	sale of sugar to Muxa de Seragusia and Daniel Farachi, Jews of Palermo
1.2.1452 c. nn	Antonio de Spatafora	5.7.0 ounces	within 4 months; paid 23.7.1452	sale of oil to Abraam de Belladeb, a Palermitan Jew
3.2.1452 c. nn	Giliberto de Auria	7.14.0 ounces	within 4 months	sale of merchandise to Graciano Calamay, a Jew in Palermo
3.2.1452 c. nn	Giliberto de Auria	6.13.0 ounces	within 4 months; paid 28.4.1452	sale of merchandise to Elia de Manuel, a Jew of Palermo
5.2.1452 c. nn	Gerardo Lomillino	5.22.0 ounces	within 5 months	sale of cloth to Salamon de Simon, a Jew
18.2.1452 c. nn	Giuliano de Bes	2 ounces		sale of goods to Brachono Panichellu, a Jew in Palermo
23.2.1452 c. nn	Antonio Aglata	39 ounces	within 6 months	sale of cloth to Abraam Abudarcham, a Palermitan Jew

26.2.1452 c. nn	Antonio de Pedivillano	3.2.0 ounces	within a month	sale of purple dye to Sadono Sala, a Jew of Palermo
1.3.1452 c. nn	Filippo Aglata	2 ounces	within 4 months	sale of linen to Muxa and Abraam Ysac, Jews of Palermo
4.3.1452 c. nn	Iacob and Donato de Mussutu, Jews of Monte San Giuliano	3 ounces		sale of a mule
12.3.1452 c. nn	Iacobo de Panichello	41 ounces	within 3 months; paid 1.6.1452	sale of cloth to Iosep Balbu, a Jew
28.9.1450 c. nn	Antonio de Casafranca	8 ounces	within 4 months; paid 18.4.1451	sale of cloth to Xibiten Gibel, a Palermitan Jew
28.9.1450 c. nn	Berengario Ademar	4.12.0 ounces	within 4 months; paid 18.4.1451	sale of cloth to Xibiten Gibel, a Palermitan Jew
28.9.1450 c. nn	Antonio de Casafranca	14.4.7 ounces	within 4 months; paid 10.4.1451	sale of cloth to Abraam Abudarcham, a Palermitan Jew
28.9.1450 c. nn	Giovanni Cachecti	22.24.0 ounces	within 4 months; paid 9.3.1451	sale of cloth to Salamon Maltisi, a Jew of Polizzi
28.9.1450 c. nn	Antonio de Casafranca	10.8.0 ounces	within 4 months; paid 18.2.1451	sale of cloth to Salamon Maltisi, a Jew of Polizzi
30.9.1450 c. nn	Bernardo de Spule	16.10.0 ounces	within 4 months; paid 8.2.1451	sale of cloth to Gaudio de Anello, a Jew of Agrigento
30.9.1450 c. nn	Antonio Aglata	5.24.0 ounces	within 2 months at Florence	sale of gold wire to Muxa de Daniele, a Jew of Messina
30.9.1450 c. nn	Berengario Ademar	6 ounces	within 4 months; paid 9.2.1451	sale of cloth to Gaudio de Anello, a Jew of Agrigento

30.9.1450 c. nn	Bartholomeo Fibixero	13 ounces	within 4 months; paid 28.4.1451	sale of cloth to Gaudio de Anello, a Jew of Agrigento
30.9.1450 c. nn	Arnaldo Pomar	15 ounces	within 4 months; paid .2.1451	sale of cloth to Gaudio de Anello, a Jew of Agrigento
3.10.1450 c. nn	Simone de Risignano	2.18.15 ounces	within 4 months	sale of iron to Merdoc Vignuni, a Palermitan Jew
3.10.1450 c. nn	Iaimo Sermono	8.16.16 ounces	within 4 months; paid 4.11.1451	sale of merchandise to Salamon de Muxa, a Jew
3.10.1450 c. nn	Pietro Amar	6.15.0 ounces	within 4 months	sale of cloth to Xibiten Gibel, a Jew in Palermo
3.10.1450 c. nn	Guglielmo Barollo	9.240 ounces	within 4 months; paid 9.2.1451	sale of cloth to Gaudio de Anello, a Jew of Agrigento
4.10.1450 c. nn	Pistura, wife of Bartholomeo de mastro Antonio	9.2.0 ounces	within 4 months	sale of goods to Muxa de Daniele, a Jew in Palermo
4.10.1450 c. nn	Antonio de Casafranca	5.9.0 ounces	within 4 months; paid 29.11.1451	sale of cloth to Bellomo Sacerdoto, a Jew of Palermo
4.10.1450 c. nn	Arnaldo Pomar	3.9.15 ounces	within 6 months; paid 29.4.1451	sale of cloth to Bellomo Sacerdoto, a Jew of Palermo
5.10.1450 c. nn	Pino Amar	16.12.7 ounces	within 4 months; paid 10.8.1451	sale of woollen cloth (*frixoni*) to Bellomo Sacerdoto, a Jew of Palermo
5.10.1450 c. 77r	Gasparino de Moroxini	14.18.0 ounces	within 6 months; paid 27.1.1451	sale of merchandise to Nissim Azaruti, a Jew of Palermo
5.10.1450 c. nn	Pasquale de Leo	2 ounces		sale of goods to Bracha Minachem, a Palermitan Jew

5.10.1450 c. nn	Antonio Casafranca	16.4.10 ounces	within 4 months; paid 8.5.1451	sale of cloth to Onorato de Gaudio, a Palermitan Jew
5.10.1450 c. nn	Antonio Casafranca	7.6.0 ounces		sale of merchandise to Onorato de Gaudio, a Palermitan Jew
5.10.1450 c. nn	Antonio Casafranca	5.2.0 ounces		sale of cloth to Xibiten Vignuni, a Jew of Palermo
6.10.1450 c. nn	Guglielmo Barollo	2.10.0 ounces	within a month; paid 18.10.1451	sale of linen to Merdoc Malti, a Jew in Palermo
6.10.1450 c. 83r	Iaimo Cadumo	6.15.0 ounces	within 4 months; paid 13.3.1451	sale of daggers to Salamon de Muxa, a Jew of Palermo
6.10.1450 c. nn	Antonio Casafranca	4.28.0 ounces	within 4 months; paid 4.1.1451	sale of cloth to Abraam de Sangallo, alias Abuganell, a Jew of Palermo
7.10.1450 c. nn	Guglielmo Barollo	9 ounces	within 4 months; paid 9.2.1451	sale of oil to Iosep Binasar, a Palermitan Jew
7.10.1450 c. nn	Arnaldo Pomar	36.9.0 ounces	within 4 months; paid 25.8.1451	sale of cloth to Onorato de Gaudio, a Jew of Palermo
7.10.1450 c. 87r	Iacobo Aglata	2.29.0 ounces	within 4 months	sale of gold wire to Nissim Azaruti, a Palermitan Jew
7.10.1450 c. 87v	Arnaldo Pomar	9.19.0 ounces	within 4 months; paid 13.6.1451	sale of cloth to Moyse Sacerdotu alias Cuyno, a Palermitan Jew
10.10.1450 c. 91r	Pietro Gaytano	2.24.0 ounces	within 4 months; paid 16.6.1451	sale of gold wire to Xamueli Sacerdoto, a Palermitan Jew
11.10.1450 c. 92r	Pietro Amar	7 ounces	within 4 months; paid 17.3.1451	sale of cloth to Iosep de Iona, a Jew of Monte San Giuliano

11.10.1450 c. 93r	Antonino and Bartholomeo Aglata	5.18.0 ounces	within 4 months; paid 15.9.1451	sale of cloth to Farchono Nifusi, a Jew of Palermo
11.10.1450 c. 93v	Guglielmo Barollo	6.27.8 ounces	by April; paid 11.4.1451	sale of cloth to Rubino Gibra and Mussuto Binna, Jews of Palermo
11.10.1450 c. 93v	Antonino and Bartholomeo Aglata	11.6.0 ounces	by February; paid 17.11.1451	sale of cloth to Sabeti Liuni and Bulchayra Frisisa, Jews of Palermo
11.10.1450 c. 94r	Guglielmo Barollo	4.8.0 ounces	paid 14.2.1451	sale of cloth to Azarono Minzill, a Jew of Palermo
13.7.1451 c. nn	Cristofaro Caspiani	2.12.0 ounces		sale of merchandise to Isac de Isac, a Jew of Palermo
18.7.1451 c. nn	Sabeti Cuyno, a Palermitan Jew	2.15.18 ounces	by October; paid 19.2.1452	sale of goods to Sabeti Malti, a Jew in Palermo
18.7.1451 c. nn	Antonio Lomellino	2.15.0 ounces	within a month	sale of wool to Gaudeo de Lu Medicu, a Palermitan Jew
21.7.1451 c. nn	Iusep de La Magna, a Jew of Palermo	12 ounces	within 4 months; paid 13.11.1451	sale of goods
9.8.1451 c. nn	Iacobo de Mazaria	1.7.0 ounces	within a month	sale of iron to Xibiten de Minichi, a Palermitan Jew
17.11.1451 c. nn	Bernardo [...]	15 ounces	within 6 months; paid 5.9.1454	sale of cloth to Abraam and Isac Brixa, Jews in Palermo
19.11.1451 c. nn	Pietro Amato	58.2.0 ounces	within 6 months	sale of cloth to Chayrono Balbo, a Jew of Mazara

21.11.1451 c. nn	[...] Amichello	9.22.0 ounces	within 6 months	sale of cloth to Chayrono Malti and Iosep de Minichi, Jews of Palermo
23.11.1451 c. nn	Chayrono Balbu, a Jew of Mazara			sale of tunny
28.11.1451 c. nn	Pietro Aurifichi	1.15.0 ounces	within 6 months	sale of cloth to Farchono Sala, a Jew of Palermo
29.11.1451 c. nn	Iacobo de Pisa	7.24.0 ounces	within a month; paid 4.4.1454	sale of merchandise to Xamuel Xacharono, a Jew of Palermo
2.12.1451 c. nn	Bellomo Ximeni, a Jew in Palermo			sale of rabbit skins
5.12.1451 c. nn	Antonio de Bonconte	2.15.0 ounces	within a month	sale of merchandise to Bracha Calabresi, a Palermitan Jew
13.12.1451 c. nn	Muxa de Vanni alias Lu Kumutu, a Jew of Palermo	exchange for salt		sale of a mule
20.12.1451 c. nn	Iosep de La Cana, a Palermitan Jew	8.12.0 ounces	within a month; paid 13.4.1452	sale of merchandise
20.12.1451 c. nn	Arnaldo Pillizeri	3.23.0 ounces	within 6 months; paid 31.12.1452	sale of cloth to Merdoc Liuni, a Jew in Palermo
24.12.1451 c. nn	Andrea de Orio	4.24.0 ounces	within 4 months	sale of goods to Busac and Elia de Xaul, Jews of Palermo
24.12.451 c. nn	Farchono Sala, a Palermitan Jew	4 ounces		sale of a mule
3.1.1452 c. nn	Azarono de Monuchatulo, a Jew of Marsala	21 ounces	within 12 days; paid 24.8.1452	sale of wheat

3.1.1452 c. nn	Antonino Blancu	12.9.0 ounces	within a month; paid 21.3.1452	sale of cloth to Xamueli Caru, a Jew in Palermo
3.1.1452 c. nn	Pietro Amatu	12.25.0 ounces	within 3 months; paid 10.12.1454	sale of rice (*risi*) to Salamon Boniasu, a Jew in Palermo
8.1.1452 c. nn	Antonio de Calogero	1.11.0 ounces	by February	loan to Bulchayra de Vannis, a Jew of Palermo
20.1.1452 c. nn	Gerardo de Lomellino	27.10.0 ounces	within 4 months; paid 22.5.1453	sale of gold wire to Muxa de Iusep, a Jew of Palermo
20.1.1452 c. nn	Gerardo de Lomellino	15.18.15 ounces	within 4 months; paid 22.6.1453	sale of gold wire to Donato de Bonaventura, a Jew of Palermo
20.1.1452 c. nn	Gerardo de Lomellino	15.8.0 ounces	within 4 months; paid 22.6.1452	sale of gold wire to Donato de Bonaventura, a Jew of Palermo
22.1.1452 c. nn	Salvatore de Auria	5.12.0 ounces	within 4 months; paid 14.11.1451	sale of gold wire to Xibiten de Minichi, a Palermitan Jew
27.1.1452 c. nn	Nicola de Morsu	20 *tarì* a table	within a month	sale of Venetian tables to Busacca Naguay, a Palermitan Jew

Source: ASP, Not. Giacomo Comito, reg. 848

Date and Page	Debtor	Amount	Reason	Remarks
7.2.1438 c. 10v	Marino de Graciano	sum agreed	outstanding debt	creditor: Nissim Azara, a Palermitan Jew
10.2.1438 c. 14r	Salamon de Minichi, a Jew of Palermo	5 ounces	unpaid debt	creditor: Antonio Parisio; to be paid within 2 months

28.4.1438 c. 173v	Salamon Azara, a Jew of Palermo	22 *tarì*	unpaid debt	creditor: Antonio Maylla; to be paid within a year
25.10.1452 c. 80r	Brachono Sayd alias Arano, a Jew	10 *tarì*	balance for the sale of sugar cane	creditor: Antonio Bayamonte; to be paid in 4 months, in instalments
8.11.1452 c. 101r	Sabet de Vignuni, a Palermitan Jew	6 ounces	unpaid debt	creditor: Sadono de Medico, a Jew of Palermo; to be paid within 6 months
15.11.1438 c. 119v	Iosep de Tripuli, a Palermitan Jew	6 ounces	guarantee for Brachono Sidoti, a Jew	creditor Giovanni; to be paid by May
12.12.1452 c. 167v	Sabet Russo, a Jew of Palermo	25 ounces	debt of rental long overdue	creditor: Vito de Fasola of Mazara; to be paid within a year
18.12.1452 c. 144r	Chayrono de Xaul, a Jew of Mazara	6 ounces	oustanding debt	creditor: Vito Contilecto, a Genoese merchant; to be paid with grain of the new harvest
24.1.1453 c. 222v	Iuda de Minichi, a Palermitan Jew	5 ounces	unpaid debt	creditor: Antonio Manganaro; to be paid on demand
17.7.1453 c. 316v	Raffael Chirusu, a Jew of Trapani	bedcover, bedsheets and linen	undelivered goods	creditor: Xamuel de Xacca, a Jew; to be delivered as soon as possible
25.7.1453 c. 322r	Farchono Sala, a Jew of Palermo, for Andrea cONA	2 OUNCES	UNPAID loan	creditor: Gerardo Carbona; paid 27.6.1455
3.8.1453 c. 346r	Busacca Actuni, a Jew of Palermo	15 *tarì*	settlement of accounts	creditor: Andreotta Gintili; to be paid within 6 months

Date and Page	Lender or Seller	Amount	Payment	Remarks
8.8.1453 c. 351v	Sabatino de Bindira, a Jew of Palermo	8 ounces	settlement of accounts	creditor: Tommaso de Impendi; to be paid within a month and a half; paid 28.9.1454
8.8.1453 c. 351v	Sabatino de Benedicto, a Palermitan Jew	8 ounces	settlement of acounts	creditor: Antonio de Imperiali, a Genoese merchant; to be paid in one and a half months
8.8.1453 c. 351v	Iosep Levi, a Jew of Messina	2.14.0 ounces	balance of 39.14.0 ounces owed for the purchase of cloth	creditor: Nicolò de Guzzardo, a Genoese merchant; to be paid in 4 months; paid 3.8.1455
11.3.1454 c. 111r	Elia Sabuchi, a Jew of Trapani	4 ounces	balance of debt	creditor: Mariano Aglata, to be paid within 2 months; paid 8.11.1454
22.3.1454 c. 132v	Iosep de Brachono on behalf of Manuel Chetibi, Jews in Palermo	3 ounces	bill of exchange	creditor: Giovanni de La Matina
Date and Page	**Lender or Seller**	**Amount**	**Payment**	**Remarks**
5.2.1438 c. 8r	Mussutu Minzili, a Jew of Ciminna	4 ounces	paid	sale of cheese to Dionisio Montuni
12.2.1438 c. 18r	Iacobo Aglata	5 ounces	within 4 months	sale of goods to Salamon Aurifichi
13.2.1438 c. 18r	Costantino Grixono	11 ounces	by April; paid 5.6.1438	sale of linen to Xamuel Sindichi, a Jew of Palermo
18.2.1438 c. 18r	Dionisio Marchini	4.12.0 ounces	within 4 months	sale of a harness to Merdoc de Assuni and Xamuel Binna, Jews of Palermo

18.2.1438 c. 26r	Dionisio Marchini	5.18.15 ounces	within 4 months	sale of merchandise to Vita Amar, a Jew in Palermo
18.2.1438 c. 27r	Mussutu Minzil, a Jew of Termini	6.10.0 ounces	within 3 months	sale of 108 *salme* of barley to Dionisio Marchini
27.2.1438 c. 39v	Iacobo de Anzalono	6.24.0 ounces	within 8 months	sale of gold wire to Salamon Bindira, a Jew of Palermo
6.3.1438 c. 67r	Dionisio Marchini	4 months	on demand	sale of merchandise to Merdoc de Mussutu and Xibiten Misiria, Palermitan Jews
10.3.1438 c. 76r	Giovanni Damiani	23 *tarì*	within 2 months; paid 18.2.1439	sale of gold wire to Merdoc de Mussutu and Xibiten Misiria, Palermitan Jews
24.3.1438 c. 96r	Mariano Cusintino	3.7.10 ounces	within 3 months	sale of gold wire to Muxa de Daniel, a Jew
24.3.1438 c. 97v	Dionisio Marchini	1.15.0 ounces	within 2 months	sale of linen to Chayrono de Xamuel, a Jew
26.3.1438 c. 101v	Cristofaro Manialupo	2.23.0 ounces	by June	sale of wheat to Merdoc de Abramellu, a Jew of Sciacca
27.3.1438 c. 102v	Chayrono de Xaull, a Jew of Mazara	25 *tarì*	by April	sale of barley to Guglielmo Bonfilio
27.3.1438 c. 103r	Salamon Minzili, a Jew of Palermo	12 ounces	paid	sale of goods to Antonio de Soprano
31.3.1438 c. 108v	Chayronello Balbu, a Jew of Mazara	22 *tarì* a *salma*	by April	sale of wheat to Antonio de Soprano
3.4.1438 c. 120r	Bundo de Pandino	3.11.0 ounces	within a month and a half; paid 18.8.1438	loan to Gallufo de Charusio, a Jew of Sciacca

24.4.1438 c. 160r	Manuel de Aram, a Jew in Palermo	11 ounces	on delivery	sale of wheat to Giovanni Panto
28.4.1438 c. 170v	Muxa Sidoti, a Jew of Palermo	1.6.0 ounces	within 2 months	sale of gold wire to Francesco de Crispo
5.9.1452 c. 11r	Ambrogio de Puchio	4 ounces	within a month	sale of gold wire to Muxa Siddita, a Jew of Palermo
5.9.1452 c. 11v	Pino Lu Gauiusu	5.12.0 ounces	by May	sale of cloth to Sabet de Liuni, a Palermitan Jew
18.9.1452 c. 46v	Valluni Xummixi, a Jew of Syracuse	2 ounces	within a month	sale of hides to Giovanni de Ferrino
20.9.1452 c. 48v	Busacca Chansini, a Jew of Agrigento	1 ounce	paid	sale of decorated white sheets to Blasia, wife of Iacobo de Naro
17.10.1452 c. 52r	Iuliano de Momblino	2.18.0 ounces	within 3 months	sale of red cloth to Gaudio Adila, a Jew of Palermo
19.10.1452 c. 58r	Cristofaro Torpiano	5 ounces	within 4 months	sale of gold chains to Bracha de Bundo, a Jew of Palermo
20.10.1452 c. 60r	Agostino Lagiroffo, a Genoese merchant	26 ounces	by August; paid 5.3.1454	sale of gold wire to Ysac de Bonanno, a Jew in Palermo
30.10.1452 c. 88r	Azarono Aglata	23 *tarì*	within a month	sale of a *salma* of wheat to Chanino Balbu, a Jew of Mazara
1.11.1452 c. 95r	Xibiten Vignuni, a Jew in Palermo		delivery within a month	sale 21 *salme* of barley to Pino de Marchisio
13.11.1452 c. 113v	Azarono de Minachem, a Jew of Marsala	agreed price		sale of 30 harnesses to Giovanni de Vinaya, a Genoese merchant

6477

1.12.1452 c. 144r	Ambrogio Lanza	6.12.0 ounces	within 4 months	sale of cloth to Xibiten de Minichi, a Palermitan Jew
7.12.1452 c. 155r	Gerardo Lomillina	7 ounces	by May	sale of assorted goods to Iosep La Cana, a Palermitan Jew
15.12.1452 c. 170v	Bartholomeo de La Oliva, a Genoese merchant	2.15.0 ounces	within a month	sale of gold wire to Iosep de La Cana, a Palermitan Jew
22.12.1452 c. 178v	Pietro de Gerardo, a Genoese merchant	27 *tarì*	shortly	sale of wine to Sabet Vignuni, a Jew of Palermo
22.12.1452 c. 180v	Filippo de Vitali	2.15.0 ounces	by June	sale of merchandise to Iosep Xalom and Farchono Sala, Jews of Palermo
2.1.1453 c. 184v	Bartholomeo de Oliva, a Genoese merchant	6 ounces	within 2 months	sale of gold wire to Muxa Barbuto, a Jew of Palermo
11.1.1453 c. 192r	Giovanni Lanza	6 ounces	within 7 months	sale of 66 barrels of inferior tunny parts (*buzunaglia*) to Leone Amar, a Palermitan Jew
18.1.1453 c. 210r	Bartholomeo de Oliva	8.11.15 ounces	within 4 months	sale of cloth to Iuda Beniosep, a Jew of Palermo
23.1.1453 c. 219v	Bartholomeo de Oliva, a Genoese merchant	9.9.15 ounces	within 4 months	sale of gold wire to Iosep de La Cana, a Jew in Palermo
1.2.1453 c. 237v	Giovanni de Adam	12.11.0 ounces	within 10 months	sale of assorted goods to Ysach Sala, a Palermitan Jew
6.2.1453 c. 241r	Giovanni de Adam, a Catalan merchant	3.23.0 ounces	within 8 months	sale of cloth to Iosep de Brachono and Sabatino de Minichi, Jews of Palermo

6478

6.2.1453 c. 242v	Andrea Mazari	1.14.0 ounces	within a month	sale of cloth to Elia de Mazara and Iosep Lu Medicu, Jews of Monte San Giuliano
12.2.1453 c. 257r	Antonio Valdaura, a Genoese	3 ounces	by August; paid 12.9.1454	sale of 2 paper bales to Muxa de Lu Medicu and Ysach de Anello, Jews of Palermo
15.6.1453 c. 279r	Gerardo Lomellino, a Genoese merchant	4 ounces	by November	sale of gold wire to Iosep de La Cana, a Palermitan Jew
21.6.1453 c. 289r	Dionisio Livatino	1 ounce	by January	sale of wine to Sabet and Nixim Malti, Palermitan Jews
30.6.1453 c. 309r	Giaimo de Salvo	2 ounces	within 4 months; paid 12.4.1454	sale of bedsheets to Mussutu Binna, a Jew of Palermo
17.7.1453 c. 314v	Xamuel de Vita, a Jew of Syracuse	25.27.0 ounces	within 5 months	sale of linen to Elia, son of the late Muxa Cuyno, a Jew of Trapani
8.8.1453 c. 349v	Andreotta Gentili	1.3.0 ounces	within 5 months; paid 23.6.1460 [!]	sale of merchandise to Vita Azara, a Palermitan Jew
8.8.1453 c. 350v	Antonio de Casafranca, a merchant of Barcelona	2.12.0 ounces	within 2 months; paid 15.12.1459	sale of cloth of Barcelona to Onorato de Gaudeo, a Jew of Palermo
8.8.1453 c. 350v	Masio Paris, a merchant of Majorca	6.15.0 ounces	within 6 months	sale of cloth to Bulchayra Sansono, a Jew of Palermo
9.8.1453 c. 352r	Iosep Levi, a Messinese Jew	8.25.10 ounces	within 5 months	sale of silk veils (*xindati*) to Simon Benassay, a Palermitan Jew

9.8.1453 c. 353v	Nicolò de Guchardo, a Pisan merchant	15.21.10 ounces	within 8 months	sale of cloth to Iosep Levi, a Messinese Jew
18.8.1453 c. 362r	Cristofaro Palau	1.25.0 ounces	within 2 months; paid 18.11.1459 [!]	loan to Sadia Siddoti
22.8.1453 c. 370r	Bonu de Iachinto	1 ounce	3 instalments of 10 *tarì*	sale of linen to Mussuto de Siracusia, a Jew
27.8.1453 c. 370v	Pino Cusintino	7.27.0 ounces	within 7 months	sale of cloth to Iosep de Abudaram, a Jew
7.9.1453 c. 9v	Antonio de Corderas, a Genoese merchant	50.29.0 ounces	within 8 months; paid 119.1454	sale of thick wool to Muxa Xunina and Muxa Taguil, Palermitan Jews
17.9.1453 c. 22r	Bernardo de Tabasai, Majorcan merchant	14.20.0 ounces	within a month	sale of linen to Muxa de Siracusa, acting for David Ferachi, Jews in Palermo
17.9.1453 c. 24r	Antonio Cortes	14.19.0 ounces	within 3 months	sale of cloth to Busacca Actuni and his son Azarono, Palermitan Jews
28.9.1453 c. 44v	Bernardo Chalalou	10.22.0 ounces	within 2 months	sale of linen to Iacob Taguil, a Jew of Palermo
11.1.1454 c. 70v	Raynaldo Pallazaru	3 ounces	within 7 months	sale of cloth to Abram Bass, a Palermitan Jew
16.1.1454 c. 78r	Cristofaro Torpiano, a Genoese merchant	3.15.0 ounces	within 6 months	sale of goods to Azarono Azara, a Jew in Palermo
15.3.1454 c. 119r	Nicolò de Lomellino	5 ounces	within a month	sale of gold wire to Muxa Ysach, a Jew of Palermo
15.3.1454 c. 119v	Nicolò de Lomellino	5.6.0 ounces	within a month	sale of merchandise to Iosep Sillac, a Palermitan Jew

6480

Date and Page	Tenant/Owner	Location and Description	Rent and Duration	Remarks
27.3.1454 c. 140v	Iacobo de Trapano	7.12.0 ounces	within 9 months	sale of spices and pepper to Gimilono Naguay, a Palermitan Jew
5.5.1454 c. 145r	Antonio Blundo	18 *tarì*		sale of wine to Iosep Malasu, a Jew of Polizzi
12.5.1454 c. 153v	Nicolò de Lomellino	7.24.0 ounces	within 6 months	sale of cloth to Xamuel Xaccharono, a Jew of Palermo
22.5.1454 c. 157r	Antonio Cardillo	2.12.0 ounces	within 2 months	sale of doublets to Bulchayra de Vignuni, a Palermitan Jew
3.4.1455 c. 6r	Francesco Spano	2.12.0 ounces	within a month	sale of oil to Busacca Sala, a Jew of Palermo
3.4.1455 c. 13r	Angelo de Rizono	2.13.0 ounces	within 2 months	sale of oil to Muxa and Xamuel Isach and Salamon Magaseni, Jews in Palermo
11.10.1455 c. 38r	Giovanni de Diana, a Venetian merchant	7.2.0 ounces	within 2 months	sale of hides to Vita de Policio, a Jew of Palermo
12.10.1455 c. 38v	Xamuel de Anello, a Jew of Agrigento	21.24.0 ounces	paid	sale of wheat to Francesco Aglata
Date and Page	**Tenant/Owner**	**Location and Description**	**Rent and Duration**	**Remarks**
9.7.1455 c. 164v	Thomeo de Sema	Monreale, contrada Di Lu Tambuni; 2 vineyards with garden	sale for 25 ounces	vendor: Salamon Azaru, a Jew of Palermo

Source: ASP, Not. Giacomo Comito reg. 849

Date and Page	Debtor	Amount	Reason	Remarks
12.3.1455 c. 96v	Bernardino de Andriolo of Naro	2.25.0 ounces	guarantee	creditor: Abram Bass, a Palermitan Jew; to be paid on demand
28.3.1455 c. 121v	Iosep Chamusu, a Jew of Palermo	2 ounces	unpaid loan	creditor: Giovanni de Raynaldo; to be paid within 2 months
7.5.1455 c. 141v	Minto de Muxarella, a Jew of Marsala	2 ounces	unpaid debt	creditor: Antonio de Noto; to be paid at vintage time
6.11.1456 c. 39r	Minto de Muxarella, a Jew of Marsala	1.10.0 ounces	unpaid purchase	creditor: Xibiten Asara, a Jew of Polizzi; to be paid shortly
18.11.1456 c. 52v	Mussuto Minzil, a Palermitan Jew	8 ounces	balance of 10 ounces owed for purchase of tunny	creditor: Antonio Aglata, a Pisan merchant; to be paid by July
11.3.1457 c. 90v	Abram Bass, a Palermitan Jew	15 ounces	unpaid loan	creditor: Giovanni de Aldobrandini through Guglielmo Valdaura; to be paid by April
1.4.1457 c. 123r	Iosep Xalom, a Jew of Palermo	4 ounces	unpaid loan	creditor: Antonio Spatafora
12.4.1457 c. 127r	Ysdrael Chanino, a Jew of Palermo	2 ounces	unpaid loan	creditor: Michele de Marino; to be paid within 6 months
21.7.1457 c. 152v	Salamon de R[..]	5.6.0 ounces	unpaid debt	creditor: Giovanni de Bononia; to be paid within 6 months
6.10.1457 c. 24r	Vita Xamuel, a Jew in Palermo	21 *tarì*	unpaid debt	creditor: Giovanni Labati; to be paid within 4 months

Date and Page	Lender or Seller	Amount	Payment	Remarks
[5.2.].1455 c. 1r	Sabet Russo, a Palermitan Jew	4 ounces	3.21.0 ounces on account, balance on delivery	sale of black slave girl
5.2.1455 c. 1v	Giovanni Comes	2.24.0 ounces	paid	sale of 2 casks of wine to Fariono Sala, a Palermitan Jew
7.2.1455 c. 9r	Iosep La Cana, a Jew in Palermo	21 *tarì*	within a month	sale of playing cards (*naybis*) to Guglielmo de Venuti
21.2.1455 c. 27r	Antonio Consili	1.18.0 ounces	by Easter	sale of salt to Ysach Sala, a Palermitan Jew
3.3.1455 c. 55v	Luchino de Aurea, a Genoese merchant	13 ounces	within 4 months	sale of gold wire to Abram Bass, a Jew of Palermo
5.3.1455 c. 65v	Muxa and Manuel Aurifici, Palermitan Jews	22 ounces	by April	sale of sugar to Giovanni de Bayamonte
11.3.1455 c. 76r	Pietro Amato, Catalan merchant	1.18.0 ounces	by June	sale of a mule to Ysach Sala, a Palermitan Jew
12.3.1455 c. 88r	David Nachon, a Jew of Palermo	9 ounces	paid	sale of a black slave to Pietro Comites, a Catalan merchant
12.3.1455 c. 88v	Merdoc Vignuni, a Jew of Palermo			sale of a black slave girl to Pietro Comites
Note: Doc. defective.				
13.3.1455 c. 90r	Giovanni de Bonconte	5 ounces	as soon as possible	loan to Abram Bass, a Palermitan Jew
20.3.1455 c. 109r	Gerardo de Lomellino	9.6.0 ounces	by August	sale of gold wire to Chanino Balbu, a Jew of Mazara

31.3.1455 c. 124v	Gerardo de Lomellino, a Genoese merchant	7.24.0 ounces	by 15.5	sale of 3 pounds of gold wire to Iacob de Lu Presti, a Jew of Palermo
1.4.1455 c. 126v	Matheo de Andrea	5 ounces	by August	sale of silk to David Millac, a Palermitan Jew
1.4.1455 c. 126v	Gerardo de Lomellino	3.10.0 ounces	in instalments	sale of white cloth to Minto Xiffuni, a Jew of Palermo
2.4.1455 c. 137r	Matheo de La Manna, a Pisan merchant	5 ounces	by July	sale of two barrels of lead carbonate to Iosep de La Cana, a Jew of Palermo
19.5.1455 c. 164r	Francesco Allegra	1.25.0 ounces	within 6 months	sale of assorted goods to Iosep Chamusu, a Jew of Palermo
20.5.1455 c. 169v	Antonio Palatino, a Florentine merchant	cows and calves	by July	sale of 5 kantars and 80 *rotoli* of iron ingots (*virzillini*) to Sabet Malti, a Jew in Palermo
21.5.1455 c. 171v	Antonio Palatino, a Florentine merchant	31.24.0 ounces	within a month	sale of Florentine cloth to Chayronello Balbu, a Jew of Mazara, acting for Chanino Balbu, a Jew
21.5.1455 c. 172r	Antonio Palatino, a Florentine merchant	32.3.0 ounces	with wheat at harvest time	sale of Florentine cloth to Manuel de Vita, a Jew of Mazara
21.5.1455 c. 173v	Antonio La Matina	10.6.3 ounces	within 6 months	sale of clothes to Salamon Taguil, a Jew of Palermo
3.6.1455 c. 191v	Damiano Spinola, a Genoese merchant	4.16.11 ounces	within 6 months	sale of assorted goods to Salamon Taguil, a Jew of Palermo

9.6.1455 c. 208v	Giovanni de Campo	21 ounces	by August	sale of barrels of tunny to Gaudeo Abdile, a Jew of Palermo
11.6.1455 c. 211r	Antonio de Palatino, a Florentine merchant	7 ounces	monthly instalments of 1 ounce	sale of Florentine cloth to Iuda de Pantelleria, a Jew of Marsala
12.6.1455 c. 216r	Abram Daru, a Jew of Palermo	8 *tarì* a pound	50 ducats on account, balance by 15.7	sale of iron to Antonio Tadera, a Genoese merchant
13.6.1455 c. 222r	Georgio Buychello	8.24.8 ounces	within 2 months	sale of 5 bales of writing paper to Farchono Ysach, a

Palermitan Jew; to be paid to Tommaso Spinola, a Genoese merchant.

13.6.1455 c. 222v	Pietro Dari, a Majorcan merchant	64.15.0 ounces	25 ounces on demand, the balance in 8 months in 2 instalments	sale of cloth to Abram Bass, a Jew of Palermo
8.8.1455 loose leaf	Rosa, wife of Sadono Benassay, a Jewess of Palermo	2 ounces		sale of 2,000 ropes for tunny to Giovanni de Homodeo
8.8.1455 loose leaf	Rachila widow of Muxa Contenti, a Jewess	15 *tarì*		sale of 500 ropes for tunny to Giovanni de Homodeo
8.8.1455 loose leaf	Altadonna, wife of Mussuto Minachem, a Jewess of Palermo	1 ounce		sale of 1,000 ropes for tunny to Giovanni de Homodeo

8.8.1455 loose leaf	Stella, widow of Cimixi de Amato, a Jewess of Palermo	1 ounce		sale of 1,000 ropes for tunny to Giovanni de Homodeo
8.8.1455 loose leaf	Stella, widow of Sayti de Trapani, a Jewess of Palermo	2 ounces		sale of 2,000 ropes for tunny to Giovanni de Homodeo
9.8.1455 loose leaf	Sufeni Misiria, a Palermitan Jew	2 ounces		sale of 1,000 heavy ropes for tunny and 1,000 light ones to Giovanni de Homodeo
9.8.1455 loose leaf	Sadia Azaruti, a Palermitan Jew	2 ounces		sale of 1,000 heavy ropes for tunny and 1,000 light ones to Giovanni de Homodeo for his plant in San Giorgio
28.8.1455 c. 226r	Iosep Balbu, a Jew of Mazara	12 *tarì* a *salma*	paid 4.5.1455	sale of wheat to Michele La Manna
9.9.1455 c. 40r	Antonio Palatino, a Florentine merchant	23 ounces	by 15.10	sale of cloth to Iuda de Pantelleria, a Jew of Marsala
10.9.1455 c. 46r	Iacob Melaxino, a Genoese merchant	2.17.10 ounces	within 4 months	sale of bands to Brachono Panichello, a Jew in Palermo
12.9.1455 c. 49v	Iacob Melaxino, a Genoese merchant	15.6.0 ounces	within 4 months	sale of gold wire and low quality silk (*terzanellarum*) to Iosep de La Cana, a Jew of Palermo
17.9.1455 c. 55r	Gerardo Lomellino	2 ounces	within 2 months	sale of gold wire to Iosep de La Cana, a Jew of Palermo

Date	Person	Amount	Term	Transaction
18.9.1455 c. 58v	Antonio Aglata	9 ounces	by 15.11	sale of buttons (*buctunellorum*) to Mussuto Minzil, a Palermitan Jew
2.10.1455 c. 78r	Muxa Xifuni, a Palermitan Jew	33.12.15 ounces	within 4 months; paid 12.12.1456	sale of cheese to Giacomo Imperlaxino, a Genoese merchant
3.10.1455 c. 81v	Giacomo Imperlaxino, a Genoese merchant	2.9.0 ounces	within 5 months	sale of gold wire to Muxa Xifuni, a Palermitan Jew
11.10.1455 c. 97r	Iosep Balbu, a Jew of Mazara	40 ounces	by June	sale of 80 *salme* of wheat to Galvano de Auria, a Genoese merchant
11.10.1455 c. 97v	Chayrono Balbu, a Jew of Mazara	40 ounces	by July	sale of 80 *salme* of wheat to Galvano de Auria, a Genoese merchant
11.10.1455 c. 98r	Raffael de Vita, a Jew of Mazara	1.15.0 ounces	paid	sale of 3 *salme* of wheat to Iosep Balbu, his Jewish fellow citizen.
12.10.1455 c. 100v	Damiano Spinula	8.15.0 ounces	monthly instalments of 12 *tarì*	sale of assorted goods to Nixim Cathanisi, a Jew in Palermo
14.10.1455 c. 105v	Andrea Failuta, a Genoese merchant	25 *tarì*	within a month	sale of gold wire to Fraym Ysach, a Jew of Palermo
27.10.1455 c. 123r	Bartholomeo Rizono, a Genoese merchant	10.15.0 ounces	within a year	sale of cloth to Bulchayra de Vignuni, a Palermitan Jew
27.10.1455 c. 124r	Giaimo Falco, a Catalan merchant	1.15.0 ounces	by January	sale of cloth to Asisa, wife of Pasquale Sidoti, a Jewess of Palermo

1.11.1455 c. 129v	Giaimo Falco, a Catalan merchant	2.12.0 ounces	within 6 months; paid 12.4.1456	sale of cloth to Vita Busiti, a Jew of Palermo
3.11.1455 c. 134r	Giaimo Bonfili	1.14.0 ounces	within 1 month; paid 24.4.1456	sale of cloth to Leone Benny, a Jew
4.11.1455 c. 136v	Tommaso Spinula	5.11.9 ounces	within 1½ months	sale of silk to Xibiten de Minichi, a Palermitan Jew
4.11.1455 c. 137r	Dionisio Risoto, a Genoese merchant	3.10.0 ounces	within 3 months	sale of knives to Fraym Ysach, a Jew in Palermo, acting also for Iosep Beniosep, his fellow Jew
18.11.1456 c. 54r	Filippo de La Mantia of Monreale	1.9.0 ounces	by November; paid 16.12.1456	sale of 1½ quintals of grapes to Fariono Sala
18.11.1456 c. 86r	Luca Lu Castellanu	4 ounces	within 4 years	sale of a tunic to Muxa and Vita Sabuchi, Jews of Palermo
1.7.1457 c. 130v	Chayrono Xalom, a Palermitan Jew	1.10.0 ounces		sale of merchandise to Pachio de Faragono
1.7.1457 c. 134v	Agostino de Egidio	13.10.0 ounces		sale of iron to Gaudeo de Mezano, a Jew in Palermo
16.7.1457 c. 142r	Sabet Cuyno, a Palermitan Jew	18.1710 ounces	within a year; paid 18.6.1458	sale of sugar to Nicolò Costantino
18.7.1457 c. 146r	Graciano Tachariato and Elia Lu Pisau, Jews of Polizzi	2 ounces	paid	sale of empty wine casks to Iuppe Calzaranu
1.8.1457 c. 151r	Andrea Fogletti	1.11.0 ounces	within 4 months; paid 5.7.1460 [!]	sale of Florentine cloth to Xibiten Vignuni, a Jew of Palermo

Date and Page		Location and Description	Rent and Duration	Remarks
8.8.1457 c. 165v	Gauiusa, widow of Sadono de Pulisi, a Jewess	20 *tarì*	paid	sale of 1,000 ropes for tunny to Giovanni Homodeo
23.9.1457 c. 14r	Antonio de Aglo	1.15.0 ounces	as soon as possible	sale of wine to Sadono de Tripuli, a Jew of Palermo

Date and Page	Tenant/ Parchaser	Location and Description	Rent and Duration	Remarks
24.4.1459 c. 147r	Iuda de Minichi, a Palermitan Jew	*xirba* in Palermo, *contrada* Pixi de Birxatamuri	sale for 9.6.10 ounces	vendor: Antonio Pinesi
7.8.1459 c. 339r	Iaimo de Racaffa	warehouse in Palermo	3.6.0 ounces, for one year	landlord: Sadono Maltisi, a Jew

Source: ASP, Not. Giacomo Comito, reg. 850

Date and Page	Debtor	Amount	Reason	Remarks
4.9.1457 c. 19r	Lia de Missina, a Jew of Palermo	10.15.0 ounces	unpaid debt	creditor: Calzarano Aquilo, a Catalan merchant; to be paid within 4 months
29.11.1457 c. 53r	Merdoc and Azarono Vignuni and Mussutu Binna, Jews of Palermo	40 ounces	unpaid debt	creditor: Benedetto de Palmerio; to be paid by 25.12
8.2.1458 c. 60r	Sadono Xaccharono and Abram Bass, Jews of Palermo	7.12.0 ounces	unpaid loan	creditor: Iacobo de Masticochario
21.3.1458 c. 116r	Xibiten Malti, a Jew of Nicosia	7 ounces	unpaid debt	creditor; Alfonso Saladino; in monthly instalments of 25 *tarì*

16.5.1459 c. 105r	Nixim Fitira, a Jew of Palermo	18 *tarì*	unpaid loan	creditor: Giovanni de Lista; to be paid within a month
6.4.1459 c. 138v	Lia Ubi and Mactutu Actuni, Jews of Palermo	6.0 ounces	unpaid price for 13 dozen swords	creditor: Egidio de Mizano, a Genoese merchant
11.5.1459 c. 165r	Mussuto Binna, a Palermitan Jew	2 ounces	unpaid loan	creditor: Geronimo de Venuto, a Genoese merchant; to be paid on arrival of a Venetian vessel at Palermo
1.6.1459 c. 193r	Xamuel Nikisen, a Jew in Palermo	10 *tarì*	unpaid balance of purchase price of goods	creditor: Benedetto Rizocto, a Genoese merchant; to be paid within 2 months
2.6.1459 c. 194v	Xamuel Russo, a Jew of Palermo		unpaid loan	creditor: Giliberto de Milano; to be paid by July
18.6.1459 c. 223r	Busacca Sala, a Jew of Palermo	2.6.0 ounces	balance of price for cloth	creditor: Nicolò Insula; to be paid within 2 months
26.10.1459 c. 62r	Chaym de Tripuli, a Palermitan Jew	6.10.0	unpaid loan	creditor: Iacobo de Capua; to be paid by April
18.2.1460 c. 181r	Xamuel de Cabaylla, a Jew of Naro	1.9.0 ounces	unpaid debt for purchase of goods	creditor: Giuliano Tumminia
25.4.1460 c. 205r	Salamon de Muxa, a Jew of Palermo	4 ounces	unpaid loan	creditor: Aloysio de mastro Angilo; to be paid in a month; paid 4.6.1460
28.4.1460 c. 206r	Abram Bass, a Jew of Palermo	1 ounce	unpaid loan	creditor: Antonio Spatafora; to be paid by August
3.4.1460 c. 232r	Abram Bass, a Jew of Palermo		undelivered Venetian tables	creditor: Giovanni Falcono; to be delivered on time

Sicily

Date and Page	Lender or Seller	Amount	Payment	Remarks
23.8.1457 c. 12r	heirs of Giovanni de Bononia	1.6.10 ounces	by October	sale of doublets to Salamon Coffer, a Jew of Palermo
4.9.1457 c. 16v	Geronimo de Oria, a Genoese merchant	12.4.0 ounces	within a month	sale of thick wool to Sabet Cuyno, a Jewish miller in Palermo, and his wife Iannusa
4.9.1457 c. 21v	Pietro Maduchono, a merchant of Barcelona	5.21.0 ounces	2 ounces within a month, balance by December	sale of cloth to Gaudeo Taguil, a Jew of Palermo
15.9.1457 c. 38v	Benedetto Sigitor	8.20.0 ounces	within 4 months	sale of cloth to Lia, son of Sabet Cuyno, a Jew of Trapani
16.9.1457 c. 42v	Leonardo Bertolino, a Florentine merchant	25.15.12 ounces	by January	sale of cloth to Lia, son of Sabeti Cuyno, a Jew of Trapani
9.2.1458 c. 63r	Aloysio de Vinaldo, a Genoese merchant	11 ounces	within 3 months	sale of merchandise to Chayrono Romano, a Palermitan Jew
16.2.1458 c. 77r	Antonio Aglata	2.10.0 ounces	within 4 months	sale of cloth to Sabet Levi and Iosep Xalom, Palermitan Jews
17.2.1458 c. 78v	Egidio de Ruzono	3.2.15 ounces	within 5 months	sale of doublets to Xamuel Caru, a Jew in Palermo
3.3.1458 c. 93v	Minto Soffer, a Jew of Palermo	15 *tarì*	*paid*	sale of goods to Gregorio de Marino
4.3.1458 c. 97r	Perconte Boves, a Genoese merchant	13 ounces	by May	sale of cloth to Sabet Cuyno, a Jew of Palermo

7.3.1458 c. 97v	Nicolò de Galiuni	13 ounces	by 18.9	sale of cloth to Muxa Xifuni, a Jew of Palermo
7.3.1458 c. 98r	Luchino de Lomellino, a Genoese merchant	2 ounces	by April	sale of gold wire to Graciano Minachem, a Jew of Palermo
13.3.1458 c. 106v	Bartholomeo de Grimaldi, a Genoese merchant	2 ounces	by 15 May	sale of cloth to Sabet Russo, a Jew in Palermo
14.3.1458 c. 109v	Benedetto de Cassona, a Genoese merchant	25.22.10 ounces	by April	sale of gold wire to to Salamon Taguil, a Palermitan Jew
23.3.1458 c. 118r	Xamuel de La Pantelleria, a Jew of Marsala	8.13.0 ounces	within 3 months	sale of 11 *salme* of wheat to Marco de Iona, a Jew
7.4.1458 c. 132v	Bartholomeo de Grimaldi, a Genoese merchant	7.12.0 ounces	within a year	sale of 4 dozen of *indixani* [!] to Gabriel Lu Medicu, a Palermitan Jew
13.4.1458 c. 140v	Benedetto Rizocto	7.2.5 ounces	within 4 months	sale of 2 bales of writing paper and 2 bales of waste paper to Iosep Lu Medicu, a Jew of Palermo
9.9..1458 c. 10r	Raffaello Spinula, a Genoese merchant	9.13.8 ounces	within 4 months	sale of wine to Muxa de Palermo, a Jew of Nicosia
9.9.1458 c. 15r	Benedetto Rizocto	3.12.15 ounces	paid 15.11.1458	sale of velvet and linen to Moyse and Gallufo de Benedicto, Jews
9.10.1458 loose leaf	Stella, wife of Salamon de Missina, a Jewess of Palermo	1 ounce	15 *tarì* on account	sale of 1,000 ropes for tunny to Giovanni de Homodei for his plant in San Giorgio

9.10.1458 loose leaf	Stella, wife of Sansono de Gauyo, a Jewess of Palermo	20 *tarì*	9.15 *tarì* on account	sale of 1,000 ropes for tunny to Giovanni de Homodei for his plant in San Giorgio
9.10.1458 loose leaf	Contissa, wife of Ferrugio Sichiliano, a Jewess od Palermo	1 ounce		sale of 1,000 ropes for tunny to Giovanni de Homodei for his plant in San Giorgio
9.10.1458 loose leaf	Rachila wife of Muxa Contentu, a Jewess of Palermo	15 *tarì*	paid	sale of 500 ropes for tunny to Giovanni de Homodei for his plant in San Giorgio
9.10.1458 loose leaf	Mela, wife of Iuda Millac, a Jewess of Palermo	1 ounce		sale of 1,000 ropes for tunny to Giovanni de Homodei for his plant in San Giorgio
9.10.1458 loose leaf	Stella, wife of Merdoc Sacerdoto, a Jewess of Palermo	1 ounce	paid	sale of 1,000 ropes for tunny to Giovanni de Homodei for his plant in San Giorgio
9.10.1458 loose leaf	Rachila, wife of Muxa Contentu, a Jewess of Palermo	1.15.0 ounces	15 *tarì* on account	sale of 1,500 ropes for tunny to Giovanni de Homodei for his plant in San Giorgio
9.10.1458 loose leaf	Czachara, wife of Iosep Iummarra, a Jewess of Palermo	1 ounce		sale of 1,000 ropes for tunny to Giovanni de Homodei for his plant in San Giorgio
9.10.1458 loose leaf	Graciosa, wife of Luce de Momo, a Jewess of Palermo	1 ounce	15 *tarì* on account	sale of 1,000 ropes for tunny to Giovanni de Homodei for his plant in San Giorgio

9.10.1458 loose leaf	Chaguena, wife of Sadono Barbaruso, a Jewess of Palermo	15 *tarì*		sale of 500 ropes for tunny to Giovanni de Homodei for his plant in San Giorgio
9.10.1458 loose leaf	Ricca wife of Vita Maltisi, a Jewess of Palermo	2 ounces	20 *tarì* on account	sale of 2,000 ropes for tunny to Giovanni de Homodei for his plant in San Giorgio
9.10.1458 loose leaf	Stella Amar, a Jewess of Palermo	2 ounces		sale of 2,000 ropes for tunny to Giovanni de Homodei for his plant in San Giorgio
9.10.1458 loose leaf	Chaguena wife of Momo Merdoc, a Jewess of Palermo	2 ounces		sale of 2,000 ropes for tunny to Giovanni de Homodei for his plant in San Giorgio
24.10.1458 c. 39v	Benedetto Rizocto	3 ounces	within 4 months	sale of assorted merchandise to Iuda Beniosep, a Palermitan Jew
25.10.1458 c. 42r	Salamon Farachi, a Palermitan Jew	1 ounce	paid	sale of grapes to Muxa de Policio, a Jew of Palermo
12.12.1458 c. 52r	Giovanni Garibaldo, a Genoese merchant	3 ounces	within 2 months	sale of cloth/clothes to Abram Brissa, a Jew of Polizzi
22.12.1458 c. 55r	Consalvo Delnova	10 ounces	within 6 months	sale of cloth/clothes to Iosep de Medico, a Palermitan Jew
5.1.1459 c. 66r	Raffaello Spinola, a Genoese merchant	14.2.0 ounces	within 8 months	sale of black cloth/clothes to Abram Bass, a Palermitan Jew

12.1.1459 c. 74r	Mazullo Spagnolo, a Jew of Palermo	9 *tarì* a *salma*		sale of wheat and other cereals to Vinchiguerra de Vinales
5.5.1459 c. 110v	Pietro Valles, a merchant of Barcelona	6 ounces	by Easter	loan to Abram Bass, a Jew of Palermo, through Bernardo Catafano
9.5.1459 c. 114r	Gabriele Lochimura, a Catalan	1 ounce a hundredweight	3 ounces on account	sale of all the fish produced during the current season by the tunny plant of Francesco de Moxia to Iacob Sabatino, a Jew of Palermo
16.5.1459 c. 167r	Giovanni de Patroni	14 ounces	within 5 months	sale of silk and coarse wool to Robino de Muxarella, a Palermitan Jew
5.6.1459 c. 200v	Giordano de Giovanni, a Venetian merchant	27 ounces	on demand; paid 5.10.1459	sale of cloth/clothes to David Xunina, a Jew of Palermo
12.6.1459 c. 213r	Francesco Falco	14 *tarì*	within 15 days	sale of coarse wool to Salamon Farachi, a Jew in Palermo
13.6.1459 c. 215r	Giaimo Falco son of Francesco, a Catalan merchant	3 ounces	on demand	sale of coarse wool to Iacob Tavormina, a Jew of Palermo
14.6.1459 c. 217v	Valeriano Li Calsi, a Catalan merchant	6 ounces	within 2 months	sale of saffron to Iosep Lu Medicu, a Palermitan Jew
14.6.1459 c. 217v	Giaimo Falco, a Catalan merchant	2.8.0 ounces	within 4 months	sale of *albaxi* to Iosep Lu Medicu, a Palermitan Jew

15.6.1459 c. 222r	Guido Salvagio, a Genoese merchant	2 ounces	by 25.8	sale of cloth/clothes to Mussuto Balam, a Jew of Trapani
19.6.1459 c. 225r	Giovanni Monblanc, a Catalan merchant	6 ounces	within 6 months	sale of cloth/clothes to Busacca Sala, a Jew in Palermo
9.7.1459 c. 244v	Giaimo Falcono	23 *tarì*	by August	sale of coarse wool to Salamon Farachi, a Jew of Palermo
14.7.1459 c. 250v	Guido Salvagio, a Genoese merchant	11.18.0 ounces	within 6 months; paid 6.2.1460	sale of fabric to Iacob Ladib, a Jew of Palermo
17.7.1459 c. 257v	Guido Salvagio, a Genoese merchant	25.5.0 ounces	by January; paid 17.7.1460	sale of gold wire to Sabet Azaru, a Palermitan Jew
26.7.1459 c. 291r	Aron Farachi, a Palermitan Jew	2.3.18 ounces	within a year	sale of assorted merchandise to Michael Rabibi and Muxa Rustico, Jews of Palermo
8.8.1459 c. 303v	Giaimo Sanipoli	3.2.0 ounces	within a month	sale of cloth/clothes to Fariono Sala, a Jew in Palermo
9.8.1459 c. 304r	Iosep Chirusi	40.20.15 ounces	during current month; paid 18.10.1459	sale of Venetian tables to Bonsignoro Canet, a Palermitan Jew
6.9.1459 c. 8v	Busacca de Iochi, a Jew of Marsala	1.15.10 ounces	within 15 days	sale of wheat to Benedetto Falcono, a Catalan merchant
12.9.1459 c. 22r	Merdoc Bulfarachi, a Jew of Trapani	5 ounces	within 6 months	sale of wheat to Bartolo Bongiorno

4.10.1459 c. 40r	Chaym de Murxocti and Iosep Lu Presti, Jews of Marsala	6 *tarì* a *salma*	to be deducted from price of cloth sold them	sale of wheat to Aloysio de Sancto Angilo
11.10.1459 c. 49r	Giaimo Falcono	11.27.0 ounces	within a month	sale of velvet to Sabatino de Girachio, a Jew in Palermo
5.11.1459 c. 72r	Pinesi de Aron, Mussuto Michisen and Samuel Galifa, Jews of Palermo	15 grana a *salma*		sale of olive pips to Masio de Lanza
9.11.1459 c. 81v	Rixono de Rugila, a Jew of Mazara	6.15.0 ounces	within a month	sale of 60 *salme* of wheat to Pasquale Lomellino
8.1.1460 c. 134r	Iosep de Brachono and Xua Chetibi, Jews of Palermo	12 ounces	on delivery	sale of red [dye/colour] of bilberry to Abram Bass, a Jew of Palermo
9.1.1460 c. 134r	Giovanni de Rossoligno	6.10.0 ounces	within 6 months	sale of wine to Salamon Cuyno, a Jew of Trapani
9.1.1460 c. 134v	Bernardo Ros, a merchant of Barcelona	2 ounces	within a month	sale of spices to Muxa Levi, a Jew of Palermo
10.1.1460 c. 135v	Iacob de Bundo	8 ounces	1 ounce on account, balance on delivery	sale of wheat Mussuto Minachem, a Jew of Palermo
24.1.1460 c. 156r	Daniel Xunina, a Jew of Palermo	6.24.0 ounces	within a month	sale of cheese to Georgio de Burixello, a Genoese merchant
29.1.1460 c. 158r	Iacob Galifa, a Palermitan Jew	20 *tarì*		sale of firewood to Iacobo de Strano for use in his sugar refinery

6.2.1460 c. 164v	Guglielmo Nigro, a merchant of Barcelona	47.12.0 ounces	within 6 months	sale of cloth of Barcelona to Abram Bass, a Palermitan Jew
13.2.1460 c. 171v	Giovanni Lo Porcaro	3.12.0 ounces	within 5 months	sale of wine to Iosep de Brachono, a Jew of Palermo
13.2.1460 c. 171v	Giovanni de Ganxio	25.10.0 ounces	within 8 months	loan to Abram Bass, a Jew of Palermo
5.3.1460 c. 197r	Giuliano Rizocto	24.28.0 ounces	within 2 months	sale of wine to Xalom Marsili, a Jew of Palermo
23.4.1459 c. 204r	Benedetto Falcono, a Catalan merchant	9 ounces	within 5 months; paid 12.4.1461	sale of Majorcan cloth to Daniel Provinzano, Merdoc Vignuni and Iacob Sabatino, Jews of Giuliana
2.4.1460 c. 231v	Nissim Farmuni, a Palermitan Jew	21 ounces	by the end of August	sale of a Berber slave girl to Nicolò Virgilio
16.4.1460 c. 237v	Aloysio de Sancto Angilo	1.8.0 ounces	within 2 months; paid 19.6.1460	sale of iron to Brachono Simaeli and Muxa Ysach, Jews in Palermo
16.4.1460 c. 240r	Muxa Calabrisi, a Palermitan Jew	1.24.0 ounces	paid	sale of a horse with harness and reins to Michilono Ysach, a Jew of Palermo
21.5.1460 c. 273v	Antonio Visconto	25.3.4 ounces	within a month	sale of linen and cloth to Salamon Taguil, a Palermitan Jew
5.6.1460 c. 289r	Giovanni de Catanzario	24 *tarì*	at vintage time	sale of half a kantar of grapes to Sadono Verru, a Jew in Palermo
21.6.1460 c. 297r	Chiminto de Vitali, a Genoese merchant	2.7.0 ounces	within 6 months	sale of gold wire to Muxa de Minto, a Jew of Palermo

Date and Page		Amount		
26.6.1460 c. 308r	Antonio de Cunza	18.15.0 ounces	within a month; paid 27.8.1460	sale of merchandise to Abram Bass, a Palermitan Jew
17.7.1460 c. 330r	Iosep Lu Medicu, a Jew in Palermo	1.10.0 ounces	on delivery	sale of barley Gregorio de Pertininga

Source: Not. Giacomo Comito, reg. 851

Date and Page	Debtor	Amount	Reason	Remarks
15.1.1461 c. 57r	Sadia Balbu, a Jew of Trapani	4 ounces	amount entrusted to him by the Jewish community in Trapani	creditor: Enrico Burgisi
4.7.1461 c. 246r	David Farachi, a Palermitan Jew		undelivered goods	creditor: Giusto de San Cristofaro; to be delivered by August
26.10.1461 c. 19v	Muxa de Girgenti, a Jew of Sciacca	8 *tarì*	balance of price for the tanning of some hides	creditor: Giacomo de Provinzano, a Genoese merchant; to be paid within 3 months
29.10.1461 c. 47r	Iosep Lu Medicu, a Jew of Palermo	1.12.0 ounces	unpaid loan	creditor: Giaimo de Bonfiglo, a Catalan merchant; to be paid in a month; paid 10.11.1461
22.6.1461 171r	Xibiten Pilau and Abdila Xunina, Jews in Palermo	14.3.0 ounes	balance of price of goods	creditor: Lauro de Fermo; to be paid in a year
Date and Page	Lender or Seller	Amount	Payment	Remarks
23.11.1460 c. 6r	Francesco de Lu Kippu	2 ounces	on delivery; paid 20.10.1461	sale of salt and other goods to Gallufo Taguil, a Palermitan Jew

1.12.1460 c. 20r	Giovanni Russo, a cleric of Marsala	20 ounces	on delivery	sale of 50 *salme* of wheat to Gaudeo Abdila, a Jew in Palermo
8.12.1460 c. 24v	Donato de Bonaventura, a Jew of Palermo	3.6.0 ounces	with 10 *salme* of coal, a cask of wine and cash by vintage time	sale of 2 quintals of grapes from his vineyard in the *contrada* Gabellis to Iacobo de Bonnano
13.12.1460 c. 20r	Filippo de Pagano	3.6.0 ounces at 8 *tarì* a *salma*	by April	sale of 12 *salme* of salt to Sadono de Vita, a Palermitan Jew
18.12.1460 c. 36r	Antonio Ienna of Pollina	15 *tarì*	by April	sale of pips to Sadono de Vita, a Palermitan Jew
17.12.1460 c. 36v	Iacobo de Fresco	10 *tarì*	by January	sale of salt to Sadono de Vita, a Palermitan Jew
11.1.1461 c. 41r	Sadono Vita, a Palermitan Jew	1.15.15 ounces	within 6 months; paid 18.5.1462	sale of iron to Pino de Campustino and Iacobo Cornu
3.2.1461 c. 67r	Pino de Bencolli, a Pisan merchant	4.24.0 ounces	by Easter	sale of velvet to Merdoc Binna, a Jew in Palermo
15.2.1461 c. 71r	Antonio Sini	11.20.0 ounces	by April	sale of tunny to Elia Amar and Xalom Marzoch, Palermitan Jews
3.3.1461 c. 91v	Iacobo de Bonnano	6.24.0 ounces	by July	sale of 4 casks of wine to Robino Muxarella, a Jew of Palermo
28.3.1461 c. 129r	Antonio Spatafora	11 ounces	by September; paid 1.4.1462	sale of Malmsey wine to Ysach Bass, a Jew in Palermo

30.3.1461 c. 130r	Michel de Parisio	27 ounces	by June	sale of cloth to David Salamon, a Jew
7.4.1461 c. 144v	Giusto de Lu Bandilumonte	8.26.3 ounces	within 2 months; paid 10.11.1462	sale of gold wire to Iosep Lu Medicu, a Jew of Monte San Giuliano
7.4.1461 c. 147v	Matheo de Placentia	20.9.0 ounces	within 2 months	sale of merchandise to Abram Bass, a Jew of Palermo
28.5.1461 c. 199v	Giovanni de Polito	22 ounces	by December	sale of casks of wine to Muxa de Medico, a Palermitan Jew
20.7.1461 c. 261r	Raffaele de Garifa, a Genoese merchant	16 ounces	within 4 months; paid 4.1.1462	sale of gold wire to Zudo and and Minto de Liucio, father and son, Jews in Palermo
9.8.1461 c. 282v	Raffaele de Garifa, a Genoese merchant	4.28.15 ounces	within 4 months	sale of assorted merchandise to Sabet Russo, a Jew in Palermo
23.10. 1461 c. 3v	Giovanni Matto	22 *tarì*	by 29.10	sale of tallow candles to Gabriel Balbu, a Jew of Palermo
19.3.1461 loose leaf	Giaimo Bonfiglo	36 ounces	within 8 months	sale of Majorcan cloth to Sadia de Agra, a Jew of Agrigento
18.3.1461 c. 127v	Giaimo Bonfiglo	36.2.0 ounces	by August	sale of fabric amd cloth to Sadia Datu, a Jew of Palermo
20 5.1461 c. 139v	Giaimo Bonfiglo	10.28.0 ounces	within a month	sale of cloth to Xamuel Bono, a Jewish tailor in Palermo

Source: ASP, Not. Giacomo Comito, reg. 852

Date and Page	Debtor	Amount	Reason	Remarks
7.9.1462 c. nn	Siminto de Bonnano, a Palermitan Jew	4 ounces	unpaid pice of goods	creditor: Alfonso de Martino; to be paid within 3 months
25.10.1462 c. 165r	Sadia Cuyno and his son Iosep, Jews of Trapani	2 ounces	unpaid debt	creditor: Attardo La Canigla; to be paid within 3 months
3.11.1462 c. 173v	Isabella, wife of Salvatore de Tristano	6.18.0	unpaid goods	creditor: Xamuel Russo, a Jew of Polizzi; paid by the husband
12.11.1462 c. 195v	Bernardo de La Maritata		unpaid debt	creditors: Axuni de Tripuli, a Jew of Mazara, and
				Chichono de Balbu, a Jew of Ciminna; paid through the bank of Pilaya
11.1.1463 c. 265r	Iuda de Minichi, a Jew of Palermo	3 ounces	unpaid debt	creditor: Antonio de Petralia; to be paid by 13.2
14.6.1463 c. 431r	Francisco Pennino	6.1.0 ounces	debt	creditor: Busacca Panichello, a Jew of Palermo; paid with bill of exchange
14.6.1463 c. 431v	Aron Abdila, a Jew of Palermo	1.6.0 ounces	unpaid price of cloth	creditor: Thomeo de Graciano; to be paid within 6 months

Date and Page	Lender or Seller	Amount	Payment	Remarks
8.10.1462 c. 243r	Salvato de Risguardo	2 ounces	within 4 months	loan to Salamon Cuyno, a Jew of Trapani
21.10.1462 c. 164r	Sadia de Girachio, a Jew of Caltabellotta	18 *tarì*	3 *tarì* on account, balance on delivery; paid 1.12.1463	sale of manure to Sadono Ubi, a Jew of Palermo

27.10.1462 c. 166r	Benedetto Chaseni, a Palermitan Jew	7.6.0 ounces	within 5 months; paid 24.3.1463	sale of a certain quantity of casks of wine to Raffaele de Campo, a Genoese merchant
29.10.1462 c. 167v	Cristofaro Trupiano, a Genoese merchant	6.9.15 ounces	weekly instalments of 1 ounce	sale of linen to Xibiten Vignuni and Abram Ximmexi, Jews in Palermo
12.11.1462 c. 196r	Iuliano de Bonconte	2.14.0 ounces	within 2 months	sale of a vest to Liucio de Sabatino, son of Iacob de Sabatino, a Jew of Palermo
22.11.1462 c. nn	Antonio Lu Furmentu	1.6.0 ounces	22 *tarì* on account, balance at vintage time	sale of grapes to Sadono Xerra, a Palermitan Jew
29.11.1462 c. nn	Pino de Sanctu Faru	2.20.10 ounces	as soon as possible	sale of gold wire to Merdoc de Liucio, a Jew of Palermo
1.12.1462 c. 225v	Pino de Sanctu Faru	1.20.0 ounces	within 6 months	sale of gold wire to Iuda Boniosep, a Jew of Palermo
8.12.1462 c. 231v	Iuda de Minichi, a Palermitan Jew	4 ounces	3 ounces on account	sale of grapes to Iacobo de La Corte
23.12.1462 c. 239r	Giuliano de Ricco	1 ounce	at vintage time	sale of grapes to Sabatino Ubi, a Jew of Palermo
11.1.1463 c. 244r	Antonio de Iordano	24 *tarì*	within 4 months	sale of gold wire to Merdoc Rizu, a Jew of Palermo
11.1.1463 c. 264r	Antonio Chona, a Genoese merchant	2.24.0 ounces	within 4 months	sale of gold wire to Muxa de Rizu, a Jew of Palermo
11.1.1463 c. 264r	Salamon de Graciano, a Jew of Caltabellotta	2 ounces	paid	sale of oil to Nicolò de Sancta Rocca, a Genoese merchant

6503

11.1.1463 c. 265r	Sadia de Guillelmo, a Jew of Caltabellotta	12 ounces		sale of 30 kantars of iron to Sabet Ubi, a Palermitan Jew
12.1.1463 c. 265v	Merdoc de Martorana, a Jew of Palermo	18 *grana* the case	6 *tarì* on account	sale of manure to Guglielmo de Matheo
19.1.1463 c. nn	Mussutu Minzil, a Jew of Palermo	4.20.0 ounces	on delivery	sale of silk (*xindarelli*) to Giovanni de Homodeo
23.3.1463 c. nn	Antonio Aleppo	2.15.0 ounces	3 monthly instalments	sale of assorted merchandise to Merdoc Rizu, a Jew in Palermo
29.3.1463 c. nn	Abram Bass, a Palermitan Jew	11 ounces	within 6 months	sale of 11 kantars of sugar to Nicola de Liofante, for Giovanni de Adam
14.4.1463 c. nn	Francesco Pernizola, a Genoese merchant	5.17.0 ounces	3 monthly instalments	sale of gold wire to Xibiten de Minichi, a Palermitan Jew
15.4.1463 c. nn	Iacobo de Manilia, a Genoese merchant	5.22.10 ounces	within 6 months	sale of silk veils (*tercianellorum cindellarum*) to Elia de Manueli, a Jew of Palermo
15.4.1463 c. nn	Guglielmo de Bonnano	2.24.0 ounces	by September	sale of wine to Merdoc Mira, a Jew in Palermo
15.4.1463 c. nn	Iacobo de Manilia	3.17.0 ounces	as soon as possible	sale of velvet to Abram Xunina, a Jew of Palermo
27.4.1463 c. 326r	Francesco Pernizola, a Genoese merchant	5.12.0 ounces	by October	sale of 2 pounds of gold wire to Elia Ubi, a Palermitan Jew

28.4.1463 c. 326v	Thomeo Pernomo, a Genoese merchant	7.4.11 ounces	within 3 months	sale of iron to Merdoc Vignuni, a Jew of Palermo
3.5.1463 c. nn	Francesco Pernizola	2.24.0 ounces	within 3 months	sale of gold wire to Iosep Beniosep, a Jew of Palermo
4.5.1463 c. nn	David Dragna, a Jew of Caltabellotta	10 *tarì* a kantar	1.12.0 ounces on account, balance by 15.5	sale of 20 kantars of *pecorino* cheese to Sadono Ubi, a Jew in Palermo
10.5.1463 c. nn	Chonino de Giaimo, a Genoese merchant	20.25.0 ounces	within 4 months	sale of gold wire to Graciosa, wife of Xamuel Talo, a Jewess of Palermo
11.5.1463 c. nn	Giovanni de Nicolosi	1.24.0 ounces	by August	sale of grapes to Salamon Cuyno, a Jew in Palermo
11.5.1463 c. nn	Thomeo de Graciano, a Genoese merchant	6.1.6 ounces	within 6 months	sale of gold wire to Xibiten Xaxilicto, a Jew of Palermo
11.5.1463 c. nn	Matheo de Modica	24 ounces	within 4 months	sale velvet to Muxa Ysach, a Palermitan Jew
16.5.1463 c. 405r	Thomeo de Graciano, a Genoese merchant	3.7.0 ounces	within 3 months	sale of gold wire to Xamuel Lombardo, a Jew of Palermo
17.5.1463 c. 406r	Thomeo de Graciano, a Genoese merchant	1.11.0 ounces	within 3 months	sale of gold wire to Busacca de Bono, a Jew of Palermo
18.5.1463 c. 409r	Sabet and Merdoc Cuyno, Palermitan Jews	56 ounces	bill of exchange	sale of cloth to Iacobo de Manilia

20.5.1463 c. 411r	Trupiano de Girella, a Genoese merchant	3 ounces	within 6 months	sale of cloth to Aron and Sadono Cuyno, Jews of Palermo
30.6.1463 c. 283v	Thomeo de Graciano, a Genoese merchant	10 ounces	within 6 months	sale of Pisan iron to David Chaguela, a Palermitan Jew
11.7.1463 c. 295r	Antonio de Lizu	4.24.0 ounces	within 6 months	sale of velvet to Merdoc Rizu, a Jew of Palermo
28.7.1463 c. 315r	Thomeo de Chirchilecha	1.9.0 ounces		sale of a tunic to Iuda de Minichi, a Palermitan Jew
2.8.1463 c. 318r	Thomeo de Graciano, a Genoese merchant	5.23.0 ounces	within 6 months	sale of assorted merchandise to Samuel Lombardo, a Jew of Palermo
3.8.1463 c. 320r	Mariano Aglata	3.12.0 ounces	within 2 months	sale of heavy Dutch fabric to Minto de Liucio, a Jew in Palermo
12.8.1463 c. 320v	Mariano Aglata	3.4.0 ounces	within 2 months	sale of heavy Dutch fabric to Xibiten de Tripuli, a Jew in Palermo
12.8.1463 c. 336v	Antonio de Rizzo	6.28.0 ounces	within 4 months	sale of silk (*xillini!*) to Merdoc Vignuni, a Jew of Palermo
18.8.1463 c. 340v	Thomeo de Graciano, a Genoese merchant	2 ounces	within 4 months	sale of fabric to Brachono Farmuni, a Jew of Palermo
20.8.1463 c. 343r	Francesco Aglata	2.9.0 ounces		sale of iron to David Chaguela, a Jew of Palermo
22.8.1463 c. 347v	Thomeo de Graciano, a Genoese merchant	1.10.0 ounces	within 4 months	sale of iron to Busacca Panichello, a Jew in Palermo

22.8.1463 c. 354r	Thomeo de Graciano, a Genoese merchant	1.4.0 ounces	within 5 months	sale of iron to Salamon Gibell, a Palermitan Jew
13.10.1463 c. 6v	Thomeo de Graciano, a Genoese merchant	1.25.0 ounces	within 2 months	sale of gold wire to Gaudeo de Gaudeo, a Jew of Palermo
24.10.1463 c. 19v	Simone de Cardella, a Genoese merchant	8 ounces	within a month	sale of fabric to Samuel de Caro, a Palermitan Jew
25.10.1463 c. 22v	Michilono Ysach, a Jew of Palermo	1.5.0 ounces	15 *tarì* on account, balance by December	sale of a horse to Antonio Rizzo, royal *porterio*
2.11.1463 c. 33v	Tommaso de Nigrono	1 ounce	within a month	sale of goods to Busacca and Nissim de Minachettulo, Jews of Palermo
3.1.1464 c. 63r	Iacobo de Mindalaro	26 ounces	within a month	sale of linen to Gauio Muxara, a Jew of Palermo
4.1.1464 c. 64v	Donato de Bonaventura, a Jew of Palermo	1.12.0 ounces a quintal, total 4.6.0 ounces	a cask of wine on account, balance at vintage time; paid 24.10.1464	sale of 3 quintals of grapes to Iacobo de Bonnano

Source: ASP, Not. Giacomo Comito, reg. 853

Data and Page	Debtor	Amount	Reason	Remarks
14.2.1466 c. 257r	Iuda de Vita and Chayronello Balbu, Jews of Mazara		unpaid bill for cloth	creditor: Battista Aglata; to be paid in April
24.5.1466 c. 353r	Suffeni de Minichi, a Jew of Palermo		unpaid debt	creditor: Giovanni de La Turri; to be paid by May; paid 5.9.1466

Date and Page	Lender or Seller	Amount	Payment	Remarks
17.9.1465 c. 28r	Manuel Bulfarachi, a Jew of Palermo	15 *tarì*	paid	sale of wheat to Gallufo Ammara, a Jew of Palermo
23.9.1465 c. 39r	Surano de Caccabo		1 ounce on account, balance on delivery and not later than November	sale of 50 *salme* of pips to Sadono Sadia, a Jew of Palermo
8.10.1465 c. 71r	Antonio Perdichizi	2 ounces		sale of assorted merchandise to Gimilono Naguay and Deulusa Boniacu, Jews in Palermo
15.10.1465 c. 82r	Manuel Benassay, Gallufo Amar and Muxa Soffer, Jews of Palermo	2 ounces	paid	sale of a horse to Simone Tarbo
24.10.1465 c. 99r	Sadono de Verru and Elia Cuyno, Palermitan Jews	16 *tarì* for cowhides and 10 *tarì* for calf hides		sale of all the hides produced in the vendors' abattoir until the end of May to Pasquale de Lipari
28.11.1465 c. 153v	Ysach Sala, a Jew of Palermo	3 ounces	15 *tarì* on account, balance in instalments; paid 12.12.1465	sale of a mule to Antonio Bulza
2.1.1466 c. 190r	Parruchio Lu Medicu, a Jew of Palermo	3 ounces	monthly instalments until April	sale of a mule to Minto de Alfonso
13.1.1466 c. 201v	Battista de Vilardo, a Genoese merchant	1.27.0 ounces	within 6 months	sale of iron to Gallufo Amarano and Iuda Caskecti, Jews in Palermo

14.1.1466 c. 201v	Battista de Vilardo, a Genoese merchant	1.24.0 ounces	within 6 months	sale of tables to Gallufo Amarano and Iuda Caskecti, Jews in Palermo
23.1.1466 c. 207r	Francesco Punzo, a Genoese merchant	5 ounces	by Easter; paid 5.6.1466	sale of cloth to Brachono Xaffu, a Jew of Palermo
6.2.1466 c. 233v	Guglielmo Sales	6.18.0 ounces	within 4 months; paid 27.7.1466	sale of linen to Brachono Lu Medicu and Benedetto Sidoti, Jews of Palermo
6.2.1466 c. 233v	Bernardo Careni	8 ounces	within 5 months	sale of cloth to Muxa Sadono, a Palermitan Jew
6.2.1466 c. 234v	Pietro Pardo, a Catalan merchant	5.12.0 ounces	within 6 months; paid 21.6.1467	sale of textiles and velvet to Benedetto Sidoti, a Jew of Palermo
6.2.1466 c. 235r	Francesco de Spule, a Catalan merchant	3.18.0 ounces	within 4 months; paid 7.5.1467	sale of cloth/clothes and other goods to Nissim Binna, a Palermitan Jew
7.2.1466 c. 238r	Iuda de Vita and Chaynello Balbu, Jews of Mazara	9 *tarì* a *salma*, totalling 15 ounces	1 ounce on account, balance on delivery	sale of 50 *salme* of wheat to Antonio de Scopino
7.2.1466 c. 241r	Giovanni Damiani	3.6.0 ounces	monthly instalments of 20 *tarì*	sale of iron to Abram de Vignuni, a Palermitan Jew
7.2.1466 c. 241r	Bernardo Sindonia, a merchant of Barcelona	6.6.0 ounces	within 5 months; paid 17.9.1466	sale of iron to Abram de Amarono and Bulchayra de Benedicto, Jews of Mazara
7.2.1466 c. 242r	Bernardo Sindonia, a merchant of Barcelona	5.7.0 ounces	within 5 months; paid 10.4.1466	sale of iron to Iuda Cusintinu, a Jew of Mazara

8.2.1466 c. 242v	Giovanni Bardo, a Pisan merchant	11.17.15 ounces	within 6 months	sale of Florentine cloth to Iuda de Vita and Chaym Balbu, Jews of Mazara
8.2.1466 c. 243v	Bernardo Perna	3.16.10 ounces	within 4 months; paid 30.7.1466	sale of cloth to Abram de Muxarella, a Jew of Marsala
8.2.1466 c. 244r	Bernardo Sindonia, a merchant of Barcelona	8.9.0 ounces	by Easter	sale of cloth to Iosep Abudaram, a Palermitan Jew
8.2.1466 c. 244v	Guglielmo Sialis, a merchant of Tripoli	8.3.0 ounces	within 4 months; paid 12.10.1466	sale of cloth to Mussuto and Busacca Michon, Jews of Palermo
8.2.1466 c. 245r	Bernardo Sindonia	5.24.0 ounces	within 5 months; paid 27.8.1466	sale of cloth to Busacca Michon, a Jew of Palermo
8.2.1466 c. 245r	Giovanni Prestia, a Pisan merchant	8.1.85 ounces	within 5 months	sale of cloth to Brachono de Lu Presti, a Jew of Mazara
8.2.1466 c. 246v	Bernardo Amari, a merchant of Barcelona	17.8.0 ounces	within 6 months	sale of linen to Busacca Sala, a Palermitan Jew
9.2.1466 c. 247v	Bernardo Sindonia, a merchant of Barcelona	6.24.18 ounces	within 5 months	sale of cloth to Salamon de Muxa, a Jew of Palermo
10.2.1466 c. 252v	Battista Aglata	2 ounces	within a month; paid 19.10.1466	sale of iron to Merdoc Vignuni, a Palermitan Jew
13.2.1466 c. 252v	Giovanni de Risignano	15.18.0 ounces	within 5 months; paid 2.7.1466	sale of assorted merchandise to Iuda de Vita and Chaynorello Balbu, Jews of Mazara

13.2.1466 c. 254v	Guglielmo Sialia, a merchant of Tripoli	8.28.15 ounces	within 6 months; paid 18.10.1466	sale of goods to Samuel Sidita, a Jew in Palermo
13.2.1466 c. 254v	Giaimo de Risignano	18.12.0 ounces	within 5 months	sale of velvet to Saduchi Ladib, a Jew of Mazara
13.2.1466 c. 256r	Francesco de Sole, a merchant of Barcelona	1.10.10 ounces	within 5 months; paid 24.3.1467	sale of cloth to Iuda de Vita and Chayronello Balbu, Jews of Mazara
15.2.1466 c. 260r	Giovanni Trabona, a merchant of Barcelona	1.21.0 ounces	within a month; paid 11.6.1466	sale of pepper to Iuda de Vita and Chayronello de Balbu, Jews of Mazara
16.2.1466 c. 261r	Giaimo de Sindonia	2.17.0 ounces	monthly instalments of 6 *tarì*	sale of light coloured bricks to Iosep Chamusi, a Jew of Palermo
17.2.1466 c. 264r	Bernardo Virdi	20.3.0 ounces	within 4 months; paid 8.5.1466	sale of cloth to Geremia Cuyno, a Jew in Palermo
17.2.1466 c. 264v	Bernardo Sutor	33.21.15 ounces	within 4 months; paid 16.11.1466	sale of linen to Iacob Xunina, a Palermitan Jew
22.4.1466 c. 277v	Verardo de Sutera	2.15.0 ounces		sale of tables to Iosep de Amoruso, a Jew in Palermo
21.5.1466 c. 297v	Gaudeo Abdila, a Jew of Palermo	11 *tarì* a *salma*, totalling 5.14.0 ounces	5.10.5 ounces on account	sale of wheat to Tommaso Simeti
21.5.1466 c. 298r	Gaudeo Abdila, a Jew of Palermo	11 *tarì* a *salma*, totalling 9.5.0 ounces		sale of 25 *salme* of wheat to Andrea de Martino
2.5.1466 c. 319v	Guglielmo de Summa, a Genoese merchant	10.6.0 ounces	within 2 months	sale of cloth to Iosep Abudaram, a Palermitan Jew

6.5.1466 c. 327r	Iacobo de Perlimani	7.15.0 ounces	by August	sale of gold wire to Muxa Abudaram, a Jew in Palermo
7.5.1466 c. 330r	Benedetto Milari, a Pisan merchant	2.24.15 ounces	within 2 months	sale of pips to Muxa Siddoti, alias Cuyno, a Jew
13.5.1466 c. 331r	Battista Milari, a Pisan merchant	6.22.10 ounces	within a month; paid 1.11.1466	sale of gold wire to Muxa de Danieli, a Jew of Palermo
14.5.1466 c. 332r	Pino de Pasquali, a Pisan merchant	2.15.0 ounces	monthly instalments of 15 *tarì*; paid 7.10.1466	sale of goods to Merdoc and Xillebi de Rustico, Jews of Palermo
16.5.1466 c. 337v	Omodeo de Rizu	4.10.0 ounces	within a month	sale of olive oil to Xannono de Niyar and Muxa Siddoti, Jews of Palermo
24.5.1466 c. 353r	Arnaldo Ferro, a merchant of Barcelona	5.4.10 ounces	by June	sale of goods to Daniel Ysach, a Jew in Palermo
27.5.1466 c. 361v	Arnaldo Ferro, a merchant of Barcelona	24 *tarì*	by June	sale of cloth to Iosep de Bandino, a Jew in Palermo
17.6.1466 c. 373r	Battista Aglata	21.10.0 ounces	within a month; paid 31.7.1466	sale of gold wire to Manuel and Muxa Aurifichi, a Jews of Palermo
18.6.1466 c. 377r	Manuel Ubi, a Palermitan Jew	2 ounces	paid	sale of a horse to Antonio Guardalaxu
25.6.1466 c. 418r	Thomeo de Parisio	2 ounces	within a month	sale of gold wire to Busacca Panichello, a Jew of Palermo
21.7.1466 c. 421r	Tommaso de Nigrono, a Genoese merchant	4.12.6 ounces	within 2 months	sale of cloth to Xamuel de Caro, a Jew of Palermo
1.8.1466 c. 439r	Chayrono Brixa, a Jew of Marsala	agreed price		sale of all the cheese produced on vendor's farm to Bartholomeo de Isfar

4.8.1466 c. 441v	Lupo de Sevigla	6.6.0 ounces	4 monthly instalments	sale of cloth to Abram Bass, a Palermitan Jew
13.8.1466 c. 454r	Thomeo de Grignano, a Genoese merchant	6.6.13 ounces	within 4 months	sale of merchandise to Merdoc Vignuni, a Palermitan Jew
22.8.1466 c. 461r	Giovanni de Homodei	2.2.0 ounces	by 4.9	sale of tunny to Benni Planza, a Jew in Palermo
25.8.1466 c. 465r	Antonio Salvatu	11.15.0 ounces	within 6 months	sale of cloth to Robino and Nixim Gibra, father and son, Jews

Source: ASP, Not. Giacomo Comito, reg. 854

Date and Page	Debtor	Amount	Reason	Remarks
24.7.1463 c. 163v	Xamuel Actuni, a Jew of Palermo		unpaid debt	creditor: master Xamuel Machelli, a Jewish physician in Palermo

Date and Page	Lender or Seller	Amount	Payment	Remarks
7.10.1461 c. 10v	Giovanni Bayamonte	19.15.0 ounces	11.15.0 ounces on account, balance in a month	sale of 100 sugar loaves to Manuel and Muxa Aurifichi, a Palermitan Jews
28.5.1462 c. 45r	Giovanni Antonio de Filosto, a Genoese merchant	3.20.0 ounces	by April	sale of 3 barrels of tunny to Michilono Xunina, a Jew of Palermo
28.5.1462 c. 45v	Giovanni Antonio de Filosto, a Genoese merchant	5.21.0 ounces	by 13.10; paid 12.1.1463	sale of goods to Abram Xunina, a Jew of Palermo

2.6.1462 c. 53r	Paolo de Valdina	1.12.0 ounces	by August	sale of gold wire to Xibiten Rabbi, a Palermitan Jew
3.6.1462 c. 55r	Michele Cathanisi of Messina	2.20.0 ounces	1.12.0 ounces on account, balance at vintage time	sale of *muscatella* grapes to Muxa Millac, a Jew of Palermo
4.6.1462 c. 56r	Muxa de Nixo, a Jew of Palermo	3 ounces		sale of cloth to Muxa Xammati, a Jew of Palermo
14.11.1462 c. 13r	Bernardo Melori	6 ounces	within 6 months; paid 23.5.1462	sale of clothing to Sisa, wife of Pasquale Sidoti, and Isdraeli Chamuchi, Jews of Palermo
15.11.1462 c. 14r	Iacu Sufi, a Jew of Termini	22.10.0 ounces	on delivery; paid 21.11.1462	sale of wheat to Michele Pillicano
21.11.1462 c. 22v	Giovanni Penzo, a Genoese merchant	1.13.10 ounces	within 5 months	sale of cloth to Muxa Farmuni, a Palermitan Jew
31.1.1463 c.71v	Aron Xunina, a Jew of Palermo	4.12.0 ounces	by June	sale of merchandise to Farchono Niffusi, a Jew of Palermo
28.5.1463 c.93r	Salamon Cuyno, a Jew of Palermo	10 ounces	half by June and half by July; paid 30.5.1465	sale of oil and other goods to Michel de Lacarta
7.6.1463 c.101r	Iosep Chamuso, a Palermitan Jew	1.21.0 ounces	within 4 months	loan to Gaspare de Marino; pawn: 6 silver rings studded with precious stones, a gold ring and other articles
28.6.1463 c.112v	Antonio Romano of Alcamo	2.4.0 ounces	within 4 months	sale of wheat to David Chaguela, a Palermitan Jew
1.7.1463 c. 119v	Salamon de Cuyno, a Jew of Palermo	2.12.0 ounces	within 4 months; paid 10.6.1464	sale of Florentine cloth to Giuliano de Lista

6514

3.7.1463 c. 123v	Antonio Romano of Alcamo	2.10.0 ounces	within 4 months	sale of wheat to Muxa de Minichi, a Palermitan Jew
3.7.1463 c. 123v	Antonio Romano of Alcamo	1.15.0 ounces	within 5 months	sale of wheat to Ysach Rabbibi, a Jew of Palermo
5.7.1463 c. 126v	David Ysach, a Palermitan Jew	3.15.0 ounces	within 5 months	sale of assorted goods to Xamuel Nixiffi, a Jew of Gozo
17.7.1463 c. 145r	Ambrogio de Burghisi	1.9.0 ounces	within 5 months	sale of linen to Nachono Millaya, a Jew of Mazara
17.10.1463 c. 2r	Arnaldo Poma, a merchant of Barcelona	1.20.0 ounces	within 5 months	sale of cloth to Xibiten de Yona, a Jew of Alcamo
17.10.1463 c. 2v	Antonio de Constancia	18 *tarì*	within a month	sale of cloth to Xibiten de Yona, a Jew of Alcamo
17.10.1463 c. 3r	Antonio de Saperlano, a Pisan merchant	1.24.0 ounces	within 3 months	sale of cloth to Xibiten de Yona, a Jew of Alcamo
20.10.1463 c. 8r	Antonio Custanisa, a merchant of Majorca	28.24.0 ounces	within 5 months; paid 8.5.1464	sale of cloth to Iosep Maltisi, a Jew of Polizzi
21.10.1463 c. 9v	Iacobo Aglata	10.15.0 ounces	weekly instalments of 1 ounce	sale of gold wire to Salamon Benassay, a Palermitan Jew
24.10.1463 c. 21r	Antonio de Stefano	7.6.0 ounces	within 4 months	sale of merchandise to Iosep de Abudaram, a Jew of Palermo
29.10.1463 c. 25v	Arnaldo de Orta, a merchant of Barcelona	15 ounces	by January	sale of cloth to Iosep Abudaram, a Jew of Palermo

31.10.1463 c. 31v	Arnaldo de Orta, a merchant of Barcelona	1.25.15 ounces	within 3 months	sale of cloth to Iosep de Aurifichi, a Jew of Palermo
4.11.1463 c. 36v	Iacob Xunina, a Jew of Palermo	30 ounces	within 6 months	sale of assorted merchandise to Leone Romano, a Jew of Palermo
6.11.1463 c. 42v	Dionisio Mestu	2.9.5 ounces	within 3 months	sale of cloth to Vita Ammara, a Jew in Palermo
20.11.1463 c. 47v	Antonio de Septimo	5.10.0 ounces	within 5 months	sale of cloth to Brachono Taguil, a Jew of Palermo
20.11.1463 c. 47v	Antonio de Septimo	5.15.0 ounces	within 5 months	sale of olives to Nissim Binna, a Palermitan Jew
26.11.1463 c. 47v	Carmelo [...]			sale [...] to Muxa de Medico, acting for Siminto de Muxarella, [Jews]

Note: Doc. defective.

23.11.1463 c. 3r	Antonio de Iohanne	2.15.0 ounces	within 4 months	sale of gold wire to Xamuel Ysach, a Jew of Palermo
23.11.1463 c. 8r	Antonio Bartholomeo de Milacio, *secreto* of Corleone	21.6.0 ounces	within a month	sale of cloth to Xamuel Castiglione, a Jew of Palermo
15.12.1463 c. 45r	Giuliano de Marinis, a Genoese merchant	1.16.6 ounces	within 4 months	sale of silk to Nixim Azaruti, a Jew of Palermo

Date and Page	Tenant	Location and Description	Rent and Duration	Remarks
27.6.1467 c. 115v	Marino de Layarda	Cassaro, *vanella* Moyses Chetibi; group of houses with small garden and pergola	6 *tarì* annually	landlords: Salamon Farachi and his wife Stella, Palermitan Jews

Source: ASP, Not. Giacomo Comito, reg. 855

Date and Page	Debtor	Amount	Reason	Remarks
13.11.1466 c. 86v	Chayrono Xunina, a Jew of Palermo	5.21.10 ounces	unpaid price for wheat	creditor: Francesco Aglata; paid 7.8.1467
29.7.1467 c. 152v	Samuel Bambalo, a Jew of Palermo	2.6.0 ounces	unpaid price for assorted goods	creditor: Giovanni Ferro; to be paid in monthly instalments of 8 *tarì*
28.10.1467 c. 62v	Sabet Cuyno, a Jew of Palermo	2.14.0 ounces	unpaid debt	creditor: Strugo de Amarano, a Jew of Trapani; to be paid by November
13.11.1467 c. 126r	Xibiten Barbuto, a Palermitan Jew	2.8.10 ounces	unpaid loan	creditor: Simone de Risignano; to be paid within 6 months
10.12.1467 c. 162v	Jewish community in Trapani		unpaid debt	creditor: Leone Aurifichi, a Jew of Palermo; paid
24.10.1468 c. 46r	Iosep de Yona, a Jew of Monte San Giuliano		unpaid debt	creditor: Antonio de Septimo; to be paid within 8 days
19.10.1469 c. nn	Sabet Russo, a Palermitan Jew	5 ounces	unpaid rent	creditor: Matheo de [...]; to be paid within 5 months; paid 27.11.1470

Date and Page	Lender or Seller	Amount	Payment	Remarks
18.10. 1466 c. 24r	Lupo Aglata, a Genoese merchant	12.24.0 ounces	within 2 months	sale of gold wire to Muxa Siddoti, a Jew of Palermo
22.10. 1466 c. 32r	Antonio de Blundo	11.12.0 ounces	within 7 months	sale of cloth to Gimilono Naguay, a Jew in Palermo
24.10.1466 c. 53v	Daniele Xunina, a Jew of Palermo	50 ounces	on demand	loan to his son Chayrono

10.11.1466 c. 72r	Durante de Nucho	7 *tarì* a kantar	3 ounces on account; paid 12.8.1467	sale of all the cheese produced on vendor's farm until Lent to Ysach Sala, a Palermitan Jew
10.11.1466 c. 73v	Vita, widow of Mariano Aglata	22.21.0 ounces	within 4 months	sale of Dutch fabric to Bonsignuri de Camuto, a Jew in Palermo
11.12.1466 c. 115r	Michele de Cammarata	1.15.0 ounces		sale of 2,000 ropes for tunny to Salamon Cusintino, a Palermitan Jew
23.7.1467 c. 146r	Simone de San Filippo	8 *tarì* a wagonload	1 ounce on account, balance on delivery	sale of 250 wagonloads of stone to Muxa and Merdoc Ammarono and Siminto de Gaudeo, Palermitan Jews
20.8.1467 c. 181v	Manuel Actuni, a Jew of Palermo	22 *tarì*	within a month	sale of a kantar of olive oil to Giovanni Antonio de Sancto Giovanni
24.9.1467 c. 28r	Iacobo de Augustino, a Genoese merchant	2.12.0 ounces	within 3 months	sale of gold wire to David de Liuzo, a Jew in Palermo
3.10.1467 c. 41r	Ubertino de Guchardino	9 *tarì* a kantar totalling 30 ounces	17.10.0 ounces and 2 pounds of gold wire, balance on 15.4; paid 21.7.1468	sale of *caciocavallo* to Chayrono Azeni, a Jew of Palermo
7.10.1467 c. 45r	Muxa Millac, a Jew of Palermo	5 ounces	by November	sale of a band and other articles to Mussuto Binna, a Jew of Palermo
7.10.1467 c. 46r	Elia Talbi, a Jew of Palermo	2 ounces		sale of barley to Giovanni de Pandino

8.10.1467 c. 46v	Francesco de Martino of Trapani	11.2.0 ounces	by January	sale of 200 Venetian tables and other goods to Muxa Xunina, a Jew of Palermo
21.10.1467 c. 56r	Andrea de Antelamo	16.22.10 ounces	by August	sale of assorted merchandise to Abram Bass, a Palermitan Jew
30.10.1467 c. 64r	Pietro de Bandilomunti, a Florentine merchant	8.10.0 ounces	within 6 months	sale of Dutch fabric to Benedetto de Girachio and Iacu Dinar, Jews of Palermo
23.11.1467 c. 95v	Iacobo de Formentu	3 ounces	within 4 months	sale of gold wire to Moyses Barbuto, a Jew of Palermo
23.11.1467 c. 96r	Iacobo de Formentu	33 ounces	by June	sale of assorted goods to Chanino Balbu, a Jew of Mazara
27.11.1467 c. 101r	Simone Cavallero	2.18.0 ounces	within a month	sale of berets to Aron Xilios, a Jew in Palermo
27.10.1467 c. 102r	Antonio de Septimo	2.10.0 ounces	by July	sale of salt tunny to Salamon Levi, a Jew of Termini
5.11.1467 c. 111r	Antonio Aglata	5.18.0 ounces	half in a month and half within 4 months	sale of gold wire to Iosep Sillach, a Palermitan Jew
5.11.1467 c. 112r	Iacobo de Xillino	7.18.11 ounces	within 6 months	sale of linen to Salamon Russo, a Jew of Palermo
10.11.1467 c. 111r	Pietro Valle	13.19.8 ounces	within 6 months	sale of cloth to Iosep Sillach, a Jew in Palermo
13.11.1467 c. 126r	Iacobo de Francesco de Chillino	8.11.0 ounces	half in 2 months and half within 4 months	sale of linen to Iosep Sillach, a Jew in Palermo

17.11.1467 c. 130r	Iacobo de Virgillito	33 ounces	within 6 months	sale of cloth to Azarono de Minachem, a Jew of Palermo
19.11.1467 c. 134v	Bernardo Oliva, a merchant of Barcelona	3.27.0 ounces	on demand; paid 17.4.1475 [!]	sale of hides to Bulchayra Frisisa and Xibiten Gibell, Jews of Palermo
19.11.1467 c. 135r	Chillino de Septimo	2.18.0 ounces	within 5 months	sale of silk to Ysach de La Magna, a Jew of Palermo
19.11.1467 c. 135v	Filippo de Amabile	4.28.10 ounces	within 5 months; paid 30.4.1475 [!]	sale of cloth to Bulchayra Frisisa and Xibiten Gibell, Jews of Palermo
11.12.1467 c. 164v	Francesco Aglata	1.1.5 ounces	on demand	sale of salt to Ysrael de Minichi, a Jew of Palermo
30.12.1467 c. 183v	Mazullo de Bonafide	13 ounces	within a year	loan to Charono Xunina, a Jew of Palermo
3.1.1468 c. 187r	Merdoc Sala, a Jew of Palermo	unspecified amount	15 *tarì* on account, balance on demand	sale of tow for tunny barrels to Lupo de Sivigla, owner of the tunny plant in San Giorgio
4.2.1468 c. c. 222r	Antonio La Matina	6.2.7 ounces	within 6 months	sale of coarse wool to Aron Anaffi, a Catalan Jew
12.8.1468 c. 353r	Benedetto Spagnolo, a Jew of Nicosia	10 ounces	5 ounces on account and 5 ounces by September; paid 22.12.1468	sale of a black slave named Ali, 25 years old, to Iacob Sabatino, a Jew of Palermo
25.8.1468 c. 366v	Stigliano Perdimani, a Genoese merchant	17 ounces	within 2 months	sale of assorted merchandise to Aron Anaffi, a Jew in Palermo

9.10.1468 c. 11v	Antonino de Septimo	7.13.0 ounces	half in 2 months and half within 4 months	sale of velvet to Muxa de Danieli, a Jew of Palermo
15.10.1468 c. 32v	Giovanni Amabile, a merchant of Barcelona	16 ounces	within 2 months	sale of cloth to Nixim Azaruti, a Jew of Palermo
16.10.1468 c. 33v	Antonio Villar, merchant of Barcelona	10.1.8.0 ounces	within 5 months	sale of cloth to Nixim Azaruti, a Jew of Palermo
22.10.1468 c. 39v	Giovanni de Maiano, a Pisan merchant	1.24.0 ounces	within 4 months	sale of 2 kantars of tinplated iron and 28 kantars of Pisan iron to Merdoc Magaseni, a Jew of Palermo
22.10.1468 c. 40r	Antonio de Septimo	2.24.0 ounces	by 1.11	sale of tow to Strugu Bumato, a Catalan Jew of Perpignan
24.10.1468 c. 45r	Giovanni Damiani	1.8.0 ounces	monthly instalments of 20 *tarì*	sale of gold wire to Muxa de Xilla, a Jew of Palermo
26.10.1468 c. 47r	Giovanni de Sivigla	10.7.4 ounces	by February; paid 28.6.1472	sale of iron to Leone Siddoto, a Jew of Palermo
13.11.1468 c. 50r	Azarello Soffer, a Palermitan Jew	13 *tarì*	10.7 *tarì* on account; balance in 2 months	sale of a harness for animals to Vinchio de Bardi
20.12.1468 c. 86v	Xamuel Russo, a Jew of Palermo	15 ounces	within 3 months	sale of a black slave girl to Bartholomeo Viscardo
20.12.1468 c. 88v	Andrea Sindicu	1.10.0 ounces	within a month	sale of gold wire to Iacob Cuyno and Sadia Abdila, Jews of Palermo
15.3.1469 c. 125r	Azara Rustico, a Palermitan Jew	3.6.0 ounces	1.6.0 ounces on account; balance later	sale of a mule with saddle and reins to Xibiten Tranu, a Jew of Palermo

18.3.1469 c. 130v	Merdoc Xaynila, a Jew of Palermo	15 *tarì*	paid	sale of a quintal of sugar cane to Andrea Gibilaro
13.10.1469 c. nn	Antonio Carbona	13.25.15 ounces	within a month; paid 7.11.1470	sale of linen to Giovanni Percordia and Muxa Fitira, a Palermitan Jew
21.10.1469 c. nn	Galvano de Orea, a Genoese merchant	26 ounces	within a year	sale of cloth to Graciano Dinar and Iacob Ladib, Palermitan Jews
Date and Page	**Tenant/Owner**	**Location and Description**	**Rent and Duration**	**Remarks**
11.8.1467 c. 162v	Federico de Diana	Cassaro of Palermo, *vanella* leading to purchaser's mansion and bordering on the house of Nixim Fitira, a Jew; row of single storey and *solerata* houses	sale for 40 ounces	vendors: Gallufo Minichi, a Palermitan Jew, also on behalf of his wife and his son, Xibiten
23.9.1467 c. 26v	Federico de Diana	Cassaro of Palermo, in front of purchaser's mansion; row of houses	sale for 23.15.5 ounces	vendor: Iosep Yattuni, a Jew of Palermo
29.10.1467 c. 63v	Bartholomeo de Miglacio	Cassaro of Palermo, *ruga* San Cataldo, bordering on shop of Ianna, wife of Pino de Castro; house	sale for 9 ounces	vendor: Salamon de Liucio, a Jew of Palermo
22.12.1467 c. 179r	Leone Aurifichi, a Jew of Trapani	Trapani, *ruga* Fadaluni; row of houses	15 *tarì* annually and 5 ounces for the lease	landlady: Zacharona wife of Elia Cuyno, a Palermitan Jewess

24.1.1467 c. 210r	Iacob Cuyno, a Jew of Palermo	Cassaro of Palermo, Platea Marmorea; shop with attic, bordering on shop of Manuel Aurifichi, a Jew	4 ounces for 2 years	landlord: Graciano Dinar, a Palermitan Jew
19.3.1468 c. 269v	Alessandro de Septimo	Lu Burgo quarter in Palermo; warehouse	until August for 1.12.0 ounces	landlord: Farchono de Simone, a Palermitan Jew
23.5.1468 c. 287v	Nicolò de La Chimia of Naro	Palermo, *contrada* Lactarini, bordering on shop of Michilono Xunina; shop	a year for 1 ounce	landlord: master Perrachio de Medico, a Jewish physician of Palermo

Source: ASP, Not Giacomo Comito, reg. 856

Date and Page	Debtor	Amount	Reason	Remarks
6.11.1469 c. 10v	Salamon de Cuyno, a Jew of Palemo	2 ounces	unpaid purchase	creditor: Salvato de Bandino; to be paid 23 *tarì* by January, balance within 4 months
14.11.1469 c. 22v	Sabet Rugila, a Palermitan Jew	15 ounces	unpaid debt	creditor: Giuliano de Ponticorona
3.7.1470 c. 121v	Iuda Muxarella, a Jew of Naples	7.2.0 ounces	unpaid loan	creditor: Doriano de Pernano; to be paid within 6 months
13.1.1471 c. 82v	Vita Xageni, a Jew of Nicosia	1.6.0 ounces	unpaid purchase	creditor: Giovanni Lu Partutu for Federico de La Lauria
30.4.1471 c. 129r	Sadia de Capua, a Jew of Palermo		unpaid purchase of Genoese iron	creditor: Bartholomeo de Pagano

6523

10.1.1472 c. 107v	Andrea Cusanza	1 ounce	down payment for wine sold by Giovanni de Vincenzio	creditor: Muxa Millac, a Palermitan Jew
3.2.1472 c. 122r	Nissim de Leone, a Jew	6.2.0 ounces	unpaid debt	creditor: Amato de Augusta; paid 6.12.1475
3.7.1472 c. 227r	Chola Xillia of Pollina		undelivered merchandise	creditor: Muxa Ubi, a Jew of Palermo; to be paid by August
18.7.1472 c. 237r	Iosep de Liuni, a Palermitan Jew	1 ounces	unpaid price of oil	creditor: Salamon Millac, a Jew of Palermo; as soon as possible; Xibiten Lu Presti, a Jew, had stood surety

Date and Page	Lender or Seller	Amount	Payment	Remarks
6.11.1469 c. 13r	Pietro de Lu Muntiliuni	8.28.0 ounces	within 2 months; paid 13.2.1470	sale of grapes to Xamuel Caro, a Jew of Palermo
13.11.1469 c. 19r	Muxa Millac, a Palermitan Jew	18.21.0 ounces		sale of grapes to Muxa Minachem, a Jew of Palermo
14.11.1469 c. 50r	Iosep Bonu, a Jew of Palermo	for a quantity of grapes	delivery by 18.11	sale of a mule to Guglielmo Cappa
21.11.1469 c. 56v	Braxono de Pantelleria, a Jew of Marsala	24 *tarì*	10 *tarì* on account	sale of seals to Salamon Naguay, a Jew
28.11.1469 c. 63v	Michele de Contissa	2.21.0 ounces	15 *tarì* on account, balance half by August and half by November	sale of a mule to Sabet Millac, a Jew
29.11.1469 c. 64r	Muxa Copiu, a Palermitan Jew	24.12.10 ounces	within 4 months	sale of cheese to Nixim Medui, a Jew
29.11.1469 c. 64v	Iacobo de Valenti of Agrigento	24 *tarì*	paid	sale of a mule to Nixim Malti, a Jew

2.12.1469 c. 66r	Xidedi Azara and Asisa, wife of Pasquale Sacerdoto, Jews of Palermo	3 ounces	paid	sale of a mule to Graciano Puleio
3.12.1469 c. 69v	Francesco Rampulla	16 *tarì*		sale of grapes to Xaym Frisisa, a Jew, in exchange for charcoal
10.12.1469 c. 76r	Cono de Magda	1.9.0 ounces	on delivery	sale of grapes to Aron Sacerdoto, a Palermitan Jew
10.12.1469 c. 76r	Pietro Cannata	1.15.0 ounces	on delivery	sale of grapes to Aron Sacerdoto, a Palermitan Jew
13.12.1469 c. 82v	Salamon Azara, a Palermitan Jew	2.24.0 ounces	1 ounce by June, balance by September	sale of a mule to Thomeo de Pino
16.12.1469 c. 88r	Nicolò de Odo	1.6.0 ounces	delivery at vintage time	sale of grapes to Lia Xunina, a Jew
19.12.1469 c. 92v	Leonardo Campisi	2.20.0 ounces	within 6 months; paid 26.11.1470	sale of oil to Nixim Sansono, a Jew
6.2.1470 c. 108v	Giovanni Cusintino	5.2.10 ounces	within 5 months; paid 5.7.1470	sale of garments to Iosep Riczu
26.6.1470 c. 113v	Fraym and Nixim Gazu, father and son, Palermitan Jews	2 ounces	in exchange for *disa* and salt	sale of rope for tunny to Alessandro de Septimo
27.6.1470 c. 116r	Francesco de Putiglianu	7.5.0 ounces	within 5 months; paid 25.4.1472	sale of casks of wine to Xibiten Malti, a Jew in Palermo

5.7.1470 c. 124v	Pasquale Sacerdoto, his wife Sisa, and his son Iuda, Palermitan Jews	20 *tarì* for 1,000 heavy ropes, 1 ounce for 1,000 light ropes, totalling 45 ounces	during fishing season	sale of 30,000 heavy ropes for tunny and 15,000 light ones to Alessandro de Septimo in exchange for fresh and salted tunny
18.11.147 c. 5r	Ambrogio de Lomellino, a Genoese merchant	17.12.0 ounces	within 6 months	sale of cloth to Xamuel Caru, a Palermitan Jew
18.12.1470 c. 36r	Pietro de Pagano, a Genoese merchant	7.6.0 ounces	within 5 months	sale of cloth to Leono Bricha, a Jew in Palermo
8.1.1471 c. 69r	Ansalono de Bonu, a Genoese merchant	5.27.0 ounces	within 6 months	sale of cloth to Leono Bricha, a Jew in Palermo
13.1.1471 c. 81r	Giovanni Cammarat de Moxia	7.28.10 ounces	daily instalments of 3 *tarì*	sale of bee honey to master Vita de La Bonavogla, a Jewish physician of Messina
16.1.1471 c. 86r	Adam Picti		12 *tarì*	sale of wheat to Siminto Xaccaruni, a Jew
16.1.1471 c. 91v	Bartholomeo Pagano	26 *tarì*	monthly instalments	sale of Genoese iron to Sadia de Capua, a Jew in Palermo
28.3.1471 c. 99r	Cristofaro de Cateno	2.15.0 ounces	within 4 months; paid 22.9.1471	sale of olive oil to Daniel Ysach, a Jew of Palermo
9.4.1471 c. 109v	Bartholomeo Portugallo	3.6.0 ounces	by July	sale of cloth to Aron Anaffi, a Jew of Palermo
16.4.1471 c. 124v	Bartholomeo Portugallo	4.15.8 ounces	within a month	sale of olives to Azaro Rustico for his brother Nixim, Palermitan Jews

16.4.1471 c. 125v	Pietro de Virgillito	1.19.0 ounces	within 3 months	sale of goods to Iosep de Chamusi, a Jew of Palermo
30.4.1471 c. 126v	Bartholomeo Rizono	1.5.5 ounces	within 2 months; paid 14.6.1471	sale of Genoese iron to Salamon de Bundo for Isdrael Camudi, Palermitan Jews
30.4.1471 c. 129r	Bartholomeo Pagano, a Genoese merchant	27 *tarì*	within 3 months	sale of iron to Sadia de Capua, a Jew of Palermo
3.5.1471 c. 138r	Bartholomeo Pagano	2.10.0 ounces	within 2 months	sale of Genoese iron to Aron Misiria, a Jew of Palermo
10.5.1471 c. 144r	Aloysio Gallo, a Majorcan merchant	12 ounces	within 6 months	sale of cloth to Abram Bass, a Palermitan Jew; Abram Azara, a Jew, stands surety
2.9.1471 c.1v	Bartholomeo de Rao of Marsala for Iosep Lu Presti, a Jew of Marsala	7.8.0 ounces		sale of wheat to Doriano de Naumachia, a Genoese merchant
29.10.1471 c. 20r	Muxa Millac, a Palermitan Jew	1.15.0 ounces	by February; paid 3.6.1472	sale of wine to Iacobo de Miglacio
29.10.1471 c. 20v	Luna, wife of Elia de Furmento, a Palermitan Jewess	1 ounce	18 *tarì* on account	sale of rope for tunny to Giovanni de Homodeo
29.10.1471 c. 21r	Sisa, wife of Zullo de Belladeb and Gaudiosa, wife of Merdoc Chamusi, Jewesses of Palermo	20 *tarì* a thousand	12 *tarì* on account	sale of rope for tunny to Giovanni de Homodeo for his plant at San Giorgio

29.10.1471 c. 21v	Perna, wife of Salamon de Seracusia, a Palermitan Jewess	20 *tarì* a thousand	8 *tarì* on account	sale of rope for tunny to Giovanni de Homodeo
29.10.1471 loose leaf	Channa, wife of Vita Cathanisi, a Jewess in Palermo	20 *tarì* a thousand		sale of rope for tunny to Nicolò de Playa and Nicolò de Castello
29.10.1471 loose leaf	Altadonna, wife of Gabriel Misiria, a Jewess in Palermo	15 *tarì*		sale of rope for tunny to Giovanni de Homodeo
29.10.1471 loose leaf	Channa Ammara, a Palermitan Jewess	1 ounce		sale of 1,000 ropes for tunny to Giovanni de Homodeo
29.10.1471 loose leaf	Gauiusa, wife of Azarono Bambalu, a Jewess in Palermo	20 *tarì*		sale of rope for tunny to Giovanni de Homodeo
29.10.1471 loose leaf	Luna, wife of Channono Millac, a Jewess of Palermo	1 ounce		sale of rope for tunny to Giovanni de Homodeo
29.10.1471 loose leaf	Gracia, wife of Gallufo Balbu, a Jewess of Palermo	20 *tarì*		sale of rope for tunny to Giovanni de Homodeo
29.10.1471 loose leaf	Stella, widow of Raffael Rugila, a Palermitan Jewess	20 *tarì*		sale of rope for tunny to Giovanni de Homodeo

6528

29.10.1471 loose leaf	Rachila, wife of Minto Romano, a Jewess of Palermo	20 *tarì*		sale of 500 ropes for tunny to Giovanni de Homodeo
29.10.1471 loose leaf	Channa, wife of Iosep Chicula, a Jewess of Palermo	20 *tarì*		sale of 500 ropes for tunny to Giovanni de Homodeo
4.11.1471 c. 29r	Bussaca Tavormina	4.20.0 ounces	18 *tarì* on account	sale of 7,000 ropes for tunny to Giovanni de Homodeo
7.11.1471 c. 36r	Muxa Marzoctu, a Jew in Palermo	2.16.10 ounces	18 *tarì* on account	sale of a horse to Giovanni Bayamonte
7.11.1471 c. 36v	Salamon Argentu, a Jew	1 ounce		sale of 1,000 ropes for tunny to Giovanni de Homodeo
7.11.1471 c. 37v	Angilo de Lomellino	21.10 *tarì*	within 4 months; paid 6.12.1472	sale of goods to Gaudeo de Abdila, a Jew in Palermo
12.11.1471 c. 42r	Matheo Valeri	10.15.0 ounces	5 ounces on account	sale of cloth to Muxa Xunina and Muxa Maltisi, Palermitan Jews
13.11.1471 c. 44v	Xibiten Bonu, a Jew of Palermo	15 *tarì* a box		sale of soap to Abram Gallifa, a Jew of Palermo
14.11.1471 c. 45r	Francesco Luxardo of Pollina	10 *grana* a *tumino*		sale of all cheese produced by vendor's herd during the current season to Muxa de Leo, a Jew in Palermo
21.11.1471 c. 46r	Giovanni de Milia	18.10 *tarì* a kantar totalling 6.5.0 ounces	1 ounce on account; by November; paid 10.12.1473	sale of 10 kantars of olive oil to Muxa Millac, a Palermitan Jew

27.11.1471 c. 58r	Sisa, widow of Chayrono Malti, a Palermitan Jewess	20 *tarì*		sale of 500 ropes for tunny to Giovanni de Homodeo
27.11.1471 c. 58v	Rosa, widow of Salamon Rustico, a Palermitan Jewess	12 *tarì*		sale of 20 bundles of ropes for tunny to Giovanni de Homodeo
3.12.1471 c. 69v	Mazeo Anderono	3.20.0 ounces	paid	sale of 20 ounces of barley to Muxa Millac, a Palermitan Jew
12.12.1471 c. 77r	Sadia de Graciano, a Jew of Caltabellotta	8 *tarì* a kantar	2 ounces on account	sale of all the cheese produced by the vendor's herd during the current year to Antonio Pepi
13.12.1471 c. 78r	Antonio Nusti	11.11.0 ounces	half on account and half within a month; paid 3.4.1472	sale of cloth to Xua de Rustico, a Jew of Trapani
20.1.1472 c. 111v	Aron Anaffi, a Jew of Palermo	70 ounces	half in 2 months and half in 4 months; paid 6.12.1475	sale of cloth and other goods to Donato Spagnolo and Salamon Binna, Jews of Palermo
2.4.1472 c. 164v	Angilo de Lomellino	6.2.0 ounces	within 6 months	sale of 2 bales of paper to Sema Cuyno and Ysaya Vignuni, Jews of Palermo
3.4.1472 c. 167v	Xamuel Caro, a Jew in Palermo	14 *tarì* a *salma*		sale of barley and other cereals to Angilo de Lomellino
8.4.1472 c. 174v	Antonio de Salvato	6.10.0 ounces	by October	sale of tunny to Leone Chamuel, Xamuel Azaruti, Mazullo Azaruti and Nissim Malti, Jews of Palermo

Date	Name	Amount	Terms	Description
15.4.1472 c. 180v	Angelo de Lomellino	5.18.0 ounces	by August	sale of velvet to Sema Cuyno, a Palermitan Jew
8.5.1472 c. 200v	Angelo de Lomellino	1.20.0 ounces	within 3½ months	sale of fringes (*franze de rexia*) to Xamuel Ysach, a Jew of Palermo
16.6.1472 c. 216v	Nicolò La Chimia	20 *tarì* a *rotolo*	12 *tarì* on account, balance by November	sale of 4 kantars and 50 rotoli of olive oil to Muxa Millac, a Palermitan Jew
23.6.1472 c. 225v	Iacobo de Sadono, a Jew of Trapani	1.6.0 ounces	paid	sale of heavy cloth to Federico de Vitali
13.7.1472 c. 232v	Asisa, wife of Pasquale Sacerdoto, her husband and son, Jews of Palermo	11 ounces	5.15.0 ounces by Passover, balance in instalments for 6 months	sale of a white slave girl named Magira to Alessandro de Septimo
27.8.1472 c. 260v	Abram Dixon, a Jew of Palermo	2.21.0 ounces	within 6 months	sale of 3 barrels of tunny to Vita Ginni, a Jew in Palermo
15.1.1473 c. 61r	Mastro Blasio de Barrangono and his son Antonio	12 ounces	3 ounces on account; the balance in exchange for olive oil valued at 1.10.0 ounces the kantar, to be delivered at Lent	sale of 10 quintals of grapes to Iacob and Abram Cuyno, Jewish brothers in Palermo
18.1.1473 c. 64v	Antonio Pernagallo	1.7.10 ounces	within 2 months	sale of iron wire to Xamuel Azaruti, a Palermitan Jew
4.2.1473 c. 87v	Antonio de Allegra, a Genoese merchant	3.6.16 ounces	instalments; paid 20.8.1473	sale of a bale of Genoese heavy fabric to David de Liucio, a Jew of Palermo

6531

11.3.1473 c. 114r	Angelo de Lomellino	1.25.0 ounces	within 2 months	sale of goods to Xamuel Ysach, a Palermitan Jew
24.3.1473 c. 140r	Giovanni Demma, a Venetian merchant	2 ounces	within 6 months	sale of tables to Graciano Dinar, a Jew of Palermo
1.4.1473 c. 149v	David de Lu Medicu, a Palermitan Jew	11 ounces	cash, wheat and silver articles	sale of a black slave girl called Fatima to Iosep de Donato, a Jew of Palermo
2.4.1473 c. 154r	Muxa Sabuxi, a Jew of Palermo	1 ounce	18 *tarì* on account, balance half in a month and half by May	sale of cloth to Pagirino Fagni
12.5.1473 c. 185v	Angelo de Lomellino	8.23.0 ounces	within 6 months; paid 16.10.1476	sale of fabric to Mussuto Binna and his son Manuel, Jews of Palermo
13.5.1473 c. 186v	Nerono de Nisio	29.10.0 ounces	within a year	sale of cloth to Xua de Messana, a Jew of Trapani
14.5.1473 c. 189r	Antonio Orsino, a Genoese merchant	2.25.0 ounces	half by June and half by July	sale of cloth to Chaym Nifusi, a Jew in Palermo; Fariono Nifusi, a Jew, stands surety
25.5.1473 c. 193v	Abram de Grixon also for his father Nixim, Jews of Palermo	1 ounce for 1,000 heavy ropes and 20 *tarì* for 1,000 light ropes	3 kantars of tunny on account	sale of ropes for tunny to Lupo de Sivigla
8.7.1473 c. 220r	Aron Aseni, a Palermitan Jew	13 *tarì* a kantar, totalling 8.13.0 ounces	1 ounce on account, balance on delivery	sale of cheese to Angelo de Lomellino

Date and Page	Tenant	Location and Description	Rent and Duration	Remarks
22.4.1472 c. 192v	Iacob Cuyno, a Palermitan Jew	Cassaro of Palermo, Platea Marmorea, *vanella* Li Sancti; shop and attic	2 years, 4 ounces a year	landlord: Graciano Dinar, a Palermitan Jew

Source: ASP, Not. Giacomo Comito, reg. 857

Date and Page	Debtor	Amount	Reason	Remarks
5.7.1477 c. 313r	Merdoc Vignuni, a Jewish smith of Palermo	1.21.13 ounces	unpaid loan	creditor: Giuliano Inchenso; to be paid in 6 months
5.7.1477 c. 314v	Cola de Magali of Tusa	26 *tarì*	balance of price for a lined vest and other clothes	creditor: Iuda Salvatu, a Palermitan Jew; to be paid within 2 months
18.1.1478 c. 309v	Muxa Xillini, a Jew of Sciacca	5 ounces	unpaid loan	creditor: Nicolò de Anifra; to be paid by March; paid 12.10.1483
24.1.1480 c. 331r	Salamon Maltisi, a Jew of Palermo	6 ounces	balance of price for purchase of cloth	creditor: Guglielmo Scalis, a merchant of Majorca; to be paid within 5 months; paid 6.6.1481
26.1.1480 c. 336r	Abram Siddotu, a Jew of Palermo		undelivered linen sacks	creditor: Martino de Liberto for Giovanni Sollima
2.5.1480 c. nn	Abram Grixon, a Palermitan Jew	1.7.4 ounces	surety stood for third party	creditor: Giovanni Corsini, a Genoese merchant; to be paid within 2 months

22. 12.1475 c. nn	Pinesi de Aron, a Jew of Palermo	2 *tarì*	unpaid balance of 2 ounces for purchase	creditor: Angelo de Giordano
15.2.1476 c. nn	Muxa Fitira, a Jew of Palermo		undelivered clothing sold for a certain amount	creditor: Nicolò de Pilaya
4.11.1473 c. nn	Elya Cuyno, a Jew of Palermo	2.13.0 ounces	unpaid balance of the purchase price of goods	creditor: Masi de Lomellino; to be paid by April; paid 10.9.1478
20.4.1474 c. 278v	Muxa de Ammara for Gallufo de Minichi, Palermitan Jews	1 ounce	unpaid price of clothes	creditor: Giovanni de Vaccha; to be paid on demand; paid 8.5.1475
20.4.1474 c. 278v	Iuliano Beninato	3 ounces	unpaid price of cloth	creditor: Salamon Cuyno, a Palermitan Jew; to be paid the following month
Date and Page	**Lender or Seller**	**Amount**	**Payment**	**Remarks**
20.8.1477 c. nn	Rosa, wife of Siminto Azaruti, a Jew of Palermo	16.10 *tarì*	paid	sale of 1,000 ropes for tunny to Abneri Grixon, a Jew of Palermo
20.8.1477 c. nn	Chino Spina, also for his mother	agreed price	18.25.0 ounces on account	sale of all the *caciocavallo* produced by the vendor's cows to Graciano Naguay, a Jew of Palermo
20.8.1477 c. nn	Alfonso de Castro	1.20.0 ounces	paid by a loan	sale of a quintal of grapes to Salamon Russo, a Palermitan Jew
20.8.1477 c. nn	Busacca Maltisi, a Jew of Palermo	19 *tarì*	14 *tarì* on account	sale of 1,000 ropes for tunny to Abneri Grixon, a Palermitan Jew

20.8.1477 c. nn	Perna Azeni and his wife Luna, Jews of Palermo	14 *tarì* a 1,000	7 *tarì* on account	sale of 2,000 ropes for tunny to Abneri Grixon, a Jew of Palermo
22.8.1477 c. nn	Bartholomeo de Ferro and Andrea Catanzaru	18 *tarì* a kantar	5 Venetian ducats on account, balance by November	sale of 3 kantars of olive oil to Abneri Grixon, a Palermitan Jew
23.8.1477 c. nn	Xibiten Abbati and his wife Gazalle, Jews of Palermo	18 *tarì*	6 *tarì* on account	sale of 1,000 ropes for tunny to Abneri Grixon, a Jew of Palermo
23.8.1477 c. nn	Pietro de Vinaldis	7.11.10 ounces	within 20 days; paid 15.2.1478	sale of cloth to David Liucio, a Jew in Palermo
23.8.1477 c. nn	Gauiu de Gastigla	10 *tarì* a kantar	paid	sale of 4 kantars of cheese to Geremia Cuyno, a Jew of Palermo
23.8.1477 c. nn	Xibiten de Benedicto, a Jew of Palermo	20 *tarì*	on 6.9	sale of a Sicilian crisp almond sweet (*cubayte*) to Raynaldo de Salamone
27.8.1477 c. nn	Pietro de Pectinaro	4.10.0 ounces	within 5 months in monthly instalments of 24 *tarì*; paid 10.4.1478	sale of goods to Ayeti Nifusi, a Jew of Palermo
27.8.1477 c. nn	Sabet Missilecti, a Jew in Palermo	1.16.0 ounces	23 *tarì* on account	sale of a beast of burden to Fraym Sermeni, a Jew in Palermo
27.8.1477 c. nn	Vita Aurifichi, a Jew of Palermo	2 ounces	by Christmas	sale of 8 barrels of tunny to Filippo Iamfodi of Petralia Sottana and Guglielmo Pasta of Palermo
28.8.1477 c. nn	Aron Azeni, a Jew of Palermo	28.17.0 ounces	on demand	sale of 2 *salme* and 1 *tumino* of wheat to Altadonna, wife of

			Raffael de Missina, Perna, wife of Iacob Lu Vichuzu and Gimilona, widow of Lia de Minichi, Jewesses of Palermo	
29.8.1477 c. nn	Xibiten [torn] alias Maniagnellu and Busacca Ammara, Jews of Palermo	9 *tarì*	paid	sale of half a kantar of olive oil to Raffaele de Danieli, a Jew in Palermo
5.7.1477 c. 315v	Iuliano Vinchiarellu	2 ounces	16 *tarì* on account, balance in instalments until December	sale of a mule to Iuda Salvatu, a Jew of Palermo
1.8.1477 c. 339r	Andrea de Mortido, a Genoese merchant	5.9.0 ounces	within a month; paid 18.7.1479	sale of cloth to Siminto de Policio, a Jew of Palermo
5.8.1477 c. 343v	Andrea de Mortido, a Genoese merchant	2.15.18 ounces	within 5 months; paid 3.8.1478	sale of assorted goods to Muxa Taguil, a Palermitan Jew
5.8.1477 c. 343v	Andrea de Mortido, a Genoese merchant	2.16.16 ounces	within 6 months	sale of cloth to Azara Taguil, a Jew of Palermo
16.1.1478 c. nn	Antonio de Septimo	5.25.0 ounces	within 5 months; paid 22.8.1481	sale of deerskin to to Iosep Choru, a Jew of Palermo
16.1.1478 c. nn	Guglielmo Siltor, a Majorcan merchant	16.21.0 ounces	within 5 months; paid 14.6.1481	sale of wool to Iosep de Tripuli and Busacca Medui, Palermitan Jews
17.1.1478 c. nn	Antonio Vidal	21.20.0 ounces	within 5 months; paid 31.7.1481	sale of deerskin to Xamuel Gedidia, a Jew in Palermo
17.1.1478 c. nn	Antonio de Septimo	5.25.0 ounces	within 5 months; paid 31.5.1482	sale of deerskin to Xibiten Gibel and Brachono Farmuni, Palermitan Jews

18.1.1478 c. nn	Giovanni Damiani, a Pisan merchant	2.8.8 ounces	by February; paid 13.7.1481	sale of a bale of cloth (*crisinarum*) to Muxa Levi and Azarono Rizu, Jews in Palermo
18.1.1478 c. 309r	Guglielmo Scalis, a Majorcan merchant	13.6.16 ounces	within 5 months	sale of 18 *rotoli* of decorations (*adornari*) to Manuel de Aram, a Jew of Palermo
19.1.1478 c. 311r	Bernardo Xerra	18.24.0 ounces	by June; paid 10.6.1482	sale of assorted merchandise to Muxa de Xillini, a Jew of Sciacca
19.1.1478 c. 311v	Raysio de Risignano	1 ounce	within 2 months; paid 26.4.1482	sale of gold wire to Merdoc Vignuni, a Jew of Palermo
20.1.1478 c. 318r	Antonio de Septimo	8.15.0 ounces	within 8 months; paid 8.6.1482	sale of velvet and brocade to Elia Nissim, a Jew of Sciacca
20.1.1478 c. 319r	Providu Salvatu	16.18.0 ounces	by June	sale of cloth to Muxa Xillino, a Jew of Sciacca
20.1.1478 c. 321v	Salvagno Sales, a merchant of Barcelona	4.24.0 ounces	within 5 months	sale of embroidered cloth to Leone Amar, a Jew of Palermo
20.1.1478 c. 321v	Francesco de Spule, a merchant of Barcelona	9.20.0 ounces	within 5 months	sale of assorted goods to Salamon Maltisi, a Jew of Palermo
20.1.1478 c. 322v	Antonio de Septimo	4.18.0 ounces	within 5 months	sale of cloth to Iuda Rabibi and Iosep de Benedicto, Jews of Palermo
23.1.1480 c. 326v	Antonio de Septimo	13.24.0 ounces	by July; paid 6.1.1481	sale of cloth to Muxa Xillino, a Jew of Sciacca

23.1.1480 c. 327v	Francesco de Spule, a merchant of Barcelona	2.8.0 ounces	within 4 months; paid 6.1.1481	sale of cloth to Salomon Maltisi, a Palermitan Jew
23.1.1480 c. 328r	Battista Aglata, a Pisan merchant	7.22.14 ounces	monthly instalments of 28 *tarì*	sale of textiles to Daniel Ysac, a Palermitan Jew
24.1.1480 c. 331v	Battista Aglata, a Pisan merchant	7.15.6 ounces	monthly instalments of 23 *tarì*	sale of lead (*plumellorum*) to Fraym Xaccaruni, a Jew of Palermo
24.1.1480 c. 332v	Bernardo de Cangio, a Genoese merchant	5.6.0 ounces	monthly instalments of 15 *tarì*	sale of silk veils (*xindati*) to Graciano Naguay and Muxa de Danieli, Jews of Palermo
25.1.1480 c. 333v	Arnaldo Garau, a Genoese merchant	3.12.0 ounces	by May; paid 10.7.1481	sale of cloth to Muxa Xillaru, a Jew of Sciacca
26.1.1480 c. 336r	Battista Aglata	5.18.0 ounces	by February; paid 14.8.1481	sale of wire of metal ingots (*fili virzillini*) to Muxa Canziri, a Jew of Giuliana
12.2.1480 c. 341v	Provido Sindonia, a merchant of Barcelona	15 ounces	within 5 months	sale of cloth to Gallufo de Cherno, a Jew of Sciacca
30.1.1480 c. 343v	Battista Aglata, a merchant of Pisa	3.25.0 ounces	within 2 months; paid 27.7.1481	sale of goods to Muxa Mactuti, a Jew in Palermo
30.4.1480 c. nn	Giliberto Vitali	20 *tarì* a kantar	within 2 months	sale of rye (*sigilini dactilis*) to Sadono Russo, a Jew of Palermo

2.5.1480 c. nn	Nicolò Cernida, a sugar merchant, and Michele de Campo of Syracuse	1.18.0 ounces a quintal, totalling 3.6.0 ounces	21 *tarì* on account, balance at vintage time	sale of grapes to Iacob Cuyno, a Jew of Palermo
6.5.1480 c. nn	Riccardo de Permillario	3.15.0 ounces	1.6.0 on account, balance by July	sale of 5 *salme* of barley and 2 *salme* of wheat to Xibiten Gibey, a Jew of Palermo
10.5.1480 c. nn	Andrea de Moltido, a Genoese merchant	5.16.0 ounces	within 4 months	sale of goods to Bulchayra Frisisa and his son Nixim, Jews of Palermo
11.6.1480 c. nn	Angelo de Morso of Polizzi	1.5.0 ounces	within 6 months	sale of olive oil to Salamon Maniapani and Xamuel Ysac, Jews of Palermo
30.1.1476 c. nn	Angelo de Morso of Polizzi	1.6.0 ounces	within 4 months	sale of olive oil to Merdoc Vignuni, a Jew of Palermo
30.1.1476 c. nn	Matheo de Carastono	20 *tarì* a kantar, totalling 40 ounces	20 ounces in a month, balance on delivery	sale of olive oil to Muxa Millac, a Palermo Jew
5.3.1476 c. nn	Pino Cathalano of Monte San Giuliano	7 *tarì* a kantar	1 ounce on account	sale of all of the sheep and cow cheese produced by the vendors's herd to Iosep de Benedicto, a Jew of Palermo
1.1.1476 c. nn	Manfrido de La Muta	20 *tarì* a kantar, totalling 13.10.0 ounces	10.20.0 ounces on account, balance on delivery; paid 12.6.1475	sale of olive oil to Muxa Millac, a Palermitan Jew

3.1.1476 c. nn	Giovanni de Cerula of Monreale	8 *tarì* a kantar for cheese and 12 *tarì* a kantar for *caciocavallo*	6 ounces on account	sale of all the cheese produced by the vendor's herd during the X Indiction to Muxa Xunina, a Palermitan Jew
13.1.1476 c. nn	Angelo Strumentu	2 ounces		sale of a pair of white bed sheets to Muxa de Benedicto, a Jew of Palermo
11.1.1476 c. 129r	Giovanni de Adam	1.10.0 ounces	within 6 months	sale of tables to Nixim Tiolo, a Jew in Palermo
11.1.1476 c. 129v	Giovanni Antonio de Diana	10.10.0 ounces	within 8 months; paid 12.1.1478	sale of tables to Graciano Dinar, a Jew of Palermo
18.1.1476 c. 145v	Giovanni Cassaruto of Caltagirone	3.10.0 ounces	by Easter; paid 18.6.1476	sale of bee honey to Xibiten de Benedicto, a Palermitan Jew
25.1.1476 c. 149v	Francesco Aglata	293.0 ounces	by August	sale of cloth to Aron Anaffi, Iosep de Benedicto and Pinesi de Aron, Jews of Palermo
16.10.1475 c. nn	Andrea de Moltido, a Genoese merchant	4.6.5 ounces	within 4 months	sale of myrtle to Michilono Xunina, a Palermitan Jew
16.10.1475 c. nn	Garlando de Xibilia	2.24.0 ounces		sale of barrels of salted fish to Iosep Abindara, a Jew in Palermo
19.10.1475 c. nn	Elia Ubi, a Jew of Palermo	18.10.0 ounces	by March	sale of olive oil to Masi de Rinzono
19.10.1475 c. nn	Bartholomeo de Calvitto and Masio de Naczaro	42.8.0 ounces		sale of 100 *salme* of wheat to Nixim Millac, a Palermitan Jew

23.10.1475 c. nn	Giovanni Antonio de Diana, a Venetian merchant	1.10.0 ounces	monthly instalments of 6 *tarì*	sale of Venetian tables to Muxa Levi, a Jew of Palermo
30.10.1475 c. nn	Giaimo de Salvatu, farmer of the *gabella fumi* [of the Jewish community in Palermo]	27 *tarì*		sale of tax for the current year to Abram Russo, a Jew of Palermo
30.10.1475 c. nn	Giovanni Antonio de Diana, a Venetian merchant	2.10.0 ounces	monthly instalments of 6 *tarì*	sale of tables to Muxa Russu, a Jew in Palermo
6.11.1475 c. nn	Pietro de Carastono	20 *tarì* a kantar, totalling 6.20.0 ounces	paid 30.4.1476	sale of 10 kantars of olive oil to Muxa Millac, a Jew of Palermo
9.11.1475 c. nn	Giovanni Antonio de Diana, a Venetian merchant	1.10.0 ounces	within 6 months; paid 7.5.1477	sale of tables to Busacca Malki, a Jew of Palermo
20.11.1475 c. nn	Andrea de Moltido, a Genoese merchant	2.19.0 ounces	within 4 months; paid 8.6.1476	sale of canvas to Muxa Taguil, a Palermitan Jew
20.11.1475 c. nn	Andrea de Moltido, a Genoese merchant	2.24.0 ounces		sale of canvas to Azara Taguil, a Palermitan Jew
20.11.1475 c. nn	Andrea de Moltido, a Genoese merchant	3.15.0 ounces	within 3 months; paid 23.10.1476	sale of linen to Iacob de Liucio, a Palermitan Jew

20.11.1475 c. nn	Giovanni Antonio de Diana, a Venetian merchant	1.10.0 ounces	monthly instalments of 6 *tarì*	sale of tables to Cara, wife of Iosep de Gaudeo, a Palermitan Jewess
29.11.1475 c. nn	Giovanni Antonio de Diana	1.10.0 ounces	monthly instalments of 6 *tarì*	sale of tables to Galifa de Benedicto, a Palermitan Jew
20.2.1476 c. nn	Andrea de Moltido, a Genoese merchant	3.12.0 ounces	within 4 months	sale of velvet to Abram and Busacca Fitira, Jews of Palermo
22.2.1476 c. nn	Guglielmo de Failla	1.23.10 ounces	within 2 months	sale of Pisan iron to Xibiten de Lu Presti, a Jew of Palermo
13.3.1476 c. nn	Pietro de Cannaro	28.10.0 ounces	by Easter	sale of cloth to Chicono de Minichi, a Palermitan Jew
1.12.1476 c. nn	Giovanni Antonio de Diana	2.15.0 ounces	within 3 months	sale of assorted merchandise to Iosep Coczu, a Jew of Palermo
23.12.1476 c. nn	Giovanni Antonio de Diana	1.25.0 ounces	monthly instalments of 6 *tarì*	sale of tables to Muxa Ysac, a Palermitan Jew
23.12.1476 c. nn	Andrea de Moltido, a Genoese merchant	8.22.0 ounces	half in 15 days and half in a month	sale of assorted merchandise to Geremia Azeni, a Jew of Palermo
30.12.1476 c. nn	Pietro de Calanzano	25 ounces	paid	sale of an infidel slave girl to Salamon Cuyno, a Jew of Palermo
2.1.1477 c. nn	Antonio de Pietro	20 ounces	18 ounces on account, balance on delivery	sale of 60 kantars of salted tunny in barrels to Abram Grixon, a Palermitan Jew

5.1.1477 c. nn	Pietro de Orto	6.14.15 ounces	within a month	sale of wheat to Abneri Grixon, a Jew of Palermo
10.10.1473 c. nn	Andrea de Moltido, a Genoese merchant	8.17.0 ounces	within 8 months	sale of Genoese cloth to Aron Anaff, a Jew of Palermo
17.10.1473 c. nn	Giovanni de Vacca, a Venetian merchant	1.27.0 ounces	within a month; paid 16.12.1477	sale of tables to Muxa Ysrael, a Jew of Palermo
20.10.1473 c. nn	Andrea de Moltido, a Genoese merchant	2.10.13 ounces	within 6 months	sale of cloth to Nixim Catalano, a Jew of Palermo
1.9.1473 c. nn	Giovanni de Vacca, a Venetian merchant	2.6.0 ounces	monthly instalments of 15 *tarì*	sale of cow hides to Xamuel de Gallifa and Xamuel Summatu, Jews of Sciacca
30.9.1473 c. nn	Giovanni Capizu	2.23.0 ounces	paid	sale of a horse to Muxa Amarano and Muxa de Furmento, Jews in Palermo
6.10.1473 c. nn	Mario de Naczaro	7.10 0 ounces	by June	sale of a mule and other goods to Muxa Millach and Aron Azeni, Palermitan Jews
16.8.1474 c. nn	Nicolò Bonfanti	1 ounce	at vintage time	sale of a quintal of grapes to Manuel Russo, a Jew in Palermo
27.7.1474 c. nn	Abneri Grixon, a Jew of Palermo	1 ounce a thousand heavy ropes and 20 *tarì* a thousand light ones	partly paid in exchange for tunny valued at 18 *tarì* a kantar and albacore valued at 2.10.0 ounces a quintal	sale of 30,000 ropes for tunny to Lupo de Sivigla

28.7.1474 c. nn	Busacca Sacerdoto, a Jew of Palermo	3.6.0 ounces		sale of a pair cushions (*cuxinellorum*) of crimson (*carmixini*) velvet to Manuel de Innixa, a Jew of Palermo
3.8.1474 c. nn	Giovanni Vacca, a Venetian merchant	2.8.0 ounces	within a month	sale of tables to Gallufo de Benedicto and his son Bracha, Jews of Palermo
8.8.1474 c. nn	Martino de Persico	4.19.10 ounces	within a month	sale of heavy cloth to Busacca Frisisa, a Jew of Palermo
11.5.1474 c.nn	Iacobo de Morso, a Genoese merchant	1.6.6 ounces	by August	sale of goods to Xibiten Summatu, a Jew in Palermo
4.6.1474 c. 468v	Guarnero de Barbutu and his mother Florencia	21 *tarì* a kantar, totalling 3.18.0 ounces	18 *tarì* on account, balance in a month; paid 19.9.1474	sale of tallow to Minto Cuyno, a Palermitan Jew
3.6.1474 c. 319r	Bracha de Liucio, a Jew of Palermo	4 ounces	paid	sale of a mule to Battista de Vuturo, a Genoese merchant
7.6.1474 c. 324v	Iacobo de Martino, a Genoese merchant	1.26.0 ounces	within 2 months; paid 13.2.1475	sale of assorted goods to Gaudeo Ysach, a Jew of Palermo
28.3.1474 c. nn	Muxa and Vita Sabuchi, Jews of Palermo	9 *tarì*	paid	sale of tow for tunny barrels to Alessandro de Septimo
1.4.1474 c. nn	Iacobo de Galiffa and his wife Gaudiosa, Jews in Palermo	16 *tarì* a thousand		sale of 3,000 ropes for tunny to Lupo de Sivigla
13.4.1474 c. nn	Chayrono de Misiria and his wife Disiata, Jews in Palermo	21 *tarì* a thousand	paid	sale of 1,000 heavy ropes for tunny to Alfonso de Girona

13.4.1474 c. 270r	Xanguena, widow of Mussutu Migleni, a Palermitan Jewess	1.10.5 ounces	on delivery	sale of 1,500 of ropes [for tunny] to Alfonso de Girona
14.4.1474 c. 270r	Gaudiosa, wife of Sabeti Formentini, a Jewess of Palermo	1.12.0 ounces	on delivery	sale of 2,000 ropes for tunny to Alfonso de Girona
14.4.1474 c. 271r	Busacca de Pasquale and his wife Meme, Palermitan Jews	12 *tarì*		sale of 500 ropes for tunny to Alfonso de Girona
14.4.1474 c. 271v	Ricca, wife of Brachono Ismaeli, a Palermitan Jewess	13 *tarì*	paid	sale of 500 ropes for tunny to Alfonso de Girona
14.4.1474 c. 272r	Disiata, wife of Iacob Amaru, a Jewess of Palermo	21 *tarì*	on delivery	sale of 1,000 ropes for tunny to Alfonso de Girona
27.4.1474 c. 281r	Giovanni Vacca	10.20.0 ounces	within 6 months	sale of deerskin to Abram de Aron and his son Nissim, Palermitan Jews
28.4.1474 c. 282r	Giovanni Vacca	1.28.0 ounces	monthly instalments of 7 *tarì*	sale of hides to Gallufo de Benedicto and his sons Bracha and Muxa, Jews of Palermo
28.4.1474 c. 282v	Giuliano de Resymito	1 ounce	by May	sale of a horse to Merdoc Millac, a Jew of Palermo

2.5.1474 c. 283v	Francesco Bono, a Genoese merchant	2.13.0 ounces	by August; paid 7.10.1474	sale of two bales of paper to Busacca Frisisa, a Palermitan Jew
5.5.1474 c. 288v	Angelo de Martino	2.8.6 ounces	by June	sale of cloth to Gaudeo Abdila, a Jew in Palermo
1.3.1474 c. nn	Giovanni Vacca	5.10.0 ounces	within 6 months	sale of cow hides to Manuel de Tripuli, a Palermitan Jew
1.3.1474 c. nn	Giovanni Vacca	1.10.0 ounces	within 45 days	sale of cow hides to Sabeti Marsili, a Jew of Palermo
12.3.1474 c. nn	Muxa Xiraeli, a Jew of Palermo	1.13.0 ounces	on delivery	sale of ropes for tunny to Francesco Sivigla
28.3.1474 c. nn	Muxa Canchila, a Jew of Salemi	12 *tarì*		sale of 500 ropes for tunny to Lupo de Sivigla
5.9.1473 c. nn	Dionisio Zaccaria, a merchant of Barcelona	7.12.0 ounces	within 5 months	sale of cloth to Abram de Muxarella, a Jew of Marsala
12.9.1473 c. nn	Francesco de maystru Capellaru	2.15.0 ounces	within 6 months; paid 10.10.1475	loan to Mussuto, a Jew of Castrogiovanni
13.9.1473 c. nn	Dionisio Zaccaria, a merchant of Barcelona	18.15.0 ounces	monthly instalments of 18 *tarì*	sale of iron to Iosep Sillac and Muxa de Muxa, Palermitan Jews
18.9.1473 c. nn	Antonio Bono	13.20.0 ounces	within a month	sale of cloth to Onorato de Gaudeo and Abram Abaynello, Jews in Palermo
22.10.1473 c. nn	Giovanni Antonio Floccari of Messina	1.15.0 ounces	1 ounce on account, balance on completion of delivery	sale of grapes to Xibiten Xunina, a Palermitan Jew

27.10.1473 c. nn	Giovanni Vacca	3.10.0 ounces	within 5 months; paid 29.10.1474	sale of hides to Nixim Furmeni, a Jew of Palermo
4.11.1473 c. nn	Iacobo de Moltido, a Genoese merchant	2.24.0 ounces	monthly instalments of 1 ounce	sale of myrtle
5.11.1473 c. nn	Francesco de Lovinio, a Genoese merchant	5.23.12 ounces	within 4 months	sale of 5 bales of paper to Deulusa Boniach, a Jew in Palermo
9.11.1473 c. nn	Giovanni Vacca	1.16.0 ounces	weekly instalments of 2 *tarì*	sale of hides to Merdoc de Lu Munti and his daughter Stella, widow of Iacob de Liuzu, Jews in Palermo
10.11.1473 c. 89r	Francesco de Lovinio, a Genoese merchant	6.10.0 ounces	within 4 months	sale of gold wire to Sadia Abdila, a Jew of Palermo
10.11.1473 c. 89v	Giovanni Vacca	7.6.0 ounces	monthly instalments	sale of leather to Abram de Mona and his wife, Jews of Palermo
16.11.1473 c. 93v	Giovanni Vacca	5.20.0 ounces	within a month	sale of leather to Vita Abbati, a Jew in Palermo
16.11.1473 c. 94v	Francesco Lovinio	1.7.4 ounces	within 4 months	sale of gold wire to Xamuel Actuni, a Palermitan Jew
16.11.1473 c. nn	Giovanni Vacca	2.10.0 ounces	within 6 months	sale of women's clothes to Abram Nifusi, a Jew of Palermo
4.1.1474 c. nn	Iacob Marzullo and his wife Luna, Jews in Palermo	11 *tarì*		sale of 500 ropes for tunny to Alfonso de Girona

4.1.1474 c. nn	Disiata, wife of Gimilono Achina, a Jewess in Palermo	21 *tarì*		sale of 1,000 ropes for tunny to Alfonso de Girona
4.1.1474 c. nn	Cara, wife of Muxa Nifusi, a Jewess in Palermo	21 *tarì*		sale of 1,000 ropes for tunny to Alfonso de Girona
4.1.1474 c. nn	Merdoc and Laudata Sidita, Jews of Palermo	21 *tarì* a thousand, totalling 2.13.0 ounces	paid	sale of 3,000 ropes for tunny to Alfonso de Girona
4.1.1474 c. nn	Disiata, wife of Michilono Ysach, a Palermitan Jewess	21 *tarì* a thousand, totalling 2.24.0 ounces	1 ounce on account	sale of 4,000 ropes for tunny to Alfonso de Girona
4.1.1474 c. nn	Luna, wife of Merdoc de Minichi, a Jewess of Palermo	21 *tarì*	6 *tarì* on account	sale of 1,000 ropes for tunny to Alfonso de Girona
4.1.1474 c. nn	Abram Lu Presti and his wife Xanna, Jews of Palermo	21 *tarì*		sale of 1,000 ropes for tunny to Alfonso de Girona
4.1.1474 c. nn	Farachi Sichilianu and his wife Contissa, Jews of Palermo	21 *tarì*		sale of 1,000 ropes for tunny to Alfonso de Girona
4.1.1474 c. nn	Ricca, wife of Merdoc Chagueli, a Jewess of Palermo	21 *tarì* a thousand	20 *tarì* on account	sale of 2,000 ropes for tunny to Alfonso de Girona

4.1.1474 c. nn	Vita, widow of Iuda Ingelli, a Jewess of Palermo	21 *tarì*		sale of 1,000 ropes for tunny to Alfonso de Girona
4.1.1474 c. nn	Mazucta Trapanisi, widow of Graciano Pulisi, a Jewess of Palermo	21 *tarì* a thousand, totalling 3.15.0 ounces	1.15.0 ounces on account	sale of 5,000 ropes for tunny to Alfonso de Girona
4.1.1474 c. nn	Cara, wife of Chaym de Liucio, a Jewess in Palermo	1.12.0 ounces		sale of 2,000 ropes for tunny to Alfonso de Girona
4.1.1474 c. nn	Agnixia, wife of Minto Bricha, a Jewess of Palermo	21 *tarì*		sale of 1,000 ropes for tunny to Alfonso de Girona
4.1.1474 c. nn	Disiata, wife of David Misiria, a Jewess of Palermo	21 *tarì*	6 *tarì* on account	sale of 1,000 ropes for tunny to Alfonso de Girona
4.1.1474 c. nn	Gaudiosa, wife of Salamon Lu Presti, a Jewess in Palermo	21 *tarì* a thousand, totalling 1.12.0 ounces	12 *tarì* on account	sale of 1,000 ropes for tunny to Alfonso de Girona
4.1.1474 c. nn	Chillucha, wife of Abram Sabuchi, a Jewess of Palermo	1.12.0 ounces		sale of 1,000 ropes for tunny to Alfonso de Girona
4.1.1474 c. nn	Luna, wife of Iosep de Castrogiovanni, a Jewess in Palermo	21 *tarì* a thousand, totalling 8.12.0 ounces	2 ounces on account	sale of 8,000 ropes for tunny to Alfonso de Girona

Date and Page	Tenant/Owner		Rent and duration	Remarks
4.1.1474 c. nn	Stella, wife of Iuda Sidoti, a Palermitan Jewess	21 *tarì*		sale of 1,000 ropes for tunny to Alfonso de Girona
17.1.1474 c. 168r	Bulfarachi, a Jew of Caltabellotta			exchange of mules with Antonio de Grimaldo
17.1.1474 c. 179r	Giovanni Solis, a Genoese merchant	4.8.0 ounces	within 2 months; paid 15.6.1474	sale of heavy linen to Nixim Catalano, a Palermitan Jew
27.1.1474 c. 180v	Giovanni de Sole, a Genoese merchant	4.7.18 ounces	within 2 months; paid 5.7.1474	sale of heavy linen to Busacca Frisisa, a Jew of Palermo
28.1.1474 c. 180v	Giovanni de Vacca, a Venetian merchant	2.15.0 ounces	weekly instalments of 3 *tarì*; paid 11.5.1475	sale of sheepskin to Salamon Sanu and Benedicto Rugila, Jews in Palermo
18.2.1474 c. nn	Iaimo de Bonfiglo, a merchant of Barcelona	2.18.0 ounces	by April; paid 1.12.1474	sale of woollen cloth to Daniel and Xibiten Xunina, Jews of Palermo

Date and Page	Tenant/Owner	Location and Description	Rent and duration	Remarks
20.8.1477 c. nn	Ubertino de Luna and Pietro Aragonese, barbers	Cassaro of Palermo, *vanella* leading to the monastery Martorana, bordering on others shops of Muxa and the tavern of Giovanni de Palermo; groundfloor shop	1 ounce a year, for 6 years	landlord: Muxa Taguil, a Palermitan Jew
20.8.1477 c. nn	Michele de Maynerio	Cassaro of Palermo, *vanella* of the dwelling of Muxa Aurifichi, a Jew, with an entrance in the *vanella* leading to the house of Bundo de Campo, bordering on the house of Sabatino de Minichi, a Jew, and next to the house of Donato Aurifichi, another Jew; row of small houses	1.15.0 ounces annually	landlord: Parisio de Homodei

29.8.1477 c. nn	Nardo de Lixandro	Cassaro of Palermo, Platea Marmorea, bordering on the shop of Geronimo Laniroxa and that of the landlord; groundfloor shop	2.18.0 ounces a year for 7 years	landlord: Xibiten Xaccarono, a Palermitan Jew
6.5.1480 c. nn	Salamon Rubeo, a Jew of Palermo	*ruga* S. Maria de La Nova, in the Conciaria quarter, bordering on the storehouse of Sadono Ubi [a Jew]; storehouse with attic	2.6.0 ounces annually, for 2 years	landlord: Lupo de Sivigla
22.8.1474 c. nn	Iosep Cathalano, a Palermitan Jew	Trapani; half a row of houses	1 ounce annually	landlords: Muxa de Contilissa, his wife and his children Merdochay, Sisa and Gaudiosa, Jews of Trapani
30.8.1474 c. nn	Lupo de Sivigla	Piano di S. Iacomo de Maritima, bordering on the salt mill of the landlords and the storehouse of Nicolò de Laudano; a storehouse *solerato*	1.15.0 ounces [annually]	landlord: Bracha Cuyno and his wife, Jews of Palermo

23.3.1474 c. 267r	Angrinixa, widow of Chayrono Cuyno and her sons Busacca and Salamon, Jews in Palermo	Cassaro of Palermo, *vanella* Li Panitichelli, under the *darbo* containing the house of Iosep Aurifichi, a Jew; a row of *solerata* houses	15 ounces	sold to Iosep Cuyno, a Palermitan Jew
20.12.1473 c. nn	Blasio de Costancio of Naples	house bordering of that of Bracha Cuyno, a Jew of Palermo	2.12.0 ounces annually for 5 years starting in January 1474	landlords: Manuel and Muxa Ubi, Jews of Palermo

Source: ASP, Not. Giacomo Comito, reg. 858

Date and Page	Debtor	Amount	Reason	Remarks
4.9.1476 c. nn	Gabriel Cathalano, a Jew of Palermo	1.15.0 ounces	unpaid loan	creditor: Xua de Missina, a Jew of Palermo; to be repaid shortly
25.9.1476 c. 230r	Michele Cathanesi		undelivered grapes	creditor: Aron Aseni, a Jew of Palermo; to be delivered during the coming month
15.11.1476 c. nn	Enrico de Bizula	1.18.0 ounces	unpaid price of deerskin	creditor: Iuda Boniosep, a Jew of Palermo; paid 22.1.1478
4.12.1476 c. 301r	Elia Ubi, a Palermitan Jew	10.3.0 ounces	unpaid debt for heavy cloth	creditor: Iosep de Benedicto, a Jew in Palermo, for Giuliano de Irnerio
4.12.1476 c. 301r	Iosep de Policio, a Jew	10 ounces	unpaid debt	creditor: Elia Ubi, a Jew of Palermo, for Giuliano de Irnerio; to be paid by May

Date and Page	Lender or Seller	Amount	Payment	Remarks
17.4.1477 c. 168r	Gabriel Cathalano, a Jew of Palermo	1 ounce	unpaid loan	creditor: Andrea Spingardo
17.7.1477 c. 214v	Elia Ubi, a Jew of Palermo	4.11.8 ounces	unpaid loan	creditor: Nicolò de Giuliano; to be paid by October
18.7.1477 c. 215v	Xibiten Xua, a Jew of Palermo	2 ounces	unpaid loan	creditor: Nicolò de Bononia; to be paid by October
15.10.1477 c. 39v	Busacca Frisisa, a Jew of Palermo	1 ounces	unpaid balance of debt	creditor: Mariano Zapparuti; to be paid in a day
3.11.1477 c. 116r	Antonio de Bonnano	2 ounces	settlement of accounts	creditor: Sabet Xunina, a Palermitan Jew; to be paid with coal
28.11.1477 c. 143r	Moyse Azeni, a Palermitan Jew	26 ounces	debt arising out of a commercial contract signed in April	creditor: Battista de Lumbardo; to be paid within 4 months
10.4.1478 c. 178v	Antonio de Girachio and Abneri Grixon, a Jew of Palermo	20 ounces	surety stood for Angelo de Girgenti	creditors: Nicola Pepi and Geronimo Bello; promise to the castellan Salvatore de Markisio to pay by 8.6.1478
30.7.1478 c. 219r	Giovanni de Pasquali	4 ounces	settlement of accounts of transaction involving sale of olive oil	creditor: Muxa Millac, a Palermitan Jew; to be paid by April
4.8.1478 c. 225r	Merdoc Frisisa, a Jew of Palermo	27 *tarì*	balance of payment for a black suit	creditor: Raynaldo de Cristofalo; to be paid in a month
Date and Page	**Lender or Seller**	**Amount**	**Payment**	**Remarks**
4.9.1476 c. nn	Antonio de Lumbardo	2.10.0 ounces	by October; paid 9.12.1477	sale of Dutch cloth to Sabeti de Benedicto, a Jew in Palermo

20.9.1476 c. 225v	Antonio Conlitiso	1.3.2 ounces	by December	sale of tow to David Benzanzan, a Jew in Palermo
1.10.1476 c. 232r	Paolo de Valditaro, a Genoese merchant	1.13.0 ounces	within 20 days	sale of cloth to Merdoc Frisisa, a Jew of Palermo
9.10.1476 c. 241r	Abram Grixon, a Palermitan Jew	1 ounce a thousand, totalling 22 ounces		sale of 22,000 ropes for tunny to Giovanni Homodei, owner of the tunny plant of Solanto
22.10.1476 c. nn	Antonio de Moltido, a Genoese merchant	3.8.6 ounces	within 6 months; paid 12.5.1478	sale of velvet to Ysrael de Danieli, a Jew of Palermo
24.10.1476 c. nn	Antonio de Moltido, a Genoese merchant	3.6.0 ounces	monthly instalmenst for 4 months; paid 14.5.1477	sale of 2 kantars of *roxuni* to Merdoc Russo, a Jew of Termini
24.10.1476 c. nn	Muxa Leone, a Jew of Palermo	78.22.15 ounces	within a year	sale of 50 kantars of sugar to Paolo de Salvatu, a Genoese merchant
25.10.1476 c. nn	Andrea de Moltido, a Genoese merchant	17.29.0 ounces	within 5 months; paid 4.8.1477	sale of cloth to Muxa Taguil, a Palermitan Jew
15.11.1476 c. nn	Andrea de Moltido, a Genoese merchant	5.17.0 ounces	within 8 months	sale of a bale of paper *ad opus scribendi* to Merdochay Sufi, a Jew of Termini
20.11.1476 c. nn	Abram Russo, a Palermitan Jew	1 ounce a thousand		sale of 10,000 ropes for tunny to Antonio Blundo, owner of the tunny plant at Castellammare del Golfo

28.11.1476 c. nn	Abramellu Xunina, a Jew of Palermo	1.2.0 ounces	10 *tarì* and a piece of velvet on account	sale of a mule to Muxa Millac, his fellow Jew
4.12.1476 c. nn	*Raysi* Chicco Lu Salatu and *Raysi* Giovanni Lu Pagleru of Trapani	19 *tarì* a kantar for tunny and 10 *tarì* a kantar for Albacore		sale of all the fish produced by the vendors in their tunny plant during the present season to Salamon Russo, a Palermitan Jew
4.12.1476 c. 302r	Natale de Costanzu	6.20.0 ounces	half in 4 months and half in 8 months; paid 15.1.1478	sale of cloth to Ysac Commachino and Xibiten Xunina, Jews in Palermo
4.12.1476 c. 121r	Federico Cavalariu of Cefalù	3.10 *tarì* a sack	1.25.0 worth of French iron on account, balance on delivery	sale of 20 sacks of coal to Busacca de Tripuli, a Palermitan Jew
30.12.1476 c. nn	Francesco de Frisco	19.23.0 ounces	within 6 months; paid 9.10.1477	sale of Genoese cloth to Robino Xamueli, a Jew of Palermo
17.4.1477 c. 166v	Antonio de Ruzolono	market price	3.15.0 ounces on account, balance on delivery	sale of 15 *salme* of wheat to Muxa Millac, a Palermitan Jew
17.4.1477 c. 167r	Giovanni Pasquali and Nicolò La Chimia	6 *tarì* a *salma*, totalling 2.12.0 ounces	partly with half a quintal of grapes; paid 22.8.1478	sale of 12 *salme* of barley to Muxa Millac, a Palermitan Jew
17.4.1477 c. 167v	Giovanni Pasquali	1 ounce		sale of 2 *salme* of wheat to Muxa Millac, a Palermitan Jew
28.4.1477 c. 172r	Andrea de Moltido, a Genoese merchant	5 ounces	within 6 months; paid. 4.5.1478	sale of canvas to Azara Taguil, a Palermitan Jew
22.5.1477 c. 196v	Muxa Millac, a Jew of Palermo	2.10.0 ounces	by 15.7	sale of a cask of wine to Giovanni Pasquali

9.7.1477 c.199v	Francesco de Flore	20 *tarì* a kantar, totalling 4.20.0 ounces	by 15.11	sale of 7 kantars of olive oil to Iacob Cuyno, a Jew of Palermo
15.7.1477 c. 204r	Andrea de Moltido	7.12.0 ounces	within 6 months	sale of goods to Siminto de Policio, a Jew in Palermo
16.7.1477 c. 204v	Andrea de Moltido, a Genoese merchant	5.6.5 ounces	2 instalments in 3 and 6 months	sale of canvas to Fraym Xiffuni, a Jew of Palermo
1.8.1477 c. 252r	Giovanni Puyades, *bombarderius*	17.10 *tarì*	during current month	sale of tunny to Nixim Rustico, a Jew in Palermo
5.8.1477 c. 258v	Antonio de Carzona of Corleone	balance of 50 ounces		sale of cereals to Chayrono Xunina, a Jew of Palermo
28.8.1477 c. 274r	Muxa Millac, a Jew of Palermo	9.3.0 ounces	within 3 months	sale of assorted merchandise to Nixim Minachem, a Jew in Palermo
5.9.1477 c. 7v	Busacca Frisisa, a Jew of Palermo	28 *tarì* a thousand heavy ropes and 26 *tarì* a thousand light ones, totalling 18.9.0 ounces	9.4.0 ounces during the current month, balance at the *tagliata* of the tunny plant; paid 10.4.1478	sale of 14,000 heavy ropes for tunny and 6,000 light ones to Lupo de Sivigla
11.9.1477 c. 13r	Iacobo de Banni	2 ounces the quintal	by Christmas; paid 8.7.1478	sale of 2 quintals of grapes of the new vintage to Muxa and Manuel Verru, Jews of Palermo
18.9.1477 c. 22v	Muxa Millac, a Palermitan Jew	4 ounces	half by Christmas and half by May	sale of grapes to Michele Cathanisi
1.10.1477 c. 26r	Paolo Lu Lisu of Messina	20 *tarì* a kantar	20 *tarì* on account, balance on delivery	sale of 4 kantars and 8 *cafisi* of olive oil to Muxa Millac, a Palermitan Jew

7.10.1477 c. 30v	David Azaruti, a Jew of Palermo	15 ounces	3 ounces on account	sale of 18,000 heavy ropes for tunny and 9,000 light ones to Lupo de Sivigla
14.10.1477 c. 38r	Vinichio de Taxu of Palermo	18 ounces	2 ounces on account, balance on delivery	sale of 50 kantars of tunny to Donato Spagnolo and Vita Aurifichi, Palermitan Jews
22.10.1477 c. 43r	Muxa Xunina, a Palermitan Jew	2.13.10 ounces	within a month	sale of tunny to Manuel Iagnotto of Corleone
22.10.1477 c. 46r	Raymondo Bellomo	10.10.0 ounces	by May; paid 8.2.1480	sale of 12 *salme* of wheat to Manuel and Muxa Verru, Jews in Palermo
22.10.1477 c. 47r	Manuel and Muxa Ubi, Jews of Palermo	10 ounces		sale of 10½ *salme* of wheat to Baldassare de Sancto Iaimo
27.10.1477 c. 104r	Paolo Valdina, a Genoese merchant	1.2.6 ounces	within 2 months	sale of cloth to Iosep de Padua, a Palermitan Jew
30.10.1477 c. 104v	Enrico Demme of Monreale	15 *grana* a *salma*	8 *tarì* on account	sale of 12 *salme* of coal to Xamuel Russo, a Jew of Palermo
19.11.1477 c. 130r	the brothers Iacobo and Nicola de Lu Ficu	2.20.0 ounces a quintal	2 ounces on account, balance in a month	sale of grapes to Abneri Grixon, a Palermitan Jew
24.11.1477 c. 132r	Giovanni Vennuchi	1.1.0 ounces a quintal		sale of grapes to Ysaia Romano and Xibiten Xunina, Jews of Palermo
20.2.1478 c. 148v	Muxa Millac, a Jew in Palermo	1.12.0 ounces	within 2 months	sale of olive oil to Pietro de Nastasio
23.2.1478 c. 148v	Geremia Cuyno, a Jew of Palermo	3 ounces		sale of tunny to Giovanni Stratella

23.2.1478 c. 150v	Paolo Valdaura, a Genoese merchant	10.27.0 ounces	in instalments; paid 28.11.1478	sale of assorted merchandise to Braxa and Minto de Liucio, Jews of Palermo
25.2.1478 c. 152r	Salamon Russo, a Palermitan Jew	18 *tarì* a kantar	on delivery	sale of 50 kantars of *caciocavallo* to Tommaso Mallo
3.3.1478 c. 153v	Agostino de Bonivento	1.17.0 ounces	within 3 months; paid 24.11.1478	sale of heavy cloth to Benedetto de Ray and Xibiten de Rabbi Iacob, Jews of Palermo
10.3.1478 c. 155v	Paolo Valdaura, a Genoese merchant	2.12.0 ounces	by 25.3; paid 26.9.1478	sale of gold wire to Benedetto de Ray and Xibiten de Rabbi Iacob, Jews of Palermo
17.3.1478 c. 157v	Rachile Cathanisi	1.18.0 ounces	at vintage time	sale of grapes to Muxa Millac, a Palermitan Jew
1.4.1478 c. 167v	Paolo Lu Loscu	20 *tarì* a kantar, totalling 3.10.0 ounces	by 15.11	sale of 5 kantars of olive oil to Muxa Millac, a Palermitan Jew
1.4.1478 c. 168r	Paolo Valdaura, a Genoese merchant	8 ounces	within 2 months; paid 23.11.1478	sale of gold wire to Bracha de Liucio, a Jew of Palermo
13.4.1478 c. 180r	Paolo Valdaura, a Genoese merchant	25.16.0 ounces	within 6 months; 1.12.1478	sale of 18 bales of paper to Salamon de Xeni, a Palermitan Jew
15.4.1478 c. 183v	Paolo Valdaura, a Genoese merchant	22.29.13 ounces	within a year; paid 27.7.1479	sale of velvet to Salamon de Xeni, a Palermitan Jew
20.4.1478 c. 186r	Tommaso Mallo, a Catalan merchant	7 ounces	by November; paid 3.12.1479	sale of 2 embroidered white curtains to Iosep de Padua, a Jew of Palermo

24.4.1478 c. 189v	Muxa Millac, a Palermitan Jew	1.18.0 ounces	at vintage time	sale of grapes to Pietro de Panictera
5.5.1478 c. 196r	Andrea de Moltido, a Genoese merchant	5.2.6 ounces	within 4 months	sale of a bale of canvas to Muxa Taguil, a Jew of Palermo
15.7.1478 c. 210v	Andrea de Moltido, a Genoese merchant	2.10.8 ounces	within 5 months; paid 15.11479	sale of assorted goods to Michilono Xunina, a Jew of Palermo
16.7.1478 c. 211r	Raynaldo de Cristofaro	1.10.0 ounces	within 4 months	sale of velvet to Muxa de Medico, a Jew in Palermo
17.7.1478 c. 214r	Andrea de Moltido, a Genoese merchant	6.16.2 ounces	within 4 months; paid 3.3.1479	sale of heavy cloth to Muxa Taguil, a Jew of Palermo
20.7.1478 c. 215r	Damiano Spinula, a Genoese merchant	1.25.10 ounces	by January	sale of linen to Manuel Binna, Jew of Palermo
7.8.1478 c. 227r	Stella, wife of Merdoc Rugila, a Jewess of Palermo	13 *tarì* a thousand		sale of 1,500 ropes for tunny to Lupo de Sivigla
7.8.1478 c. 228v	Cara de Minichi, a Jewess of Palermo	22 *tarì* a thousand	8 *tarì* on account	sale of 2,000 ropes for tunny to Lupo de Sivigla
7.8.1478 c. 228v	Luna, sister of Cara de Minichi, a Jewess of Palermo	22 *tarì* a thousand		sale of 2,000 ropes for tunny to Lupo de Sivigla
7.8.1478 c. 229r	Fadale, wife of Ysac de Minichi, a Jewess of Palermo	22 *tarì* a thousand		sale of 1,000 ropes for tunny to Lupo de Sivigla

Date and Page		Amount		Remarks
7.8.1478 c. 229v	Millecta, daughter of Stella de Sancto Marco, a Jewess in Palermo	22 *tarì* a thousand		sale of 1,000 ropes for tunny to Lupo de Sivigla
7.8.1478 c. 234v	Muxa de Messina, a Palermitan Jew	11 *tarì*		sale of 500 ropes for tunny to Lupo de Sivigla
7.8.1478 c. 237r	David de Messina, a Jew of Palermo	11 *tarì*		sale of 500 ropes for tunny to Lupo de Sivigla

Date and Page	Tenant	Location and Description	Rent and Duration	Remarks
5.7.1481 c. 222r	Muxa Millac, a Palermitan Jew	Cassaro of Palermo, in the *darbo* called Lu Biffardo, bordering on the property of Sidoti Suffi, a Jew; a row of *solerata* houses	3 ounces for 2 years	landlady: Amor, widow of Nixim Grixon, a Palermitan Jewess

Source: ASP, Not. Giacomo Comito, reg. 859

Date and Page	Debtor	Amount	Reason	Remarks
2.10.1479 c. 19v	Aron de Xirelli, a Palermitan Jew	15 *tarì*	unpaid balance of loan	creditor: Dionisio Saduna, a merchant of Barcelona; to be paid within 20 days
12.10.1480 c. 29r	Chicco de Xirello	1.18.10 ounces	balance of unpaid debt for goods	creditor: Muxa Millac, a Palermitan Jew; to be paid in instalments

9.10.1480 c. 49v	Sadono Sala, a Jew of Trapani	6 ounces	unpaid debt	creditor: Ysac Sala, debtor's brother; to be paid by 15.8; paid 2.1.1482
15.10.1480 c. 61v	Salamon Cuyno, a Jew of Palermo	1 ounce	unpaid debt arising out of commercial transaction	creditor: Nicolino Spinola, a Genoese merchant; to be paid within a month
23.10.1480 c. 76r	Salamon Cuyno, a Jew in Palermo	5 ounces	unpaid loan	creditor: Francesco Aglata; to be paid within 2 months; paid 28.11.1481
3.12.1480 c. 121v	Iosep de Padua, a Jewish inhabitant of Palermo	1 ounce	guarantee in favour of Mario Mallo, a Genoese merchant	creditor: Salamon Cuyno, a Palermitan Jew; to be paid within 3 months
23.12.1480 c. 142r	Muxa Taguil, a Jew of Palermo	40 ounces	return of advance	creditor: Andrea de Moltido, a Genoese merchant
25.1.1481 c. 167v	Minto de Liucio, a Jew of Palermo	5 ounces	balance of debt for business transaction	creditor: Iacob Baldinotte, cashier of the bank Li Maystri
24.2.1481 c. 187v	Aron Aseni, a Jew of Palermo		balance of debt for business transaction	creditor: Francesco Farfagla; paid

Date and Page	**Lender or Seller**	**Amount**	**Payment**	**Remarks**
24.9.1479 c. 2r	Giovanni de Castelli	27.27.0 ounces	by February; paid 24.4.1484 [!]	sale of cloth to Fortunato de Anello, a Jew of Alcamo
26.9.1479 c. 3v	Antonio de Septimo	26.6.0 ounces	by June	sale of assorted merchandise to Salamon Maltisi, a Jew of Palermo
27.9.1479 c. 6v	Antonio de Septimo	9.23.0 ounces	within 2 months; paid 9.11.1479	sale of cloth to Salamon Maltisi, a Jew of Palermo

1.10.1479 c. 17v	Antonio de Septimo	27 ounces	shortly	loan to Chayrono de Xaulo, a Jew of Mazara; guarantor: his brother Iosep
2.10.1479 c. 21r	Pino de Bramello	6.10.0 ounces	2 instalments within 2 and 4 months	sale of olive oil to Elia de Nixim, a Jew in Palermo
3.10.1479 c. 21v	Giaimo de Mazzaruli	30.12.0 ounces	within 9 months	sale of cloth to David Magaseni, a Jew of Palermo
3.10.1479 c. 22r	Giuliano Iacobo de Perconti	27.13.5 ounces	by July	sale of some bales of paper for writing and for scrap (*ad usum scribendi et straczandi*) to Salamone Attaro, a Jew
17.10.1479 c. 36r	Antonio de Septimo	9.18.0 ounces	within 3 months	sale of cloth to Graciano Timpariano and Salamon Benassay, Jews in Palermo
17.10.1479 c. 37v	Antonio Aglata	18.29.0 ounces	within 6 months; paid 12.6.1484 [!]	sale of cloth to Elia Cuyno, a Palermitan Jew
18.10.1479 c. 40r	Gabriele de Igillo, a Majorcan merchant	44.21.0 ounces	within 4 months; paid 22.10.1484	sale of cloth to Elia Cuyno, a Palermitan Jew
6.9.1480 c. 3v	Bartholomeo Virgillito	9 ounces	2 ounces on account, balance on delivery	sale of half a quintal of grapes to Sabet Millac, a Jew in Palermo
12.9.1480 c. 3v	Bartholomeo Caraffa and Antonio Lu Giumpu of Corleone	12 ounces		sale of all the cheese produced by the vendors' herd during the current season to Xibiten Gibell, a Jew in Palermo
11.10.1480 c. 27v	Giovanni Marino	1.18.0 ounces	1 ounce on account, balance on delivery	sale of grapes to Muxa Millac, a Jew in Palermo

12.10.1480 c. 28r	Tommasino Oliva, a Genoese merchant	24 ounces	2 instalments in a month and in 2 months; paid 4.4.1481	sale of cloth to Aron Taguil, a Jew of Palermo
13.10.1480 c. 30r	Tommaso Mallo, a Catalan merchant	2.15.10 ounces	within 6 months	sale of cloth to David Spagnolo, a Jewish tailor of Seville in Palermo
13.10.1480 c. 30v	Muxa Millac, a Jew of Palermo	6.15.0 ounces	within 6 months	sale of cloth to Azara Taguili, a Jew of Palermo
13.10.1480 c. 30v	Muxa Millac, a Jew of Palermo	3.24.0 ounces	within 2 months	sale of assorted merchandise to Azara Taguili, a Jew of Palermo
15.10.1480 c. 34r	Michele de Penichello	7 ounces	4 ounces on account; balance in a month	sale of half a quintal of grapes to Muxa Millac, a Palermitan Jew
19.10.1480 c. 34v	Lorenzo de Nazario	1 ounce		sale of a quintal of grapes to Muxa Millac, a Palermitan Jew
16.10.1480 c. 65r	Cola and Giovanni Xilla of Polizzi	7 *tarì* a kantar	1 ounce on account	sale of 36 kantars of *filini*[!] *salatis* to Sadono Ubi, a Jew of Palermo
22.10.1480 c. 75r	Abram Bass, a Palermitan Jew	80 ouncs	in instalments	sale of cloth to Iacobo de Xixo
25.10.1480 c. 83r	Ubertino de Guchardino	21 *tarì*	paid	sale of grapes to Muxa Millac, a Jew in Palermo
30.10.1480 c. 91v	Poldo Quartarocta of Naro	1 *tarì* a *salma*	15 *tarì* on account	sale of 30 *salme* of Cammarata salt to Iuda de Tripuli, a Jew of Palermo
8.11.1480 c. 95r	Bernardo de Bellina	1.18.0 ounces	paid	sale of a quintal of grapes to Muxa Millac, a Jew of Palermo

3.12.1480 c. 121r	Tommaso Oliva, a Genoese merchant	2.5.0 ounces	within 3 months; paid 18.7.1481	sale of paper to Busacca Frisisa, a Jew of Palermo
9.12.1480 c. 127r	Lauro de Nanzano and Giulio Bayamonte	1.12.0 ounces for the grapes	12 *tarì* on account, balance by 15.6	sale of a quintal of grapes and a *salma* of barley to Muxa Millac, a Jew of Palermo
10.12.1480 c. 128r	Filippo de Trapano alias de Bonura	*calabrese* grapes for 2 ounces a quintal, *guarnaccio* and local grapes for 1.18.0 ounces a quintal	9 ounces on account; balance at vintage time	sale of 1 quintal of red *calabrese* grapes, 2 quintals of *guarnaccia* grapes and 6 quintals of local ones to Muxa Millac, a Jew of Palermo
22.12.1480 c. 136v	Bartholomeo Andrea, a Catalan	exchange for corals and a white bedspread		sale of a mule with saddle and harness to Xamuel Cuyno, a Palermitan Jew
18.1.1481 c. 158v	Pietro de Vinaldes	97.6.7 ounces	within a year	sale of silk and other fabrics to Benedetto Conti, a Jew of Palermo
21.1.1481 c. 159v	Pietro La Penictera	2.12.0 ounces	some goods from the purchaser's shop on account	sale of 1½ quintals of grapes to Muxa Millac, a Jew of Palermo
24.1.1481 c. 164r	Cipriano de Giliberto, a Genoese merchant	12 ounces	within 6 months	sale of bales of paper to Gabriel Vignuni, a Palermitan Jew
26.1.1481 c. 167v	Tommaso de Oliveri, a Genoese merchant	7.2.0 ounces	monthly instalments of 9 *tarì*	sale of textiles and other goods to Ysach de Virgnono, a Jew of Palermo
26.1.1481 c. 169r	Tommaso Mallo	7.21.0 ounces	within a month	sale of Dutch fabric to Minto de Liucio and Crixi de Canet, Jews in Palermo

26.1.1481 c. 169v	Muxa Millac, a Palermitan Jew	3 ounces	by February; paid 24.10.1481	sale of a beast of burden to Michele de Panichello
23.2.1481 c. 187r	Lupo de Sivigla	2 ounces	within a month	sale of 4 barrels of salted albacore to Abram de Girachio and Chicono de Tripuli, Jews of Palermo
24.2.1481 c. 187v	Michele de Penichello	3 ounces	30 *quartare* of wine in casks on account	sale of grapes to Muxa Millac, a Palermitan Jew
28.2.1481 c. 191v	Tommaso Oliva, a Genoese merchant	1.10.0 ounces	within 3 months; paid 1.6.1481	sale of cloth to Bulchayra de Girachio, a Jew of Palermo
2.3.1481 c. 195r	Sabet Ramuxi, a Jew of Giuliana	5.10.0 ounces	paid	sale of 2 mules to Giovanni de Giuramendu
15.3.1481 c. 201r	Lupo de Sivigla	5.22.0 ounces	by April; paid 7.7.1481	sale of salted albacore in barrels to Busacca Frisisa, a Jew of Palermo
29.3.1481 c. 206r	Richardo de Pedivillano	current price	1 ounce on account	sale of 2 *salme* of wheat and 3 of barley to Xibiten Gibey, a Jew in Palermo
5.4.1481 c. 211r	Giovanni Magirono and Bartholomeo de La Rocca	1.12.0 ounces	13 *tarì* on account, balance at vintage time	sale of a quintal of grapes to Muxa Millac, a Palermitan Jew
14.4.1481 c. 215r	Masio Mallo	8.7.4 ounces	by June; paid 14.9.1481	sale of Dutch fabric to Xibiten Soffer, a Jew of Palermo
2.6.1481 c. 243r	Paolo de Valdita, a Pisan merchant	2.12.15 ounces	by July	sale of assorted merchandise to Donato de Iamicto, a Jew in Palermo
7.3.1481 c. 252r	Arnaldo de Partis, a merchant of Barcelona	3.22.10 ounces	within 5 months	sale of cloth to Sabeti Sala, a Jew of Trapani

7.3.1481 c. 252v	Arnaldo de Partis	36.3.10 ounces	within 3 months	sale of embroidered cloth to Muxa Chamuti, a Jew of Palermo
23.6.1481 c. 255v	Tommasino de Oliverio, a Genoese merchant	4.14.0 ounces	within 4 months; paid 22.1.1482	sale of cloth to Elia Ubi, a Palermitan Jew
11.7.1481 c. 269v	Iaimo Bonfiglo, a Catalan merchant	5.10.0 ounces	monthly instalments of 1 ounce	sale of cloth to Iacob de Liucio, a Jew of Palermo
26.7.1481 c. 273r	Muxa Millac, a Palermitan Jew, acting also for Arono Azeni, his Jewish fellow citizen	10 *tarì* a *salma*	within 8 months	sale of 100 *salme* of wheat to Mariano Zapparuti
1.8.1481 c. 280v	Tommasino de Oliverio, a Genoese merchant	4.15.0 ounces	within 6 months; paid 8.8.1482	sale of *filorum riordorum* [!] to Iosep de Policio
27.3.1481 c. 158r	Giovanni Partis *bombardero*	2.22.0 ounces	monthly instalments of 14 *tarì* starting Easter	sale of iron to Mussuto Balam, a Jew of Trapani
28.3.1481 c. 159r	Bartholomeo Cannata and Giovanni Magaseni	9.24.0 ounces	by December	sale of 7 quintals of grapes to Muxa Millac, a Palermitan Jew
28.3.1481 c. 159v	Giovanni Partis *bombardero*	4.25.13 ounces	within 3 months; paid 16.7.1481	sale of iron to Abram de Minichi, a Jew in Palermo
2.4.1481 c. 161r	Martino Lamparolis, a Genoese merchant	2.28.0 ounces	within 5 months; paid 3.6.1482	sale of heavy cloth to Muxa Xeni, a Jew of Palermo

9.4.1481 c. 166r	Adamo Contirione, a Genoese merchant	5.18.0 ounces	half within 2 months, balance within 4 months	sale of silk to the brothers Muxa and Elia Xunina, Palermitan Jews
16.4.1481 c. 172r	Adamo Contirione, a Genoese merchant	11.6.0 ounces	half within 3 months and half within 6	sale of heavy cloth and linen to Busacca Frisisa, a Palermitan Jew
30.4.1481 c. 176r	Giacomo Rizzo, a Genoese merchant	1.12.10 ounces	within 2 months	sale of iron to Crixi de Canet and his son Donato, Palermitan Jews
9.5.1481 c. 179r	Abram Rustico, a Jew of Palermo	10 *tarì* a barrel	1 ounce on account, balance by 11.6.1482	sale of 60 barrels of salted tunny and albacore to Andrea de Morano of Naples
15.5.1481 c. 185r	Giovanni Partis *bombardero* of Palermo	23 *tarì*	by June	sale of iron to Nixim Sala, a Jew of Palermo
25.5.1481 c. 191r	Abram Rustico, a Palermitan Jew	30 ounces	on delivery; paid 12.8.1481	sale of salted tunny and albacore to Andrea de Morano of Naples
1.6.1481 c. 195r	Giovanni Partis *bombardero* of Palermo	1.10.0 ounces	by July; paid 14.7.1481	sale of iron to Abram Cuyno, a Jew of Palermo
19.6.1481 c. 208r	Giovanni Partis *bombardero* of Palermo	1.0 ounces	within 2 months; paid 9.9.1481	sale of iron to Brachono Fitira, a Jew in Palermo
11.7.1481 c. 227r	Aron Azeni, a Jew of Palermo	21 ounces	within 45 days	sale of 25 barrels of salted tunny to Giovanni de Sparti
16.7.1481 c. 237r	Giovanni Partis *bombardero* of Palermo	2.12. ounces	by September; paid 9.4.1482	sale of iron to Abram de Minichi and Muxa Levi, Jews in Palermo

17.7.1481 c. 242r	Giovanni Partis *bombardero* of Palermo	3.22.0 ounces	within 3 months	sale of iron to Busacca Aurifichi, a Jew of Alcamo; Abram de Minichi, a Jew, acted as guarantor
7.8.1481 246v	Iacobo and Agostino de Benedicto	4.2.0 ounces	within 4 months	sale of harness and reins to Busacca Frisisa, a Palermitan Jew
27.8.1481 c. 259r	Agostino and Iacobo de Benedicto	3.10.12 ounces	within 3 months	sale of assorted goods to David Minzil, a Palermitan Jew

Date and Page	Tenant	Location and Description	Rent and Duration	Remarks
5.7.1481 c. 222r	Muxa Millac, a Palermitan Jew	Cassaro, *darbo* Lu Biffardo, bordering on on the house of Sidoti Suffi; row of *solerata* houses	2 years for 3 ounces annually	landlord: Amor Grixon, widow of Nixim Grixon, a Jewess of Palermo

Source: ASP, Not. Giacomo Comito, reg. 860

Date and Page	Debtor	Amount	Reason	Remarks
29.11.1481 c. 72r	Sabet Millac, a Palermitan Jew, acting for Nicolò de Restivo of Corleone	2 ounces	debt of 7 ounces to Azara Taguil arising out of a business transaction	balance within a month; paid 1.4.1482
2.4.1482 c. 135v	Muxa, son of the late Simone Ysac, a Jew in Palermo	2.12.0 ounces	unpaid loan made by Giaimo Terrazu	by 20th of current month; paid 6.8.1484

1.6.1482 c. 181r	Muxa Levi, a Jew of Sardinia		unpaid debt to Adamo Portinari, a Genoese merchant	paid
7.6.1482 c. 187r	Abram Frisisa, a Jew in Palermo	2.14.0 ounces	unpaid balance of purchase price for assorted goods owed Martino de Riparoli, a Genoese merchant	monthly instalments of 6 *tarì*
[1482] c. 53r	Salamon de Sancto Marco, a Palermitan Jew, also on behalf of his wife Graciosa, at the request of Asisa, wife of Pasquale Sacerdoto, Jews		delivery of rope for tunny	in weekly instalments
5.7.1482 c. 63r	Mario Mori	20 *tarì*	unpaid rent for a house let by Salamon Millac, a Palermitan Jew	by August
7.8.1482 c. 72v	Manfrido de La Muta, a convert	1.3.0 ounces	undelivered 3 *salme* of wheat to Sabet Calabrisi, a Palermitan Jew	by 12 September
7.1.1483 c. 64v	Crispo de Rundinella of Monreale		undelivered half a kantar of olive oil purchased by Chanino Amar, a Jew of Palermo	2 *cafisi* a month
10.7.1483 c. 164v	Busacca Chandarello, a Jew of Palermo	5.15.0 ounces	unpaid contractual debt to Francesco de Li Parti, a Genoese merchant	by August

Date and Page	Lender or Seller	Amount	Payment	Remarks
13.2.1483 c. 83v	Nicolò de La Chimia		a quintal of grapes, balance of price for wine sold by Muxa Millac, a Jew in Palermo	at next vintage time
30.10.1483 c. 35v	Lorenzo de Namizone	2.12.0 ounces	unpaid balance of purchase price for assorted goods	grapes for 1.18.0 ounces and wheat for the balance
28.9.1481 c. 25v	Giovanni Partis	4.6.0 ounces	by December	sale of French iron to Xibiten Tranu, a Jew in Palermo
8.10.1481 c. 40v	Giovanni de Albara, a Genoese merchant	5.6.10 ounces	within 4 months	sale of cloth to Abram Xamuel, a Jew in Palermo
12.10.1481 c. 43r	Muxa Pulisi, a Palermitan Jew	2 ounces	paid	sale of 3 *kantars* of olive oil to Rinaldo Callari
8.11.1481 c. 52r	Lorenzo de Ranzano		by coming vintage time	sale of grapes to Muxa Millac, a Jew of Palermo
28.11.1481 c. 70r	Giovanni Partis	3.6.10 ounces	by 15.2.1482	sale of iron to Muxa Lu Presti, a Palermitan Jew; guarantor: Xamuel Actuni, his Jewish fellow citizen
5.12.1481 c. 79r	Sabet Millac, a Palermitan Jew	25 *tarì* a *kantar*, totalling 3.10.0 ounces	2.20.0 ounces on account, balance on delivery	sale of 4 *kantars* of olive oil to Martino de Viro
7.2.1482 c. 103v	Ambrogio de Iohanne	1.12.0 ounces the quintal	1.18.0 ounces on account paid with various articles including a napkin and a skirt, balance at vintage time	sale of 1.5 quintals of grapes to Muxa Millac, a Palermitan Jew

[.].3.1482 c. 117r	Guglielmo de Negronis, a Genoese merchant	6 ounces	monthly instalments of 1 ounce	sale of albacore (*albaxorum*) to Xamuel de Medico and Aron Aurifichi, Jews of Palermo
20.3.1482 c. 124v	Bartholomeo Spinula, a Genoese merchant	16.8.0 ounces	monthly instalments of 2 ounces	sale of wool to Xibiten Tranu and Nixim Rustico, Palermitan Jews
27.3.1482 c. 130r	Giovanni Partis	2.6.0 ounces	by May; paid 1.9.1482	sale of iron to Brachono Fitira, a Jew of Palermo
12.4.1482 c. 140v	Bartholomeo Spinula, a Genoese merchant	50.12.0 ounces	on request; paid 5.5.1483	sale of iron to Gallufo Zel, a Jewish ironmonger/smith of Palermo
15.4.1482 c. 143v	Don Antonio de la Castellana on behalf of the countess de Infuxa in Castellammare	20 *tarì*	monthly instalments of 3 *tarì*	sale of beast of burden to Xibiten Sivena [a Jew in Palermo]
16.4.1482 c. 145v	Giovanni Prades	2.27.13 ounces	within 3 months	sale of iron to Merdoc Fadali, a Palermitan Jew
2.5.1482 c. 158r	Giovanni Sinordus, a clergyman	4 ounces	within 8 months	sale of 65 *kantars* of olive oil to Iosep de Policio, a Jew in Palermo
6.5.1482 c. 159r	Antonio de Riparola, a Genoese merchant	6.2.0 ounces	weekly instalments of 8 *tarì*	sale of heavy cloth to Busacca and Leone Frisisa, Jewish brothers in Palermo
7.6.1482 c. 185r	Giovanni Tarantino	1.18.0 ounces	at vintage time	sale of 1.5 quintals of grapes to Gallufo Levi, a Palermitan Jew

7.6.1482 c. 186v	Enrico de la Francesca, a Pisan	50 ounces	within 8 months	sale of assorted goods including textiles to Muxa de Missina, a Jew of Castellammare del Golfo
18.6.1482 c. 193r	Martino de Riparolo	1.27.7 ounces	monthly instalments of 10 *tarì*	sale of cloth to Leone and Muxa Anaffi, Jews of Palermo
16.7.1482 c. 200v	Tommaso Mallo	31 ounces	within 6 months; paid 30.10.1483	sale of cloth to Muxa Taguil and Elia Ubi, Palermitan Jews
16.7.1482 c. 201r	Bartholomeo Spinula, a Genoese merchant	4.4.0 ounces	by October; paid 11.1.1483	sale of iron to David Lu Presti, a Jew in Palermo
19.8.1482 c. 215r	Sallimbeni de Pace and Xamuele Azeni, a Palermitan Jew	2 ounces a cartload	with grapes at next vintage time	sale of 10 cartloads of cane from Xamuele's plantation to Giovanni de Partis
[1482] c. 47r	Nicolò Picara	23 *tarì*		sale of half a quintal of grapes to Manuel de Termini, a Jew of Palermo
[1482] c. 51v	Antonio de Maxali, royal *porterio*	3 ounces	1 ounce on account; balance later	sale of a mule to Xibiten Tranu, a Palermitan Jew
[1482] c. 52r	Tobia de Liucio, a Jew in Palermo	12 *tarì*	paid	sale of half a *kantar* of olive oil to Ayrono Assuni, a Palermitan Jew
9.7.1482 c. 65v	Luna, wife of Xanino Fusuturri, and Rayla, wife of Natale de Tripuli, Palermitan Jewesses	10 *tarì* the bundle	12 *tarì* on account	sale of 5,000 ropes for tunny to Iuda de Minichi, a Jew in Palermo

10.7.1482 c. 66r	Muxa Mizoc, a Jew in Palermo	11 *tarì*		sale of *disa* rope for tunny to Iuda de Minichi, a Palermitan Jew
10.7.1482 c. 67r	Contissa, wife of Simaeli Tudisco, a Jewess of Palermo	10 *tarì* a thousand		sale of rope for tunny to Iuda de Minichi, a Jew in Palermo
17.7.1482 c. 69r	Thomeo de Homodei	2.3.10 ounces	by September; paid 25.10.1482	sale of a new doublet (*dublecti*) and some napkins to Graciano de Benedicto, a Jew of Palermo
7.8.1482 c. 73r	Iosep Talo, a Jew of Palermo	1.6.0 ounces	monthly instalments of 5 *tarì*	sale of Barcelona cloth to Francesco de Visi of Calabria and Iacobo de Maxuri of Cefalù
[1]5.8.1482 c. 73v	Iacob Levi and his wife Desiata, Jews of Palermo	20 *tarì* a thousand, totalling 4 ounces	1 ounce on account with barrels of tunny	sale of 6,000 ropes for tunny to Iuda de Minichi, a Jew in Palermo
22.8.1482 c. 77v	Merdoc Maymuni and his wife Luna, Palermitan Jews	20 *tarì* a thousand, totalling 2 ounces	24 *tarì* on account	sale of 3,000 ropes for tunny to Iuda de Minichi, a Jew of Palermo
25.8.1482 c. 79r	Tuta, widow of Merdoc Millac, a Palermitan Jewess	20 *tarì* a thousand	15 *tarì* on account, balance on delivery	sale of 6,000 ropes for tunny to Aloisio de Girono
25.8.1482 c. 80r	Vita and Rosa de Tripuli, Jews of Palermo	20 *tarì* a thousand	15 *tarì* on account	sale of 1,000 ropes for tunny to Aloisio de Girono

23.8.1482 c. 80r	Abram Todaroczu Spagnolu and his wife Vintura. Jews of Palermo	20 *tarì* a thousand	15 *tarì* on account	sale of 1,000 ropes for tunny to Aloisio de Girono
23.8.1482 c. 81r	Xibiten Xunina and his wife Xanna, Palermitan Jews	20 *tarì* a thousand		sale of 1,000 ropes for tunny to Aloisio de Girono
23.8.1482 c. 82v	Ricca, widow of Salamon de Messana, a Jewess in Palermo	20 *tarì* a thousand, totalling 4 ounces	22 *tarì* on account	sale of 6,000 ropes for tunny to Aloisio de Girono
28.8.1482 c. 84r	Humana, wife of Iuda Provinzano, a Jewess in Palermo	20 *tarì* a thousand, totalling 1.10.0 ounces	22.10 *tarì* on account	sale of 2,000 ropes for tunny to Aloisio de Girono
28.8.1482 c. 84v	Rayla, widow of Nixim Migluni, a Jewess of Palermo	20 *tarì* a thousand	10 *tarì* on account	sale of 2,000 ropes for tunny to Aloisio de Girono
28.8.1482 c. 85r	Muxa Romano and his wife Rosa, Palermitan Jews	20 *tarì* a thousand	6.10 *tarì* on account	sale of 2,000 ropes for tunny to Aloisio de Girono
7.8.1482 c. [1r]	Manfrido La Muta, a convert	11 *tarì* a *salma*	monthly instalments of 6 *tarì*	sale of 3 *salme* of wheat to Sabet Calabrisi, a Palermitan Jew
16.10.1482 c. 29v	Xibiten de Minichi and Salamon Naguay, Jew of Palermo	50 ounces	3 ounces of account	sale of merchandise to Tommaso Mallo, a merchant

16.10.1482 c. 30r	Martino de Reparola (Ripasola)	5.18.0 ounces	weekly instalments of 2 *tarì*	sale of linen cloth to Busacca Frisisa and his son Salamon, Jews of Palermo
17.10.1482 c. 30v	Tommaso Mallo, a Catalan merchant	2.15.0 ounces	within 3 months	sale of iron to David Lu Presti, a Palermitan Jew
26.10.1482 c. 34v	Giovanni Partis, a *bombardiere* in Palermo	1.9.0 ounces	monthly instalments of 9 *tarì*	sale of iron to Salamon de Lu Medicu, a Palermitan Jew
11.11.1482 c. 40r	Pietro de la Penictera	current price	2 ounces on account in cash and 1 ounce in articles	saloe of wheat to Muxa Millac, a Jew of Palermo
25.11.1482 c. 46r	Francesco Nicolò de Chirchi of Florence	5.21.0 ounces	monthly instalments of 1 ounce	sale of gold wire to Minto de Liucio, a Jew of Palermo
18.12.1482 c. 57r	Stefano de Marcherilli	3 ounces	12 *tarì* on account	sale of 2 kantars of grapes and 1 kantar of olive oil to Muxa Millac, a Palermitan Jew
28.1.1483 c. 73r	Tommaso Mallo, a Catalan merchant	4.12.0 ounces	within 2 months	sale of Spanish iron to Busacca Lu Presti, a Jew in Palermo
17.2.1483 c. 85r	Stefano de Seragusia	1.12.0 ounces	at next vintage time	sale of 1 quintal of grapes to Muxa Millac, a Jew in Palermo
18.2.1483 c. 88r	Masino Oliva, a Genoese merchant	2.18.10 ounces	by May	sale of paper to Iosep de Policio, a Palermitan Jew
25.2.1483 c. 96r	Pino de La Motta of Corleone	9.12 *tarì* a kantar	1 ounce on account	sale of all the cheese produced on his farm to Sabet Millac, a Jew of Palermo

10.3.1483 c. 99v	Antonio Archemo, a Genoese merchant	4.19.0 ounces	within a month	sale of assorted goods to Sabet Millac, a Jew of Palermo
13.3.1483 c. 103r	Andrea de Moltido, a Genoese merchant	1.18.0 ounces	within 4 months	sale of paper to Xamuel and Muxa Ysac, Jewish brothers in Palermo
13.3.1483 c. 103r	Andrea de Moltido, a Genoese merchant of Savona	1.18.0 ounces	within 4 months	sale of writing paper to Iona and Muxa Russo, Palermitan Jews
17.3.1483 c. 109r	Andrea de Moltido, a Genoese merchant of Savona	1.2.5 ounces	within 4 months	sale of a bale of paper *ad opus scribendi* to Daniel and Ysrael Ysac, Jews in Palermo
17.3.1483 c. 109r	Andrea de Moltido, a Genoese merchant of Savona	1.4.8 ounces	within 4 months	sale of a bale of paper *ad opus scribendi* to Xamuel Azaru, a Jew in Palermo
17.3.1483 c. 109v	Andrea de Moltido, a Genoese merchant of Savona	3.18.6 ounces	within 4 months	sale of writing paper to Abram Frisisa, a Palermitan Jew
19.3.1483 c. 110r	Andrea de Moltido, a Genoese merchant	4.24.0 ounces	within 4 months; paid 10.12.1483	sale of writing paper to Benedetto Beniosep and Busacca Xunina, Jews of Palermo
21.3.1483 c. 110v	Andrea de Moltido, a Genoese merchant	1.24.0 ounces	within 4 months	sale of a bale of writing paper to Sabet Millac and Muxa Russu, Jews of Palermo

15.5.1483 c. 116r	Nicolino de Barnabo	1.15.10 ounces	within 3 months	sale of some goods to Muxa Ysac, a Jew of Palermo
4.6.1483 c. 146v	Andrea de Moltido, a Genoese merchant	3.16.0 ounces	within 4 months	sale of bales of writing paper to Busacca and Leone Frisisa, Jewish brothers in Palermo
4.6.1483 c. 147r	Andrea de Moltido, a Genoese merchant	1.4.0 ounces	within 4 months	sale of a bales of writing paper to Nixim Frisisa, a Jew of Palermo
4.6.1483 c. 147v	Giovanni de Partis, *bombardiere* in Palermo	5.4.4 ounces	by July	sale of 14 *rotoli* of French iron to David Lu Presti, a Palermitan Jew in Castronovo
18.6.1483 c. 153r	Andrea de Moltido, a Genoese merchant	1.18.0 ounces	within 4 months; paid 29.9.1484	sale of paper to Salamon Romano, a Palermitan Jew
29.7.1483 c. 178r	Andrea de Moltido, a Genoese merchant	5.4.2 ounces	on demand	sale of heavy cloth to Muxa Taguil and Elia Ubi, Jews of Palermo
30.7.1483 c. 178v	Andrea de Moltido, a Genoese merchant	7.6.5 ounces	on demand	sale of heavy cloth and paper to Xamuel Azeni, a Jew in Palermo
13.8.1483 loose leaf	Vincenzo de Riparola	7.12.0 ounces	within a month	sale of sugar to Sabet Millac, a Palermitan Jew
18.8.1483 c. 185r	Antonio de Simento of Naples	53 ounces	within 4 months; paid 7.10.1484	sale of material for the making of books to Abram de Fano, a Jewish bookseller in Palermo

21.8.1483 c. 186r	Andrea de Moltido, a Genoese merchant	1.5.0 ounces		sale of heavy cloth to Muxa Anaffi, a Jew in Palermo
12.9.1483 c. 7v	Minto Collura of Prizzi	12 *tarì* a kantar, totalling 8 ounces	1.10.0 ounces on account, balance by Christmas	sale of 20 kantars of cheese to Aron Azeni, a Palermitan Jew
13.9.1483 c. 8r	Xibiten Sofer, a Palermitan Jew	10 ounces	with cow and calf leather at 9 *tarì* a piece	sale of London cloth to Salamon Bass, a Palermitan Jew
17.9.1483 c. 11v	Nixim de Liucio and his wife, Jews of Palermo	18 *tarì* a thousand	12 *tarì* on account, balance on delivery	sale of 6,000 ropes for tunny to Giuliano de Ponticorona
28.9.1483 c. 14r	Giovanni de Vuozo	8 *tarì* a *salma*	12 *tarì* on account	sale of 2 *salme* wheat to Benedetto Canet, a Palermitan Jew
8.10.1483 c. 18v	Antonio de Vernigla	1 ounce	at vintage time	sale of a quintal of grapes to Iacob Cuyno, a Palermitan Jew
8.10.1483 c. 19v	Iosep de Seragusia, a Jew of Palermo	6.12.0 ounces	by November	sale of 4 quintals of grapes to Antonio de Agrigento
9.10.1483 c. 19v	Andrea de Moltido, a Genoese merchant	9.3.0 ounces	within 6 months	sale of assorted merchandise to Muxa Taguil, a Palermitan Jew
9.10.1483 c. 20r	Andrea de Moltido, a Genoese merchant	1.4.0 ounces	within 4 months	sale of heavy cloth to Muxa Anaffi, a Jew of Palermo
12.10.1483 c. 20v	Andrea de Moltido, a Genoese merchant	4.16.5 ounces	within 6 months; paid 5.1.1485	sale of canvas to Nixim Cathalano, a Palermitan Jew

15.10.1483 c. 26v	Andrea de Moltido, a Genoese merchant	8 ounces	within a month	sale of paper to Muxa Millac, a Jew in Palermo
17.10.1483 c. 31v	Andrea de Moltido, a Genoese merchant	1.24.0 ounces	within 4 months	sale of a bale of paper to Abram Frisisa, a Jew in Palermo
23.10.1483 c. 32v	Andrea de Moltido, a Genoese merchant	10.12.0 ounces		sale of Cammarata salt to Muxa Millac, a Palermitan Jew
12.11.1283 c. 49r	Muxa de Millac, a Palermitan Jew		1½ quintals of grapes to be paid: 1 quintal at vintage time, balance in wine	sale of goods (*raubis*) to Giovanni de Marino
17.11.1483 c. 53v	Andrea de Moltido, a Genoese merchant	1.16.0 ounces	within 4 months; paid 28.4.1486	sale of paper and canvas to Abram Sivena, a Palermitan Jew
28.11.1483 c. 63r	Muxa Millac, a Jew of Palermo		at vintage time	sale of 1 quintal of grapes to Filippo Panichello
3.12.1483 c. 65r	Alfonso de Vitali	1 ounce	10 *tarì* on account	sale of grapes to Muxa Millac, a Jew of Palermo
8.1.1484 c. 79v	Filippo Panichello and Manfrido de Simone	20 *tarì*		sale of a quintal of grapes to Muxa Millac, a Jew of Palermo
22.1.1484 c. 84r	Andrea de Moltido, a Genoese merchant	6.4.0 ounces	within 6 months	sale of Cammarata salt to Muxa Taguil, a Jew of Palermo
22.1.1484 c. 84v	Andrea de Moltido, a Genoese merchant	6.15.5 ounces	within 6 months	sale of Cammarata salt to Elia Ubi, a Palermitan Jew

3.2.1484 c. 87r	Cola La Chimia	1 ounce	paid	sale of a quintal of grapes to Muxa Millac, a Jew of Palermo
11.2.1484 c. 88v	Masio Insimina	2.8.14 ounces	within 2 months	sale of cloth to Abram de Medico, a Jew of Palermo
11.2.1484 c. 88v	Stefano de Micheli	1.6.0 ounces	12 *tarì* on account, balance later	sale of a quintal of grapes to Muxa Millac, a Jew of Palermo
17.3.1484 c. 100r	Giuliano de Ponticorona	1 ounce	by 19 March	sale of assorted goods to Xibiten de Liucio, a Jew of Palermo
28.4.1484 c. 123r	Antonio de Iohanne	1.6.0 ounces	by vintage time	sale of 1½ quintals of grapes to Muxa Millac, a Palermitan Jew
15.5.1484 c. 126r	Salamon Formusa, a Palermitan Jew	14 *tarì* a kantar	by June; paid 3.4.1485	sale of *pecorino* to Antonio Bonimonti, a Genoese merchant
11.6.1484 c. 146r	Giacomo Costa of Trapani	7.10 *tarì* a *salma*	20 *tarì* on account	sale of 2 kantars of salt to Manuel de Muxa, a Jew of Palermo

Date and Page	Tenant	Location and Description	Rent and Duration	Remarks
11.7.1482 c. 68r	Muxa de Farrugio, a Palermitan Jew	*ruga* de Lu Daptilu in Palermo; warehouse	13 *tarì* a month; a year	landlord: Muxa Ysac son of Simon, a Jew of Palermo
18.7.1482 c. 69r	Aloisio de Girachio	Cassaro in *ruga* Magna, bordering on the house of Mardochai; a house	23 *tarì* annually; 7 years	landlord: Abram de Noto, a Palermitan Jew, acting also for Mardochai de Liucio, a Jew

28.8.1482 c. 83v	Vita de Seragusia, a Jew of Palermo	Cassaro in his courtyard in the *ruga* Moyses Chetibi, bordering on the house of Lia Sacerdoto, a Jew; house with well	26 *tarì* annually; 2 years	landlord: Iacob Lu Presti, a Palermitan Jew
31.10.1482 c. 37r	Muxa Millac, a Jew of Palermo	*contrada* Colli in Palermo; vineyard	2 ounces [annually]	landlords: Laurencio de Provinzano and Muxa Nifusi, a Jew

Source: ASP, Not. Giacomo Comito, reg. 861

Date and Page	Debtor	Amount	Reason	Remarks
13.9.[1459] c. nn	Muxa Xillebi, a Jew of Palermo	3.15.0 ounces	balance of debt of 5 ounces to Francesco de Iacobo result of business transaction	to be paid within a month; paid 9.3.[1459]
9.9.[..] c. nn	Sabet Cuyno, a Jew of Palermo		paid mortgage	removal of lien on his property by Dionisio de Nigrono
15.8.1473 c. nn	Conino de La Iudeca, a Palermitan Jew	22 *tarì*	balance of price for Florentine cloth owed Benedetto de Percomanno, a Florentine merchant	to be paid within 23 months
12.1.[1482] c. nn	Robino de Xamueli, a Jew in Palermo	1.14.0 ounces	balance of price for Majorcan cloth owed by Giovanni de Galeuni	to be paid within 6 months

Date and Page	Lender or Seller	Amount	Payment	Remarks
28.2.[1482] c. nn	Muxa Levi, a Jew of Palermo		undelivered rope for tunny promised Antonino de Vicazini, a convert	to be delivered to Giuliano Ponticorona, creditor of Antonino
20.3.1477 c. nn	Ysac Vignono, a Jew of Palermo	3.12.0 ounces	balance of price for heavy cloth owed Giovanni de Stratella, a Genoese merchant	to be paid within 6 months; paid 15.1.1478
23.2.1477 c. nn	Merdoc Sillac, a Jew of Palermo	16 *tarì*	unpaid debt to Dionisio Inmegni	to be paid within 2 months
22.4.1477 c. nn	Iuda de Minichi, a Jew in Palermo	22.17.0 ounces	unpaid debt to Salamon Niffusi, a Jew in Palermo	to be paid on demand
Date and Page	**Lender or Seller**	**Amount**	**Payment**	**Remarks**
11.9.[1459] c. nn	Antonio de Flores	2 ounces	20 *tarì* on account	sale of 2 quintals of grapes to Bulchayra Vignuni, a Palermitan Jew
18.9.[1459] c. nn	Giaimo Quartilocto	6 ounces	within 6 months	sale of merchandise to Farchono Sala, a Jew of Palermo
26.9.[1459] c. nn	Chillino de Septimo	12.2.9 ounces	by 15 October	sale of cloth to Muxa de Muxa, a Palermitan Jew
1.9.[..] c. nn	Iacobo de Crispo	1.12.0 ounces	within a month	sale of cloth to Fariono and Vita Sabbatino and Muxa Brixa, Palermitan Jews
2.9.[..] c. nn	Brachono Bambalu alias Barbucza, a Palermitan Jew	5 *tarì* a cow hide, 6.17 *tarì* a young cow hide and 8 *tarì* a calf hide	20 ounces on account	sale to Nicolò Bono di Gangi of all the hides produced in the abattoir of the Jewish community in Palermo until August

11.9.[..] c. nn	Filippo and Cola Friscia of Prizzi	9 *tarì* a kantar, totalling 9 ounces	1 ounce on account	sale of cheese and *caciocavallo* to Iacob Taguil, a Jew in Palermo
25.9.[..] c. nn	Graciano Ysac, a Jew of Palermo	12 *tarì* a kantar	paid	sale of 25 kantars of cheese to Bartholomeo Graniti
6.9.[..] c. nn	Giovanni de Maiano	3.18.0 ounces	monthly instalments of 15 *tarì*	sale of clothes to Muxa de Samuele, a Jew of Palermo
10.9.[1467] c. nn	Pietro Aglata	5.15.0 ounces	within 5 months	sale of cloth to Summato de Muxarella, a Jew of Marsala
11.9.[1467] c. nn	Conino de mastro Antonio	4 ounces	2 ounces by Christmas, balance later	sale of yarn (?) (*flandini*) to Suffeni and Merdoc de Minichi, Jews of Palermo
11.9.[1467] c. nn	Giovanni de Flores	39 ounces	monthly instalments of 2 ounces	sale of cloth to Summato de Muxarella, a Jew of Marsala
12.9.[1467] c. nn	Conino di mastro Antonio	4.12.0 ounces	within 2 months; paid 27.7.[1468]	sale of cow leather to Xua Amar, a Palermitan Jew
12.9.[1467] c. nn	Pietro Aglata	44.10.0 ounces	within 5 months; paid 18.4.[1468]	sale of deerskin to Muxa Siddoti, Salamon de Messina, Graciano Siddoti, Iosep Chonu, Xibiten Gibey and Brachono Frisisa, Palermitan Jews
13.9.[1467] c. nn	Pietro Mesala, a merchant of Barcelona	6.4.0 ounces	within 5 months	sale of deerskin to Xirello de Seracusia, a Jew of Palermo
22.9.[1467] c. nn	Pietro Catalano, a merchant of Barcelona	10.10.0 ounces	within 5 months; paid 14.8.[1468]	sale of deerskin to Xamuel Gididia, a Palermitan Jew

25.9.[1467] c. nn	Antonio Costanisi	18.6.0 ounces	within 6 months	sale of cloth to Elia Cuyno, a Jew in Palermo
30.9.[1467] c. nn	Pietro Mesala	10.18.0 ounces	within 5 months; paid 18.4.[1468]	sale cloth to Muxa Siddoti, a Jew of Palermo
1.10.[1467] c. nn	Sadia Ionti, a Jew of Palermo	1 ounce a thousand	on delivery	sale of 6,000 ropes for tunny to Giovanni de Martorana
12.10.[1467] c. nn	Battista Rizu, a Genoese merchant	8.15.0 ounces	within 4 months	sale of deerskin to Ysac de La Magna, a Jew of Palermo
26.10.[1467] c. nn	Galvano de Auria, a Genoese merchant	34 ounces	within 2 months	sale of embroidered silk to Ysac de La Magna, a Jew of Palermo
13.10.[1466] c. nn	Antonio de Castilla, a Genoese merchant	1.27.0 ounces	within 2 months; paid 18.1.[1467]	sale of assorted merchandise to Gaudeo de Medico, a Jew in Palermo
23.9.[1466] c. nn	Guiscardo de Lomellino, a Genoese merchant	2.10.10 ounces	within 2 months	sale of cloth to Iosep de La Cona, a Jew of Palermo
23.9.[1466] c. nn	Guiscardo de Lomellino, a Genoese merchant	8 ounces	within 3 months; paid 3.1.[1467]	sale of heavy linen cloth and other cloth to Salamon Boniacu, a Jew of Palermo
23.9.[1466] c. nn	Galvano de Auria, a Genoese merchant	3.16.0 ounces	within 2 months; paid 17.4.[1467]	sale of gold wire to Muxa Siddoti, a Jew of Palermo
27.9.[1466] c. nn	Giovanni de Monblanco, a Catalan merchant	2.27.15 ounces	by June; paid 1.7.[1467]	sale of iron to Busacca de Ysac, a Palermitan Jew

3.10.[1466] c. nn	Guglielmo de Giuliano	11 *tarì* a kantar	8 ounces on account, balance in monthly instalments; paid 11.1.[1467]	sale of 100 kantars of wool (*frixonati*) to Iacob Taguil, a Palermitan Jew
13.10.[1466] c. nn	Benedetto de Percomanno, a Florentine merchant	1.10.0 ounces	within 6 months	sale of finished cloth to Leono de Iordano (?), a Jew of Palermo
15.10.[1466] c. nn	Antonio de Aycardi	3.15.0 ounces	within 6 months; paid 3.5.[1474]	sale of canvas to Michilono Xunina, a Jew in Palermo
15.8.1473 c. nn	Benedetto de Percomanno, a Florentine merchant	2.2.0 ounces	within 6 months	sale of iron to Merdoc de Vizini, a Jew in Palermo
15.8.1473 c. nn	Andrea Moltido, a Genoese merchant	2.10.0 ounces	during current month; paid 21.6.1474	sale of cloth to Chanino Farmono, a Palermitan Jew
15.8.1473 c. nn	Andrea Moltido, a Genoese merchant	1.10.0 ounces	within 5 months	sale of sheepskin to Zudo de Liuzo, a Jew in Palermo
20.8.1473 c. nn	Giovanni Partis	3.5.0 ounces	within 5 months; paid 20.4.1474	sale of deerskin to Mussuto Binna, a Jew in Palermo
22.10.1473 c. nn	Aginolfo de Alfonso, a Pisan merchant	12.13.10 ounces	within 6 months; paid 23.11.174	sale of Florentine cloth to David Abayle and Muxa de Mussuto, Palermitan Jews
22.10.1473 c. nn	Giovanni de Aprea	1.20.0 ounces	within 4 months	sale of iron to Nixim Millac, a Jew in Palermo
25.10.1473 c. nn	Pietro Guchardi	6.12.0 ounces	on demand; paid 15.3.1474	sale of cloth to Iosep Abudarcham, a Jew

22.10.1473 c. nn	Antonio Ayrordi, a Florentine merchant	1.27.12 ounces	by 20 June	sale of a bale of writing paper to Vita Azaru, a Jew of Palermo
2.11.1473 c. nn	Benedetto de Prothomasio, a Florentine merchant	34.21.0 ounces	within 6 months; paid 8.7.1474	sale of velvet to Siminto de Muxarella, a Jew of Marsala
2.11.1473 c. nn	Benedetto de Prothomasio, a Florentine merchant	23.6.0 ounces	within 6 months; paid 10.5.1474	sale of cloth to Iosep Provinzanu alias Puzuni, a Jew of Giuliana
13.12.[1481] c. nn	Mariano Aglata, a Pisan merchant	10 *tarì* a *salma*	by June; paid 30.1.[1483]	sale of wheat to Sabet Daidono, a Jew of Marsala
15.12.[1481] c. nn	Antonio Aglata	8.5.0 ounces	by 15 August	sale of cloth to Sabet Daidono, a Jew of Marsala
13.12.[1481] c. nn	Filippo and Antonio Aglata	12.22.10 ounces	by August	sale of cloth to Sadia Siracusano, a Palermitan Jew
23.12.[1481] c. nn	Gallufo Aurifichi, a Palermitan Jew	4 ounces	within 2 months	sale of sugar to Aloysio Bonet, a Palermitan spice merchant
28.12.[1481] c. nn	Giovanni Amodeo de Lana	2.15.10 ounces	within 4 months	sale of cloth to Vita Lu Medicu, a Jew in Palermo
14.1.[1482] c. nn	Ricca and Giovanni Buchista	1 ounce	by 25th of current month	sale of cow leather to Muxa Rubeo (Rosso), a Jew of Palermo
30.1.[1482] c. nn	Francesco de Frisco, a Genoese merchant	21.5.8 ounces	within 6 months	sale of cloth to Aron Anaffi, a Palermitan Jew
3.2.[182] c. nn	Giovanni Homodei, owner of tunny plant at Solanto	10 *tarì* a kantar	5 ounces on account	sale of 50 kantars of tunny to Vita Aurifichi, a Palermitan Jew

26.2.[182] c. nn	Giovanni Homodei, owner of tunny plant at Solanto	10 *tarì* a kantar	5 ounces on account	sale of another 50 kantars of tunny to Vita Aurifichi, a Palermitan Jew
3.3.[1482] c. nn	Giovanni Stratella	3.3.0 ounces	within 6 months	sale of heavy cloth to Isaya de Vignono, a Jew of Palermo
5.3.[1482] c. nn	Giovanni Stratella	3.16.0 ounces	within 6 months	swale of heavy cloth to Busacca Frisisa, a Jew in Palermo
8.3.[1482] c. nn	Iosep de Benedicto, a Palermitan Jew	2.10.0 ounces	1 ounce with grapes on account, balance later	sale of a mule with saddle and reins to Paolo de La Rocca
18.3.[1482] c. nn	Giovanni Battista de Lavinio, a Genoese merchant	3.10.0 ounces	within 2 months	sale of woollen cloth to Merdochay Sufi, a Jew in Palermo
19.3.[1482] c. nn	Sabatino Campisi, a Jew of Agrigento	5 ounces	1 ounce on account, balance on delivery	sale of 20 *salme* of Cammarata salt
18.3.1477 c. nn	Agostino de Banquisto, a Genoese merchant	9.6.0 ounces	within 6 months	sale of assorted goods to Iacob Malti, Benedetto Aurifichi and Xibiten de Rabbi Iacob, Palermitan Jews
18.3.1477 c. nn	David Azaruti, a Jew of Palermo	20 *tarì* a thousand	2 ounces with barrels of tunny on account; paid 13.11.1477	sale of 20,000 ropes for tunny to Lupo de Sivigla
19.3.1477 c. nn	Giovanni de Stratella, a Genoese merchant	7.10.0 ounces	by September; paid 15.10.1477	sale of heavy cloth to Ysac Frisisa, a Jew of Palermo
19.2.1477 c. nn	Bernardo de Flores, a Pisan merchant	12 ounces	on Easter; paid 12.7.1479	sale of myrtle to Vita Amar, a Palermitan Jew

19.2.1477 c. nn	Bernardo de Risignano	2.3.0 ounces	within 2 months	sale of cinnamon (*cinnamorum*) to
				Leone La Iudeca, a Jew of Palermo
23.2.1477 c. nn	Dionisio Inmegni, a Florentine merchant	4.10.0 ounces	within 4 months	sale of buttons (*buctinorum*) to Busacca Sala, a Jew
23.2.1477 c. nn	Antonio de Cona	6.8.10 ounces	by July	sale of assorted goods to Leone
				de La Iudeca, a Palermitan Jew
23.2.1477 c. nn	Narazzo de Villa, a merchant of Barcelona	11.15.0 ounces	within 6 months	sale of pepper to Chayrono and Xamuel Russo, Jews in Palermo
23.2.1477 c. nn	Pietro Gimol	19.6.0 ounces	within 4 months	sale of cloth to Minto de Muxarella, a Jew of Marsala
23.2.1477 c. nn	Pietro Corachis, a merchant of Valencia	5.12.0 ounces	by September	sale of cloth to Iosep Abudaram, a Jew of Palermo
23.2.1477 c. nn	Pietro Concilla, a merchant of Barcelona	14.24.0 ounces	within 4 months; paid 22.6.1479	sale of Barcelona cloth to Nixim de Cathania, a Jew of Caltabellotta
25.2.1477 c. nn	Salamon de Minichi, a Jew of Palermo			sale of 9 *salme* of salt to Bettino de Ventimiglia
25.2.1477 c. nn	Guglielmo de Spuches	42.5.0 ounces	within 5 months	sale of cloth to Minto de Muxarella, a Jew of Marsala
25.2.1477 c. nn	Andreocta Gentili, a Genoese merchant	5.22.0 ounces	within 2 months	sale of cloth to Xibiten Binna and Benedetto Azeni, Palermitan Jews
1.3.1477 c. nn	Nicolò Guchardo	1.26.0 ounces	within 6 months	sale of 2 bales of cloth (*azari de raxia*) to Iacob Xunina, a Jew of Palermo

6588

1.3.1477 c. nn	Narasso de Bondello, a merchant of Barcelona	6.24.0 ounces	within 6 months; paid 19.5.1479	sale of merchandise to Vita Azaru, a Jew in Palermo
23.4.1477 c. nn	Nardo de Vita	18 *tarì*		sale of tunny to Iuda de Minichi, a Palermitan Jew
30.4.1477 c. nn	Iacob de Seragusia, a Jew of Palermo	7.10 *tarì* a kantar, totalling 17 ounces	4 ounces on account, balance on delivery	sale of salted tunny to Gauio de Rabbi, a Jew in Palermo
6.5.1477 c. nn	Giovanni de Bayamonte	30 ounces	by 15 June	sale of 51 kantars of sugar to Manuel and Muxa Aurifichi, Palermitan Jews
9.5.1477 c. nn	Simone de Sparti, a Pisan merchant	25 ounces	within 2 months; paid 20.8.1479	sale of Florentine cloth to Chayrono Xunina, a Jew of Palermo
14.5.1477 c. nn	Muxa Millac, a Palermitan Jew	11.10.0 ounces	within 6 months	sale of almonds to Xamuel Sacerdoto, a Jew in Palermo
9.9.1468 c. nn	Giovanni Damiani, a Pisan merchant	6.6.0 ounces	monthly instalments of 12 *tarì*	sale of gold wire to Salamon Benassay, a Jew of Palermo
15.9.1468 c. nn	Pietro de Pasquali, a merchant of Barcelona	21.23.0 ounces		sale of cloth to Xibiten Azaru, a Palermitan Jew
21.9.1468 c. nn	Giovanni Bellachera	1.10.0 ounces	by 21.11	sale of grapes to Graciano Tachariato, a Palermitan Jew
28.2.[1469] c. nn	Alfonso Saladino	8.10.0 ounces	by June	sale of 20 *salme* of salt to Salamon Lu Presti, a Jew in Palermo
28.2.[1469] c. nn	Pietro Comes, a merchant of Barcelona	4.9.0 ounces	weekly instalments of 6 *tarì*	sale of oil to Vanni Sabuchi, a Palermitan Jew

4.10.[1469] loose leaf	Iacob de Ysaia, a Jew of Caltabellotta	2 ounces	wthin a month	sale of a mule to Nicolò de Odo
4.10.[1469] loose leaf	Benedetto de Procopio	1 ounce		sale of oil to Gimilono Naguay, a Palermitan Jew
23.2.14[..] loose leaf	Guglielmo de Scales, a Majorcan merchant	7.8.0 ounces	within 6 months; paid 12.3.14[..]	sale of cloth to Muxa Cuyno, a Jew in Palermo
[..].[..].14[..] loose leaf	Nastasio de Benedicto	19.6.0 ounces		sale of cloth to Iosep Maltisi, a Jew of Polizzi
30.10.14[..] loose leaf	Pino Zapparuto	10 *grana* a *salma*, totalling 20 *tarì*	on delivery	sale of 40 *salme* of cane to Muxa de Medico, a Jew of Palermo
3.7.14[..] loose leaf	Francesco de Ribes, a merchant of Barcelona	12.10.0 ounces	within 6 months	sale of cloth to Muxa de Chazuni, a Jew of Mozia

Date and Page	Tenant or Buyer	Location and Description	Rent/price and Duration	Remarks
20.3.1477 c. nn	Manuel and Muxa Ubi, Palermitan Jews	Platea S. Iacobi de Maritima in the Conciaria quarter, bordering on the warehouse of 2 other Jews and on that of Giovanni di lu Brandino; warehouse	2 years	landlady: Violante de Inperatore, widow of Michele de Blundo, also on behalf of her children
4.10.1469 loose leaf	Sabet de Minichi, a Jew of Palermo	*Contrada* Ferraria in Palermo, bordering on the shop of Salamon Ubi, a Jew, and on that of Profachi Musili; ironmonger's shop; subject to an annual ground rent of 1.6.0 due to Conino de Mayda	sale for 9.24.0 ounces	vendor: Salomon de Minichi, his fellow Jew

Not. Antonino de Melina

Note: The register consists of over 3,000 unbound and unnumbered pages.

Palermo, [...].14[..]

Source: ASP, Not. Antonino de Melina, reg. 937, c. nn.

Release of Raffael de Daniel, a Jew, by Iosep and Fariono de Medico, the latter in Trapani, Jews, from the guarantee in regard to a debt of 5.6.0 ounces to Antonio de La Matina. Antonio had sold Iosep and Fariono six kantars of oil by a deed drawn up by the Jewish notary Daniel Yagegi. If Raffael had to pay, the would compensate him immediately.

Palermo, [...].14[..]

Source: ASP, Not. Antonino de Melina, reg. 937, c. nn.

Nissim Millac, a Jewish citizen of Palermo, entrusts Muxa Rubeo, his Jewish fellow citizen, with two ounces ex causa et nomine accomanda ad negociandum salvos in terra [Doc. incomplete].

Palermo, [...].14[..]

Source: ASP, Not. Antonino de Melina, reg. 937, c. nn.

Deed of sale whereby Isdrael Farachi and Muxa de Siracusia, Jewish citizens of Palermo, sell the couple master Belinguerio and Distule de Falco a curtain for 4.24.0 ounces. The couple promise to pay with grapes worth 2.12.0 ounces at the coming vintage, and undertake to pay the balance by February.

Palermo, 16 September 1428/9

Source: ASP, Not. Antonino de Melina, reg. 937, c. nn.

Mussutu de Messana and Yanuni Nazani, Jewish citizens of Palermo, set up a joint venture for a year to work iron. Mussutu undertakes to invest his labour in his shop/workshop and divide expenses with Yanuni.

Palermo, [....]

Source: ASP, Not. Antonino de Melina, reg. 937, c. nn.

Iosep Abudaram, a shoemaker and Issiele Vital, Jews, nominate arbitrators to decide a dispute between them. Iosep had been awarded a sum of money against Issiele by the pretor's court in Palermo, and contests the verdict. The arbitrators selected are the notaries Urbano de Sinibaldo and Giovanni de Vetero [the Doc. breaks off at this point].

Palermo, [December, 1430]

Source: ASP, Not. Antonino de Melina, reg. 937, c. nn.

Xibiten de Barbuto, a Jewish citizen of Palermo, cedes to Stefano de Pizuto of Castelvetrano all his rights with reference to the brothers Pietro and Francesco de Inverato of Castelvetrano in regard to 22 sacks of corkwood charcoal and other goods. Stefano promises to deliver the articles to Xibiten's home by January [rest of Doc. washed out].

Palermo, 22 December, 1430

Source: ASP, Not. Antonino de Melina, reg. 937, c. nn.

Paolo Chimuntutu of Monreale sells Sabeti Gillebi, a Jewish citizen of Palermo, half a kantar of white grapes from his vineyard for 22 tarì, *paid immediately.*

Palermo, [July 1429]

Source: ASP, Not. Antonino de Melina, reg. 937, c. nn.

Salamon Rugila and Merdoc Actuni, Jewish citizens of Palermo, hire themselves out to Pietro Calandra to work as builders in Carini and Palermo until August for 1 tarì *a day. David Rugila, a Jew, stands surety.*

Palermo, 6 July [1429]

Source: ASP, Not. Antonino de Melina, reg. 937, c. nn.

Notarial protest lodged by Iarono Rubeus and his brothers, Palermitan Jews, againt the notary Giovanni de Vetero [the Doc. breaks off at this point].

Palermo, 16 May 14[31]

Source: ASP, Not. Antonino de Melina, reg. 937, c. nn.

Isolda de lu Re and another woman gave Busacca Sacerdoto, a Jewish public vendor and citizen of Palermo, two togas worth 1.20.0 ounces, for sale. Busacca left Palermo without paying them. Leone, Busacca's son, comes to an agreement with Enrico, Isolda's nephew, whereby Leone is to pay the debt in instalments [Doc. incomplete].

Palermo, 6 July 1431

Source: ASP, Not. Antonino de Melina, reg. 937, c. nn.

Caym Levi, a Jewish citizen of Palermo, and two other Jews hire themselves out to Nissim de Siracusia and Nayuni Yabirra, their Jewish fellow citizens, to fertilize the sugar cane plants of Masi de Crispis during the entire season for 15 grana *a day.*

Palermo, 6 July 1431

Source: ASP, Not. Antonino de Melina, reg. 937, c. nn.

Simon Besicti, a Jewish citizen of Palermo, hires himself out to Masi de Crispis to cultivate his sugar cane during the whole season for 10 grana *a day.*

Palermo, 6 July 1431

Source: ASP, Not. Antonino de Melina, reg. 937, c. nn.

Bunetto de Siracusa, Malluzo Trapanese, Iacob Maltense and Bennibu de Tripuli, Jewish citizens of Palermo, hire themselves out to Masio de Crispis to fertilize his sugar cane during the whole season for 15 grana *a day each. They are paid four* tarì *each on account*

6593

Palermo, [...1431]

Source: ASP, Not. Antonino de Melina, reg. 937, c. nn.

[...] Carastono, acting for [Ubertino de Marinis] archbishop of Palermo, sells Busacca de Tripuli, Gallufo Sansuni and Vita Amar, Palermitan Jews, the tenth of the revenues of the tunny plant in Arenella during the current season, to which the archbishop is entitled as decima. *The price is 14 ounces. Carastono and the Jews also set up a joint venture for the processing and sale of tunny.*

Note: Doc partly washed out.

Palermo, 9 June [1430]

Source: ASP, Not. Antonino de Melina, reg. 937, c. nn.

Contract whereby Fariono Pulchi, a Jewish citizen of Palermo, indentures his son David to Gallufo Camuti, a Jewish smith, his fellow citizen, for two years. David is to be paid 1.18.0 ounces plus food and shoes.

Palermo, 13 June [1430]

Source: ASP, Not. Antonino de Melina, reg. 937, c. nn.

Deed of sale whereby Nardo Mazarella sells pro *indiviso Schamueli Rubeo, a Jewish citizen of Palermo, half of his 90 cows, valued at 15 ounces, and half of his six horses and a foal for 5.25.0 ounces, to be paid by July. The two also set up a joint venture for the management of the herd.*

Palermo, 3 May [1431]

Source: ASP, Not. Antonino de Melina, reg. 937, c. nn.

Meni, widow of Tubia Trabysi, a Jewess, lodges a notarial protest against Sadia Yactan, her fellow Jew, to see to the rebuilding of a collapsed joint wall.

Palermo, 4 May [1431]

Source: ASP, Not. Antonino de Melina, reg. 937, c. nn.

Muxa Actuni, a Jewish citizen of Palermo, lodges a notarial protest against Sadia Yactan, her fellow Jew, to see to the rebuilding of a collapsed joint wall.

Palermo, 14 May [1428?]

Source: ASP, Not. Antonino de Melina, reg. 937, c. nn.

Brayono Sunina, a Jewish citizen of Palermo, hires to David Aram, a dyer, his Jewish fellow citizen, acting for Chanchio Raimundo, a cauldron until September for 7.10 tarì *a month.*

Palermo, 17 May [1428?]

Source: ASP, Not. Antonino de Melina, reg. 937, c. nn.

Muxa de Sacerdoto, a Jewish citizen of Palermo, declares that he received from Vita Catalano, his Jewish fellow citizen, 27 tripods worth 24 tarì *each for sale until June* ex causa accomande ad vendendum salvos in terra. *He is to hand Vita half the proceeds. If not all of the tripods are sold, Muxa is to pay Vita 1.10.0 ounces.*

Palermo, 4 November [1428?]

Source: ASP, Not. Antonino de Melina, reg. 937, c. nn.

Agreeement between Sadono Ubi and Robino Gibra, Jewish citizens of Palermo, to select arbitrators and abide by their decision in regard to their dispute over the hiring of a mule. The arbitrators are Pietro de Berliono, a doctor of law, and Giovanni de Gactalluxio.

Palermo, 10 November [1428?]

Source: ASP, Not. Antonino de Melina, reg. 937, c. nn.

Final accounting between Matheo de Carastono, a citizen of Palermo, and Gallufu Levi, his Jewish fellow citizen, in regard to past business transactions. It transpires that Gallufu owes Matheo four ounces.

Palermo, 11 November [1428?]

Source: ASP, Not. Antonino de Melina, reg. 937, c. nn.

Czullu Miquiseu, a Jewish citizen of Palermo, hires hinself out to Busacca de Tripuli, his Jewish fellow citizen, to sell wine in Czullu's tavern until all the wine in stock is sold.

Palermo, [11 November 1428?]

Source: ASP, Not. Antonino de Melina, reg. 937, c. nn.

Claim by the Jewish brothers Xidedi and Merdoc Azara, Jewish citizens of Palermo, of master Gaudio Chetibi, their Jewish fellow citizen, for expenses, damages and interest in connection with the sale of a beast of burden. As a result master Gaudio was imprisoned. Matheo Abudera, a Jew, promises to pay the brothers 1.21.0 ounces to settle their claim.

Palermo, 17 November [1428]

Source: ASP, Not. Antonino de Melina, reg. 937, c. nn.

Deed whereby Gaspare de Iorlando, a citizen of Palermo, and Mordoc Simael, his Jewish fellow citizen, set up a joint venture for the management of some land and an orchard belonging to Gaspare. The profit is to be divided in equal shares.

Palermo, 23 November [1428]

Source: ASP, Not. Antonino de Melina, reg. 937, c. nn.

Agreement between Nissim Millac and Muxa Rubeo, Jewish citizens of Palermo, whereby Nissim invests two ounces in a joint business venture with Muxa. The profits are to be divided between the parties.

Palermo, 5 December [1428]

Source: ASP, Not. Antonino de Melina, reg. 937, c. nn.

Deed of sale whereby Iosep Abudaram, a Palermitan Jewish citizen, sells to Giovanni de Cordario hooded vests: duarum chopparum panni catalaniski coloris gambillini et alterius chilestrem, *for 1.6.0 ounces. Giovanni also receives in* accomanda *3 togas:* togas duas unam coloris virdi infoderatam panni de blankiecto et aliam panni de gambillina infoderatam panni de bleni, *worth 1.6.0 ounces. He promises to sell them, or else return them to Iosep.*

Palermo, 24 November [1428]

Source: ASP, Not. Antonino de Melina, reg. 937, c. nn.

Agreement whereby Federico de Sinibaldo cedes to Nissim Millac, a Jewish citizen of Palermo, 18 tarì *owed him by Pinesi Sacerdoto, also a Jew of Palermo, for oil. Pinesi had failed to pay Federico.*

Palermo, 21 September [1429]

Source: ASP, Not. Antonino de Melina, reg. 937, c. nn.

Notarial protest lodged by Schamuel Rossi, a Jewish citizens of Palermo, against his brother, Yarono, for having refused to render accounts, especially in regard to some caciocavallo *cheese which Schamuel claims as his own.*

Palermo, 11 September [1429]

Source: ASP, Not. Antonino de Melina, reg. 937, c. nn.

Notarial protest lodged by Iosep Aurifichi, a Jewish citizen of Palermo, against Azarellu, a Jewish butcher, in regard to the non-delivery of tallow.

Palermo, 2 September [1429]

Source: ASP, Not. Antonino de Melina, reg. 937, c. nn.

Donato de Aram, a Jewish dyer of Palermo, replies to the protest of Thommasio de Geremia in regard to the tax on dyeing (gabella tintorie). *He claims that he is not subject to it.*

Palermo, [ca. 1429]

Source: ASP, Not. Antonino de Melina, reg. 937, c. nn.

Pinesi Sacerdotu, master builder, a Jewish citizen of Palermo, hires himself out to Aloisio de Ast to work as builder for a minimum [ad scansas] *of 1.10* tarì. *He is paid a* salma *of wheat and eight* tarì *on account.*

· Palermo, [ca. 1429]

Source: ASP, Not. Antonino de Melina, reg. 937, c. nn.

Master Metus Cavalerio, a citizen of Palermo, and Iuda Sivena, his Jewish fellow citizen, set up a partnership for running the tavern belonging to Sabet de Minichi, their Jewish fellow citizen. The partnership is to last two years. The tavern had been let to Metus by Sabet. The agreement spells out the terms for the supply of wine to the tavern and other expenses, as well as the division of profits.

Palermo, [ca. 1429]

Source: ASP, Not. Antonino de Melina, reg. 937, c. nn.

Graciosa, widow of Vita Calbi, a Jewish citizen of Palermo, and, by Palermitan custom (consuetudinis urbis Panormi), *guardian of their minor daughter Marzucca, has the property of her late husband inventoried in the presence of Antonio de Arano, judge* ydeota *of the court in Palermo. The husband had died intestate*

Palermo, [ca. 1429]

Source: ASP, Not. Antonino de Melina, reg. 937, c. nn.

Vanni de Terminis, a Jewish citizen of Palermo, lodges a notarial protest against Bulchayra de Termini, his Jewish fellow citizen, demanding the return of a bedcover valued at four ounces. Bulayra rejects the protest, arguing that he was given the bedcover as the result of having had to pay a debt of Vanni for which he had stood surety.

Palermo, 19 July 1430

Source: ASP, Not. Antonino de Melina, reg. 937, c. nn.

Francesco de Pascina, a Palermitan citizen, promises Yanino Formone, his Jewish fellow citizen, to treat 65 deerskin and other hides for 12 tarì. *He is paid six* tarì *on account.*

Palermo, [ca. 1429]

Source: ASP, Not. Antonino de Melina, reg. 937, c. nn.

Braya de Liucio, a Jew of Alcamo, indentures his son Schalamon to Sadono Ubi, a Jewish citizen of Palermo, as an apprentice smith (famulus fabri) *for a year. Sadono is to provide Schalamon with food and lodging, shoes and a salary of 18* tarì.

Palermo, [ca. 1429]

Source: ASP, Not. Antonino de Melina, reg. 937, c. nn.

Siminto Maltensis and Musutu Cusintino, Jewish citizens of Palermo, hire themselves out to Nissim Siracusia and Nayuni Yabirra, their Jewish fellow citizens, to fertilize the sugar cane plants of Tommaso de Crispis during the entire season for 15 grana *a day.*

Palermo, 1 September [1429]

Source: ASP, Not. Antonino de Melina, reg. 937, c. nn.

Sabet Misiria, a Jewish citizen of Palermo, indentures his son Musutu to Yua de Chiffuni, his Jewish fellow citizen, as apprentice (famulus et discipulus) *in his shoemaking business for a year. Yua promises to pay Musutu 1.9.0 ounces and a pair of shoes.*

Palermo, 25 September [1429]

Source: ASP, Not. Antonino de Melina, reg. 937, c. nn.

Matheo de Scalia, a canon of Palermo, declares that received his due from Busacca de Tripuli, a Jewish citizen of Palermo, on account of their joint venture for the sale of tunny belonging to the archbishopric on account of the tithe.

Palermo, 19 June [1428]

Source: ASP, Not. Antonino de Melina, reg. 937, c. nn.

Injunction by Samuel Sala, a Jew, against Daniele Chagegi, notary of the Jews in Palermo. Chagegi holds the documents of his predecessor in office, the late master Xibiten [empty space], including the nuptial contract between Asisa, daughter of the late Farrugio de Medico, and Moyse son of Samuele Chetibi. Sala demands that the notary give him a complete copy of the document, rather than the brief extract he furnished him with.

Palermo, November [1428]

Source: ASP, Not. Antonino de Melina, reg. 937, c. nn.

Master Sadono de Medico, a Jewish physician, citizen of Palermo, leases in perpetuity to Iacob, son of the late Muxa de Terminis, his Jewish fellow citizen, a solerata *house in the Cassaro of Palermo. The house borders on that of Muxa and of master Azarono de Medico. The annual rent is one ounce.*

Palermo, 30 October [1428]

Source: ASP, Not. Antonino de Melina, reg. 937, c. nn.

Perna, wife of master shoemaker Abraham Baidu, a Jewish citizen of Palermo, indentures her son Muxa, aged 13, to her husband as apprentice for three years to train as shoemaker. He is to be paid two ounces, food and clothes.

Note: Muxa appears to have been Perna's son from another marriage.

Palermo, 8 November [1428]

Source: ASP, Not. Antonino de Melina, reg. 937, c. nn.

Deed of sale whereby Musutu Binna, a Jewish citizen of Palermo, sells Siminto de Missina, his Jewish fellow citizen, seven casks containing 16 quartara *of wine. The wine is to be sold for two* grana *a* quartuccio *in Musutu's tavern, let to Siminto.*

Note: The *quartara* was equal to 13¾ litres and contained 16 *quartucci*.

Palermo, 13 November [1428]

Source: ASP, Not. Antonino de Melina, reg. 937, c. nn.

Agreement between the brothers Xidedi and Mardoc Azara, Jewish citizens of Palermo, and Matheo Abudera, their Jewish fellow citizen. Magister Gaudio Chetibi, father-in-law of Matheo, is in prison on account of the damage he caused to the brothers resulting from the sale of a beast of burden. Matheo promises to pay the brothers 1.21.0 ounces in weekly instalments of 15 tarì.

Palermo, 13 November [1428]

Source: ASP, Not. Antonino de Melina, reg. 937, c. nn.

Declaration by Chayrono Levi, a Jewish citizen of Palermo, dropping charges in the captain's court in Palermo against Elia de Melita, his Jewish fellow citizen.

Palermo, 17 November [1428]

Source: ASP, Not. Antonino de Melina, reg. 937, c. nn.

Merdoc and Stilla, as well as Fadalono, Stilla's husband, claim their share in the dowry of their late mother, Ricca. She had been the widow of Muxa Lu Faxillaru and had subsequently married Abraham Birda. They reach an agreement with Ricca's second husband over the division of her estate, especially a house in the Cassaro of Palermo.

Palermo, [November, 1428]

Source: ASP, Not. Antonino de Melina, reg. 937, c. nn.

Gaspare de Orlando cedes to Giovanni de Ferrio his rights in the joint venture with Mordoc Simael, his Jewish fellow citizen. Gaspare and Mordoc had agreed on the joint cultivation of some farmland belonging to Gaspare in the contrada *Chabirligi in Palermo.*

Palermo, 29 November [1428]

Source: ASP, Not. Antonino de Melina, reg. 937, c. nn.

Paolo Maltensi promises Busacca Actuni, a Jewish citizen of Palermo and collector of the taxes of Jewish community, to bind over and imprison Jews listed by Busacca [for failing to pay their due]. Paolo is to work three days a week for a year for 1.12.0 ounces.

Palermo, 1 December [1428]

Source: ASP, Not. Antonino de Melina, reg. 937, c. nn.

Contract between Merdoc Semal and Simon di la Iudeca, Jewish citizens of Palermo, and Sabbatino de Augusta, a Jewish smith in Palermo, for the joint management of a smithy. Among other articles, they are to make bells.

Palermo, 7 December [1428]

Source: ASP, Not. Antonino de Melina, reg. 937, c. nn.

Master Gaudio Francus, a Majorcan Jew, declares that he owes Antonio de

Surrenti of Palermo 18 tarì *for the purchase of four casks of wine, which Gaudio promises to pay* in litore maris *on his return to Calabria.*

Palermo, 7 December [1428]
Source: ASP, Not. Antonino de Melina, reg. 937, c. nn.

Guarnerio de Ventimiglia, owner of half the revenues from the gisia *of the Jewish community in Palermo, and Salamon Azara,* protho *of the Jewish community, settle accounts in regard to the* gisia. *Nissim Ysac, Jewish tax collector, undertakes to pay Guarnerio part of the debt. David Nazar, another Jew, stands surety.*

Palermo, 7 December [1428]
Source: ASP, Not. Antonino de Melina, reg. 937, c. nn.

Maseo de Anselmo of Palermo undertakes to deliver to Busacca Yayaruni, a Jewish citizen of Palermo, half a quintal of white grapes for 18 tarì *at vintage time.*

Palermo, 7 December [1428]
Source: ASP, Not. Antonino de Melina, reg. 937, c. nn.

Nissim Ysac, a Jewish citizen of Palermo, collector of the tax on wine of the Jewish community, presents his accounts to the prothi *Raffael Daniel and Busacca de Guglielmo.*

Palermo, 7 December [1428]
Source: ASP, Not. Antonino de Melina, reg. 937, c. nn.

Agreement whereby Leone de Medico, a Jewish citizen of Palermo, hires himself out to work as parator cannamellis *in the sugar refinery of Enrico de Vaccarellis during the entire season.*

Palermo, 1 March [1429]
Source: ASP, Not. Antonino de Melina, reg. 937, c. nn.

Graciano Tayaratus, a Jewish citizen of Palermo, inherited from his father Tobias two ounces which Stefano Columba owed him. Graciano makes a present of the credit to Nicolò de Oliveri, a notary.

Palermo, 1 March [1429]

Source: ASP, Not. Antonino de Melina, reg. 937, c. nn.

Lease whereby Simone de Chilino of Ciminna lets to Lia de Missina alias Picta, a Jewish citizen of Palermo, a solerata house in Ciminna in the piano S. Maria for 24 tarì. Half the rent is paid on account and the balance in two instalments of 6 tarì.

Palermo, 2 March [1429]

Source: ASP, Not. Antonino de Melina, reg. 937, c. nn.

Deed of sale whereby Simone de Chilino of Ciminna sells Lia de Missina, alias Picta, a Jewish citizen of Palermo, two salme and three tumini of wheat from the new harvest for 15 tarì, to be delivered at Lia's house in July. Lia pays three tarì on account and promises to pay the balance on delivery.

Palermo, 2 March [1429]

Source: ASP, Not. Antonino de Melina, reg. 937, c. nn.

Vita Nazam, a Jewish citizen of Palermo, hires himself out as a builder to Gallufo Binna, his Jewish fellow citizen, for 16 grana a day.

Palermo, 2 March [1429]

Source: ASP, Not. Antonino de Melina, reg. 937, c. nn.

Busacca de Amato, a Jewish citizen of Palermo, hires himself out to Samueli Schalom, his Jewish fellow citizen, to work in his ironmonger shop for 18 grana a day until the end of June. He is to start work after Passover.

Palermo, 2 March [1429]

Source: ASP, Not. Antonino de Melina, reg. 937, c. nn.

Gallufo Zel, a Jewish citizen of Palermo, purchased oil for 1.6.0 ounces from

Antonio de Gimbesio. On Gallufo's death, his son Sabet refused to honour his late father's obligation toward Antonio. Sabet now agrees to pay the debt in two instalments.

Palermo, 3 March [1429]

Source: ASP, Not. Antonino de Melina, reg. 937, c. nn.

Deed of sale whereby Aloisio de Monaco, a citizen of Palermo, sold Vita Catalano, his Jewish fellow citizen, cow hides for 7.2.10 ounces, to be paid in two instalments, one in May and the other in August.

Palermo, 4 March [1429]

Source: ASP, Not. Antonino de Melina, reg. 937, c. nn.

Deed of sale whereby Xibiten Gazu and Sufen de Misiria, Jewish citizens of Palermo, sell Muxa Actuni, their Jewish fellow citizen, olive oil (olei olivarum boni novi clari resisi et tramutati a fecce et gruppis cantarum unum ad generalem cantarum et mensuram olei Panormi) *for 18 tarì, which Muxa pays immediately.*

Palermo, 4 March [1429]

Source: ASP, Not. Antonino de Melina, reg. 937, c. nn.

Agreement whereby Iasiel Vivanti, a Jew of Lombardy in Palermo, hires himself out to Antonio Cheva, acting for Francesco Ventimiglia, to cultivate his sugarcane during the current season for 15 grana *a day. Salamon Bumat, a Jewish citizen of Palermo stands surety.*

Palermo, 4 March [1429]

Source: ASP, Not. Antonino de Melina, reg. 937, c. nn.

Deed of sale whereby Enrico and Antonio de Molidia of Alcamo sell Schamueli Schalono, a Jewish citizen of Palermo 48 sacks of cork wood charcoal for three ounces. Schamueli paid 1.6.0 ounces on account.

Sicily

Palermo, 15 March [1429]

Source: ASP, Not. Antonino de Melina, reg. 937, c. nn.

Agreement whereby Nissim Busiti, a Jewish citizen of Palermo, hires himself out to Yacob de Carastono, his fellow citizen, as labourer until August for 15 tarì *a day.*

Palermo, 13 April [1429]

Source: ASP, Not. Antonino de Melina, reg. 937, c. nn.

Contract whereby Nissim de Liucio, a Jew of Alcamo, indentures his son Fariono with Schamuel Schilono, a Jewish smith and citizen of Palermo, for 15 grana *a day.*

Palermo, 27 April [1429]

Source: ASP, Not. Antonino de Melina, reg. 937, c. nn.

Enrico de Alongi, a Palermitan citizen, lodges a protest against Charono Russo, his Jewish fellow citizen, for having failed to take back his cows. A partnership between them had been dissolved.

Palermo, 27 April [1429]

Source: ASP, Not. Antonino de Melina, reg. 937, c. nn.

Contract wherby Azarello de Rustico, a Jewish citizen of Palermo, hires himself out to Pino de Alfano, his fellow citizen, to slaughter meat in the Jewish abattoir of Palermo until the end of August for 15 tarì *and two* rotoli *of meat*

Palermo, 27 April [1429]

Source: ASP, Not. Antonino de Melina, reg. 937, c. nn.

Master Moyse Chetibi, a Jewish physician and citizen of Palermo, lets Salvatore Strogili, his fellow citizen, a solerata *house and courtyard, situated in the* contrada *Lactinorum in the Conciaria quarter, for two ounces a year.*

Palermo, 3 May [1429]

Source: ASP, Not. Antonino de Melina, reg. 937, c. nn.

Contract whereby Schamuel Zafarana, a Jew of Calabria, hires himself out to Iasiel Vivanti, a Jew in Palermo, to fertilize the sugarcane of Francesco Ventimiglia for 15 grana *a day.*

Palermo, 3 May [1429]

Source: ASP, Not. Antonino de Melina, reg. 937, c. nn.

Deed of sale whereby Antonio Matina sells Brayono Taguil, a Jewish citizen of Palermo, 10 kantars of oil. Brayono promises to pay Antonio within four months. Master Moyse Chetibi stands surety for Brayono.

Palermo, 11 May [1429]

Source: ASP, Not. Antonino de Melina, reg. 937, c. nn.

Agreement whereby Vanni Subbusiu, a Jewish citizen of Palermo, promises Salamone Sofer, his Jewish fellow citizen, to fertilize the sugarcane plants of Giovanni Omodei on the usual terms.

Palermo, 19 May [1429]

Source: ASP, Not. Antonino de Melina, reg. 937, c. nn.

Agreement whereby Vita Nada, a Jewish citizen of Palermo, hires himself out to Pietro de Calandra as carpenter for a month for 15 tarì.

Palermo, 8 November [1429]

Source: ASP, Not. Antonino de Melina, reg. 937, c. nn.

Agreement whereby Sabet Misiria, a Jewish citizen of Palermo, indentures his son Musuto, with Amuruso Gilebbi, his Jewish fellow citizen, in his shoe shop (famulus apotece corbeserie) *for a year for 1.3.0 ounces and a pair of leggings valued at two* tarì.

Palermo, 16 November [1429]
Source: ASP, Not. Antonino de Melina, reg. 937, c. nn.

Contract whereby Xibiten de Misiria and Brayono, with the consent of his mother Bella, widow of Sadono Cusintino, Jewish citizens of Palermo, hire themseleves out to Salomon Yammara, their Jewish fellow citizens, to work as paratores *in the sugar refinery of Iacobo de Bononia for one ounce a month. Sabutu Medui, a Jew, stands surety.*

Palermo, 16 November [1429]
Source: ASP, Not. Antonino de Melina, reg. 937, c. nn.

Contract whereby Gallufo Cuyno, a Jewish citizen of Palermo, hires out his slave Abdalla to master Giovanni de Galluro for a month to work as builder for 20 tarì.

Palermo, 15 February [1430]
Source: ASP, Not. Antonino de Melina, reg. 937, c. nn.

Settlement of accounts by Pino de Alfano of Palermo with Muxa Achina, a Jewish citizen of Palermo, in regard to the moneys, hides and other items of the Jewish abattoir in Palermo. As a result it transpires that Pino owes Muxa 4.27.0 ounces, which Pino promises to pay by 21 May. On the other hand Pino is owed 2.6.0 ounces by Simone de Puglisio which Muxa has ceded to Pino.

Palermo, 20 February [1430]
Source: ASP, Not. Antonino de Melina, reg. 937, c. nn.

Notarial protest by Busacca de Tripuli, a Jewish citizen of Palermo, against Sadia Ysac, his Jewish fellow citizen, in the matter of two beasts of burden belonging to Busacca which Benedetto Bono had hired to Sadia. Busacca alleges that Sadia is causing him damage.

Palermo, 13 March [1430]
Source: ASP, Not. Antonino de Melina, reg. 937, c. nn.

Nissim de Syracusia, a Jewish citizen of Palermo, hires two beasts of burden from

Yacob Pappa, his fellow citizen, for the portage and sale of red earth. They are to divide the profits.

Palermo, 28 March [1430]

Source: ASP, Not. Antonino de Melina, reg. 937, c. nn.

Undertaking by Benedetto Gibra, a Jewish builder (fabricator) *and citizen of Palermo, with the consent of his brother Muxa, to Nicolò Passafiume, squire* (scutifero) *of Aloisio de Ast, to carry out work for the latter in Palermo and elsewhere for a daily wage of 1.10* tarì.

Palermo, 31 March [1430]

Source: ASP, Not. Antonino de Melina, reg. 937, c. nn.

Lease whereby Nissim Millac, a Jewish citizen of Palermo, with the consent of his brother Muxa, lets Gallufo de Minichi, his Jewish fellow citizen, a press situated in the Ferraria Iudeorum, to be used as shop for the sale of saddles and harnesses, or coal. The rent is 25 tarì.

Palermo, 7 April [1430]

Source: ASP, Not. Antonino de Melina, reg. 937, c. nn.

Agreement whereby Vignaminu de Girachio, a Jewish citizen of Palermo, hires himself out to Busacca de Tripuli, his Jewish fellow citizen, to work in the tunny plant of Rogerio de Paruta, Giovanni de Caltagirone and Giovanni de Carastono for 18 tarì. *He is paid six* tarì *on account.*

Palermo, 3 May [1430]

Source: ASP, Not. Antonino de Melina, reg. 937, c. nn.

Contract for the setting up of a partnership between Bartholomeo de Gactalluxio, a Palermitan citizen, and Yarono Malti, his Jewish fellow citizen, for the production of candles and their sale. The venture is to last until Easter 1431.

Palermo, 3 May [1430]

Source: ASP, Not. Antonino de Melina, reg. 937, c. nn.

Deed of gift by Nissim Millac, a Jewish citizen of Palermo, also on behalf of his wife Gazella and of his children, makes a present to his bother Bulchaira in consideration of brotherly love and services rendered. The object of the gift is a press and some shops in the contrada *Ferraria Hebreorum, bordering on the* hilba seu viridariolum nobilis Henrici de Gactalluxio ex una parte occidentis et secus apotecam Gallucii bardarii ex parte altera, viam publicam et alios confinos.

Palermo, 4 September [1430]

Source: ASP, Not. Antonino de Melina, reg. 937, c. nn.

Xibiten Schammara, Iacob Tunisinu, Sabet Yaguisi and Iosep Ammara, also on behalf of Salomone Rugila, all Jewish citizens of Palermo, hire themselves out to master Nicto de Cavalleria and Iuda Sivena, a Jew, their fellow citizens, to tread out the grapes and make the wine at their tavern for 25 tarì *a thousand (i.e. 10 quintals) of grapes.*

Palermo, 4 September [1430]

Source: ASP, Not. Antonino de Melina, reg. 937, c. nn.

Agreement whereby Nicolò de Monaco, a Palermitan citizen, hires himself out to Yarono Rubeo (Rossi) his Jewish fellow citizen, to work as butcher tempus staxionis trappetorum cannamellis *for 16* tarì *a month and two* rotoli *of meat a week. He is paid nine* tarì *on account.*

Palermo, 5 September [1430]

Source: ASP, Not. Antonino de Melina, reg. 937, c. nn.

Contract whereby the brothers Salamon and Caym de Leone, Jewish brothers of Castroreale, and their partners promise Enrico de Vaccarellis to transport sugarcane (gendiras, cannamellis et stirpones) *to his sugar refinery for six* tarì *a hundred* salme. *They undertake to use four big beasts of burden. Gaudio Gibel, another Jew, stands surety.*

Palermo, 6 September [1430]

Source: ASP, Not. Antonino de Melina, reg. 937, c. nn.

Agreement whereby David Ysac, a Jewish citixen of Palermo, indentures his son with Yanino Formono, a master shoemaker, his Jewish fellow citizen, for two years for 12 tarì *a year and lodging. He is to learn the shoemaker's trade.*

Palermo, 6 September [1430]

Source: ASP, Not. Antonino de Melina, reg. 937, c. nn.

Simon Schalomo, a Jewish citizen of Palermo, demands of Muxa Gazella, his Jewish fellow citizen, the part of the shop which Muxa had let him for 14.10 tarì *and for which he had made a down payment of one* tarì. *The shop is situated in the Ferraria of Palermo, near the abattoir of the Jews.*

Palermo, 13 September [1430]

Source: ASP, Not. Antonino de Melina, reg. 937, c. nn.

Injunction by fra Pietro de Marocta against Shamuele Rubeo, a Jewish citizen of Palermo, to refrain from slaughtering the cows which Pietro had sold him, since Shamuele had failed to pay him the price agreed on between them.

Palermo, 22 September [1430]

Source: ASP, Not. Antonino de Melina, reg. 937, c. nn.

Notarial protest by Muxa Levi and Lia Sofer, Jewish citizens of Palermo, together with Azarono Ricio, their Jewish fellow citzen, against Merdoc de Tripuli, also a Jewish citizen of Palermo, who is alleged to have pressed their grapes, bought from Ubertino de Abbatellis and stored in Merdoc's house. Merdoc is either to press the grapes [again] or give the protesters two casks of wine.

Palermo, 22 September [1430]

Source: ASP, Not. Antonino de Melina, reg. 937, c. nn.

Busacca and Muna Calabrensi, relatives of Vita Calabrensi, and David, Vita's brother, all Jews in Palermo, undertake to pay the debt owed by Vita to Safila de Buccuni for the purchase of linen. In return Vita is to be released from prison.

Source: ASP, Not. Antonino de Melina, reg. 937, c. nn.

Statement by David Abramuni, a Jew, that he had received his share of the herd of cows which he had owned in partnership with the late Paolo de Alexandro. On Alexandro's death, his son Giovanni had inherited his father's estate and had dissolved the partnership.

Palermo, 26 October [1430]

Source: ASP, Not. Antonino de Melina, reg. 937, c. nn.

Deed of sale whereby Isdrael Medui, a Jewish citizen of Palermo, sold master Giovanni Spina, smith and his Palermitan fellow citizen, an anvil, a pedestal and a pair of bellows.

Palermo, 7 November [1430]

Source: ASP, Not. Antonino de Melina, reg. 937, c. nn.

Agreement between Nissim de Catania, a Jew in Palermo, and David Calabrensi, a Jewish citizen of Palermo, whereby Nissim undertakes to work with two of David's beasts of burden during the entire sugarcane season. The profits are to bedivided between the two. Nissim is responsible for feeding the animals.

Palermo, 7 November [1430]

Source: ASP, Not. Antonino de Melina, reg. 937, c. nn.

Gallucio de Minichi, a Jewish citizen of Palermo, demands damages from Vanne de Terminis, his Jewish fellow citizen. Gallucio had rented a storehouse in the Cassaro to store there some myrtle. Rainwater had infiltrated the storehouse and had caused damage to the myrtle.

Palermo, 7 November [1430]

Source: ASP, Not. Antonino de Melina, reg. 937, c. nn.

Deed of sale whereby Busacca de Tripoli, a Jewish citizen of Palermo, sells David de Cipriano, his Jewish fellow citizen, two brown coated beasts of burden and harness for two ounces. David pays three tarì *on account and promises to pay the balance in instalments.*

Palermo, 24 November [1430]

Source: ASP, Not. Antonino de Melina, reg. 937, c. nn.

Agreement whereby Minto Chaela, a Jewish citizen of Palermo, hires himself out to Schamuel Schalomo, a Jewish smith and fellow citizen, as smith and assistant (faber et famulus faber) *for 18* grana *a day, starting 27 December.*

Palermo, 28 November [1430]

Source: ASP, Not. Antonino de Melina, reg. 937, c. nn.

Agreement whereby Schalomus Rugila, a Jewish citizen of Palermo, hires himself out to Yanino Formono, his Jewish fellow citizen, as assistant and apprentice (famulus et discipulus) *in his shoemaker's business for a year for 1.27.0 ounces.*

Palermo, 27 March [1431]

Source: ASP, Not. Antonino de Melina, reg. 937, c. nn.

Contract whereby Nissim de Syracusia and Nayuni Yabirra, Jewish citizens of Palermo, hire themselves out together with 13 men to Masio de Crispis, their fellow citizen, to fertilize his sugarcane for 14 tarì *a thousand plants.*

Palermo, 27 March [1431]

Source: ASP, Not. Antonino de Melina, reg. 937, c. nn.

Agreement whereby Gaudio de Sacca, a Jew, hires himself out to Nissim de Syracusia and Nayuni Yabirra, Jewish citizens of Palermo, to fertilize the sugar cane of Thomasio de Crispis during the entire season for 15 grana *a day. He is paid 4.10* tarì *on account.*

Palermo, 28 March [1431]

Source: ASP, Not. Antonino de Melina, reg. 937, c. nn.

Notarial protest by Busacca Romano, a Jewish citizen of Palermo, against Ysac

Perpignana, a Jew in Palermo, demanding the immediate return to work of Muxa and David, Ysac's sons. Ysac had indentured his sons with Busacca as apprentices and assistants (discipulos et famulos) *with Busacca to train as tailors.*

Palermo, 9 April [1431]

Source: ASP, Not. Antonino de Melina, reg. 937, c. nn.

Contract whereby master Paolo La Magra, an inhabitant of Palermo, hires himself out to Salamone Zafarana, a Jewish citizen of Palermo, until the end of May, to make a sublimate and water to separate silver and gold (in faciendum sollematum et in faciendum aquam separandi argentum et orum), *for 12* tarì.

Palermo, 21 April [1431]

Source: ASP, Not. Antonino de Melina, reg. 937, c. nn.

Agreement whereby Ianino Fusaru, a Jew of Catania, hires himself to Vita de Minichi, a Jewish citizen of Palermo, as saddler, until August for 2.2.10 ounces.

Palermo, 21 April [1431]

Source: ASP, Not. Antonino de Melina, reg. 937, c. nn.

Agreement whereby Muxa Bonus, a Jewish citizen of Palermo, hires himself out to Andrea Ferrerio of Palermo, as miller until August for 18 tarì *a month.*

Palermo, 3 January [1431]

Source: ASP, Not. Antonino de Melina, reg. 937, c. nn.

Agreement whereby Machono Iardinello hires himself out to Panchella Marsiglia, a Jewish citizen of Palermo, to work as saddler in his service until August for 11 grana *a saddle.*

Palermo, 1 February [1431]

Source: ASP, Not. Antonino de Melina, reg. 937, c. nn.

Agreement whereby Antonio de La Dagna promises to David Abramuni, [a Jew], to transport to his storehouse with the help of three animals all the cheese and wool produces by his herd for 15 grana *a kantar. He is paid 18* tarì *on account.*

Palermo, 20 February [1430]

Source: ASP, Not. Antonino de Melina, reg. 937, c. nn.

Contract between Charono Rubeo, a Jewish citizen of Palermo, and Giovanni de Messina whereby the white grapes which Charono sold to Giovanni are to be delivered on the following dates: six salme *and 2½* frise [!] *at the coming vintage and a similar quantity at the the subsequent vintage.*

Palermo, 1 February [14..]

Source: ASP, Not. Antonino de Melina, reg. 937, c. nn.

Agreement whereby Siminto Gilfa and Lia Amoranu, Palermitan Jews, acting for Pietro de Speciali, promise Iohannicio de Maxaru to carry out a building job at his farm for 3.10 tarì *a* canna. *Iohannino is to supply the building materials. They are paid 15* tarì *on account.*

Palermo, 28 February [14..]

Source: ASP, Not. Antonino de Melina, reg. 937, c. nn.

Agreement whereby Muxa Meme and Xileri Azan alias Rustico, Palermitan Jews, hire themselves out to Minto Giberi, their fellow Jew, to work in his sugar refinery for a year for one ounce a month. They are paid one ounce on account.

Palermo, 29 May [14..]

Source: ASP, Not. Antonino de Melina, reg. 937, c. nn.

Contract whereby Vita de Aram and Donato Spagnolo, Jewish citizens of Palermo, set up a joint dyeing business (arte tintorie) *to last a year, starting 1 September.*

Palermo, 9 June [14..]

Source: ASP, Not. Antonino de Melina, reg. 937, c. nn.

Agreement whereby Iosep de Ragusia and Vita Firreri, Palermitan Jews, hire themselves out to Gabriele de Imperatore to cultivate his sugarcane plantation in Ficarazzi for a year for one tarì *a day.*

Palermo, 27 June [14..]

Source: ASP, Not. Antonino de Melina, reg. 937, c. nn.

Sabet Russo, a Palermitan Jew, attorney for Sadia Sibisi, a fellow Jew, creditor of Benedetto Girachio, also a Jew, for 2.10.0 ounces, grants Benedetto a postponement on the payment of the debt. They agree that Benedetto pay 24 tarì *in 15 days and the balance within a month. Salamone de Simon, a Jew, stands surety for Benedetto.*

Palermo, 1 December [14..]

Source: ASP, Not. Antonino de Melina, reg. 937, c. nn.

Agreement whereby Mardoc Xasermini, a Palermitan Jew, hires himself out to Biscardo to work in his sugar refinery at Ficarazzi during the entire season for a monthly wage of 20 tarì.

Palermo, 10 January [14..]

Source: ASP, Not. Antonino de Melina, reg. 937, c. nn.

As the result of the settlement of a financial dispute between Iosep Brachono and David Collino, Palermitan Jews, David declares that he owes Iosep 2.1.0 ounces.

Palermo, 7 November [1429]

Source: ASP, Not. Antonino de Melina, reg. 937, c. 54r.

Quittance by Xibiten Yassuni, a Jew of Nicosia, to Benedetto Misiria, a Jewish citizen of Palermo, in regard to the amount owed him on the strength of a contract drawn up by the notary Andrea Isganga of Nicosia.

Palermo, 7 November [1429]

Source: ASP, Not. Antonino de Melina, reg. 937, c. 54v.

Contract whereby Schirello Formoni, a Jewish citizen of Palermo, hires out his slave Mayumeto to Pietro Pinzavalli for a month to work as a building labourer (ut manualis marammatis) for 18 tarì.

Palermo, 4 September [1430]

Source: ASP, Not. Antonino de Melina, reg. 937, c. 9v.

Deed of sale whereby Guglielmo de Sinibaldo sells Sophen de Iacob, a Jewish citizen of Palermo, wheat for 12 tarì.

Palermo, 4 September [1430]

Source: ASP, Not. Antonino de Melina, reg. 937, c. 9v.

Deed of sale whereby Guglielmo de Sinibaldo sells wheat to Muxa and Gauyusa de Termini, Jewish citizens of Palermo for 1.2.0 ounces. They promise to pay within two months.

Source: ASP, Not. Antonino de Melina, reg. 937

Date and Page	Principal	Attorney	Purpose	Remarks
24.11.[..] c. nn	Bulchaira Ubi, a Palermitan Jew	Gallufo Coyno, a Palermitan Jew	to safeguard Bulchaira's rights in regard to the lease of 2 shops in the Ferraria Iudeorum of Palermo against Nissim Millac, their fellow Jew	
12.9.1430 c. nn	Iacob Taguil, a Jew of Palermo	Gallufu Taguil, a Jew of Palermo	to collect the sums owed him	
3.11.1430 c. nn	Iacob Taguil, a Palermitan Jew	Gallufu Taguil, his brother	To collect the sums owed him	

6616

Date and Page	Debtor	Amount	Reason	Remarks
2.1.[..] c. nn	Siminto Briga, a Jew of Palermo	6 ounces	payments made to various creditors by Benedetto Sacerdoto, a Jew of Palermo	to be paid to Benedetto in annual instalments of 1 ounce
[...] c. nn	Vita Catalano, a Palermitan Jew	4 ounces	unpaid debt on account of joint venture	creditor: Merdoc Malti, Vita's son-in-law
29.5.[..] c. nn	Thomeo de Zamparono	1 ounce	debt for sale of a curtain	creditor: Vita Cathalano, a Jew of Palermo; to be paid by October
28.4.1429 c. nn	Andrea Damiata	1.18.0 ounces	unpaid debt	creditor: Busacca de Tripuli, a Palermitan Jew; to be paid by May by Alesssandro and David Abramuni, Jews of Palermo
23.4.1429 c. nn	Xibiten Zel, a Jew of Palermo	1.18.0 ounces		creditor: Guglielmo Siniscalco; to be paid in annual instalments of 9.4. *tarì*; guarantor: Merdoc Vignuni, a Jew
23.9.1429 c. nn	Xibiten Zel, a Jew of Palermo	1.12.0 ounces	unpaid price of tunny	creditor: convent of S. Maria di Monte Carmelo; to be paid in annual instalments of 12.10 *tarì*
28.10.1429 c. nn	Giovanni de Mineo and Antonio de Sallucio of Castelvetrano	37 double sacks of cork tree charcoal	residual quantity of 52 double sacks	creditor: Xibite de Barbuto, a Palermitan Jew; following court action, Giovanni and Antonio promise to deliver the goods
7.11.1429 c. nn	Xibiten Yassuni, a Jew of Nicosia		debt by deed of the notary Andrea Isganga of Nicosia	creditor: Benedetto Misiria, a Jew of Palermo

Date and Page	Lender or Seller	Amount	Payment	Remarks
29.5.14[..] c. nn	Giuliano de Liveri	20 *tarì*	debt for sale of a foal	creditor: Conino Riccio, a Palermitan Jew; to be paid by August to Conino or his nephew, Siminto
9.11.1430 c. nn	Minto Aguel, a Jew of Palermo		unpaid rent of a shop	creditor: Nissim Millac, a Jew in Palermo
15.7.1460 c. nn	Lia Xibiten, a Jew of Palermo	17.3.0 ounces	unpaid debt	creditor: Iacobo de Seri Guglielmo
12.9.1430 c. nn	Nayuni Yairra, a Jew of Palermo	1 ounce	paid 19.10.1430	creditor: Antonio Gimbesio, for oil; moratorium of 3 months; Czullu Markecti, another Jew, stood surety
9.11.1429 c. nn	Minto Aguel, a Jew of Palermo	rent of shop	paid	creditor: Nissim Millac, another Jew; return of pawn sequestered by the Pretorian court
18.11.1429 c. nn	Filippo Testavirdi of Monreale		debt for string (*disa*)	creditor: Isdrael Medui, a Jew in Palermo; paid
Date and Page	**Lender or Seller**	**Amount**	**Payment**	**Remarks**
[...].14[..] c. nn	Muxa Achina and Busacca de Tripoli, Palermitan Jews	1.2.0 ounces	16 *tarì* paid on 4.3	sale of soles to Iacob de Bellassai, a Palermitan Jew
[...].14[..] c. nn	Iosep de Minichi, a Jew of Palermo	19 *tarì*	settlement of debt	sale of beast of burden to Chicco de notario Simone, creditor
16.9.[1428] c. nn	Stire, wife of master Moyse de Gaudio, a Jewess of Palermo	12 ounces	within 7 months	sale

16.9.[1428] c. nn	Xamuele Schilomo, a Palermitan Jew	2.24.0 ounces	within 4 months; paid 8.3.1429	sale of 3 kantars and 23 *rotoli* of Genoese iron to Mussuto de Messina, a Jew of Palermo
[1428] c. nn	Antoniu de Maydaro	22.10 *tarì*	18 *tarì* on account, balance on delivery at vintage time	sale of half a quintal of white grapes to the partners Daniele Rugila and Merdoc Vignuni, Jews of Palermo
[1428] c. nn	Muxa Sacerdotu, a Palermitan Jew	1.12.0 ounces	instalments	sale of a nag to Benedetto Carioso
8.2.[1431?] c. nn	Antonius Rubeus, alias Giordano of Castelvetrano	2 ounces	1 ounce on account, balance in 2 instalments on delivery; paid 12 *tarì* on 20.2., balance on 18.6	sale of 32 double sacks of coal to Isdrael Medui, a Jew of Palermo
8.4.[..] c. nn	Antonio Gimbesio	1.7.0 ounces	paid 24.10	sale to Sufen de Iacob, a Jew of Palermo
[...] c. nn	Bundus de Campis	1.6.0 ounces	12 *tarì* on account, 12 *tarì* by Easter, balance by Pentecost	sale to Lucio Sacerdoto, a Jew in Palermo
28.7.[..] c. nn	Carlo de Spiruverio	13.10.10 ounces	weekly instalments of 11.5 *tarì*; paid 1.9	sale to Musa Rubeo, a Jew in Palermo
29.7.[..] c. nn	Nicolò de Castrogiovanni	1.12.0 ounces	24 *tarì* on account, balance by August; paid 11.9	sale to Schamuele Schalono, a Jew of Palermo
22.12.[..] c. nn	Paolo Miniritu	21 *tarì*	paid	sale to Sabeti Gillebi, a Jew in Palermo
6.7.[..] c. nn	Giovanni de Mirabella	24 *tarì*	11 *tarì* on account; paid	sale of half a quintal of white grapes to Daydono Riccio, a Jew of Palermo

[...] c. nn	Nicolò Rubeo	1.21.0 ounces	1 ounce on account; 9 *tarì* on 10.4., balance on 9.1; paid 9.1	sale of a quintal of red Calabrian grapes to Nissim Lu Cribaru, a Jew of Palermo
22.6.[..] c. nn	Girardo de Castronovo	1 ounce	paid	sale of 16 double sacks of coal to Isdrael Medui, a Palermitan Jew
29.5.[1430?] c. nn	Iuliano de Ansaldo	8 *tarì*	paid	sale to Schamueli Schalono, a Jew of Palermo
30.5.[1430?] c. nn	Federico de Sinibaldis	2.12.0 ounces	by September	sale to Czullu Makekti, Sadono Rugila and Salamon Rugila, Jews of Palermo
1.6.[1430] c. nn	Pietro de Azulino of Monreale	19.10 *tarì*	paid	sale of half a quintal of white grapes to Nissim Frisisa, a Jew in Palermo
2.6.[1430?] c. nn	Vita Catalano, a Jew in Palermo	1 ounce	within 5 months	sale to Daniel de Raffael, a Jew of Corleone
7.6.[1430?] c. nn	Antonio de Matina	2 ounces	within a month	interest free loan to Siminto Maltensis, a Jew of Palermo; guarantor: Yarono Maltensis, son of Siminto
7.6.[1430?] c. nn	Antonio de Bechino	1.7.0 ounces	by December	sale of a quintal of white grapes to Iacob Levi, a Palermitan Jew
7.6.[1430?] c. nn	Vita Catalano, a Jew of Palermo	1.6.0 ounces	by October	sale to Manuel Yalla, a Jew of Palermo
9.6.[1430?] c. nn	Nicolò de Neapoli	1 ounce	within 4 months	sale to Muxa de Butera, a Jew of Palermo

9.6.[1430?] c. nn	David Ysac and David Myar, Jews of Palermo	2 ounces	with grapes and oil	sale
[.].5.[1431?] c. nn	Antonio Gimbesio	1.18.0 ounces	within 4 months	sale to Amoroso Gibesi and Xibiten Ysac, Palermitan Jews
14.5.[1431?] c. nn	Antonio Rubeus	2.9.7.3 ounces	by June; paid	sale to Isdrael Medui, a Jew in Palermo
14.5.[1431?] c. nn	Isdrael Medui, a Jew of Palermo	all debts [for unspecified reasons]		to Muxa de Butera, a Jew of Palermo
14.5.[1431?] c. nn	Giuliano de Grisafi	15 *tarì*	paid	sale of quarter quintal of white grapes to Vita Azaro, a Jew of Palermo
22.5.[1431?] c. nn	Filippo Calandra	15.10 *tarì*	paid	sale to Sabeti Gillebi, a Palermitan Jew
23.5.[1431?] c. nn	Sabet Gillebi, a Jew of Palermo	17 *tarì*	within 2 months; paid: September	sale
24.5.[1431?] c. nn	Pietro de Chicco and Giovanni Camardus	1.23.10 ounces	8 *tarì* on account	sale to Daydono Riccio, a Jew of Palermo
29.10.[..] c. nn	Antonio Gimbesio	1.6.0 ounces	by 24 March	sale to Yaruna; guarantor: her husband, Vannis Mindoli, a Jew in Palermo
29.10.[..] c. nn	Michael de Placia	2.3.0 ounces	1.10.0 ounces by Carnival time, 1.1.10 ounces on 20.6; paid: 6.10	sale to Yarono Medui, a Jew of Palermo
8.11.[..] c. nn	Matheo de Sancto Georgius		paid	sale to Bulchayra Sansuni, a Jew of Palermo
10.11.[..] c. nn	Pietro de Marco	26.15 *tarì*	weekly instalments of 1.10 *tarì*; paid 13.2.[..]	sale to Manuel Verru, a Jew in Palermo

16.11.[..] c. nn	Giovanni de Puleyo of Nicosia	8.10 *tarì* a kantar	15 *tarì* on account; paid 13.6	sale of 10 kantars of cheese and the rest of the cheese produced by the
		herd of Francesco de Ventimigla to Vita Catalano, a Palermitan Jew; Chaym Talbi, a Jew of Marsala, stands surety		
17.11.[..] c. nn	Nardo de Muzarella	1 ounce	within 4 months; paid 6.5	sale 3 *salme* of wheat to Vanni de Sabuchi, a Jew of Palermo
17.11.[..] c. nn	Chicco de La Brama	1.3.18 ounces	within 4 months; paid 21.6	sale of goods to Liuciu Sacerdoto, a Jew in Palermo [Doc. damaged]
18.11.[..] c. nn	Nicola de Scanduri and Giovanni de Milacio	20 *tarì*	8 *tarì* on account; paid 1.2	sale to Sabeti Gillebi, a Palermitan Jew
19.11.[..] c. nn	Sufen Misiria and Salamon [...], Jews	1.6.0 ounces	by November; paid 22.11	sale
19.11.[..] c. nn	Mannus de Gramatico		19 *tarì* on account, balance on delivery; paid 31.1	sale to Isdrael Medui, a Jew
23.11.[..] c. nn	Nissim Millac, a Palermitan Jew	3 ounces	within 4 months; paid 29.4	sale of 3 kantars of Pisan iron to Muxa and Iosep Ammara, Jews of Palermo
24.11.[..] c. nn	Federico Sinibaldis	10 *tarì*	paid	sale; payment by Missim Millac, a Jew
24.11.[..] c. nn	Rosa de Simenti and her son Francesco	1.24.0 ounces	by November	sale to Iacob Levi
26.11.[..] c. nn	Vita Catalano, a Palermitan Jew	1.20.0 ounces	instalments; paid 4.11 of following year	sale of soles to Fariono S[..], a Jew of Palermo [Doc. damaged]

30.12.[..] c. nn	Antonio de Matina	16.0 ounces	within 6 months; paid 8.9 two years later	sale to Isdrael N [..], a Jew in Palermo; guarantor: Iannono Calabrensis
[...] c. nn	Federico de Sinibaldis	1.6.0 ounces	by October; paid 17.10	sale of oil to Azarono de Medico, a Jew in Palermo
2.1.[..] c. nn	Ruggero de Ursone	1.21.0 ounces	23 *tarì* on account, balance by January; paid 13.2	sale to Xibiten Barbuto, a Palermitan Jew
24.3.[..] c. nn	Antonio Rubeus and Antonio Sallucio of Castelvetrano	2 ounces	1 ounce on account; balance on delivery; paid 29.5	sale of 36 double sacks of coal to Xibiten Barbuto, a Palermitan Jew
29.9.[..] c. nn	Pietro de Montalbano	1 ounce	instalments	sale to Muxa Ysac, a Jew in Palermo
[...] c. nn	Giovanni de la Marra	2 ounces	12 *tarì* on account, balance on delivery	sale of 4 kantars of tallow to Siminto Aurifichi, a Jew of Palermo
[...] c. nn	Nicolò de Senna and Masio de Brancato	2 ounces	21 *tarì* on account, balance on delivery	sale 20 *salme* of myrtle to Muxa Sacerdoto and Sabet Furmuni, Palermitan Jews
2.9.[..] c. nn	master Pietro de Montalbano	1.30 ounces	instalments	sale to Xibiten de Lu Presti, a Jew in Palermo
2.9.[..] c. nn	Philippo de Carbonello	1.24.0 ounces	instalments; paid 22.11	sale of grapes to Salamon Benassai, a Jew of Palermo
12.5.[..] c. nn	Giovanni Rubeo	1.3.0 ounces	within 6 months; paid 24.10	sale of 1 kantar of oil to Manuel de Doharicu, a Jew of Palermo

[.].1.[..] c. nn	Federico Sinibaldis	30 *tarì*, i.e. 1 ounce	on demand; instalments; 18 *tarì* paid by 10.11, balance to be paid by Christmas	loan to Czullu Market, a Palermitan Jew
24.1.[..] c. nn	Antonio Matina	3 ounces	by January of following year	sale to Muxa and Sabucu Millac, a Jew of Palermo
[...] c. nn	Merdoc de Malti, a Jew of Palermo	4 ounces	within 18 months	loan
[...] c. nn	Muxa Rubeus, a Jew in Palermo	2.21.16 ounces	by October	sale
[..].5.[..] c. nn	Musarella Adila, a Jew of Piazza	1.6.0 ounces	paid	sale to Azaccaria Achina, a Jew of Palermo
2.1.[..] c. nn	Antonio Gimbesio	1.10.0 ounces	paid	sale to Abram Calabrensi
2.1.[..] c. nn	Simon de Manganello and Allegrancia	2.24.0 ounces		sale to Nissim Ysac, a Jew of Palermo
[...] c. nn	Antonio Matina	1.5.0 ounces	by May; paid 5.8	sale to Cribario Braya, a Jew of Palermo; Nissim de Terminis, a Jew, stood surety
[...] c. nn	Antonio Gimbesio	1.5.0 ounces	paid	sale to Muxa de Butera, a Jew in Palermo
1.9.[..] c. nn	Enrico Gactalluxio	1 ounce	within 3 months	sale 2 *salme* and 8 tumini of wheat to Iacobo Fitira and Xibiten Medui, Palermitan Jews
1.9.[..] c. nn	Filippo de Calandra	25 *tarì*		sale of grapes to Iuda Sivena, a Palermitan Jew [Doc. damaged]

1.9.[..] c. nn	Muxa Chua and Busacca de Tripuli, Jews of Palermo	1.2.0 ounces	16 *tarì* on account	sale
25.9.[..] c. nn	Marco de Salem	2.3.0 ounces	instalments; paid	sale to Amoroso Gibesi, a Jew in Palermo
25.9.[..] c. nn	Marco de Salem	1.3.0 ounces	instalments	sale to Missira Sufen, a Jew in Palermo
5.7.[..] c. nn	Antonio Bentivegna	17.3 *grana* a *salma*	9 *tarì* on account, balance on delivery	sale of 25 *salme* of string (disa) for tunny to Siminto Aurifichi, a Jew of Palermo
8.7.[..] c. nn	Iacobo de Angelo and Filippo de Blanco	17.3 *grana* a *salma*	12 *tarì* on account, balance on delivery	sale of 40 *salme* of string (disa) for tunny to Siminto Aurifichi, a Jew of Palermo
8.7.[..] c. nn	Isdrael Medui, a Palermitan Jew	6 ounces	1 *tarì* on account, balance in monthly instalments of 8 *tarì*	sale of an anvil (*ancunia*) to Leone Sacerdoto, a Jew in Palermo; the anvil is available for use only in the evening: *per*
			facere operam in dicta ancunia in apoteca ipsius *Leonis a primo sero usque ad mediam nocte*	
11.11.1428 c. nn	David Farachi and Muxa de Siracusa, Jews of Palermo	8.21.0 ounces	instalments; paid 18.3.1429	sale of silk to Busacca de Alamagna and Muxa de Siragusia, Jews of Palermo
28.10.1428 c. nn	Filippo de Girardo	24 *tarì*	paid	sale of half a quintal of grapes to Xibiten Ysac, a Jew of Palermo
24.10.1428 c. nn	Benedetto de Girachio, a Jew of Palermo	1.18.0 ounces	12 *tarì* on account, balance in 6 weeks; paid 13.1	sale of grapes to Iuliano Grillo and to Tobias Sirug, a Jew of Catania

18.10.1428 c. nn	Andrea de Alamanno	1.6.0 ounces	paid	sale of 2 quintals of oil to Benedetto de Girachio, a Jew of Palermo
18.10.1428 c. nn	Filippa and her son Nicola de Naro	3 ounces	2 ounces on account, balance within a month; paid 18.11	sale of 2 quintals of grapes to Benedetto Chazen, a Palermitan Jew
18.10.1428 c. nn	Nicola Grillo	1.24.0 ounces	by Christmas, paid 10.1.1429	sale 6 kantars of iron to Xibiten Barbutu, a Jew of Palermo
30.10.1428 c. nn	Enrico de Alamanna	21 *tarì*	paid	sale of half a kantar of grapes to Ayrono Xalom, a Jew of Palermo
30.10.1428 c. nn	Paolo Chimminitu of Monreale		paid	sale of a quintal of grapes to Ayrono Xalom, a Jew of Palermo [Doc. damaged]
30.10.1428 c. nn	Giovanni Buctuchella	24 *tarì*	paid	sale of a quintal of white grapes to Daydono Riccio, a Jew of Palermo
30.10.1428 c. nn	Nicola de Tropea	1.18.0 ounces	1 ounce on account, balance within 10 days; paid 18.11.1428	sale of a quintal of white grapes to Brachono Bambalo, a Jew in Palermo
30.10.1428 c. nn	Salvo de Liocta	3 ounces	1.12.0 ounces on account, balance of delivery	sale of 2 quintals of white grapes to Sadono Obi, a Jew of Palermo
8.11.1428 c. nn	Saladino de Modica	1.6.0 ounces	within 4 months; paid 19.3.1429	sale of 1 kantar of oil to Sabet Minichi, a Palermitan Jew
8.11.1428 c. nn	Pietro Zambaglia	3 ounces	instalments; 27.11.1428	sale of 2 quintals of white grapes to Brachono Bambalo, a Jew in Palermo

6626

12.11.1428 c. nn	Antonio de Bruna	2 ounces	on demand	interest free loan to Nissim Grixon, a Jew of Palermo
12.11.1428 c. nn	Sabet Xaccarrono, a Jew of Palermo	26.10 *tarì*	paid	sale of 1,000 ropes for tunny to Ayrono Xalom, a Jew in Palermo
12.11.1428 c. nn	Saladino de Modica	1.7.0 ounces	half in 2 months, balance in another 2 months; paid 4.5.1429	sale of soles to Xibiten de Marzuc, a Jew of Palermo
12.11.1428 c. nn	Antonio Meliorato	2.8.0 ounces	within 4 months	sale of 2 kantars of oil to Xamuel Gididia and Elia de Malta, Jews of Palermo
12.11.1428 c. nn	Flos Binante, widow of Mordochai Binante, a Jewess of Palermo	1.6.0 ounces		sale [Doc. damaged]
13.11.1428 c. nn	Iacob Xunina, a Palermitan Jew	4.1.16 ounces	by February 1429	sale of 27 *canne* of Calabrian heavy cloth to Fariono Sivena, a Jew in Palermo
17.11.1428 c. nn	Pietro Carecta	1.3.0 ounces	by February 1429; paid 11.2.1429	sale of 3 *salme* of barley to Ayrono Xalom, a Jew in Palermo
17.11.1428 c. nn	Gaspar de Iorlando and Mardoc Simael, Jews in Palermo	1 ounce		sale
21.11.1428 c. nn	Matheo de Girachio	14 *grana* a *salma*	4.10 *tarì* on account, balance in instalments	sale of 60 *salme* of string (*disa*) to Manuel de Doharicu, a Jew in Palermo

1.12.1428 c. nn	Pietro de Mule	2.24.0 ounces	2 ounces on account, balance on delivery; paid	sale of a quintal of red grapes to Nissim Binna, a Jew of Palermo
1.12.1428 c. nn	Filippo de Bove	1.6.0 ounces	6 *tarì* on account, balance on delivery; paid 23.12.1429	sale to Vita Catalano, a Jew of Palermo
7.12.1428 c. nn	Antonio Surrenti	18 *tarì*	on debtor's return to Calabria	sale to master Gaudio Francus of Majorca, a Jew in Palermo
7.12.1428 c. nn	Mazeo de Anselmo	18 *tarì*	paid	sale of half a quintal of white grapes to Busacca Yacaruni, a Jew of Palermo
7.12.1428 c. nn	Antonio de Archide	27 *tarì*	paid	sale to Schamueli Schalono, a Jew in Palermo
12.12.1429 c. nn	Morando de Iandinota	10.15 *tarì*	5.15 *tarì* on account; paid	sale of 14 *salme* of string (disa) for tunny to Sadia Yactan, a Palermitan Jew
14.12.1429 c. nn	Giovanni de Genova	4 ounces	2 ounces on account, balance on delivery	sale to Isdrael Medui, a Jew of Palermo
14.12.1429 c. nn	Iacob Levi, a Jew in Palermo	1.2.0 ounces	within six months; paid 16.6.1430	sale
16.12.1429 c. nn	Antonio de Matina	1.5.0 ounces	within 6 months; paid 23.3.1430	sale of a kantar of oil to Muxa de Matera, a Jew in Palermo; Merdoc Vignuni, a Palermitan Jew, stands surety
16.12.1429 c. nn	Antonio de Matina	1.5.0 ounces	by May 1429; paid 29.8.1430	sale of a kantar of oil to Busacca Sala, a Jew of Palermo

16.12.1429 c. nn	fra Ubertino of the convent S. Maria del Monte Carmelo	1.24.0 ounces	by Easter	sale of 6 casks of tunny to Sabet Zel, a Palermitan Jew
16.12.1429 c. nn	Antonio Matina	1.5.0 ounces	by May 1430; paid 30.5.1430	sale of a kantar of oil to Sabutu Marchili, a Palermitan Jew
16.12.1429 c. nn	Antonio Matina	1.5.0 ounces	by middle of May; paid 7.11.1430	sale of a kantar of oil to Vita Minichi, a Jew in Palermo
19.12.1429 c. nn	Paolo Chiminnito and Giovanni Lu Stalicu of Monreale	1.2.10 ounces	6 *tarì* on account, balance on delivery; paid 1.2.1431	sale of 50 *salme* of string for tunny to Vita Ammara, a Jew in Palermo
19.12.1428 c. nn	Iuda Sivena, a Jew in Palermo	20.24.9 ounces	instalments; paid 26.9.1429	sale of 16 casks of wine to Nicolò de Merabella
19.12.1428 c. nn	Filippo de Testaverdi and Paolo Gittardo of Monreale	13 *tarì*	paid	sale of 20 *salme* of string to Isdrael Medui, a Jew in Palermo
22.12.1428 c. nn	Pietro de Azulino of Monreale	18 *tarì*	paid	sale of half a quintal of grapes to Nissim Frisisa, a Jew in Palermo
22.12.1428 c. nn	Giovanni Drago and Nerio de Donato of Alcamo	2 ounces	1 ounce on account, balance on delivery; paid 16.2.1429	sale of 32 double sacks of cork tree charcoal and 2 *salme* of chestnuts to Isdrael Medui, a Jew in Palermo
22.12.1428 c. nn	Pietro de Francesco de Interrato of Castelvetrano	1 ounce	paid	sale of 16 double sacks of cork tree charcoal and 1 *salma* of chestnuts to Xibiten Barbuto, a Jew of Palermo

23.12.1428 c. nn	Pietro de Interrato of Castelvetrano	1 ounce	paid	sale of 17 double sacks of cork tree charcoal to Isdrael Medui, a Jew in Palermo
23.12.1428 c. nn	Masio de La Falchi of Monreale	18.10 *tarì*	paid	sale of 30 *salme* of string for tunny to Xibiten Barbuto, a Jew of Palermo
23.12.1428 c. nn	Paolo Musillo	18 *tarì*	12 *tarì* on account, balance by August; paid 25.10	sale of 30 *salme* of string for tunny to Schamuel Schalomo, a Jew of Palermo
23.12.1428 c. nn	Antonio de Matina	1.5.0 ounces	by April 1429	sale of a kantar of oil to Graciano Tayariatu, a Jew in Palermo
2.10.1428 c. nn	Antonio de La Matina	2.6.0 ounces	1.3.0 ounces by Carnival time, 1.3.0 ounces by August; paid 22.9.1429	sale of a quintal of white grapes to Liucio Sacerdoto, a Palermitan Jew
3.10.1428 c. nn	master Pietro de Martino	1.27.0 ounces		sale of a quintal of white grapes to Iacob Levi, a Jew in Palermo
[.].10.1428 c. nn	Antonio de Gimbesio	1.5.0 ounces	within 4 months; paid 20.12.1428	sale of 1 kantar of oil to Muxutu de Missina, a Jew of Palermo
1.12.1428 c. nn	Nardo de Muzzarella, a notary	2 ounces	within 6 months	sale of 2 kantars of iron to Merdoc Semal and Vanni de Termini, Jews in Palermo
28.2.1429 c. nn	Giovanni de Inguaiato of Monreale	11.5 *tarì*	paid	sale of 15 *salme* of string for tunny to Sadia Yactan, a Jew of Palermo

28.2.1429 c. nn	Azaccaria Achina, a Palermitan Jew	4.15.0 ounces	at vintage time; paid 19.2.1430	sale of a silk covered curtain to Costanza, widow of Antonio Russo of Monreale; pietro de Cannata of Monreale stands surety
28.2.1429 c. nn	Lia Sivena, a Palermitan Jew	1 ounce	by Easter	loan to Graciosa, wife of Vita Sivena, a Palermitan Jewess; she pawns some articles part of her *ketubbah* to be returned after payment.
28.2.1429 c. nn	Muxa de Tripuli, a Jew in Palermo	21 *tarì*	paid 2.1.1430	sale of 1 kantar of oil; Xibiten Sammara, a Jew of Palermo, stands surety
1.3.1429 c. nn	Mayaluffo Cuzuza and Iosep Grecu, Jews of Trapani	15 ounces	9 ounces by April, balance by December; paid 6.2.1430	sale of cheese to Nicola de Ruma of Trapani
9.3.1429 c. nn	Antonio de Gimbesio	1.6.0 ounces	within 4 months; paid 15.2.1430 by Matheo de Messana, a Jew	sale of a kantar of oil to Muxa de Bulgiti and his son Natale, Jews in Palermo
10.3.1429 c. nn	Nicolò de Leonardo	10 *tarì*	paid	sale of 1,000 white bricks to Lia Sivena, a Jew in Palermo
10.3.1429 c. nn	Pino de Naso of Monreale	1.9.0 ounces	24 *tarì* on account, balance on 23.3.1430	sale of a quintal of grapes to Brayono Siragusano also on behalf of Isdrael Benassai, Jews of Palermo

Date	Name	Amount	Terms	Description
10.3.1429 c. nn	Pietro de Monaco and master Nicolò de Leonardo	24 *tarì*	2 *tarì* on account, balance on delivery	sale of 1,000 roof tiles to Benedetto Sacerdoto, a Jew; Sabet Schayaruni and Benedetto Cavisi, Jews of Palermo
11.3.1429 c. nn	Simon de Guzardo	13 *tarì*	6 *tarì* on account, balance on delivery	sale of 20 *salme* of string for tunny to Busacca de Tripuli, a Palermitan Jew
11.3.1429 c. nn	Antonio Gimbesio	2.13.0 ounces	within 4 months; paid 20.12.1430	sale of 2 kantars of oil to Merdoc Levi, a Palermitan Jew; Natale Bulgiti, his Jewish fellow citizen, stands surety
14.3.1429 c. nn	Friderico de Monaco	1.18.0 ounces	1.6.0 ounces on account, balance at vintage time	sale of a quintal of white grapes to Fariono Niquiseu, a Jew in Palermo
14.3.1429 c. nn	Giovanni Pugnuduru of Monreale	16.13 *tarì*	12 *tarì* on account, balance by August; paid in August	sale of 25 *salme* of string for tunny to Schamuel Schalomo, a Jew in Palermo
14.3.1429 c. nn	Thomeo Damiano of Monreale	21 *tarì*	21 *tarì* on account	sale of a quintal of white grapes to Sabet Gillebi, a Palermitan Jew
14.3.1429 c. nn	Merdoc Calabrensis, a Palermitan Jew	1.12.0 ounces	15 *tarì* on account, balance on 15.4; paid 6.4	sale
17.3.1429 c. nn	Antonio de mastro Angelo	21 *tarì*	paid	sale of half a quintal of white grapes to Aydono Riccio, a Jew of Palermo
17.3.1429 c. nn	Aloisio de Ast	18.10 *tarì*	within 6 months	sale of half a kantar of oil to to Benedetto Gibra and Pinesio Sacerdoto, Jews of Palermo

17.3.1429 c. nn	Antonio Gimbesio	2.12.0 ounces	within 4 months	sale of 2 kantars of oil to Brachono Mizoc, a Palermitan Jew
18.3.1429 c. nn	Angilo de Michio	9 *tarì*	paid	sale of 2½ *salme* of white grapes to master Abram Chualena, a Jew of Palermo
18.3.1429 c. nn	Pietro de Luntanu of Monreale	18 *tarì*	paid	sale of half a quintal of white grapes to Nissim Adoroti, a Jew in Palermo
18.3.1429 c. nn	Nissim Millac, a Jewish smith in Palemo	1.18.0 ounces	by April	loan to Busacca de Amato, a Jew of Nicosia in Palermo; deed drawn up by Graciano Naguay, notary of the Jewish community in Palemro
22.3.1429 c. nn	Antonio de Anselmo	3.15.0 ounces	instalments until Pentecost; paid 30.5.1429	sale of 1½ quintals of white grapes to Sadia Yactan, a Palermitan Jew
23.3.1429 c. nn	Antonio Czinziri	18.15 *tarì*	7.10 *tarì* on account, balance on delivery	sale of 25 *salme* of string (*disa*) for ropes for tunny to Siminto Aurifichi, a Jew in Palermo
11.4.1429 c. nn	Antonio de Antonius de Amare, a canon	2.18.0 ounces	1.12.0 ounces on account, balance by June	sale of a mule to Nissim Millac, a Palermitan Jew
13.4.1429 c. nn	Aloysio de Pasquale, a Palermitan citizen	18.15 *tarì*	6 *tarì* on account, balance on delivery	sale od 25 *salme* of string for tunny ropes to Sadia Yactan, a Palermitan Jew
14.4.1429 c. nn	Iohanne Sadoc, a Palermitan Jew	22 *tarì*	paid	sale

15.4.1429 c. nn	Enrico and Antonio de La Mulidia of Alcamo	5 ounces	2.18.0 ounces on account, balance on delivery	sale of 80 double sacks of cork tree charcoal to Schamuel Schalomo, a Jew of Palermo
15.4.1429 c. nn	Iacobo de Antonio	1.4.0 ounces		sale of oil to Busacca de Syracusia, a Jew in Palermo
18.4.1429 c. nn	Matheo de Carastono	14 ounces	instalments until 14.6.1430; paid 14.9.1431	sale of 12 kantars of oil to Lia de Barbuto, a Palermitan Jew
19.4.1429 c. nn	Pietro de Azulino of Monreale	19.10 *tarì*	paid	sale of a quarter of a quintal of white grapes and another of red grapes to Nissim Frisisa, a Jew in Palermo
19.4.1429 c. nn	Antonio de Gimbesio	1.6.0 ounces	within 5 months	sale of 1 kantar of oil to Maymuni Virra and Salamon Rugila, Jews of Palermo
19.4.1429 c. nn	Antonio de Ausilio	21 *tarì*	18 *tarì* on account, balance on demand	sale to Sadia Yactan, a Palermitan Jew
21.4.1429 c. nn	Salamon Azara, a Jew in Palermo	2 ounces	1 ounce at vintage time, the other at the following vintage time	sale to Muxa Medui, Vita Luristivu, son of Busacca Calabrensi, and Merdoc di Liucio, Palermitan Jews
22.4.1429 c. nn	Antonio and Masio La Corsa	1.10.10 ounces	22.10 *tarì* on account; balance in kind; paid 28.6.1429	sale of a quintal of grapes to Siminto Benassai, a Jew in Palermo
28.4.1429 c. nn	Antonio Angilo	18 *tarì*	paid	sale to Daydono Ricio, a Jew of Palermo
3.5.1429 c. nn	Francesco de Pastina	25 *tarì*	21 *tarì* on account	sale of half a kantar white grapes to Sabeti Gillebi, a Jew in Palermo

3.5.1429 c. nn	Francesco de Trapani	1.21.0 ounces	3 *tarì* on account; paid 15.3.1430	sale of a quintal of grapes to Muxa de Butera, a Jew of Palermo
4.5.1429 c. nn	Xibite Vignuni, a Palermitan Jew	1.27.11½ ounces	within a month	sale of 51 *rotoli* of processed tin to Muxa Ysac, a Palermitan Jew;
	surety by Muxa de Buggeya, a Jew in Palermo			
6.5.1429 c. nn	Vita Azara, a Jew in Palermo	1.3.15 ounces	2 *tarì* a month until August	sale to Yacob Ficira, a Jew of Palermo
8.5.1429 c. nn	Bartholomeo de Consatori	2.15.0 ounces	2.10 *tarì* on account	sale to Vannis de Missina, a Jew of Palermo
12.5.1429 c. nn	Lia Isaya, a Palermitan Jew	2.15 tari	15 *grana* on account, balance on delivery	sale to Gallufo Minichi, a Jew in Palermo
12.5.1429 c. nn	Azaccaria Achina, a Palermitan Jew	2.2.0 ounces	within 2 months	sale to Sabatino de Policio, a Jew of Caccamo
20.5.1429 c. nn	Giovanni de Ganchio	8 ounces	1.12.0 ounces on account, balance after deduction of expenses; paid 4.8.1429	sale to David Abramuni, a Jew of Palermo
22.5.1429 c. nn	Giovanni de Bivona	13 *tarì* a kantar until August	5 + 7 *tarì* on account, balance on delivery	sale of all the tallow produced in the abattoir of Palermo to Muxa Achina, a Jew in Palermo
30.10.1429 c. nn	Antonio de Matina	1.1.10 ounces	by May 1430; paid 27.7.1430	sale of 9 *cafisi* of oil to Gallufu de Minichi, a Jew in Palermo
30.10.1429 c. nn	Iacob Levi, a Jew of Palermo, acting for master Bartholomeo Ciru	9 ounces	paid	sale of a white Circassian slave girl named Milica to Matheo de Carastono

30.10.1429 c. nn	Ubertino de Imperatore	29 *tarì*	paid 30.5.1430	sale to Yanino Formono, a Jew of Palermo
30.10.1429 c. nn	Nicolò Scanduri of Monreale and Simon de Fina, a Jew of Palermo	16.5 *tarì*	8.10 *tarì* on account, balance by August	sale of 25 *salme* of string for tunny to Isdrael Medui, a Jew of Palermo
8.11.1429 c. nn	Daunisio de Ragusa of Cammarata	24 *tarì*	within 7 weeks; paid 4.6.1431	sale 2 *salme* of Cammarata salt to Gallufo Mayurana, a Jew in Palermo; Iosep Trinuti of Cammarata stands surety
8.11.1429 c. nn	Nissim Binna, a Jew of Palermo	2.9.0 ounces	6 *tarì* on account; balance in in weekly instalments of 6 *tarì*; paid 13.2.1430	sale of 6 kantars of cheese to Nissim de Benedetto, a Palermitan Jew
14.11.1429 c. nn	Mazeo de Messana, a Jew of Palermo	3.3.0 ounces	instalments; paid 19.5.1430	sale
14.11.1429 c. nn	Antonio de Matina	1.15.0 ounces	by April	sale to Nissim Millac, a Jew of Palermo
16.11.1429 c. nn	Antonio de Matina	3.3.0 ounces	by December; paid 7.4.1430	sale of 3 kantars of oil to Marzoco Binna, a Palermitan Jew
16.11.1429 c. nn	Faczino de Pulchellis	1.12.0 ounces	6 *tarì* on account, balance on delivery; paid 9.12.1429	sale of a quintal of white grapes to Xibite Barbuto, a Palermitan Jew
16.11.1429 c. nn	Xibiten Gazu, a Jew in Palermo	3.24.0 ounces	paid	sale of 4 kantars of oil to Enrico de Gactalluxio
16.11.1429 c. nn	Antonio de Matina	1.5.0 ounces	by March 1430; paid 17.4.1431	sale of 1 kantar of oil to Luna, wife of Sabeti Schayaruni, a Jewess of Palermo

6636

17.11.1429 c. nn	Giovanni de Alessandro and David Abramuni, a Palermitan Jew	24 ounces	instalments until 2.6.1430	sale to Busacca de Tripoli, a Jew of Palermo
18.11.1429 c. nn	Pietro de Afflicto	10 ounces	instalments	sale of 5 kantars of olive oil to Nissim de Benedetto, a Jew of Palermo
18.11.1429 c. nn	Pietro de Afflicto	4 ounces	paid	sale of olive oil to Nissim de Benedetto, a Jew of Palermo
18.11.1429 c. nn	Isdrael Medui, a Jew in Palermo	26 *tarì*	24 *tarì* on account; balance on demand	sale of 40 *salme* of string for tunny ropes to Simon de Guzardo
18.11.1429 c. nn	Filippo de Testavirdi	19.10 *tarì*	3 *tarì* on account, balance on 16.10	sale of 30 *sale* of string to Isdrael Medui, a Jew in Palermo
18.11.1429 c. nn	Francesco de Pastina	1.18.0 ounces with leather	by vintage time	sale of 1 quintal of grapes to Sabeti Gillebi, a Jew in Palermo
18.11.1429 c. nn	Filippo de Testavirdi and Filippo Girardo	27 *tarì*	paid	sale of 30 *sale* of string to Isdrael Medui, a Jew in Palermo
18.11.1429 c. nn	Antonius de Traina	6.10.0 ounces	paid	sale to Yarono Taguil, a Jew of Monreale
22.11.1429 c. nn	Iacob Levi, a Palermitan Jew	10.15.0 ounces	instalments; paid 5.1.1430	sale
22.11.1429 c. nn	Chirello Finiolu	26.13 *tarì*	20 *tarì* on account, balance on delivery	sale to Xibiten Barbuto, a Jew of Palermo
22.11.1429 c. nn	Antonio de Matina	2.10.0 ounces	within 6 months; paid 1.6.1430	sale to Salamon Rugila alias Nasca, a Palermitan Jew

23.11.1429 c. nn	C[..] and Angelo de Vizzini	1.2.10 ounces	13 *tarì* on account, balance in 2 instalments by June 1430	sale of 50 *salme* of string to Isdrael Medui, a Palermitan Jew
23.11.1429 c. nn	Antonio and Pietro Carecta	1.10.0 ounces	1 ounce on account, balance on delivery	sale of 60 *salme* of string to Xibite Barbuto, a Jew in Palermo
24.11.1429 c. nn	Antonio de Matina	1.6.0 ounces	instalments until July 1430; paid 7.8.1430	sale of a kantar of oil to Salamon Actuni, a Palermitan Jew
14.2.1430 c. nn	Constancia, wife of Antonio Russo	1.21.0 ounces	1.15.0 ounces on account; balance on delivery	sale 1½ quintals of grapes to Azaccaria Achina, a Palermitan Jew
14.2.1430 c. nn	Guillelmu de Vita	18.10 *tarì*	paid	sale of half a quintal of grapes to Daydono Riccio, a Jew of Palermo
15.2.1430 c. nn	Antonio de Matina	2.10.0 ounces	within 6 months	sale of 2 kantars of oil to Muxa and Sabutu Millac, Jewish brothers of Palermo
17.2.1430 c. nn	Pietro de Afflicto	3.6.0 ounces	within 4 months; paid 17.11.1430	sale of pieces of silk of various colours to Lia de Messana alias Picta, a Jew of Palermo
17.2.1430 c. nn	Matheo de Murrecta	3.5 *tarì* each	12 *tarì* on account, balance on delivery	sale of 30 sheepskins to Nissim Frisisa, a Jew in Palermo
20.2.1430 c. nn	Frederico Sinibaldis	20 *tarì*	by the feast of St. John (27.12); paid 3.7.1430	sale to Sabatino Calabrensis, a Jew of Palermo; Busacca de Tripuli, another Palermitan Jew, stood surety

Date	Seller	Price	Payment	Description
22.2.1430 c. nn	Antonio Russo of Castelvetrano	1 ounce	paid 27.6.1431	sale of 18 double sacks of coal to Xibiten Barbuto, a Palermitan Jew; Antonio is to deliver another 12 double sacks on account of an earlier sale
27.2.1430 c. nn	Ileria, widow of Covino de Simone, and her children Garite and Francesco	5.2 *tarì* a kantar	2.12.0 ounces on account, balance in instalments; paid	sale of all the cow cheese produced on their farm during May to Vita Catalano, a Jew in Palermo
1.3.1430 c. nn	Pietro de Mazzulino	18 *tarì*	paid	sale of half a quintal of white grapes to Nissim Frisisa, a Jew of Palermo
2.3.1430 c. nn	Antonio Gimbesio	1 ounce	within 6 months; paid 7.11.1430	sale of a woan's tunic to Bella, wife of Copiu, a Jewess of Palermo; guarantors: her son Muxa Copiu and Isdrael Ysac, Jews of Palermo
14.3.1430 c. nn	Pietro de Chicco of Monreale	18 *tarì*	paid	sale of half a quintal of white grapes to Nissim Binna, a Palermitan Jew
15.3.1430 c. nn	Iacobo de Ioya of Monreale	18 *tarì*	paid	sale of half a quintal of grapes to Xibite Barbuto, a Palermitan Jew
15.3.1430 c. nn	Nardo Freza, acting for Pietro Afflicto	3.20.0 ounces	2 *tarì* on account; balance on payment of a debt of 3.18.0 ounces of Merdoc Vivanti, [a Jew]; paid 14.11.1430	sale of 5 pieces of silk (veils) to Nissim Agruti, a Jew of Palermo
15.3.1430 c. nn	Schamuel Schalono, a Palermitan Jew	2.26.0 ounces	within 6 months	sale to Muxa Vignuni, a Jew in Palermo

Date	Name	Amount	Terms	Description
24.3.1430 c. nn	Enrico de Gactalluxio	12 *tarì*	instalments; paid 4.8.1430	sale to Czullu Marchecti, a Jew of Palermo
24.3.1430 c. nn	Giovanni Russo	1.6.0 ounces	within 6 months; paid 24.10.1430	sale of 1 kantar of oil to Brayono Grecu, a Palermitan Jew; Manuel de Doharicu, a Jew, stood surety
24.3.1430 c. nn	Antonio de Matina	2.25.0 ounces	by August; paid 13.11.1430	sale of 2½ kantars of oil to Vita Ysac, a Palermitan Jew
24.3.1430 c. nn	Antonio de Matina	1 ounce	within 2 months; paid 11.8.1430	sale of 1 kantar of oil to Nissim Millac, a Jew in Palermo; Sabuto Millac, a Jew, stands surety
27.3.1430 c. nn	Angelo Demma and his wife Pasqua	16½ *tarì*	paid	sale of half a quintal of white grapes to Nissim Frisisa, a Jew of Palermo
27.3.1430 c. nn	Aloysio Lombardo and his wife Ventura	1.10.0 ounces	9 *tarì* on account, balance by July; paid 24.10.1430	sale of 10 *salme* of barley to Isdrael Medui, a Jew in Palermo
29.3.1430 c. nn	Siminto Aurifichi, a Palermitan Jew	1.1.0 ounces	by July	sale of 500 heavy ropes and 500 light ropes for tunny to Antonio de Rigio
29.3.1430 c. nn	Federico de Sinibaldis	2.12.0 ounces	by September; paid 26.9.1430	sale of 2 kantars of oil to Samuel and Busacca Sala, Jews in Palermo
3.4.1430 c. nn	Giovanni Yalesi of Monreale	14 *tarì*	6 *tarì* on account; balance on delivery; paid 6.9.1430	sale of 20 *salme* of string to Sadia Yactan, a Jew of Palermo

3.4.1430 c. nn	Pietro de Alba of Monreale	9.15 *tarì*	4 *tarì* on account; balance on delivery	sale of 15 *salme* of string to Sadia Yactan, a Jew of Palermo
3.4.1430 c. nn	Pino de Bove	1.6.0 ounces	13 *tarì* on account, balance on delivery; paid 24.10	sale of 1 quintal of white grapes to Isdrael Medui, a Jew in Palermo
4.4.1430 c. nn	Pietro de Leontino of Monreale	16.10 *tarì*	paid	sale of half a quintal of white grapes to Leone Sacerdoto, a Jew of Palermo
4.4.1430 c. nn	Antonio de Matina	1.2.0 ounces	by August; paid 1.9.1430	sale of 1 kantar of oil to Xibiten de Syracusia alias mastru Pino, a Jew of Palermo
4.4.1430 c. nn	Antonio de Matina	1.2.0 ounces	by August; paid 13.9.1430	sale of 1 kantar of oil to Daniel de Raffaeli, a Jew of Sciacca;

Xibiten de Siracusia and Lia Banbulu, Palermitan Jews, stand surety

6.4.1430 c. nn	Tuchio de Lu Castelluczu of Ciminnna	10.10 *tarì*	paid	sale of 5 *salme* of white and red must to Lia de Messana, a Palermitan Jew
7.4.1430 c. nn	Vita Catalano, a Palermitan Jew	2.12.0 ounces	1 ounce on account; balance within 3 months	sale of a silk covered curtain to Diamante, wife of Giovanni de Comite Virardi of Mazara in Palermo; Benedetto di Mazara in

Palermo stands surety

10.4.1430 c. nn	Iacobo de Ioya of Monreale	9 *tarì*	paid	sale a quarter quintal of grapes to Xibite Barbuto, a Palermitan Jew
11.4.1430 c. nn	Nicola Charchara and Benedetto Chanchilleri	20 *tarì*	8 *tarì* on account, balance on delivery	sale of 30 *salme* of string for ropes to Sadia Yactan, a Jew of Palermo

14.4.1430 c. nn	Vita Catalano, a Palermitan Jew	1.2.0 ounces	by October; paid 5.10	sale of a kantar of oil to Laudatu de Mariano
14.4.1430 c. nn	Vita Catalano, a Palermitan Jew	1.2.0 ounces	by October	sale of a kantar of oil to Busacca Guctuz, a Jew of Palermo
14.4.1430 c. nn	Benedetto Sacerdoto, a Palermitan Jew	3.12.0 ounces	1.6.0 ounces on account, balance in instalments; paid 13.8.1430	sale of cattle to Giovanni Fatarcha of Palermo
20.4.1430 c. nn	Enrico Spiridiu	1 ounce	paid	sale of nag with saddle and harness to Iacobo Danieli, a Jew of Palermo
27.4.1430 c. nn	Andrea Yamami of Monreale	21 *tarì*	11 *tarì* on account; balance at vintage time	sale of half a quintal white grapes to Xibite Barbuto, a Jew in Palermo
24.4.1430 c. nn	Simone de Sikiki	20 *tarì*	paid	sale of 6 cow hides to Merdoc Semal and Vanni de Termini, Jews
3.5.1430 c. nn	Nicolò Susinni of Monreale	18 *tarì*	paid	sale of half a quintal of white grapes to Nissim Frisisa, a Jew of Palermo
3.5.1430 c. nn	Pino de La Falchi and Antonio de Lupo of Monreale	20 *tarì*	9 *tarì* on account, balance in instalments by June	sale of 30 *salme* of string for ropes to Sadia Yactan, a Jew of Palermo
4.5.1430 c. nn	Antonio de Matina	3.15.0 ounces	by August; paid 22.9.1430	sale of 3½ kantars of oil to master Yarono Taguil, a Palermitan Jew
5.5.1430 c. nn	Fulco Palumba	1 ounce	by July	sale of 1 kantar of oil to Muxa Cardamono, a Jew of Palermo;

Muxa pawns a garment with Fulco, returned
on payment of debt

8.5.1430 c. nn	Friderico de Porchello, barber	2 ounces	by August; paid 25.10	sale of 2 kantars of oil to the smith Lia Cusinu, alias Sacerdoto, a Palermitan Jew
9.5.1430 c. nn	Isdrael Medui, a Jew in Palermo		at harvest time; paid 23.11.1430	interest free loan of 2 *salme* and 8 *tumini* of wheat to Giovanni de Prisa
4.9.1430 c. nn	Guglielmo de Siniscalco	12 *tarì*	within 6 months	sale of 1½ *salme* of oil to Sophen de Yacob, a Jew of Palermo
4.9.1430 c. nn	Guglielmo de Siniscalco	1.2.0 ounces	within 6 months	sale of 4 *salme* of oil to Muxa de Terminis and his wife Gauyusa, Jews of Palermo
6.9.1430 c. nn	Grazona wife of Chilino	2 ounces a quintal	within a month; paid 24.9.1430	sale of all the grapes produced by her vineyard to Schamueli Sacerdoto, a Jew of Palermo
7.9.1430 c. nn	Isdrael Medui, a Jew of Palermo		paid	sale of merchandise
4.9.1430 c. nn	Marco de Salem	2.18.0 ounces	weekly instalments of 9.5 *tarì*; paid	sale of 1 quintal of white grapes from his vineyard to Gallufo Sano, a Jew of Palermo
11.9.1430 c. nn	Enrico de Bellordono	1.9.0 ounces	weekly instalments; paid 16.10.1431	sale of 1 quintal white grapes to Xibiten Ysac, a Palermitan Jew
11.9.1430 c. nn	Manuel di Doharico, a Jew in Palermo	1 ounce	by January 1431; paid	sale of 1 kantar of oil to Giovanni de Prisa

11.9.1430 c. nn	Enrico de La Manna	21 *tarì*	20 *tarì* on account	sale of half a quintal of grapes from his vineyard to Manuel de Doharico, a Jew of Palermo
11.9.1430 c. nn	Guglielmo de Siniscalco	6.13.0 ounces	within 4 months; paid 20.3.1431	sale of goods to Azaronu Ricio and Robino Gibra, Palermitan Jews
[...].1430 c. nn	Antonio de Gimbesio	1 ounce	by March	sale of half a quintal of white grapes to Merdoc de Tripuli, a Jew of Palermo
13.9.1430 c. nn	Giovanni Rubeo	2.8.0 ounces	within 4 months; paid 22.6.1431	sale of 2 kantars of oil to Iacob Taguil, a Jew of Palermo; Brayono Taguil, his brother, stood surety
13.9.1430 c. nn	Antonio de Gimbesio	1.7.0 ounces	within 4 months; paid 28.6.1431	sale of oil to the brothers Muxa and Pasquale Sacerdoto, Palermitan Jews
13.9.1430 c. nn	Marco de Salem	2.18.0 ounces	weekly instalments of 1.10 *tarì*; paid 26.10.1431	sale of a quintal of white grapes to Amuroso Gillebi and Merdoc Malti, Palermitan Jews
22.9.1430 c. nn	Vita Catalano, a Palermitan Jew	6.6.0 ounces	by March; paid 25.9.1431	sale of 6 kantars of oil to Andrea de la Matina
22.9.1430 c. nn	Giovanni Scarchella	20 *tarì*	by November; paid 25.5.1431	sale of 100 pairs of soles to Vanni di Termini, a Jew in Palermo
25.9.1430 c. nn	the brothers Siminto and Yua Aurifichi, Jews of Palermo	7.22.10 ounces	by April 1431	sale of 5 kantars of Tunisian oil and 500 forms for sugar to Thomeo de magistro Antonio

6644

25.9.1430 c. nn	Paolo Musillino	24 *tarì*	23.10 *tarì* on account; balance on delivery	sale of half a kantar of white grapes to Schamueli Schalomo, a Palermitan Jew; Ruggero de Severino stands surety
25.9.1430 c. nn	Ruggero de Severino	24 *tarì*	12 *tarì* on account; balance on delivery	sale of half a quintal of white grapes to Schamueli Schalono, a Palermitan Jew
25.9.1430 c. nn	Ruggero de Severino			sale of *disa* to Schamueli Schalomo, a Palermitan Jew
26.9.1430 c. nn	Giuliano and Domenico de Ansaldo			sale to Schamueli Schalomo, a Palermitan Jew
26.9.1430 c. nn	Antonio de Ansaldo, a clergyman, and after his death his heirs Giuliano and Domenico Ansaldo			sale of half a quintal and 6 *pisa* of grapes to Benedetto Yaseni, a Palermitan Jew; Giuliano and Domenico de Ansaldo stood surety
26.9.1430 c. nn	Antonio de Ansaldo, a clergyman, and after his death his heirs Giuliano and Domenico Ansaldo			sale of 8 *salme* and 3 *pisa* of grapes to Benedetto Yaseni
26.9.1430 c. nn	Israel Medui, a Palermitan Jew	1.8.0 ounces	by August	sale of an anvil to master Giovanni Spina, a smith
22.10.1430 c. nn	Nerio de Donato of Alcamo	1 ounce	24 *tarì* on account; balance on delivery	sale of 16 double sacks of cork tree charcoal to Israel Medui, a Palermitan Jew

31.10.1430 c. nn	notary Chicco son of notary Simon	4 ounces	paid	sale of 2½ quintals of grapes to Nissim Binna, a Jew in Palermo
2.11.1430 c. nn	Giovanni Rubeo	1.5.0 ounces	within 4 months; paid 6.9.1431	sale of goods to Sadia Ysac, a Jew of Palermo
7.11.1430 c. nn	Giovanni Rubeo	1 ounce	within 6 months	sale of 1 kantar of oil to Manuel de Doharicu, a Jew of Palermo
7.11.1430 c. nn	Busacca de Tripuli, a Palermitan Jew	2 ounces	by May 1431; paid 3.7.1431	sale of tunny to Vita Ammara alias Pancza, a Jew of Palermo; Sadia Ysac, another Jew, stood surety
7.11.1430 c. nn	Busacca de Tripuli, a Palermitan Jew	2 ounces	weekly instalments of 8.10 *tarì*	sale of 2 beasts of burden and an interest free loan of 3 *tarì* to David Chipriano, his fellow Jew
8.11.1430 c. nn	Leone Sacerdoto, a Jew of Palermo	3 ounces	paid	sale of an anvil to Israel Medui, a Palermitan Jew
9.11.1430 c. nn	Antonio Gimbesio	1.6.0 ounces	monthly instalments of 1.10 *tarì*; paid 12.2.1433	sale of goods to Xibiten Zel, a Jew of Palermo; Gallufu Mayurana, another Jew, who stood surety, paid Antonio
9.11.1430 c. nn	Nicolò de Nanni	1.24.0 ounces	1 ounce on account, balance by Christmas; paid 12.12.1430	sale of a quintal of white grapes to David Schacaruni, a Jew of Palermo
[..].11.1430 c. nn	Giovanni Rubeo	1.5.0 ounces	paid 21.9.1431	sale of 1 kantar of oil to Sadia Ysac, a Palermitan Jew; Vita Ammara, alias Pancza, and his son Leone, Jews, stood surety

13.11.1430 c. nn	Chanchiu de Raimundo	2 ounces	instalments; paid 5.6.1431	sale of 30 double sacks of coal to Israel Medui, a Palermitan Jew
14.11.1430 c. nn	Antonio Gimbesio	1.6.0 ounces	within 4 months; paid 26.10.1431	sale of a kantar of oil to Iacob Maltese, his wife Nesa and Pasquale Sacerdoto, Jews of Palermo
21.11.1430 c. nn	Pietro de Afflicto	2.15.0 ounces	by December	sale of cloth to Lia de Messina, alias Picca, a Palermitan Jew
23.11.1430 c. nn	Israel Medui, a Jew in Palermo			sale of goods to Thomeo de Crutone in Castelvetrano
23.11.1430 c. nn	Israel Medui, a Jew in Palermo	12 *tarì*	by December; paid 1.2.1431	sale of 2 *salme* of barley to Giovanni de Prisa
29.11.1430 c. nn	Enrico de Bellordono	1.3.0 ounces	weekly instalments of 4 *tarì*	sale of a nag to Merdoc di Minichi alias Santo Marco, a Jew of Palermo
1.12.1430 c. nn	master Marino de Ianrubeo	2 ounces	within 2 months; paid 5.3.1431	sale of pepper and ginger to Benedetto Sacerdoto,
			a Palermitan Jew; Siminto Briya stood surety	
4.12.1430 c. nn	Antonio Gimbesio	18 tari	within 4 months; paid 20.11.1433	sale of half a kantar of oil to Minto Iaela, a Jew of Palermo
4.12.1430 c. nn	Ruggero de Iannello	1.18.0 ounces	paid 11.10.1431	sale of a quintal of white grapes to Iuda Sivena, a Palermitan Jew; Nicolò Corvo stood surety
4.12.1430 c. nn	Antonio Gimbesio	18 *tarì*	within 4 months	sale of half a kantar of oil to Muxa Copiu, a Jew of Palermo;
			Brayono de Policio, a Jew of Palermo, stood surety	

4.12.1430 c. nn	Antonio Gimbesio	24 *tarì*	monthly instalments of 2 *tarì*	sale of 8 *cafisi* of oil to Ysac de Tripuli, a Palermitan Jew
7.12.1430 c. nn	Angelo de Polito	24 *tarì*	paid	sale of half a quintal of white grapes to Xibite Barbuto, a Jew in Palermo
11.12.1430 c. nn	Giovanni Rubeo	9 *tarì*	with half a kantar of oil by October 1431	loan to Sabet Schayaruni, a Jew of Palermo
11.12.1430 c. nn	Pietro de Chicco	24 *tarì*	paid 16.1.1431	sale of half a quintal of white grapes to Nissim Binna, a Palermitan Jew
11.12.1430 c. nn	Nicolò de Lamanno and his wife Victoria	1.18.0 ounces	27 *tarì* on account, balance within 10 days; paid	sale of a kantar of white grapes to Israel Medui, a Palermitan Jew
11.12.1430 c. nn	Pietro de Raia	2 ounces	paid	sale of a kantar of white grapes to Nissim Binna, a Jew of Palermo
12.12.1430 c. nn	Cristofalo Scarparo	1.18.0 ounces	paid	sale of a kantar of white grapes to Iuda Sivena, a Palermitan Jew
12.12.1430 c. nn	Muxa Sacerdotu, a Jew in Palermo	1.20.0 ounces	1.11.10 ounces on account, balance within 8 days; paid 20.12.1430	sale of a kantar of white grapes to Israel Medui, a Palermitan Jew
14.12.1430 c. nn	Iuda Sivena, a Jew in Palermo	16.27.8 ounces	2 ounces on account; paid	sale of red and white wine in 9 casks and 12 *quartaria* to master Nicola de Cavalerio; Nicola is to pay the tax on Jewish (i.e. kosher) wine

15.12.1430 c. nn	Antonio de Damiata of Monreale with the consent of his guardian Andrea de Damiata, a priest	24 + 20 *tarì*	1.6.0 ounces on account, balance within 6 days; paid 20.12.1430	sale of half a quintal of white wine and a kantar of olive oil to Israel Medui, a Palermitan Jew
15.12.1430 c. nn	Antonio Gimbesio	2.10.0 ounces	within 4 months; paid 3.9.1431	sale of 4 kantars of honey to Lia de Benedetto, a Palermitan Jew
18.12.1430 c. nn	Fulco Palumba	1.6.0 ounces	instalments alabour	sale to Iarono Malti, a Jew in Palermo
19.12.1430 c. nn	Corrado de Vizini of Monreale			sale of half a quintal of white grapes to Nissim Frisisa, a Palermitan Jew
28.3.1431 c. nn	Giovanni Carastono son of Nicola	7.4.10 ounces	2 ounces by April; balance in August	sale of strings for bows (*balestra*) to Merdoc Vivanti, a Jew of Palermo
29.3.1431 c. nn	Pietro de Agati	1.24.0 ounces	paid	sale of a quintal of white grapes to David Ysac and David Nigar, Jews of Palermo
9.4.1431 c. nn	Schamuel Schalomo, a Jew of Palermo	3.12.0 ounces	by January; paid 20.6.1431	sale of a certain quantity of grapes to Vita Catalano, a Jew of Palermo
9.4.1431 c. nn	Andrea and Mazeo de Mantea, father and son of Monreale	24 *tarì*	paid	sale half a quintal of white grapes to Nissim Frisisa, a Palermitan Jew

9.4.1431 c. nn	master Masio de Balestreri	10 *tarì*		sale of a quarter of a quintal and 2 *pisa* of white grapes to Xibite Barbuto, a Jew in Palermo
10.4.1431 c. nn	Pino Bensa and his wife Isolda	24 *tarì*	paid	sale of half a quintal of white grapes to Israel Medui, a Palermitan Jew
10.4.1431 c. nn	Vita Catalano, a Jew of Palermo	2.6.0 ounces	by October; paid 4.2.1432	sale of Napolitan cloth and a kantar of oil to Vita Isac, a Jew of Palermo
10.4.1431 c. nn	Vita Catalano, a Jew of Palermo	1.3.0 ounces	within 6 months; paid 10.1.1432	sale of a kantar of oil to Lia Migleni, a Jew of Palermo; guarantor: Muxa Missina, a Jew
12.4.1431 c. nn	Tubia Strugu, a Palermitan Jew	28.10 *tarì*	by May	sale of rope for tunny to Rasio Abitudo
12.4.1431 c. nn	Pino de La Manna	24 *tarì*	12 tari on account, balance on delivery	sale of a quintal of white grapes to Daniel Rugila, a Jew of Palermo
12.4.1431 c. nn	Richello Luchido	1.16.0 ounces	by June; paid	sale of 6 *salme* of wheat to Nissim Binna, a Palermitan Jew
12.4.1431 c. nn	Richello Luchido and his son Michael	2.15.0 ounces	paid	sale of 10 *salme* and 8 *tumini* of barley and 4 *salme* of wheat to Isdrael Medui, a Jew of Palermo
16.4.1431 c. nn	Nicola de Bizolo	1.20.0 ounces	within 4 months; paid	sale of a kantar and 87 *rotoli* of iron to Musutu de Missina and Schannuni Ayar, Jews of Palermo

17.4.1431 c. nn	Angelo Gaytano and Girardo de Castronovo in Alcamo	2 ounces	1 ounce on account, balance on delivery	sale of 33 double sacks of cork tree charcoal to Isdrael Medui, a Jew of Palermo
17.4.1431 c. nn	Friderico de Turturichi	1.24.0 ounces	24 *tarì*, balance in instalments; paid 1.6.1431	sale of a quintal of white grapes to Sabeti Formone, a Jewish shoemaker of Palermo
18.4.1431 c. nn	master Mazeo de Vizini of Corleone	8.10.0 ounces	3 ounces on account; paid	sale of 50 kantars of cow cheese to Vita Catalano, a Palermitan Jew
18.4.1431 c. nn	master Francesco de Castellammare	17 *tarì*	by October	put in order machine and press (*conczatura machine et trappetti*) for Momo Gaczo, a Palermitan Jew
23.4.1431 c. nn	Amuroso de Marsiglia, a Jew of Trapani	3.13.0 ounces	by September; paid 2.11.1431	sale of curtain to Cormonisio de Provinzano, a master barber, and his wife Bonura
24.4.1431 c. nn	Angelo de Pulito	24 *tarì*	15 *tarì* on account, balance within 15 days	sale of a quintal of white grapes to Xibite Barbuto, a Jew in Palermo
24.4.1431 c. nn	Nicolò de Roma	2.10 *tarì* an animal	3 *tarì* on account	sale of 30 sheep to Yanino Formone and Yue Sifuni, Jews of Palermo
[...].1438 c. nn	Gauyusa, widow of Simone Benasam, a Jewess of Palermo	22 *tarì*	paid	sale of 1,000 ropes for tunny to Vita Amar, a Palermitan Jew, acting also on behalf of Giovanni de Amodeo
[...].1438 c. nn	Giovanni de Marringo of Corleone	7.10 *tarì* a kantar	9 kantars on account, balance on delivery	sale of cheese to Salamone Azara and Gallufo Cuyno, Jews of Palermo

6651

Date and Page	Tenant Purchase	Location and Description	Rent and Duration/Price	Remarks
[...].1438 c. nn	Siminto and Xua Aurifichi, Jews of Palermo	3.8.0 ounces		sale of 5 kantars of iron to Chicco de Ambroxano and his sons Nicola and Giovanni
[...].1438 c. nn	Bundo de Campo	1.3.0 ounces	within a year	sale of goods to Sabeto Sagnarono, a Jew of Palermo
12.11.[..] c. nn	mastro Ianino de Monte	Palermo, Cassaro, Platea Marmorea, bordering on the property of Ursone and shops and houses of Muxa; *solerata* house and shop	2.12.0 ounces annually for 8 years	landlord: Muxa Bulgidi, a Palermitan Jew
10.2.[..] c. nn	Xibite Barbuto, a Palermitan Jew	Palermo, Ferraria, bordering on Xibite's house; a small building	11 *tarì* annually for 3 years	landlord: Sabutu Baracta, a Jew of Palermo
18.11.1428 c. nn	Salamone Zafarana, a Palermitan Jew	Palermo, Cassaro, bordering on Steri hospice, house of Nayumi Yalla, a Jew, and a public square; a shop	1 ounce annually for 15 years	landlady: Francesca Iuveges
14.4.1429 c. nn	Nissin Ysac, a Palermitan Jew	Cassaro, Palermo; *solerata* house	1 ounce annually	landlady: Caterina de Neapoli alias La Santa; ground rent of 24 *tarì* is due to the tenant for life

18.11.1429 c. nn	Yanino Yua, a Jew of Palermo	Cassaro, Palermo, near the church of S. Ippolito, bordering on the house of the Jews Simone de Medico, Salamon Levi and Simone Ysac; *solerata* house and small building	sold for 3 ounces	owner: Vita Ricio and Gauyusa his wife, Palermitan Jews
3.4.1430 c. nn	Iohanne Rubeo	Cassaro, Palermo, bordering on house of Nicolò de Spigandio and public road; ground floor house	18 *tarì* annually for 18 years	landlord: Manuel de Doharicu, a Jew in Palermo
19.9.1430 c. nn	Benedetto Robino, a Palermitan Jew	Palermo, Platea Marmorea, bordering on landlord's property and public road; 3 shops	1.11.0 ounces annually	landlord: Zafarono de Zafarono
21.11.1431 c. nn	Busacca de Tripuli, a Jew of Palermo	Palermo; warehouse and orchard	1 ounce annually	landlord: Fridericus de Vaccarellis

1.12.1447 c. nn	Gallufo Aurifichi, a Jew of Palermo	Cassaro, Palermo, via Tagliavia, bordering on house of Gallufo and of the heir of the late Lia, Jews, and public road; *solerata* house	9 ounces	owner: Benedetto Xammara, a Jew of Palermo
21.5.1460 c. nn	Xua Summato, a Jew of Palermo	Cassaro, Palermo; upper floor of a house	22 *tarì*, 1 year	landlord: Xua de Messina, a Palermitan Jew

Not. Manfrido La Muta

Palermo, 11 February 1429
Source: ASP, Not. Manfrido La Muta, reg. 415, cc. 28v–29r.

Notarial protest by Galluffo de Hilfa and Sabatino de Ragusia, Jews of Syracuse, against Francesco Prixoneri, a Catalan merchant. They had purchased 24 kantars of dates from Giovanni Castell, a Catalan merchant in Syracuse and had dispatched the dates to Palermo on Francesco's boat. Francesco had failed to make delivery and the protesters demand that he do so forthwith.

Palermo, 3 May, XV Indiction [1422/1437]
Source: ASP, Not. Manfrido La Muta, reg. 415, cc. 94v–96v.

Last will and testament of Ricca, wife of Simone de Lu Medicu, a Jewish girurgicus. *She leaves most of her property to her husband and to her children Iosep and Sisa. Ricca dowry is described in her* ketubah *drawn up by Daniel Chagegi, notary of the Jewish community of Palermo. She leaves half to her husband and the children Iosep and Sisa, and half to the grandchildren, the children of Iosep and Sisa. If her granchildren die, that half is to be divided between the grandchildren of her husband: Perna, heiress of Fariono de Lu Medicu, Quahena, heiress of Brachono de Lu Medicu, and master Azarono de Lu Medicu. She also makes other bequests to Perna, Stira, Quahena and Azarono. She leaves 30 ounces to her husband for repairs to their home. On the husband's death the house is to be divided among the other heirs: the children Iosep and Sisa are to receive half and the grandchildren Stira, Quahena and Azarono the other half. She also leaves Sisa two* rotoli *of raw silk, owed her by Gimeni Azeni, and an embroidered bedspread, three Florentine coats, some napkins and other items. Witnesses: Merdoc Xillac, Azaronus Cusintinus, Sufen de Medicu, Sabeti Busicta, Vannes de Messana, Iacob Puliti, Iacob Xunina, Salamon Levi and Xabeti Gillebi.*

Bibliography: Bresc, *Arabi*, pp. 135, Tabella (who has 1421), 204, 346, n. 968.

Source: ASP, Not. Manfrido La Muta, reg. 415

Date and Place	Lender or Seller	Amount	Payment	Remarks
[.].1.1429 c. 59r	Guglielmo Argentario	6 ounces	within 2 months; paid 18.5.1429	sale of saffron to Salamon Muxa and Muxa de Siragusa, Jews
[.].1.1429 c. 58r	Andreotta Gentile, a Genoese merchant	4 ounces	within 2½ months with cow leather	sale of 9 pieces of cloth (*buccaxinis*) to Vanni de Termini and Mardoc Samuel, Jews
[.].1.1429 c. 56v	Agninolfo de Fornaio of Pisa	7.21.0 ounces	monthly instalments of 2.12.0 ounces; paid 22.6.1429	sale of Bordeaux cloth to Salamon de Muxa alias Saracinu, a Jew
31.1.1429 c. 48v	Raynerio Aglata, a Pisan merchant	8 ounces	within 6 months; paid 11.8.1429	sale of cloth to Senia de Partanna, a Jew of Sciacca
31.1.1429 c. 47v	Leonardo Bertolini, a Florentine merchant	1.12.0 ounces		sale of a box of coloured glass pearls to Vita Sivena, a Jew
31.1.1429 c. 45v	Sferando Palau, a merchant of Tortosa	15.24.0 ounces	within 4 months; paid 18.5.1429	sale of 6 pieces of Barcelona cloth to Senia di Partanna, a Jew
31.1.1429 c. 45v	Yaimo Sinid, a merchant of Barcelona	4 ounces	within 2 months; paid 4.7.1429	sale of 50 deerskins to Aron Ricio, a Palermitan Jew
31.1.1429 c. 28v	Yaimo Sinid	19.6.0 ounces	within 4 months; paid 8.7.1429	sale of 8 pieces of fine lambswool to Iosep Maltisi, a Jew of Polizzi
[.].2.1429 c. 28v	Francesco Prixaner, a merchant of Barcelona	7.6.0 ounces	within 2 months; paid 7.9.1429	sale of 4 pieces of Perpignan cloth to Iosep Maltisi, a Jew of Polizzi

[.].2.1429 c. 27r	Enrichetto Brina	4.15.0 ounces	within 4 months	sale of assorted goods to Musutu Bricha, a Palermitan Jew
21.5.[1422] c. 76v	Leucius de Gentile	4 florins		loan to Elia Sala, a Jew
25.2.[14..] c. 133r	Lia Ficira and Merdoc de Meba, Jews of Sciacca	9.15.0 ounces		sale of black slave girl

Not. Nicolò Marotta

Palermo, 3 January 14[..]

Source: ASP, Not. Nicolò Marotta, reg. 938, c. nn.

Contract whereby Marchono Iardinello, a citizen of Palermo, hires himself out to Panchello Marsiglia, his Jewish fellow citizen, to make saddles in Panchello's shop until Easter for 16 grana *a large saddle and 11* grana *a small one. He is paid 15* tarì *on account.*

Note: The register contains few dates. Bresc, *Un Monde Méditerranéen*, p. 27, suggests 1431–1440. And see below, tables. Cf. supra, pp. 6613, 6614, where some of these deeds were drawn up by the notary de Melina.

Palermo, 14[..]

Source: ASP, Not. Nicolò Marotta, reg. 938, c. nn.

Contract whereby Antonio de la Dagna, a citizen of Palermo, hires himself out to David Abramuni, his Jewish fellow citizen, to transport or cause to transport all the cheese produced by David's cow herds to David's storehouse in Palermo. The price will be determined by the distances covered. David pays Antonio 18 tarì *on account. The balance is due on completion of the job.*

Palermo, 14[..]

Source: ASP, Not. Nicolò Marotta, reg. 938, c. nn.

Deed of sale whereby Chicco de Oddo de Castelbuono sells David Abramuni, a Palermitan Jew, a certain quantity of cheese bono, mercantibili et staxunato *for 6.10* tarì *a kantar. The cheese is to be supplied until May.*

Sicily

Palermo, 14[..]

Source: ASP, Not. Nicolò Marotta, reg. 938, c. nn.

Giovanni di Messina, a citizen of Palermo, was unable to supply to Charono Rubeo (Rossi) the two quintals of grapes which he sold him by notarial deed of sale. The parties agree that Giovanni supplies Charono the grapes from the next two vintages.

Source: ASP, Not. Nicolò Marotta, reg. 938

Date and page	Lender or seller	Amount	Payment	Remarks
5.12.1430 c. 109v	Antoniu de Anselmo	1.15.0 ounces	1.9.0 ounces on account, balance on delivery	sale of goods to Sadia Chaten, a Palermitan Jew
1.2.1432 c. 152v	Pirrono de Luc[..]	1.8.0 ounces	immediate	sale of a quintal of white grapes to Daydono Riczu, a Jew of Palermo
1.2.1432 c. 153v	Chicco de Oddo of Castelbuono	6.10 *tarì* a kantar	by June	sale of cheese to David Abramuni, a Jew in Palermo; delivery in May or June at David's warehouse in Palermo
26.2.1430 c. 191r	Chicco de La Bua	18 *tarì*	by November	sale of 1 kantar of oil to Tobia Strugu, a Jew of Palermo; delivery in November
7.3.1430 c. nn	Leone Fuchilla alias Figlu Dublella, a Palermitan Jew	20 *tarì*	by October	sale of 1 kantar of oil to Liuni Sacerdoto, a Jew of Palermo; delivery by October; guarantor: Lia Chagi, a Jew

6659

Not. Luigi Terranova

Palermo, 26 July 1431

Source: ASP, Not. Luigi Terranova, reg. 1063, c. 20r.

Agreement between Cristofaro Scarpario, a citizen of Palermo, and Sabet de Doherico, his Jewish fellow citizen, in which they alter the terms of a deed of sale, whereby Sabet had sold Cristofaro a curtain embroidered with silk for 4.6.0 ounces. Cristofaro made a down payment of 2.18.0 ounces and promised to pay the balance by December. Lia Sivena, another Jew stood surety for Cristofaro. The parties now agree that the guarantor pay Sabet and Cristofaro compensate him with grapes. In the margin: settled in October 1431.

Palermo, 26 July 1431

Source: ASP, Not. Luigi Terranova, reg. 1063, c. 20r-v.

Notarial protest by Isdrael Medui, a Jewish citizen of Palermo, acting for Mena, a Jewess, against Xallufo Sarratanu, their Jewish fwllow citizen, for having made alterations to his house and opened a window overlooking Mena's house. Isdrael demands that Xallufo restore the status quo ante.

Palermo, 25 September 1431

Source: ASP, Not. Luigi Terranova, reg. 1063, c. 11r.

Deed of sale whereby Simone Lupo, an inhabitant of Carini, sells Lia Barbuto, a Jewish citizen of Palermo, all the caciocavallo *produced by his herd for 8.10* tarì *a kantar to be delivered at Lent. Lia pays 15* tarì *on account and promises to pay the balance on delivery. They also agree that if Lia wants Jewish (i.e. kosher) cheese and* caciocavallo, *he must provide Simone with a young Jew to curdle the milk. Simone will provide for his upkeep. The cheese is to be sent to Lia's storehouse in Palermo. Delivered and paid up 3.12.1432.*

Sicily

Palermo, 25 September 1431

Source: ASP, Not. Luigi Terranova, reg. 1063, c. 11r-v.

Contract for the setting up of a partnership for the transpost of red earth by Lia Barbuto and Vita Farzuni, Jewish citizens of Palermo. The partnership is to last until Lia is called to curdle milk for cheese making. Lia invests two donkeys and Vita invests his labour. The two are to share expenses and profits.

Palermo, 10 October 1431

Source: ASP, Not. Luigi Terranova, reg. 1063, c. 20r.

Notarial protest by Sabet de Doherico, a Jewish citizen of Palermo, against Busacca Actuni, tax collector of the Jewish community, his Jewish fellow citizen. Busacca bound over Sabet for a debt owed Manuel de Doherico, claiming that Sabet had stood surety for Manuel. Sabet demands that Busacca return the pledges taken from him, unless Busacca can show proof that Sabet had indeed stood surety for Manuel.

Palermo, 10 October 1431

Source: ASP, Not. Luigi Terranova, reg. 1063, c. 20r.

Deed of sale whereby Cristofaro Scarpario, a citizen of Palermo, sells Daydono Ricio, his Jewish fellow citizen, one and a half quintals of white grapes from his vineyard for 2.15.0 ounces. Daydono makes a down payment of 12 tarì. The balance is to be paid at vintage time.

Palermo, 10 October 1431

Source: ASP, Not. Luigi Terranova, reg. 1063, c. 22r.

Agreement whereby Lia Sofer, a Jewish citizen of Palermo, undertakes to harvest the olives of Giovanni de Vaccarellis, a canon, during the entire season for 12 tarì a month ad scarsas. *He may rest on Saturdays, but his rest days are to be deducted from his wages. He is paid six* tarì *on account.*

Palermo, 10 October 1431

Source: ASP, Not. Luigi Terranova, reg. 1063, c. 22v.

Agreement whereby Iosep de Minichi, a Jewish citizen of Palermo, undertakes to harvest the olives of Angelo de Sorronia, a knight, during the entire season for 12 tarì *a month* ad scarsas. *He may rest on Saturdays, but his rest days are to be deducted from his wages. He is paid five* tarì *on account.*

Palermo, 10 October 1431

Source: ASP, Not. Luigi Terranova, reg. 1063, c. 24v–25r.

Agreement between Garita, widow of Antonio de Lucarollu, and Xibiten Barbuto, a Jewish citizen of Palermo, whereby the widow and her son promise to supply Xibiten the grapes she owes him from future vintages. Her late husband had sold Xibiten one and a half quintals of grapes, but the widow was unable to deliver more than six salme.

Palermo, 15 October 1431

Source: ASP, Not. Luigi Terranova, reg. 1063, c. 25r-v.

Settlement of accounts between Sabet Gillebi, a Jewish citizen of Palermo, and Francesco de la Pasta, his fellow citizen, in regard to the sale of leather by Sabet to Francesco. The result: Francesco still owes Sabet 2.15.0 ounces. He promises to pay 25 tarì *by November, another 25 by January and the balance by Easter.*

Palermo, 16 October 1431

Source: ASP, Not. Luigi Terranova, reg. 1063, c. 25v–26r.

Deed of sale whereby Giovanni de Alessandro, a Palermitan citizen, sells Lia Barbuto and Marzuco Binna, his Jewish fellow citizens, the caciocavallo *produced by his herd, estimated at between 90 and 300 kantars, for 8.10* tarì *a kantar. He is paid two ounces on account and the balance in monthly instalments of 1.18.0 ounces. Giovanni is to deliver the merchandise to the storehouses of the purchasers.*

Palermo, 27 November 1431

Source: ASP, Not. Luigi Terranova, reg. 1063, c. 45v–46r.

Agreement whereby Xibiten Gaczu, Iairuni Gaczu, Fariuni Gaczu and Manuel Darmuna, Jewish citizens of Palermo, hire themselves out to Masio de Crispis, their fellow citizen, to work, together with another Jew to be chosen by them, as paratores *in Masio's sugar refinery during the entire season. They are to be paid 27* tarì *a month* ad scarsas. *Masio makes a down payment of 27* tarì *through the bank of Pietro Gaytano.*

Palermo, 2 March 14[..]

Source: ASP, Not. Luigi Terranova, reg. 1063, c. 2v.

Notarial protest by Graciano Tachariato, a Jewish citizen of Palermo, against Benedetto Xaseni, a maggiorente *of the Jewish community in Palermo, demanding that Benedetto prevent Daniele, husband of Graciano's daughter, from leaving town during the hearing of the divorce proceedings between his daughter and Daniele.*

Palermo, 5 March 14[..]

Source: ASP, Not. Luigi Terranova, reg. 1063, c. 5r-v.

Agreement whereby Gallufo Romano, a Jewish citizen of Palermo, undertakes to work as parator *in the sugar refinery of Thomeo de mastro Antonio during the entire season, on the terms agreed on with Fariono de Berni, Xalomo Buxa and Iuda Cuchilla, also Jews.*

Palermo, 7 March 14[..]

Source: ASP, Not. Luigi Terranova, reg. 1063, c. 16v.

Undertaking by Begnamino Sillica, a Jew, to clean all the barrels of Gallufello Maxurano, another Jew, for 22 denari *apiece. He is paid six* tarì *on account.*

Palermo, 18 March 14[..]

Source: ASP, Not. Luigi Terranova, reg. 1063, c. 5r-v.

Deed of sale whereby Filippo de San Filippo sells Muxa Sofer, a Jew, a mule, with saddle and harness, for 3.6.0 ounces, to be paid in instalments.

Palermo, 18 March 14[..]

Source: ASP, Not. Luigi Terranova, reg. 1063, c. 18v.

Undertaking by Braxono de Leone, a Jew, to repair the barrels of Gallufello Maxurano for 21 tarì *apiece. He is paid six* tarì *on account.*

Palermo, 19 March 14[..]

Source: ASP, Not. Luigi Terranova, reg. 1063, c. 19r.

Agreement whereby the Jews Iuda Cuchilla and Gallufo Romano, also acting on behalf of Busacca Malki, a Jew, undertake to press the wine of Vita Catalano, their fellow Jew, at the coming vintage for three tarì *a quintal. The are paid six* tarì *on account.*

Palermo, 22 March 14[..]

Source: ASP, Not. Luigi Terranova, reg. 1063, c. 21r.

Contract whereby Chayrono Levi and Muxa de Tripuli, Jews, promise Marino de Ianrusso to fertilize his sugar cane plants, gididas et striponas, *during the entire season for 26.10* tarì *a thousand. They are given six* tarì *on account.*

Palermo, 22 March 14[..]

Source: ASP, Not. Luigi Terranova, reg. 1063, c. 21v–22r.

Deed of sale whereby Antonio de Meliorato sells Lia Malki, a Jew, two canne *and two* palmi *of Florentine cloth for 2.6.0 ounces to be paid for in instalments.*

Palermo, 23 March 14[..]

Source: ASP, Not. Luigi Terranova, reg. 1063, c. 22r-v.

Notarial protest by Antonio de Messina against Merdoc de Minichi, a Jew, that he not been given a nag valued at 1.6.0 ounces for which he had made a down payment of six tarì. *The nag was being kept in a storehouse and has nearly died. If the nag goes on being kept there, it would be at Merdoc's risk.*

Palermo, 1 April 14[30]

Source: ASP, Not. Luigi Terranova, reg. 1063, c. 22v–23r.

Contract whereby Iosep de Minichi, Iuda de Minichi and Salamon Missina, Jews, promise Lia Sivena, another Jew, to transport at vintage time 10 quintals of grapes, including two quintals from the vineyard of Fariono Sala, in the contrada Sisa, *one quintal from the vineyard of Samuele Balbu, in the same* contrada, *and one quintal from the vineyard of Iuda Sivena, in the contrada* Cartusiorum, *all Jews. The price agreed on is 2.3.0 ounces. They are paid one ounce on account, drawn on the bank of Mario Bonconte.*

Palermo, January 1433

Source: ASP, Not. Luigi Terranova, reg. 1063, c. 1r.

Settlement of accounts between Gallufo Levi, a Jewish citizen of Messina, and Xamuele Sacerdoto, a Jewish fellow citizen. As a result Gallufo remains owing Xamuele two tarì, *which he is to pay Xamuele on demand.*

Palermo, 9 February 1433

Source: ASP, Not. Luigi Terranova, reg. 1063, c. 21r-v.

Notarial protest by Zullu Malki, a Jewish citizen of Palermo, against Bartholomeo Gactaluxio, his fellow citizen. Bartholomeo had sold Zullu a certain quantity of wine for 12 ounces to be sold by Zullu in Bartholomeo's tavern. Following differences of opinion between the two, Zullu had been forced to sell some of the wine in another tavern which he had to rent. He claims his rights against Bartholomeo.

Palermo, 9 February 1433

Source: ASP, Not. Luigi Terranova, reg. 1063, c. 21v.

Deed of sale whereby Consulo Bellachera of Monreale sells Nissim Binna, a Jewish citizen of Palermo, some white grapes from his vineyard for 1.22.0 ounces. The deed is cancelled on 15.10.1434.

Palermo, 9 February 1433

Source: ASP, Not. Luigi Terranova, reg. 1063, c. 21v.

Ilaria de Simone, a citizen of Palermo, sells Gallufello Maxurano, her Jewish fellow citizen, one and three quarter quintals of white grapes from her vineyard in the contrada *Sabuchie for two ounces. The deed is cancelled on 26.2.1434.*

Palermo, February 14[..]

Source: ASP, Not. Luigi Terranova, reg. 1063, c. 3r.

Notarial protest by Ubertino Bonioanne against Nissim Sansono, a Jew, who has sold him a cask of wine, which had turned out to be of inferior quality. Ubertino wishes to safeguard his rights.

Palermo, 4 March 1449

Source: ASP, Not. Luigi Terranova, reg. 1063, cc. 15v–16r.

Final accounting between the Jews Xanino Xairono and Braxono de Amarono in regard to the sale of a calapodium. *It transpires that Braxono owes Xanino 18* tarì, *which he promises to pay in monthly instalments of three* tarì *starting after Easter. Gaudio de Minichi, a Jew, stands surety for Braxono.*

Note: *Calapodium* may mean lectern or stool.

Palermo, 5 March 1449

Source: ASP, Not. Luigi Terranova, reg. 1063, c. 18r.

Contract whereby Isdrael Ysac and Siminto Aurifichi, Jews, undertake to dig a well for supplying water to the houses of Antonio de Maria, a clergyman and Francesco La Chimia. The job is to be completed by March and is to cost 1.12.0 ounces. A down payment of 12 tarì *is made to Isdrael and Siminto.*

Palermo, 6 March 1449

Source: ASP, Not. Luigi Terranova, reg. 1063, c. 20r-v.

Contract between Federico de Vaccarellis and Sabatino de Lentini, a Jew, for setting up a joint venture for the production of manure. Federico invests a donkey and one ounce and Sabatino his labour. Federico is to feed the donkey and Sabatino is to provide surety. The profits are to be divided between them in equal shares.

Palermo, 10 March 1449

Source: ASP, Not. Luigi Terranova, reg. 1063, c. 23v.

Agreement whereby Iosep Ammara, Yaymi de Liucio, Vita Maltensis, Gallufo Amar, Jews, hire themselves out to Lia de Sadia and to his partner, Iacob de Termini, Jews, to tread their grapes at vintage time. They are also to carry out other work, such as: faciendo pedes, stringendo in stringitorio, lavando vegetes, impostando tenas et vegetes et eluverare(!) caricatoi(!), *and to clean up. They are paid 4.5* tarì *a quintal and receive a down payment of eight* tarì. *They are to get another four* tarì *at Easter.*

Palermo, 11 March 1449

Source: ASP, Not. Luigi Terranova, reg. 1063, c. 25r-v.

Agreement whereby Muxa Marzoc, a Jew, undertakes to transport to Palermo all the produce of the herd belonging to Cattaldo Cappitella for 19 grana *the kantar. Muxa is to make use of four beasts of burden. He is paid 12* tarì *on account.*

Palermo, 11 March 1449

Source: ASP, Not. Luigi Terranova, reg. 1063, c. 25v.

Notarial protest by Iuda Puglisi, a Jew, against Sabet de Minichi, his fellow Jew, in the matter of an alleged breach of contract. Iuda claims that Sabeti let him a mill called "de lu Sali". Under the terms of the contract, Sabet was to provide a mill and a storehouse and to see to it that the owner of the mill did not require payment from Iuda. Sabet had not fulfilled these terms. Sabet replies that he undertook only to provide spare parts if the mill failed to function, that he never included the storehouse in the contract, and that Iuda was bound by the terms of the mill's lease.

Palermo, 17 March 1449

Source: ASP, Not. Luigi Terranova, reg. 1063, c. 32r.

Contract whereby Galfuni de Rumania and Salamon de Messina, Jews, undertake to transport for Nissim Sansono, their fellow Jew, the grapes of his various vineyards in and around Palermo for seven tarì the quintal. They are paid three tarì *on account.*

Palermo, 17 March 1449

Source: ASP, Not. Luigi Terranova, reg. 1063, c. 32r.

Contract whereby Iosep de Siragusia, a Jew, promises Xilomo Galifa, his fellow Jew, to fertilize during the entire season the sugar cane plants of Gerardo Aglata and Federico Migliacio for 16 grana *a day. He is paid four* tarì *on account.*

Palermo, 19 October 14[..]

Source: ASP, Not. Luigi Terranova, reg. 1064, c. nn.

Deed of sale whereby Xididi Aczara, a Jew, sells to Andrea de Ianca, a mule pili morelli cum barda et capistro *for 4.6.0 ounces and two* salme *of wood to be paid in instalments over a year. In the margin: On 10 April Xididi cedes his credit with Andrea to his brother Salamon.*

Palermo, 19 October 14[..]

Source: ASP, Not. Luigi Terranova, reg. 1064, c. nn.

Notarial protest lodged by Sabet de Minichi, a Jew, against Sabet Sacerdoto, another Jew, for having done shoddy work in coating (stalglare) *a pavement* (astraco) *of his and for not having completed the job. He demands that Sacerdoto fulfil his commitments, or pay damages.*

Palermo, 14[..]

Source: ASP, Not. Luigi Terranova, reg. 1064, c. nn.

Agreement whereby Sansono Candioto, a Jewish citizen of Palermo, hires himself out to work in the oil press of Braxa Calabrisi, his Jewish fellow citizen, to work in Braxa's olive press during the entire season. He is to do the pressing for 16 tarì *a month plus food and drink.*

Source: ASP, Not. Luigi Terranova, reg. 1063

Date and Page	Debtor	Amount	Reason	Remarks
15.6.14[..] c. 269v	Vita de Minichi, a Jew	1.6.0 ounces	unfulfilled obligation to Nissim Isac, a Jew, for improvements to a vineyard bought by Vita	to be paid by Christmas
20.2.14[..] c. nn	Merdok Nikiseu, a Jew	all the money he owes Antonio de Gimbesio	not given	paid
11.2.14[..] c. nn	Agnesia, widow of David de Minichi, a Jewess	3 ounces	not given	1.21.0 ounces on account to Samueli and Muxa sons of Lia Romani and grandsons of the creditor, the late Xibiten Cunti
3.2.1433 c. nn	master Antonio de Scorridato	24 *tarì*	unpaid price of a cape	creditor: Iosep Abudaram, a Palermitan Jew; court order to pay;
			Antonia, widow of master Antonio de Luconte, debtor's mother, stands surety for debt to be paid within a year	
12.2.1433 c. nn	Antonio de Andrea	2 ounces	debt of of 1 ounce, balance of 2 ounces the price of a curtain	creditor: Sabet Gillebi, a Jew; to be paid within 3 months
18.3.14[..] c. nn	Merdoc and Sabet Malti, father and son, Jews	1.16.10 ounces	balance of debt for a brown tunic and a toga	creditor: Ubertinello de Marinis, acting for Tura de Imperatore; to be paid within 7 days
Date and page	Lender or seller	Amount	Payment	Remarks
12.7.1431 c. nn	Fiduchio de Urso	3 ounces	paid	sale to Xirello; Farmuni, a Jew

16.7.1431 c. 16r	Vita Cathalano, a Palermitan Jew	1.2.0 ounces	within 4 months; paid 10.2.1432	sale of oil to Muxa Bivera, a Jew in Palermo; Mardoc Vignuni, another Jew, stands surety
26.7.1431 c. nn	Cristofaro Scarpario	2.6.0 ounces	paid 1.2.1432	sale to Lia Sivena, a Palermitan Jew
26.7.1431 c. nn	Cristofaro Scarpario	2.6.0 ounces	paid	sale of a quintal of white grapes to Lia Sivena, a Jew of Palermo; to be delivered at the coming vintage
13.8.1431 c. nn	Antonio de Rosata of Monreale	10 *tarì*	2 *tarì* on account	sale of half a kantar of oil to Mussutu Binna, a Jew of Palermo; delivery in October
13.8.1431 c. nn	Andrea de Regina of Cammarata	1.12.0 ounces	paid	sale of 2 beasts of burden to Gallufo Maiorana, a Jew of Palermo
12.9.1431 c. nn	Giovanni de Castrogiovanni	2.6.0 ounces	paid	sale 3 kantars of oil to Vita Catalano, a Jew
12.9.1431 c. nn	Marco de Salem	15 *tarì*	monthly instalments	sale half a kantar of grapes to Zullo Marchisen, a Jew of Palermo; guarantor: his brother Merdoc
12.9.1431 c. nn	Marco de Salem	4.15.0 ounces	2 ounces on account, monthly instalments; paid by December 1432	sale of grapes to Muxa Xeba, a Jew of Palermo
12.9.1431 c. nn	Marco de Salem	2.6.0 ounces	monthly instalments of 5.12½ *tarì*; paid by 30.10.1432	sale of grapes to Lia Xaseni, a Jew of Palermo
12.9.1431 c. nn	Marco de Salem	3 ounces	monthly instalments of 7.10 *tarì*; paid by 10.12.1432	sale of grapes to Pachino Marsili, a Jew

2.10.1431 c. nn	Michele Maiali	1.3.0 ounces	paid	sale of a nag to Xibiten Bambuli, a Jew
8.10.1431 c. nn	Consulo de Ioya	1.1.10 ounces	paid	sale of 1½ kantars of oil to Vita Isac, a Palermitan Jew, acting for Solucenta; Andrea de Michele stands surety
8.10.1431 c. nn	Nicco Finiolu and Giovanni Bellachera	1.23.6 ounces	1.10 ounces on account, balance within 2 months; paid March 1432	sale of 80 salme of string (*disa*) to Xibiten Barbuto, a Palermitan Jew; Chirello, Nicco's father, promises to make up a deficiency and to pay expenses
10.10.1431 c. nn	Muxa Vignuni, a Jew of Palermo	2 ounces	within 3 months; paid 19.2.1432	sale of 2 kantars of oil to Marino de Ianrusso
10.10.1431 c. nn	Muxa Achina, a Jew	2 ounces	within 3 months; paid 31.12.1431	sale of 2 kantars of oil to Marino de Ianrusso
[..].10.1431 c. nn	Masio de Gilberto	2.20.0 ounces		sale of 20 *terzaroli* of tunny to Muxa Achina, a Jew
25.10.1431 c. nn	Iacobo Xunina, a Jew of Palermo	12 ounces	3 ounces by May; balance by August; paid up 7.6.1432	sale of a silk curtain to Enrico de Ventimiglia
30.10.1431 c. nn	Perino de Naso of Monreale	24.12 *tarì*	2.10 *tarì* on account, balance on delivery; paid 8.11.1431	sale of 6 *salme* of grapes to Isdrael Medui, a Jew of Palermo
30.10.1431 c. nn	Masio Gictardo	3 ounces	1.20.0 ounces on account; balance by Christmas; paid 9.1.1432	sale of a quintal and half of grapes to Salamon de Minichi, a Jew
7.11.1431 c. nn	Nardo de Raxa	7.10 *tarì* a kantar	2 ounces by Christmas; balance on delivery	sale of cheese to Lia Barbuto and Musutu Binna, Jews of Palermo

7.11.1431 c. nn	Enrico de Ranzano	1.18.0 ounces	12 *tarì* on account	sale of a quintal of grapes to Daidono Ricio, a Palermitan Jew
8.11.1431 c. nn	Vita Samuel, a Jew of Corleone	27 *tarì*	following day; paid 9.11.1431	sale of a nag to Isdrael Medui, a Palermitan Jew
8.11.1431 c. nn	Vita Maltesi, a Jew of Palermo			sale of 8 and 5 bundles of rope for tunny to Isdrael Medui, a Palermitan Jew
12.11.1431 c. nn	Antonio de Gimbesio	2.3.0 ounces	within 4 months	sale of 3 kantars of honey to Lia de Benedetto, a Jew in Palermo
14.11.1431 c. nn	Pietro de Galati	24 *tarì*	7.10 *tarì* on account	sale of grapes to Daidono Ricio, a Jew
19.11.1431 c. nn	Thomeo de Damiano	1.12.0 ounces	paid	sale of quintal of grapes to Muxa Copiu, a Jew of Palermo; Sabet Gilebet, another Jew, stands surety
19.11.1431 c. nn	Giovanni de Viviano	9 *tarì*	paid	sale of 2 *salme* of white grapes to Xibiten Barbuto, a Jew
29.11.1431 c. nn	Isdrael Medui, a Jew in Palermo	1.18.0 ounces	instalments; balance by December	sale of a nag to Ruggero Perricaro; to be paid to Muxa Tornerio, a Jew in Palermo
[.]1.1432 c. nn	Braxa Calabrisi, a Jew of Palermo	1.10.0 ounces	paid	sale of 2 kantars of oil to Antonio de Gimbesio; Fariono de Axan, a Jew of Palermo, stands surety

6672

10.3.[..] c. nn	Giovanni de Palma	25.10 *tarì*	paid	sale of half a quintal of grapes to Benedetto Chaseni, a Jew
15.3.[..] c. nn	Nicolò de Cammarata	27 *tarì*	paid	sale of half a quintal of grapes to Lia de Minichi, a Jew
15.3.[..] c. nn	Berto de Falco	1.18.0 ounces	within 8 days; paid	sale of half a quintal of grapes to Lia de Minichi, a Jew
15.3.[..] c. nn	Gallufo de Lu Presti, a Jew	1.21.0 ounces	paid	sale of a quintal of grapes to Gallufello de Mayurana, a Jew
15.3.[..] c. nn	Marchono Rindichella and Giovanni de Traina	22 *tarì*	by April; paid	sale of 2 *salme* of saltpetre to Gallufello Mayurana, a Jew
15.3.[..] c. nn	Rinaldo Meczatesta	25.10 *tarì*	paid	sale of half a quintal od grapes to Gallufello Mayurana, a Jew
17.3.[..] c. 269r	Belingario de Falco	2.12.0 ounces	paid	sale of 1½ quintals of grapes to Leone Amar, a Jew of Palermo
18.3.[..] c. nn	Buxacca de Termini, a Jew	3.12.0 ounces	paid	sale of 2 quintals of grapes to master Iosep Abudaram, a Jew
19.3.[..] c. 271r	Leucio Arnao	1.15.0 ounces	by June; paid	sale of 3 *salme* of barley to Minto Vignuni, a Jew
19.3.[..] c. 271r	Giovanni Serventi, a Pisan merchant	12.15.0 ounces	within 4 months; paid 17.12	sale to Muxa Sacerdotu, a Jew
19.3.[..] c. nn	Giovanni Serventi	27.25.7 ounces	within 4 months; paid 17.12	sale

22.3.[..] c. 273v	Antonio de Meliorato	1 ounce	on demand	loan to Lia Malki, a Jew
22.3.[..] c. 273v	Giovanni de Canfora	24 *tarì*	paid	sale of half a quintal of white grapes to Merdoc Chaseni, a Jew
5.4.[..] c. nn	Zullo Abramuni, a Jew	1.12.0 ounces	by June; paid 13.7	sale of a nag to Masia, wife of Giovanni de Angelo
7.4.[..] c. 279v	Giovanni de Oddo	24 *tarì*	paid	sale of half a quintal of white grapes to Benedetto Xaseni, a Jew; delivery at harvest time
16.4.[..] c. 298r	Pietro Lu Russu	1.24.0 ounces	by first week in June	sale to Braxono Sacerdotu, a Jew; guarantors: Lia Malki and Fadalono Nifusi, Jews
[.].1.1433 c. nn	Gallufu Levi, a Jew of Messina	1 ounce	paid with kerchiefs and silk veils	sale of a mule to Xamuele Sacerdotu, a Jew
16.1.1433 c. nn	Michilono Nachuay, a Jew of Palermo	1.4.0 ounces	17 *tarì* by carnival time, balance within 6 months; paid 8.9.1435	sale of 3 kantars of cheese to Merdoc de Minichi, a Jew
19.1.1433 c. nn	Antonio de Gimbesio	2.10.0 ounces	within 4 months; paid 14.10.1433	sale of 2 kantars of oil to Muxa Sacerdoto and Xairono Niiar, Jews
22.1.1433 c. nn	Azarono Ricio, a Jew	1.15.15 ounces	within a month and a half; paid 13.3.1433	sale
26.1.1433 c. nn	Bullara, widow of Iosep Achina, a Jewess	1.8.0 ounces	within 2 months; paid 11.1433	sale of 1 kantar and 2 *cafisi* of oil to Braxono Susa, a Jew of Caccamo; Vita de Minichi, another Jew, stands surety

6674

26.1.1433 c. nn	Accursio Mataroczo	1.10.0 ounces	24 *tarì* on account, balance on delivery	sale of 2 kantars of oil to Braxono Xunina, a Palermitan Jew
[.].2.1433 c. nn	Perrino Lu Vechu of Corleone	7 *tarì* a kantar	2 ounces on account	sale of sheep cheese to Vita Cathalano, a Jew of Palermo
9.2.1433 c. nn	Zullu Mark[et]i and Braxono de Amarano, Palermitan Jews	1 ounce	2 *tarì* on account; balance on delivery; paid	sale of 1½ kantars of oil to Giovanni Rubeo
10.2.1433 c. nn	Giovanni Firriolo	13.2. *grana* a *salma*	7 *tarì* on account; balance on delivery; paid 8.1.1436 [!]	sale of string (*disa*) to Vita Amar, a Jew
10.2.1433 c. nn	Muxa Actuni, a Jew	6 ounces	cession of credit with Bernardo Curti	sale of female deerskin to Muxa and Sabet Levi, father and son
11.2.1433 c. nn	Azarono Ricio, a Jew of Palermo	2.1.0 ounces	24 *tarì* on account, balance by Easter; paid 12.5	sale of 4 dozen treated sheep skin to master Donato Rubeo
[..].2.1433 c. nn	Consulo Bellachera of Monreale	1.22.0 ounces	paid	sale of quintal of white grapes to Nissim Binna, a Palermitan Jew
[..].2.1433 c. nn	Ilaria de Simone	3.15.0 ounces	2.5.0 ounces on account, balance on delivery and vintage time	sale of 1¾ quintals of grapes to Gallufello Mayurana, a Jew
[..].2.1433 c. nn	Sabet Gillebi, a Jew of Palermo	15 *tarì*	within 2 months	sale of hides to Giovanni de Girachio
16.2.1433 c. nn	Matheo de Mediola	27 *tarì*	paid	sale of half a quintal of white grapes to Vita Catalano, a Jew of Palermo

23.2.1433 c. nn	Iacobo de Ianrusso	2 ounces	11 *tarì* on account, balance on delivery; paid 3.1433	sale of 24 double sacks of cork wood charcoal to Xannono Niiar, a Jew of Palermo
23.2.1433 c. nn	Nicolò de lu Monaco	13 *tarì* a kantar	12 *tarì* on account; balance on delivery	sale to Muxa Achina, a Jew, of all the tallow the vendor produces at his butcher's shop from Carnival until Easter
25.2.1433 c. nn	Pietro de Palermo	1.18.0 ounces	1 ounce on account; balance on demand; paid 16.10	sale of a quintal of white grapes to Vita Catalano, a Jew
25.2.1433 c. nn	Nicolò Perraturi	24 *tarì*	paid	sale of half a quintal of grapes to Michilono Nachuay, a Jew
27.2.1433 c. nn	Iacob Taguil, a Palermitan Jew	6.2.0 ounces	4.11.0 ounces on account; paid	sale of silk bedspread embroidered with gold and Genoese borders
19.2.14[34] c. 252v	Lia de Minichi, a Jew	1 ounce plus 2.10 *tarì*	1 ounce with Cammarata salt; balance on demand	sale of 1 kantar of oil and expenses respectively to Merdoc Safar, a Jew
19.2.1434 c. nn	Merdoc Achina, a Jew	11½ *grana* a *rotolo*	1 ounce on account; balance on delivery	sale of material for ornamental iron for carriages to Calzerano Laficara
20.2.14[..] c. 254v	Valente de Sparverio	1.18.0 ounces	paid	sale of 1 quintal of white grapes to Lia Siveni, a Jew
27.2.14[..] c. nn	Leone Amar, a Jew	2.24.0 ounces	18 *tarì* on account, balance to be defrayed by debt owed by Rubia Gibel	sale 1½ quintals of grapes to Muxa Rubeo, a Jew

28.2.14[..] c. nn	Gimilono Nachui, a Jew	16.10 *tarì* a kantar	1 ounce on account; balance on delivery	sale of tallow to Minto de Victi purchased from Gimilono de Merdok Actuni, a Jew
5.3.14[..] c. nn	Marco de Salem, attorney for Thomeo Lupicturatu	1.18.0 ounces	24 *tarì* on account; balance in weekly instalments of 15 *tarì*	sale of a quintal of white grapes to Lia de Manueli
6.3.14[..] c. nn	Michilono Minachem, a Jew	1.18.0 ounces	by August	sale of a beast of burden to Antonio Gambera
11.3.14[..] c. nn	Federico de Virardo	1.12.0 ounces	paid	sale of grapes from several vineyards to Benedetto Xaseni
13.3.14[..] c. nn	Vita Sivena, a Jew	4.3.0 ounces	within 15 days; paid 9.5	sale of ornamental tin to master Angelo Coppola and return of borrowed tin
13.3.14[..] c. nn	Antonio d'Angelo	9.2.0 ounces	at vintage time	sale to Fadalono Xabena, a Jew, of a toga consigned by David Isac, a Jew
18.3.14[..] c. nn	Muxa Xassuni, a Jew of Nicosia	2.24.0 ounces	2.1.0 ounces on account, balance on delivery	sale of 2 mules to Nicolò Caramanno
4.2.14[..] c. nn	Filippo de Gilberto	3.6.0 ounces	24 *tarì* on account; balance in monthly instalments of 9 *tarì*	sale to Busacca de Anzalono, a Jew
4.2.14[..] c. nn	Mauro de Lumia and Filippo de Iacono	10 *tarì* a kantar	4 ounces on account, balance on delivery	sale of *caciocavallo* to Gimilono Naguay, a Jew
4.2.14[..] c. nn	Leone de Girachio, a Jew	10 *grana* a *rotolo*	1 ounce on account	sale of iron

Date and Page	Tenant	Location and description	Rent and duration	Remarks
13.2.1433 c. nn	Samuele Sacerdotu, a Palermitan Jew	Cassaro of Palermo, bordering on the tavern of Martino de Marini, a shop of the heirs of Filippo de Gimbesio and public road; shop	18.15. *tarì* a year for 3 years	
19.2.14[..] c. 252v	Vita and Sadono Rugila, Jews	Cassaro of Palermo, *contrada* S. Salvatore, bordering on house of Fariono Farrugio and Bulchayra Millac, Jews; house and courtyard	3 ounces for 3 years	landlord: Giuliano de Bononia, acting for his mother Flora
21.2.14[..] c. 255r	Giuliano de Bononia	Cassaro of Palermo, next to the shop of Lia Sivena, a Jew; shop	2.15.0 ounces for 1 year	landlady: Chaguena Sivena, widow of Vita, a Jewess
5.11.14[..] c. nn	Iosep Gaczo	Palermo, contrada Ferrarie, bordering on house of David Sirruni, a Jew, Federico [...], Merdoc Vignuni, a Jew, and public road; perpetual lease of house	1 ounce a year	landlord: Sabatino Abramello, a Jew; property subject to ground rent of 24 *tarì* a year to the monastery S. Maria degli Angeli

Source: ASP, Not. Luigi Terranova, reg. 1064

Date and Page	Lender or seller	Amount	Payment	Remarks
31.8.14[..] c. nn	Muxa Sacerdotu and Vita Polizi, Palermitan Jews	8 ounces	within 4 months; paid 23.2	sale
18.[...] c. nn	prior of the church in Monreale	6.10.0 ounces a kantar	10 ounces on account; balance on delivery	sale of cheese to Abitella and Daniele Xunina, Jews
[...] c. nn	Salimbeni de Italia	2.6.0 ounces	by August	sale to Fariono Nifusi, a Palermitan Jew
[...] c. nn	Marco de la Valle	1 ounce	by Christmas	sale to Sabet Russu, a Jew of Palermo
[...] c. nn	Marco de la Valle	1 ounce	by Christmas; paid 13.2	sale to Iuda Rabibi, a Jew
[...] c. nn	Giovanni de Anzelmo	24 *tarì*	paid	sale to Muxa Sacerdotu, a Jew
17.10.14[..] c. nn	Simon de Abunda and Paolo Guilla	3.18.0 ounces	2 ounces on account; paid May	sale to Gallufello Maxurana, a Jew
22.10.14[..] c. nn	Antonio de Meliorato	1.6.0 ounces	within 5 months	sale to Fariono and Liucio Gaczu, Jewish brothers
19.10.14[..] c. nn	Pietro de Liuciu	2.16.0 ounces	within 3 months	sale to Bracha Minacham and David Nicat, Jews
19.10.14[..] c. nn	Nissim Grisoria, a Jew of Palermo	1.6.0 ounces	within 5 months; paid 21.4	sale
19.10.14[..] c. nn	Pietro Pirricola	3 ounces	1 ounce on account; balance on delivery	sale to Levi Sacerdotu and Muxa Xaguela, Jews

19.10.14[..] c. nn	Gallufello Maxurana, a Jew	9 ounces	2 ounces on account; balance by January; paid in instalments until 20.1	sale
19.10.14[..] c. nn	Federico Gautarello	1.24.0 ounces	by November; paid 15.11	sale to Gallufello Maxurana, a Jew
28.11.14[..] c. nn	Pietro Lombardo	1.9.0 ounces	within 2 months; paid 1.1	sale to David Catalano, a Jew
28.11.14[..] c. 90v	Enrico Montono	4.6.0 ounces	within 6 months; paid 14.6	sale to Samuel Gididia, a Jew
29.11.14[..] c. 91v	Farrugio Sivena, a Jew	1 ounce	instalments of 10 *tarì* starting within 3 months; paid 30.5	sale to Iacob Susi, a Jew
29.1.14[..] c. nn	Benedetto Cafisa, Salamon de Missina and Sabet Busacca, Jews	1.4.10 ounces	paid	sale

Not. Pietro Castelli

Palermo, 17 June 1432

Source: ASP, Not. Pietro Castelli, reg. 1044, cc. 24r–25r.

Agreement whereby Iosep Ammari and Iacob Tunisini, Jewish citizens of Palermo, hire themselves out to Bundo de Campo, acting for Aloisio de Campo, to work as labourers and builders for 18 grana *a day. They are paid nine* tarì *each on account.*

Palermo, 17 July 1432

Source: ASP, Not. Pietro Castelli, reg. 1044, c. 40r-v.

Moratorium of eight months granted by Giovanni de Miro to Samuel Mixiti, a Jewish inhabitant of Palermo, on the payment for a kantar of drugs/sweetmeat (confectionum). *Salamon Zafara, another Jew, stood surety.*

Palermo, 3 March 1434

Source: ASP, Not. Pietro Castelli, reg. 1044, cc. 107v–108r.

Contract between Sadia de Lia, a Jew of Trapani, and Muxa de Daniele, a Jew of Messina, for a partnership nomine accomande ad medietatem lucri. *Sadia declares that he received from Muxa assorted merchandise consisting of textiles, velvet, silk handkerchiefs, corals and articles made of gold worth 30 ounces. Sadia is to trade in Palermo and elsewhere. He is to render daily accounts when in Palermo.*

Source: ASP, Not. Pietro Castelli, reg. 1044

Date and page	Principal	Attorney	Purpose	Remarks
9.12.1433 c. nn	Gaudio de Ram, a Messinese Jew	Nicolò de Fessaletta	to collect a debt of 22 ounces	
11.3.1434 c. nn	Gaudio Francu, a Jew of Calabria	Antonio Villa	to collect various debts in Palermo	Gaudio is in prison in Palermo

Date and Page	Debtor	Amount	Reason	Remarks
[..].10.1436 c. 148v	Iacob Fitira	1 ounce	debt for soles	creditor: Antonio Bartolone; payment forthwith

Date and page	Lender or seller	Amount	Payment	Remarks
19.3.1434 cc. 138v–139r	Sufen Gillebi, a Jew	24 *tarì*	instalments, including 16 empty barrels	sale of a horse to Matheo de San Giovanni
18.10.1436 c. 150r-v	Andrea Caputo	2 ounces	within 2 months; paid 3.1437	sale of sweet white grapes to Salamon Gibel, a Jewish master locksmith in Palermo
18.10.1436 c. 150v	Andrea Caputo	2.12.0 ounces	by September 1437; 1 ounce paid 22.3.1437	sale of sweet white grapes to Muxa Sufer, a Jew; guarantor: Salamon Gibel, another Jew
31.10.1436 c. 158r	Bartholomeo de Blanco	3.4.10 ounces	balance of 3 ounces within 4 months	sale of 6 *palmi* of velvet silk cloth to Lia de Missina, a Jew
31.7.1432 c. nn	Mariano de Benedetto	26 *tarì*	by February; paid 4.1433	sale of a light anchor (*ancorecte*) to master Muxa de Butera, a Palermitan Jew

Date and page	Tenant	Location and description	Rent and duration	Remarks
1.7.1432 c. nn	Xamuele Zumbo, a Palermitan Jew	Palermo, Albergaria quarter, *contrada* Ballarò, bordering on sugar refinery of the late Antonio Chagi; a butcher's stall	1 year for 4 ounces	

Not. Pietro Goffredo

Palermo, 19 February 1434

Source: ASP, Not. Pietro Goffredo, reg. 1076, c. nn.

Notarial protest lodged by Nissim Crivaru, a Jewish citizen of Palermo, against Galluffo Chochen Sacerdoto, ordinary judge of the Jews (Iudicem ordinarium Iudeorum). *Galluffo had sequestered a curtain from Salamon Levi, Nissim's father-in- law, who had been sued by Giovanni Rubeo on account of a debt of one ounce. Salamon had asked Nissim to pay the ounce and redeem the pawn. The pawn had not been returned.*

Palermo, 22 February 1434

Source: ASP, Not. Pietro Goffredo, reg. 1076, c. nn.

Response of Galluffo Chochen Sacerdoto, Jewish judge in Palermo, to the protest lodged by Nissim Crivaru, for not having had a pawn returned to him. In Galluffo's absence, Graziano [Naguay], notary of the Jewish court, had received the ounce which Nissim paid on behalf of Salamon Levi, his father-in law, but had retained the pawn. Subsequently Salamon offered to pay Nissim the ounce which he had advanced for Salamon and claimed the curtain for himself. The judge asks Nissim to withdraw his protest.

Palermo, 24 March 1434

Source: ASP, Not. Pietro Goffredo, reg. 1076, cc. 32v–33r.

Fariuni de Lerni, Busac Actuni, Sabet Busac, Sabuc Marsiglia, Brachono Sicilianu and Garrono Gazu, Jewish citizens of Palermo, hire themselves out to Bartholomeo Columba to fertilize his sugar cane for 18 tarì *a thousand plants. They are paid one ounce on account to be shared in equal parts.*

Bibliography: Ashtor, *Palermitan Jewry*, p. 224, n. 49.

6684

Palermo, 14 April 1434

Source: ASP, Not. Pietro Goffredo, reg. 1076, cc. 48v–49r.

Agreement between fra Paolo de Iordano, abbot of the monastery S. Maria degli Angeli in Palermo, and Vanni de Termini, a Jewish citizen of Palermo, in regard to the rent for some houses belonging to the monastery, situated in the Cassaro, in the ruga *Luxeri. Vanni had leased the property from the monastery in perpetuity. The dispute over the rent had been heard by the Pretorian court and by the* Magna Regia Corte. *Under the terms of the accord Vanni promises to pay by August 1.6.0 ounces rent for the years of the XI and XII indiction.*

Palermo, 23 April 1434

Source: ASP, Not. Pietro Goffredo, reg. 1076, c. nn.

Xibiten Balbu, a Jewish citizen of Palermo, hires himself out to Gallufo de Seson to render to him servicia tam urbana quam rusticana tam Panormi quam extra sibi possibilia et specialiter exercicium bordunarie *for two ounces.*

Palermo, 27 April 1434

Source: ASP, Not. Pietro Goffredo, reg. 1076, c. nn.

Alamagna, a Jewess of Palermo, widow of Xallu Gibili, appoints Ximinto de Geraci, a Jew of Polizzi, her attorney to collect for her the estate of her sister, the late Stira, a Jewess of Polizzi, who had made Alamagna her principal heir.

Palermo, 28 April 1434

Source: ASP, Not. Pietro Goffredo, reg. 1076, c. nn.

Brachono Sofer, a Jewish citizen of Palermo, hires himself out to Giovanni de Veteri, a notary, to seal wine barrels for 3.2 grana *each and put in stoppers for 10* grana *each* (magister aptator seu stringitor vegetum).

Palermo, 23 May 1434

Source: ASP, Not. Pietro Goffredo, reg. 1076, c. nn.

Sabeti de Minichi, a Jewish citizen of Palermo, hires himself out to Giovanni

Patronello for a year to work in his mill for a total of six ounces and a tumulo *of flour a week. He is paid two ounces on account. He is to start on the 1st of September, and to work continously except on Saturdays.*

Palermo, 8 June 1434

Source: ASP, Not. Pietro Goffredo, reg. 1076, c. nn.

Daniel de Avirra, a Jewish citizen of Palermo, hires himself out to Elia Barbuto, his Jewish fellow citizen, as muledriver to transport stone and earth and to dig trenches: cum duobus animalibus lapides et terras rubeas et facere fossiata et alia servicia sibi possibilia necessaria marammatis dictis conductoris.

Palermo, 17 June 1434

Source: ASP, Not. Pietro Goffredo, reg. 1076, c. nn.

The children of the late Sadono and Muxa and his children appoint Ximinto Romano, husband of Mariuma, daughter of Sadono, to obtain possession of the estate of the late Muxa Rubeo (Rossi), father of Sadono and Muxa. Muxa Rubeo senior had died intestate, and his widow, Gimula, had been appointed guardian of the (then) minor Sadono and Muxa and administratrix of the estate. Some probi *Jews had stood surety for her. Sadono, since deceased, and Muxa never obtained possession of the estate.*

Palermo, 19 May 1435

Source: ASP, Not. Pietro Goffredo, reg. 1076, c. nn.

Contract between Gaudio de Gabriele, a Jew of Salemi, and Sadono de Medico, another Jew, to set up a partnership to trade (ex causa et nomina accommande) *in certain goods for four months and to divide the profit between them. Gaudio invests 11.17.0 ounces and a mule, which he is to have back on the termination of the partnership.*

Palermo, 20 May 1435

Source: ASP, Not. Pietro Goffredo, reg. 1076, c. nn.

Notarial protest lodged by Sabet Rubeo, a Jewish citizen of Palermo, against

master Thomeo Catulla. *The two had sold some sugar and had bought ten and a*
half pieces of cloth with the proceeds. Sabet demands that Thomeo hand over to
him half the cloth.

Palermo, 21 May 1435

Source: ASP, Not. Pietro Goffredo, reg. 1076, c. nn.

The sacristans of the Jewish community in Palermo lodge a notarial protest
against Amico de Gregorio and Michael de Terranu, for having trespassed on the
cemetery, the property of the community. They had sown barley and wheat on
the land. They are warned to stop forthwith on pain of a fine.

Notum facimus et testamur quod Sabet Dinar, Xannino Aurifichi et Simon
Isac Iudei, cives Panormi, et sacristani muskite seu sinagoge Iudayce
urbis eiusdem presentes coram nobis, animo et intentioni de protestandi
requirendi iusque dicte Iudayce in posterum illesum conservandum
adversus et contra Amicum de Gregorio presentem et audientem, nec non
contra et adversus Michaelem de Terranu perquisitum et non inventum,
ut nobis dicti protestantes asseruerunt cives per eiusdem exposuerunt,
dicantes quod cum prefata Iudayca habeat, teneat et possideat extra
muros urbis eiusdem quendam locum, sei quoddam territorium in quo
cadavera Iudeorum morturum sepeliri [empty space], qua Iudayca tenente
et possidente pacifice et quiete dum est et de presenti tamquam vera et
libera domina et patrona loci predicti, nemine contradicente. Nunc autem
prefatus Amicus et Michael protestati, auctoritate propria et de facto
absque licencia et consensu Iudayce prefate, non in modicum preiudicium
et lesionem iuris eiusdem Iudayce in dicto loco et terreno eorum ordeum
pisare presumerint et ayrem in eodem fecerint et faciant de presenti tam
ordea et frumenta in eorum pisandi. Propterea dicti sacrestani Iudayce
prefate volentes cautius et sicure agere, per presentis protestacionis et
requisicionis seriem et tenorem requisiverunt et requirunt instanter et
instantissime ex parte regia, sub pena unciarum auri quinquaginta regio
fisco inremissibiliter applicandarum, et sub pena unciarum auri decem
regie curie capitani et iusticiari urbis prefate, quod inmediate a dicto
territorio et loco dictam aerem delevare debeant et minime amplius
in eodem territorio presument facere aliquod exercicium et signanter
artem prefatam, alias se secus fecerit in premissis, vel circa premissa, ex
nunc pro tunc et equo dictas penas sibi denunciaverunt et denunciant
contra eosdem protestatos et quemlibet eorum in solidum extorquendas

tociens quociens contrafactum fuerit in premissis et circa premissa. Et nichilominus preter contra eosdem de omnibus dampnis, interesse et expensis passis et passuris ob culpam et defectum dictorum protestatorum nolentes forte premissa adimplere constituentes eosdem in dolo, mora et culpa hanc eorum protestacionem nomine dicte Iudayce sibi facientes, etc. Testes: Angelus de Leucio, Aloysius de Lapi, Iohannis de Favra et Aloysius de Cullaza.

Bibliography: Bresc, *Un Monde Méditerranéen*, p. 634, n. 269; Id., *Arabi*, p. 118, n. 612.

Palermo, 27 May 1435

Source: ASP, Not. Pietro Goffredo, reg. 1076, c. nn.

Agreement between master Moyse Chetibi, widower of the late Manuella, and Ioseph and Stira, Manuella's children from her marriage to Michael de Brachono. Ioseph and Stira cede all their rights to master Moyse.

Palermo, 28 May 1435

Source: ASP, Not. Pietro Goffredo, reg. 1076, c. nn.
Publication: Ashtor, *Palermo*, pp. 242f.

Some 132 members of the Jewish community in Palermo lodge a notarial protest against Iacob Xunina, Xaninu Aurifichi and Sabet Dinar, sacristans of the community, and Benedetto Chazen, Ximinto Aurifichi and David Diffuti, prothi. *They demand that the officials take action in the matter of the dispute with Olivo de Sottile. The land of the synagogue borders on that of Olivio. The community and Olivio had made an agreement between the parties, formulated by the notary Nicolò Aprea, delimiting the boundaries between their properties. Nonetheless, Olivo had dismantled part of the boundary wall and had appropriated some of the community's land. The officials are called upon to safeguard the rights of the synagogue.*

Note: Ashtor misread some of the names, e.g. Granus = Gracianus, Cachariatus = Tachariatus, etc.

Palermo, 29 May 1435

Source: ASP, Not. Pietro Goffredo, reg. 1076, c. nn.

Salamon Levi, a Jewish citizen of Palermo, lodges a notarial protest against Minto Romano and Sabet Russo, his fellow Jews, who had hired him to work their sugar cane plantation, for having failed to abide by the terms of the contract between them.

Note: See below on this page.

Palermo, 30 May 1435

Source: ASP, Not. Pietro Goffredo, reg. 1076, c. nn.

Iuda Chirusi, a Jew of Monte San Giuliano, and Nissim de Sidita, a Jew of Caccamo, hire themselves out to Pietro de Calandra for 24 days to work in his vineyard for 20 tarì *each. Iacobo de [..]llus and Muxa de Termis stand surety.*

Palermo, 31 May 1435

Source: ASP, Not. Pietro Goffredo, reg. 1076, c. nn.

Brachono Mizoc, a Jewish citizen of Palermo, lodges a notarial protest against Effraim Caccamia, attorney for Minto Mizoc, his Jewish fellow citizens, to hand over to him half the house which Minto had sold him. He also demands the rent of the property from the date of the sale onward. Effraim replies that he no longer represents Minto.

Palermo, 31 May 1435

Source: ASP, Not. Pietro Goffredo, reg. 1076, c. nn.

Following the final accounting of a partnership between Daniel Avirra and Muxa Sacerdoto, Jewish citizens of Palermo, Daniel remains owing Muxa 1.22.0 ounces, which Daniel promises to pay with manure. They also set up a new partnership for a year, in which Muxa invests a beast of burden and its upkeep, and Daniel his labour in a sugar refinery.

Palermo, 1 June 1435

Source: ASP, Not. Pietro Goffredo, reg. 1076, c. nn.

Ximinto Romano, a Jewish citizen of Palermo, lodges a notarial protest against Salamon Levi, his Jewish fellow citizen, for having failed to abide by the terms of a contract between them whereby Salamon hired himself out to Ximinto as aptator zuccari. *Ximinto claims damages.*

Palermo, 10 June 1435

Source: ASP, Not. Pietro Goffredo, reg. 1076, c. nn.

Iacob de Andarello and Galluffo Mayurana, Jewish citizens of Palermo, set up a joint venture for exercising the trade of muledrivers. Iacob invests his labour and Galluffo provides two animals and their upkeep. During the vintage season Galluffo is to employ a further two beasts of burden. Iacob is to report to Galluffo daily and to pay him his share.

Palermo, 15 June 1435

Source: ASP, Not. Pietro Goffredo, reg. 1076, c. nn.

Contract whereby Muxa Malti, a Jew of Polizzi, hires himself out to Pietro de Calandra as a manual labourer for 24 continuous days, to work every day until 23 hours (i.e. 5.00 p.m.) and on Fridays until 22 hours. He is to be paid 20 tarì *alla* scarsa, *and is given six* tarì *on account.*

Palermo, 17 June 1435

Source: ASP, Not. Pietro Goffredo, reg. 1076, c. nn.

Sabet de Minichi, a Jewish citizen of Palermo, lodges a notarial protest against Nicolò de Iaconia and Blandinu de Lu Presti, farmers of the tax on mills in Palermo. Sabet had recently bought a mill. They were charging him seven tarì *based on turnover instead of the customary tax.*

Palermo, 17 June 1435

Source: ASP, Not. Pietro Goffredo, reg. 1076, c. nn.

Contract whereby Salamon de Messana hires out his son Galluffo to Xibiten Barbuto, all Jewish citizens of Palermo, for 10 years. During the first five years Galluffo is to be entitled to upkeep and clothing, including clothes for Saturdays: et sic promisit esum et potum et indumenta et calciamenta necessaria, indumenta vero de panno finarisi et togam viam aut clamidem de panno colorato pro diebus sabbatis. *During the following five years he is to be paid two ounces.*

Palermo, 6 March 1438

Source: ASP, Not. Pietro Goffredo, reg. 1076, c. nn.

Sansono Candiono, a Jewish citizen of Palermo, hires himself out to Salamon Ximara, Salamon de Messina and Marzuc Binna, his Jewish fellow citizens, to work day and night (tam de die quam de nocte) *as a wine treader* (stringitorii uvarum) *for 10 tarì a month, and is paid three tarì on account.*

Palermo, 7 March 1438

Source: ASP, Not. Pietro Goffredo, reg. 1076, c. nn.

Salamon de Messina, a Jewish citizen of Palermo, lodges a notarial protest against Marino de Ianrusso for having failed to give him the keys to a warehouse owned by Elia alias Picca, Salamon's father. In the warehouse were stored 110 sugar loaves belonging to Marino. Salamon was to see to their refining, and to barter the refined sugar for mastic. Salamon demands the keys.
In the margin: *Marino replies that he deposited the sugar in the warehouse. It should remain there until it sold. He does not understand Salamon's protest.*

Palermo, 10 March 1438

Source: ASP, Not. Pietro Goffredo, reg. 1076, c. nn.

David Rugila, Leone Nichilli, Elia de Gazella e Chabrellus Calabresi, Jewish citizens of Palermo, hire themselves out to Marzuc Binna, their Jewish fellow citizen, to press his grapes: calcare et pistare omnes et singulas quantitates uvarum bene, sollicite, fideliter et legaliter, *for three tarì a quintal of grapes. They are paid 12 tarì on account.*

Palermo, 10 March 1438

Source: ASP, Not. Pietro Goffredo, reg. 1076, c. nn.

Iosep Copiu, a Jewish citizen of Palermo, acknowledges receipt from Chaim Monsor, his Jewish fellow citizen, of all the articles, except a mattress, promised Iosep by Chaim as dowry on the occasion of Iosep's marriage to Chaim's sister. The contract between the parties had been drawn up by the Jewish notary Abram Abeladeb: vigore cuiusdam note publice celebrate manu notari Abrahe Abeladeb, Iudeorum dicte urbis notarius, preter materacium unum purpurignum plenum lana.

6691

Palermo, 10 March 1438

Source: ASP, Not. Pietro Goffredo, reg. 1076, c. nn.

Deed of sale whereby Sabet Azara, a Jewish citizen of Palermo, sells Isaya de Isaya, his Jewish fellow citizen, a red-coated mule for 2.6.0 ounces. Sabet pays one ounce on the spot and promises to pay the balance within 40 days, provided the mule does not show signs of disease or hidden blemishes.

Palermo, 2 April 1438

Source: ASP, Not. Pietro Goffredo, reg. 1076, c. nn.

Agreement between Busac de Tripuli and Fariono Nifusi, prospective son-in-law and father-in-law, Jewish citizens of Palermo, setting out the terms of the dowry promised by Fariono to Busac on his marriage to Stira, Fariono's daughter. Fariono pays Busac six ounces in cash and a herd of 150 sheep valued at six ounces. The sheep are to be delivered by August.

Palermo, 4 April 1438

Source: ASP, Not. Pietro Goffredo, reg. 1076, c. nn.

Quittance by Xamuele Sala to Elia de Benedetto, Jewish citizens of Palermo, of one ounce on account of the rent for a shop and a warehouse. He expects to receive another ounce after Passover.

Palermo, 21 April 1438

Source: ASP, Not. Pietro Goffredo, reg. 1076, c. nn.

Salamon Azara and Isac de Guillelmo, Jewish citizens of Palermo, promise to release from slavery Aniderachame, their Saracen slave. He undertakes to pay them 21 ounces for his manumission: six ounces in the first year in monthly instalments of 15 tarì, and the remaining 15 ounces over the course of the following three years. During these four years the slave must not escape or commit a crime.

Palermo, 28 April 1438

Source: ASP, Not. Pietro Goffredo, reg. 1076, c. nn.

Promise by Brachono Taguil, a Jew of Termini, to Moyse de Medico and Iuda

Siveni, prothi *of the Jewish community in Palermo, to obtain from the king confirmation of a privilege granted the Jews by King Peter. The* prothi *give him the text of the document, and Brachono is to make three copies of it. Brachono is also to obtain the implementation order* (esecutoria) *by the viceroy. He is to be paid 10 ounces, including expenses.*

Note: The Doc. does not state which King Peter is being referred to.

Palermo, 30 April 1438

Source: ASP, Not. Pietro Goffredo, reg. 1076, c. nn.

Salamon Rabibi, a Jewish citizen of Palermo acknowledges receipt from Salamon Azara, his Jewish fellow citizen, of 12 ounces, paid the preceding September, to trade with. This sum included 1.2.0 ounces which Azara paid on behalf of Sabet Dinar as rent of the shop in which Rabibi stored his merchandise. Rabibi must pay Azara the invested capital and half the profit. If profitable business opportunities offer themselves, Azara is prepared to invest an additional eight ounces for half the profit.

Palermo, 5 May 1438

Source: ASP, Not. Pietro Goffredo, reg. 1076, c. nn.

The three judges of the Jewish community in Palermo, Iacob Xunina and David Xiffuni, acting also on behalf of the absent Sabet Dinar, lodge a notarial protest against Benedetto Chazeni and Isac de Guillelmo, sacristans of the community. The judges accuse the sacristans of interfering with their jurisdiction in spiritual matters. In their reply, the sacristans reject the judges' protest, and complain that on the contrary, the judges encroach on their authority.
In the margin: *On 6 May the parties had still not come to an agreement.*

1. Eodem. Notum facimus et testamur quod Iacob Xunina et David Xiffuni, Iudei cives Panormi, presentes coram nobis, tam pro eis et eorum propriis nominibus quam nomine et pro parte Sabet Dinar absentis, iudices in civilibus et spiritualibus Iudayce dicte urbis, animo et intentione sibi protestandi in quoque officii eorumdem prelibatam in posterum conservandi, contra et adversus Benedictum Chazeni et Isac de Guillelmo, Iudeos eorum concives, sacristas Iudayce prelibata presentes et audientes, exposuerunt dicentes quod cum prefati exponentes fuerint et

sint iudices in civilibus et spiritualibus Iudayce prefate, ipsique protestati presumant se impedire de iurisdicione spirituali et rebus protestatis et eorum officii non competentibus et non pertinentibus legitime, non in modicum preiudicium, lesionem et detrimentum iurisdicionis officii eorundem exponentium, prout noviter intellexirunt, ea propter dicti exponentes eosdem protestatos ex parte regia sub pena unciarum auri L^{ta} regio fisco applicandarum et ab eisdem inremissibiliter extorquendarum instanter et instantissime requisiverunt et requirunt quod nullimodo ipsi pretendant de cetero impedire se debeant de rebus et negociis spiritualibus eis legitime imcompetentibus et impartenentibus. Et nichilominus si forte dicti protestati aliqualem auctoritatem legitimam se impediendum de rebus et negociis spiritualibus, ut predicitur, habeant, quod non credunt, oppositam ipsam auctoritatem exerceant iuxta eorum legitimam auctoritatem, quam auctoritatem demonstrent et demonstrare debeant seu ostendant, qua auctoritate legitima deinde ut supra aversa per quam auctoritatem possint legitime se impedire de rebus et negociis spiritualibus, quod eo nunc statim et incontinenti presens protestacio sit et esse debeat nulla, irrita et cassa, ac se minime facta fuisset, alias si secus fecerint quod incidant et incidere debeant in penam prelibatam, quam ex nunc pro tunc regio denunciaverint et denunciant hanc eorum protestacione sibi facientes suis loco et tempore valituram. Ad quam quidam protestacionem et requisicionem prefati protestati immediate cum omni qua decet responsio respondeberint quod habita copia eis consultis responsionem pro nunc sibi facientis.

Testes: Brachonus Bambula, Busac de Tripuli, Viticchius Mulini et Muxa Marsili.

2. Eodem. Notum facimus et testamur quod Benedictus Chazeni et Isac de Guillelmo, Iudei cives Panormi, sacriste Iudayce predicte urbis, presentes coram nobis, sponte requisiverunt et requirunt instanter et instantissime Iacob Xuninam et David Xiffuni, Iudeos eorum concives, presentes et audientes, ex parte regia sub pena uncias auri centum pro quolibet ipsorum regio fisco applicandarum et ab eisdem insolidum inremissibiliter extorquendarum, quod nullimodi se impedire debeant, nec presumant, seu contradicant facto dicto nec opere de officio eorundem requirentium et iuribus ac iurisdicionibus eisdem officii prout et sic eisdem requirentibus per Iudaycam prelibatam fuit commissum et ordinatum, alias si secus fecerunt, quod incidant et incidere debeant in penam prelibatam, quam ex nunc pro tunc regio eis et cuilibet ipsorum denunciaverunt et denunciant habita eorum requisitionem sibi facientes. Ad quam quidem requisitionem prefati Iacob et David prout sibi facientes

immediate cum omnia qua expedit responsio respondiderunt quod habita copia respondebunt consulte. Et Nichilominus idem David requisivet et requirit eosdem Benedictum et Isac quod demostrent seu ostendent quam auctoritatem habent, cum fuerint et sint paratus ipsi obedire habita eorum responsionem prout sibi facientes.

Testes ut supra.

Palermo, 6 May 1438

Source: ASP, Not. Pietro Goffredo, reg. 1076, c. nn.

Manumission of Machamet, slave of Nissim Millac, a Jewish citizen of Palermo, by his master, provided the slave or someone on his behalf pays Nissim 16 ounces in weekly instalments of 2.10 tarì. Only on completed payment of this sum may the slave consider himself a freedman. If Machamet escapes or tries to, he is to remain a slave.

Palermo, 6 May 1438

Source: ASP, Not. Pietro Goffredo, reg. 1076, c. nn.

Agreement whereby Xalem Alluxi and Xibiten Gazu, Jewish citizens of Palermo, stand surety for Fariono Gazu, their Jewish fellow citizen. The latter had guaranteed the payment of rent owed by Xibiten Virdi, another Jew, to Iacob Xunina, also a Jew. The rent had not been paid, and Xunina had Fariono put in prison.

Palermo, 12 May 1438

Source: ASP, Not. Pietro Goffredo, reg. 1076, c. nn.

David Machazeni, a Jewish citizen of Messina and Gallufo Cuyno, a Jewish citizen of Palermo, express their willingness to emancipate Ali, their Saracen slave, provided he pays them 20 ounces in monthly instalments of 15 tarì.

Palermo, 14 May 1438

Source: ASP, Not. Pietro Goffredo, reg. 1076, c. nn.

Iosep de Vitali, a Jewish citizen of Palermo, grants a moratorium of five years to

6695

Xibiten Ysac and to the latter's guarantor, master Sadono de Obbi , his Jewish fellow citizens, on a debt of 10 ounces. They are to pay them in annual instalments of two ounces. The debt arose out of the terms of a partnership in which Fariono Cuyno also took part. Fariono had paid Ioseph 10 out of the 20 ounces due to him.

Palermo, 15 May 1438

Source: ASP, Not. Pietro Goffredo, reg. 1076, c. nn.

Agreement between Anzalono Actuni, a Jewish citizen of Palermo, and Antonio de Sinibaldis whereby Anzalono undertakes to tan a certain quantity of hides for 23 tarì, *and is paid three* tarì *on account.*

Palermo, 17 May 1438

Source: ASP, Not. Pietro Goffredo, reg. 1076, c. nn.

Deed of sale whereby Farrugio Isac, a Jewish citizen of Palermo, sells to Sabet Sabatino, his Jewish fellow citizen, a certain quantity of doublets for 2.18.0 ounces. Sabet promises to pay Farrugio by August. Paid on 27 November.

Palermo, 17 May 1438

Source: ASP, Not. Pietro Goffredo, reg. 1076, c. nn.

Ysac de magistro Moyse, a Jew of Tuscany, hires himself out to Muxa Sacerdoto, a Jewish citizen of Palermo, for a year starting the first of June. He undertakes to carry out: omnia et singula servicia que sibi idem conductor commiserit et mandaverit faciendum in eadem urbe sibi congrua et possibilia, *in return for:* esu et potu et cubili ad opus dormiendum et solaturis necessariis ac duobus paribus antepedium de dayno et pro solvendo unciarum auri unius et tr. XVIII p. g.

Palermo, 7 January 1444

Source: ASP, Not. Pietro Goffredo, reg. 1076, c. nn.

Contract between Antonio Quanupani and Brachono Bambalo, a Jewish citizen of Palermo. Antonio undertakes to transport all the grapes produced in Brachono's vineyard during the coming vintage season for two ounces a thousand, i.e. ten quintals. Xidedi Azara, a Jew, stands surety.

Palermo, 5 February 1444

Source: ASP, Not. Pietro Goffredo, reg. 1076, c. nn.

Agreement between Simone de Bankerio, acting for his absent brother, Leonardo, and Bracha Sacerdoto, a Jewish citizen of Palermo. Simone agrees that if Bracha returns to Leonardo 13 ounces and the rent of a solerata *house within five years, he would forego the lien* (subiugatio) *on the house.*

Palermo, 5 February 1444

Source: ASP, Not. Pietro Goffredo, reg. 1076, c. nn.

Contract for the setting up of a partnership between Muxa Sacerdoto, a Jewish citizen of Palermo. and Nicolò Banno, his fellow citizen, to last eight years, for winemaking. Muxa is to invest a building (un fundacum situm et positum in Contrata buchirie Iudeorum prope miskitam) *worth seven ounces, some tools, straw and other items:* tantam quantitatem palae ac licterias duas fulcitas raubas et ... vegetes XII et duos caratellos nanos ac tenam et apparatorem ad opus pistandi uvas... *worth 4 ounces. Both are to invest their labour. The proceeds are to be divided into three parts: two thirds are to go to Muxa in return for the investment of 11 ounces and his labour, and one third is to be Nicolò's in return for his labour.*

Bibliography: Bresc, *Arabi*, p. 265, and n. 1283.

Palermo, 5 February 1444

Source: ASP, Not. Pietro Goffredo, reg. 1076, c. nn.

Chayrono Gazu, a Jewish citizen of Palermo, hires himself out to Ubertino de Imperatore to work as paratore *in his sugar refinery for one ounce, and is paid three* tarì *on account.*

Palermo, 5 February 1444

Source: ASP, Not. Pietro Goffredo, reg. 1076, c. nn.

Agreement between Muxa Actuni, a Jewish citizen of Palermo, and Antonio de Villanova to pay a debt of three ounces in weekly instalments of 1.10 tarì. In return Antonio has Muxa released from prison.

Palermo, 7 February 1444

Source: ASP, Not. Pietro Goffredo, reg. 1076, c. nn.

Declaration by Adario de Lu Presti of Palermo that contrary to the assertion in another deed, Bulchayra de Termini, a Jewish citizen of Palermo is not involved in the debt which Adario owes Elena de Cataldo for oil.

Palermo, 7 February 1444

Source: ASP, Not. Pietro Goffredo, reg. 1076, c. nn.

Master Michele de Limisi, a surgeon, and Xamuel Gididia, a Jewish citizen of Palermo, set up a partnership for the purchase of 51 deerskins, their tanning and sale. Michele invests 4.15.0 ounces. The proceeds are to be divided between the partners in equal shares, after deduction of expenses. Gaudiosa, Xamuel's wife, pledges her ketubbah *as surety for Xamuel.*

Palermo, 12 February 1444

Source: ASP, Not. Pietro Goffredo, reg. 1076, c. nn.

Salamon de Ragusia, Farrugio Sichiliano, Ximinto Candioto and Vita Maltense, Jewish citizens of Palermo, hire themselves out to Marino de Ianrusso to transport his sugar cane straw for 16 grana a day each.

Palermo, 27 February 1444

Source: ASP, Not. Pietro Goffredo, reg. 1076, c. nn.

Brachono Bambalo and Elia Miglieni, Jewish citizens of Palermo, set up a partnership for the making of wine and its sale in a tavern for a year. Brachono is to buy grapes for 23.5.0 ounces a thousand (i.e. 10 quintals), whereas Elia is to sell the wine in the tavern. Brachono had rented the tavern from Moyse de Medico, another Jew. The proceeds were to be divided between the partners in equal shares, after deduction of expenses.

Palermo, 6 November 1447

Source: ASP, Not. Pietro Goffredo, reg. 1076, c. nn.

Deed recording that on 9 September Isac de Guillelmo, a Jewish citizen of Palermo, read out to a large number of Jews congregated in the synagogue of Palermo the royal order providing for the abolition of the office of dienchelele, *and the viceregal order of implementation. The notary authenticated the text of both documents. The royal order was dated 10.2.1447 and that of the viceroy was given on 1.10.1447.*

Note: See above, Docs. 2850 and 2860. The royal order presented to the congregation in Palermo is dated 1.2.1447, whereas the one addressed to the Jewish community in Messina is dated 16.1.1447. There are minor differences in the wording. The viceregal *executoria* presented in Palermo are dated 1.10.1447, whereas those directed to Messina are dated 23.5.1447.

Palermo, 6 November 1447

Source: ASP, Not. Pietro Goffredo, reg. 1076, c. nn.

Deed recording that on 9 September Isac de Guillelmo, a Jewish citizen of Palermo, read out to a large number of Jews congregated in the synagogue of Palermo the royal confirmation on 14.8.1447 of the concessions granted the Jewish communities by the viceroy Lopes Ximen Durrea on 9.5.1447. The notary authenticated the text of both documents.

Note: See above, Docs. 2857 and 2869. In addition viceregal *executoria* of the royal confirmation, dated 4.9.1447, are quoted.

Palermo, 5 July 1448

Source: ASP, Not. Pietro Goffredo, reg. 1076, c. nn.

Manumisson of Ganima, a slave girl, by master Sadono de Medico, a Jewish physician, citizen of Palermo, following payment of the last instalments of 16 ounces, the price agreed on for her emancipation.

Palermo, 30 March 1451

Source: ASP, Not. Pietro Goffredo, reg. 1076, c. nn.

Agreement by Iuda de Minichi, a Jewish citizen of Palermo, and the notary Berto de Trapano whereby Iuda undertakes to transport must from the notary's vineyards to his tavern in Palermo during vintage time. He is to transport 50 quartari *with four animals for four* tarì *a trip. Iuda is paid three* tarì *on account by Brachono Sacerdoto, a Jewish publican, on behalf of Berto. He is promised the balance on completion of the transport.*

Palermo, 2 April 1451

Source: ASP, Not. Pietro Goffredo, reg. 1076, c. nn.

Agreement between Guglielmo de Albergo of Naso and master Salamon Gibel, a Jewish citizen of Palermo, whereby Guglielmo is to supply 60 salme *of coal to the shore of Naso in the* contrada Mirabitu, *and Salamon is to transport the coal to Palermo and sell it there. The proceeds are to be divided in equal shares between the two.*

Palermo, 7 June 1458

Source: ASP, Not. Pietro Goffredo, reg. 1076, c. nn.

Giuliano de Raimundo promises Brachono Bambulo, a Jewish citizen of Palermo, to transport three and a half quintals of grapes from his vineyard to his home for 24.7 tarì. *He is also to do likewise for Minto de Minichi, another Jew, on the strength of a different contract.*

Palermo, 13 June 1458

Source: ASP, Not. Pietro Goffredo, reg. 1076, c. nn.

Iuda Isac, a Jewish citizen of Palermo, apprentices his son Nissim with David de Malta, his Jewish fellow citizen, for five years. David is to train Nissim in carpentry and teach him Hebrew. David is also to provide Nissim with upkeep and clothing. If David is unable to abide by these terms he is to pay Nissim two ounces. David is also to provide Nissim with enough ironware to make a large gate.

Sicily

Palermo, 13 June 1458

Source: ASP, Not. Pietro Goffredo, reg. 1076, c. nn.

Muxa de Tripuli, a Jewish citizen of Palermo, grants a moratorium to Fariono Gazu, his Jewish fellow citizen, on the paymet of the price for a certain quantity of tunny. Fariono is unable to pay at present.

Palermo, [..]June 1458

Source: ASP, Not. Pietro Goffredo, reg. 1076, c. nn.

Bracha de Liucio, a Jewish citizen of Palermo, hires himself out to Salamon de Bumachi, his fellow Jew, for one year for four ounces.

Note: Doc. largely washed out.

Source: ASP, Not. Pietro Goffredo, reg. 1076

Date and Page	Principal	Attorney	Purpose	Remarks
27.4.1434 c. nn	A[..] Gibil, a Jew of Palermo	Ximinto de Girachi, a Jew of Palermo	to collect debts and take suitable steps against those unable to pay	
19.5.1434 c. nn	Xibiten Barbutu, a Jew of Palermo	Matheo Sacerdoto, a Jew of Palermo	to collect debts	Matheo may keep a third of the sums collected
27.5.1435 c. nn	Iosep Brachono, a Jew of Palermo	Moise Chetibi, a Jew of Palermo	to administer all his property	
31.3.1451 c. nn	Sadono de Medico, a Jew of Palermo	Pinesi de Aron, a Jew of Palermo	to go to Syracuse to trace a white slave girl named Terna	Pinesi is to sell her or emancipate her for a suitable sum of money

| 31.3.1451 c. nn | Vita Amara, a Palermitan Jew | Battista de Gilberto | to collect debts from Antonio de Sikiki and Giovanni de Sinibaldis | |

Date and Page	Debtor	Amount	Reason	Remarks
2.6.1434 c. nn	Mardoc de Rustico, a Palermitan Jew	1 ounce		creditor: Simon Rugila, a Jew of Palermo; guarantor: Salamone de Rustico, both Jews of Palermo; to be paid in 4 months
28.3.1438 c. nn	Brachono Candila, a Palermitan Jew	1.6.0 ounces	rent for a house	creditor: Thoma Gilberto; guarantors: Salamon Gibel and Muxa Galluxi, Jews; to be paid within a year
1.4.1438 c. nn	Brachono Rubeo [Rossi], a Jew of Palermo	1.7.0 ounces		creditor: Leone Abbate, a Jew of Palermo; guarantor: Rubeo de Lombardo, a Jew
6.2.1444 c. nn	Muxa Actuni, a Jew of Palermo	3 ounces		creditor: Antonio de Villanova; to be paid in weekly instalments of 1 *tarì*
14.2.1444 c. nn	Vita Siveni, a Jew in Palermo	1 ounce		creditor: Antonio de Gimbesio; 5 *tarì* on account, balance later

Date and Page	Lender or Seller	Amount	Payment	Remarks
21.2.1434 c. nn	Antonia de Paramides	24 *tarì*	3 *tarì* in September, balance within 4 months	sale of a woman's skirt to Xidedi Azara, a Jew of Palermo
25.2.1434 c. nn	Antonio Sambataru	2.24.0 ounces	15 *tarì* on account; paid 8.6	sale of *caciocavallo* cheese to Ximinto Romano, a Palermitan Jew

25.2.1434 c. nn	Stefano Sambataru	6.26.0 ounces	3.1.0 ounces on account, balance in a month; paid 20.4	sale of linen to Leone de Medico, a Jew of Palermo
3.3.1434 c. nn	Zullu Bramuni and Gallufu Chamari, Jews of Palermo	1 ounce	3 *tarì* on account; balance in 3 days	sale of a horse
4.3.1434 c. nn	Isabella, wife of Giovanni Vitale	1.3.0 ounces	within 4 months	sale of linen to Daniele Abramello, a Jew of Palermo
16.3.1434 c. nn	Pietro de Raia	27 *tarì*	paid	sale of grapes to Nissim Binna, a Jew in Palermo
23.3.1434 c. nn	Guarnerio de Alfano	2.10.0 ounces	15 *tarì* on account	sale of myrtle to Daidono Rizo, a Palermitan Jew
24.3.1434 c. nn	Giovanni Anchellu	7 florins	paid	sale of grapes to Elia Sivena, a Jew of Caltanissetta
6.4.1434 c. nn	Iacobo Castellar	4½ *tarì* a pound	1 ounce on account; balance in weekly instalments of 1 ounce; paid 4.2.1435	sale of silk to Xamuel Sacerdoto and Abramo Laude, Jews of Palermo
12.4.1434 c. nn	Elia Barbuto, a Jew of Palermo	4 ounces	paid	sale of *caciocavallo* cheese
12.4.1434 c. nn	Antonio Lupilulu	7 ounces	paid 12.6	sale of cheese to Elia Barbuto, a Palermitan Jew
22.4.1434 c. nn	Nicolò de La Panictera	1 ounce	27 *tarì* on account, balance later	sale of grapes to Xua Marsili, a Jew in Palermo
23.4.1434 c. nn	master Nardo de Li Calci	1.18.0 ounces	paid 3.2.1435	sale of a quintal of white grapes to Iuda Siveni, a Jew of Palermo

25.4.1434 c. nn	Stefano Promisto	9.26.0 ounces	within 4 months; paid 14.9	sale of linen to Xamuel Sacerdoto, a Jew of Palermo
19.5.1434 c. nn	Giovanni Porcatu	24 *tarì*	3 *tarì* on account	sale of wheat to Marzucco Binna, a Jew in Palermo
19.5.1434 c. nn	Iacobo Grasso			sale of grapes to Daidono Rizu, a Jew of Palermo
20.5.1434 c. nn	Antonio Buccheri	1 ounce	paid	sale of a horse to Vita Amar, a Jew of Palermo
21.5.1434 c. nn	Antonio Rubeus (Rossi)		12 florins on account	sale of grapes to Sofen de Minichi, a Jew of Palermo
24.5.1434 c. nn	Antonio Strazapilato	12 *tarì*	paid	sale of grapes to Xibiten Barbuto, a Jew in Palermo
2.6.1434 c. nn	Matheo de Manfre	20 ounces	12 *tarì* on account, balance on delivery; paid 30.4.1435	sale of coal to Xibiten Barbuto, a Jew of Palermo
2.6.1434 c. nn	Simon Rugila, a Palermitan Jew	1 ounce	within 4 months	loan to Mardoc de Rustico, a Jew of Palermo; Salamone de Rustico, another Jew, stands surety
2.6.1434 c. nn	Giovanni de Carabelli	10.18.0 ounces	12 and 7.10 *tarì* on account, balance by 1.6; paid	sale of a Saracen slave to Levi Xanto, a Palermitan Jew
4.6.1434 c. nn	Antonio La Calcara	2 ounces		sale of coal to Xibiten Barbuto, a Jew of Palermo
22.6.1434 c. nn	Galluffo de Mirmichi, a Jew of Palermo	1.18.0 ounces	24 *tarì* by the middle of July, 24 *tarì* by October; paid 15.12.1435	sale of beast of burden

23.6.1434 c. nn	Giovanni de Vine	2.3.0 ounces	within 2 months	sale of soap to Busacca de Tripuli, a Jew in Palermo
23.6.1434 c. nn	Andrea Gentili	4 ounces	paid 13.7.1435	loan to Merdoc Samuel and Boninu de Termini, Palermitan Jews
1.7.1434 c. nn	Giovanni de Tusa		12 *tarì* on account	sale of grapes to Muxa Achivo, a Palermitan Jew
1.7.1434 c. nn	Salamon Rusticu, a Palermitan Jew	2 ounces		sale of an anvil weighing 132 *rotoli*; guarantor: Muxa Xeba, a Jew of Palermo
1.7.1434 c. nn	Bertino de Imperatore	1.6.0 ounces		loan of an anvil to Muxa Xeba, a Jew of Palermo
1.7.1434 c. nn	Stefano Promiti	3.13.2 ounces	by 1.8; paid 19.8	sale of linen to Salamon de Muxa, a Jew of Palermo
1.7.1434 c. nn	Stefano Promiti	3.22.4 ounces	by 1.8	sale of linen to Benedetto Azara, a Jew of Trapani;
			guarantor: Galluffo Palermo	Maiorana, a Jew of
16.5.1435 c. nn	Antonio de Gimbesio			sale of grapes to Musuto Binna, a Jew in Palermo
17.5.1435 c. nn	Nicolò de Buccanesi	1.13. 0 ounces	paid	sale of oil to Vita Amar, a Palermitan Jew; guarantor: Sadia Isac, a Jew of Palermo
18.5.1435 c. nn	Frederico de Monteleone	1 ounce	6 *tarì* on account, balance on delivery	sale of coal to Muxa Rubeo and Simon Xalom, Palermitan Jews

20.5.1435 c. nn	Domenica, wife of Ficcaglu	1.13.10 ounces	6 *tarì* on account, balance a week later; paid 9.1.1436	sale of grapes to Salamone de Mermichi, a Jew of Palermo
20.5.1435 c. nn	Giovanni Marabella	1.7.10 ounces	15 *tarì* on account	sale of string (*disa*) to Busac de Tripuli, a Jew of Palermo
20.5.1435 c. nn	Giovanni Balvis	1 ounce	21.10 *tarì* on account, balance in November on delivery	sale of half a kantar of oil to Chanino Farmono, a Jew of Palermo
23.5.1435 c. nn	Prono de Bertulino and Nicolò Vernigla	1.7.10 ounces	3 and 12 *tarì* on account, balance on delivery	sale of string (*disa*) to Muxa de Tripuli, a Jew in Palermo
24.5.1435 c. nn	Guarnerio de Alfano and Matheo de Gigla	2.0.17 ounces	12 *tarì* on account	sale of myrtle and myrtle wood to Musuto Binna, a Palermitan Jew
24.5.1435 c. nn	Giovanni de Angelo	21 *tarì*		sale of grapes to Isdrael Strugu, a Palermitan Jew
25.5.1435 c. nn	Xua Aurifichi, a Jew in Palermo	1.18.0 ounces	within 4 months	sale of 2 oxen to Manfridu de Lombardo
27.5.1435 c. nn	Xamuel Sacerdotu, a Jew of Palermo	1.18.0 ounces	18 *tarì* on account, balance at vintage time	sale of a mule to Ioseph Minichi, a Jew in Palermo
1.6.1435 c. nn	Siminto Achanino, a Palermitan Jew	2.15.0 ounces	within 6 months	sale of silk cocoons to Natale Bugil
1.6.1435 c. nn	Merdoc Sacerdoto, a Jew of Marsala	2.15.0 ounces	by the middle of July; paid 18.7	sale of merchandise
2.6.1435 c. nn	Nicolò de Dunzello	1.24.0 ounces	24 *tarì* on account; balance at vintage time	sale of grapes to Marzuc Binna, a Palermitan Jew
2.6.1435 c. nn	Giovanni Mairana	16 *tarì*	6 *tarì* on account, balance later	sale of a youg animal to Chaim Gazo, a Jew

8.6.1435 c. nn	Salamon de Muxa, a Palermitan Jew	1.20.0 ounces	4 *tarì* on account; balance within 3 months	sale of fabric
8.6.1435 c. nn	Galluffo Maiurana, a Jew of Palermo	24 *tarì*	by November	sale of a donkey to Brachono Zacharo, a Jew in Palermo
10.6.1435 c. nn	Giovanni Carbonello	1.3.0 ounces	paid	sale of a beast of burden to Busacca de Tripuli, a Jew of Palermo
10.6.1435 c. nn	Nicolò de Latora	10 ounces	4 ounces during the current month, balance by July	sale of castrated animals to Chaim Gazo, a Jew of Palermo
15.6.1435 c. nn	Giovanni Mussillo and Manfrido Bellachera	1/7/10 ounces	15 *tarì* on account, balance on delivery	sale of string (*disa*) to Busac de Tripuli, a Palermitan Jew
17.6.1435 c. nn	Siminto Achanino, a Jew of Palermo	2.24.0 ounces	by September	sale of brass (*auribelli*) to Muxa de Gaudio, a Jew in Palermo
20.6.1435 c. nn	Filippo de Minuchio	3.3.0 ounces	1.16.0 ounces and 17 *tarì* on account, balance on demand	sale of grapes to Salamon de Minichi, a Jew in Palermo
21.6.1435 c. nn	Giovanni de Vitale	3.1.5 ounces	within a year	sale of myrtle to Mardoc Levi, a Jew of Palermo
21.6.1435 c. nn	Giovanni de Vitale	2.15.0 ounces	within a year	sale of myrtle to Fariono Nifusi, a Jew of Palermo
21.6.1435 c. nn	Giovanni de Vitale	2 ounces	within a year	sale of myrtle to Mussuto Binna, a Jew of Palermo
21.6.1435 c. nn	Pietro de Surdo	14 ounces	paid	sale of a black slave girl to Onorato de Gaudio, a Palermitan Jew

21.6.1435 c. nn	Antonio Bartulono	1.5.0 ounces	by September	sale of leather to Muxa Casamini, a Jew in Palermo
6.3.1438 c. nn	Musuto Binna, a Palermitan Jew	2 ounces	by April	sale of leather
6.3.1438 c. nn	Enrico Lumbardu	2 ounces	1 ounce on account; balance on delivery	sale of coal to Brachono de Panichello, a Jew in Palermo
6.3.1438 c. nn	Muxa Achina, a Jew in Palermo	18 *tarì*		sale of tallow
6.3.1438 c. nn	Salamon Ximara and Salamon de Missina, Jews of Palermo	18.10 *tarì*		sale of a vice to Marzuc Binna, a Jew of Palermo
6.3.1438 c. nn	Azarono Ricio and Fariono Nifusi, Jews of Palermo	1.19.10 ounces	by the middle of May	sale of hides
7.3.1438 c. nn	Muxexi de Agnati	8 ounces	by August	sale of silk to Rabbi Levi de Xentob, a Palermitan Jew
7.3.1438 c. nn	Muxa Achina, a Jew in Palermo	15 *tarì*	4 *tarì* on account, balance by August	sale of tallow to Antonio de Loci
10.3.1438 c. nn	Brachono Xuffi, a Jew of Palermo			sale of 100 roof tiles
10.3.1438 c. nn	Masio Zaparuni	same as earlier sale	2.18.0 ounces on account, balance on delivery	sale of 1.5 quintals of grapes to Nissim Serritanu, a Palermitan Jew
10.3.1438 c. nn	Sabet Azara, a Jew of Palermo	2.6.0 ounces	1 ounce on account, balance by Easter	sale of a mule to Isaia de Isaia, a Palermitan Jew

10.3.1438 c. nn	Nicolò Perraturi	22 *tarì*		sale of grapes to Salamuni Actuni, a Jew of Palermo
14.3.1438 c. nn	Giovanni de Lavuri	9 ounces	paid	sale of a black slave girl to Iacob Sabatino, a Jew of Palermo
17.3.1438 c. nn	Thomeo de Damiano	21 *tarì*	paid	sale of grapes to Bulchayra Frisisa, a Jew of Palermo
17.3.1438 c. nn	Ventura, widow of Pietro Firreri	3.12.0 ounces		sale of grapes to Sabet Xunina, a Jew of Palermo
19.3.1438 c. nn	Nicolò de Carissimo	1.18.0 ounces		sale of grapes to Salamon Actuni, a Jew of Palermo
20.3.1438 c. nn	Pietro de Raia and Michilono Minacham, a Jew of Palermo	5 ounces a hundred	5 ounces on delivery, a third by Christmas, balance by Easter	sale of sheep
21.3.1438 c. nn	Giovanni de Calandrino	22 *tarì*		sale of a horse to Elia de Benedetto, a Jew of Palermo, guarantor: Zullo Markeki, a Jew in Palermo
24.3.1438 c. nn	Xamuele Sacerdoto, a Palermitan Jew	1.25.0 ounces	by Easter	sale of heavy and light rope
24.3.1438 c. nn	Angelo de Pulito	8.18.0 ounces	paid	sale of grapes to Zudo Abramuni, a Jew in Palermo
24.3.1438 c. nn	Elia de Benedetto, a Palermitan Jew	1.9.0 ounces	half by May and half at vintage time	sale of a horse
28.3.1438 c. nn	Antonio Zafarana	24 *tarì*		sale of grapes to Zudo Abramuni, a Jew of Palermo

28.3.1438 c. nn	Luca de Muraturi	1.18.0 ounces	paid	sale of grapes to Vita Amara, a Jew in Palermo
4.4.1438 c. nn	Rubino Muxarella, a Jew of Palermo	1.6.0 ounces		loan
4.4.1438 c. nn	Abraam Abeladeb, a Palermitan Jew	6 ounces	paid	sale of goods to Axeri Manu and Muxa Minachim, Jews of Marsala
7.4.1438 c. nn	Nardo de Giovanni Terxi	15 *tarì*	7.10 *tarì* on account	sale of new white roof tiles to Deulusa Salvi, a Jew of Palermo
8.4.1438 c. nn	Mardoc Xaul, a Jew in Palermo	2 ounces	annual instalments of 12 *tarì*	sale of tools, including an anvil, pincers and a hammer to Nissim Millac, a Palermitan Jew
8.4.1438 c. nn	Brachono Cappello	1.18.0 ounces	18 tari on account	sale of grapes to Muxa Achina, a Jew in Palermo
8.4.1438 c. nn	Nario de Naro of Castelvetrano	6.20.0 ounces	2 ounces on account, balance on delivery; paid	sale of corktree charcoal to Xibiten Barbuto, a Palermitan Jew
8.4.1438 c. nn	Antonio Calandrino			sale of 2 grave stones to Moise Sacerdoto, a Jew of Palermo
9.4.1438 c. nn	Nacum Avirra, a Palermitan Jew	24 *tarì*		sale of goods to Rabbi [Abraam] Abeladeb, a Jew of Palermo
21.4.1438 c. nn	Benedetto Chazeni, a Jew of Palermo	3.6.0 ounces	paid	sale of a third (*terciae integre partis pro indiviso*) of a Saracen slave
22.4.1438 c. nn	Giovanni Costanatu	27 *tarì*	12 *tarì* on account	sale of grapes to David Xaccarono, a Palermitan Jew

23.4.1438 c. nn	Antonio de Guctardo, Matheo de Manfre and Pietro de Pulacta	2 ounces	24 *tarì* on account	sale of corktree charcoal to Xibiten Barbuto, a Jew in Palermo
28.4.1438 c. nn	Marino and Giovanni de Leo	1.15.0 ounces		sale of grapes to Salamone de Minichi, a Jew of Palermo
28.4.1438 c. nn	Garita, wife of Guglielmo de Maurichio	1.12.0 ounces	22.10 *tarì* on account; paid 2.10	sale of grapes to Muxa Achina, a Jew in Palermo
28.4.1438 c. nn	Elia de Missina, a Jew of Palermo	3 ounces	by October	sale of mastic
28.4.1438 c. nn	Busacca de Tripuli, a Jew of Palermo	10 ounces	paid	sale of a Saracen slave to Galluffo Maiurana, a Jew in Palermo
28.4.1438 c. nn	Galluffu Maiurana, a Jew of Palermo	10.9.0 ounces		sale of a Saracen slave to Onorato de Gaudio and
				Benedetto Gazeni, Jews of Palermo; witnesses: Graciano de Medico, Iacob Levi and Galluffo Sanu, Jews of Palermo
29.4.1438 c. nn	Nicolò Marotta	1.7.0 ounces	by August	sale of oil to Leone and Vita Vitrani, Palermitan Jews
29.4.1438 c. nn	Guillelmo de Raffo	1 ounce	12 *tarì* on account	sale of straw to Mardoc de Minichi, a Jew of Palermo
30.4.1438 c. nn	Angelo de Pasquali	21 *tarì*	paid	sale of grapes to Galluffo Maiurana, a Jew of Palermo
[30].4.1438 c. nn	Filippo de Minuchio	4.15.0ounces	paid	sale of grapes to Salamone de Minichi, a Jew of Palermo
30.4.1438 c. nn	Enrico Lu Barberi	2 ounces	1 ounce on account	sale of coal to Brachono Panichello, a Jew in Palermo

30.4.1438 c. nn	Xibiten de Bonavogla, a Jew in Scicli	15 ounces		sale of half (*medietatem integram pro indiviso*) of a black slave to Salamone de Azara, a Palermitan Jew
1.5.1438 c. nn	Rubino Muxarella, a Jew of Marsala	15 *tarì*	by August	sale of a calf
2.5.1438 c. nn	Pino de Alammana	22.10 *tarì*	paid	sale of grapes to Bulchaira Iusise, a Jew of Palermo
2.5.1438 c. nn	Antonio de Marnichio	1 ounce	24 *tarì* on account; balance later	sale of barley straw to Mardoc Minichi, a Jew of Palermo
5.5.1438 c. nn	Giovanni Pompa	1.21.0 ounces	paid	sale of grapes to Galluffo Sansono, a Jew in Palermo
7.5.1438 c. nn	David Machazeni, a Messinese Jew	2.24.0 ounces	1 ounce on account; 18 *tarì* in 2 months, balance in 4 months	sale of a mule
7.5.1438 c. nn	Simone de Siniscalcho	1.19.10 ounces	by September	sale of oil to Aiete Cuinu alias Sacerdoto, a Jew of Palermo
12.5.1438 c. nn	Nicolò Cuzu	5 ounces	2 ounces in 8 days, 3 ounces by August	sale of linen to Vita Siveni, a Palermitan Jew
12.5.1438 c. nn	Salamone Azara, a Jew of Palermo	4.25.10 ounces	within 5 weeks	sale of goods to Xibiten Azara, a Palermitan Jew
12.5.1438 c. nn	Sabatino Muxa, a Palermitan Jew	2 ounces	paid	sale of a mule to Chanino Formano, a Jew of Palermo
12.5.1438 c. nn	Xibiten Muxa, a Jew of Piazza	10 ounces	paid	sale of a Saracen slave to David Machazeni, a Messinese Jew, and Galluffo Cuino, a Palermitan Jew

23.5.1438 c. nn	Vita Siveni, a Jew of Palermo	1.18.0 ounces	monthly instalments of 6 *tarì*	sale of a horse
14.5.1443 c. nn	Xamuel Grecu, a Jew of Trapani	25 *tarì*	within 6 weeks after delivery	sale of wheels to Isdraele Medui, a Jew of Palermo
25.5.1443 c. nn	Enrico de Simone	9.25.16 ounces	part by August, balance within 4 months; paid 11.2.1444	sale of French paper to Sabet Cuinu, a Palermitan Jew
15.5.1443 c. nn	Filippo Aglata	18 ounces	within 4 months; paid	sale of 50 deer to Iosep and Daniel Miri, Palermitan Jews
15.5.1443 c. nn	Enrico de Simone	9.24.0 ounces	within 8 months	sale of French paper to Iosep Sillac, a Jew in Palermo
15.5.1443 c. nn	Giovanni de Carastono	4.10.0 ounces	within 6 months	sale of oil to Mardoc Levi, a Jew of Palermo
16.5.1443 c. nn	Xidedi Azara, a Jew in Palermo	1.12.0 ounces	weekly instalments of 1.10 *tarì*	sale of a horse
17.5.1443 c. nn	Farrugio Isac, a Jew of Palermo	2.18.0 ounces	by August	sale of doublets to Sabet Sabatino, a Jew of Palermo
17.5.1443 c. nn	Iacobo de Salvo	3 ounces	within 6 months	sale of footwear and leggings to Busacca Isac and Somma, a Jewish couple of Palermo
20.5.1443 c. nn	Salvo de Salvo	41.2.0 ounces	by 16.7	sale of canvas borders and linen to Salamon Muxa and Muxa de Muxa, Palermitan Jews
20.5.1443 c. nn	Salmerio de Silvestro	1.6.0 ounces	within 2 months	sale of myrtle to Xibiten Isac, a Jew of Palermo

22.5.1443 c. nn	Iacob de Bracha, a Jew of Messina	3.3.0 ounces	half by vintage time and half by Lent	sale of a mule to Salamon, son of Fariono de Missina, a Jew in Palermo
22.5.1443 c. nn	Cristoforu Scarpario	24 *tarì*	paid	sale of grapes to Daidono Ricio, a Jew of Palermo
27.5.1443 c. nn	Xalon Minsel	2.27.0 ounces	within 4 months	sale of soles to Xamuel Gididia, a Jew of Palermo
27.5.1443 c. nn	Antonio de Pachi	1.18.0 ounces	paid	sale of grapes to Iacob Taguil, a Jew in Palermo
27.5.1443 c. nn	Nissim de Rafael, a Jew of Sciacca	24 *tarì*	by the middle of September	sale of a horse
27.5.1443 c. nn	Antonio de Migluri	20 *tarì*	weekly instalments of 1 *tarì*	sale of cloth to Iacobo Tavormina, a Jew of Palermo
27.5.1443 c. nn	Merdoc Simael and Mordoc Chairuni, Jews of Palermo	20 *tarì*	paid	sale of oil
27.5.1443 c. nn	Zualo de Martieto	15 *tarì*		sale of oil to Muxa de Minichi, a Palermitan Jew; Xibiten Virdi, another Jew, stands surety
27.5.1443 c. nn	Nicolò de Blando	3 ounces	2 ounces on account	sale of tallow to Zaccaria Achina, a Jew of Palermo
27.5.1443 c. nn	Salamone Azara, a Jew in Palermo	15.16.10 ounces	half in 2 months, balance in 4	sale of coarse cloth to Muxa de Muxa, son of Salamone, a Palermitan Jew
30.5.1443 c. nn	Iacob Xunina, a Jew of Palermo	1.6.0 ounces	within a month	sale of linen to Xamuel Castillanu, a Jew of Palermo

7.1.1444 c. nn	Bartholomeo de Aprili and his wife	1.18.0 ounces	24 *tarì* on account, balance by February	sale of grapes to Brachono Bambulo, a Jew in Palermo
21.1.1444 c. nn	Giovanni de Vitali	6 ounces	3 ounces by Easter, another 3 by August	sale of grapes to Muxexi Marsili, a Palermitan Jew
21.1.1444 c. nn	Pietro Zambagla	22 *tarì*	paid	sale of grapes to Brachono Bambulo, a Jew in Palermo
22.1.1444 c. nn	Iosep de Medico, a Jew of Palermo	16 ounces	8 *tarì* on account	sale of embroidered silk
22.1.1444 c. nn	Giovanni de Perri	12 *tarì*	paid	sale of grapes to Brachono Xunina, a Jew of Palermo
23.1.1444 c. nn	Masio de Buzze	1.6.0 ounces	paid	sale of oil to Muxexi Marsili, a Jew of Palermo
24.1.1444 c. nn	Abraam Calabrensi, a Jew of Palermo	4.6.0 ounces	2.4.10 and 2 ounces on account, balance later	sale of black slave
24.1.1444 c. nn	Giovanni de Milacio	24 *tarì*	paid	sale of grapes to Xibiten Isac, a Jew of Palermo
3.2.1444 c. nn	Nicolò Sciacca	13 *tarì*	paid	sale of grapes to Daidono Rizo, a Palermitan Jew
3.2.1444 c. nn	Matheo de Alfano	1.18.0 ounces	paid	sale of grapes to Merdoc Minichi, a Palermitan Jew
3.2.1444 c. nn	Nicolò de Cammarata	24 *tarì*	paid	sale of grapes to Merdoc de Minichi, a Jew of Palermo
5.2.1444 c. nn	Nicolò de Angelo	1.16.0 ounces	paid	sale of grapes to Brachono Bambulo, a Jew of Palermo

5.2.1444 c. nn	Blasio Marranzanu	9.5. florins a quintal		sale of grapes to Xidedi Azara, a Jew in Palermo
7.2.1444 c. nn	Elena de Cataldo	1.6.0 ounces	within 4 months	sale of oil to Bulchaira de Termis, a Jew in Palermo
10.2.1444 c. nn	Airono Xalom, a Palermitan Jew	29.15 *tarì*	by Easter	sale of string (*disa*) to Muxexi Marsili, a Jew of Palermo
8.2.1444 c. nn	Palmerio de Leo and Grecu de Castrogiovanni	1.24.0 ounces	12 *tarì* on account	sale of string (*disa*) to Airono Xalom, a Jew of Palermo
8.2.1444 c. nn	Merdoc Vita, a Palermitan Jew	20 *tarì*	16 *tarì* on account	sale of tallow to Zaccaria Achina, a Palermitan Jew
8.2.1444 c. nn	Andrea and Benedetto Testante	1.8.0 ounces	15 *tarì* on account, balance later	sale of oil to Isac Sala, a Jew of Palermo on behalf of Asisa, a Jewess of Palermo
12.2.1444 c. nn	Iacob Xunina, a Jew of Palermo	3.21.10 ounces	within 4 months; paid 12.10.1445	sale of linen to Xamuel Sacerdotu, a Palermitan Jew
14.2.1444 c. nn	Michilono Minachem, a Jew of Palermo	1 ounce	by Easter	sale of leather
14.2.1444 c. nn	Xibiten Gazu, a Palermitan Jew	10 *tarì*		sale of oil
19.2.1444 c. nn	Minto de Minichi and Vita de Leon, Palermitan Jews	1.12.0 ounces	1.5.0 ounces on account	sale of grapes to Brachono Bambulo, a Jew in Palermo
27.2.1444 c. nn	Nicolò de Gilberto	10 ounces; 1.24.0 a quintal	8 ounces by April, balance on delivery; paid 7.10	sale of grapes to Musuto Binna, a Jew of Palermo

12.7.1448 c. nn	Elia de Manueli, a Jew of Palermo	11 ounces		sale to Gabriel de Medico, a Palermitan Jew, of rights in regard to a Saracen slave girl
1.4.1451 c. nn	Giuliano de Rigio	3.6.0 ounces	within 4 months; paid 15.3.1452	sale of spades/feldspar (*de* *spatis*) to Isac de Isac, a Jew of Palermo
2.4.1451 c. nn	Giovanni Mandaranu	1.21.0 ounces	paid	sale of grapes to Musuto Binna, a Jew in Palermo
5.4.1451 c. nn	Pietro Lutissu	2.6.0 ounces	within 3 months	sale of oil to Vita de Medico, a Jew of Palermo
8.4.1451 c. nn	Salamon Azara, a Palermitan Jew	5 ounces		loan
4.6.1458 c. nn	Filippo de Lamanna	24 *tarì*		sale of oil to Bulchaira Frisisa, a Palermitan Jew
6.6.1458 c. nn	Bracha Crivaru, a Jew of Palermo	1 ounce		sale of tunny to Vita Maltensis, a Jew of Palermo
7.6.1458 c. nn	Andrea de Griffono and Benedetto Riscolu	1 ounce	paid	sale of grapes to Elia Amara, a Palermitan Jew
13.6.1458 c. nn	Manfridu Cacecta	10 *tarì*	paid	sale of beech wood to Xamuel Sacerdoto, a Palermitan Jew
13.6.1458 c. nn	Iosep de Minichi, a Jew of Palermo			sale of beast of burden
13.6.1458 c. nn	David Mavena, a Jew of Palermo	3.18.0 ounces		sale of grapes; Xamuel Sacerdoto, a Palermitan Jew, stands surety

Date and Page				
13.6.1458 c. nn	Iacob de Musuto, a Jew of Monte San Giuliano	1 ounce	by September	sale of a mule
[..].6.1458 c. nn	Antonio de Manuele	1.4.0 ounces		sale of goods to Sadono Chanchula, a Jew of Polizzi
17.6.1458 c. nn	Andrea de Amato	1.18.0 ounces	1 ounce on account, balance by September	sale of a bedspread to Vita Minichi and Cara, wife of Gaudio de Rixio, Palermitan Jews
11.4.1459 c. nn	Iuda de Minichi, a Jew of Palermo	20 ounces	paid	sale of a carat [of gold/ precious stone] to Iacob Abeladeb, a Palermitan Jew;
			witnesses: Muxa Sacerdotu and Iacob de Terminis, Jews of Palermo	
5.1.1462 c. nn	Emanuel de Belvedere	12 ounces		sale of all rights in regard to Fatima, a Saracen slave girl, to Sadono de Medico, a Palermitan Jew
28.9.1463 c. nn	Mardoc Cathalano, a Jew	4 ounces		loan to Busacca de Chaseni, a Jew

Date and Page	Tenant	Location and Description	Rent and Duration	Remarks
14.4.1434 c. nn	Levi de Tripuli, a Palermitan Jew	Palermo, Cassaro, *ruga* Luxeri; bordering on the houses of the heirs of Enrico de Gractaluxio and Vanni de Termini, a Jew; a house	2 ounces	landlord: Satruna, a Jewess of Termini; the house is subject to a ground rent of 9 *tarì* to the monastery S. Maria degli Angeli

27.5.1435 c. nn	Iacobo de Tabernis, a notary	Palermo, Platea Marmorea, bordering on the landlord's house inhabited by Chanino, a Jew; shop	3 instalments of 1 ounce; 1 year	landlord: master Moyse Chetibi, a Jew of Palermo; 6 *tarì* on account, balance on 15.5
18.3.1438 c. nn	Iacob de Gaudio, a Jew of Palermo	courtyard of Dattilo, bordering on the well of the courtyard and on the house inhabited by Iacob Bucheri, a Jew; ground floor house	1.18.0 ounces a month	landlord: Brachono Mizoc, a Palermitan Jew
4.4.1438 c. nn	Elia de Benedetto, a Jew of Palermo	Cassaro, *ruga* del Balneo, bordering on the house of Simone, a Jew, and the house of the heir of Antonio de Speciali; a *solerata* warehouse and shop	2 ounces annually, starting 1.9.1439	landlord: Xamuel Sala, a Jew in Palermo
13.6.1458 c. nn	Ester, a Jewess of Palermo, wife of Iosep de Benedetto	Palermo; ground floor house		landlord: Brachono Mizoc, a Jew of Palermo
13.6.1458 c. nn	Iacob de Tripuli, a Jew of Palermo	a shop	12 *tarì*	landlord: Salamon Azara, a Jew of Palermo

7.6.1459 c. nn	Busacca Bono, a Jew of Palermo	Palermo, Cassaro, bordering on the house of Filippo Scolaribus, a notary, the landlord's house and the public road	2 *solerata* houses	landlord: Giovanni de Scolaribus; subject to ground rent of 24 *tarì*
3.9.1459 c. nn	Giovanni de Barrachato	Cefalù, bordering on the houses of Filippo de Pilecto and Matheo de Negla; a house		landlord: Merdoc de Liucio of Palermo, acting for his wife Rita and for the partners Iusupi and Salamone, Jews of Palermo

Indexes

Index of Persons

There follow page numbers instead of Doc. numbers, as hitherto.

[..] Amichello 6472
[..] Bonconte 6458
[..] Cusintino 6188
[..] Carastono 6594
[..] de Lu Medicu 6207
[..] de Termini 6275
[..] Suvararo 6162
A[..] Gibil 6701
Abdalla, slave 6607
Abdella Bumusa, slave 6270
Abdila Bramellu 6356
Abdila Xunina 6499
Abitella Xunina 6679
Abneri Grixon 6375, 6534, 6535, 6543, 6553, 6557
Abraam [..] 6329
Abraam Abudarcham 6467
Abraam Baylu (Baylli) 6421, 6437, 6454
Abraam Brixa (Brissa) 6471, 6494
Abraam de Sangallo, alias Abuganell 6470
Abraam Fillona 6446
Abraam Gididia 6466
Abraam Ladeb (Belladeb) 6412, 6414, 6467
Abraam Ysac 6468
Abrae Xhalifa, son of Xhilomu 6161
Abraham Baidu, master shoemaker 6600
Abraham Birda 6601
Abraham (Abram) Calabrisi (Calabrensi) 6104, 6624, 6715
Abram Abagard 6286
Abram (Abraam) Abagatel(l) (Abbaxatell) 6399, 6402, 6403, 6407, 6410, 6416, 6425, 6429, 6436, 6438, 6450, 6466

Abram Abaynello 6546
Abram Abenladep (Abeladep), notary 6080, 6691, 6710
Abram Abinazara 6460
Abram Aurifichi 6443
Abram Azara 6527
Abram Bambassu 6257
Abram Bass 6339, 6343, 6360, 6480, 6482, 6483, 6485, 6489, 6490, 6494, 6495, 6497–6499, 6501, 6504, 6513, 6519, 6527, 6563
Abram Castellanu 6175
Abram Chalena 6185
Abram Chualena (master) 6633
Abram Cuyno 6531, 6567
Abram Daru 6485
Abram de Amarono 6509
Abram de Aram 6399
Abram de Aron 6251, 6545
Abram de Fano, bookseller 6577
Abram de Girachio 6565
Abram de Grixon, son of Nixim 6532, 6533, 6542, 6554
Abram de Medico 6580
Abram de Minichi 6143, 6148, 6242, 6260, 6566–6568
Abram de Missina 6258
Abram de Mona 6547
Abram de Muxarella 6510, 6546
Abram de Noto 6580
Abram de Portugammo 6297
Abram de Siracusia (Seragusia), alias lu Raysi 6159, 61606346
Abram de Vignuni 6509
Abram Dixon 6531
Abram Fitira 6542
Abram Frisisa 6569, 6576, 6579
Abram Gallifa 6372, 6529

Geographical Index

There follow page numbers instead of Doc. numbers, as hitherto.

Subject Index

There follow page numbers instead of Doc. numbers, as hitherto.

abattoir 6154, 6156, 6157, 6508, 6582, 6605, 6607 6610, 6635, 6697

agriculture 6076–6078, 6081–6084, 6087–6090, 6092–6094, 6096, 6097, 6099, 6101, 6102, 6106, 6107, 6115, 6116, 6118–6123, 6125–6127, 6129–6131, 6135, 6136, 6141, 6144, 6146, 6147, 6149, 6150, 6152, 6153, 6159–6161, 6272, 6312, 6329, 6330, 6351, 6352, 6361, 6364, 6385, 6386, 6392, 6393, 6593, 6594, 6596, 6599, 6601, 6604–6606, 6661, 6662, 6664, 6668, 6684, 6688, 6689

albacore 6543, 6555, 6565, 6567, 6571, 6611, 6612

almonds 6217, 6411, 6589

alum 6411

anchors 6174, 6682

apprentices and apprenticeship 6367, 6376, 6594, 6598–6600, 6605, 6606, 6610, 6612, 6613, 6700

arbitrators and arbitration 6151, 6154, 6267, 6359, 6360, 6363, 6371, 6382, 6592, 6595

arms 6313

badge (Jewish) 6382

banks and bankers 6078, 6101, 6115, 6118, 6147, 6148, 6158, 6159, 6188, 6191, 6309, 6318, 6321, 6383–6385, 6394, 6403, 6502, 6561, 6665

barbers 6550, 6643, 6651

barley 6091, 6162, 6174, 6176, 6185, 6188, 6204, 6223, 6227, 6250, 6251, 6256, 6257, 6267, 6294, 6408, 6476, 6477, 6499, 6518, 6530, 6539, 6555, 6564, 6565, 6627, 6640, 6647, 6650, 6673, 6687, 6712

barter, see business

beasts of burden 6075, 6078, 6079, 6086, 6092, 6097, 6109, 6114, 6119, 6154, 6169, 6172, 6176, 6177, 6182, 6186, 6196, 6209, 6219, 6225, 6229, 6237, 6238, 6240, 6241, 6247, 6261, 6307, 6409, 6535, 6565, 6571, 6596, 6600, 6607–6609, 6611, 6612, 6618, 6646, 6661, 6666, 6667, 6670, 6677, 6689, 6690, 6704, 6707, 6717

bells 6214, 6601

Bible 6280, 6281

bills of exchange 6327–6329, 6336, 6337, 6343, 6475, 6502

biscuits 6318, 6320, 6403

bolts 6414

bombardier 6556, 6566–6568, 6575, 6577

books 6245, 6280, 6313, 6345, 6577

booksellers 6183, 6577

bows 6649

brass 6707

bricks 6171, 6187, 6211, 6223, 6225, 6227, 6511, 6631, 6632, 6708, 6710

brocade 6537

brokers and brokerage 6341, 6342, 6371, 6593

bronze 6185, 6188

building and builders 6084, 6098, 6107, 6113, 6118, 6124, 6163, 6164, 6269–6271, 6299, 6300, 6311, 6312, 6369, 6370–6373, 6377, 6380, 6389, 6592, 6597, 6603, 6607, 6608, 6614, 6616, 6666, 6668, 6681, 6686

business 6087, 6089, 6095, 6097, 6109, 6110, 6112, 6115, 6116, 6118, 6119, 6122, 6128, 6129, 6131, 6137–6139, 6143–6146, 6148, 6154, 6160–6162, 6164, 6165–6272, 6274–6300,